THEORY OF ECONOMETRICS

By the same author

MODERN MICROECONOMICS
(Second Edition)

NON-PRICE DECISIONS

THEORY OF ECONOMETRICS

An Introductory Exposition of Econometric Methods

A. KOUTSOYIANNIS

Professor of Economics
University of Waterloo, Ontario

SECOND EDITION

Foreword by C. F. CARTER

M

First edition 1973
Reprinted 1976
Second edition 1977
Reprinted 1978, 1979, 1981 (twice), 1983

Published by
THE MACMILLAN PRESS LTD
London and Basingstoke
Companies and representatives
throughout the world

ISBN 0 333 22379 9

Printed in Hong Kong

To Petros, Sotos and Ketty

Foreword

Additional textbooks require some excuse: but the reason for this one is easily stated. Most econometric textbooks are either too advanced for all but a minority of students, or achieve simplicity by leaving too many things out. Dr Koutsoyiannis set herself the difficult task of being simple and reasonably comprehensive at the same time; and, because she had a clear aim, and knows the subject intimately in every detail, she has succeeded. Furthermore, she has produced a book which is written by an economist, about the real things which ought to be the province of economics — 'a study of mankind in the ordinary business of life'. This book is not pure mathematics dressed up with a few economic names for the variables, but an effort to introduce, to a large number of economists, tools which will be of value to them in the practical business of their subject. It deserves a wide welcome.

The University of Lancaster   CHARLES F. CARTER
November 1972

Contents

PART ONE

CORRELATION THEORY
THE SIMPLE LINEAR REGRESSION MODEL

ix

PART TWO

ECONOMETRIC PROBLEMS

SECOND-ORDER TESTS OF THE ASSUMPTIONS OF
THE LINEAR REGRESSION MODEL

PART THREE

MODELS OF SIMULTANEOUS RELATIONSHIPS

Preface to the Second Edition

I have attempted in this second edition to stress the importance of the application of econometric methods to economic relationships. The structure of this edition is basically the same as that adopted in the first edition. However, the numerous comments and suggestions which I received from colleagues in several universities, reviewers and students, gave me the opportunity to rewrite many sections of the book, bearing always in mind my basic goal: the emphasis of the economic implications of the various measurement techniques. I hope, as a result, that economists will become increasingly aware of the ease with which the powerful tools of econometrics can be applied meaningfully to specific economic problems, without the heavy mathematical requirements of the other main textbooks in this field.

Complying to the many requests of teachers, instructors and students, I have added an Appendix with numerous examples and questions relating to economic applications. It is my belief that a thorough understanding of the econometric methods cannot be attained unless the student is exposed to as many examples as possible which have some degree of economic realism. Hence, I have minimised the questions which are purely theoretical, and I have concentrated on examples from economic theory which can be worked out with observations (data) of the relevant economic variables. This is a unique feature to the second edition, which, I believe, will prove most useful and will contribute to the wider use of econometric techniques.

Some of the examples have been taken from various sources and adapted to economic situations. The majority of problems, however, have been prepared by the author with the help of teaching assistants, to whom I am greatly indebted. I would like to express my thanks in this respect to A. Taher, M. Nosko, and J. Collins of the University of Waterloo. I am also grateful to D. Pallas and D. Wagg for the speed and efficiency with which they typed a difficult typescript.

A. KOUTSOYIANNIS

University of Waterloo
Ontario
May 1977

Preface to the First Edition

For a long time econometrics has been considered a highly specialised tool of research. Yet its rapid growth and increasing use in economic planning and research require its simplification and wider diffusion among students of economics and professional economists. It is the contention of the author that econometrics is much simpler than is commonly believed. It is hoped that the present textbook will substantiate this contention and, by simplifying the econometric methods, will provide a good guide to the more advanced textbooks on econometrics such as J. Johnston's *Econometric Methods,* A. Goldberger's *Econometric Theory,* or E. Malinvaud's *Statistical Methods in Econometrics.*

The thought of writing an introductory textbook on econometrics originated from the author's experience both as a student and as a teacher of econometrics. As a student, having gone through the formidable task of acquiring the background in mathematics and statistics needed for a formal course on econometrics, the author became increasingly aware that most of the ideas pertaining to the application of econometric methods may be presented clearly with the use of fairly simple mathematical and statistical notions. This conviction was strengthened by the author's teaching experience. Of course, by adopting a simple mathematical exposition, rigorous treatment is sacrificed to simplicity; but it has been the author's experience that unless students are gradually introduced to the sophisticated mathematical and statistical exposition of the standard econometric textbooks, they are often discouraged no matter how enthusiastic they are about the subject.

Recently several introductory books on econometrics have been published. However, most of these books omit many essential topics on the grounds that they are 'beyond the scope' of an introductory textbook. As a consequence these textbooks provide an incomplete treatment of the subject.

It is true that there is no substitute for the classical textbooks (such as the ones mentioned above) for the thorough understanding of econometric theory. But frequently in the advanced textbooks the economic implications of the econometric methods, which are of paramount importance for the practising economist, are shadowed by the elaborate mathematical exposition of the subject-matter. Thus even those students with an advanced background knowledge in mathematics and statistics sometimes fail to grasp the economic implications and relevance of the mathematical assumptions needed to build up the econometric methods.

The present book is an attempt to provide students of economics and professional economists, not formally trained in econometrics, with the necessary

xv

tools for econometric research in a mathematically simple way. It is intended to be a textbook of *econometrics for economists* and to serve as a stepping-stone to the more advanced books and treatises on the subject.

The book covers a range of topics similar to the classical textbooks of econometrics. The author has attempted to simplify the mathematical presentation of the econometric methods. The exposition is based on the rules of simple algebra. Matrix algebra, while allowing a neat and concise presentation, often has the effect of bewildering and discouraging the mathematically unsophisticated student for whom this book is intended. Thus the book does not assume knowledge of mathematics beyond elementary college algebra, and of statistics beyond an introductory course. The essential definitions and tools of statistics and mathematics required for the understanding of the book are summarised in two brief appendices. Mathematical proofs are mostly presented in small print so as not to interrupt the main course of exposition of the econometric techniques.

The greatest attention is given to the economic aspects of econometrics. The assumptions made in the various methods and their economic implications are treated in detail. For each method the assumptions are first explicitly stated and their economic meaning examined. Particular attention is paid to the analysis of the consequences of the violation of the assumptions on the measurements of the coefficients of economic relationships. Finally, the tools available for testing the assumptions of the econometric methods are explained and ways for improving the measurements, when the assumptions are violated, are discussed.

The book is divided in three parts.

Part One begins with a brief discussion of the procedure which must be followed in any applied econometric research. It proceeds with the examination of the theory of correlation and the simple linear regression model. In a separate chapter the method of the Analysis of Variance and its use in connection with regression analysis is developed.

Part Two is devoted to the examination of the assumptions of the linear regression model, their economic meaning, their implications for the values of the parameters of the economic relations, their tests, and the corrective action which must be adopted whenever these assumptions are violated.

Part Three includes the examination of the problems arising from the simultaneous dependence of the economic variables. The systems of simultaneous relations require the application of more elaborate econometric techniques for their measurement. An attempt is made to present the most important of these methods, starting from the simpler ones and gradually proceeding to the development of the more sophisticated maximum likelihood methods. In the final chapter the ranking of the various econometric techniques is attempted, based on the evidence provided by extensive studies generally known as Monte Carlo studies.

The author is heavily indebted to Professor C. F. Carter, Vice-Chancellor of the University of Lancaster and former Editor of the *Economic Journal*, without whose guidance, encouragement and support the project would not have been possible. I am also greatly indebted to Professor A. Goldberger of the University of Wisconsin, Professor R. J. D. Ball and Mr Renton of the London Graduate School of Business Studies, who patiently read through the typescript and made many constructive criticisms and valuable suggestions. Mr D. H. G. Trevena of the Leeds Polytechnic and Dr J. Bridge of the University of Manchester encouraged me at all stages of the project and made many helpful suggestions. Dr L. P. Mendis of the University of Lancaster and Mr G. Williams have checked through the algebra. Mr Williams also helped with the preparation of the examples and with various valuable suggestions. I am indebted to Mr T. Nguyen of the University of Lancaster for his continuous encouragement and help. Thanks are also expressed to Miss Amy Wootten and to Dr A. El-Mokadem of the University of Lancaster, and Professor J. Mars for helpful comments and encouragement. I am also greatly indebted to Professor J. Johnston of the University of Manchester for sending me several chapters of the second edition of his *Econometric Methods,* from which it became possible to enrich the contents of this book and substantially improve the exposition.

I would like to thank Katherine Kossentos for her assistance in the design of the cover of this book. I believe that the impressions of the reader of any book start from its cover. I think that Miss Kossentos's simplicity of design conveys the simplicity of approach attempted in this book.

University of Lancaster   A. KOUTSOYIANNIS
England

PART ONE

Correlation Theory
The Simple Linear Regression Model

1. Definition, Scope and Division of Econometrics

1.1. DEFINITION AND SCOPE OF ECONOMETRICS

Econometrics deals with the measurement of economic relationships. The term 'econometrics' is formed from two words of Greek origin, $οἰκονομία$ (economy), and $μέτρον$ (measure).

Econometrics is a combination of economic theory, mathematical economics and statistics, but it is completely distinct from each one of these three branches of science.

The following quotation from the opening editorial of *Econometrica* written by R. Frish in 1933 may give a clear idea of the scope and method of econometrics:

> But there are several aspects of the quantitative approach to economics, and no single one of these aspects, taken by itself, should be confounded with econometrics. Thus, econometrics is by no means the same as economic statistics. Nor is it identical with what we call general economic theory, although a considerable portion of this theory has a definite quantitative character. Nor should econometrics be taken as synonymous with the application of mathematics to economics. Experience has shown that each of these three viewpoints, that of statistics, economic theory, and mathematics, is a necessary, but not by itself sufficient, condition for a real understanding of the quantitative relations in modern economic life. It is the *unification* of all three that is powerful. And it is this unification that constitutes econometrics.

Thus econometrics may be considered as the integration of economics, mathematics and statistics for the purpose of providing numerical values for the parameters of economic relationships (for example, elasticities, propensities, marginal values) and verifying economic theories. It is a special type of economic analysis and research in which the general economic theory, formulated in mathematical terms, is combined with empirical measurement of economic phenomena. Starting from the relationships of economic theory, we express them in mathematical terms (i.e. we build a model) so that they can be measured. We then use specific methods, called *econometric methods,* in order to obtain numerical estimates of the coefficients of the economic relationships. Econometric methods are statistical methods specifically adapted to the peculiarities of economic phenomena. The most important characteristic of economic relationships is that they contain a random element, which, however, is ignored by

3

economic theory and mathematical economics which postulate exact relationships between the various economic magnitudes. Econometrics has developed
methods for dealing with the random component of economic relationships.

An example will make the above clear. Economic theory postulates that the
demand for a commodity depends on its price, on the prices of other commodities,
on consumers' income and on tastes. This is an exact relationship, because it
implies that demand is completely determined by the above four factors. No
other factor, except those explicitly mentioned, influences the demand. In
mathematical economics we express the above abstract economic relationship
of demand in mathematical terms. Thus we may write the following demand
equation

$$Q = b_0 + b_1 P + b_2 P_0 + b_3 Y + b_4 t$$

where Q = quantity demanded of a particular commodity
        P = price of the commodity
        P_0 = prices of other commodities
        Y = consumers' income
        t = tastes
        b_0, b_1, b_2, b_3, b_4 = coefficients of the demand equation.

The above demand equation is exact, because it implies that the only determinants of the quantity demanded are the four factors which appear in the
right-hand side of the equation. Quantity will change only if some of these
factors change. No other factor may have any effect on demand. Yet it is
common knowledge that in economic life many more factors may affect
demand. The invention of a new product, a war, professional changes, institutional changes, changes in law, changes in income distribution, massive population
movements (migration), etc., are examples of such factors. Furthermore, human
behaviour is inherently erratic. We are influenced by rumours, dreams, prejudices,
traditions and other psychological and sociological factors, which make us
behave differently even though the conditions in the market (prices) and our
incomes remain the same. In econometrics the influence of these 'other' factors
is taken into account by the introduction into the economic relationships of a
random variable, with specific characteristics, which will be discussed in later
chapters. In our example the demand function studied with the tools of
econometrics would be of the (stochastic) form

$$Q = b_0 + b_1 P + b_2 P_0 + b_3 Y + b_4 t + u$$

where u stands for the random factors which affect the quantity demanded.

It is essential to stress that econometrics presupposes the existence of a body
of economic theory. Economic theory should come first, because it sets the
hypotheses about economic behaviour which should be tested with the application of econometric techniques. In testing a theory we start from its mathematical
formulation, which constitutes *the model* or the *maintained hypothesis*. In our

example of the demand function the maintained hypothesis is

$$Q = b_0 + b_1 P + b_2 P_0 + b_3 Y + b_4 t + u$$

The next step is to confront the model with observational data referring to the actual behaviour of the economic units — consumers or producers. The aim of this stage is to establish whether the theory can explain the actual behaviour of the economic units, i.e. whether the theory is compatible with the facts. If the theory is compatible with the actual data, we accept the theory as valid. If the theory is incompatible with the observed behaviour, we either reject the theory or, in the light of the empirical evidence of the data, we may modify it. In the latter case one needs additional new observations in order to test the revised version of the theory.

The procedure to be followed when testing a theory may be schematically presented as in Figure 1.1.

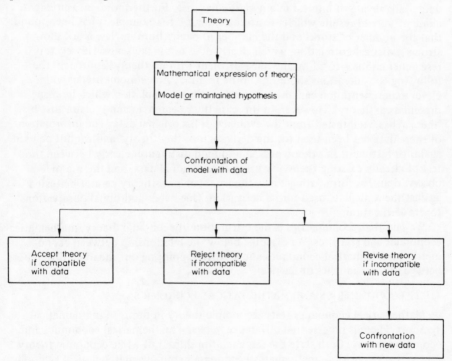

Figure 1.1

The procedure outlined above is not intended to imply that when testing a theory the researcher should restrict himself only to factors suggested by economic theory. If these factors do not provide a satisfactory explanation of economic behaviour, the research worker is certainly entitled to look for other factors. Experimentation with alternative formulations, each including various explanatory factors, has proved a most valuable guide to the revision and restatement of the hypotheses of economic theory. Econometrics, by establishing the usefulness or the insignificance of factors suggested by economic theories, has given new insight into various fields of economics and often provided evidence which has led to a reshaping of theoretical economics. One of the most striking examples in this respect is the investment function. (See M. K. Evans, *Macroeconomic Activity*, Harper & Row, 1969, Chapters 4–8.)

Various writers have argued that there is no need for a pre-existing body of theory: one may start with a set of observed data and from this derive a behavioural theory. This argument is known as 'measurement with no theory'. Such an approach seems absurd given that economics in its present state does provide a large number of hypotheses which may be tested empirically. A pre-existing body of theory saves a lot of time by showing which of the mass of · data available are of interest in any particular case. Furthermore, measurement alone may yield results which are not meaningful; for example it has been found that the number of storks and the number of babies born in New York show a strong statistical correlation, which clearly does not make sense. However, if the researcher chooses to adopt the 'measurement with no theory' approach, the following considerations should be borne in mind. An econometrician with clever experimentation can always arrive at some formulation which he may present as a 'theory'. However, in this case the researcher cannot claim that his 'theory' has been tested from the evidence of his original data. The information of these data has been used for the derivation of the 'theory' and cannot be used again for testing it. In other words, one should distinguish clearly between the test of already existing theory by using observational data, and the use of observations for formulating a new theory. Such new theory cannot be tested against the same data used for its derivation. One needs additional observations for its verification.

We said that econometrics is the integration of economic theory, mathematical economics and statistics. We examine below the relationship between econometrics, mathematical economics and statistics, pointing out the main differences between these branches of science.

1.1.1. ECONOMETRICS AND MATHEMATICAL ECONOMICS

Mathematical economics states economic theory in terms of mathematical symbols. There is no essential difference between mathematical economics and economic theory. Both state the same relationships, but while economic theory uses verbal exposition, mathematical economics employs mathematical symbolism. Both express the various economic relationships in an exact form. Neither economic theory nor mathematical economics allows for random elements which might affect the relationship and make it stochastic. Furthermore, they do not provide numerical values for the coefficients of the relationships.

Econometrics differs from mathematical economics. Although econometrics presupposes the expression of economic relationships in mathematical form, like mathematical economics it does not assume that economic relationships are exact. On the contrary, econometrics assumes that relationships are not exact. Econometric methods are designed to take into account random disturbances which create deviations from the exact behavioural patterns suggested by economic theory and mathematical economics. Furthermore, econometric methods provide numerical values of the coefficients of economic phenomena. For example, economic theory suggests that the demand for a product which covers a basic human need is inelastic, provided the commodity does not have close substitutes. This information is of little assistance to policy-makers, because the coefficient of elasticity may assume any value between 0 and 1. Econometrics can supply precise estimates of elasticities and other parameters of economic theory.

1.1.2. ECONOMETRICS AND STATISTICS

Econometrics differs both from mathematical statistics and economic statistics. An economic statistician gathers empirical data, records them, tabulates them or charts them, and then attempts to describe the pattern in their development over time and perhaps detect some relationship between various economic magnitudes. Economic statistics is mainly a descriptive aspect of economics. It does not provide explanations of the development of the various variables and it does not provide measurement of the parameters of economic relationships.

Mathematical (or inferential) statistics deals with methods of measurement, which are developed on the basis of controlled experiments in laboratories. Statistical methods of measurement are not appropriate for economic relationships, which cannot be measured on the basis of evidence provided by controlled experiments, because such experiments cannot be designed for economic phenomena. In physics and some other sciences the researcher can hold all other conditions constant and change only one element in performing an experiment. He can then record the results of such a change and apply the classical statistical methods to deduce the laws governing the phenomenon being investigated. In studying the economic behaviour of human beings one cannot change only one factor while keeping all other factors constant. In the real world all variables change continuously and simultaneously, so that controlled experiments are impossible. We cannot change only incomes, keeping prices, tastes and other factors constant, because the latter will change as a result of income changes.

Econometrics uses statistical methods after adapting them to the problems of economic life. These adapted statistical methods are called econometric methods. In particular, econometric methods are adjusted so that they become appropriate for the measurement of economic relationships which are stochastic, that is they include random elements. The adjustment consists primarily in specifying the stochastic (random) elements that are supposed to operate in the real world and enter into the determination of the observed data, so that the latter can be interpreted as a (random) sample to which the methods of statistics can be applied.

1.2. GOALS OF ECONOMETRICS

We can distinguish three main goals of econometrics: (1) analysis, i.e. testing of economic theory; (2) policy-making, i.e. supplying numerical estimates of the coefficients of economic relationships, which may be then used for decision-making; (3) forecasting, i.e. using the numerical estimates of the coefficients in order to forecast the future values of the economic magnitudes. Of course, these goals are not mutually exclusive. Successful econometric applications should really include some combination of all three aims.

1.2.1. ANALYSIS: TESTING ECONOMIC THEORY

In the earlier stages of the development of economic theory economists formulated the basic principles of the functioning of the economic system using verbal exposition and applying a deductive procedure. The earlier economic theories started from a set of observations concerning the behaviour of individuals as consumers or producers. Some basic assumptions were set regarding the motivation of individual economic units. Thus in demand theory it was assumed that the consumer aims at the maximisation of his satisfaction (utility) from the expenditure of his income, given the prices of the commodities. Similarly, producers were assumed to be motivated by maximisation of their profits. From these assumptions the economists by pure logical reasoning derived some general conclusions (laws) concerning the working processes of the economic system. Economic theories thus developed in an abstract level were not tested against economic reality. In other words no attempt was made to examine whether the theories explained adequately the actual economic behaviour of individuals.

Econometrics aims primarily at the verification of economic theories. In this case we say that the purpose of the research is *analysis*, i.e. obtaining empirical evidence to test the explanatory power of economic theories, to decide how well they *explain* the observed behaviour of the economic units. Today any theory, regardless of its elegance in exposition or its sound logical consistency, cannot be established and generally accepted without some empirical testing.

1.2.2. POLICY-MAKING: OBTAINING NUMERICAL ESTIMATES OF THE
COEFFICIENTS OF ECONOMIC RELATIONSHIPS FOR POLICY SIMULATIONS

In many cases we apply the various econometric techniques in order to obtain reliable estimates of the individual coefficients of the economic relationships from which we may evaluate elasticities or other parameters of economic theory (multipliers, technical coefficients of production, marginal costs, marginal revenues, etc.). The knowledge of the numerical value of these coefficients is very important for the decisions of firms as well as for the formulation of the economic policy of the government. It helps to compare the effects of alternative policy decisions.

For example, the decision of the government about devaluing the currency will depend to a great extent on the numerical value of the marginal propensity to import, as well as on the numerical values of the price elasticities of exports and imports. If the sum of price elasticities of exports and imports is less than one in absolute value, the devaluation will not help in eliminating the deficit in the balance of payments.

Similarly, if the price elasticity of demand for a product is less than one (inelastic demand), it does not pay the manufacturer to decrease its price, because his receipts would be reduced.

In a competitive market with linear demand and supply curves of the usual type (downward-sloping demand and upward-sloping supply), the government should not impose a specific excise tax (per unit of output) if its aim is to curb price increases, because such a tax would raise the price, although less than the amount of the tax per unit, *ceteris paribus*.

Such examples show how important is the knowledge of the numerical values of the coefficients of the economic relationships. Econometrics can provide such numerical estimates and has become an essential tool for the formulation of sound economic policies.

1.2.3. FORECASTING THE FUTURE VALUES OF ECONOMIC MAGNITUDES

In formulating policy decisions it is essential to be able to forecast the value of the economic magnitudes. Such forecasts will enable the policy-maker to judge whether it is necessary to take any measures in order to influence the relevant economic variables.

For example, suppose that the government wants to decide its employment policy. It is necessary to know what is the current situation of employment as well as what the level of employment will be, say, in five years' time, if no measure whatsoever is taken by the government. With econometric techniques we may obtain such an estimate of the level of employment. If this level is too low, the government will take appropriate measures to avoid its occurrence. If the forecast value of employment is higher than the expected labour force, the government must take different measures in order to avoid inflation.

Forecasting is becoming increasingly important both for the regulation of developed economies as well as for the planning of the economic development of underdeveloped countries.

1.3. DIVISION OF ECONOMETRICS

Econometrics may be distinguished into two branches, theoretical econometrics and applied econometrics.

Theoretical econometrics includes the development of appropriate methods for the measurement of economic relationships. As mentioned above, econometric techniques are basically statistical techniques which have been adapted to the particular characteristics of economic relationships. Two features of economic reality render the pure methods of mathematical statistics inappropriate for the measurement of economic phenomena. Firstly, the data which are used for the measurement of economic relationships are observations of actual life and are not derived from controlled experiments. In economic life laboratory experiments are not possible, because most of the economic magnitudes change contemporaneously and each influences and is influenced by all the other magnitudes. Accordingly, econometric methods have been developed for the analysis of non-experimental data. Secondly, the economic relationships are not exact, as economic theory and mathematical economics assume them to be. Economic behaviour is to a certain extent erratic, being influenced by unpredictable events. The effects of such factors are taken into account by econometricians through the introduction in the relationship being studied of a special random variable, whose nature will be examined in subsequent chapters.

Econometric methods may be classified into two groups: (1) single-equation techniques, which are methods that are applied to one relationship at a time; and (2) simultaneous-equation techniques, which are methods applied to all the relationships of a model simultaneously. In this book we shall develop various methods of measurement of economic phenomena.

Applied econometrics includes the applications of econometric methods to specific branches of economic theory. It examines the problems encountered and the findings of applied research in the fields of demand, supply, production, investment, consumption, and other sectors of economic theory. Applied econometrics involves the application of the tools of theoretical econometrics for the analysis of economic phenomena and forecasting economic behaviour.

2. Methodology of Econometric Research

Applied econometric research is concerned with the measurement of the parameters of economic relationships and with the prediction (by means of these parameters) of the values of economic variables.

The relationships of economic theory which can be measured with one or another econometric technique are causal, that is, they are relationships in which some variables are postulated as causes of the variation of other variables. In this sense definitional equations do not require any measurement. For example the equation $Y = C + I + G$ is the mathematical expression of the definition of national income of economic theory. It does not explain the determination of the level of income or the causes of its variations. We stress this point because in many instances researchers tend to 'measure' a relationship which actually is a simple definition and does not express any causal relationship among the variables involved.

In any econometric research we may distinguish four stages.

Stage A. The first step in any econometric research is the specification of the model with which one will attempt the measurement of the phenomenon being analysed. This stage is also known as the formulation of the *maintained hypothesis.*

Stage B. After the formulation of the model one should obtain estimates of its parameters, that is, the second stage includes the estimation of the model by means of the appropriate econometric method. This stage is known as the testing of the maintained hypothesis.

Stage C. Once the model has been estimated, one should proceed with the evaluation of the estimates, that is to say decide on the basis of certain criteria whether the estimates are satisfactory and reliable.

Stage D. The final stage of any econometric research is concerned with the evaluation of the forecasting validity of the model. Estimates are useful because they help in decision making. A model, after the estimation of its parameters, can be used in forecasting the values of economic variables. The econometrician must ascertain how good the forecasts are expected to be, in other words he must test the forecasting power of the model.

Stages A and C are the most important for any econometric research. They require the skills of an economist with experience of the functioning of the economic system. Stages B and D are technical and require knowledge of theoretical econometrics.

In this chapter we will discuss in some detail these four stages of econometric research.

11

2.1. STAGE A. SPECIFICATION OF THE MODEL

The first, and the most important, step the econometrician has to take in attempting the study of any relationship between variables, is to express this relationship in mathematical form, that is to specify the model, with which the economic phenomenon will be explored empirically. This is called the specification of the model or formulation of the *maintained hypothesis*. It involves the determination of: (1) the dependent and explanatory variables which will be included in the model; (2) the *a priori* theoretical expectations about the *sign* and the *size* of the parameters of the function. These *a priori* definitions will be the theoretical criteria on the basis of which the results of the estimation of the model will be evaluated; (3) the mathematical form of the model (number of equations, linear or non-linear form of these equations, etc.).

The specification of the econometric model will be based on economic theory and on any available information relating to the phenomenon being studied. Thus the specification of the model presupposes knowledge of economic theory as well as familiarity with the particular phenomenon being studied. The econometrician must know the general laws of economic theory, and furthermore he must gather any other information relevant to the particular characteristics of the relationship as well as all studies already published on the subject by other research workers.

2.1.1. VARIABLES OF THE MODEL

From the above sources of information the econometrician will be able to make a list of the variables (regressors) which might influence the dependent variable (regressand). Economic theory indicates the general factors which affect the dependent variable in any particular case. For example, suppose that the econometrician wants to study the demand for a particular product. The first source of his information is the static theory of demand which suggests that the determinants of the demand for any product are its price, the prices of other goods (mainly of substitutes and complements), the level of the income of consumers, and their preferences. On the basis of this information we may write the demand function in the general form

$$Q_z = f(P_z, P_0, Y, T)$$

where Q_z = quantity demanded of commodity z
   P_z = price of commodity z
   P_0 = price of other commodities
   Y = consumers' income
   T = a suitable measure of consumers' tastes.

Apart from general economic theory, studies already published in any particular field provide additional knowledge about the factors determining the dependent variable. Thus published results of econometric research on the demand for various products provide evidence that, apart from the above four factors suggested by economic theory, the demand is affected by other factors such as the level of income earned in previous periods $(Y_{t-1}, Y_{t-2}, \text{etc.})$, the taxation and credit policy of the government (G), and the distribution of income (Y_d). Thus the demand function becomes

$$Q_z = f(P_z, P_{0,,}Y, T, Y_{t-1}, Y_{t-2}, G, Y_d)$$

Finally the information about the individual conditions in a particular case, and the actual behaviour of the economic agents (consumers or producers) implements the knowledge of theory and of applied research. If we study the demand for exports of a product, in addition to the above factors we must take into account dumping policies, tariffs of country-buyers, foreign currency restrictions in these countries, etc.

It should be clear that the number of variables to be included in the model depends on the nature of the phenomenon being studied and the purpose of the research. Usually we introduce explicitly in the function only the most important (four or five) explanatory variables. The influence of less important factors is taken into account by the introduction in the model of a random variable, usually denoted by u. The values of this random variable cannot be actually observed like the values of the other explanatory variables. We thus have to guess at the pattern of the values of u by making some plausible assumptions about their distribution. The statement of the assumptions about the random variable is part of the specification of the model (see Chapter 4).

2.1.2. SIGNS AND MAGNITUDE OF PARAMETERS

The same sources of knowledge — theory, other applied research and information about possible special features of the phenomenon being studied — will contain suggestions about the *sign* of the parameters and possibly of their *size*.

For example assume that we investigate the demand function for a given product

$$Q_z = b_0 + b_1 P_z + b_2 P_j + b_3 Y + u$$

We should expect, according to the general theory of demand, the following findings.

The parameter b_1 is expected to have a negative sign, given the 'law of demand' which postulates an inverse relationship between quantity demanded and price.

The parameter b_3 related to the variable Y is expected to appear with a positive sign, since income and quantity demanded are positively related, except in the case of inferior goods.

The parameter b_2 of the variable P_j is expected to have a positive sign if commodity j is a substitute of commodity z, and a negative sign if the two commodities are complementary.

As regards the magnitude of the parameters we note the following. The b's are either elasticities, propensities or other marginal magnitudes of economic theory, or are components of these parameters. In a linear demand function, such as the one in our example, the b's are components of the relevant elasticities.[1] Now the theory of demand suggests that the size of the elasticities depends mainly on the nature of the commodity and the existence of substitutes. If the product is a 'necessity', price and income elasticities are expected to be small, if it is a 'luxury' these elasticities will be high assuming that the commodity has no close substitutes. The cross elasticity of demand for commodity z with respect to the price of commodity j, depends on how close a substitute or a complement commodity j is with respect to commodity z. If j is a very close substitute of commodity z the cross elasticity of demand will be very high. Thus, given the units of measurement of the variables, the b's are expected to assume values which would give rise to elasticities of the appropriate theoretical magnitude.

As another example let us examine the simple version of the consumption function which states that consumption (C) depends on the level of income (Y)

$$C = b_0 + b_1 Y + u$$

In this function the coefficient b_1 is the marginal propensity to consume and should be positive with a value less than unity ($0 < MPC < 1$), while the constant intercept (b_0) of the function is expected to be positive. The meaning of this positive constant is that even when income is zero, consumption will assume a positive value: people will spend past savings, will borrow or find other means for covering their needs.

To decide in any particular case whether a good is normal or inferior, a 'necessity' or a 'luxury' item, whether it has substitutes and how close these substitutes are, one should know the conditions of the market being studied. For example a television set is a 'necessity' in the United Kingdom, while it is a 'luxury' product in under-developed countries.

Determination of the variables to be included or excluded from a function may be viewed as imposition of zero and non-zero restrictions on the parameters of the variables of the model. That is, once we decide to exclude a variable from a function we actually impose the restriction that its parameter be zero in that function. Similarly if we decide to include a variable in the function this means that we impose the restriction that its parameter assumes a value different from zero. Of course the measurement of the relation may show that some of the included in the function variables are not significant, in which case we may modify our initial hypothesis by excluding these variables. Thus the number of variables to be initially included in the model depends on the nature of the economic phenomenon being studied, while the number of variables which will finally be retained in the model depends on whether the parameter estimates related to the variables pass the economic, statistical and econometric criteria, which we will discuss below.

2.1.3. MATHEMATICAL FORM OF THE MODEL

Economic theory may or may not indicate the precise mathematical form of the relationships, or the number of equations to be included in the economic

[1] See pp. 66–7.

model. For example, the theory of demand does not determine whether the demand for a particular commodity should be studied with a single-equation model or with a system of simultaneous equations. Furthermore economic theory does not say whether the demand function will be of a linear or a nonlinear form; demand curves are drawn as straight downward-sloping lines or as curves. However, demand theory contains some information about the mathematical form of a demand function. Static demand theory is based on the assumption that the behaviour of consumers is rational and that they do not suffer from money illusion. This assumption implies that if all prices and incomes change by the same proportion, the rational consumer will not change his consumption patterns, that is he will not change his demand for the various commodities. Thus the demand function should assume a mathematical form which will take into account the rationality assumption of demand theory. In technical jargon we say that the demand function is homogeneous of degree zero. (There are various ways for expressing the rationality assumption of the theory of demand. See L. R. Klein, *An Introduction to Econometrics,* Prentice-Hall International, London 1962, pp. 19–24.)

In most cases economic theory does not explicitly state the mathematical form of economic relationships. It is often helpful to plot the actual data on two-dimensional diagrams, taking two variables at a time (the dependent and each one of the explanatory variables in turn). In most cases the examination of such scatter diagrams throws some light on the form of the function and helps in deciding upon the choice of the mathematical form of the relationship connecting the economic variables. In view of the vagueness of economic theory in this respect it has become a usual practice for the econometrician to experiment with various forms (linear, nonlinear) and then choose from among the various results the ones that are judged as the most satisfactory on the basis of certain criteria which will be discussed below.

Nonlinearities are usually taken into account by a polynomial form, for example

$$Y = b_0 + b_1 X + b_2 X^2 + u$$

or

$$Y = b_0 + b_1 X + b_2 X^2 + b_3 X^3 + u$$

and so on. The number of nonlinear terms which will be retained in the function is decided upon tests of their significance (see Chapter 8).

We should finally note that economic theory does not explicitly state whether a particular phenomenon should be studied with a single equation model or with a multi-equation model. It is the econometrician who must decide whether the phenomenon being studied can be adequately described by a single equation or by a system of simultaneous equations. If an economic relationship is complex and we attempt to approximate it by a single-equation model, we are almost certainly bound to obtain incorrect estimates of the parameters. Taking into account the complexity of the real world one should hardly expect to study economic phenomena satisfactorily by using single-equation models. Yet an important part of applied econometric research is based on single-equation models and it measures their coefficients by single-equation techniques. This may not be the appropriate procedure, as we shall later see. We note here that the number of equations, that is the size of the model, depends on the complexity of the phenomenon being studied, the purpose for which the model is estimated (forecasting, or obtaining accurate individual values for particular coefficients), the availability of data and the computational facilities available to the research worker. In some cases the model is simplified by dropping some of its equations for lack of data, money or time.

As a final remark we note that the specification is the most important and the most difficult stage of any econometric research. It is often the weakest point of most econometric applications. Some of the reasons for incorrect specification of economic models are easy to see: (1) the imperfection, looseness of statements in economic theories; (2) the limitation on our knowledge of the factors which are operative in any particular case; (3) the formidable obstacles presented by data requirements in the estimation of large models. The most common *errors of specification* are the omission of some variables from the functions, the omission of some equations and the mistaken mathematical form of the functions. It should be noted that almost all the econometric methods are sensitive to errors of specification, that is the estimates of the coefficients obtained from most econometric methods will be incorrect or unreliable if the model is not correctly specified. (See Theil, *Economic Forecasts and Policy*, North-Holland, Amsterdam 1965, pp. 204—40. See also Chapter 11.)

2.2. STAGE B. ESTIMATION OF THE MODEL

After the model has been specified (formulated) the econometrician must proceed with its estimation, in other words he must obtain numerical estimates of the coefficients of the model.

The estimation of the model is a purely technical stage which requires knowledge of the various econometric methods, their assumptions and the economic implications for the estimates of the parameters.

The stage of estimation includes the following steps.

(1) Gathering of statistical observations (data) on the variables included in the model.

(2) Examination of the identification conditions of the function in which we are interested.

(3) Examination of the aggregation problems involved in the variables of the function.

(4) Examination of the degree of correlation between the explanatory variables, that is, examination of the degree of multicollinearity.

(5) Choice of the appropriate econometric technique for the estimation of the function and critical examination of the assumptions of the chosen technique and of their economic implications for the estimates of the coefficients.

We will attempt to give some idea of the problems involved in each of the above steps, but their full understanding will be possible only after reading the whole book.

2.2.1. GATHERING DATA FOR THE ESTIMATION OF THE MODEL

The data used in the estimation of a model may be of various types.

Time series

Time series data give information about the numerical values of variables from period to period. For example the data on gross national income in the period 1950–65 forms a time series on the variable 'income'.

Cross-section data

These data give information on the variables concerning individual agents (consumers or producers) at a given point of time. For example a cross-section sample of consumers is a sample of family budgets showing expenditures on various commodities by each family, as well as information on family income, family composition and other demographic, social or financial characteristics. Cross-section data may also refer to aggregate variables of different countries (or other regional entities) referring to the same time. Such data are usually called cross-nation (or cross-country) samples and are used for international comparative studies.

Panel data

These are repeated surveys of a single (cross-section) sample in different periods of time. They record the behaviour of the same set of individual micro-economic units over time.

Engineering data

These data give information about the technical requirements of the method of production (productive processes) employed (by a firm or an industry, or the economy as a whole) for producing a certain commodity. These are collected from the producers of the commodity and are used in studies of production (production functions, input–output relationships, etc.). For example, we can obtain information from the steel firms about the engineering characteristics of their method of steel production and the volume of their output. This information will enable us to find the proportions in which the several methods are employed, and thus we can make a close approximation to the relationship between steel output and input requirements.

Legislation and other institutional regulations

Some models can be estimated from direct information about the nature of the relationship involved. This is particularly true for institutional functions, like tax functions. For example, in most countries the taxation of cigarette consumption is determined by law. Taking into account the various tax coefficients for the various brands of tobacco products as well as the volume of consumption of each tobacco brand, it is possible to estimate the tax burden on tobacco. Suppose that this information shows that tobacco is taxed, on the average, at 65 per cent of its retail value. The tax revenue function from tobacco would be related to expenditure on tobacco by the function

$$T = 0.65 \, C$$

where T = government revenue from tobacco consumption
        C = expenditure on tobacco manufactures.

This is a function 'estimated' by reference to the information of the tax legislation; it is an 'institutional' function.

Data constructed by the econometrician: Dummy variables

In many cases some factors affecting the dependent variable cannot be measured in any of the above conventional data, because they are qualitative factors. For example profession, religion, sex, are factors affecting the consumption of particular items, like bread, meat, cosmetics. Such qualitative attributes can be approximated by the introduction in the function of 'dummy variables', that is, indexes which we construct with considerable arbitrariness, but in a way relevant to the influence of the factor concerned. For example if we study the demand for bread with cross-section data, the factor 'sex' could be represented by a dummy variable, which might be assigned the value of one when the individual is a male and the value of zero when the consumer is a female. In this case the coefficient of the dummy variable will be positive if in the real world females consume less bread. As another example suppose we want to estimate the demand for petrol from a cross-section sample. The main determinant of the demand in this case will be the ownership of a car. We may approximate the factor "car-ownership" with a dummy variable which would take the value of zero if an individual consumer does not own a car and the value of unity if the consumer does own a car.

It should be noted that various problems arise from the use of the one or the other type of data for the estimation of a given econometric model. For example, the meaning of the estimates of the coefficients is different according to whether we use time series or cross-section data. Furthermore, in some cases there is need for pooling together various types of data for the estimation of a model. Such problems will be discussed in detail in subsequent chapters.

2.2.2. EXAMINATION OF THE IDENTIFICATION CONDITION OF THE FUNCTION

Identification is the procedure by which we attempt to establish that the coefficients which we shall estimate by the application of some appropriate econometric technique are actually the true coefficients of the function in which we are interested. This may sound strange at this stage, but there are cases in which we may obtain estimates for which we cannot be certain as to which function they belong: they may either belong to the function on which our interest is focused, or they may belong to some other function which happens to have the same statistical form (that is it has the same variables as the one which we are studying), or they may be some mixture of coefficients belonging to various functions. For example, suppose we want to estimate the demand function for a product for a period over which incomes and other factors except price have remained constant. Thus both the demand and the supply will depend on the price of the commodity

$$Q_d = f(P) \quad \text{and} \quad Q_s = f(P)$$

Assume that we wish to estimate the demand function by using time series of market data. Such data record the quantity demanded at a certain price; but the quantity bought is at the same time the quantity sold ($D \equiv S$) at the market price P. Thus when using the recorded market data on Q and P we do not know whether we are estimating the parameters of the demand function or of the supply function. There are some rules by means of which we may establish identification of the coefficients of a function. These rules are analysed in Chapter 15. We note here that the job of identification is most important since it determines whether a relationship, although theoretically plausible, can be statistically estimated or not.

2.2.3. EXAMINATION OF THE AGGREGATION PROBLEMS OF THE FUNCTION

Aggregation problems arise from the fact that we use aggregative variables in our functions. Such aggregative variables may involve:

(a) *Aggregation over individuals.* For example, total income is the sum of individual incomes; total output is the sum of the output of individual firms, and so on.

(b) *Aggregation over commodities.* We may aggregate over the quantities of various commodities (using appropriate quantity indexes), or over the prices of a group of commodities (using some appropriate price index). For example, if we want to estimate the demand function for 'food', with explanatory variables 'total income', 'the price of food', and 'the price of other commodities', all variables will include a certain level of aggregation.

(c) *Aggregation over time periods.* In many cases statistical sources publish data which refer to a time period different (longer or shorter) than the unit time period required in theory for the functional relationship among the economic variables. For example, the production of most manufacturing commodities is completed in a period shorter than a year. If we use annual figures there may be some error in the coefficients of the production function.

(d) *Spatial aggregation.* For example the population of towns, counties, regions; or, product of regions, of the whole country, of the world as a whole, and so on.

The above sources of aggregation create various complications which may impart some 'aggregation bias' in the estimates of the coefficients. It is important to examine the possibility of such sources of error before estimating the function, and to adjust the aggregative variables or the model accordingly whenever possible. (See R. G. D. Allen, *Mathematical Economics*, Macmillan, London, 1956, chapter 20. Also L. R. Klein, *An Introduction to Econometrics*, Prentice-Hall International, London 1962, pp. 64–6, 86–7, 104–5.)

2.2.4. EXAMINATION OF THE DEGREE OF CORRELATION AMONG THE EXPLANATORY VARIABLES

Most economic variables are correlated, in the sense that they tend to change simultaneously during the various phases of economic activity. Income, employment, consumption, investment, exports, imports, taxes, tend to grow in booms and decline in periods of depression. Thus a certain degree of multicollinearity is inherent in the economic variables due to the growth and technological progress. If, however, the degree of collinearity is high, the results (measurements) obtained from econometric applications may be seriously impaired and their use may be greatly misleading, because in these conditions it may not be computationally possible to separate the influence of each one explanatory variable. For example, prices and wages tend to increase together. If we include both these variables in the set of explanatory variables in a demand function, it is most probable that the estimated values of the coefficients will be inaccurate and will show a distorted influence of each individual explanatory variable on demand. The problem of multicollinearity is discussed in Chapter 11.

2.2.5. CHOICE OF THE APPROPRIATE ECONOMETRIC TECHNIQUE

The coefficients of economic relationships may be estimated by various methods which may be classified in two main groups:

(i) *Single-equation techniques.* These are techniques which are applied to one equation at a time. The most important are: the Classical Least Squares or Ordinary Least Squares method, the Indirect Least Squares or Reduced-form technique; the Two-stage Least Squares method, the Limited Information Maximum Likelihood method and various methods of Mixed Estimation.

(ii) *Simultaneous-equation techniques.* These are techniques which are applied to all the equations of a system at once, and give estimates of the coefficients of all the functions simultaneously. The most important are the Three-stage Least Squares method and the Full Information Maximum Likelihood technique.

Which technique will be chosen in any particular case depends on many factors, such as: (a) The nature of the relationship and its identification condition. If we study a simple phenomenon which can be satisfactorily approximated with a single-equation model the method of ordinary least squares will usually be chosen for its considerable advantages (see Chapter 4). If, however, the particular function in which we are interested belongs to a system of simultaneous equations we may use any one of the above techniques, depending primarily on the identification condition of the function. If the function is identified, as we shall see in Chapter 15, we have ample choice among various of the above techniques. Choosing among them we shall take into consideration some of the following factors. (b) The properties of the estimates of the coefficients obtained from each technique. In Chapter 6 we shall see that a 'good' estimate should possess the properties of unbiasedness, consistency, efficiency, sufficiency or a combination of such properties. If one method gives an estimate which possesses more of these desirable characteristics than any other estimate from other methods, then the former technique is preferred to the others. We shall return to this point again. (c) However, which of these desirable characteristics is the most important, depends on the purpose of the econometric research. It is usually argued that if the purpose of the model is forecasting, the property of minimum variance is very important, bias being less important in predicting the values of economic variables; but if the purpose of the research worker is analysis or policy-making, in which case he is interested in obtaining good estimates of individual coefficients, the degree of bias becomes crucial. (d) In some cases the simplicity of the method is used as a criterion of choice: a method may be preferred to another because the first involves simpler computations and has less data requirements than the other. (e) Finally, the time and cost requirements of the various methods are often important criteria for the choice of the technique for the estimation of the parameters of a model.

From the above discussion we conclude that the estimation of a model can be managed with several econometric methods, but in most cases only one would be, theoretically, the most appropriate for the problem being studied. However, the theoretically most appropriate econometric technique may not be applicable due to non-availability or to defects (e.g. multicollinearity) of the relevant statistical data and other information. Thus it becomes necessary to choose another less suitable technique, given the data limitations. In most empirical research data-limitations restrict seriously the possibilities of employing the theoretically most suitable econometric technique and render inevitable the use of a less appropriate method. In this case one should interpret the results of the estimation taking into account the effects and possible errors introduced into the estimates by the use of the less appropriate technique.

For example the demand function for most goods should be estimated with a complete model which would take into account the whole working mechanism of the market of this product. There should be included in this model a demand equation, a supply equation, a price equation as well as other relevant equations (tax functions) because it is common knowledge that in all markets the quantities demanded, the quantities supplied, the price and the taxation policy are interdependent, each one of these factors influencing and at the same time being influenced by the others. However, for simplicity, econometricians tend to use single-equation demand models, sacrificing to a certain extent the accuracy of the estimates in order to facilitate the estimation. Taking into account the interdependence of quantity and price, however, it is obvious that the estimates will include some error, which should be taken into account when interpreting the results of the calaculations.

After choosing the econometric technique for the estimation of his model, the econometrician should state explicitly the assumptions of this technique and examine their implications for the estimates of the parameters. Strictly speaking the assumptions relate (a) to the form of the distribution of the random variable u and (b) to the relationships among the explanatory variables. They are assumptions concerning the variables of the model and not the particular method which is applied for the estimation of the model. However, they are usually stated as assumptions of the particular technique. In any case the explicit statement of these assumptions is a very important task; if these assumptions are violated, either the estimates of the parameters will be biased, or it will not be possible to assess their reliability, or both. On the basis of the assumptions of each method the econometrician determines the econometric criteria, which will be used for the evaluation of the results of the computations (see section 2.3 below).

2.2.5. 'EXPERIMENTAL APPROACH' VERSUS 'ORTHODOX APPROACH'

In applying econometric methods for the estimation of economic models two approaches have been developed, the 'orthodox approach' and the 'experimental approach'.

The 'orthodox' econometric approach consists in formulating a mathematical model on *a priori* theoretical grounds, and attempting to measure the parameters of that model on the basis of the best available data. Data deficiencies might lead to minor modifications of the model before it could be tested statistically, but broadly speaking, having established his model the 'orthodox' econometrician would tend to stick to it, despite unfavourable statistical results. In other words, following the orthodox approach of econometric research one would proceed as follows:

(1) Collect all information, from theory or from practice, relevant to the phenomenon being studied.

(2) Decide on *a priori* reasoning on the particular mathematical expression of the model.

(3) Estimate the model with the available statistical data.

The model constructed on *a priori* assumptions is considered by the orthodox econometrician as the only true model, irrespective of the results obtained. If these results are 'unfavourable', that is the signs and size of the parameters do not conform to *a priori* knowledge, the econometrician will not reject the model, but would try to explain the results by attributing them to data deficiencies mainly. The initial model is considered as 'correct' and would not be revised.

It is obvious that such a rigid approach to applied econometric research is not commendable. First of all in order to stick to an initial formulation of the model, one should be certain that he commands perfect knowledge of all the aspects of the phenomenon being analysed. Such a pretention would be outrageous, given the complexity of economic phenomena and the loose exposition of economic theory. Furthermore, one may pretend to have followed the orthodox approach, while in reality one has experimented to a considerable extent, before settling for the model, which one may present afterwards as being compiled by the most orthodox econometric methodology.

Today most econometric research is attempted by the experimental approach. Experimentation with various models has been facilitated by the expansion of the use of electronic computers. In following the experimental approach one starts with simple models containing a small number of equations and variables. These models are formulated on *a priori* considerations, like the models of the orthodox approach, but they are not considered as being rigid. On the contrary, they are modified gradually, on the basis of the statistical evidence accruing from the computations. The econometrician starts from a simple model, which on *a priori* grounds is believed to contain the most important factors of the relationship being analysed. Then additional variables are added, and perhaps the formulation is given a more complex appearance (non-linear forms, etc.). In other words the econometrician experiments with various theoretically plausible models including various variables and/or various mathematical formulations.

The experimental approach combines the theoretical considerations (*a priori* criteria) with the empirical observations available and is designed to extract the maximum of information from the available data. As calculations are carried out by adding other explanatory variables in various combinations, or by adding other equations, or by changing the mathematical form of the functions, or by using alternative econometric methods for the estimation of the models, the econometrician is able to observe the effects of such changes in an attempt to achieve the best model, the best explanation of the phenomenon being analysed. Each time a new variable (or any other change) is introduced because it is thought to improve the explanation of the phenomenon, three statistical effects on the model will normally result.

(1) The new variable (or change) will have some effect, minor or major, on the systematic part of the relation. In other words, the new variable will or will not be shown to explain a significant part of the variation in the dependent variable.

(2) It will affect the non-systematic (residual) part of the relationship, for example because of errors of measurement in this new variable.

(3) It will have some minor or major effect upon the coefficients of the variables already included in the equation (model). We should notice that if an important variable is omitted, not only will the overall fit of the relation be worse, but the coefficients of the included variables may well be distorted from the values which would be obtained from a complete analysis. In this case the introduction of the new variable will 'correct' the value of the coefficients of the other explanatory variables.[1]

It is obvious from the above discussion that the experimental approach to econometric analysis has more advantages in comparison to the orthodox approach. In particular it renders possible a better use of the available data and information. The experimentation may involve models with (a) various variables,

---

[1] See R. Stone, 'The Analysis of Market Demand', *Journal of the Royal Statistical Society*, Great Britain 1945, vol. CVIII. See also Chapter 11.8.

(b) various mathematical forms, (c) various numbers of equations, (d) various econometric methods. The process of choosing between the various models involves both the *a priori* and economic-theoretical considerations of the 'orthodox' econometrician, and also a sifting of the statistical evidence given by the experimental approach.

We should note that both the alternative lines of approach have a certain degree of arbitrariness: the orthodox approach makes *a priori* assumptions, while the second makes *a posteriori* choice. What matters is that the investigator should give a full description of his method of research, so that one can judge how much reliability can be attached to the results obtained.[1]

Some authors have criticised the experimental approach on the grounds that (a) the degree of subjective judgement it involves is higher than in the orthodox approach, and (b) the use of the same sample of data for the estimation of various models implies a loss of degrees of freedom which is overlooked in most cases. The meaning of 'degrees of freedom' is discussed briefly in Appendix I.

We agree that the experimental approach is not *the* perfect approach. There is a considerable realism in the argument that if an econometrician is clever and persistent he can always find an equation that fits the data satisfactorily. What is worse, he may argue that his equation is theoretically plausible, i.e. he may attempt to revise economic theory on the basis of his results, a procedure which may not always be justifiable.

The argument of loss of degrees of freedom is often referred to as '*the problem of data mining*'. (See M. Friedman, in 'Conference on Business Cycles', Universities NBER (New York, 1951), pp. 107–14. Also C. F. Christ, *Econometric Models and Methods,* Wiley 1966, New York, pp. 8–9.) This argument is based on purely statistical considerations and runs as follows. The reliability of the estimates is judged on the basis of statistical tests of significance (discussed in Chapter 5), which assume that the maintained hypothesis (the model which we test against the data) is known with certainty. In the experimental approach the maintained hypothesis is not known with certainty, but is chosen because it gives the best fit to the available sample data. This decision implies that in the hypothetical repeating sampling procedure on which the classical tests of significance are based, we use not all possible samples, but only those samples that fit the data well: in this way we introduce a non-random factor in the process for selecting samples, which restricts our freedom of choice. This loss of degrees of freedom should be taken into account in order to adjust the test procedure, otherwise the tests will not be valid. In most cases, however, the appropriately adjusted statistical test is not known. Thus researchers tend mostly to ignore the problem completely. Some writers have suggested a new method of research which incorporates actual numerical *a priori* knowledge in the model, a fact that reduces the need for experimentation to a great extent.

[1] See A. Koutsoyiannis, *An Econometric Study of the Leaf Tobacco Market of Greece,* 1962, Papadimitropoulous Press, pp. 8–9.

This method is known as 'mixed estimation' and will be discussed in Chapter 17. It is the author's belief that the 'data mining' problem is not important for econometrics. Statistical considerations may become highly restrictive for the purposes of econometrics. Some 'loose' interpretation of statistical rules is at times essential if econometrics is to be helpful in testing economic theory and in measuring economic relationships.

2.3. STAGE C. EVALUATION OF ESTIMATES

After the estimation of the model the econometrician must proceed with the evaluation of the results of the calculations, that is with the determination of the reliability of these results. The evaluation consists of deciding whether the estimates of the parameters are theoretically meaningful and statistically satisfactory. For this purpose we use various criteria which may be classified into three groups. Firstly, economic *a priori* criteria, which are determined by economic theory. Secondly, statistical criteria, determined by statistical theory. Thirdly, econometric criteria, determined by econometric theory.

2.3.1. ECONOMIC *'A PRIORI'* CRITERIA

These are determined by the principles of economic theory and refer to the sign and the size of the parameters of economic relationships.

As we have already mentioned, the coefficients of economic models are the 'constants' of economic theory: elasticities, marginal values, multipliers, propensities, etc. Economic theory defines the signs of these coefficients and in broad lines their magnitude. In econometric jargon we say that economic theory imposes restrictions on the signs and values of the parameters of economic relationships.

For example, let us examine the liquidity preference function of an economy. The Keynesian theory of liquidity preference postulates that the main determinants of the demand for money are the level of income (Y) and the rate of interest (i). This theory suggests that there is a positive relationship between the demand for money (M) and the level of income: the larger the income, the larger the amount of money held in the form of cash balances, because the larger the income, the larger the amount required to carry out the transactions. On the contrary, there is a negative relationship between the demand for money and the rate of interest: the higher the rate of interest, the lower the amount of money demanded (to hold in idle balances), because (a) the loss from not lending the money is high, and (b) because a high i implies a low price of bonds and other securities, a fact that makes the purchase of such securities attractive in the expectation of reselling them at a higher price later and thus having capital gains. The liquidity preference function may be expressed in the mathematical form

$$M = b_0 + b_1 Y + b_2 i + u$$

On the basis of the above theory the *a priori* criteria to be used for the evaluation of the estimates of the liquidity preference function may be stated as follows.

The sign of b_1 is expected to be positive while the sign of b_2 is expected to be negative. As regards the magnitude of these parameters not much information is provided by the theory of liquidity preference. However, knowledge of the habits of firms and individuals of an economy may help in setting *a priori* limits to the sizes of b_1 and b_2.

If the estimates of the parameters turn up with signs or size not conforming to economic theory, they should be rejected, unless there is good reason to believe that in the particular instance the principles of economic theory do not hold. In such cases the reasons for accepting the estimates with the 'wrong' sign or magnitude must be stated clearly. However, in most cases the wrong sign or size of the parameters may be attributed to deficiencies of the empirical data employed for the estimation of the model.[1] In other words either the observations are not representative of the relationship, or their number is inadequate, or some assumptions of the method employed are violated. In general, if the *a priori* theoretical criteria are not satisfied, the estimate should be considered unsatisfactory.

2.3.2. STATISTICAL CRITERIA: FIRST-ORDER TESTS

These are determined by statistical theory and aim at the evaluation of the statistical reliability of the estimates of the parameters of the model. The most widely used statistical criteria are the *correlation coefficient* and *the standard deviation* (or standard error) *of the estimates.* These criteria will be explained in subsequent chapters, but a few comments are appropriate here.

The estimates of the parameters of the model are obtained from a sample of observations of the variables included in the relationship. The sampling theory of statistics prescribes some tests for finding out how accurate these estimates are.

The square of the correlation coefficient is a statistical number, computed from the data of the sample, which shows the percentage of the total variation of the dependent variable being explained by the changes of the explanatory variables. It is a measure of the extent to which the explanatory variables are responsible for the changes in the dependent variable of the relationship (see Chapter 5).

The standard deviation or standard error of the estimates is a measure of the dispersion of the estimates around the true parameter. The larger the standard error of a parameter, the less reliable it is, and vice versa (see Chapter 5 and Appendix I).

It should be noted that the statistical criteria are secondary only to the *a priori* theoretical criteria. The estimates of the parameters should be rejected in general if they happen to have the 'wrong' sign (or size) even though the correlation coefficient is high, or the standard errors suggest that the estimates are statistically significant. In such cases the parameters, though statistically satisfactory, are theoretically implausible, that is to say they make no sense on the basis of the *a priori* theoretical-economic criteria.

[1] See, for example, J. Johnston, *Statistical Cost Analysis*, McGraw-Hill, 1962, for a discussion of the data problems in estimating cost functions.

The importance of the statistical criteria in evaluating the results of the estimates of the coefficients is further discussed in Chapter 5.

2.3.3. ECONOMETRIC CRITERIA: SECOND-ORDER TESTS

These are set by the theory of econometrics and aim at the investigation of whether the assumptions of the econometric method employed are satisfied or not in any particular case. The econometric criteria serve as second-order tests (as tests of the statistical tests); in other words they determine the reliability of the statistical criteria, and in particular of the standard errors of the parameter estimates. They help us establish whether the estimates have the desirable properties of unbiasedness, consistency, etc. (see Chapter 6).

If the assumptions of the econometric method applied by the investigator are not satisfied, either the estimates of the parameters cease to possess some of their desirable properties (for example become biased) or the statistical criteria lose their validity and become unreliable for the determination of the significance of these estimates.

We said that the econometric criteria aim at the detection of the violation or validity of the assumptions of the econometric method employed in any particular application. The assumptions of the various econometric techniques differ and hence there are various econometric criteria for each method. These will be discussed in connection with the various techniques. Some examples may illustrate the meaning of the econometric criteria.

All econometric techniques listed in page 20 have the common assumption that the values of the random variable included in the model are not connected one to the other. This is known as the assumption of non-autocorrelated random disturbances (see Chapters 4 and 10). If this assumption is violated the standard errors of the parameters are not a reliable criterion for the evaluation of the statistical significance of the coefficients. To test the validity of the assumption of non-autocorrelated disturbances, we may compute a statistic, known as the 'Durbin–Watson d statistic', from the names of the inventors (see Chapter 10). The 'd' statistic is an econometric criterion used in the evaluation of the results of the estimates.

Another example is the 'test' aiming at establishing the identification conditions of a relationship. All econometric methods assume that the function to which they are applied is identified, since otherwise the estimation of the coefficients is meaningless. The application of the formal rules of identification, which will be developed in Chapter 15, consists of an econometric test, aiming at the detection of the fulfilment of one of the basic assumptions of all econometric techniques.

From the above discussion it should be clear that the evaluation of the results obtained from the estimation of the model, is a very complex procedure. The econometrician must use all the above criteria, economic, statistical and econometric, before he can accept or reject the estimates.

When the assumptions of an econometric technique are not satisfied it is customary to respecify the model (e.g. introduce new variables or omit some others, transform the original variables, etc.) so as to produce a new form which meets the assumptions of the econometric theory. We then proceed with re-estimation of the new model and with re-application of all the tests. This process of re-specification of the model and re-estimation will continue until the results pass all the economic, statistical and econometric tests. (See E. Kane, *Economic Statistics and Econometrics,* Harper & Row, International edition, 1969, pp. 352–3.)

2.4. STAGE D. EVALUATION OF THE FORECASTING POWER OF THE ESTIMATED MODEL

We have said that the objective of any econometric research is to obtain good numerical estimates of the coefficients of economic relationships and to use them for the prediction of the values of economic variables. Forecasting is one of the prime aims of econometric research.

Before using an estimated model for forecasting the value of the dependent variable we must assess by some way or another the predictive power of the model. It is conceivably possible that the model is economically meaningful and statistically and econometrically correct for the sample period for which the model has been estimated, yet it may very well not be suitable for forecasting due, for example, to rapid change in the structural parameters of the relationship in the real world.

The final stage of any applied econometric research is the investigation of the stability of the estimates, their sensitivity to changes in the size of the sample. We must establish whether the estimated function performs adequately outside the sample of data, whose 'average' variation it represents. Extra-sample performance is an important and independent test of the results obtained by applying an econometric technique. It is a test independent of the statistical and econometric tests applied in the previous stage.

One way of establishing the forecasting power of a model is to use the estimates of the model for a period not included in the sample. The estimated value (forecast value) is compared with the actual (realised) magnitude of the relevant dependent variable. Usually there will be a difference between the actual and the forecast value of the variable, which is tested with the aim of establishing whether it is (statistically) significant. If after conducting the relevant test of significance, we find that the difference between the realised value of the dependent variable and that estimated from the model is statistically significant, we conclude that the forecasting power of the model, its extra-sample performance, is poor.

Another way of establishing the stability of the estimates and the performance of the model outside the sample of data from which it has been estimated, is to re-estimate the function with an expanded sample, that is a sample including additional observations. The original estimates will normally differ from the new estimates. The difference is tested for statistical significance with appropriate methods. Such tests will be developed in Chapters 8 and 20.

There may be various reasons for a model's poor forecasting performance. (a) The values of the explanatory variables used in the forecast may not be accurate. (b) The estimates of the coefficients ($\hat{b}$'s) may be poor, due to deficiencies of the sample data. (c) The estimates are 'good' for the period of the sample, but the structural background conditions of the model may have changed from the period that was used as the basis for the estimation of the model, and therefore the old estimates are not 'good' for forecasting. In this event the whole model needs re-estimation before it can be used for prediction.

We shall discuss the problems of the forecasting performance of estimated models in Chapter 20, but for the moment we give a simplified example of the forecasting procedure. Suppose that we estimate the demand function for a given commodity with a single equation model using time series data for the period 1950–68, as follows

$$\hat{Q}_t = 100 + 5 \ Y_t - 30 \ P_t$$

This equation is then used for 'forecasting' the demand of the commodity in the year 1970, a period outside the sample data.

Given $Y_{1970} = £1000$ and $P_{1970} = 5$ shillings

$$\hat{Q}_t = 100 + 5 \ (1000) - 30 \ (5) = 4,950 \text{ tons}$$

If the actual demand for this commodity in 1970 is 4,500 tons, there is a difference of 450 tons between the estimated from the model and the actual market demand for the product. This difference can be tested for significance by various methods (see Chapters 8 and 20). If it is found significant, we try to find out what are the sources of the error in the forecast, in order to improve the forecasting power of our model.

2.5. DESIRABLE PROPERTIES OF AN ECONOMETRIC MODEL

An econometric model is a model whose parameters have been estimated with some appropriate econometric technique.

The 'goodness' of an econometric model is judged customarily according to the following desirable properties.

(1) *Theoretical plausibility*. The model should be compatible with the postulates of economic theory. It must describe adequately the economic phenomena to which it relates.

(2) *Explanatory ability*. The model should be able to explain the observations of the actual world. It must be consistent with the observed behaviour of the economic variables whose relationship it determines.

(3) *Accuracy of the estimates of the parameters*. The estimates of the coefficients should be accurate in the sense that they should approximate as best as possible the true parameters of the structural model. The estimates should if possible possess the desirable properties of unbiasedness, consistency and efficiency discussed in Chapter 6.

(4) *Forecasting ability.* The model should produce satisfactory predictions of future values of the dependent (endogenous) variables.

(5) *Simplicity.* The model should represent the economic relationships with maximum simplicity. The fewer the equations and the simpler their mathematical form, the better the model is considered, *ceteris paribus* (that is to say provided that the other desirable properties are not affected by the simplifications of the model).

The more of the above properties a model possesses, the better it is considered for any practical purpose. (See C. Christ, *Econometric Models and Methods*, pp. 4—6. Also H. Theil, *Economic Forecasts and Policy*, North-Holland, Amsterdam 1965, pp. 204—8.)

EXERCISES

Exercises relating to the material of this chapter are included in Appendix III.

3. Correlation Theory

3.1. GENERAL NOTES

There are various methods for measuring the relationships existing between economic variables. The simplest are correlation analysis and regression analysis. We shall start from correlation analysis, because, although it has serious limitations and throws little light on the nature of the relationship existing between variables, it will make the student familiar with the correlation coefficient, which is an essential statistic of regression analysis.

Correlation may be defined as the degree of relationship existing between two or more variables. The degree of relationship existing between two variables is called simple correlation. The degree of relationship connecting three or more variables is called multiple correlation. In this chapter we shall examine only simple correlation, postponing the discussion on multiple correlation until a later chapter, after the examination of regression analysis. (Actually the multiple correlation coefficient cannot be interpreted without reference to the multiple regression analysis.)

Correlation may be *linear,* when all points (X, Y) on a scatter diagram seem to cluster near a straight line, or *nonlinear,* when all points seem to lie near a curve.

Two variables may have a positive correlation, a negative correlation, or they may be uncorrelated. This holds both for linear and nonlinear correlation.

Positive correlation. Two variables are said to be positively correlated if they tend to change together in the same direction, that is, if they tend to increase or decrease together. Such positive correlation is postulated by economic theory for the quantity of a commodity supplied and its price. When the price increases the quantity supplied increases, and conversely, when price falls the quantity supplied decreases. The scatter diagram of two variables positively correlated appears in figure 3.1. All points in the scatter diagram seem to lie near a line or a curve with a positive slope. If all points lie *on* the line (or curve) the correlation is said to be *perfect positive.*

Negative correlation. Two variables are said to be negatively correlated if they tend to change in the opposite direction: when X increases Y decreases, and vice versa. For example, the quantity of a commodity demanded and its price are negatively correlated. When price increases, demand for the commodity decreases and when price falls demand increases. The scatter diagram appears in figure 3.2; the points cluster around a line (or curve) with a negative slope. If all points lie on the line (or curve) the correlation is said to be *perfect negative.*

No correlation, or, zero correlation. Two variables are uncorrelated when

(a) Positive linear correlation

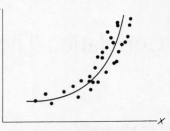

(b) Positive nonlinear correlation

Figure 3.1

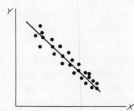

(a) Negative linear correlation

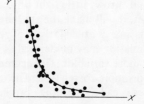

(b) Negative nonlinear correlation

Figure 3.2

they tend to change with no connection to each other. The scatter diagram will
appear as in figure 3.3. The points are dispersed all over the surface of the *XY*
plane. For example one should expect zero correlation between the height of
the inhabitants of a country and the production of steel, or between the weight
of students and the colour of their hair.

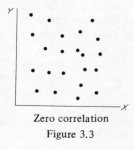

Zero correlation

Figure 3.3

3.2. MEASURE OF LINEAR CORRELATION: THE POPULATION
CORRELATION COEFFICIENT ρ, AND ITS SAMPLE ESTIMATE r

In the light of the above discussion it appears that we can determine the
kind of correlation between two variables by direct observation of the scatter
diagram. In addition, the scatter diagram indicates the *strength* of the relationship between the two variables. If the points lie close to the line, the correlation

is strong. On the other hand a greater dispersion of points about the line implies weaker correlation. Yet inspection of a scatter diagram gives only a rough idea of the relationship between variables X and Y. For a precise quantitive measurement of the degree of correlation between Y and X we use a parameter which is called *the correlation coefficient* and is usually designated by the Greek letter ρ, having as subscripts the variables whose correlation it measures. ρ refers to the correlation of all the values of the population of X and Y. Its estimate from any particular sample (the sample statistic for correlation) is denoted by r with the relevant subscripts. For example if we measure the correlation between X and Y the population correlation coefficient is represented by ρ_{XY} and its sample estimate by r_{XY}. We will establish that the sample correlation coefficient is defined by the formula

$$r_{XY} = \frac{\Sigma x_i y_i}{\sqrt{\Sigma x_i^2} \sqrt{\Sigma y_i^2}} \tag{3.1}$$

where $x_i = X_i - \overline{X}$ and $y_i = Y_i - \overline{Y}$. (Throughout this book lower-case letters will denote deviations from the mean of the variables and capital letters the observed values, unless otherwise stated.)

We will use a simple example from the theory of supply. Economic theory suggests that the quantity of a commodity supplied in the market depends on its price, *ceteris paribus*. When price increases the quantity supplied increases, and *vice versa*, when the market price falls producers offer smaller quantities of their commodity for sale. In other words economic theory postulates that price (X) and quantity supplied (Y) are positively correlated.

Our problem is to define a measure with which we will determine the correlation between price X and quantity supplied Y. Our first task is to gather observations of prices and quantities supplied during a given time period. A set of hypothetical observations appears in table 3.1.

Table 3.1

Time period (in days)	Quantity supplied Y_i (in tons)	Price X_i (in shillings)
1	$Y_1 = 10$	$X_1 = 2$
2	$Y_2 = 20$	$X_2 = 4$
3	$Y_3 = 50$	$X_3 = 6$
4	$Y_4 = 40$	$X_4 = 8$
5	$Y_5 = 50$	$X_5 = 10$
6	$Y_6 = 60$	$X_6 = 12$
7	$Y_7 = 80$	$X_7 = 14$
8	$Y_8 = 90$	$X_8 = 16$
9	$Y_9 = 90$	$X_9 = 18$
10	$Y_{10} = 120$	$X_{10} = 20$
$n = 10$	$\sum_i^n Y_i = 610$	$\sum_i^n X_i = 110$

By plotting the above observations on a rectangular co-ordinate system, we get the scatter diagram of figure 3.4.[1]

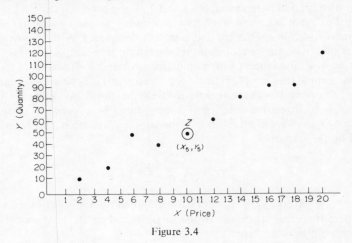

Figure 3.4

Each point of the scatter diagram represents a pair of price—quantity in a given period. For example, point Z represents the pair (X_5, Y_5), that is the price, which is 10 shillings and the quantity supplied, which is 50 tons, during the 5th period. Looking at the diagram we see that the points tend to cluster around a line with a positive slope. This suggests that there exists a positive linear correlation between price and quantity. In order to find the exact measure of correlation we work as follows.

(1) We compute the mean value of the variables

$$\overline{X} = \frac{\Sigma X_i}{n} = \frac{110}{10} = 11 \quad \text{and} \quad \overline{Y} = \frac{\Sigma Y_i}{n} = \frac{610}{10} = 61$$

(2) We draw the perpendiculars $\overline{X}\overline{X}$ and $\overline{Y}\overline{Y}$ from the means, $\overline{X}$ and $\overline{Y}$, thus dividing the area of the rectangular co-ordinate system into four quadrants: I, II, III and IV (figure 3.5).

(3) We next take the deviation of each value of X and Y from their mean and denote this difference by lower case letters

$$x_i = (X_i - \overline{X}) \quad \text{and} \quad y_i = (Y_i - \overline{Y})$$

Examining the deviations of the values of the variables X and Y from their means, we observe that their products can provide a measure of the correlation between the variables X and Y.

[1] It is necessary to start correlation analysis by plotting the sample observations on a scatter diagram, in order to see whether the relationship is linear or nonlinear. Because if the relationship between X and Y exists, but is nonlinear, the formulae which will be developed in the present chapter break-down (see below, page 43).

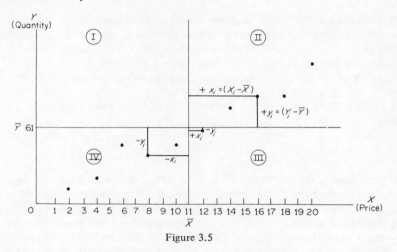

Figure 3.5

(a) In quadrants II and IV the product $(X_i - \overline{X})(Y_i - \overline{Y}) = x_i y_i$ is positive, because both deviations x_i and y_i have the same sign, both being either positive or negative.

(b) In quadrants I and III the product $(X_i - \overline{X})(\overline{Y}_i - \overline{Y}) = x_i y_i$ is negative, because the deviations of the x_i's have the opposite sign of the deviations of the y_i's lying in the same quadrants.

Thus if most observations fall in quadrants II and IV, the correlation between Y and X is positive. If on the other hand most of the quantity—price pairs fall in quadrants I and III, the correlation between Y and X will be negative. If the observations are scattered at random all over the four quandrants, the positive and negative products $x_i y_i$ will tend to cancel each other out, and the sum of products will tend to approach zero. If the sum of all products of the deviations of variables X and Y from their means is positive, the correlation between X and Y will be positive, while if the sum of the products of deviations is negative, the correlation between X and Y will be negative. Symbolically

if
$$\sum_{i}^{n}(X_i - \overline{X}_i)(Y_i - \overline{Y}_i) = \sum_{i}^{n} x_i y_i > 0$$

the correlation between X and Y is positive;

if
$$\sum_{i}^{n}(X_i - \overline{X}_i)(Y_i - \overline{Y}_i) = \sum_{i}^{n} x_i y_i < 0$$

the correlation between X and Y is negative.

Thus the sum of the products of the deviations $\Sigma x_i y_i$ provides a measure of the association between X and Y. However, this measure has two basic defects. Firstly, it is affected by the number of observations. The greater the number of observations, the greater the number of products will be, and therefore the value of the sum $\Sigma x_i y_i$ will be different. Thus if X and Y are positively related, an increase in the number of observations would make the correlation appear stronger, without this being necessarily true. Secondly, the sum $\Sigma x_i y_i$ is affected by the units of measurement of the variables X and Y. For example, the correlation in the above case would appear higher if the supply was measured in kilograms and the price in pence although the observations would be exactly the same.

To correct the first defect we divide the sum $\Sigma x_i y_i$ by the number of observations n

$$\frac{\Sigma x_i y_i}{n} = S_{XY}.$$

This expression is the *covariance* of X and Y and is obviously a better measure of correlation than the simple sum $\Sigma x_i y_i$, because it will not change directly with the number of observations in the sample. However, it still has the defect of being influenced by the units in which the variables X and Y are measured. To correct this defect we divide the covariance by the standard deviations of the variables, which are measured in the same units as the variables themselves, so that the ratio becomes a pure number, independent of any change in the units of measurement of X and Y. The resulting ratio is the sample *correlation coefficient r*, which is an estimate of the population correlation coefficient ρ.

$$r = \frac{\sum_{i}^{n} x_i y_i}{n S_X S_Y} = \frac{S_{YX}}{S_X S_Y} \tag{3.2}$$

where $S_{XY} =$ covariance of X and $Y = (\Sigma x_i y_i)/n$

$$S_X = \text{standard deviation of } X, \; S_X = \sqrt{\frac{\Sigma(X_i - \overline{X})^2}{n}} = \sqrt{\frac{\Sigma x_i^2}{n}}$$

$$S_Y = \text{standard deviation of } Y, \; S_Y = \sqrt{\frac{\Sigma(Y_i - \overline{Y})^2}{n}} = \sqrt{\frac{\Sigma y_i^2}{n}}$$

Substituting the values of S_{XY}, S_X and S_Y in expression 3.2 we find

$$r = \frac{\Sigma x_i y_i}{n \sqrt{(\Sigma x_i^2/n)(\Sigma y_i^2/n)}} = \frac{\Sigma x_i y_i}{\sqrt{(\Sigma x_i^2)(\Sigma y_i^2)}} \tag{3.3}$$

This formula is expressed in deviations of the variables from their means. If we want to use the actual values of the observations we use the following form:

$$r = \frac{n \Sigma(X_i Y_i) - (\Sigma X_i)(\Sigma Y_i)}{\sqrt{n \Sigma X_i^2 - (\Sigma X_i)^2} \sqrt{n \Sigma Y_i^2 - (\Sigma Y_i)^2}} \tag{3.4}$$

This formula is derived from (3.3) through the following transformations:

Given,

$$r = \frac{\Sigma x_i y_i}{\sqrt{\Sigma x_i^2} \sqrt{\Sigma y_i^2}}$$

(1) The numerator can be expanded as follows

$$\Sigma xy = \Sigma(X - \overline{X})(Y - \overline{Y}) = \Sigma(XY - Y\overline{X} - X\overline{Y} + \overline{XY}) = \Sigma XY - \overline{X}\Sigma Y - \overline{Y}\Sigma X + n\overline{XY}$$

$$= \Sigma XY - \frac{\Sigma X}{n}\Sigma Y - \frac{\Sigma Y}{n}\Sigma X + n\frac{\Sigma X}{n}\frac{\Sigma Y}{n}$$

$$= \frac{n\Sigma XY - \Sigma X\Sigma Y}{n}. \tag{3.5}$$

(2) From the denominator of expression (3.3) we get

$$\Sigma x^2 = \Sigma(X - \overline{X})^2 = \Sigma(X^2 - 2X\overline{X} + \overline{X}^2) = \Sigma X^2 - 2\overline{X}\Sigma X + n\overline{X}^2$$

$$= \Sigma X^2 - 2\overline{X}\Sigma X + nX\frac{\Sigma X}{n}$$

$$= \Sigma X^2 - \overline{X}\Sigma X$$

$$= \Sigma X^2 - \frac{(\Sigma X)^2}{n} \tag{3.6}$$

$$= \frac{n\Sigma X^2 - (\Sigma X)^2}{n} \tag{3.7}$$

Similarly

$$\Sigma y^2 = \frac{n\Sigma Y^2 - (\Sigma Y)^2}{n} \tag{3.8}$$

(3) Substituting (3.5), (3.6) and (3.8) in (3.3) we get

$$r = \frac{\{n\Sigma XY - (\Sigma X)(\Sigma Y)\}/n}{\sqrt{\{n\Sigma X^2 - (\Sigma X)^2\}/n}\sqrt{\{n\Sigma Y^2 - (\Sigma Y)^2\}/n}} = \frac{n\Sigma XY - (\Sigma X)(\Sigma Y)}{\sqrt{n\Sigma X^2 - (\Sigma X)^2}\sqrt{n\Sigma Y^2 - (\Sigma Y)^2}}$$

The above formulae of the correlation coefficient have two points of interest:
(1) The formulae are symmetric with respect to X and Y, that is $r_{YX} = r_{XY}$.
(2) The formulae are applicable only for linear relationships. Expressions for nonlinear relationships will be developed in Chapter 7 in connection with regression analysis.

3.3. NUMERICAL VALUES OF THE CORRELATION COEFFICIENT

The correlation coefficient is a measure of the degree of covariability of the variables X and Y. The values that the correlation coefficient may assume vary from -1 to $+1$. When r is positive, X and Y increase or decrease together. $r = +1$ implies that there is perfect positive correlation between X and Y. Diagrammatically, all the observations on Y and X lie on a straight line with a positive slope (figure 3.6).

When r is negative, X and Y move in opposite directions. If $r = -1$, there exists a perfect negative correlation between X and Y. Diagrammatically, all the observations of Y and X lie on a line with a negative slope (figure 3.7).

When r is zero, then the two variables are uncorrelated.

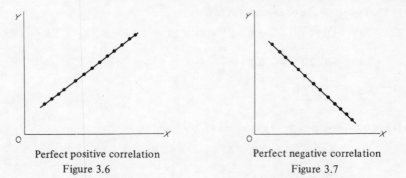

Perfect positive correlation   Perfect negative correlation
Figure 3.6   Figure 3.7

We shall prove that the *r* will assume the value of unit when the two variables are perfectly linearly correlated. In this case all the observations will lie on a line with a positive or negative slope according to whether the correlation is positive or negative.

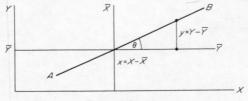

Figure 3.8

In figure 3.8 we picture the case of perfect positive correlation between *X* and *Y*. The line depicting the relation forms an angle θ with the parallel $\overline{YY}$ to the horizontal axis. From elementary trigonometry it is known that $\tan \theta = y/x$. Therefore $\{(x) . (\tan \theta)\} = (y)$. Substituting this result in the formula of the correlation coefficient we find

$$r = \frac{\sum xy}{\sqrt{\sum x^2 \sum y^2}} = \frac{\sum x(x) . (\tan \theta)}{\sqrt{\sum x^2 \sum \{(x).(\tan \theta)\}^2}}$$

$$r = \frac{(\tan \theta) . (\sum x^2)}{\sqrt{(\sum x^2) . (\tan \theta)^2 . (\sum x^2)}} = \frac{(\tan \theta) (\sum x^2)}{\sqrt{(\tan \theta)^2 (\sum x^2)^2}} = 1$$

In practice, we almost never observe either perfect correlation or zero correlation. Usually *r* assumes some value between zero and one. The closer that value is to one, the greater is the degree of covariability, that is the closer will the scatter of points approach a straight line. On the other hand, the greater the scatter of points in the diagram, the closer *r* is to zero.

We said that *r* is the sample estimate of the population correlation coefficient ρ. As a statistical estimate *r* is inevitably subject to some error and should be tested for its reliability. Tests of significance for *r* are explained in Chapters 5 and 8.

Example. Suppose we want to compute the correlation coefficient between the variables *Y* (quantity supplied) and *X* (price) with the observations included in table 3.1.

Table 3.2 Data for the estimation of the sample correlation coefficient r_{YX}

n	Y_i	X_i	$x_i = X_i - \bar{X}$	$y_i = Y_i - \bar{Y}$	x_i^2	y_i^2	x_iy_i	X_iY_i	X_i^2	Y_i^2
1	10	2	−9	−51	81	2,601	459	20	4	100
2	20	4	−7	−41	49	1,681	287	80	16	400
3	50	6	−5	−11	25	121	55	300	36	2,500
4	40	8	−3	−21	9	441	63	320	64	1,600
5	50	10	−1	−11	1	121	11	500	100	2,500
6	60	12	+1	−1	1	1	−1	720	144	3,600
7	80	14	+3	+19	9	361	57	1,120	196	6,400
8	90	16	+5	+29	25	841	145	1,440	256	8,100
9	90	18	+7	+29	49	841	203	1,620	324	8,100
10	120	20	+9	+59	81	3,481	531	2,400	400	14,400
$n = 10$	$\Sigma Y_i = 610$	$\Sigma X_i = 110$	$\Sigma x_i = 0$	$\Sigma y_i = 0$	$\Sigma x_i^2 = 330$	$\Sigma y_i^2 = 10,490$	$\Sigma x_iy_i = 1,810$	$\Sigma X_iY_i = 8,520$	$\Sigma X_i^2 = 1,540$	$\Sigma Y_i^2 = 47,700$

Computation of r *using deviations from the means*

$$r = \frac{\Sigma x_i y_i}{\sqrt{\Sigma x_i^2} \sqrt{\Sigma y_i^2}}$$

We need compute the terms $\Sigma x_i y_i$, Σx_i^2, Σy_i^2 which appear in the formula. The computations are given in table 3.2.

We see that $\Sigma xy = 1,810$, $\Sigma x^2 = 330$, $\Sigma y^2 = 10,490$. Substituting

$$r = \frac{1,810}{\sqrt{330} \sqrt{10,490}} = 0\cdot975$$

Computation of r *using actual observations*

$$r = \frac{n\Sigma XY - \Sigma X \Sigma Y}{\sqrt{n\Sigma X^2 - (\Sigma X)^2} \sqrt{n\Sigma Y^2 - (\Sigma Y)^2}}$$

From the formula we see that we need compute the terms

$$\Sigma XY \quad \Sigma X^2 \quad \Sigma Y^2 \quad \Sigma X \quad \Sigma Y \quad (\Sigma X)^2 \quad (\Sigma Y)^2$$

The computations are shown in table 3.2. Substituting we find

$$r = \frac{(10).(8,520) - (610).(110)}{\sqrt{(10).(1540) - 12,100} \sqrt{(10).(47,700) - 372,100}} = 0.975$$

3.4. THE RANK CORRELATION COEFFICIENT

The formulae of the linear correlation coefficient developed in the previous section are based on the assumption that the variables involved are quantitative and that we have accurate data for their measurement. However, in many cases the variables may be qualitative (or binary variables) and hence cannot be measured numerically. For example, profession, education, preferences for particular brands, are such categorical variables. Furthermore, in many cases precise values of the variables may not be available, so that it is impossible to calculate the value of the correlation coefficient with the formulae developed in the preceding section. For such cases it is possible to use another statistic, the *rank correlation coefficient* (or Spearman's correlation coefficient). We rank the observations in a specific sequence, for example in order of size, importance, etc., using the numbers $1, 2, \ldots, n$. In other words we assign *ranks* to the data and measure the relationship between their ranks instead of their actual numerical values. Hence the name of the statistic as rank correlation coefficient. If two variables X and Y are ranked in such way the rank correlation coefficient may be computed by the formula

$$r' = 1 - \frac{6\Sigma D^2}{n(n^2 - 1)} \tag{3.9}$$

where D = difference between ranks of corresponding pairs of X and Y
         n = number of observations.

The values that r' may assume range from $+1$ to -1. (For a test of significance of r' see Chapter 6.)

Two points are of interest when applying the rank correlation coefficient. Firstly, it does not matter whether we rank the observations in ascending or descending order. However, we must use the same rule of ranking for both variables. Second, if two (or more) observations have the same value we assign to them the *mean rank*. Some examples will illustrate the application of the rank correlation coefficient.

Example 1. The following table shows how ten students were ranked according to their performance in their class work and their final examinations. We want to find out whether there is a relationship between the accomplishments of the students during the whole year and their performance in their exams.

Students →	A	B	C	D	E	F	G	H	I	J
Ranking based on class work	2	5	6	1	4	10	7	9	3	8
Ranking based on exam marks	1	6	4	2	3	7	8	10	5	9

The differences between the two rankings is given in the following table.

D	1	−1	2	−1	1	3	−1	−1	−2	−1	
D^2	1	1	4	1	1	9	1	1	4	1	$\Sigma D^2 = 24$

The rank correlation coefficient is

$$r' = 1 - \frac{6 \Sigma D^2}{n(n^2 - 1)} = 1 - \frac{6(24)}{10(10^2 - 1)} = 0 \cdot 855$$

The high value of the rank correlation coefficient indicates that there is a close relationship between class work and exam performance: students with good record all over the year do well in their examinations and *vice versa*.

Example 2. A market researcher asks two smokers to express their preference for twelve different brands of cigarettes. Their replies are shown in the following table.

Brands of cigarettes	A	B	C	D	E	F	G	H	I	J	K	L
Smoker Z	9	10	4	1	8	11	3	2	5	7	12	6
Smoker W	7	8	3	1	10	12	2	6	5	4	11	9

The differences of preferences of the two smokers are shown below

D	2	2	1	0	−2	−1	1	−4	0	3	1	−3	
D^2	4	4	1	0	4	1	1	16	0	9	1	9	$\Sigma D^2 = 50$

The rank correlation coefficient

$$r' = 1 - \frac{6 \Sigma D^2}{n(n^2 - 1)} = 1 - \frac{6(50)}{12(12^2 - 1)} = 0 \cdot 827$$

shows a marked similarity of preferences of the two consumers for the various brands of cigarettes.

3.5. PARTIAL CORRELATION COEFFICIENTS

A partial correlation coefficient measures the relationship between any two variables, when all other variables connected with those two are kept constant. For example, let us assume that we want to measure the correlation between the number of hot drinks (X_1) consumed in a summer resort and the number of tourists (X_2) coming to that resort.[1] It is obvious that both these variables are strongly influenced by weather conditions, which we may designate by X_3. On *a priori* grounds we expect X_1 and X_2 to be positively correlated: when a large number of tourists arrive in the summer resort one should expect a high consumption of hot drinks and *vice versa*. The computation of the simple correlation coefficient between X_1 and X_2 may not reveal the true relationship connecting these two variables, however, because of the influence of the third variable, weather conditions (X_3). In other words the above positive relationship between number of tourists and number of hot drinks consumed is expected to hold *if weather conditions can be assumed constant*. If weather changes, the relationship between X_1 and X_2 may be distorted to such an extent as to appear even negative. Thus if the weather is hot, the number of tourists will be large, but because of the heat they will prefer to consume more cold drinks and ice-cream rather than hot drinks. If we overlook weather and look only at X_1 and X_2 we will observe a negative correlation between these two variables which is explained by the fact that hot drinks as well as number of visitors are affected by heat. In order to measure the true correlation between X_1 and X_2 we must find some way of accounting for changes in X_3. This is achieved with the partial correlation coefficient between X_1 and X_2 when X_3 is kept constant. The partial correlation coefficient is determined in terms of the simple correlation coefficients among the various variables involved in a multiple relationship. In our example there are three simple correlation coefficients

r_{12} = correlation coefficient between X_1 and X_2
r_{13} = correlation coefficient between X_1 and X_3
r_{23} = correlation coefficient between X_2 and X_3

There are two partial correlation coefficients

$r_{12.3}$ = partial correlation coefficient between X_1 and X_2 when X_3 is kept constant

$$r_{12.3} = \frac{r_{12} - (r_{13})(r_{23})}{\sqrt{(1 - r_{13}^2)(1 - r_{23}^2)}} \tag{3.10}$$

and

[1] The example is taken from J. E. Freund and F. J. Williams, *Modern Business Statistics*, Pitman, London 1959.

$r_{13 \cdot 2}$ = partial correlation coefficient between X_1 and X_3 when X_2 is kept constant

$$r_{13 \cdot 2} = \frac{r_{13} - (r_{12})(r_{23})}{\sqrt{(1 - r_{12}{}^2)(1 - r_{23}{}^2)}}$$

The proof and rationalisation of these formulae will be given in Chapter 7, by which time the reader will have become familiar with regression analysis. The formula for the partial correlation coefficient can be directly extended to relationships involving any number of explanatory variables (see Chapter 7).

3.6. LIMITATIONS OF THE THEORY OF LINEAR CORRELATION

Correlation analysis has serious limitations as a technique for the study of economic relationships.

Firstly. The above formulae for r apply only when the relationship between the variables is linear. However, two variables may be strongly connected with a nonlinear relationship.

It should be clear that zero correlation and statistical independence of two variables (X and Y) are not the same thing. Zero correlation implies zero covariance of X and Y so that

$$r = \frac{\Sigma x_i y_i}{\sqrt{\Sigma x^2} \sqrt{\Sigma y^2}} = 0$$

Statistical independence of X and Y implies that the probability of X_i and Y_i occurring simultaneously is the simple product of the individual probabilities

$$P(X \text{ and } Y) = P(X) \cdot P(Y)$$

(For a discussion of this result see Appendix I.)

Independent variables do have zero covariance and are uncorrelated: the linear correlation coefficient between two independent variables is equal to zero (figure 3.9). However, zero linear correlation does not necessarily imply independence. In other words uncorrelated variables may be statistically dependent. For example if X and Y are related so that the observations fall

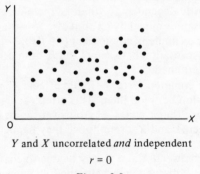

Y and X uncorrelated *and* independent

$r = 0$

Figure 3.9

on a circle or on a symmetrical parabola (as in figures 3.10 and 3.11) the relationship is perfect but not linear. The variables are statistically dependent, although their covariance and the linear correlation coefficient are zero. Absence

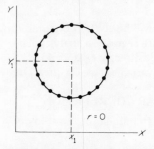

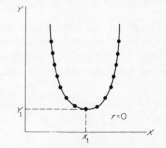

Y and X uncorrelated but dependent.
Their function is

$$(X - X_1)^2 + (Y - Y_1)^2 = a^2$$
$$r = 0$$

Figure 3.10

Y and X uncorrelated but dependent.
Their function is

$$(X - X_1)^2 = 4a(Y - Y_1)^2$$
$$r = 0$$

Figure 3.11

of linear correlation does not imply absence of any dependence. (See A. Goldberger, *Econometric Theory,* Wiley, New York 1964, pp. 61–2. Also C. Christ, *Econometric Models and Methods,* p. 146.)

Secondly. The second limitation of the theory is that although the correlation coefficient is a measure of the covariability of variables it does not necessarily imply any functional relationship between the variables concerned. Correlation theory does not establish, and/or prove any causal relationship between the variables. It seeks to discover if a covariation exists, but it does not suggest that variations in, say, Y are 'caused' by variations in X, or *vice versa*. Knowledge of the value of r, alone, will not enable us to predict the value of Y from X. A high correlation between variables Y and X may describe any one of the following situations:

(1) Variation in X is the cause of variation in Y,

(2) Variation in Y is the cause of variation in X.

(3) Y and X are jointly dependent, or there is a two-way causation, that is to say Y is the cause of (is determined by) X, but also X is the cause of (is determined by) Y. For example in any market $Q = f(P)$, but also $P = f(Q)$, therefore there is a two-way causation between Q and P, or in other words P and Q are simultaneously determined.

(4) There is another common factor (Z), that affects X and Y in such a way as to show a close relation between them. This often occurs in time series, when two variables have strong time trends (i.e. grow over time); in this case we find a high correlation between Y and X, even though they happen to be causally independent.

(5) The correlation between X and Y may be due to chance.

To illustrate the above discussion, we cite the following examples.

Example 1. Suppose we look at the marks a student gains in his examinations (Y) and his hours of work in a shop (X). By gathering information on the performance of the student in various exams and the hours he worked in the shop during terms, we compute the correlation coefficient which assumes, say, the value of -0.9. This value of r is not enough evidence to prove that there exists actually an inverse causal relationship between grades (Y) and hours of outside work (X). More information is required before we can establish such a functional (causal) relationship, since any one of the following situations is conceivably possible: (1) A causal relationship exists ($Y = f(X)$): due to long hours of working at the shop the grades scored at exams are low. (2) The opposite may be true, ($X = f(Y)$): because of low grades it may be that the student cannot get a scholarship and as a result he has to do outside work. (3) There may be a third factor, affecting both X and Y in such a way that they show a close relation, that is it may be that the student has to support his ailing parents, who are causing him to get low grades and engage in extra outside work for money. (4) The correlation of X and Y may be due to chance: the student who works in a shop may be a bad examinee in general, scoring low marks in examinations.

Example 2. Correlations are sometimes observed between quantities that could not conceivably be causally related. For example, if a high correlation is found between the number of births and the number of murders in a country, this should not obviously provide a proof that the births of babies are determined by the number of murders! Also the fact that statisticians have observed a high correlation between births of babies and arrivals of storks does not mean that births are determined by stork movements! It simply shows that storks and babies show time trends. These are examples of what is called *spurious correlation* (or chance correlation), in other words correlation which does not show any causal relationship between the variables involved.

Example 3. Consumption (C) and income (Y) are jointly dependent variables, since $C = f(Y)$ according to the simple Keynesian theory, but also $Y = f(C)$. Similarly price (P) and quantity demanded are two jointly dependent variables, since $D = f(P)$ but also $P = f(D)$.

It follows from the above discussion that correlation theory does not establish a functional relationship, that is to say it does not prove which is the dependent and which is the explanatory variable. Only through a more thorough investigation using economic theory can we come to some conclusion as to whether or not X is the cause of Y. Furthermore, correlation analysis does not give numerical values for the coefficients of the relationship, that is it does not give estimates for the slope and the constant intercept of the function. A given value of the correlation coefficient is consistent with an infinite number of straight lines. In figures 3.12 and 3.13 the correlation between X and Y is positive and perfect, all observations lie on the lines, but the lines are completely different, having different slopes and intercepts.

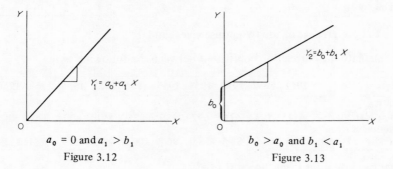

$a_0 = 0$ and $a_1 > b_1$ $b_0 > a_0$ and $b_1 < a_1$

Figure 3.12   Figure 3.13

In summary, the linear correlation coefficient measures the degree to which the points cluster around a straight line, but it does not give the equation for the line, that is it does not assign numerical values to the parameters of the function which is represented by this line. These parameters are elasticities (or components of elasticities), or propensities and multipliers as far as economic theory is concerned, and the knowledge of their numerical value is of particular interest both to entrepreneurs and to policy-makers.

To estimate the parameters of the relationship we may apply various methods. We will start by the development of the method of Ordinary Least Squares regression, because it is the simplest of all and, furthermore, it forms the basis of most of the other, more elaborate, econometric techniques.

EXERCISES

1. Calculate the correlation coefficient between the following series:

	1961	1962	1963	1964	1965	1966	1967	1968	1969	1970
Road accidents	155	150	180	135	156	168	178	160	132	145
Consumption of beer (in tons)	70	63	72	60	66	70	74	65	62	67

	1961	1962	1963	1964	1965	1966	1967	1968	1969	1970
Road accidents	155	150	180	135	156	168	178	160	132	145
Wages and salaries (in £m)	15,500	14,500	19,300	15,600	16,400	19,300	25,600	25,000	26,900	27,850

Interpret your results.

2. The following table includes the rankings of the preferences of two housewives for ten different brands of soap.

Brands of soap	A	B	C	D	E	F	G	H	I	J
Ranking by Mrs *X*	3	5	8	10	7	9	1	4	6	2
Ranking by Mrs *Z*	5	6	4	9	8	3	1	2	10	7

Are the preferences of the two housewives similar?

3. Calculate the correlation coefficient between the following series

	1951	1952	1953	1954	1955	1956	1957	1958	1959	1960
Deaths from cancer (in 1000)	612	583	671	692	689	835	891	800	923	982
Production of steel (in millions of tons)	66·6	84·9	88·6	78·0	96·8	105·2	93·2	111·6	88·3	117·0

What can you infer from the value of *r*?

4. Suppose that a firm had the following profits and investment expenditures in each year from 1961−1970.

	1961	1962	1963	1964	1965	1966	1967	1968	1969	1970
Profits (£1000)	100	200	300	400	500	600	700	800	900	1000
Investment expenditure (£1000)	40	45	50	65	70	70	80	85	85	95

(a) Estimate the correlation coefficient between profits and investment expenditures.

(b) On the basis of the observed correlation coefficient, researcher A claims that profits determine the level of investment, while researcher B claims that investment determines the profitability of the firm. Who of the two researchers is right?

5. It is often suggested that the research expenditure of a firm is related to the level of its profits. Do the following data substantiate this hypothesis?

	1955	1956	1957	1958	1959	1960	1961	1962	1963	1964
Research expenditure	10	10	8	8	8	12	12	12	11	11
Profits (£1000)	100	150	200	180	250	300	280	310	320	300

6. Show algebraically that the correlation coefficient between n observations on

$$Y_i^* = aY_i + b \qquad \text{and} \qquad X_i^* = cX_i + d$$

(where a, b, c, d are constants) is equal to the correlation coefficient between the simple observations Y_i and X_i.

7. Repeat exercise 6 with

$$Y_i^* = \frac{Y_i - a}{b} \qquad \text{and} \qquad X^* = \frac{X_i - c}{d}$$

8. Generalise the results of exercises 6 and 7 to show that the value of the correlation coefficient is independent of the scale and origin of measurement of Y and X, and hence the burden of calculation of r is most reduced if a, b, c, d are chosen to make Y^* and X^* as simple as possible.

Note. Additional exercises are included in Appendix III.

4. The Simple Linear Regression Model
The Ordinary Least Squares Method

There are various econometric methods that can be used to derive estimates of the parameters of economic relationships from statistical observations. In this chapter we shall examine the method of ordinary least squares (OLS) or classical least squares (CLS). The reasons for starting with this method are many. Firstly, the parameter estimates obtained by ordinary least squares have some optimal properties which will be discussed in Chapter 6. Secondly, the computational procedure of OLS is fairly simple as compared with other econometric techniques and the data requirements are not excessive. Thirdly, the least squares method has been used in a wide range of economic relationships with fairly satisfactory results (see Chapter 21), and, despite the improvement of computational equipment and of statistical information which facilitated the use of other more elaborate econometric techniques, OLS is still one of the most commonly employed methods in estimating relationships in econometric models. Fourthly, the mechanics of least squares are simple to understand. Fifthly, OLS is an essential component of most other econometric techniques. In fact, as we will see later, with the exception of the Full Information Maximum Likelihood method, all other techniques involve the application of the least squares method, modified in some respects.

We shall start by the simple linear regression model, that is, by a relationship between two variables, one dependent and one explanatory, related with a linear function. Subsequently we will examine the multiple regression analysis, which refers to the relationship between more than two variables..

4.1. THE SIMPLE LINEAR REGRESSION MODEL

An example

We will illustrate the meaning of the method of least squares by referring to our earlier example from the theory of supply. The theory of supply in its simplest form postulates that there exists a positive relationship between the quantity supplied of a commodity and its price, *ceteris paribus*. When the price rises the quantity of the commodity supplied increases and *vice versa*. Following the econometric procedure outlined in Chapter 2, our first task is the specification of the supply model, that is, the determination of the dependent (regressand) and the explanatory variables (regressors), the number of equations of the model and their precise mathematical form, and finally the *a priori* expectations concerning the sign and the magnitude of the coefficients. Economic theory provides the following information with respect to the supply function.

48

(1) The dependent variable is the quantity supplied and the explanatory variable is the price

$$Y = f(X)$$

where Y = quantity supplied
X = price of the commodity.

(2) Economic theory does not specify whether the supply should be studied with a single-equation model or with a more elaborate system of simultaneous equations. In view of this indeterminacy we choose to start our investigation with a single-equation model. In later stages we may study more elaborate models.

(3) Economic theory is not clear about the mathematical form (linear or nonlinear) of the supply function. In textbooks the supply is sometimes depicted by a straight upward-sloping line, or by an upward-sloping curve. The latter implies a nonlinear relationship between quantity and price. Again the econometrician has to decide the form of the supply function. We start by assuming that the variables are related with the simplest possible mathematical form, that is, the relationship between quantity and price is linear of the form

$$Y_i = b_0 + b_1 X_i$$

This form implies that there is a one-way causation between the variables Y and X: price is the cause of changes in the quantity supplied, but not the other way around.

The parameters of the supply function are b_0 and b_1, and our aim is to obtain estimates of their numerical values, $\hat{b}_0$ and $\hat{b}_1$.

As regards the sign and size of the constant intercept $\hat{b}_0$, we note that it should be either zero (in which case its meaning is that the quantity is zero when price is zero) or positive (in which case its meaning is that some quantity is supplied even when the price drops to zero). Normally $\hat{b}_0$ should not be negative in the case of a supply function. If $\hat{b}_0$ turns up with a negative sign we should ignore the negative part of the supply function, since a negative quantity does not make sense in economics. However, the sign of $\hat{b}_0$ is crucial in determining the price elasticity of supply, as we will presently see.

Regarding the value of $\hat{b}_1$, we note that in the particular case of a supply function we expect the sign of $\hat{b}_1$ to be positive ($\hat{b}_1 > 0$), since a supply curve is normally upward-sloping.

It is important to examine the relationship between the price elasticity of supply and the coefficients $\hat{b}_0$ and $\hat{b}_1$. Recall that the elasticity is defined by the expression

$$\eta_p = \frac{dQ}{dP} \cdot \frac{P}{Q} = \frac{dY}{dX} \cdot \frac{X}{Y}$$

From the supply function it is obvious that

$$\frac{dY}{dX} = b_1$$

In computing the elasticity from a regression line, we use the estimate $\hat{b}_1$ and the mean values of price $(\bar{X})$ and quantity $(\bar{Y})$ in the sample. Thus

$$\hat{\eta}_p = \hat{b}_1 \cdot \frac{\bar{X}}{\bar{Y}}$$

But, as we will show on page 63,

$$\bar{Y} = \hat{b}_0 + \hat{b}_1 \bar{X}$$

Thus, substituting for $\bar{Y}$ in the expression of the elasticity, we obtain

$$\hat{\eta}_p = \frac{\hat{b}_1 \bar{X}}{\hat{b}_1 \bar{X} + \hat{b}_0}$$

Given that $\hat{b}_1 > 0$, it follows that

    (i)   the supply will be elastic $(\eta_p > 1)$ if $\hat{b}_0$ is negative $(\hat{b}_0 < 0)$
    (ii)   the supply will be inelastic $(\eta_p < 1)$ if $\hat{b}_0$ is positive $(\hat{b}_0 > 0)$
    (iii) the supply with have unitary elasticity if $\hat{b} = 0$.

Thus the elasticity of a supply curve (with positive slope) depends on the sign of the constant intercept, $\hat{b}_0$.

(4) The above form of the supply function implies that the relationship between quantity and price is *exact,* that is that all the variation in Y is due solely to changes in X, and that there are no other factors affecting the dependent variable. If this were true all the points of price—quantity pairs, if plotted on a two-dimensional plane, would fall on a straight line. However, if we gather observations on the quantity actually supplied in the market at various prices and we plot them on a diagram we see that they do not fall on a straight line (or any other smooth curve for that matter). Suppose that we have the ten pairs of observations on X and Y shown in table 4.1. The scatter

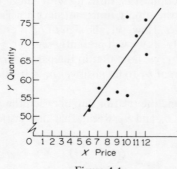

Figure 4.1

diagram of these observations shows that the relationship between price and quantity supplied has a form roughly similar to a straight line (figure 4.1).

The deviations of the observations from the line may be attributed to several factors.

(1) *Omission of variables from the function*

In economic reality each variable is influenced by a very large number of factors. For instance, the consumption pattern of a family is determined by family income, prices, the composition by age and sex of the family, the past levels of the family income, tastes, religion, social and educational status, wealth, and so on. One could compile an almost non-ending list of such factors. However, not all the factors influencing a certain variable can be included in the function for various reasons. (a) Some of the factors may not be known even to the person most aquainted with the relationship being studied. This lack of knowledge is to a great extent due to incomplete theory about the variation of economic variables in general. (b) Even when known to be relevant, some factors cannot be measured statistically. These are mainly psychological factors, or, in general, qualitative factors (tastes, expectations, religion) which cannot even be approximated satisfactorily with dummy variables. (c) Some factors are random, appearing in an unpredictable way and time, so that their influence cannot be taken satisfactorily into account (e.g. epidemics, earth-quakes, wars). (d) Some factors may have, each individually, a very small influence on the dependent variable. Thus their parameter is so small that it cannot be measured in a reliable way (due to rounding errors of the computa-tions). All these factors together, however, may account for a considerable part of the variation of the dependent variable. (e) Even if all factors are known, the available data most often are not adequate for the measurement of all factors influencing a relationship. This is particularly so when we use time series, which are usually short. Thus in most cases only the most important three or four variables are explicitly included in the function. The lack of

Table 4.1

Number of observations	Y Quantity	X Price
1	69	9
2	76	12
3	52	6
4	56	10
5	57	9
6	77	10
7	58	7
8	55	8
9	67	12
10	53	6
11	72	11
12	64	8

adequate number of observations creates a problem of 'degrees of freedom', which impairs the application of the traditional tests of significance. (See Chapter 5 and Appendix I.)

(2) *Random behaviour of the human beings.* The scatter of points around the line may be attributed to an erratic element which is inherent in human behaviour. Human reactions are to a certain extent unpredictable and may cause deviations from the 'normal' behavioural pattern depicted by the line. For example in a moment's whim a consumer may change his expenditure pattern, although income and prices did not change.

(3) *Imperfect specification of the mathematical form of the model.* We may have linearised a possibly nonlinear relationship. Or we may have left out of the model some equations. The economic phenomena are much more complex than a single equation may reveal, no matter how many explanatory variables it contains. In most cases many variables are simultaneously determined by a system containing many equations. For example price determines and is determined by the quantity supplied. Under such circumstances if we attempt to study the phenomenon with a single-equation model, we are bound to commit an error, which is due to the imperfect specification of the form of the model, that is, of the number of its equations.

(4) *Errors of aggregation.* We often use aggregate data (aggregate consumption, aggregate income), in which we add magnitudes referring to individuals whose behaviour is dissimilar. In this case we say that variables expressing individual peculiarities are missing. For example, in a production function for an industry we add together the factor inputs and outputs of dissimilar entrepreneurs. Changes in the distribution of total output among firms are important in the determination of total output. However, such distributional variables are often missing from the function. There are other types of aggregation which introduce error in the relationship. For example, aggregation over time, spatial aggregation, cross section aggregation, and so on.

(5) *Errors of measurement.* The deviations of the points from the line may be due to errors of measurement of the variables, which are inevitable due to the methods of collecting and processing statistical information.

The first four sources of error render the form of the equation wrong, and they are usually referred to as *error in the equation* or *error of omission.* The fifth source of error is called *error of measurement* or *error of observation.* It is usual of course to have both these types of error simultaneously in the function.

In order to take into account the above sources of error we introduce in econometric functions a random variable which is usually denoted by the letter u and is called *error term* or *random disturbance term* or *stochastic term* of the function, so called because u is supposed to 'disturb' the exact linear relationship which is assumed to exist between X and Y. By introducing this random variable in the function the model is rendered stochastic of the form

$$Y_i = (b_0 + b_1 X_i) + (u_i)$$

The true relationship which connects the variables involved is split into two parts: a part represented by a line and a part represented by the random term u. The meaning of these two parts may be explained by looking at figure 4.2. The

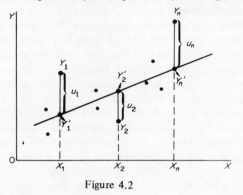

Figure 4.2

scatter of observations represents the true relationship between Y and X. The line represents the exact part of the relationship and the deviations of the observations from the line represent the random component of the relationship. Were it not for the errors in the model, we would observe the points on the line $Y'_1, Y'_2, \ldots, Y'_n$, corresponding to $X_1, X_2, \ldots, X_n$. However, because of the random disturbances, we observe $Y_1, Y_2, \ldots, Y_n$, corresponding to $X_1, X_2, \ldots, X_n$. These points diverge from the regression line by quantities $u_1, u_2, \ldots, u_n$, where u_i is the random error associated with Y_i. In other words the values of Y corresponding to a value of X will on the average fall on a line, but each individual Y_i will deviate from the line depending on the value of u_i. Hence each $Y_i (i = 1, 2, \ldots, n)$ can be expressed in terms of two components, one component due to X_i and a second component due to the influences included in the random term u_i

$$Y_i \quad = \quad \underbrace{b_0 + b_1 X_i} \quad + \quad \underbrace{u_i}$$

$$\begin{bmatrix} \text{Variation} \\ \text{in } Y_i \end{bmatrix} = \begin{bmatrix} \text{Systematic} \\ \text{variation} \end{bmatrix} + \begin{bmatrix} \text{Random} \\ \text{variation} \end{bmatrix}$$

or

$$\begin{bmatrix} \text{Variation} \\ \text{in } Y_i \end{bmatrix} = \begin{bmatrix} \text{Explained} \\ \text{variation} \end{bmatrix} + \begin{bmatrix} \text{Unexplained} \\ \text{variation} \end{bmatrix}$$

The first component in brackets is the part of the variation in Y explained by the changes in X and the second is the part of the variation not explained by any specific factor, that is to say the variation in Y is due to the random influence of u.

Seen in this light the random term u seems to have a meaning related to the *ceteris paribus* clause of economic theory. Economic theory assumes that the functional relationships between variables are exact under the *ceteris paribus* clause. For example, the demand function $D = b_0 + b_1 P$ postulated by economic theory implies that the quantity of a particular commodity is a linear function of its price alone, 'other things remaining equal'; that is, the price—quantity relationship holds provided that all other factors not appearing explicitly in the function (for example tastes, income, other prices) remain unchanged. However, theories are simplifications of the complex relationships which exist in the real world, so that the *ceteris paribus* clause is very seldom fulfilled. When we collect data on the quantities of a commodity purchased at various prices we do not observe the quantity that would be bought if all 'other things' were constant, but rather the quantities purchased while the prices of other goods, incomes, tastes and other factors have all been changing.

In econometrics we may read the true relationship connecting the variables as follows. Y is connected with X by a linear relationship, *ceteris paribus.* If factors other than X remain unchanged then changes in Y would be fully explained by changes in X. However, other factors do not remain equal; hence we introduce u into the function to account for the changes in other variables not included in it explicitly.

We may now look at the final form of our equation $Y_i = b_0 + b_1 X_i + u_i$ in another way. For a given value of X, Y may assume various values depending on the particular (positive or negative) value that u happens to assume. To each value of X corresponds a distribution of various values of u, and therefore Y's. This situation is pictured in figure 4.3. For example if the price of the commodity is equal to X_1, the quantity which will be supplied at this price may assume any value between Y_1' and Y_1'', depending on the value of u in this period. If, for instance, there is a strike of lorry drivers, or a power cut, which delays the delivery of the commodity (these situations being examples of chance events), the quantity will not be Y_1, as the linear equation suggests, but a smaller quantity Y_1^*, due to the above factors which give a value u_1^* to the random term. If, however, there is a rumour of a fall in prices of substitutes or of a new product being developed, the supplier may offer all the stock, which

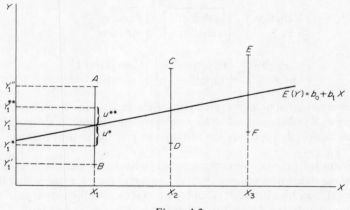

Figure 4.3

he otherwise would offer in future periods, so that at the price X_1 the quantity supplied would be Y_1^{**}, because the change in expectations caused u to assume the value u_1^{**}.

To estimate the coefficients b_0 and b_1 we need observations on X, Y and u. Yet u is never observed like the other explanatory variables,[1] and therefore in order to estimate the function $Y_i = b_0 + b_1 X_i + u_i$, we should 'guess' the values of u, that is we should make some reasonable (plausible) assumptions about the shape of the distribution of each u_i (its mean, variance and covariance[2] with other u's). These assumptions are guesses about the true, but unobservable, values of u_i.

4.2. ASSUMPTIONS OF THE LINEAR STOCHASTIC REGRESSION MODEL

The linear regression model is based on certain assumptions, some of which refer to the distribution of the random variable u, some to the relationship between u and the explanatory variables, and finally some refer to the relationship between the explanatory variables themselves. We will group the assumptions in two categories, (a) stochastic assumptions, (b) other assumptions.

4.2.1. STOCHASTIC ASSUMPTIONS OF ORDINARY LEAST SQUARES

These are assumptions about the distribution of the values of u. They are crucial for the estimates of the parameters and will be explained in detail in subsequent chapters (see Chapters 9–12). It is these assumptions about the random term u that adapt the least squares method, which is a statistical method, to the stochastic nature of economic phenomena. At this stage we will state these assumptions without attempting to explain their implications for the parameter estimates.

Assumption 1 u_i is a random real variable.

The value which u_i may assume in any one period depends on chance; it may be positive, negative or zero. Each value has a certain probability of being assumed by u in any particular instance.

Assumption 2 The mean value of u in any particular period is zero.

This means that for each value of X, u may assume various values, some greater than zero and some smaller than zero, but if we considered all the possible values of u, for any given value of X, they would have an average value equal to zero. With this assumption we may say that $Y_i = b_0 + b_1 X_i$ gives the relationship between X and Y *on the average*, that is, when X

---

[1] As we shall see readily, we can get an estimate of the u's after the estimation of the regression line and the computation of the residual deviations of the observations from this line.

[2] The covariance of the u's measures the way in which the u's of different periods tend to covary. The covariance of u's and X's measures the way in which the values of u's of different periods tend to vary with the values of X in these periods. (See Appendix I.)

assumes the value X_i the dependent variable will on the average assume the value Y_i (on the line), although the actual value of Y observed in any particular occasion may display some variation: sometimes the value of the dependent variable (corresponding to the given value of X) will be bigger than Y_i, and at other times it will be smaller than the Y_i (on the line). Yet on the average the value of Y will be equal to Y_i when X assumes the value X_i. That is, on the average u is equal to zero.

Assumption 3 The variance of u_i is constant in each period.

The variance of u_i about its mean is constant at all values of X. In other words for all values of X, the u's will show the same dispersion round their mean. In figure 4.3 this assumption is denoted by the fact that the values that u may assume lie within the same limits, irrespective of the value of X: for X_1, u can assume any value within the range AB; for X_2, u can assume any value within the range CD which is equal to AB and so on.

Assumption 4 The variable u_i has a normal distribution.

The values of u (for each X_i) have a bell-shaped symmetrical distribution about their zero mean.

The above four assumptions about the behaviour (distribution) of the values of u may be summarised by the expression

$$u \sim N(0, \sigma_u^2)$$

and are pictured in figure 4.4.

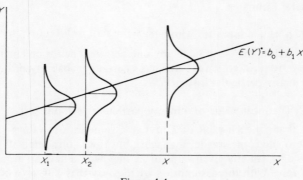

Figure 4.4

Assumption 5   The random terms of different observations (u_i, u_j) are independent.

This means that all the covariances of any u_i with any other u_j are equal to zero. The value which the random term assumed in one period does not depend on the value which it assumed in any other period.

Assumption 6 u is independent of the explanatory variable(s).

The disturbance term is not correlated with the explanatory variable(s). The u's and the X's do not tend to vary together; their covariance is zero. Symbolically

$$\text{cov}(Xu) = E\{[X_i - E(X_i)] [u_i - E(u_i)]\} = 0$$

It is, however, conceptually easier and computationally more convenient to make an alternative assumption which ensures zero covariance of the u's and X's.

Assumption 6A   The X_i's are a set of fixed values in the hypothetical process of repeated sampling which underlies the linear regression model.

This means that, in taking a large number of samples on Y and X, the X_i values are the same in all samples, but the u_i values do differ from sample to sample, and so of course do the values of Y_i. For example, assume that every day in a market we choose the same prices $X_1, X_2, \ldots, X_n$, and we record the quantities Y_i's sold each day at these prices. The X's do not vary, they are a set of fixed values; while the Y_i's vary for each day due to different random influences. Clearly, under these conditions the covariance of the (fixed) X's and the u's is zero. Because

$$
\begin{aligned}
\text{cov}(Xu) &= E\{[X_i - E(X_i)] [u_i - E(u_i)]\} \\
&= E\{[X_i - E(X_i)] u_i\} \qquad \text{given } E(u_i) = 0 \\
&= E(X_i u_i) - E(X_i)E(u_i) \\
&= E(X_i u_i) \\
&= X_i E(u_i) \qquad \text{given that the } X_i\text{'s are fixed} \\
&= 0
\end{aligned}
$$

In the remainder of this book we will mostly use Assumption 6A, that the explanatory variables are fixed.

Assumption 7   The explanatory variable(s) are measured without error.

u absorbs the influence of omitted variables and possibly errors of measurement in the Y's. That is, we will assume that the regressors are error-free, while the Y values may or may not include errors of measurement.

4.2.2. OTHER ASSUMPTIONS OF ORDINARY LEAST SQUARES

Assumption 8 The explanatory variables are not perfectly linearly correlated.

If there is more than one explanatory variable in the relationship it is assumed that they are not perfectly correlated with each other. Indeed the regressors should not even be strongly correlated, they should not be highly multicollinear.

Assumption 9 The macrovariables should be correctly aggregated.

Usually the variables X and Y are aggregative variables, representing the sum of individual items. For example, in a consumption function $C = b_0 + b_1 Y + u$, C

is the sum of the expenditures of all consumers and Y is the sum of all individual incomes. It is assumed that the appropriate aggregation procedure has been adopted in compiling the aggregate variables.

Assumption 10 The relationship being estimated is identified.

It is assumed that the relationship whose coefficients we want to estimate has a unique mathematical form, that is it does not contain the same variables as any other equation related to the one being investigated. Only if this assumption is fulfilled can we be certain that the coefficients which result from our computations are the true parameters of the relationship which we study.

Assumption 11 The relationship is correctly specified.

It is assumed that we have not committed any specification error in determining the explanatory variables, that we have included all the important regressors explicitly in the model, and that its mathematical form (number of equations and their linear or nonlinear nature) is correct.

4.3. THE DISTRIBUTION OF THE DEPENDENT VARIABLE Y

In this section we will establish that the dependent variable Y has a normal distribution with mean

$$E(Y_i) = b_0 + b_1 X_i \tag{4.1}$$

and variance

$$\text{var}(Y_i) = E[Y_i - E(Y_i)] = E(u_i^2) = \sigma_u^2 \tag{4.2}$$

Proof 1. The mean of $Y_i = E(Y_i) = b_0 + b_1 X_i$.
   By definition the mean of Y_i is its expected value.

Given $Y_i = b_0 + b_1 X_i + u_i$

Taking expected values we find

$$E(Y_i) = E[b_0 + b_1 X_i + u_i]$$
$$= E(b_0 + b_1 X_i) + E(u_i)$$

Given that b_0 and b_1 are parameters and by Assumption 6A the values of X_i's are a set of fixed numbers (in the process of hypothetical repeated sampling)

$$E(b_0 + b_1 X_i) = b_0 + b_1 X_i$$

Furthermore, by Assumption 2

$$E(u_i) = 0$$

Therefore,

$$E(Y_i) = b_0 + b_1 X_i$$

Proof 2. The variance of $Y_i = E[Y_i - E(Y_i)]^2 = \sigma_u^2$.
   Substitute $Y_i = b_0 + b_1 X_i + u_i$ and $E(Y_i) = b_0 + b_1 X_i$ in the definition of the variance

$$E[Y_i - E(Y_i)]^2 = E[b_0 + b_1 X_i + u_i - b_0 - b_1 X_i]^2 = E(u_i)^2$$

But, by Assumption 3, the u_i's are homoscedastic, that is, they have the constant variance σ_u^2

$$E(u_i^2) = \sigma_u^2 \text{ constant}$$

Therefore,

$$\text{var}(Y_i) = E[Y_i - E(Y_i)]^2 = \sigma_u^2$$

Proof 3. The distribution of Y_i is normal.

The shape of the distribution of Y_i is determined by the shape of the distribution of u_i, which is normal by Assumption 4. Clearly b_0 and b_1, being constants, do not affect the distribution of Y_i. Furthermore the values of the explanatory variable, X_i, are a set of constant values by Assumption 6A and therefore do not affect the shape of the distribution of Y_i.

4.4. THE LEAST SQUARES CRITERION AND THE 'NORMAL' EQUATIONS OF OLS

Thus far we have completed the work involved in the first stage of any econometric application, namely we have specified the model and stated explicitly its assumptions. The next step is the estimation of the model, that is, the computation of the numerical values of its parameters.

The linear relationship $Y_i = b_0 + b_1 X_i + u_i$ holds for the population of the values of X and Y, so that we could obtain *the* numerical values of b_0 and b_1 only if we could have all the conceivably possible values of X, Y, and u which form the population of these variables. Since this is impossible in practice, we get a sample of observed values of Y and X, we specify the distribution of the u's and we try to get satisfactory estimates of the true parameters of the relationship. This is done by fitting a regression line through the observations of the sample, which we consider as an approximation to the true line. The true relationship between X and Y is

$$Y_i = b_0 + b_1 X_i + u_i$$

the true regression line is

$$E(Y_i) = b_0 + b_1 X_i$$

the estimated relationship is

$$Y_i = \hat{b}_0 + \hat{b}_1 X_i + e_i$$

and the estimated regression line is

$$\hat{Y}_i = \hat{b}_0 + \hat{b}_1 X_i$$

where $\hat{Y}$ = estimated value of Y, given a specified value of X

$\hat{b}_0$ = estimate of the true intercept b_0

$\hat{b}_1$ = estimate of the true parameter b_1

e = estimate of the true value of the random term u.

The true and the estimated regression lines are shown in figure 4.5. In our example of the supply function, in order to compute the numerical values of the

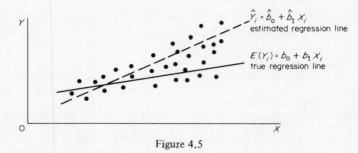

Figure 4.5

true parameters b_0 and b_1 we should have all the conceivable values of quantities supplied at all conceivable prices, which of course is impossible. Consequently we take a sample of observed prices and quantities sold over some period of time and we attempt to obtain the best possible estimate of the supply function.

The snag in this procedure is that from a given sample we may obtain an infinite number of estimated regression lines, by assigning different values to the parameters b_0 and b_1. In figure 4.6 we have drawn two such lines, AA' and BB'. When we assign to the parameters the values b_0^* and b_1^* we get the line $AA' = b_0^* + b_1^* X$, while if the parameters are given the values $\hat{b}_0$ and $\hat{b}_1$, the line will be $BB' = \hat{b}_0 + \hat{b}_1 X$, and so on. It is clear, however, that the deviations of the actual sample observations from each line are different. For example point z is closer to line AA', while point z' is nearer to line BB'. In other words if we choose the upper line $Y^* = b_0^* + b_1^* X$, point z will deviate by e, while if we take the line $BB'(\hat{Y} = \hat{b}_0 + \hat{b}_1 X)$, the same point z will deviate from it by a greater distance equal to $e'(e' > e)$.

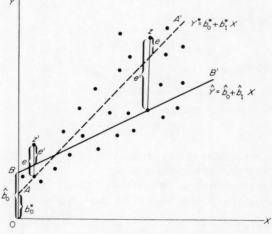

Figure 4.6

Clearly the deviations of the observations from the lines depend on their constant intercept (b_0) and their slope (b_1). The choice among all possible lines is done on the basis of what is called *the least squares criterion*. The rationale of this criterion is easy to understand. It is intuitively obvious that the smaller the deviations from the line, the better the fit of the line to the scatter of observations. Consequently from all possible lines we choose the one for which the deviations of the points is the smallest possible. The *least squares criterion* requires that the regression line be drawn (i.e. its parameters be chosen) in such a way as to minimise the sum of the squares of the deviations of the observations from it.

The first step is to draw the line so that the sum of the simple deviations of the observations is zero — some observations will lie above the line and will have a positive deviation, some will lie below the line, in which case they will have a negative deviation, and finally the points lying on the line will have a zero deviation. In summing these deviations the positive values will offset the negative values, so that the final algebraic sum of these residuals will equal zero by definition $(\Sigma e \equiv 0)$. This of course does not mean that the deviations disappear when we fit the least squares line, but that their algebraic sum is by construction equal to zero. How then, can one minimise a quantity which is by definition zero? The best solution is to square the deviations and minimise the sum of the squares, (Σe_i^2). The reason for calling this method *the least squares method* should now be clear: the method seeks the minimisation of the *sum of the squares* of the deviations of the actual observations from the line.

Our next task is to express the residual deviations $(e$'s$)$ in terms of the observed values of Y and X in our sample. In figure 4.7 the estimated line is $\hat{Y} = \hat{b}_0 + \hat{b}_1 X$. As already mentioned the sign $(^\wedge)$ on top of the dependent variable indicates the estimated (predicted) value of the dependent variable, as distinguished from the observed value of this variable, which is represented by

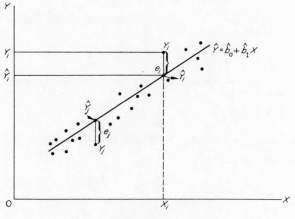

Figure 4.7

the simple letter Y_i. If $\hat{b}_0$ and $\hat{b}_1$ are numerically known, from the estimated line we can obtain a prediction of Y, that is, an 'estimated' value of the dependent variable ($\hat{Y}_i$) which corresponds to a given value of the explanatory variable (X_i). That is, for each given X, the corresponding $\hat{Y}$ lies on the line. For example when X assumes the value X_i, the equation predicts that the dependent variable will assume the (estimated) value $\hat{Y}_i$. However, the actually observed value of the dependent variable which corresponds to X_i, is Y_i, and not $\hat{Y}_i$ as the line predicts. In other words, the actual observations of Y may not lie on the estimated line. It is apparent that the equation does not predict the values of the dependent variable with perfect accuracy. We have denoted by e_i the difference between the observed value Y_i and its estimated value $\hat{Y}_i$, that is

$$e_i = Y_i - \hat{Y}_i$$

Substituting $\hat{Y}_i$ we find

$$e_i = Y_i - \hat{b}_0 - \hat{b}_1 X_i$$

Squaring these deviations and taking their sum we obtain

$$\sum_{i=1}^{n} e_i^2 = \sum_{i=1}^{n} (Y_i - \hat{Y}_i)^2 = \sum_{i=1}^{n} (Y_i - \hat{b}_0 - \hat{b}_1 X_i)^2$$

The sum of squared residual deviations is to be minimised with respect to $\hat{b}_0$ and $\hat{b}_1$. Following the minimisation procedure we get the *normal equations*

$$\Sigma Y = n\hat{b}_0 + \hat{b}_1 \Sigma X \tag{4.3}$$
$$\Sigma XY = \hat{b}_0 \Sigma X + \hat{b}_1 \Sigma X^2 \tag{4.4}$$

Formal derivation of the normal equations

We have to minimise the function

$$\Sigma e_i^2 = \Sigma(Y_i - \hat{b}_0 - \hat{b}_1 X_i)^2$$

with respect to $\hat{b}_0$ and $\hat{b}_1$. The necessary condition for a minimum is that the first derivatives of the function be equal to zero

$$\frac{\partial \Sigma e^2}{\partial \hat{b}_0} = 0 \quad \text{and} \quad \frac{\partial \Sigma e^2}{\partial \hat{b}_1} = 0$$

To obtain the above derivatives we apply the 'function of a function' rule of differentiation. According to this rule if $y = f(w)$ and $w = f(x)$,

then
$$\frac{dy}{dx} = \frac{dy}{dw} \cdot \frac{dw}{dx}$$

In the case of the above function we let $(Y_i - \hat{b}_0 - \hat{b}_1 X_i) = w$. Thus we have:

Partial derivative with respect to $\hat{b}_0$

$$\frac{\partial \Sigma e^2}{\partial \hat{b}_0} = \frac{\partial \Sigma(Y_i - \hat{b}_0 - \hat{b}_1 X_i)^2}{\partial \hat{b}_0} = 0$$

$$2\Sigma(Y_i - \hat{b}_0 - \hat{b}_1 X_i) \cdot (-1) = 0$$

$$\Sigma(Y_i - \hat{b}_0 - \hat{b}_1 X_i) = 0 \tag{4.5}$$

Partial derivative with respect to b_1

$$\frac{\partial \Sigma e^2}{\partial \hat{b}_1} = \frac{\partial \Sigma (Y_i - \hat{b}_0 - \hat{b}_1 X_i)^2}{\partial \hat{b}_1} = 0$$

$$2\Sigma (Y_i - \hat{b}_0 - \hat{b}_1 X_i) . (-X_i) = 0$$

$$\Sigma (Y_i X_i - \hat{b}_0 X_i - \hat{b}_1 X_i^2) = 0 \tag{4.6}$$

Combining equations (4.5) and (4.6) and performing the summations we get

$$\Sigma Y_i - \Sigma \hat{b}_0 - \Sigma \hat{b}_1 X_i = 0$$

$$\Sigma Y_i X_i - \Sigma \hat{b}_0 X_i - \Sigma \hat{b}_1 X_i^2 = 0$$

Applying the usual summation rules (see Appendix I) we obtain the 'normal' equations of OLS

$$\Sigma Y_i = \hat{b}_0 n + \hat{b}_1 \Sigma X_i$$

$$\Sigma Y_i X_i = \hat{b}_0 \Sigma X_i + \hat{b}_1 \Sigma X_i^2$$

Solving the normal equations for $\hat{b}_0$ and $\hat{b}_1$ we obtain the least squares estimates[1]

$$\hat{b}_0 = \frac{\Sigma X^2 \Sigma Y - \Sigma X \Sigma XY}{n\Sigma X^2 - (\Sigma X)^2} \tag{4.7}$$

$$\hat{b}_1 = \frac{n\Sigma XY - \Sigma X \Sigma Y}{n\Sigma X^2 - (\Sigma X)^2} \tag{4.8}$$

It is clear that $\hat{b}_0$ and $\hat{b}_1$ can be estimated by substituting the terms n, ΣX, ΣY, ΣXY and ΣX^2, whose values can be obtained from the sample observations.

The above formulae are expressed in terms of the original sample observations on X and Y. It can be shown that the estimates $\hat{b}_0$ and $\hat{b}_1$ may be obtained by the following formulae which are expressed in deviations of the variables from their means:

$$\hat{b}_0 = \overline{Y} - \hat{b}_1 \overline{X} \tag{4.9}$$

$$\hat{b}_1 = \frac{\Sigma x_i y_i}{\Sigma x_i^2} \tag{4.10}$$

Proof

(1) In Chapter 3 we established that $\Sigma x_i y_i = (n\Sigma XY - \Sigma X \Sigma Y)/n$. (This is the expression 3.5 on p. 37.)

(2) Similarly we have proved (expression 3.6 of Chapter 3) that

$$\Sigma x_i^2 = \frac{n\Sigma X^2 - (\Sigma X)^2}{n}$$

(3) Substituting in the expression for $\hat{b}_1$ we find

$$\hat{b}_1 = \frac{\Sigma x_i y_i}{\Sigma x_i^2} = \frac{(n\Sigma XY - \Sigma X \Sigma Y)/n}{(n\Sigma X^2 - (\Sigma X)^2)/n} = \frac{n\Sigma XY - \Sigma X \Sigma Y}{n\Sigma X^2 - (\Sigma X)^2}$$

---

[1] The solution of a system of equations may be obtained by the use of various methods. In Appendix II we explain the method of determinants which is conceptually the simplest of all.

Table 4.2. Worksheet for the estimation of the supply function of commodity Z

n	Y_i Quantity (in tons)	X_i Price (in £ per ton)	X_i^2	X_iY_i	y_i $(Y_i - \bar{Y})$	x_i $(X_i - \bar{X})$	x_iy_i	x_i^2 $(X_i - \bar{X})^2$	$\hat{Y}_i = \hat{b}_0 + \hat{b}_1 X_i$	e_i $(Y_i - \hat{Y}_i)$	e_i^2
1	69	9	81	621	+ 6	0	0	0	63.00	6.00	36.00
2	76	12	144	912	+13	+3	39	9	72.75	3.25	10.56
3	52	6	36	312	−11	−3	33	9	53.25	− 1.25	1.56
4	56	10	100	560	− 7	+1	−7	1	66.25	−10.25	105.06
5	57	9	81	513	− 6	0	0	0	63.00	− 6.00	36.00
6	77	10	100	770	+14	+1	14	1	66.25	10.75	115.56
7	58	7	49	406	− 5	−2	10	4	56.50	1.50	2.25
8	55	8	64	440	− 8	−1	8	1	59.75	− 4.75	22.56
9	67	12	144	804	+ 4	+3	12	9	72.75	− 5.75	30.06
10	53	6	36	318	−10	−3	30	9	53.25	− 0.25	0.06
11	72	11	121	792	+ 9	+2	18	4	69.50	2.50	6.25
12	64	8	64	512	+ 1	−1	−1	1	59.75	4.25	18.06
$n = 12$	$\Sigma Y_i = 756$	$\Sigma X_i = 108$	ΣX_i^2 $= 1,020$	ΣX_iY_i $= 6,960$	$\Sigma y_i = 0$	$\Sigma x_i = 0$	Σx_iy_i $= 156$	$\Sigma x_i^2 = 48$	$\Sigma \hat{Y}_i$ $= 756.0$	$\Sigma e_i = 0$	Σe_i^2 $= 383.98$

$\bar{Y} = 63$

$\bar{X} = 9$

$\hat{\bar{Y}} = 63$

Dividing the first normal equation through by n we obtain

$$\frac{\Sigma Y}{n} = \frac{\hat{b}_0 n}{n} + \frac{\hat{b}_1 \Sigma X}{n}$$

or
$$\overline{Y} = \hat{b}_0 + \hat{b}_1 \overline{X}$$

that is the regression line passes through the point defined by the means of the variables. This is a very useful result which we will use often in subsequent chapters.

Example. To illustrate the use of the above formulae we will estimate the supply function of commodity z using the data in table 4.2.

We substitute the computed values from table 4.2 into the formulae for $\hat{b}_0$ and $\hat{b}_1$.

(1) *Using the original sample observations*

$$\hat{b}_0 = \frac{\Sigma X^2 \Sigma Y - (\Sigma X)(\Sigma XY)}{n\Sigma X^2 - (\Sigma X)^2} = \frac{(1,020)(756) - (108)(6,960)}{(12)(1,020) - (108)^2} = \frac{19,440}{576} = 33 \cdot 75$$

$$\hat{b}_1 = \frac{n\Sigma XY - \Sigma X \Sigma Y}{n\Sigma X^2 - (\Sigma X)^2} = \frac{(12)(6,960) - (756)(108)}{(12)(1,020) - (108)^2} = \frac{1,872}{576} \approx 3 \cdot 25$$

(2) *Using the deviations of the variables from their means*

$$\hat{b}_1 = \frac{\Sigma xy}{\Sigma x^2} = \frac{156}{48} = 3 \cdot 25$$

$$\hat{b}_0 = \overline{Y} - \hat{b}_1 \overline{X} = 63 - (3 \cdot 25)(9) = 33 \cdot 75$$

Thus the estimated supply function is

$$\hat{Y}_i = 33 \cdot 75 + 3 \cdot 25 X_i$$

4.5 ESTIMATION OF A FUNCTION WHOSE INTERCEPT IS ZERO

In some cases economic theory postulates relationships which have a zero constant intercept, that is, they pass through the origin of the XY plane. For example linear production functions of manufactured products should normally have zero intercept, since output is zero when the factor inputs are zero. In this event we should estimate the function

$$Y = b_0 + b_1 X + u$$

imposing the restriction $b_0 = 0$. The formula for the estimation of $\hat{b}_1$ then becomes

$$\hat{b}_1 = \frac{\Sigma XY}{\Sigma X^2}$$

which involves the actual values of the variables, and not their deviations, as in the case of unrestricted value of b_0.

Proof. We want to fit the line $Y = b_0 + b_1 X_1 + u$, subject to the restriction $b_0 = 0$. This is a restricted minimisation problem: we minimise

$$\Sigma e^2 = \Sigma (Y - \hat{b}_0 - \hat{b}_1 X)^2$$

subject to $\hat{b}_0 = 0$. Following the minimisation procedure for a constrained function, we form the composite function

$$\phi = \Sigma(Y - \hat{b}_0 - \hat{b}_1 X)^2 - \lambda \hat{b}_0,$$

where λ is a Lagrange multiplier, and we minimise it with respect to $\hat{b}_1$ and $\hat{b}_0$:

$$\frac{\partial \phi}{\partial \hat{b}_0} = -2\Sigma(Y - \hat{b}_0 - \hat{b}_1 X) - \lambda = 0 \tag{1}$$

$$\frac{\partial \phi}{\partial \hat{b}_1} = -2\Sigma X(Y - \hat{b}_0 - \hat{b}_1 X) = 0 \tag{2}$$

and

$$\frac{\partial \phi}{\partial \lambda} = -\hat{b}_0 = 0 \tag{3}$$

Substituting (3) into (2) and re-arranging we obtain

$$-2\Sigma X(Y - \hat{b}_1 X) = 0$$

$$\hat{b}_1 = \frac{\Sigma XY}{\Sigma X^2}$$

It can be shown that (a) $\hat{\sigma}_u^2 = \Sigma e_i^2/(n-1)$, (b) $s_{(\hat{b}_1)} = \sqrt{\hat{\sigma}_u^2/\Sigma X^2}$, (c) $R^2 = 1 - \Sigma e_i^2/\Sigma Y_i^2$.

4.6. ESTIMATION OF ELASTICITIES FROM AN ESTIMATED REGRESSION LINE

We said that the estimated function

$$\hat{Y}_i = \hat{b}_0 + \hat{b}_i X_i$$

is the equation of a line whose intercept is $\hat{b}_0$ and its slope $\hat{b}_1$. The coefficient $\hat{b}_1$ is the derivative of $\hat{Y}$ with respect to X

$$\hat{b}_1 = \frac{d\hat{Y}}{dX}$$

and shows the rate of change in $\hat{Y}$ as X changes by a very small amount. It should be clear that if the estimated function is a linear demand or supply function the coefficient $\hat{b}_1$ is not the price elasticity, but a component of the elasticity, which is defined by the formula

$$\eta_p = \frac{dY/Y}{dX/X} = \frac{dY}{dX} \cdot \frac{X}{Y}$$

where η_p = price elasticity
Y = quantity (demanded or supplied)
X = price.

Clearly $\hat{b}_1$ is the component $\dfrac{dY}{dX}$. From an estimated function we obtain an *average* elasticity

$$\eta_p = \hat{b}_1 \cdot \frac{\bar{X}}{\bar{\hat{Y}}} = \hat{b}_1 \cdot \frac{\bar{X}}{\bar{Y}}$$

where $\bar{X}$ = the average price in the sample

$\bar{\hat{Y}}$ = average regressed value of the quantity, i.e. the mean value of the estimated from the regression $\hat{Y}_i$'s

$\bar{Y}$ = average value of the quantity in the sample.

Note that $\bar{\hat{Y}} = \bar{Y}$, that is, the mean of the *estimated* values of Y is equal to the mean of the *actual* (sample) values of Y, because

$$\hat{Y} = \hat{b}_0 + \hat{b}_1 X$$
$$\bar{\hat{Y}} = \hat{b}_0 + \hat{b}_1 \bar{X} = (\bar{Y} - \hat{b}_1 \bar{X}) + \hat{b}_1 \bar{X} = \bar{Y}$$

In our earlier example of the supply function the price elasticity of supply is

$$\eta_p = (3.25)\frac{\bar{X}}{\bar{Y}} = (3.25)\frac{9}{63} \approx 0.46$$

EXERCISES

1. Using the time series in the following table, estimate the consumption function and the savings function (in linear form) of the U.K. What is the marginal propensity to consume and the marginal propensity to save of the country? Interpret the intercepts of the two functions.

Year	Income in £m	Consumption in £m
1964	26,934	21,439
1965	28,729	22,833
1966	30,171	24,205
1967	31,781	25,307
1968	33,450	27,020

2. Assume that over the 1964–8 period direct taxation yielded the following revenues (£m):

1964	1965	1966	1967	1968
4245	5029	5518	5960	6726

Using the income figures of exercise 1 obtain the tax (linear) equation and interpret its coefficients. Plot the tax regression line.

3. A random sample of ten families had the following income and food expenditure (in £ per week):

Families	A	B	C	D	E	F	G	H	I	J
Family income	20	30	33	40	15	13	26	38	35	43
Family expenditure	7	9	8	11	5	4	8	10	9	10

Estimate the regression line of food expenditure on income and interpret your results.

4. The following results have been obtained from a sample of 11 observations on the value of sales (Y) of a firm and the corresponding prices (X).

$$\overline{X} = 519\cdot18 \quad \overline{Y} = 217\cdot82$$

$$\Sigma X_i^2 = 3,134,543 \qquad \Sigma X_i Y_i = 1,296,836 \qquad \Sigma Y_i^2 = 539,512$$

(i) Estimate the regression line of sales on price and interpret the results.

(ii) What is the part of the variation in sales which is not explained by the regression line?

(iii) Estimate the price elasticity of sales.

5. The following table gives the quantities of commodity z bought in each year from 1961–1970 and the corresponding prices.

Year	1961	1962	1963	1964	1965	1966	1967	1968	1969	1970
Quantity (in tons)	770	785	790	795	800	805	810	820	840	850
Price (in £)	18	16	15	15	12	10	10	7	9	6

(i) Estimate the linear demand function for commodity z.

(ii) Calculate the price elasticity of demand.

(iii) Forecast the demand at the mean price of the sample.

(iv) Forecast the demand at $P = 20$.

Note. Additional exercises are included in Appendix III.

5. Statistical Tests of Significance of the Least Squares Estimates: First-Order Tests

In Chapter 4 we developed the formulae for the estimation of the parameters of economic relationships by using the method of least squares. The next stage is to establish criteria for judging the 'goodness' of the parameter estimates. We divide the available criteria into three groups: theoretical *a priori* criteria, statistical criteria and econometric criteria. The theoretical criteria are set by economic theory and refer to the sign and size of the coefficients. They are defined in the first stage of econometric research, that is in the stage of the specification of the model (see Chapter 2). In this chapter we shall develop the *statistical criteria* or *first-order tests* for the evaluation of the parameter estimates. The *econometric criteria* or *second-order tests* will be examined in subsequent chapters.

The two most commonly used tests in econometrics are the following:

The first is the square of the correlation coefficient, r^2, which is used for judging the explanatory power of the linear regression of Y on X. We will prove that r^2 is a measure of the goodness of fit of the regression line to the observed sample values of Y and X.

The second test is based on the standard errors of the parameter estimates and is applied for judging the statistical reliability of the estimates of the regression coefficients $\hat{b}_0$ and $\hat{b}_1$. It provides a measure of the degree of confidence that we may attribute to the estimates $\hat{b}_0$ and $\hat{b}_1$. It enables the researcher to decide how 'good' estimates of the true parameters of the (population) relationship $\hat{b}_0$ and $\hat{b}_1$ are. In Chapter 8 we shall develop an alternative statistical technique for judging the significance of the OLS results, the *Analysis of Variance* technique.

5.1. THE TEST OF THE GOODNESS OF FIT WITH r^2

5.1.1. DEFINITION OF r^2

After the estimation of the parameters and the determination of the least squares regression line, we need to know how 'good' is the fit of this line to the sample observations of Y and X, that is to say we need to measure the dispersion of observations around the regression line. This knowledge is essential, because the closer the observations to the line, the better the goodness of fit, that is the better is the explanation of the variations of Y by the changes in the explanatory variables.

We will prove that a measure of the goodness of fit is the square of the correlation coefficient, r^2, which shows the percentage of the total variation of

69

the dependent variable that can be explained by the independent variable X. We plot the observations on a rectangular co-ordinate system. Next we compute the means

$$\overline{X} = \sum_i X_i/n \quad \text{and} \quad \overline{Y} = \sum_i Y_i/n$$

and we draw perpendiculars through the points of these means (figure 5.1).

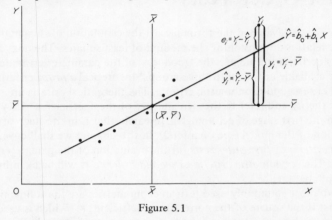

Figure 5.1

By fitting the line $\hat{Y} = \hat{b}_0 + \hat{b}_1 X$ we try to obtain the explanation of the variations of the dependent variable Y produced by the changes of the explanatory variable X. However, the fact that the observations deviate from the estimated line shows that the regression line explains only a part of the total variation of the dependent variable. A part of the variation, defined as $e_i = Y_i - \hat{Y}$, remains unexplained.

(1) We may compute the total variation of the dependent variable by comparing each value of Y to the mean value $\overline{Y}$ and adding all the resulting deviations.[1] Denoting the deviations of the values Y_i around their mean $\overline{Y}$ by lower case letters we have

$$[\text{Total variation in } Y] = \sum_i^n y_i^2 = \sum_i^n (Y_i - \overline{Y})^2 \tag{5.1}$$

Note that in order to find the total variation of the Y's we square the simple deviations, since by definition the sum of the simple deviations of any variable around its mean is identically equal to zero

$$\sum_i^n (Y_i - \overline{Y}) = \sum_i^n y_i = 0$$

[1] When we speak of changes in Y we must define the 'basis of reference', that is, a value of the variable Y, to which we compare any other value that may be assumed by this variable. As such reference value we may take the origin ($Y = 0$) or the mean value ($\overline{Y}$) or any other statistic of Y (the median, etc.). However, it is customary and computationally convenient to take the mean as reference value and express the total variation of Y's as the sum of the deviations of the Y's from their mean.

(2) In the same way we define the deviation of the regressed (that is the estimated from the line) values, $\hat{Y}$'s, from the mean value, $\hat{y}_i = \hat{Y}_i - \overline{Y}$. This is the part of the total variation of Y_i which is explained by the regression line. Thus the sum of the squares of these deviations is the total *explained by the regression line variation* of the dependent variable

$$[\text{Explained Variation}] = \sum_i^n \hat{y}_i^2 = \sum_i^n (\hat{Y}_i - \overline{Y})^2 \qquad (5.2)$$

(3) We have already defined the residual e_i as the difference $e_i = Y_i - \hat{Y}_i$, that is as the part of the variation of the dependent variable which is not explained by the regression line and is attributed to the existence of the disturbance variable u. Thus the sum of the squared residuals gives the total unexplained variation of the dependent variable Y around its mean

$$[\text{Unexplained Variation}] = \sum_i^n e_i^2 = \sum_i^n (Y_i - \hat{Y}_i)^2 \qquad (5.3)$$

In summary

$e_i = Y_i - \hat{Y}_i$ = deviation of the observations Y_i from the regression line
$y_i = Y_i - \overline{Y}$ = deviation of Y_i from its mean
$\hat{y}_i = \hat{Y}_i - \overline{Y}$ = deviation of the regressed value $\hat{Y}_i$ from the mean

Combining these expressions we obtain

$$Y_i = y_i + \overline{Y} \quad \text{and} \quad \hat{Y}_i = \hat{y}_i + \overline{Y}$$

Substituting in the expressions of the residuals we find

$$e_i = (y_i + \overline{Y}) - (\hat{y}_i + \overline{Y}) \qquad (5.4)$$

$$e_i = y_i - \hat{y}_i$$

and
$$y_i = \hat{y}_i + e_i. \qquad (5.5)$$

This equation shows that each deviation of the observed values of Y from its mean consists of two components: the first is the explained by the regression line variation and the second is the unexplained variation. This relationship is shown in figure 5.1.

Substituting 5.5 into 5.1 we obtain

$$\sum_i y_i^2 = \sum_i (\hat{y}_i + e_i)^2$$

$$= \sum_i \hat{y}_i^2 + \sum_i e_i^2 + 2\sum_i \hat{y}_i e_i$$

But $\sum_i \hat{y}_i e_i = 0$.

This can be proved as follows:
(a) We know that $y_i = \hat{Y}_i - \overline{Y}$. But $\hat{Y}_i = \hat{b}_0 + \hat{b}_1 X_i$ and $\overline{Y} = \hat{b}_0 + \hat{b}_1 \overline{X}$.
Therefore $\hat{y}_i = (\hat{b}_0 + \hat{b}_1 X_i) - (\hat{b}_0 + \hat{b}_1 \overline{X}) = \hat{b}_1 (X_i - \overline{X}) = \hat{b}_1 x_i$, where $x_i = X_i - \overline{X}$.
(b) We also know that $e_i = y_i - \hat{y}_i = y_i - \hat{b}_1 x_i$.
Therefore $\sum \hat{y}_i e_i = \sum (\hat{b}_1 x_i)(y_i - \hat{b}_1 x_i) = \hat{b}_1 (\sum x_i y_i - \hat{b}_1 \sum x_i^2)$.

But $\hat{b}_1 = \Sigma x_i y_i / \Sigma x_i^2$.
Therefore we may write:

$$\Sigma \hat{y}_i e_i = \hat{b}_1 \left(\Sigma x_i y_i - \frac{\Sigma x_i y_i}{\Sigma x_i^2} \cdot \Sigma x_i^2 \right) = 0$$

Therefore

$$\Sigma y_i^2 = \qquad \Sigma \hat{y}_i^2 + \qquad \Sigma e_i^2 \qquad\qquad (5.6)$$

or

$$\begin{bmatrix} \text{Total} \\ \text{Variation} \end{bmatrix} = \begin{bmatrix} \text{Explained} \\ \text{Variation} \end{bmatrix} + \begin{bmatrix} \text{Unexplained} \\ \text{(residual) Variation} \end{bmatrix}$$

The explained variation expressed as a percentage of total variation is $\Sigma \hat{y}^2 / \Sigma y^2$.

But $\hat{y} = \hat{b}_1 x$. Substituting we find

$$\frac{\Sigma \hat{y}^2}{\Sigma y^2} = \frac{\Sigma (\hat{b}_1 x)^2}{\Sigma y^2} = \hat{b}_1^2 \frac{\Sigma x^2}{\Sigma y^2}$$

Given that $\hat{b}_1 = \Sigma xy / \Sigma x^2$, we get

$$\frac{\Sigma \hat{y}^2}{\Sigma y^2} = \frac{(\Sigma xy)^2}{(\Sigma x^2)^2} \cdot \frac{(\Sigma x^2)}{\Sigma y^2} = \frac{(\Sigma xy)^2}{(\Sigma x^2)(\Sigma y^2)}$$

Comparing this result with the formula of the correlation coefficient developed in Chapter 3 we see that

$$\frac{\Sigma \hat{y}^2}{\Sigma y^2} = r^2 \qquad\qquad (5.7)$$

since

$$r = \frac{\Sigma x_i y_i}{\sqrt{\Sigma x_i^2} \cdot \sqrt{\Sigma y_i^2}}$$

Thus r^2 determines the proportion of the variation in Y which is explained by variations in X. For this reason r^2 is sometimes called the *coefficient of determination*. For example, if $r_{Y \cdot X}^2 = 0 \cdot 90$, this means that the regression line gives a good fit to the observed data, since this line explains 90 per cent of the total variation of the Y values around their mean. The remaining 10 per cent of the total variation in Y is unaccounted for by the regression line and is attributed to the factors included in the disturbance variable u.

5.1.2. LIMITING VALUES OF THE COEFFICIENT OF DETERMINATION, r^2

It can be proved that the coefficient of determination can assume values lying between zero and one, that is to say

$$0 \leqslant r^2 \leqslant 1$$

Proof. We have proved $\Sigma y_i^2 = \Sigma \hat{y}_i^2 + \Sigma e_i^2$. Dividing through by Σy^2 we get

$$1 = \frac{\Sigma \hat{y}^2}{\Sigma y^2} + \frac{\Sigma e^2}{\Sigma y^2} \qquad \text{or} \qquad 1 = r^2 + \frac{\Sigma e^2}{\Sigma y^2}$$

therefore
$$r^2 = 1 - \frac{\Sigma e^2}{\Sigma y^2}$$

Recall that $\Sigma e^2/\Sigma y^2$ is the proportion of the unexplained variation of the Y's around their mean $\overline{Y}$. If all the observations lie on the regression line, there will be no scatter of points; in other words the total variation of Y is explained completely by the estimated regression line, and consequently there will be no unexplained variation; that is $\Sigma e^2/\Sigma y^2 = 0$ and hence $r^2 = 1$. On the other hand, if the regression line explains only part of the variation in Y, there will be some unexplained variation, $(\Sigma e^2/\Sigma y^2 > 0)$. Therefore r^2 will be smaller than 1. Finally if the regression line does not explain any part of the variation of Y, $\Sigma e^2/\Sigma y^2 = 1$, because $\Sigma y^2 = \Sigma e^2$. Therefore in this case $r^2 = 0$.

5.1.3. RELATIONSHIP BETWEEN r^2 AND THE SLOPE $\hat{b}_1$

The relationship between the square of the correlation coefficient, r^2, and the slope of the regression line is given by the formula

$$r^2 = \hat{b}_1 \frac{\Sigma xy}{\Sigma y^2} \tag{5.8}$$

Proof. We found that

$$r^2 = \frac{(\Sigma xy)^2}{(\Sigma x^2)(\Sigma y^2)}$$

Rearranging slightly we obtain

$$r^2 = \frac{(\Sigma xy)}{(\Sigma x^2)} \cdot \frac{(\Sigma xy)}{(\Sigma y^2)}$$

But $\Sigma xy/\Sigma x^2 = \hat{b}_1$. Hence $r^2 = \hat{b}_1 \cdot (\Sigma xy/\Sigma y^2)$.

In summary, r^2 may be computed in various ways

$$r^2 = \frac{(\Sigma xy)^2}{(\Sigma x^2)(\Sigma y^2)}$$

$$r^2 = 1 - \frac{\Sigma e^2}{\Sigma y^2} \quad \text{or} \quad r^2 = \hat{b}_1 \cdot \frac{\Sigma xy}{\Sigma y^2} \quad \text{or} \quad r^2 = \hat{b}_1^2 \cdot \frac{\Sigma x^2}{\Sigma y^2}$$

Example. The coefficient of determination of the supply function estimated in Chapter 4 is found as follows.

$$\hat{Y}_i = 33.75 + 3.25\, X_i$$

$$\Sigma e_i^2 = 383.98$$

$$\Sigma y_i^2 = 894$$

Thus

$$r_{YX}^2 = 1 - \frac{\Sigma e_i^2}{\Sigma y_i^2}$$

$$= 0.570$$

5.2. TESTS OF SIGNIFICANCE OF THE PARAMETER ESTIMATES

Since $\hat{b}_0$ and $\hat{b}_1$ are sample estimates of the parameters b_0 and b_1 we must test their statistical reliability. In order to apply the standard tests of significance we must, among other things, know the mean and variance.[1] We will first develop formulae for the computation of the mean and variance of the least-squares estimates. We will next explain the procedure of the standard error test and the 't' test for judging the statistical significance of the estimates. Finally, we explain the construction of confidence intervals for the estimates $\hat{b}_0$ and $\hat{b}_1$.

5.2.1. MEAN AND VARIANCE OF THE LEAST-SQUARES PARAMETER ESTIMATES

In this section we will establish the following results
(1) Mean of $\hat{b}_0$:

$$E(\hat{b}_0) = b_0.$$ (5.9)

(2) Variance of $\hat{b}_0$:

$$\text{var}(\hat{b}_0) = E[\hat{b}_0 - b_0]^2 = \sigma_u^2 \frac{\Sigma X_i^2}{n \Sigma x_i^2}$$ (5.10)

(3) Mean of $\hat{b}_1$:

$$E(\hat{b}_1) = b_1.$$ (5.11)

(4) Variance of $\hat{b}_1$:

$$\text{var}(\hat{b}_1) = E[\hat{b}_1 - b_1]^2 = \sigma_u^2 \frac{1}{\Sigma x_i^2}$$ (5.12)

(5) Estimate of the variance of u:

$$\hat{\sigma}_u^2 = \frac{\Sigma e_i^2}{n - K}$$ (5.13)

where K = total number of parameters estimated from the regression.

5.2.2. THE MEAN OF $\hat{b}_1$

We *assume* that we draw repeated samples of size n from the population of Y and X, and for each sample we estimate the parameters $\hat{b}_0$ and $\hat{b}_1$. This is known as *hypothetical repeated sampling procedure*. If all the possible samples are taken, then the mean value of $\hat{b}_1$ will be its expected value: (mean $\hat{b}_1$) = $E(\hat{b}_1)$. To find the value of the mean in terms of the observations of our sample of Y and X we work as follows.

We established that

$$\hat{b}_1 = \frac{\Sigma x_i y_i}{\Sigma x_i^2}$$

Substituting $y_i = (Y_i - \overline{Y})$ we obtain

$$\hat{b}_1 = \frac{\Sigma x_i y_i}{\Sigma x_i^2} = \frac{\Sigma x_i (Y_i - \overline{Y})}{\Sigma x_i^2} = \frac{\Sigma x_i Y_i}{\Sigma x_i^2} - \frac{\overline{Y} \Sigma x_i}{\Sigma x_i^2}$$

But by definition the sum of the deviations of a variable from its mean is identically equal to zero, $\Sigma x_i = 0$. Therefore

$$\hat{b}_1 = \frac{\Sigma x_i Y_i}{\Sigma x_i^2} = \Sigma \left[\frac{x_i}{\Sigma x_i^2} Y_i \right]$$ (5.14)

[1] See Appendix I.

By Assumption 6A of the method of least squares, the values of X are a set of fixed values, which do not change from sample to sample. Consequently the ratio $x_i/\Sigma x_i^2$ will be constant from sample to sample, and if we denote this ratio by k_i we may write the estimate $\hat{b}_1$ in the form

$$\hat{b}_1 = \Sigma k_i Y_i.$$

By substituting the value of $Y_i = b_0 + b_1 X_i + u_i$ and rearranging the factors in the resultant expression we find

$$\hat{b}_1 = \Sigma k_i (b_0 + b_1 X_i + u_i)$$

$$= b_0 \Sigma k_i + b_1 \Sigma k_i X_i + \Sigma k_i u_i$$

But $\Sigma k_i = 0$ and $\Sigma k_i X_i = 1$.

Proof 1

$$\Sigma k_i = \frac{\Sigma x_i}{\Sigma x_i^2} = \frac{\Sigma (X_i - \overline{X})}{\Sigma x_i^2} = \frac{0}{\Sigma x_i^2} = 0$$

Proof 2

$$\Sigma \ k_i X_i = \frac{\Sigma x_i X_i}{\Sigma x_i^2} = \frac{\Sigma (X_i - \overline{X}) X_i}{\Sigma x_i^2} = \frac{\Sigma X_i^2 - \overline{X} \Sigma X_i}{\Sigma x_i^2} = 1$$

given $\Sigma x_i^2 = \Sigma X_i^2 - \overline{X} \Sigma X_i$ (see Chapter 3, expression 3.6).

Therefore

$$\hat{b}_1 = b_1 + \Sigma k_i u_i = b_1 + \frac{\Sigma x_i u_i}{\Sigma x_i^2}$$

Taking expected values, and noting that by Assumption 6A the X_i's are fixed, we obtain

$$E(\hat{b}_1) = E(b_1) + E\left[\frac{\Sigma x_i u_i}{\Sigma x_i^2}\right] = E(b_1) + \frac{\Sigma x_i E(u_i)}{\Sigma x_i^2}$$

Since b_1, the true population parameter is constant, $E(b_1) = b_1$. Furthermore by Assumption 2 the mean value of u is zero ($E(u_i) = 0$), so that the second term in the right-hand side vanishes and we have

$$\text{Mean of } \hat{b}_1 = E(\hat{b}_1) = b_1.$$

The mean of the ordinary least squares estimate $\hat{b}_1$ is equal to the true value of the population parameter b_1. This result has been established by making use of Assumption 2 and Assumption 6A.

5.2.3. THE VARIANCE OF $\hat{b}_1$

It can be proved that

$$\text{var}(\hat{b}_1) = E[\hat{b}_1 - E(\hat{b}_1)]^2 = E[\hat{b}_1 - b_1]^2 = \sigma_u^2 \frac{1}{\Sigma x_i^2}$$

Proof. We established in 5.14 that

$$\hat{b}_1 = \frac{\Sigma x_i Y_i}{\Sigma x_i^2} = \Sigma k_i Y_i$$

where $k_i = \dfrac{x_i}{\Sigma x_i^2}$ = constant weights in the process of hypothetical repeated sampling.
Therefore

$$\text{var}(\hat{b}_1) = \text{var}(\Sigma k_i Y_i) = \Sigma k_i^2 \text{ var}(Y_i)$$

given that $k_i = x_i/\Sigma x_i^2$ are constant weights, independent of the values of Y_i by Assumption 6A.
But $\text{var}(Y_i) = \sigma_u^2$ (see Chapter 4, expression 4.2). Therefore

$$\text{var}(\hat{b}_1) = \Sigma k_i^2 \ \sigma_u^2 = \sigma_u^2 \ \Sigma k_i^2$$

$$= \sigma_u^2 \ \Sigma \left(\frac{x_i}{\Sigma x_i^2} \right)^2 = \sigma_u^2 \ \frac{\Sigma x_i^2}{(\Sigma x_i^2)^2}$$

$$= \sigma_u^2 \ \frac{1}{\Sigma x_i^2}$$

5.2.4. THE MEAN OF $\hat{b}_0$

It can be proved that

$$E(\hat{b}_0) = b_0$$

Proof. We have established in Chapter 4 (expression 4.9) that

$$\hat{b}_0 = \overline{Y} - \hat{b}_1 \overline{X}$$

Substituting $\hat{b}_1 = \Sigma k_i Y_i$ we obtain

$$\hat{b}_0 = \overline{Y} - \overline{X} \Sigma k_i Y_i = \frac{\Sigma Y}{n} - \overline{X} \Sigma k_i Y_i$$

Taking Y_i as a common factor we may write

$$\hat{b}_0 = \Sigma \left[\frac{1}{n} - \overline{X} k_i \right] Y_i \tag{5.15}$$

Taking expected values

$$E(\hat{b}_0) = \Sigma \left[\frac{1}{n} - \overline{X} k_i \right] E(Y_i)$$

given that n, $\overline{X}$ and k_i are constant from sample to sample.
But in Chapter 4 (expression 4.1) we established that

$$E(Y_i) = b_0 + b_1 X_i$$

Therefore

$$E(\hat{b}_0) = \Sigma \left[\frac{1}{n} - \overline{X} k_i \right] (b_0 + b_1 X_i)$$

$$= \Sigma \left[\frac{b_0}{n} - \overline{X} k_i b_0 + \frac{b_1 X_i}{n} - \overline{X} k_i b_1 X_i \right]$$

$$= b_0 + b_1 \overline{X} - b_1 \overline{X}$$

since $\Sigma k_i = 0$ and $\Sigma k_i X_i = 1$ (see page 75). Therefore

$$E(\hat{b}_0) = b_0$$

5.2.5. THE VARIANCE OF $\hat{b}_0$

It can be proved that

$$\text{var}(\hat{b}_0) = E[\hat{b}_0 - E(\hat{b}_0)]^2 = E[\hat{b}_0 - b_0]^2 = \sigma_u^2 \frac{\Sigma X^2}{n \Sigma x^2}$$

Proof. We established in 5.15 that

$$\hat{b}_0 = \Sigma \left[\frac{1}{n} - \bar{X} k_i \right] Y_i$$

Therefore

$$\text{var}(\hat{b}_0) = \text{var} \left[\Sigma \left(\frac{1}{n} - \bar{X} k_i \right) Y_i \right]$$

$$= \Sigma \left[\frac{1}{n} - \bar{X} k_i \right]^2 \cdot \text{var}(Y_i)$$

But $\text{var}(Y_i) = \sigma_u^2$ (see Chapter 4 (expression 4.2)).
Therefore

$$\text{var}(\hat{b}_0) = \sigma_u^2 \Sigma \left[\frac{1}{n^2} - \frac{2 \bar{X} k_i}{n} + \bar{X}^2 k_i^2 \right]$$

Since $\Sigma k_i = 0$ and $\Sigma k_i^2 = \frac{1}{\Sigma x^2}$, we obtain

$$\text{var}(\hat{b}_0) = \sigma_u^2 \left[\frac{1}{n} + \frac{\bar{X}^2}{\Sigma x_i^2} \right] = \sigma_u^2 \left[\frac{\Sigma x_i^2 + n \bar{X}^2}{n \Sigma x_i^2} \right]$$

Now $\Sigma x_i^2 = \Sigma(X_i - \bar{X})^2 = \Sigma X_i^2 - n \bar{X}^2$. Therefore

$$\text{var}(\hat{b}_0) = \sigma_u^2 \frac{\Sigma X_i^2}{n \Sigma x_i^2}$$

Another convenient expression for the variance of $\hat{b}_0$ is

$$\text{var}(\hat{b}_0) = \sigma_u^2 \left(\frac{1}{n} + \frac{\bar{X}^2}{\Sigma x_i^2} \right)$$

5.2.6. THE VARIANCE OF THE RANDOM VARIABLE u

The formulae of the variance of $\hat{b}_0$ and $\hat{b}_1$ involve the variance of the random term u, σ_u^2. However, the true variance of u_i cannot be computed since the values of u_i are not observable. But we may obtain an unbiased estimate of σ_u^2 from the expression

$$\hat{\sigma}_u^2 = \frac{\Sigma e_i^2}{n - 2}$$

where $e_i = Y_i - \hat{Y}_i = Y_i - \hat{b}_0 - \hat{b}_1 X_i$

Proof. We use the device of repeated (hypothetical) sampling, through which we obtain all possible samples of size n, compute a regression line for each sample and find the values of the residuals e_i from each regression. The variance of the residuals $(e_i = Y_i - \hat{Y}_i)$ is defined as the expected value of the squared differences of e_i's from their mean, that is:

$$\text{var}(e) = E[e_i - E(e)]^2 = E(e_i^2)$$

since by definition $E(e) = 0$.

The problem is to express this variance in terms of the sample observations of X and Y. We have established in 5.4 that

$$e_i = y_i - \hat{y}_i$$

But $y_i = b_1 x_i + (u_i - \overline{u})$ (where $\overline{u}$ = mean value of u in the particular sample). Because from

$$Y_i = b_0 + b_1 X_i + u_i$$

and

$$\overline{Y} = b_0 + b_1 \overline{X} + \overline{u}$$

we get, by subtraction,

$$y_i = (Y_i - \overline{Y}) = b_1(X_i - \overline{X}) + (u_i - \overline{u}) = b_1 x_i + (u_i - \overline{u})$$

Note that while $E(u) = 0$ (that is in taking a very large number of samples we expect u to have a mean value of zero by assumption), in any particular single sample $\overline{u}$ is not necessarily zero.

Similarly $\hat{y}_i = \hat{b}_1 x_i$.

Therefore

$$e_i = b_1 x_i + (u_i - \overline{u}) - \hat{b}_1 x_i$$
$$= (u_i - \overline{u}) - (\hat{b}_1 - b_1) x_i$$

The summation over the n sample values of the squares of the residuals yields

$$\Sigma e_i^2 = \Sigma[(u_i - \overline{u}) - (\hat{b}_1 - b_1)x_i]^2$$
$$= \Sigma[(u_i - \overline{u})^2 + (\hat{b}_1 - b_1)^2 x_i^2 - 2(u_i - \overline{u})(\hat{b}_1 - b_1)x_i]$$
$$= \Sigma(u_i - \overline{u})^2 + (\hat{b}_1 - b_1)^2 \Sigma x_i^2 - 2(\hat{b}_1 - b_1)\Sigma x_i(u_i - \overline{u})$$

Taking expected values we have

$$E(\Sigma e^2) = E[\Sigma(u_i - \overline{u})^2] + E[(\hat{b}_1 - b_1)^2 \Sigma x_i^2] - 2E[(\hat{b}_1 - b_1)\Sigma x_i(u_i - \overline{u})]$$

The right-hand side terms may be rearranged as follows

(a)
$$E[\Sigma(u - \overline{u})^2] = E[\Sigma u^2 - \overline{u}\,\Sigma u_i]$$

$$= E\left[\Sigma u^2 - \frac{(\Sigma u)^2}{n}\right]$$

$$= \Sigma E(u^2) - \frac{1}{n} E[\Sigma u]^2$$

$$= n\sigma_u^2 - \frac{1}{n} E(u_1 + u_2 + \ldots + u)^2 \qquad \text{(since } E(u_2^2) = \sigma_u^2)$$

$$= n\sigma_u^2 - \frac{1}{n} E[\Sigma u_i^2 + 2\sum_{i \neq j} u_i u_j]$$

$$= n\sigma_u^2 - \frac{1}{n}\left[\Sigma E(u_i^2) + 2\sum_{i \neq j} E(u_i u_j)\right] = n\sigma_u^2 - \frac{1}{n}n\sigma_u^2 - \frac{2}{n}\Sigma E(u_i u_j)$$

$$= n\sigma_u^2 - \sigma_u^2 \qquad \text{(given } E(u_i u_j) = 0)$$

$$= \sigma_u^2(n - 1).$$

(b)
$$E[(\hat{b}_1 - b_1)^2 \Sigma x_i^2] = \Sigma x_i^2 \cdot E(\hat{b}_1 - b_1)^2$$

given that the X's are fixed in all samples. But

$$E[\hat{b}_1 - b_1]^2 = \text{var}(\hat{b}_1) = \sigma_u^2 \, \frac{1}{\Sigma x^2}$$

Therefore

$$E[(\hat{b}_1 - b_1)^2 \, \Sigma x_i^2] = \Sigma x_i^2 \, \sigma_u^2 \, \frac{1}{\Sigma x_i^2} = \sigma_u^2$$

(c) $\qquad E[(\hat{b}_1 - b_1) \, \Sigma x_i (u_i - \bar{u})] = E[(\hat{b}_1 - b_1)(\Sigma x_i u_i - \Sigma x_i \bar{u})]$.

But $\hat{b}_1 = b_1 + \Sigma k_i u_i$, from which $(\hat{b}_1 - b_1) = \Sigma k_i u_i$.

Therefore $E[(\hat{b}_1 - b_1) \, \Sigma x_i (u_i - \bar{u})] = E[(\Sigma k_i u_i)(\Sigma x_i u_i - \bar{u} \Sigma x_i)]$

$$= E[(\Sigma k_i u_i)(\Sigma x_i u_i)] \qquad (\text{given } \Sigma x_i = 0)$$

$$= E\left[\left(\frac{\Sigma x_i u_i}{\Sigma x_i^2}\right)(\Sigma x_i u_i)\right] \qquad \left(\text{since } k = \frac{x_i}{\Sigma x_i^2}\right)$$

$$= E\left[\frac{(\Sigma x_i u_i)^2}{\Sigma x_i^2}\right]$$

$$= E\left[\frac{\Sigma x_i^2 u_i^2 + 2 \sum_{i \neq j} (x_i x_j)(u_i u_j)}{\Sigma x_i^2}\right]$$

$$= \left[\frac{\Sigma x_i^2 E(u_i^2)}{\Sigma x_i^2} + \frac{2 \sum_{i \neq j} (x_i x_j) E(u_i u_j)}{\Sigma x_i^2}\right]$$

$$= \frac{\Sigma x_i^2 E(u_i^2)}{\Sigma x_i^2} \qquad (\text{given } E(u_i u_j) = 0)$$

$$= E(u_i^2) = \sigma_u^2.$$

Consequently the expected value of the sum of squares of the residuals becomes by substitution:

$$E(\Sigma e^2) = (n-1) \, \sigma_u^2 + \sigma_u^2 - 2\sigma_u^2 = (n-2) \, \sigma_u^2,$$

from which we get

$$E\left(\frac{\Sigma e^2}{n-2}\right) = \sigma_u^2$$

Defining $\hat{\theta}_u^2 = \Sigma e^2 / (n-2)$ we may write

$$E(\hat{\theta}_u^2) = \sigma_u^2$$

Thus $\Sigma e^2 / (n-2)$ is an unbiased estimate of the true variance of u.

5.2.7. THE SAMPLING DISTRIBUTION OF THE LEAST SQUARES ESTIMATES

We have found expressions for the mean and variance of the least squares estimates. Given that by Assumption 4 the random variable u is normally distributed, it can be proved that the distribution of the estimates $\hat{b}_0$ and $\hat{b}_1$ is also normal (see R. L. Anderson and T. A. Bancroft, *Statistical Theory in Research*, New York; McGraw-Hill, 1952, pp. 63–4).

These results may be stated in summary form

$$\hat{b}_0 \sim N\left(b_0, \sqrt{\sigma_u^2 \frac{\Sigma X_i^2}{n\Sigma x_i^2}}\right)$$

$$\hat{b}_1 \sim N\left(b_1, \sqrt{\sigma_u^2 \frac{1}{\Sigma x_i^2}}\right)$$

The distribution of $\hat{b}_1$ is shown in figure 5.2.

Figure 5.2

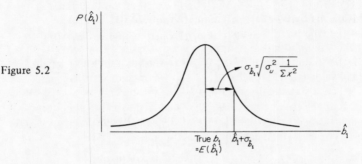

5.2.8. THE STANDARD-ERROR TEST OF THE LEAST SQUARES ESTIMATES

The least squares estimates $\hat{b}_0$ and $\hat{b}_1$ are obtained from a sample of observations on Y and X. Since sampling errors are inevitable in all estimates, it is necessary to apply tests of significance in order to measure the size of the error and determine the degree of confidence in the validity of the estimates.

There are several tests for this purpose. In the present section we will examine only one of them, namely the *standard error test* which is popular in applied econometric research.[1] This test helps us to decide whether the estimates $\hat{b}_0$ and $\hat{b}_1$ are significantly different from zero, i.e. whether the sample from which they have been estimated might have come from a population whose true parameters are zero ($b_0 = 0$ and/or $b_1 = 0$).[2] Formally we test the null hypothesis

$$H_0 : b_i = 0$$

against the alternative hypothesis

$$H_1 : b_i \neq 0$$

The standard-error test may be outlined as follows. From the formulae of the variances of $\hat{b}_0$ and $\hat{b}_1$, established in the preceding section, we compute

---

[1] In a subsequent section we will prove that the standard error test is formally equivalent to the Student's t test. Furthermore in Chapter 8 we deal with the F statistic, which is appropriate, among others, for conducting joint tests of significance, i.e. tests of the significance of all the $\hat{b}$'s in the function.

[2] Note that the null hypothesis can be generalised to allow for any *a priori* value for the true b. See pp. 83–5 and 86–9.

their standard error

$$s(\hat{b}_1) = \sqrt{\text{var}(\hat{b}_1)} = \sqrt{\hat{\sigma}_u^2 / \Sigma x^2} = \sqrt{\frac{\Sigma e^2}{(n-2)\Sigma x^2}}$$

$$s(\hat{b}_0) = \sqrt{\text{var}(\hat{b}_0)} = \sqrt{\frac{\hat{\sigma}_u^2 \Sigma X^2}{n \Sigma x^2}} = \sqrt{\frac{(\Sigma e^2)\Sigma X^2}{(n-2)n\Sigma x^2}}$$

We next compare the standard deviations with the numerical values of $\hat{b}_0$ and $\hat{b}_1$. If the standard error is smaller than half the numerical value of the parameter estimate (that is if $s(\hat{b}_i) < (\hat{b}_i/2)$, we conclude that this estimate is statistically significant. This means that we reject the null hypothesis (we reject the hypothesis that the true population parameter $b_i = 0$), which is equivalent to accepting that the true population parameter b_i is different from zero. If, on the other hand, the standard error of the parameter estimate is greater than half its numerical value (that is if $s(\hat{b}_i) > (\hat{b}_i/2)$, we conclude that the least squares estimate is not statistically significant. This means that we accept the null hypothesis that the true parameter $b_1 = 0$. In arriving at the conclusion regarding the significance or nonsignificance of $\hat{b}$ we have been using a two-tail test at the 5 per cent level of significance (see Appendix I).

Economic interpretation of the 'standard-error test'

The procedure outlined above provides a rule of thumb for deciding whether the estimates $\hat{b}_0$ and $\hat{b}_1$ are statistically reliable. The acceptance or rejection of the null hypothesis has a definite economic meaning. Namely the acceptance of the null hypothesis $b_1 = 0$ implies that the explanatory variable to which this estimate relates does not in fact influence the dependent variable Y and should not be included in the function, since the conducted test provided evidence that changes in X leave Y unaffected. In other words acceptance of H_0 implies that the relationship between Y and X is in fact $Y = b_0 + (0)(X) = b_0$, i.e. there is no relationship between Y and X.[1]

Geometric interpretation of the 'standard-error test'

We said that b_0 is the intercept of the regression line on the Y-axis, and b_1 measures the slope of the regression line.

(1) If, when conducting the above test, we find that $s(\hat{b}_0) > \hat{b}_0/2$ and accept the null hypothesis $b_0 = 0$, then the regression line passes through the origin of the axes (figure 5.3), since the relationship between Y and X is actually

$$Y_i = 0 + b_1 X_i = b_1 X_i$$

(2) Similarly, if from the test we find $s(\hat{b}_1) > \hat{b}_1/2$, we would accept the null hypothesis that $b_1 = 0$. This would imply that the relationship between Y

---

[1] Note that in this section we assumed a two-tail test of significance, conducted at the 5 per cent level of significance; that is, we allowed our conclusion to be wrong five times out of one hundred. See Appendix I, p. 563.

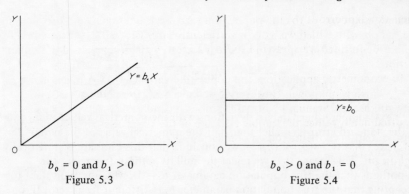

$b_0 = 0$ and $b_1 > 0$

Figure 5.3

$b_0 > 0$ and $b_1 = 0$

Figure 5.4

and X is in fact $Y = b_0$. The slope of the regression line would be equal to zero, that is the regression line would in this case be parallel to the X-axis (figure 5.4).

To facilitate the comparison of the standard errors of the estimates to their numerical value it is convenient to print the standard errors in parentheses under the parameter estimates to which they refer.

Example. The standard errors of the coefficients of the supply function, estimated in Chapter 4, are

$$s(\hat{b}_1) = \sqrt{\hat{\sigma}_u^2/\Sigma x^2} = \sqrt{38.4/48} \approx 0.9$$
$$s(\hat{b}_0) = \sqrt{(\hat{\sigma}_u^2)(\Sigma X^2)/n\Sigma x^2} = \sqrt{(38\cdot4)(1,020)/(12)(48)} \approx 8\cdot3$$

(given $\hat{\sigma}_u^2 = \Sigma e_i^2/(n-2) = 383.98/10 \approx 38.4$).

We may present the results of our regression in the compact form

$$\hat{Y}_i = 33\cdot75 + 3\cdot25\,X_i$$
$$\quad\;\; (8\cdot3) \quad\; (0\cdot9)$$

In this form a quick test of the significance of the estimates can be carried out by inspection. Clearly

$$s(\hat{b}_0) < \hat{b}_0/2 \quad \text{and} \quad s(\hat{b}_1) < \hat{b}_1/2$$

Thus both $\hat{b}_0$ and $\hat{b}_1$ are significantly different from zero at the 5 per cent level of significance (in the context of a two-tail test of significance).

We may state the statistical significance of the estimates with one of the following equivalent ways: (1) The estimates are significantly different from zero; or (2) the estimates are statistically significant; or (3) we reject the 'null hypothesis'.

Of course, each of the above statements must be accompanied by the level of significance with which the decision is made (see section 5.2.9, and Appendix I).

5.2.9. THE Z TEST OF THE LEAST-SQUARES ESTIMATES

This test is based on the Standard Normal Distribution (or Gauss Standard Normal Curve) (see Appendix I). It is applicable only if (a) the population variance is known, or (b) the population variance is unknown, and provided that the sample with which we work is sufficiently large ($n > 30$). If these conditions cannot be fulfilled we apply the student's t test, which is explained in the next section.

In econometric applications the population variance of Y is the variance of u, σ_u^2, which is unknown. However, if we have a large sample ($n > 30$) we may still use the Standard Normal Distribution and perform the Z test (approximately) since the sample estimate of the variance s^2, is a satisfactory approximation to the unknown population variance, σ^2, for large n (see Appendix I).

The Z test may be outlined as follows. We want to test the null hypothesis

$$H_0 : b_i = 0$$

against the alternative hypothesis

$$H_1 : b_i \neq 0$$

We have established that under certain assumptions regarding the values of u (namely $u \sim N(0, \sigma_u^2)$) the least squares estimates $\hat{b}_0$ and $\hat{b}_1$ have the following normal distributions

$$\hat{b}_0 \sim N\left(b_0, \sigma_{(\hat{b}_0)} = \sqrt{\sigma_u^2 \, \frac{\Sigma X^2}{n \Sigma x^2}}\right)$$

$$\hat{b}_1 \sim N\left(b_1, \sigma_{(\hat{b}_1)} = \sqrt{\sigma_u^2 \, \frac{1}{\Sigma x^2}}\right)$$

The normal distributions above can be standardised, that is they can be transformed into the units of the standard normal variable Z, which has zero mean and unit variance, $Z \sim N(0, 1)$, through the transformation formula

$$Z_i = \frac{X_i - \mu}{\sigma} \sim N(0, 1)$$

where X_i = the value of the variable which we want to normalise (transform into standard Z units)

μ = the mean of the distribution of the variable

σ = the standard deviation of the variable.

In the case of the distribution of the least squares estimates $\hat{b}_0$ and $\hat{b}_1$, the above transformation formula assumes the form:

$$Z = \frac{\hat{b}_0 - b_0}{\sigma_{(\hat{b}_0)}} = \frac{\hat{b}_0 - b_0}{\sqrt{\sigma_u^2 \Sigma X_i^2/n \Sigma x_i^2}} \sim N(0, 1) \qquad \text{for } \hat{b}_0$$

$$Z = \frac{\hat{b}_1 - b_1}{\sigma_{(\hat{b}_1)}} = \frac{\hat{b}_1 - b_1}{\sqrt{\sigma_u^2/\Sigma x_i^2}} \sim N(0, 1) \qquad \text{for } \hat{b}_1$$

With the above transformation formulae we may conduct tests of any hypothesis concerning the true value of the population parameter b. Suppose we want to test the null hypothesis that the true parameter b_1 is equal to a certain value b_1^*. Formally we wish to test the null hypothesis

$$H_0 : b_1 = b_1^*$$

against the alternative hypothesis

$$H_1 : b_1 \neq b_1^*$$

We substitute $b_1 = b_1^*$ into the above formula, and given the estimate $\hat{b}_1$ and its standard error $\sigma_{(\hat{b}_1)}$, we compute the Z^* value

$$Z^* = \frac{\hat{b}_1 - b_1^*}{\sigma_{(\hat{b}_1)}}$$

Given this 'empirical' or 'sample value' or 'observed value' of Z^*, we may calculate (from the Standard Normal distribution table on page 659, the probability of getting the estimate $\hat{b}_1$ if our basic hypothesis ($b_1 = b_1^*$) is true, as follows.

We choose a level of significance[1] for deciding whether to accept or reject our hypothesis. It is customary in econometric research to choose the 5 per cent or the 1 per cent level of significance. This means that in making our decision we allow (tolerate) five times out of a hundred to be 'wrong', that is, to reject the hypothesis when it is actually true.

In applied econometric work it has become customary to perform a two-tail test.[2] That is we choose as our critical region (C.R.) both tails of the Standard Normal distribution, and in particular that part of each tail which corresponds to half the probability of the chosen level of significance. For example, if we choose the 5 per cent level of significance, each tail will include the area (probability) 0.025 (figure 5.5). From the Standard Normal distribution table (on p. 659) we find the critical values of Z, which correspond to the probability 0.025 at each end of the curve ($Z_1 = -1.96$ and $Z_2 = 1.96$). Our final step is to compare the empirical (observed) Z^* with the above critical values of Z.

If the empirical Z^* falls in the critical region, (that is if $Z^* > 1.96$ or $Z^* < -1.96$) we reject our hypothesis that the true value of b is b^*, because the probability of observing the empirical Z^* (if our hypothesis were true) is very small (smaller than 0.025). Or, to put it in another way, it is improbable that such Z^* would be observed, if our basic hypothesis, H_0, were true. If, on the contrary, the sample value of Z^* falls outside the chosen critical region (that

---

[1] Level of significance is the probability of making the 'wrong' decision, that is the probability of rejecting the hypothesis when it is actually true or the probability of committing a type I error. See Appendix I.

[2] The choice of a two-tail test implies no *a priori* knowledge regarding the sign of the coefficient whose significance is being tested. However, a one-tail test would be more appropriate in the majority of econometric applications, since economic theory does usually provide us with *a priori* expectations regarding the sign of the coefficients of economic relations.

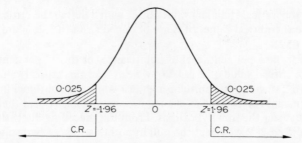

If the observed value Z^* falls in the shaded area we reject the null hypothesis H_0.

Figure 5.5. A two-tail test at the 5 per cent level of significance.

is $-1.96 < Z^* < 1.96$) we accept our basic hypothesis, $H_0(b_1 = b_1^*)$, because the probability of observing Z^* (if the hypothesis is true) is large.

For example, suppose $\hat{b} = 29.48$, $\sigma_{(\hat{b}_1)} = 36.0$ and we want to test the hypothesis $H_0 : b_1 = 25.0$. From the Z transformation formula we get

$$Z^* = \frac{\hat{b}_1 - b_1}{\sigma_{(\hat{b}_1)}} = \frac{29.48 - 25.0}{36.0} = 0.12$$

Since Z^* does not fall in the critical region ($Z^* < 1.96$) we accept our hypothesis that $b = 25.0$, because the probability of observing such a value of Z^* is large (larger than 0.05).

In applied econometrics it has become customary to test the hypothesis that the true population parameter is zero. That is, the typical form of the null hypothesis in econometrics is

$$H_0 : b_i = 0$$

and is tested against the alternative hypothesis

$$H_1 : b_i \neq 0$$

The meaning and implications of this hypothesis have been examined in the preceding section. We may summarise the discussion as follows. If we reject the null hypothesis, we say that the empirical coefficient $\hat{b}_1$ is statistically significant, or, it is significantly different from zero. If we accept the null hypothesis, then $\hat{b}_1$ is not significant and there is probably no linear relation between X and Y in the population.

To carry out the test of the above null hypothesis we set $b = 0$ in the Z transformation formula

$$Z^* = \frac{\hat{b} - b}{\sigma_{(\hat{b})}} = \frac{\hat{b} - 0}{\sigma_{(\hat{b})}} = \frac{\hat{b}}{\sigma_{(\hat{b})}}$$

Thus in the case of the test for the null hypothesis $H_0 : b_1 = 0$ the procedure of the Z test reduces to the simple step of dividing the estimated value of the parameter (b_1) by its standard deviation and then comparing the resulting Z^*

value with the theoretical (tabular) values of Z, which define the critical region of our test. The theoretical values of Z are obtained from the Standard Normal curve table (p. 659).

Given that for the 5 per cent level of significance (or the 95 per cent confidence level) the critical value of Z is 1.96, we can take this critical value as approximately equal to 2.0, and perform the rough test which was outlined in the previous section, and can now be explained in some detail. We said there that if $\sigma_{(\hat{b}_i)} > b_i/2$ we reject the null hypothesis. From the preceding discussion we concluded that if $Z^* > 2$ we reject the null hypothesis. These two statements are identical, because from the formula $Z^* = \hat{b}_i/\sigma_{(\hat{b}_i)}$ it is obvious that Z^* can be greater than 2 only if the numerator $\hat{b}_i$ is at least twice the value of the denominator, that is only if $\hat{b} > 2\sigma_{(\hat{b})}$, or $\hat{b}_i/2 > \sigma_{(\hat{b}_1)}$. Thus the statements:

    (a) we reject the null hypothesis if $Z^* > 2$; and

    (b) we reject the null hypothesis if $\sigma_{(\hat{b})} < \hat{b}/2$

are two different ways of saying the same thing. We stress that these statements assume a two-tail test conducted at the 5 per cent level of significance.

Example. Suppose that we have estimated the following supply function from a sample of 700 observations ($n = 700$)

$$Y = 100 + 4.00 X$$
$$(20) \quad (1.5)$$

We will conduct the Z-test for the slope estimate $\hat{b}_1 = 4$, given its standard error 1.5.

Since the sample is large, the estimated standard deviation of the parameters is a good approximation of the true standard deviation of these parameters. Therefore we may apply the Z test for finding the statistical significance of the estimates $\hat{b}_0$ and $\hat{b}_1$ (see Appendix I).

        Null Hypothesis: $b_1 = 0$

        Alternative Hypothesis: $b_1 \neq 0$

Computing the Z^* value, we find

$$Z^* = \frac{\hat{b}_1}{\sigma_{(\hat{b}_1)}} = \frac{4}{1.5} = 2.66$$

Since the theoretical (tabular) value of Z (at the 5 per cent level of significance) is 1.96, $Z^* > Z$.

On the evidence of our sample we conclude that it is highly improbable that the true slope b_1 is equal to zero. Our regression estimate is statistically significant.

5.2.10. THE STUDENT'S *t* TEST

We said that the Z test can be applied in the following cases only. Firstly, if the true population variance is known, irrespective of the sample size. Secondly, if the true variance of the estimates is unknown, provided the size of the sample is sufficiently large ($n > 30$), because in this case the sample estimate of the variance is a satisfactory approximation of the unknown population variance.[1]

---

[1] See T. Yamane, *Statistics*, 2nd ed., Harper & Row, Japan 1967, pp. 514–16.

In econometric applications the true variances of the estimates, $\sigma_{\hat{b}_0}^2$ and $\sigma_{\hat{b}_1}^2$, are unknown, because they involve the true variance of the random term, σ_u^2, which of course is unknown. We may, however, use the unbiased estimate $\hat{\sigma}_u^2 = \Sigma e^2/(n-K)$ and obtain estimates of the variances of the coefficients, $s_{\hat{b}_0}^2$ and $s_{\hat{b}_1}^2$. If the sample is sufficiently large $(n > 30)$ these estimates are adequate for the application of the Z transformation. However, in practice the sample is rarely sufficiently large. When the sample is small $(n < 30)$ *and provided that the population of the parameters is normal,* we can apply another transformation, based on the Student's t distribution. (See Appendix I.)

The general formula which transforms the values of any variable X into t units is similar to the Z transformation, but the t value depends in addition on the number of degrees of freedom and it includes the variance estimates s_X^2 instead of the true variance. (See Appendix I.) In the formation of the t statistic the true variance σ_X^2 is eliminated and we are left with a formula which includes its unbiased estimate $\hat{\sigma}_X^2$. (See Yamane, *Statistics,* pp. 517–19.) The t transformation formula (t statistic) is

$$t = \frac{X_i - \mu}{s_X} \qquad \text{with } n - 1 \text{ degrees of freedom}$$

where μ = value of the population mean

          s_X^2 = sample estimate of the population variance

$$s_X^2 = \Sigma(X_i - \bar{X})^2/(n-1)$$

     n = sample size.

The sampling distribution in this case, that is the distribution of the sample means, is $\bar{X} \sim N(\mu, s_{\bar{X}}^2)$ and the transformation statistic is $(\bar{X} - \mu)/\sqrt{s_X^2/n}$, and has a t distribution with $(n-1)$ degrees of freedom.

The t distribution is always symmetric, with mean equal to zero and variance $(n-1)/(n-3)$, which approaches unity when n is large. Clearly as n increases, the t distribution approaches the Standard Normal distribution $Z \sim N(0, 1)$.

The probabilities of the t distribution have been tabulated by W. S. Gosset, who wrote under the pseudonym *Student* which gave the name to the t distribution. The t distribution is reproduced in table 2 of Appendix IV (p. 660).

To perform a two-tailed test we must (a) define the null and alternative hypotheses, (b) choose the desired level of significance (5 per cent or 1 per cent customarily), (c) define the number of degrees of freedom. With this information we can define the critical region, that is the critical values of t which divide the total set of values of t in two regions, the acceptance and the rejection regions. We can define the acceptance region for t as follows. Assume we want to test the null hypothesis

$$H_0 : \mu = \mu_0$$

against the alternative hypothesis

$$H_1 : \mu \neq \mu_0$$

for a population whose variance is unknown.

Suppose that we choose the 5 per cent level of significance. The critical values of t are found from the t Table (reproduced on page 660) and are such that (with $n - 1$ degrees of freedom) each cuts off 2·5 per cent of the area of the distribution at each end. The t table differs from the Standard Normal table in that each row refers to a different number of degrees of freedom and each column corresponds to different levels of significance (that is to say a different area at the end of the distribution). For example for 10 degrees of freedom the critical values of t are found from the t table

$$t_1 = -2\cdot228 \qquad t_2 = +2\cdot228$$

Thus the acceptance region is

$$-2\cdot228 \leqslant \{t = (\bar{X} - \mu_0)/\sqrt{s_X^2/n}\} \leqslant 2\cdot228$$

The acceptance and critical regions for 10 degrees of freedom are shown in figure 5.6.

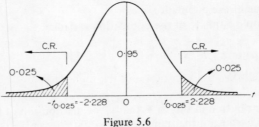

Figure 5.6

From the *sample observations* we compute $\bar{X}$ and the (observed) value of the t statistic

$$t^* = \frac{\bar{X} - \mu_0}{\sqrt{s_X^2/n}}$$

If the observed t^* value falls in the critical region we reject the null hypothesis. In summary, if

$$X \sim N(\mu, \text{unknown variance } \sigma_X^2)$$

and we have a small sample ($n < 30$) from which we obtain the estimate of the population variance

$$s_X^2 = \frac{\Sigma(X - \bar{X})^2}{n - 1}$$

then $\bar{X} \sim N(\mu, \text{with unknown variance } \sigma_X^2/n)$ and the appropriate test statistic for the sampling distribution is

$$t = \frac{(\bar{X} - \mu_0)}{\sqrt{s_X^2/n}} \qquad \text{with } (n-1) \text{ degrees of freedom}$$

In the case of the least squares estimates we have

$$\hat{b}_0 \sim N\left(b_0, \hat{\sigma}_{(\hat{b}_0)}^2 = \hat{\sigma}_u^2 \frac{\Sigma X^2}{n\Sigma x^2}\right)$$

and

$$\hat{b}_1 \sim N\left(b_1, \hat{\sigma}_{(\hat{b}_1)}^2 = \hat{\sigma}_u^2 \frac{1}{\Sigma x^2}\right)$$

It can be proved (see Appendix I) that the t statistic for $\hat{b}_i$ obtained from a single sample reduces to

$$t = \frac{\hat{b}_i - b_i^*}{\sqrt{\hat{\sigma}_{(\hat{b}_i)}^2}} \qquad \text{with } n-K \text{ degrees of freedom,}$$

where $\hat{b}_i$ = least squares estimate of b_i

b_i^* = hypothesised value of b_i $(H_0 : b_i = b_i^*)$

$\hat{\sigma}_{(\hat{b}_i)}^2$ = estimated variance of b_i (from the regression)

n = sample size

K = total number of estimated parameters ($K = 2$ in our model, since two degrees of freedom have been used up in estimating the two parameters, $\hat{b}_0$ and $\hat{b}_1$).

In econometrics the customary form of the null hypothesis is

$$H_0 : b_i = 0$$

and is tested against the alternative hypothesis

$$H_1 : b_i \neq 0$$

In this case the t statistic reduces to

$$t^* = \frac{\hat{b}_i}{\hat{\sigma}_{(\hat{b}_i)}}$$

The sample value of t^* is estimated by dividing the estimate $\hat{b}_i$ by its standard error. This value is compared to the theoretical (tabular) values of t which define the critical region in a two-tailed test, with $n - K$ degrees of freedom:

If t^* falls in the critical region we reject the null hypothesis, that is, we accept that the estimate $\hat{b}_i$ is statistically significant.

If t^* falls in the acceptance region, that is to say if $-t_{0.025} < t^* < +t_{0.025}$ (with $n - K$ degrees of freedom), we accept the null hypothesis, that is, we conclude that our estimate $\hat{b}_i$ *is not* statistically significant at the 5 per cent level of significance.

The two-tail test of the null hypothesis $H_0 : b_1 = 0$ is shown in figure 5.7.

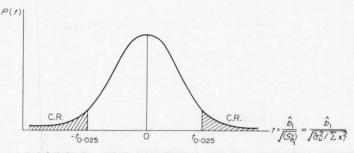

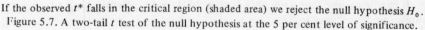

If the observed t^* falls in the critical region (shaded area) we reject the null hypothesis H_0.
Figure 5.7. A two-tail t test of the null hypothesis at the 5 per cent level of significance.

The t test can be performed in an approximate way by simple inspection. From the t table we see that the value of t changes very slowly when the degrees of freedom $(n - K)$ are more than 8. For example $t_{0.025}$ takes values between 2·30 (when $n - K = 8$) and 1·96 (when $n - K = \infty$). The change from 2·30 to 1·96 is obviously very slow. Consequently we can ignore the degrees of freedom (when $n - K > 8$) and say that the critical value of $t_{0.025}$ is 2. Thus the two-tail test of the null hypothesis (at 5 per cent level of significance) reduces to the following rule.

If the observed t^* is greater than 2 (or smaller than -2), we reject the null hypothesis.

If, on the other hand, the observed t^* is smaller than 2 (but greater than -2), we accept the null hypothesis.

Given that $t^* = \dfrac{\hat{b}_i}{s_{(\hat{b}_i)}}$, the sample value of t^* would be greater than 2 if the relevant estimate ($\hat{b}_0$ or $\hat{b}_1$) is at least twice its standard deviation. In other words

$$t^* > 2 \quad \text{if} \quad \hat{b}_i > 2s_{(\hat{b}_i)} \quad \text{or} \quad s_{(b_i)} < \hat{b}_i/2$$

Thus we see that the statements: (a) we reject the null hypothesis if $t^* > t_{0.025}$, and (b) we reject the null hypothesis is $s_{(\hat{b})} < \hat{b}/2$ are essentially the same. We repeat that this is an approximation to the formal t test and is valid only for $(n - K) > 8$.

Although the two-tail test is traditionally applied in testing the regression coefficients, a one-tail test would be appropriate in the majority of cases since economic theory provides us with *a priori* expectations regarding the sign of coefficients of economic relationships.

Example 1. Suppose that from a sample of size $n = 20$ we estimate the following consumption function

$$\hat{C} = 100 + 0.70\,Y$$
$$(75.5) \quad (0.21)$$

The figures in brackets are the standard errors of the coefficients $\hat{b}_0$ = 100 and $\hat{b}_1$ = 0·70. Since $n < 30$ we cannot apply the Z test. However, given, the stochastic assumptions about the values of u, the estimates are normally distributed, and hence we may apply the t test. For b_1 we have

$$t^* = \frac{\hat{b}_1}{\hat{\sigma}(\hat{b}_1)} = \frac{0·70}{0·21} \approx 3·3$$

We wish to test the hypothesis

$$H_0 : \hat{b}_1 = 0$$

against the alternative hypothesis

$$H_1 : \hat{b}_1 \neq 0$$

The critical values of t for $(n - K)$ = 18 degrees of freedom are

$$t_1 = -t_{0.025} = -2·10 \quad \text{and} \quad t_2 = +t_{0.025} = +2·10$$

The relevant critical region is shown in figure 5.8.

Since $t^* > t_{0.025}$ we reject the null hypothesis and conclude that $\hat{b}_1$ is different from zero.

Example 2. The standard errors and the t values for the coefficients of the supply function estimated in Chapter 4 are given below. The regression is $\hat{Y} = 33·75 + 3·25X$.

(a) The standard errors are

$$s_{\hat{b}_0} = \sqrt{\hat{\sigma}_u^2 \frac{\Sigma X_i^2}{n \Sigma x_i^2}} = 8·28 \quad \text{and} \quad s_{\hat{b}_1} = \sqrt{\hat{\sigma}_u^2 \frac{1}{\Sigma x_i^2}} = 0·89$$

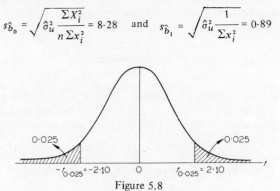

Figure 5.8

(b) The t values for the two parameter estimates are

$$t_{(\hat{b}_0)} = \frac{\hat{b}_0}{s_{\hat{b}_0}} = 4·07$$

$$t_{(\hat{b}_1)} = \frac{\hat{b}_1}{s_{\hat{b}_1}} = 3·62$$

Clearly both estimates are statistically significant.

5.3. CONFIDENCE INTERVALS FOR b_0 AND b_1

Rejection of the null hypothesis does not mean that our estimate $\hat{b}_i$ is 'the' correct estimate of the true population parameter b_i. It simply means that our estimate comes from a sample drawn from a population whose parameter b_i is different from zero.

In order to define how close to the estimate the true parameter lies, we must construct confidence intervals for the true parameter, in other words we must establish limiting values around the estimate within which the true parameter is expected to lie with a certain 'degree of confidence'. In this respect we say that with a given probability the population parameter will be within the defined *confidence interval* or *confidence limits*.

We choose a probability in advance and refer to it as *the confidence level* (or *confidence coefficient*). It is customary in econometrics to choose the 95 per cent confidence level. This means that in repeated sampling the confidence limits, computed from the sample, would include the true population parameter in 95 per cent of the cases. In the other 5 per cent of the cases the population parameter will fall outside the confidence limits.

5.3.1. CONFIDENCE INTERVAL FROM THE STANDARD NORMAL DISTRIBUTION

It has already been mentioned that the Z distribution may be employed either if we know the true standard deviation $\sigma_{(\hat{b})}$, or when we have a large sample ($n > 30$), because, for large samples, the sample standard deviation, s, is a reasonably good estimate of the unknown population standard deviation. The Z statistic for $\hat{b}_i$ is

$$Z = \frac{\hat{b}_i - b_i}{\sigma_{(\hat{b}_i)}}$$

Our first task is to choose a confidence coefficient, say 95 per cent. We next look at the standard normal table and find that the probability of the value of Z lying between -1.96 and 1.96 is 0.95. This may be written as follows

$$P\{-1.96 < Z < +1.96\} = 0.95$$

Substituting $Z = (\hat{b}_i - b_i)/\sigma_{(\hat{b}_i)}$ and rearranging slightly, we get

$$P\left\{-1.96 < \frac{\hat{b}_i - b_i}{\sigma_{(\hat{b}_i)}} < 1.96\right\} = 0.95$$

$$P\{\hat{b}_i - 1.96(\sigma_{\hat{b}_i}) < b_i < \hat{b}_i + 1.96(\sigma_{\hat{b}_i})\} = 0.95$$

Thus the 95 per cent confidence interval for b_i is

$$\boxed{\hat{b}_i - 1.96(\sigma_{\hat{b}_i}) < b_i < \hat{b}_i + 1.96(\sigma_{\hat{b}_i})}$$

or

$$\boxed{b_i = \hat{b}_i \pm (1.96) \cdot (\sigma_{\hat{b}_i})}$$

The meaning of the confidence interval is that the unknown population parameter, b_i, will lie within the defined limits 95 times out of 100.

For example, if $\hat{b} = 8.4$ and $\sigma_{(\hat{b})} = 2.2$, choosing a value of 95 per cent for the confidence coefficient, we find the confidence interval

$$b = 8 \cdot 4 \pm 1 \cdot 96 \, (2 \cdot 2)$$

or

$$8 \cdot 4 - 1 \cdot 96 \, (2 \cdot 2) < b < 8 \cdot 4 + 1 \cdot 96 \, (2 \cdot 2)$$

and

$$4 \cdot 1 < b < 12 \cdot 7$$

Thus from our single sample estimate we infer that the (unknown) true population parameter will lie between 4·1 and 12·7, with a probability of 95 per cent.

5.3.2. CONFIDENCE INTERVAL FROM THE STUDENT'S t DISTRIBUTION

The procedure for constructing a confidence interval with the t distribution is similar to the one outlined earlier with the main difference that in this case we must take into account the degrees of freedom.

The t statistic for $\hat{b}_i$ is

$$t = \frac{\hat{b}_i - b_i}{s_{(\hat{b}_i)}} \qquad \text{with } (n - K) \text{ degrees of freedom}$$

We first choose the 95 per cent confidence level (or any other confidence level) and we find from the t table the value of $\pm t_{0.025}$ with $(n - K)$ degrees of freedom. This implies that the probability of t lying between $-t_{0.025}$ and $+t_{0.025}$ is 0·95 (with $n - K$ degrees of freedom). Consequently we may write

$$P \left\{ -t_{0.025} < t < +t_{0.025} \right\} = 0 \cdot 95$$

Substituting $t = (\hat{b}_i - b_i)/s_{(\hat{b}_i)}$ in the above expression, we find

$$P \left\{ -t_{0.025} < \frac{\hat{b}_i - b_i}{s_{(\hat{b}_i)}} < + t_{0.025} \right\} = 0 \cdot 95$$

$$P \left\{ \hat{b}_i - t_{0.025} \, (s_{\hat{b}_i}) < b_i < \hat{b}_i + t_{0.025} (s_{\hat{b}_i}) \right\} = 0 \cdot 95$$

Thus the 95 per cent confidence interval for b, when we use a small sample for its estimation, is

$$\boxed{\hat{b}_i - t_{0.025} (s_{\hat{b}_i}) < b_i < \hat{b}_i + t_{0.025} (s_{\hat{b}_i})} \qquad \text{with } (n - K) \text{ degrees of freedom}$$

or

$$\boxed{b_i = \hat{b}_i \pm t_{0.025}(s_{\hat{b}_i})} \qquad \text{with } (n - K) \text{ degrees of freedom}$$

The meaning of the 95 per cent confidence interval is that there is a 0·95 probability of including the true value of the population parameter in the interval $\hat{b} \pm t_{0.025}$ (with $n - K$ degrees of freedom). For example, suppose we have estimated the following regression line from a sample of 20 observations.

$$\hat{Y} = 128 \cdot 5 + 2 \cdot 88 X \qquad (n - K) = 20 - 2 = 18.$$
$$\phantom{\hat{Y} = } (38 \cdot 2) \quad (0 \cdot 85)$$

From the t table we see that the value of $t_{0.025}$ with 18 degrees of freedom is 2·10. Hence the 95 per cent confidence interval for the parameters is:

(1) For b_0

$$b_0 = 128.5 \pm (2.10)(38.2) = 128.5 \pm 80.2$$

(2) For b_1

$$b_1 = 2.88 \pm (2.10)(0.85) = 2.88 \pm 1.79$$

Thus the value of the true intercept b_0 will lie between 48·3 and 208·7. Similarly, the value of the true parameter b_1 will lie between 1·09 and 4·67.

Another test of significance of the regression estimates (the F test) will be discussed in Chapter 8.

5.4. TEST OF SIGNIFICANCE FOR THE SAMPLE CORRELATION COEFFICIENT

The linear correlation coefficient whose formula has been derived in Chapter 3 is an estimate of the true correlation coefficient which measures the degree of interrelationship of the populations of X and Y values. Since r is a sample estimate we must test its statistical reliability by conducting some test of significance. Such tests require knowledge of the sampling distribution of r.

5.4.1. TEST OF SIGNIFICANCE OF r WHEN THE TRUE POPULATION $\rho = 0$

If the true $\rho = 0$ the sampling distribution of r is symmetric

$$r \sim N(0, \sigma_r = \sqrt{(1 - r^2)/(n - 2)})$$

and we can apply the Student's t test for establishing the significance or non-significance of the sample estimate r. The value of the t statistic is estimated from the sample correlation coefficient r, by the expression

$$t^* = \frac{r}{\sigma_r} = \frac{r}{\sqrt{(1 - r^2)/(n - 2)}} = \frac{r\sqrt{n - 2}}{\sqrt{1 - r^2}}$$

and is compared with the theoretical value of $t_{0.025}$ (for a two-tailed test at the 5 per cent level of significance) with $n - 2$ degrees of freedom.

For example, suppose that from a sample of 20 observations on prices and quantities sold we compute the correlation coefficient $r = 0.82$. We want to establish whether this estimate is statistically different from zero. That is we want to answer the question: Can we infer (at the 0·05 level of significance) that the corresponding population ρ differs from zero?

Null hypothesis $\qquad\qquad H_0: \rho = 0,$

Alternative hypothesis $\qquad\qquad H_1: \rho \neq 0,$

$$t^* = \frac{0.82 \sqrt{20 - 2}}{\sqrt{1 - (0.82)^2}} = 6.04$$

The theoretical $t_{0.025} = 2.10$ (with 18 degrees of freedom). Since $t^* > t$ we reject the null hypothesis: We conclude that $\rho \neq 0$.

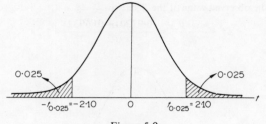

Figure 5.9

5.4.2. TEST OF SIGNIFICANCE OF r WHEN THE TRUE POPULATION $\rho \neq 0$

If the true $\rho \neq 0$ the sampling distribution of r's is not symmetric, but skewed: the higher the ρ the more skewed the sampling distribution of r. In this case Fisher has suggested the following test. (See M. Spiegel, *Statistics*, p. 247.)

The statistic

$$\omega = \frac{1}{2} \log_e \left(\frac{1+r}{1-r}\right) = 1 \cdot 1513 \log_{10} \left(\frac{1+r}{1-r}\right)$$

has an approximately normal distribution with mean

$$\mu_\omega = \frac{1}{2} \log_e \left(\frac{1+\rho}{1-\rho}\right) = 1 \cdot 1513 \log_{10} \left(\frac{1+\rho}{1-\rho}\right)$$

and standard deviation $\sigma_\omega = 1/\sqrt{n-3}$. That is

$$\omega \sim N \left\{ \frac{1}{2} \log_e \left(\frac{1+\rho}{1-\rho}\right), \sigma_\omega = \frac{1}{\sqrt{n-3}} \right\}$$

Consequently ω may be standardised

$$Z_i = \frac{\omega_i - \mu_\omega}{\sigma_\omega} \sim N(0, 1).$$

Example. From a sample of size 28 we find $r = 0 \cdot 70$. Can we reject the hypothesis that the true population $\rho = 0 \cdot 60$ at $0 \cdot 05$ level of significance?

$$H_0 : \rho = 0 \cdot 60$$
$$H_1 : \rho > 0 \cdot 60.$$

From the sample data we find

(i)
$$\omega = 1 \cdot 1513 \log_{10} \left(\frac{1 + 0 \cdot 70}{1 - 0 \cdot 70}\right) = 0 \cdot 9730$$

(ii)
$$\mu_\omega = 1 \cdot 1513 \log_{10} \left(\frac{1 + 0 \cdot 60}{1 - 0 \cdot 60}\right) = 0 \cdot 6932$$

(iii)
$$\sigma_\omega = \frac{1}{\sqrt{n-3}} = \frac{1}{\sqrt{25}} = 0 \cdot 2$$

We next find the observed value of the Z statistic

$$Z^* = \frac{\omega_i - \mu_\omega}{\sigma_\omega} = \frac{(0 \cdot 9730) - (0 \cdot 6932)}{0 \cdot 2} = 1 \cdot 28$$

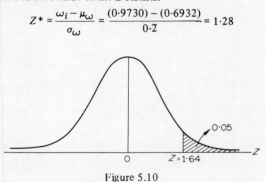

Figure 5.10

We will choose for our test the upper tail of the standard normal distribution, since the alternative hypothesis is $H_1 : \rho > 0 \cdot 60$. (See Appendix I.) From the table of the Standard Normal curve we find that $Z = 1 \cdot 64$ (at 5 per cent level of significance (figure 5.10)). Since $Z^* < Z$ we *cannot reject* the hypothesis that the population ρ is $0 \cdot 60$: We accept H_0. This implies that our estimate of r is not significantly different from $0 \cdot 60$, at the 5 per cent level of significance.

For a test of the R^2 in multiple regression see Chapter 8.

5.4.3. TEST OF SIGNIFICANCE OF THE RANK CORRELATION COEFFICIENT r'

The statistical significance of Spearman's rank correlation coefficient can be tested by the following procedure.

If the population ρ is zero, the distribution of r' can be approximated with a normal curve having the mean 0 and the standard deviation $1/\sqrt{n-1}$, that is

$$r' \sim N \left(0, \sigma_{r'} = \frac{1}{\sqrt{n-1}} \right)$$

The null and alternative hypotheses are

$$H_0 : \rho = 0 \quad \text{and} \quad H_1 : \rho \neq 0$$

Given the form of the alternative hypothesis, we apply a two-tail test. The Z statistic can be used in this test provided that the sample is large. We estimate

$$Z^* = \frac{r'}{\sigma_{r'}} = r'\sqrt{n-1}$$

We next compare Z^* with the tabular values of $Z = \pm 1 \cdot 96$, which define the critical region of a two tail test at the 5 per cent level of significance. If $-1 \cdot 96 \leqslant Z^* \leqslant 1 \cdot 96$, we accept H_0. Otherwise we reject H_0. This procedure is equivalent to the rule:

(a) We reject H_0 if $r' < \dfrac{-1\cdot96}{\sqrt{n-1}}$, or if $r' > \dfrac{1\cdot96}{\sqrt{n-1}}$

(b) We accept H_0 if $\dfrac{-1\cdot96}{\sqrt{n-1}} \leqslant r' \leqslant \dfrac{1\cdot96}{\sqrt{n-1}}$

5.5 A NOTE ON THE IMPORTANCE OF THE STATISTICAL TESTS OF SIGNIFICANCE

There is no general agreement among econometricians as to which of the two statistical criteria is more important: a high r^2, or low standard errors of the estimates.

Statistical criteria acquire great importance when one follows the experimental approach in investigating any particular problem. We said that in this approach the research takes the form of a process of computing various models with various combinations of the relevant variables, and then trying to decide which is preferable. The choice would not be difficult if one of the models produced a higher r^2 and lower standard errors. However, this is not usually the case. In most applications we obtain a high r^2, while some parameters have high standard errors. In this event some econometricians tend to attribute great importance to r^2, and to accept the parameter estimates, despite the fact that some of them are statistically insignificant. Others suggest that acceptance or rejection of the estimates which are not statistically significant depends on the aim of the model in any particular situation.

The majority of writers seem to agree that r^2 is a more important criterion when the model is to be used for forecasting, while the standard errors acquire a greater importance when the purpose of the research is the explanation (analysis) of economic phenomena and the estimation of reliable values of particular economic parameters.

A high r^2 has a clear merit only when combined with significant estimates (low standard errors). When high r^2 and low standard errors are not found contemporaneously in any particular study the researcher should be very careful in his interpretation and acceptance of the results. Priority should always be given to the fulfilment of the economic *a priori* criteria (sign and size of the estimates). Only when the economic criteria are satisfied should one proceed with the application of the first-order and second-order tests of significance.

5.6 SUMMARY OF THE ESTIMATION PROCEDURE OF OLS APPLIED TO THE TWO-VARIABLE MODEL

The estimation procedure of OLS may be expressed in a sequence of five steps, which greatly simplify the computations involved.

Step 1. Obtain $\hat{b}_1$ and $\hat{b}_0$

$$\hat{b}_1 = \frac{\Sigma x_i y_i}{\Sigma x_i^2} \qquad \hat{b}_0 = \bar{Y} - \hat{b}_1 \bar{X}$$

Step 2. Obtain r_{yx}^2

$$r_{yx} = \hat{b}_i \frac{\Sigma x_i y_i}{\Sigma y_i^2}$$

Step 3. Obtain Σe_i^2

$$\Sigma e_i^2 = (1 - r^2)\Sigma y_i^2$$

Step 4. Obtain $\hat{\sigma}_u^2$

$$\hat{\sigma}_u^2 = (\Sigma e_i^2)/(n - 2)$$

Step 5. Obtain the standard errors of $\hat{b}_1$ and $\hat{b}_0$

$$s_{(\hat{b}_1)} = \sqrt{\hat{\sigma}_u^2 \frac{1}{\Sigma x_i^2}} \qquad \text{and} \qquad s_{(\hat{b}_0)} = \sqrt{\hat{\sigma}_u^2 \frac{\Sigma X_i^2}{n\Sigma x_i^2}}$$

The following expressions are useful for the computations of the relevant terms in the above steps

(a) $\Sigma x_i^2 = \Sigma X_i^2 - n\bar{X}^2$

(b) $\Sigma y_i^2 = \Sigma Y_i^2 - n\bar{Y}^2$

(c) $\Sigma x_i y_i = \Sigma X_i Y_i - n\bar{X}\bar{Y}$

EXERCISES

1. The following table includes the gross national product (X) and the demand for food (Y) measured in arbitrary units, in an underdeveloped country over the ten-year period 1960–9.

	1960	1961	1962	1963	1964	1965	1966	1967	1968	1969
Y	6	7	8	10	8	9	10	9	11	10
X	50	52	55	59	57	58	62	65	68	70

(a) Estimate the food function

$$Y = b_0 + b_1 X + u$$

What is the economic meaning of your results?

(b) Compute the coefficient of determination and find the explained and unexplained variation in the food expenditure.

(c) Compute the standard errors of the regression estimates and conduct tests of significance at the 5 per cent level of significance.

(d) Find the 99 per cent confidence interval for the population parameters.

2. The following table shows the investment expenditure and the long-run interest rate over the ten-year period 1958–67.

	1958	1959	1960	1961	1962	1963	1964	1965	1966	1967
Y Invest-ment	656	804	836	765	777	711	755	747	696	787
r Interest	0·05	0·045	0·045	0·055	0·06	0·06	0·06	0·05	0·07	0·065

Test the hypothesis that investment is interest elastic, by fitting a regression line to the above data and conducting the relevant statistical tests of significance.

3. The following table shows the production of coal and the number of wage-earners in the coal industry over a ten-year period during which the capital equipment has remained constant.

Period	1	2	3	4	5	6	7	8	9	10
Output (mn tons)	210·8	210·1	211·5	208·9	207·4	205·3	198·8	192·1	183·9	176·8
Number of workers (000's)	706·2	703·1	701·8	699·1	697·4	695·3	692·7	630·2	602·1	531·0

(a) Estimate the production function of coal.

(b) Find the average and marginal productivity of labour.

(c) Compute the standard errors of the parameter estimates and the *t* ratios and construct 95 per cent confidence intervals for the population parameters.

4. Show algebraically the following results

(a) $\hat{b}_1 = r_{yx}^2 \cdot \dfrac{\Sigma y^2}{\Sigma xy}$

(b) $\hat{b}_1 = r_{yx} \cdot \dfrac{s_y}{s_x}$

where $s_x = \sqrt{\Sigma x_i^2/n}$ and $s_y = \sqrt{\Sigma y_i^2/n}$

Note. Additional exercises are included in Appendix III.

6. Properties of the Least Squares Estimates

We said in Chapter 4 that one of the main reasons for the widespread use of the method of ordinary least squares in the estimation of economic relationships is that the estimates of the parameters have some optimal properties. In the first section of this chapter we shall define the properties which traditional statistical theory has accepted as desirable attributes for sample estimates. In section 6.2 we shall establish that the estimates of OLS do actually possess such optimal properties.

6.1. DESIRABLE PROPERTIES OF ESTIMATORS[1]

There are various econometric methods with which we may obtain estimates of the parameters of economic relationships. How are we to choose among these methods? Clearly we shall choose the one that gives good estimates. How are we to decide whether any estimate is 'good' or whether it is 'better' than another obtained from a different method? It is evident that we need some criteria for judging the 'goodness' of an estimate. In general we would like an estimate to be close to the value of the true population parameter, to vary within only a small range around the true parameter. 'Closeness' to the population parameter is measured by the mean and variance of the sampling distribution of the estimates of the different econometric methods. We assume the usual process of hypothetical repeated sampling, that is, we assume that we get a very large number of samples each of size n; we compute the estimates $\hat{b}$'s from each sample and for each econometric method and we form their distribution. We next compare the means and variances of these distributions and we choose among the alternative estimates the one whose distribution is concentrated as close as possible around the population parameter. Closeness is judged on the basis of some traditional criteria (or desirable properties) which are listed below. We shall distinguish between estimates obtained from small samples and those obtained from large samples.[2]

---

[1] In econometric jargon the term *estimator* is used to denote the rule (method) by which we calculate the value of a parameter, while the term *estimate* is used to denote the result from applying the rule. For example, in order to calculate the sample mean we use the function (rule) $\Sigma X_i/n$, which is the *estimator* of the sample mean. The *estimate* of the mean is the number (the result) obtained after the observations $X_1, X_2, \ldots, X_n$ have been inserted in the estimator. In this book we will use both terms for denoting the result; that is, the estimated value for the population parameters.

[2] See A. Goldberger, *Econometric Theory*, pp. 115–31, for a rigorous treatment of this topic.

100

6.1.1. SMALL SAMPLE PROPERTIES OF THE ESTIMATORS

The main criteria for a good estimator obtained from a small sample are: (1) unbiasedness; (2) least-variance; (3) efficiency; (4) best, linear, unbiasedness (BLU); (5) least mean-square-error (MSE); (6) sufficiency.

Unbiased estimator

The bias of an estimator is defined as the difference between its expected value and the true parameter

$$\text{Bias} = E(\hat{b}) - b$$

An estimator is unbiased if its bias is zero, that is if $E(\hat{b}) = b$. This means that the unbiased estimator converges to the true value of the parameter as the *number of samples* (of any given finite size n) increases. An unbiased estimator gives 'on the average' the true value of the parameter. In figure 6.1 we illustrate a biased and an unbiased estimator of the true b.

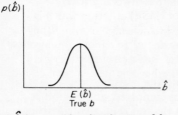
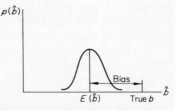

(a) $\hat{b}$ is an unbiased estimator of b (b) $\hat{b}$ is a biased estimator of b

Figure 6.1

Unbiasedness is a desirable property but not particularly important by itself. It becomes important only when combined with a small variance (see below).

Minimum-variance estimator (or best estimator)

An estimate is *best* when it has the smallest variance as compared with *any other* estimate obtained from other econometric methods. Symbolically $\hat{b}$ is best if

$$E[\hat{b} - E(\hat{b})]^2 < E[\tilde{b} - E(\tilde{b})]^2$$

or
$$\text{var}(\hat{b}) < \text{var}(\tilde{b})$$

where $\tilde{b}$ is any other (not necessarily unbiased) estimate of the true parameter b. In econometrics the term 'best' is used in this technical sense and not in the everyday meaning of 'definitely superior'. (See A. Goldberger, *Econometric Theory*, pp. 127–8.)

The minimum variance property by itself is rather meaningless. Any estimator $\hat{b}$ = a constant, has zero variance. Low variance is most desirable when combined with small bias. An estimator which has small variance but a large bias will tend to give values ($\hat{b}$'s) which will cluster closely around a value quite far from the

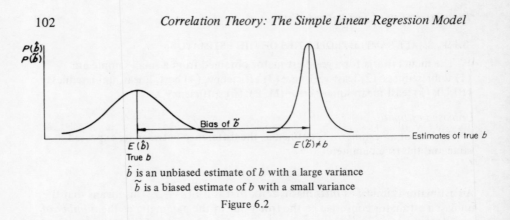

$\hat{b}$ is an unbiased estimate of b with a large variance
$\tilde{b}$ is a biased estimate of b with a small variance

Figure 6.2

true parameter b. In figure 6.2 we show the sampling distributions of two alternative estimators, $\hat{b}$ and $\tilde{b}$. $\hat{b}$ is unbiased but has a large variance, while $\tilde{b}$ is biased but has a small variance. Choice between these two alternative estimators may be based on the mean-square-error (MSE) criterion which is explained below.

Efficient estimator

An estimator is efficient when it possesses both the previous properties; that is, it is unbiased and has the minimum variance as compared with any other *unbiased* estimator. Symbolically $\hat{b}$ is efficient if the following two conditions are fulfilled

$$(a) \qquad\qquad E(\hat{b}) = b$$

and

$$(b) \qquad E[\hat{b} - E(\hat{b})]^2 < \bar{E}[b^* - E(b^*)]^2$$

where b^* is *another unbiased estimate* of the true b. In other words the efficient estimator is the minimum variance (best) estimator within the class of all unbiased estimators.

Linear estimator

An estimator is linear if it is a linear function of the sample observations; that is, if it is determined by a linear combination of the sample data. Given the sample observations $Y_1, Y_1, \ldots, Y_n$, a linear estimator will have the form

$$k_1 Y_1 + k_2 Y_2 + \ldots + k_n Y_n$$

where the k_i's are some constants.

For example, the sample mean $\overline{Y}$ is a linear estimator with $k_1 = k_2 = \ldots = k_n = \dfrac{1}{n}$. Because

$$\bar{Y} = \frac{\Sigma Y_i}{n} = \frac{1}{n} \Sigma Y_i = \frac{1}{n} (Y_1 + Y_2 + \ldots + Y_n)$$

$$= \frac{1}{n} Y_1 + \frac{1}{n} Y_2 + \ldots + \frac{1}{n} Y_n$$

In other words, in estimating the sample mean Y each observation is assigned the same weight, k, which is equal to $\frac{1}{n}$.

Best, linear, unbiased estimator (BLUE)

An estimator $\hat{b}$ is BLU if it is linear, unbiased, and has the smallest variance as compared with all other linear unbiased estimators of the true b. The BLU estimator has the minimum variance within the class of linear unbiased estimators of the true b. (See figure 6.5.)

Minimum mean-square-error (MSE) estimator

The mean-square-error criterion is a combination of the unbiasedness and the minimum variance properties. An estimator is a minimum MSE estimator if it has the smallest mean-square-error defined as the expected value of the squared differences of the estimator around the true population parameter b

$$\text{MSE}(\hat{b}) = E[\hat{b} - b]^2$$

It can be shown that the MSE is equal to the variance of the estimator plus the square of its bias

$$\text{MSE}(\hat{b}) = \text{var}(\hat{b}) + \text{bias}^2(\hat{b})$$

Proof

$$\text{MSE} = E(\hat{b} - b)^2$$
$$= E\left\{[\hat{b} - E(\hat{b}) + E(\hat{b}) - b]\right\}^2$$
$$= E[\hat{b} - E(\hat{b})]^2 + [E(\hat{b}) - b]^2 + 2E\left\{[\hat{b} - E(\hat{b})]\,[E(\hat{b}) - b]\right\}$$

But

$$E[\hat{b} - E(\hat{b})]^2 = \text{var}(\hat{b})$$
$$[E(\hat{b}) - b]^2 = \text{bias}^2(\hat{b})$$

and $E\left\{[\hat{b} - E(\hat{b})]\,[E(\hat{b}) - b]\right\} = 0$, because,

$$E\left\{[\hat{b} - E(\hat{b})]\,[E(\hat{b}) - b]\right\} = E\left\{\hat{b}E(\hat{b}) - [E(\hat{b})]^2 - \hat{b}b + bE(\hat{b})\right\}$$
$$= [E(\hat{b})]^2 - [E(\hat{b})]^2 - bE(\hat{b}) + bE(\hat{b}) = 0$$

Therefore

$$\text{MSE} = \text{var}(\hat{b}) + \text{bias}^2(\hat{b})$$

Sufficient estimator

A sufficient estimator is an estimator that utilises all the information a sample contains about the true parameter (see Yamane, *Statistics*, p. 245); it must use all the observations of the sample. This means that no other estimator can add any further information about the true population parameter which is being estimated. For example, the arithmetic mean is sufficient; it gives more information than any other measures of location, like the mode or the median. The median is not sufficient since it uses only the ranking and not the values of sample observations. Sufficiency is not by itself an important property. It is mentioned here because it is a necessary condition for efficiency.

Which is the most important of these properties is a matter on which not all the econometricians agree; to quote R. J. Ball: 'Desirable properties for estimates are a matter of choice to some extent by the statistician. There is no law that says that bias, sufficiency or efficiency should be ranked in some unique order. The most desirable characteristic in each particular study depends to a large extent on the purpose of the study.' However, the following notes should be borne in mind when considering the 'goodness' of an estimator. ·

(a) A certain estimate is considered superior to others if it possesses more of these properties than do the others.

(b) The property of minimum variance in itself is not important. An estimate may have a very small variance and a large bias: we have a small variance around the 'wrong' mean. Similarly, the property of unbiasedness by itself is not particularly desirable, unless coupled with a small variance.

(c) The BLU and MSE criteria combine both measures, the bias and the variance of an estimate, and are often preferred to other single criteria.

6.1.2. LARGE SAMPLE PROPERTIES OF ESTIMATORS: ASYMPTOTIC PROPERTIES

The criteria listed in this section refer to estimators which are obtained from large samples. Strictly speaking the application of these properties as criteria for the 'goodness' of an estimator requires the sample to be infinitely large ($n \to \infty$). This is the reason why these properties are called *asymptotic properties*. When the sample is large these properties are assumed to hold only approximately. They are: (1) Asymptotic unbiasedness. (2) Consistency. (3) Asymptotic efficiency.

Let us first introduce the concept of an asymptotic distribution (or limiting distribution).

It is helpful to use as an example the distributions of an estimate, $\hat{b}$, obtained from samples of successively increasing size

$$n_1 < n_2 < n_3 < \ldots < n_T$$

Assume a parent population of values of b. Assume that we draw a very large number of samples *all* of size n_1 (that is, we perform the usual hypothetical repeated sampling process), and we estimate the values $\hat{b}_{(n_1)}$. (The subscript denotes the sample size.) The sampling distribution of $\hat{b}_{(n_1)}$ has an expected value $E(\hat{b}_{(n_1)})$, and a variance $E[\hat{b}_{(n_1)} - E(\hat{b}_{(n_1)})]^2$.

Assume that we repeat this process with a larger sample size $n_2 > n_1$. We will obtain a distribution of the estimate $\hat{b}_{(n_2)}$, with expected value $E(\hat{b}_{(n_2)})$, and variance $E[\hat{b}_{(n_2)} - E(\hat{b}_{(n_2)})]$.

Suppose that we continue this process with successively larger samples $(n_1 < n_2 < \ldots < n_T)$, and we observe how the individual distributions from each sample size change as n_T goes to infinity.

In other words, we consider in general a sequence of random variables

$$\{ X_{(n)} \} = X_{(n_1)}, X_{(n_2)}, \ldots, X_{(n_T)}$$

each of which has its own distribution, expected value and variance. The distributions are formed from successively increasing sample size. It may be that as n_T goes to infinity these distributions converge to a certain distribution, which is called the *asymptotic distribution* or *limiting distribution* of the sequence $\{ X_{(n)} \}$.

The concept of convergence to a limiting distribution is illustrated in figure 6.3. Clearly as the sample size increases (from $n_1 = 10$ to $n_2 = 50$) the distributions come closer to the limiting (asymptotic) distribution (which is assumed to exist in this illustration).

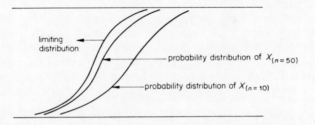

Figure 6.3. Illustration of convergence to a limiting distribution.

We will next define the mean and variance of an asymptotic distribution.[1]

The Asymptotic Expectation

The asymptotic expectation of a sequence of random variables is the mean of its asymptotic distribution.

Consider the sequence of random variables

$$\{ X_{(n)} \} = X_{(n_1)}, X_{(n_2)}, \ldots, X_{(n_T)}$$

Assume that the expected value (mean) of all individual distributions exists, so that we have the following sequence of expected values

$$\{ E(X_{(n)}) \} = E(X_{(n_1)}), E(X_{(n_2)}), \ldots, E(X_{(n_T)})$$

[1] We will confine our discussion to the limiting distributions of sequences for which the individual elements (random variables) have distributions whose expected values (means) and variances do exist and converge to finite constants as $n \to \infty$.

For other cases the reader is referred to H. Theil, *Principles of Econometrics*, chapter 8, North-Holland, 1971.

If the expected values converge to a finite constant, μ, as the sample size goes to infinity, then this constant is *the asymptotic mean* of the initial sequence of random variables. Equivalently we may say that the asymptotic mean of the sequence $\{X_{(n)}\}$ is the limit (or limiting value) of the sequence of the expectations of the individual distributions. Algebraically

$$\begin{bmatrix} \text{Asymptotic} \\ \text{expectation} \\ \text{of } \{X_{(n)}\} \end{bmatrix} = \lim_{n \to \infty} \{E(X_{(n)})\} = \mu$$

where $\lim_{n \to \infty} E(X_{(n)})$ reads: 'the limiting value of the expectations of the sequence $\{X_{(n)}\}$ as n goes to infinity'.

Asymptotic Variance

Assume that the sequence

$$\{X_{(n)}\} = X_{(n_1)}, X_{(n_2)}, \ldots, X_{(n_T)}$$

has the asymptotic expectation

$$\lim_{n \to \infty} E(X_{(n)}) = \mu$$

The sequence of variances of the individual distributions is

$$\{E[X_{(n)} - E(X_{(n)})]^2\} = E[X_{(n_1)} - E(X_{(n_1)})]^2, \; E[X_{(n_2)} - E(X_{(n_2)})]^2, \ldots$$

The asymptotic variance of the initial sequence is *not* the limiting value of the sequence of variances as $n \to \infty$, because in many cases this limiting value is zero. If in fact

$$\lim_{n \to \infty} (\text{var } X_{(n)}) \equiv \lim_{n \to \infty} E[X_{(n)} - E(X_{(n)})] = 0$$

then the distribution of $X_{(n)}$ has collapsed on a single point, and the distribution is called *degenerate*, because it is not strictly speaking a distribution. (See below.)

To avoid the difficulties of choosing among estimators which have degenerate distributions we define the variance of the asymptotic distribution (or asymptotic variance) as follows.

Instead of considering the development (behaviour) of the sequence of the variances of the individual distributions, we construct a *new sequence*, with elements the expected value of the products of the deviations $[X_{(n)} - E(X_{(n)})]$ times $\sqrt{n}$; that is, the new sequence is

$$\{E[\sqrt{n}(X_{(n)} - E(X_{(n)}))]^2\} = E[\sqrt{n_1}(X_{(n_1)} - E(X_{(n_1)}))]^2,$$
$$E[\sqrt{n_2}(X_{(n_2)} - E(X_{(n_2)}))]^2, \ldots$$

If this *new sequence* converges to a finite constant v, as n goes to infinity, that is, if

$$\lim_{n \to \infty} E[\sqrt{n}\{X_{(n)} - E(X_{(n)})\}]^2 = v$$

then the variance of the asymptotic distribution (or asymptotic variance) of the initial sequence $\{X_{(n)}\}$ is defined as

$$\begin{bmatrix} \text{Asymptotic} \\ \text{variance} \\ \text{of } \{X_{(n)}\} \end{bmatrix} = \frac{1}{n} \cdot v = \frac{1}{n} \lim_{n \to \infty} E[\sqrt{n}\{X_{(n)} - E(X_{(n)})\}]^2$$

Note that the above asymptotic moments (mean and variance)[1] may be used as approximations for the mean and variance of any finite sample of size n. Of course the approximation will be better the larger n.

In many cases the asymptotic variance depends on unknown population parameters. For example, the asymptotic variance of $\dfrac{1}{\bar{X}_{(n)}}$ is $\dfrac{\sigma_x^2}{n\mu^4}$, and both the population mean μ and variance σ_x^2 are unknown. Under certain conditions we may replace these unknowns by their sample estimates, and the thus estimated asymptotic variance can be used as an approximation to the finite sampling variance. (See H. Theil, *Principles of Econometrics*, North-Holland, 1971, pp. 377–8.) This is particularly important in cases where the exact variance for any given sample size, n, cannot be derived. (For examples of such cases see Theil, op. cit.)

We may now turn to the asymptotic properties of estimators.

Asymptotic Unbiasedness[2]

An estimator is an asymptotically unbiased estimator of the true population parameter b, if the asymptotic mean of $\hat{b}$ is equal to b. Algebraically

$$\lim_{n \to \infty} E(\hat{b}_{(n)}) = b$$

The asymptotic bias of an estimator is the difference between its asymptotic mean and the true parameter

$$\begin{bmatrix} \text{Asymptotic} \\ \text{bias of } \hat{b} \end{bmatrix} = \begin{bmatrix} \lim_{n \to \infty} E(\hat{b}_{(n)}) \end{bmatrix} - b$$

Thus, loosely speaking, an asymptotically unbiased estimator is one whose bias vanishes as the sample size becomes sufficiently large.

Note that if an estimator is unbiased (in small finite samples) it is also asymptotically unbiased; but the converse is not necessarily true.

[1] See A. Goldberger, op. cit., p. 116 (Wiley, 1964).
[2] In many books the asymptotic properties of estimators are defined by using the concept and algebra of 'probability limits'. We do not find it necessary, for the purposes of this book, to introduce probability limits.

Consistency[1]

An estimator $\hat{b}$ is a consistent estimator of the true population parameter b, if it satisfies two conditions:

(i) $\hat{b}$ must be asymptotically unbiased

$$\lim_{n \to \infty} E(\hat{b}_{(n)}) = b$$

(ii) the variance of $\hat{b}$ must approach zero as n tends to infinity

$$\lim_{n \to \infty} [\text{var}(\hat{b})] = 0$$

If the variance is zero, the distribution collapses on the value of the true population parameter b. (A distribution which is concentrated on a point and has zero variance is called a *degenerate* distribution. It is not strictly speaking a distribution, since its variance is zero. Graphically it is shown as a vertical line on the point of concentration, of height equal to unity.)

To find whether an estimator is consistent, we should examine what happens to its bias (if any) *and* to its variance as n increases. Both the bias and the variance should decrease as n becomes larger, and at the limit (as $n \to \infty$) they should be zero. The concept of consistency is illustrated in figure 6.4. As the sample size increases, both the bias of $\hat{b}$ and its variance decrease.

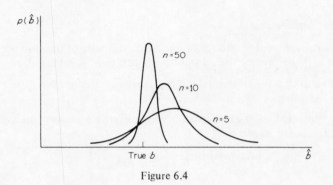

Figure 6.4

The consistency property is very attractive. It assures that with larger and larger samples which contain more information we will be able to obtain an increasingly accurate estimator. In the limiting case, if it were possible to have infinitely large samples, a consistent estimator will provide a perfect estimate of the true b.

[1] See footnote 2 on page 107.

Asymptotic Efficiency

An estimator $\hat{b}$ is an asymptotically efficient estimator of the true population parameter b, if

(i) $\hat{b}$ is consistent
(ii) $\hat{b}$ has a smaller asymptotic variance as compared with any other consistent estimator.

Symbolically we may write:

$\hat{b}$ is asymptotically efficient if

$$\left[\frac{1}{n} \lim_{n \to \infty} E\{\sqrt{n}(\hat{b}_{(n)} - b)\}^2\right] < \left[\frac{1}{n} \lim_{n \to \infty} E\{b^*_{(n)} - b\}^2\right]$$

where b^* is *any other consistent estimator* of b.

The concept of 'a smaller asymptotic variance' needs some explanation, since the variance of any consistent estimator goes to zero as the sample size grows infinite. If consistent estimators are being compared, then it is the one whose variance goes faster to zero (as n becomes sufficiently large), that is asymptotically efficient. For example, consider two estimates, $\hat{b}$ and $\tilde{b}$, whose distributions have the following mean and variance

$$E(\hat{b}) = \left(\frac{n-1}{n}\right) b \qquad \text{var}(\hat{b}) = \frac{k}{n^2}$$

$$E(\tilde{b}) = \left(\frac{n+1}{n}\right) b \qquad \text{var}(\tilde{b}) = \frac{k}{n}$$

(where k is any constant number).

It is obvious that both estimators are biased, but they are consistent, since their bias and variance becomes zero as $n \to \infty$

$$\lim_{n \to \infty} E(\hat{b}) = b \qquad \lim_{n \to \infty} \text{var}(\hat{b}) = 0$$

$$\lim_{n \to \infty} E(\tilde{b}) = b \qquad \lim_{n \to \infty} \text{var}(\tilde{b}) = 0$$

However, the variance of $\hat{b}$ goes faster to zero as $n \to \infty$; hence we say that $\hat{b}$ is asymptotically more efficient than the alternative consistent estimator $\tilde{b}$.

6.2. PROPERTIES OF THE LEAST SQUARES ESTIMATORS

In this section we will show that the least squares estimates are BLU (best, linear, unbiased) provided that the random term u satisfies some general assumptions, namely that the u has zero mean and constant variance. This proposition, together with the set of conditions under which it is true, is known as *Gauss–Markov least-squares theorem.* (See R. Wonnacott and T. Wonnacott, *Econometrics*, Wiley, New York 1970, p. 21.)

The BLU properties are shown diagrammatically in figure 6.5. Estimators of *b* may be obtained from various methods. All possible estimators are shown inside the outer border line of figure 6.5. Not all of these estimators are linear;

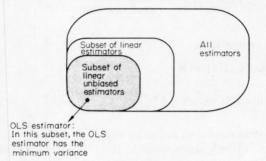

Figure 6.5

that is the linear estimators are only a subset of all estimators. Furthermore, not all linear estimators are unbiased. In other words the unbiased linear estimators are a subset of the linear estimators. Now, in the group of linear unbiased estimators the OLS estimator, $\hat{b}$, has the smallest variance. That is, the OLS estimators possess three properties: they are linear, unbiased and have the smallest variance (among the subgroup of linear unbiased estimators). The OLS estimators are BLU.

6.2.1. THE PROPERTY OF LINEARITY

The least-squares estimates $\hat{b}_0$ and $\hat{b}_1$ are linear functions of the observed sample values Y_i. The formulae derived in Chapter 4 for the estimation of the coefficients involve the variables Y and X in their first power. Given that by Assumption 6A the X_i's appear always with the same values in our hypothetical repeated sampling process, it can easily be shown that the least squares estimates depend on the values of Y only: $\hat{b}_0 = f(Y)$ and $\hat{b}_1 = f(Y)$.

Proof
  (a) We established in Chapter 5 that

$$\hat{b}_1 = \Sigma \frac{x_i}{\Sigma x_i^2} Y_i = \Sigma k_i Y_i$$

where $k_i = x_i/\Sigma x_i^2$.

By Assumption 6A the values of X are a set of fixed numbers in all samples of our hypothetical repeated sampling. Hence the k_i's are fixed constants from sample to sample, and may be regarded as constant weights assigned to the individual values of Y.

We may write

$$\hat{b}_1 = \Sigma k_i Y_i = k_1 Y_1 + k_2 Y_2 + \ldots + k_n Y_n = f(Y) \tag{6.1}$$

The estimate $\hat{b}_1$ is a linear function of the Y's, a linear combination of the values of the dependent variable.

(b) Similarly in Chapter 5 $\hat{b}_0$ was found to be

$$\hat{b}_0 = \Sigma \left[\frac{1}{n} - \bar{X} k_i \right] Y_i$$

By Assumption 6A $\bar{X}$ and k_i are fixed constants from sample to sample. Thus $\hat{b}_0$ depends only on the values of Y, that is, $\hat{b}_0$ is a linear function of the sample values of Y.

To establish the linearity property of the least squares estimates we have made use of Assumption 6A that the values of X are a set of fixed values in all hypothetical samples.

6.2.2. THE PROPERTY OF UNBIASEDNESS

The property of unbiasedness of $\hat{b}_0$ and $\hat{b}_1$ has been established in Chapter 5 where we proved that

$$E(\hat{b}_0) = b_0 \quad \text{and} \quad E(\hat{b}_1) = b_1 \tag{6.2}$$

The meaning of this property is that the estimates converge to the true value of the parameters as we increase the number of (hypothetical) samples. In other words if we take all possible samples (or a very large number of samples) of size n of observations on Y and X and compute for each sample the estimates $\hat{b}_0$ and $\hat{b}_1$, we will obtain a large number of such estimates, whose mean (expected value) will be equal to the parameters of the relationship. The distribution of the estimates will be centred on the true value b of the parameter (figure 6.6).

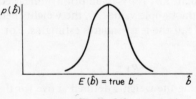

Figure 6.6

Recall that to establish the property of unbiasedness of the slope $\hat{b}_1$ and the intercept $\hat{b}_0$ we used Assumption 6A that the values of X are a set of fixed numbers, and Assumption 2, $E(u) = 0$. Therefore, if either Assumption 2 or Assumption 6A is violated in any particular instance the estimates of both parameters will be biased.

Note. If Assumption 6A is violated but Assumption 6 (that the u_i's and the X_i's are independent) is satisfied, then $\hat{b}_1$ will be unbiased even when $E(u_i) \neq 0$. However, b_0 will still be biased unless Assumption 2 is also satisfied. In other words if Assumption 2 is violated $\hat{b}_0$ will be biased, while $\hat{b}_1$ may or may not be biased, depending on whether Assumption 6 is satisfied. (See also E. Kane, *Economic Statistics and Econometrics*, Harper International Edition, Japan 1969, p. 356.)

6.2.3. THE MINIMUM VARIANCE PROPERTY

In this paragraph we will prove the Gauss—Markov Theorem, which states that the least squares estimates are *best* (have the smallest variance) as compared with *any other linear unbiased estimator* obtained from other econometric methods. This property is the main reason for the popularity of the OLS method. It should be stressed that the OLS estimates have the least variance within the class of linear unbiased estimators. It may well be that other non-linear or biased estimators from other methods have a smaller variance. However, the comparison of the OLS estimates is restricted traditionally to the class of linear unbiased estimators, which are popular because they are easy to analyse and understand. (See Wonnacott and Wonnacott, *Econometrics,* p. 21.)

Proof (1)

We found in Chapter 5 that the variance of $\hat{b}_1$ is

$$\text{var}(\hat{b}_1) = \sigma^2_{(\hat{b}_1)} = \sigma^2_u \, \frac{1}{\Sigma x_i^2}$$

We want to prove that any other linear unbiased estimate of the true parameter, for example $\tilde{b}_1$, obtained from any other econometric method, has a bigger variance than the least-squares estimate $\hat{b}_1$, that is, we want to prove that

$$\text{var}(\hat{b}_1) < \text{var}(\tilde{b}_1)$$

Firstly. The new estimator $\tilde{b}_1$ is by assumption a linear combination of the Y_i's, a weighted sum of the sample values Y_i, the weights being different from the weights $k_i \, (= x_i/\Sigma x_i^2)$ of the least-squares estimates. For example, let us assume

$$\tilde{b}_1 = \Sigma c_i Y_i$$

where $c_i = k_i + d_i$, k_i being the weights defined above for the OLS estimates, and d_i an arbitrary set of weights similar (but not the same) to the k_i's. Substituting $b_0 + b_1 X + u$ for Y_i we obtain

$$\tilde{b}_1 = \Sigma c_i(b_0 + b_1 X_i + u_i) = \Sigma(b_0 c_i + b_1 c_i X_i + c_i u_i)$$

Secondly. The new estimate $\tilde{b}_1$ is also assumed to be an unbiased estimator of the true b_1, that is $E(\tilde{b}_1) = b_1$. Taking expected values of the expression for $\tilde{b}_1$ we have

$$E(\tilde{b}_1) = E[b_0 \Sigma(c_i) + b_1 \Sigma(c_i X_i) + \Sigma(c_i u_i)]$$

Now $E(\tilde{b}_1) = b_1$ if, and only if,

$$\Sigma c_i = 0 \qquad \Sigma c_i X_i = 1 \quad \text{and} \quad \Sigma c_i u_i = 0$$

But $\Sigma c_i = 0$ implies $\Sigma d_i = 0$, because

$$\Sigma c_i = \Sigma(k_i + d_i) = \Sigma k_i + \Sigma d_i$$

which can be zero only if $\Sigma d_i = 0$, since $\Sigma k_i = 0$ as proved in Chapter 5. Similarly, $\Sigma c_i X_i = 1$ requires $\Sigma d_i X_i = 0$, since

$$\Sigma c_i X_i = \Sigma k_i X_i + \Sigma d_i X_i \quad \text{and given that} \quad \Sigma k_i X_i = 1.$$

In summary, since we are defining $\tilde{b}_1$ to be a linear unbiased estimate of b_1, with weights $c_i = k_i + d_i$, it follows that we also define

$$\Sigma c_i = 0 \qquad \Sigma d_i = 0 \qquad \Sigma c_i X_i = 1 \qquad \Sigma d_i X_i = 0$$

Thirdly. The variance of the new estimator $\tilde{b}_1$ is

$$\text{var}(\tilde{b}_1) = \text{var}(\hat{b}_1) + \sigma_u^2 \, \Sigma d_i^2$$

Proof. The procedure for the derivation of $\text{var}(\tilde{b}_1)$ is the same as that for deriving the variance of the least squares estimate $\hat{b}_1$. In Chapter 5 we found

$$\hat{b}_1 = \Sigma k_i Y_i$$

and

$$\text{var}(\hat{b}_1) = \text{var}(\Sigma k_i Y_i) = \Sigma \text{var}(k_i Y_i) = \Sigma[k_i^2 \, \text{var}(Y)] = \Sigma k_i^2 \sigma_u^2 = \sigma_u^2 \Sigma k_i^2 \qquad (6.3)$$

By analogy we may establish the variance of $\tilde{b}_1$.

$$\tilde{b}_1 = \Sigma c_i Y_i$$

and

$$\text{var}(\tilde{b}_1) = \text{var}(\Sigma c_i Y_i) = \Sigma c_i^2 \, \text{var}(Y_i)$$

given that the c_i's are constant weights, independent of the Y_i's. But

$$\text{var}(Y_i) = \sigma_u^2 \qquad \text{(see Chapter 4)}$$

Therefore

$$\text{var}(\tilde{b}_1) = \sigma_u^2 \, \Sigma c_i^2$$

Now

$$\Sigma c_i^2 = \Sigma(k_i + d_i)^2 = \Sigma k_i^2 + \Sigma d_i^2 + 2 \Sigma k_i d_i = \Sigma k_i^2 + \Sigma d_i^2$$

given that

$$\Sigma k_i d_i = \Sigma \frac{x_i}{\Sigma x_i^2} d_i = \frac{\Sigma(X_i - \bar{X}) d_i}{\Sigma x_i^2} = \frac{\Sigma d_i X_i - \bar{X} \Sigma d_i}{\Sigma x_i^2} = 0$$

(from the conditions $\Sigma d_i X_i = 0$ and $\Sigma d_i = 0$, set above). Substituting, we find

$$\text{var}(\tilde{b}_1) = \sigma_u^2 (\Sigma k_i^2 + \Sigma d_i^2) = \sigma_u^2 \Sigma k_i^2 + \sigma_u^2 \Sigma d_i^2$$

But $\sigma_u^2 \Sigma k_i^2 = \text{var}(\hat{b}_1)$; therefore

$$\text{var}(\tilde{b}_1) = \text{var}(\hat{b}_1) + \sigma_u^2 \, \Sigma d_i^2$$

Given that the d_i's are defined as arbitrary constant weights not all of them zero, the second term is positive ($\sigma_u^2 \, \Sigma d_i^2 > 0$).

(Since $c_i = k_i + d_i$, if all d_i were zero then $c_i = k_i$, which would make $\tilde{b}_1 = \hat{b}_1$, contrary to our assumption that $\tilde{b}_1$ is a new estimator different from $\hat{b}_1$.)

Therefore

$$\text{var}(\tilde{b}) > \text{var}(\hat{b}_1)$$

Thus in the group of linear unbiased estimates of the true b_1, the least-squares estimate has minimum variance.

Proof (2)

In a similar way we can prove that the least-squares constant intercept $\hat{b}_0$ has minimum variance.

Firstly. We take a new estimator $\tilde{b}_0$, which we assume to be a linear function of the Y_i's, with weights $c_i = k_i + d_i$, as before. Recall that the least squares $\hat{b}_0$ was found

$$\hat{b}_0 = \Sigma \left[\frac{1}{n} - \overline{X} k_i \right] Y_i$$

By analogy

$$\tilde{b}_0 = \Sigma \left[\frac{1}{n} - \overline{X} c_i \right] Y_i = f(Y)$$

Secondly. We want $\tilde{b}_0$ to be an unbiased estimator of the true b_0, that is, $E(\tilde{b}_0) = b_0$. We substitute for $Y_i = b_0 + b_1 X_i + u_i$ in $\tilde{b}_0$

$$\tilde{b}_0 = b_0 \left[1 - \overline{X} \Sigma c_i \right] + b_1 \left[\overline{X} - \overline{X} \Sigma c_i X_i \right] + \Sigma \left[\frac{1}{n} - \overline{X} c_i \right] u_i$$

Taking expected values we find

$$E(\tilde{b}_0) = b_0 \left[1 - \overline{X} E(\Sigma c_i) \right] + b_1 \left[\overline{X} - \overline{X} E(\Sigma c_i X_i) \right] + E \left[\Sigma \left(\frac{1}{n} - \overline{X} c_i \right) u_i \right]$$

Now $E(\tilde{b}_0) = b_0$ if, and only if,

$$\Sigma c_i = 0, \qquad \Sigma c_i X_i = 1 \quad \text{and } \Sigma c_i u_i = 0$$

These conditions imply

$$\Sigma d_i = 0 \quad \text{and} \quad \Sigma d_i X_i = 0$$

Thirdly. The variance of $\tilde{b}_0$ will be

$$\text{var}(\tilde{b}_0) = E(\tilde{b}_0 - b_0)^2 = \sigma_u^2 \Sigma \left[\frac{1}{n} - \overline{X} c_i \right]^2 = \sigma_u^2 \Sigma \left[\frac{1}{n^2} + \overline{X}^2 c_i^2 - 2 \frac{1}{n} \overline{X} c_i \right]$$

$$= \sigma_u^2 \left[\frac{n}{n^2} + \overline{X}^2 \Sigma c_i^2 - 2 \overline{X} \frac{1}{n} \Sigma c_i \right] = \sigma_u^2 \left[\frac{1}{n} + \overline{X}^2 \Sigma c_i^2 - \frac{2}{n} \overline{X} \Sigma c_i \right]$$

Given that $\Sigma c_i = 0$ and $\Sigma c_i^2 = \Sigma k_i^2 + \Sigma d_i^2$, we have

$$\operatorname{var}(\tilde{b}_0) = \sigma_u^2 \left[\frac{1}{n} + \bar{X}^2 (\Sigma k_i^2 + \Sigma d_i^2) \right]$$

$$= \sigma_u^2 \left[\frac{1}{n} + \frac{\bar{X}^2}{\Sigma x^2} \right] + [\sigma_u^2 \, \bar{X}^2 \, \Sigma d_i^2]$$

But the first term is the variance of $\hat{b}_0$.

Hence

$$\operatorname{var}(\tilde{b}_0) = \operatorname{var}(\hat{b}_0) + \sigma_u^2 \, [\bar{X}^2 \, \Sigma d_i^2] \, .$$

But $\Sigma d_i^2 > 0$, because not all d's are zero.

Therefore

$$\operatorname{var}(\tilde{b}_0) > \operatorname{var}(\hat{b}_0)$$

Note that to establish the BLU properties of the OLS estimates we made use of Assumptions 1, 2, 3, 5 and 6A, but we did not require the fulfilment of Assumption 4. That is the b's have the BLU properties even if u is not normally distributed.

6.2.4. IMPORTANCE OF THE BLU PROPERTIES

The student may well ask why do econometricians attach so much importance to the BLU properties of the ordinary least-squares estimates.

The property of linearity is desirable because it facilitates the computations of the estimates. Obviously, if we have two methods and the first produced estimates which were nonlinear functions of the sample observations, while the second gave linear estimates, the latter would be simpler and hence preferable (*ceteris paribus*, that is provided that the other properties of the estimators of the various methods were the same).

The property of unbiasedness by itself is not particularly useful, since the only reassurance it gives is that if we have a very large number of samples, the estimators of the parameters obtained from these samples will *on the average* give the true value of b's. If, however, the spread of the values of the estimates around the true b is very large, the estimates from any one sample are not very helpful for inferences about the true b. Similarly, the least variance property by itself is not particularly desirable, because an estimate may have zero variance and yet have an enormous bias. However, the minimum variance property becomes desirable when combined with unbiasedness. The importance of this property is apparent when we want to apply the standard tests of significance for $\hat{b}_0$ and $\hat{b}_1$ and to construct confidence intervals for these estimates. For example, suppose we have the least-square estimate of b, $\hat{b}$, and another estimate $\tilde{b}$ obtained from another method. Assume that both estimates ($\hat{b}$ and $\tilde{b}$) are linear, unbiased estimates of the true parameter b, and also are normally distributed. However, as we have just proved, the variance of $\hat{b}$ will be smaller than the variance of $\tilde{b}$ (figure 6.7).

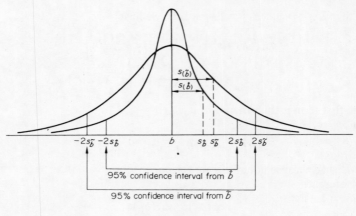

Figure 6.7

Both distributions of $\hat{b}$ and $\tilde{b}$ will be centred around the true parameter b, since both are unbiased estimates of the true b. But because of the minimum variance property of the method of least squares, $\hat{b}$ will have a smaller dispersion about b, than will the estimate $\tilde{b}$ which was obtained by some other econometric method. Thus the least squares estimates are more likely to lie in any chosen interval around the true parameter value b, than are the estimates obtained by any other method. For example, suppose we choose the interval $\{b \pm \text{ two standard deviations}\}$, as our 95 per cent confidence interval for the true value of b. This confidence interval (or any other we care to choose) will be narrower for the least squares estimates than for those obtained by any other method. From figure 6.7 it is obvious that the interval $\{\hat{b} \pm 2s_{(\hat{b})}\}$ is smaller than the interval $\{\tilde{b} \pm 2s_{(\tilde{b})}\}$. Being able to set a smaller confidence interval with least squares estimates means in effect that we are extracting more information from our sample than we would be if we were using any other method yielding unbiased estimates.

EXERCISES

Exercises relating to the material of this chapter are included in Appendix III.

7. Multiple Regression and Other Extensions of the Simple Linear Regression Model

In the first section of this chapter we shall extend the simple linear regression model to relationships with two explanatory variables. In the second section (7.2) we shall develop some practical rules for the derivation of the normal equations for models including any number of variables. In section 7.3 we shall examine the extension of the two-variable model to nonlinear relationships.

7.1. MODEL WITH TWO EXPLANATORY VARIABLES

7.1.1. THE NORMAL EQUATIONS

We shall illustrate the three-variable model with an example from the theory of demand. Economic theory postulates that the quantity demanded for a given commodity (Y) depends on its price (X_1) and on consumers' income (X_2)

$$Y = f(X_1, X_2)$$

Given that the theory does not specify the mathematical form of the demand function, we start our investigation by assuming that the relationship between Y, X_1 and X_2 is linear

$$Y_i = b_0 + b_1 X_{1i} + b_2 X_{2i} \qquad (i = 1, 2, \ldots, n)$$

This is an exact relationship whose meaning is that the variations in the quantity demanded are fully explained by changes in price and income. If this form were true any observation on Y, X_1 and X_2 would determine a point which would lie on a plane. However, if we gather observations on these variables during a certain period of time and plot them on a diagram, we will observe that not all of them lie on a plane: some will lie on it, but others will lie above or below it. This scatter is due to various factors omitted from the function and to other types of error which have been examined in Chapter 4. The influence of such factors may be taken into account by introducing a random variable u, in the function, which thus becomes stochastic

$$Y_i = \underbrace{(b_0 + b_1 X_{1i} + b_2 X_{2i})}_{\text{systematic component}} + \underbrace{(u_i)}_{\text{random component}}$$

On *a priori* grounds we would expect the coefficient $\hat{b}_1$ to have a negative sign, given the 'law of demand', while b_2 is expected to be positive, since for normal commodities the quantity demanded changes in the same direction as income.

117

To complete the specification of our simple model we need some assumptions about the random variable u. These assumptions are the same as in the single-explanatory-variable model developed in Chapter 4. That is:

Assumption 1 (Randomness of u)

The variable u is a real random variable.

Assumption 2 (Zero mean of u)

The random variable u has a zero mean value for each X_i,

$$E(u_i) = 0$$

Assumption 3 (Homoscedasticity)

The variance of each u_i is the same for all the X_i values

$$E(u_i^2) = \sigma_u^2 \qquad \text{constant}$$

Assumption 4 (Normality of u)

The values of each u_i are normally distributed

$$u_i \sim N(0, \sigma_u^2)$$

Assumption 5 (Nonautocorrelation or serial independence of the u's)

The values of u_i (corresponding to X_i) are independent from the values of any other u_j (corresponding to X_j)

$$E(u_i u_j) = 0 \qquad \text{for} \qquad i \neq j$$

Assumption 6 (Independence of u_i and X_i)

Every disturbance term u_i is independent of the explanatory variables

$$E(u_i X_{1i}) = E(u_i X_{2i}) = 0$$

This condition is automatically fulfilled if we assume that the values of the X's are a set of fixed numbers in all (hypothetical) samples. This is *Assumption 6A*.

Assumption 7 (No errors of measurement in the X's)

The explanatory variables are measured without error.

Assumption 8 (No perfect multicollinear X's)

The explanatory variables are not perfectly linearly correlated.

Assumption 9 (Correct aggregation of the macro-variables)

The appropriate 'aggregation bridge' has been constructed between the aggregate macro-variables used in the function and their individual components (micro-variables).

Assumption 10 (Identifiability of the function)

The relationship being studied is identified.

Assumption 11 (Correct specification of the model)

The model has no specification error in that all the important explanatory variables appear explicitly in the function and the mathematical form is correctly defined (linear or nonlinear form and number of equations in the model).

These assumptions will be examined in detail in Chapters 9–12. Having specified our model we next use sample observations on Y, X_1 and X_2 and obtain estimates of the true parameters b_0, b_1 and b_2:

$$\hat{Y}_i = \hat{b}_0 + \hat{b}_1 X_{1i} + \hat{b}_2 X_{2i}$$

where $\hat{b}_0$, $\hat{b}_1$, $\hat{b}_2$ are estimates of the true parameters b_0, b_1 and b_2 of the demand relationship.

As before, the estimates will be obtained by minimising the sum of squared residuals

$$\sum_{i=1}^{n} e^2 = \sum_i^n (Y_i - \hat{Y}_i)^2 = \sum_i^n (Y_i - \hat{b}_0 - \hat{b}_1 X_{1i} - \hat{b}_2 X_{2i})^2$$

A necessary condition for this expression to assume a minimum value is that its partial derivatives with respect to $\hat{b}_0$, $\hat{b}_1$ and $\hat{b}_2$ be equal to zero:

$$\frac{\partial \Sigma (Y_i - \hat{b}_0 - \hat{b}_1 X_{1i} - \hat{b}_2 X_{2i})^2}{\partial \hat{b}_0} = .0$$

$$\frac{\partial \Sigma (Y_i - \hat{b}_0 - \hat{b}_1 X_{1i} - \hat{b}_2 X_{2i})^2}{\partial \hat{b}_1} = 0$$

$$\frac{\partial \Sigma (Y_i - \hat{b}_0 - \hat{b}_1 X_{1i} - \hat{b}_2 X_{2i})^2}{\partial \hat{b}_2} = 0$$

Performing the partial differentiations we get the following system of three *normal equations* in the three unknown parameters $\hat{b}_0$, $\hat{b}_1$ and $\hat{b}_2$

$$\begin{aligned}
\Sigma Y_i &= n\hat{b}_0 + \hat{b}_1 \Sigma X_{1i} + \hat{b}_2 \Sigma X_{2i} \\
\Sigma X_{1i} Y_i &= \hat{b}_0 \Sigma X_{1i} + \hat{b}_1 \Sigma X_{1i}^2 + \hat{b}_2 \Sigma X_{1i} X_{2i} \\
\Sigma X_{2i} Y_i &= \hat{b}_0 \Sigma X_{2i} + \hat{b}_1 \Sigma X_{1i} X_{2i} + \hat{b}_2 \Sigma X_{2i}^2
\end{aligned} \qquad (7.1)$$

From the solution of this system (by any method, for example using determinants as explained in Appendix II) we obtain values for $\hat{b}_0$, $\hat{b}_1$ and $\hat{b}_2$.

Formal derivation of the system of normal equations

We set $w = (Y_i - \hat{b}_0 - \hat{b}_1 X_{1i} - \hat{b}_2 X_{2i})$ and use the rule of 'the function of a function', according to which

if $\qquad\qquad y = f_1(w) \quad$ and $\quad w = f_2(x)$

then $\qquad\qquad \dfrac{dy}{dx} = \dfrac{dy}{dw} \cdot \dfrac{dw}{dx}.$

1. Partial derivative with respect to $\hat{b}_0$

$$\frac{\partial \Sigma e_i^2}{\partial \hat{b}_0} = \frac{\partial \Sigma(Y_i - \hat{b}_0 - \hat{b}_1 X_{1i} - \hat{b}_2 X_{2i})^2}{\partial \hat{b}_0} = 0$$

$$-2\Sigma(Y_i - \hat{b}_0 - \hat{b}_1 X_{1i} - \hat{b}_2 X_{2i}) = 0$$

$$\Sigma Y_i - \Sigma \hat{b}_0 - \Sigma \hat{b}_1 X_{1i} - \Sigma \hat{b}_2 X_{2i} = 0$$

or

$$\Sigma Y = n\hat{b}_0 + \hat{b}_1 \Sigma X_{1i} + \hat{b}_2 \Sigma X_{2i} \tag{1}$$

2. Partial derivative with respect to $\hat{b}_1$

$$\frac{\partial \Sigma e_i^2}{\partial \hat{b}_1} = \frac{\partial \Sigma(Y_i - \hat{b}_0 - \hat{b}_1 X_{1i} - \hat{b}_2 X_{2i})^2}{\partial \hat{b}_1} = 0$$

$$-2\Sigma X_{1i}(Y_i - \hat{b}_0 - \hat{b}_1 X_{1i} - \hat{b}_2 X_{2i}) = 0$$

$$\Sigma X_{1i} Y_i - \Sigma \hat{b}_0 X_{1i} - \Sigma \hat{b}_1 X_{1i}^2 - \Sigma \hat{b}_2 X_{1i} X_{2i} = 0$$

or

$$\Sigma X_{1i} Y_i = \hat{b}_0 \Sigma X_{1i} + \hat{b}_1 \Sigma X_{1i}^2 + \hat{b}_2 \Sigma X_{1i} X_{2i} \tag{2}$$

3. Partial derivative with respect to b_2

$$\frac{\partial \Sigma e_i^2}{\partial \hat{b}_2} = \frac{\partial \Sigma(Y_i - \hat{b}_0 - \hat{b}_1 X_{1i} - \hat{b}_2 X_{2i})^2}{\partial \hat{b}_2} = 0$$

$$-2\Sigma X_{2i}(Y_i - \hat{b}_0 - \hat{b}_1 X_{1i} - \hat{b}_2 X_{2i}) = 0$$

$$\Sigma X_{2i} Y_i - \Sigma \hat{b}_0 X_{2i} - \Sigma \hat{b}_1 X_{1i} X_{2i} - \Sigma \hat{b}_2 X_{2i}^2 = 0$$

or

$$\Sigma X_{2i} Y_i = \hat{b}_0 \Sigma X_{2i} + \hat{b}_1 \Sigma X_{1i} X_{2i} + \hat{b}_2 \Sigma X_{2i}^2 \tag{3}$$

Expressions (1), (2) and (3) are the three normal equations of the least squares method.

The following formulae, in which the variables are expressed in deviations from their mean, may also be used for obtaining values for the parameter estimates.

$$\left. \begin{aligned} \hat{b}_0 &= \overline{Y} - \hat{b}_1 \overline{X}_1 - \hat{b}_2 \overline{X}_2 \\ \hat{b}_1 &= \frac{(\Sigma x_{1i} y_i)(\Sigma x_{2i}^2) - (\Sigma x_{2i} y_i)(\Sigma x_{1i} x_{2i})}{(\Sigma x_{1i}^2)(\Sigma x_{2i}^2) - (\Sigma x_{1i} x_{2i})^2} \\ \hat{b}_2 &= \frac{(\Sigma x_{2i} y_i)(\Sigma x_{1i}^2) - (\Sigma x_{1i} y_i)(\Sigma x_{1i} x_{2i})}{(\Sigma x_{1i}^2)(\Sigma x_{2i}^2) - (\Sigma x_{1i} x_{2i})^2} \end{aligned} \right\} \tag{7.2}$$

These formulae can be formally derived by solving the system of *normal equations*

$$\left. \begin{aligned} \Sigma x_{1i} y_i &= \hat{b}_1 \Sigma x_{1i}^2 + \hat{b}_2 \Sigma x_{1i} x_{2i} \\ \Sigma x_{2i} y_i &= \hat{b}_1 \Sigma x_{1i} x_{2i} + \hat{b}_2 \Sigma x_{2i}^2 \end{aligned} \right\} \tag{7.3}$$

where

$$y_i = Y_i - \overline{Y}. \qquad x_{1i} = X_{1i} - \overline{X}_1 \quad \text{and} \quad x_{2i} = X_{2i} - \overline{X}_2$$

Formal derivation of the normal equations expressed in deviations

Firstly. From

$$\hat{Y} = \hat{b}_0 + \hat{b}_1 X_1 + \hat{b}_2 X_2$$

and

$$\overline{Y} = \hat{b}_0 + \hat{b}_1 \overline{X}_1 + \hat{b}_2 \overline{X}_2$$

we obtain, by subtraction

$$\hat{y}_i = \hat{Y}_i - \overline{Y} = \hat{b}_1 x_{1i} + \hat{b}_2 x_{2i}$$

Therefore

$$e_i = y_i - \hat{y}_i = y_i - (\hat{b} x_{1i} + \hat{b}_2 x_{2i})$$

Secondly. The sum of squared residuals is

$$\Sigma e_i^2 = \Sigma (y_i - \hat{y}_i)^2 = \Sigma (y_i - \hat{b}_1 x_{1i} - \hat{b}_2 x_{2i})^2.$$

Thirdly. The first conditions for a minimum require

$$\frac{\partial \Sigma e_i^2}{\partial \hat{b}_1} = 0 \quad \text{and} \quad \frac{\partial \Sigma e_i^2}{\partial \hat{b}_2} = 0$$

Carrying out the differentiation we obtain

$$\left. \begin{aligned} 2\Sigma (y_i - \hat{b}_1 x_{1i} - \hat{b}_2 x_{2i})(-x_{1i}) = 0 \\ 2\Sigma (y_i - \hat{b}_1 x_{1i} - \hat{b}_2 x_{2i})(-x_{2i}) = 0 \end{aligned} \right\} \quad (7.4)$$

Rearranging we obtain the system of normal equations

$$\Sigma x_{1i} y_i = \hat{b}_1 \Sigma x_{1i}^2 + \hat{b}_2 \Sigma x_{1i} x_{2i}$$
$$\Sigma x_{2i} y_i = \hat{b}_1 \Sigma x_{1i} x_{2i} + \hat{b}_2 \Sigma x_{2i}^2$$

Note. From 7.4 we may derive the following useful results, observing that $\hat{b}_1 x_{1i} + \hat{b}_2 x_{2i} = \hat{y}_i$,

$$\Sigma [y_i - (\hat{b}_1 x_{1i} + \hat{b}_2 x_{2i})] (x_{1i}) = \Sigma (y_i - \hat{y}_i)(x_{1i}) = 0$$

and

$$\Sigma [y_i - (\hat{b}_1 x_{1i} + \hat{b}_2 x_{2i})] (x_{2i}) = \Sigma (y_i - \hat{y}_i)(x_{2i}) = 0$$

or

$$\left. \begin{aligned} \Sigma e x_{1i} = 0 \\ \Sigma e x_{2i} = 0 \end{aligned} \right\} \quad 7.5$$

7.1.2. THE COEFFICIENT OF MULTIPLE DETERMINATION (OR THE SQUARED MULTIPLE CORRELATION COEFFICIENT) $R^2_{Y.X_1 X_2}$

When the explanatory variables are more than one we talk of multiple correlation. The square of the correlation coefficient is called the *coefficient* of *multiple determination* or squared multiple correlation coefficient. The coefficient of multiple determination is denoted by capital R^2, with subscripts the variables whose relationship is being studied. For example in the three-variable model the squared multiple correlation coefficient is $R^2_{Y.X_1 X_2}$. As in the two-variable model, R^2 shows the percentage of the total variation of Y explained by the regression plane, that is, by changes in X_1 and X_2

$$R^2_{Y.X_1 X_2} = \frac{\Sigma \hat{y}^2}{\Sigma y^2} = \frac{\Sigma (\hat{Y} - \overline{Y})^2}{\Sigma (Y - \overline{Y})^2} = 1 - \frac{\Sigma e^2}{\Sigma y^2} = \frac{\Sigma y^2 - \Sigma e^2}{\Sigma y^2}$$

We have established that $e_i = y_i - \hat{y}_i$ and

$$\hat{y}_i = \hat{b}_1 x_{1i} + \hat{b}_2 x_{2i}$$

The squared residuals are

$$
\begin{aligned}
\Sigma e_i^2 &= \Sigma e_i (y_i - \hat{y}_i) \\
&= \Sigma e_i (y_i - \hat{b}_1 x_{1i} - \hat{b}_2 x_{2i}) \\
&= \Sigma e y_i - \hat{b}_1 \Sigma e_i x_{1i} - \hat{b}_2 \Sigma e_i x_{2i}
\end{aligned}
$$

But from 7.4 we know $\Sigma e_i x_{1i} = 0$ and $\Sigma e_i x_{2i} = 0$.
Therefore

$$
\begin{aligned}
\Sigma e_i^2 &= \Sigma e_i y_i \\
&= \Sigma (y_i - \hat{y}_i) y_i \\
&= \Sigma y_i (y_i - \hat{b}_1 x_1 - \hat{b}_2 x_2) \\
&= \Sigma y_i^2 - \hat{b}_1 \Sigma y x_1 - \hat{b}_2 \Sigma y x_2
\end{aligned}
$$

By substituting in the formula of $R^2_{Y.X_1 X_2}$ we get

$$R^2_{Y.X_1 X_2} = \frac{\Sigma y_i^2 - (\Sigma y_i^2 - \hat{b}_1 \Sigma y_i x_{1i} - \hat{b}_2 \Sigma y_i x_{2i})}{\Sigma y_i^2}$$

or

$$R^2_{Y.X_1 X_2} = \frac{\hat{b}_1 \Sigma y_i x_{1i} + \hat{b}_2 \Sigma y_i x_{2i}}{\Sigma y_i^2} \tag{7.6}$$

The value of R^2 lies between 0 and 1. The higher R^2 the greater the percentage of the variation of Y explained by the regression plane, that is, the better the 'goodness of fit' of the regression plane to the sample observations. The closer R^2 to zero, the worse the fit.

The above formula for R^2 does not take into account the loss of degrees of freedom from the introduction of additional explanatory variables in the function. An 'adjusted' expression for R^2 will be discussed later in this chapter.

7.1.3. THE MEAN AND VARIANCE OF THE PARAMETER ESTIMATES $\hat{b}_0$, $\hat{b}_1$, $\hat{b}_2$

The mean of the estimates of the parameters in the three-variable model is derived in the same way as in the two-variable model. The estimates $\hat{b}_0$, $\hat{b}_1$, $\hat{b}_2$ are unbiased estimates of the true parameters of the relationship between Y, X_1 and X_2: their mean expected value is the true parameter itself

$$E(\hat{b}_0) = b_0 \qquad E(\hat{b}_1) = b_1 \qquad E(\hat{b}_2) = b_2$$

The variances of the parameter estimates are obtained by the following formulae

$$\text{var}(\hat{b}_0) = \hat{\sigma}_u^2 \left[\frac{1}{n} + \frac{\bar{X}_1^2 \Sigma x_2^2 + \bar{X}_2^2 \Sigma x_1^2 - 2\bar{X}_1 \bar{X}_2 \Sigma x_1 x_2}{\Sigma x_1^2 \Sigma x_2^2 - (\Sigma x_1 x_2)^2} \right]$$

$$\text{var}(\hat{b}_1) = \hat{\sigma}_u^2 \, \frac{\Sigma x_2^2}{\Sigma x_1^2 \Sigma x_2^2 - (\Sigma x_1 x_2)^2}$$

$$\text{var}(\hat{b}_2) = \hat{\sigma}_u^2 \, \frac{\Sigma x_1^2}{\Sigma x_1^2 \Sigma x_2^2 - (\Sigma x_1 x_2)^2}$$

where $\hat{\sigma}_u^2 = \Sigma e^2/(n-K)$, K being the total number of parameters which are estimated. In the three-variable model $K = 3$.

7.1.4. TESTS OF SIGNIFICANCE OF THE PARAMETER ESTIMATES

The traditional test of significance of the parameter estimates is the standard error test, which is equivalent to the Student's t test. Both tests have been explained in detail in Chapter 5. We summarise the main procedures so that the student has an opportunity to become familiar with the concepts involved in hypothesis testing.

Traditionally in econometric applications, researchers test the null hypothesis $H_0: b_i = 0$ for each parameter, against the alternative hypothesis $H_1: b_i \neq 0$.[1] This type of hypothesis implies a two-tail test (see Appendix I) at a chosen level of significance, usually at the 5 per cent (and more rarely at the 1 per cent level).

1. The standard error test

We print the standard errors $(s_{\hat{b}_i} = \sqrt{\text{var}(\hat{b}_i)})$ underneath the respective estimates and compare them with the numerical values of the estimates.

(a) If $s_{(\hat{b}_i)} > \frac{1}{2}\hat{b}_i$ we accept the null hypothesis; that is, we accept that the estimate b_i is not statistically significant at the 5 per cent level of significance for a two-tail test.

(b) If $s_{(\hat{b}_i)} < \frac{1}{2}\hat{b}_i$ we reject the null hypothesis, in other words we accept that our parameter estimate is statistically significant at the 5 per cent level of significance for a two-tail test.

The smaller the standard errors, the stronger is the evidence that the estimates are statistically significant,

We stress that the standard error test is an approximate test and implies a two-tail test conducted at the 5 per cent level of significance.

2. The Student's test of the null hypothesis

We compute the t ratio for each $\hat{b}_i$

$$t^* = \frac{\hat{b}_i}{s_{(\hat{b}_i)}}$$

This is the observed (or sample) value of the t ratio, which we compare with the theoretical value of t obtainable from the t-table (page 660) with $n - K = n - 3$

---

[1] For tests of other hypotheses $(H_0: b_i = b_i^*)$ see pp. 83–5 and 87–9.

degrees of freedom. The theoretical values of t (at the chosen level of significance) are the critical values that define the critical region in a two-tail test, with $n - K$ degrees of freedom.

(a) If t^* falls in the acceptance region; that is, if $-t_{0.025} < t^* < t_{0.025}$ (with $n - K$ degrees of freedom), we accept the null hypothesis; that is, we accept that $\hat{b}_i$ is not significant (at the 5 per cent level of significance) and hence the corresponding regressor does not appear to contribute to the explanation of the variations in Y.

(b) If t^* falls in the critical region we reject the null hypothesis, and we accept the alternative one: $\hat{b}_i$ is statistically significant.

Clearly the greater the value of t^* the stronger is the evidence that $\hat{b}_i$ is significant. (Note that t^* and the $s_{(\hat{b}_i)}$ are inversely related.) For a number of degrees of freedom higher than 8 the crucial value of t (at the 5 per cent level of significance) for the rejection of the null hypothesis is approximately 2.

Example. Table 7.1 contains observations on the quantity demanded (Y) of a certain commodity, its price (X_1) and consumers' income (X_2). We will fit a linear regression to these observations and test the overall goodness of fit (with R^2) as well as the statistical reliability of the estimates $\hat{b}_0$, $\hat{b}_1$, $\hat{b}_2$. The relevant calculations are shown in table 7.1.

1. Substituting in the formulae for $\hat{b}_1$ and $\hat{b}_2$ we find

$$\hat{b}_1 = \frac{(-300)(1,580,000) - (65,000)(-5,900)}{(30)(1,580,000) - (-5,900)^2} = \frac{-90,500}{12,590} = -7.1882$$

$$\hat{b}_2 = \frac{(65,000)(30) - (-300)(-5,900)}{(30)(1,580,000) - (-5,900)^2} = \frac{180}{12,590} = 0.0143$$

Therefore

$$\hat{b}_0 = \overline{Y} - \hat{b}_1 \overline{X}_1 - \hat{b}_2 \overline{X}_2$$

$$= 80 - (-7.19)(6) - (0.0143)(800) = 111.69$$

2. The unadjusted coefficient of multiple determination $R^2_{Y \cdot X_1 X_2}$ may be computed by the expression

$$R^2 = \frac{\hat{b}_1 \Sigma y x_1 + \hat{b}_2 \Sigma y x_2}{\Sigma y^2}$$

$$= \frac{(-7.19)(-300) + (0.0143)(65,000)}{3,450} = 0.894$$

3. For the estimation of the standard errors of $\hat{b}_1$ and $\hat{b}_2$ we require an estimate of σ_u^2. The expression $\hat{\sigma}_u^2 = \Sigma e^2/(n - K)$ includes the sum of squared residuals, which can be obtained from the expression

$$R^2 = 1 - \frac{\Sigma e^2}{\Sigma y^2}$$

Solving for Σe^2 we find

$$\Sigma e^2 = \Sigma y^2 (1 - R^2)$$

Substituting the relevant terms Σy^2 and R^2 we find $\Sigma e^2 = (3,450)(0.106) = 365.7$. Therefore

$$\hat{\sigma}_u^2 = \frac{365.7}{10 - 3} = 52.24$$

4. The variance of $\hat{b}_1$ and $\hat{b}_2$ may be obtained by substituting the relevant terms in the

Table 7.1. Worksheet for the regression $\hat{Y} = \hat{b}_0 + \hat{b}_1 X_1 + \hat{b}_2 X_2$

n	Y Quantity demanded	X_1 Price	X_2 Income	y_i $(Y_i - \bar{Y})$	x_{1i} $(X_{1i} - \bar{X}_1)$	x_{2i} $(X_{2i} - \bar{X}_2)$	y_i^2	x_{1i}^2	x_{2i}^2	$y_i x_{1i}$	$y_i x_{2i}$	$x_{1i} x_{2i}$
1	100	5	1,000	20	−1	200	400	1	40,000	−20	4,000	−200
2	75	7	600	−5	1	−200	25	1	40,000	−5	1,000	−200
3	80	6	1,200	0	0	400	0	0	160,000	0	0	0
4	70	6	500	−10	0	−300	100	0	90,000	0	3,000	0
5	50	8	300	−30	2	−500	900	4	250,000	−60	15,000	−1,000
6	65	7	400	−15	1	−400	225	1	160,000	−15	6,000	−400
7	90	5	1,300	10	−1	500	100	1	250,000	−10	5,000	−500
8	100	4	1,100	20	−2	300	400	4	90,000	−40	6,000	−600
9	110	3	1,300	30	−3	500	900	9	250,000	−90	15,000	−1,500
10	60	9	300	−20	3	−500	400	9	250,000	−60	10,000	−1,500
$n = 10$	$\Sigma Y_i = 800$	$\Sigma X_1 = 60$	$\Sigma X_2 = 8,000$	$\Sigma y_i = 0$	$\Sigma x_{1i} = 0$	$\Sigma x_{2i} = 0$	$\Sigma y_i^2 = 3,450$	$\Sigma x_{1i}^2 = 30$	$\Sigma x_{2i}^2 = 1,580,000$	$\Sigma y_i x_{1i} = -300$	$\Sigma y_i x_{2i} = 65,000$	$\Sigma x_1 x_2 = -5,900$

$\bar{Y} = 80,$ $\quad \bar{X}_1 = 6,$ $\quad \bar{X}_2 = 800.$

formula on page 123 by the following

$$\text{var}(\hat{b}_1) = (52.24)\frac{1,580,000}{12,590,000} \approx 6\cdot53$$

$$\text{var}(\hat{b}_2) = (52.24)\frac{30}{12,590,000} = 0\cdot0001$$

$$\text{var}(\hat{b}_0) = 553\cdot69$$

Therefore the standard errors of the estimates are

$$s(\hat{b}_1) = 2\cdot55 \qquad s(\hat{b}_2) = 0\cdot01 \qquad s(\hat{b}_0) = 23\cdot5$$

5. The regression results may now be presented in the following summary form

$$\hat{Y} = 111\cdot7 - 7\cdot19\,X_1 + 0\cdot014\,X_2$$

$$s_{(b_i)}\ (23\cdot5)\quad (2\cdot55)\quad (0\cdot01) \qquad\qquad R^2 = 0\cdot894$$

$$t^*\ (4\cdot75)\quad (-2\cdot8)\quad (1\cdot28) \qquad\qquad t_{0\cdot025} = 2\cdot365$$

The variables X_1 and X_2 explain 89 per cent of the total variation in Y. The estimates $\hat{b}_0$ and $\hat{b}_1$ are statistically significant but the estimate $\hat{b}_2$ is not statistically significant at the five per cent level.

7.2. THE GENERAL LINEAR REGRESSION MODEL

In this section we will extend the method of least squares to models including any number k of explanatory variables. We will develop some rules of thumb by which we can derive (a) the normal equations, (b) the coefficient of multiple determination, (c) the variances of the coefficients, for relationships including any number of explanatory variables. In Appendix II we describe the simplest method for solving systems of equations, that is, the method of determinants known as *Cramer's rule*.

7.2.1. DERIVATION OF THE NORMAL EQUATIONS

The general linear regression model with k explanatory variables is of the form

$$Y = b_0 + b_1 X_1 + b_2 X_2 + \ldots + b_k X_k + u$$

There are K parameters to be estimated ($K = k + 1$). Clearly the system of normal equations will consist of K equations, in which the unknowns are the parameters $b_0, b_1, b_2, \ldots, b_k$, and the known terms will be the sums of squares and the sums of products of all the variables in the structural equation.

In order to derive the K normal equations without the formal differentiation procedure, we start from the equation of the estimated relationship (p. 59)

$$Y = \hat{b}_0 + \hat{b}_1 X_1 + \ldots + \hat{b}_k X_k + e$$

and we make use of the assumptions

$$\Sigma e_i = 0 \quad \text{and} \quad \Sigma e X_j = 0 \qquad (j = 1, 2, \ldots, k)$$

The normal equations for a model with any number of explanatory variables may be derived in a mechanical way, without recourse to differentiation. We will introduce a practical rule of thumb, derived by inspection of the normal equations of the two-variable and the three-variable models. We begin by rewriting these normal equations.

1. Model with one explanatory variable

Structural form $\qquad Y = b_0 + b_1 X_1 + u$

Estimated form $\qquad Y = \hat{b}_0 + \hat{b}_1 X_1 + e$

Normal equations $\qquad \begin{cases} \Sigma Y = n\hat{b}_0 + \hat{b}_1 \Sigma X_1 \\ \Sigma X_1 Y = \hat{b}_0 \Sigma X_1 + \hat{b}_1 \Sigma X_1^2 \end{cases}$

2. Model with two explanatory variables

Structural form $\qquad Y = b_0 + b_1 X_1 + b_2 X_2 + u$

Estimated form $\qquad Y = \hat{b}_0 + \hat{b}_1 X_1 + \hat{b}_2 X_2 + e$

Normal equations $\qquad \begin{cases} \Sigma Y = n\hat{b}_0 + \hat{b}_1 \Sigma X_1 + \hat{b}_2 \Sigma X_2 \\ \Sigma Y X_1 = \hat{b}_0 \Sigma X_1 + \hat{b}_1 \Sigma X_1^2 + \hat{b}_2 \Sigma X_1 X_2 \\ \Sigma Y X_2 = \hat{b}_0 \Sigma X_2 + \hat{b}_1 \Sigma X_1 X_2 + \hat{b}_2 \Sigma X_2^2 \end{cases}$

Comparing the normal equations of the above models we observe the following.

Firstly. The first normal equation is derived by summing the estimated form over all sample observations. For example, the estimated equation of the three-variable model is

$$Y = \hat{b}_0 + \hat{b}_1 X_1 + \hat{b}_2 X_2 + e$$

Summing over all sample observations and using the assumption $\Sigma e = 0$, we obtain the first normal equation

$$\Sigma Y = n\hat{b}_0 + \hat{b}_1 \Sigma X_1 + \hat{b}_2 \Sigma X_2$$

Secondly. The second normal equation is derived by multiplying the estimated form of the model by X_1 and summing over all sample observations. For example in the three-variable model premultiplying the estimated form by X_1 we find

$$YX_1 = \hat{b}_0 X_1 + \hat{b}_1 X_1^2 + \hat{b}_2 X_1 X_2 + e X_1$$

Summing over the n sample observations and using the assumption $\Sigma e X_1 = 0$, we obtain the second normal equation

$$\Sigma Y X_1 = \hat{b}_0 \Sigma X_1 + \hat{b}_1 \Sigma X_1^2 + \hat{b}_2 \Sigma X_1 X_2$$

Similarly the third normal equation of the model $Y = f(X_1, X_2)$ is obtained by multiplying the estimated form by X_2 and subsequently summing over the n sample observations.

The generalisation of this procedure to the k-variable model is straightforward.

For example the Kth equation of the model may be obtained by multiplying the estimated form of the k-variable model by X_k and then summing over all sample observations. The estimated form of the model is

$$Y = \hat{b}_0 + \hat{b}_1 X_1 + \hat{b}_2 X_2 + \hat{b}_3 X_3 + \ldots + \hat{b}_k X_k + e$$

Multiplication through by X_k yields

$$YX_k = \hat{b}_0 X_k + \hat{b}_1 X_1 X_k + \hat{b}_2 X_2 X_k + \ldots + \hat{b}_k X_k^2 + eX_k$$

and summation over the n sample observations gives the required Kth equation

$$\Sigma YX_k = \hat{b}_0 \Sigma X_k + b_1 \Sigma X_1 X_k + \hat{b}_2 \Sigma X_2 X_k + \ldots + \hat{b}_k \Sigma X_k^2$$

given that by assumption $\Sigma eX_k = 0$.

The generalisation of the linear regression model with the variables expressed in deviations from their means is the same. Thus the estimated form of the k-variable model in deviation form is

$$y = \hat{b}_1 x_1 + \hat{b}_2 x_2 + \ldots + \hat{b}_k x_k + e$$

The kth equation is derived by multiplying through the estimated form by x_k and summing over all sample observations

$$\Sigma yx_k = \hat{b}_1 \Sigma x_1 x_k + \hat{b}_2 \Sigma x_2 x_k + \ldots + \hat{b}_k \Sigma x_k^2$$

7.2.3. GENERALISATION OF THE FORMULA FOR R^2

The generalisation of the formula of the coefficient of multiple determination may be derived by inspection of the formulae of R^2 for the two-variable and three-variable models. We rewrite the expression of R^2 for these models.

1. Model with one explanatory variable

$$R^2_{Y.X_1} = \frac{\hat{b}_1 \Sigma yx_1}{\Sigma y^2}$$

2. Model with two explanatory variables

$$R^2_{Y.X_1 X_2} = \frac{\hat{b}_1 \Sigma yx_1 + \hat{b}_2 \Sigma yx_2}{\Sigma y^2}$$

By inspection we see that for each additional explanatory variable the formula of the squared multiple correlation coefficient includes an additional term in the numerator, formed by the estimate of the parameter corresponding to the new variable multiplied by the sum of products of the deviations of the new variable and the dependent one. For example, the formula of the coefficient of multiple determination for the k-variable model is

$$R^2_{Y.X_1 \ldots X_k} = \frac{\hat{b}_1 \Sigma yx_1 + \hat{b}_2 \Sigma yx_2 + \ldots + \hat{b}_k \Sigma yx_k}{\Sigma y^2}$$

7.2.4. THE ADJUSTED COEFFICIENT OF DETERMINATION: $\bar{R}^2$

It should be noted that the inclusion of additional explanatory variables in the function can never reduce the coefficient of multiple determination and will usually raise it. By introducing a new regressor we increase the value of the numerator of the expression for R^2, while the denominator remains the same (Σy^2, the total variation of Y, is given in any particular sample).

To correct for this defect we *adjust* R^2 by taking into account the degrees of freedom, which clearly decrease as new regressors are introduced in the function. The expression for the *adjusted* coefficient of multiple determination is

$$\bar{R}^2 = 1 - (1 - R^2)\frac{n-1}{n-K} \tag{7.7}$$

or

$$\bar{R}^2 = 1 - \left[\frac{\Sigma e^2/(n-K)}{\Sigma y^2/(n-1)}\right]$$

where R^2 is the unadjusted multiple correlation coefficient, n is the number of sample observations and K is the number of parameters estimated from the sample. (This formula is derived from the information of the Analysis of Variance Table, which will be explained in Chapter 8. See also D. B. Suits, *Statistics*, Chicago: Rand McNally, 1963, pp. 137–40.)

If n is large $\bar{R}^2$ and R^2 will not differ much. But with small samples, if the number of regressors (X's) is large in relation to the sample observations, $\bar{R}^2$ will be much smaller than R^2 and can even assume negative values, in which case $\bar{R}^2$ should be interpreted as being equal to zero.

7.2.5. GENERALISATION OF THE FORMULAE OF THE VARIANCES OF THE PARAMETER ESTIMATES

The generalisation of the formulae of the variances of the parameter estimates is facilitated by the use of determinants. The reader who is unacquainted with the meaning, properties and algebraic manipulation of determinants should first read Appendix II.

In the preceding sections we have developed the formulae of the variances of the estimates for models with one and two explanatory variables. We rewrite our results:

1. Model with one explanatory variable $Y = b_0 + b_1 X_1 + u$

$$\text{var}(\hat{b}_1) = \sigma_u^2 \frac{1}{\Sigma x^2}$$

2. Model with two explanatory variables $Y = b_0 + b_1 X_1 + b_2 X_2 + u$

$$\text{var}(\hat{b}_1) = \sigma_u^2 \frac{\Sigma x_2^2}{(\Sigma x_1^2)(\Sigma x_2^2) - (\Sigma x_1 x_2)^2}$$

$$\text{var}(\hat{b}_2) = \sigma_u^2 \frac{\Sigma x_1^2}{(\Sigma x_1^2)(\Sigma x_2^2) - (\Sigma x_1 x_2)^2}$$

The above expressions may be written in the form of determinants as follows. The normal equations of the model with two explanatory variables, written in deviation form, are

$$(\Sigma x_1 y) = \hat{b}_1(\Sigma x_1^2) + \hat{b}_2(\Sigma x_1 x_2)$$
$$(\Sigma x_2 y) = \hat{b}_1(\Sigma x_1 x_2) + \hat{b}_2(\Sigma x_2^2)$$

The terms in parentheses are the 'knowns' which are computed from the sample observations, while $\hat{b}_1$ and $\hat{b}_2$ are the unknowns. The known terms appearing on the right-hand side may be written in the form of a determinant

$$\begin{vmatrix} \Sigma x_1^2 & \Sigma x_1 x_2 \\ \Sigma x_1 x_2 & \Sigma x_2^2 \end{vmatrix} = |A|$$

The variance of each parameter is the product of σ_u^2 multiplied by the ratio of the minor determinant[1] associated with this parameter divided by the (complete) determinant. Thus

$$\mathrm{var}(\hat{b}_1) = \sigma_u^2 \cdot \frac{\begin{vmatrix} \Sigma x_1^2 & \Sigma x_1 x_2 \\ \Sigma x_1 x_2 & \Sigma x_2^2 \end{vmatrix}}{\begin{vmatrix} \Sigma x_1^2 & \Sigma x_1 x_2 \\ \Sigma x_1 x_2 & \Sigma x_2^2 \end{vmatrix}} = \sigma_u^2 \cdot \frac{\Sigma x_2^2}{\begin{vmatrix} \Sigma x_1^2 & \Sigma x_1 x_2 \\ \Sigma x_1 x_2 & \Sigma x_2^2 \end{vmatrix}} = \sigma_u^2 \cdot \frac{\Sigma x_2^2}{|A|}$$

$$\mathrm{var}(\hat{b}_2) = \sigma_u^2 \cdot \frac{\begin{vmatrix} \Sigma x_1^2 & \Sigma x_1 x_2 \\ \Sigma x_1 x_2 & \Sigma x_2^2 \end{vmatrix}}{\begin{vmatrix} \Sigma x_1^2 & \Sigma x_1 x_2 \\ \Sigma x_1 x_2 & \Sigma x_2^2 \end{vmatrix}} = \sigma_u^2 \cdot \frac{\Sigma x_1^2}{\begin{vmatrix} \Sigma x_1^2 & \Sigma x_1 x_2 \\ \Sigma x_1 x_2 & \Sigma x_2^2 \end{vmatrix}} = \sigma_u^2 \cdot \frac{\Sigma x_1^2}{|A|}$$

3. Model with three explanatory variables $Y = b_0 + b_1 X_1 + b_2 X_2 + b_3 X_3 + u$

The determinant of the known terms appearing in the right-hand side of the normal equations is

$$\begin{vmatrix} \Sigma x_1^2 & \Sigma x_1 x_2 & \Sigma x_1 x_3 \\ \Sigma x_1 x_2 & \Sigma x_2^2 & \Sigma x_2 x_3 \\ \Sigma x_1 x_3 & \Sigma x_2 x_3 & \Sigma x_3^2 \end{vmatrix} = |B|$$

Following the procedure outlined above for the model with two explanatory variables we may write the variances in terms of determinants as follows.

---

[1] The minor determinant for each parameter is formed by the elements of the determinant left after striking out the row and column including the parameter. See Appendix II.

$$\operatorname{var}(\hat{b}_1) = \sigma_u^2 \cdot \frac{\begin{vmatrix} \Sigma x_1^2 & \Sigma x_1 x_2 & \Sigma x_1 x_3 \\ \Sigma x_1 x_2 & \Sigma x_2^2 & \Sigma x_2 x_3 \\ \Sigma x_1 x_3 & \Sigma x_2 x_3 & \Sigma x_3^2 \end{vmatrix}}{|B|} = \sigma_u^2 \cdot \frac{\begin{vmatrix} \Sigma x_2^2 & \Sigma x_2 x_3 \\ \Sigma x_2 x_3 & \Sigma x_3^2 \end{vmatrix}}{|B|}$$

$$\operatorname{var}(\hat{b}_2) = \sigma_u^2 \cdot \frac{\begin{vmatrix} \Sigma x_1^2 & \Sigma x_1 x_2 & \Sigma x_1 x_3 \\ \Sigma x_1 x_2 & \Sigma x_2^2 & \Sigma x_2 x_3 \\ \Sigma x_1 x_3 & \Sigma x_2 x_3 & \Sigma x_3^2 \end{vmatrix}}{|B|} = \sigma_u^2 \cdot \frac{\begin{vmatrix} \Sigma x_1^2 & \Sigma x_1 x_3 \\ \Sigma x_1 x_3 & \Sigma x_3^2 \end{vmatrix}}{|B|}$$

$$\operatorname{var}(\hat{b}_3) = \sigma_u^2 \cdot \frac{\begin{vmatrix} \Sigma x_1^2 & \Sigma x_1 x_2 & \Sigma x_1 x_3 \\ \Sigma x_1 x_2 & \Sigma x_2^2 & \Sigma x_2 x_3 \\ \Sigma x_1 x_3 & \Sigma x_2 x_3 & \Sigma x_3^2 \end{vmatrix}}{|B|} = \sigma_u^2 \cdot \frac{\begin{vmatrix} \Sigma x_1^2 & \Sigma x_1 x_2 \\ \Sigma x_1 x_2 & \Sigma x_2^2 \end{vmatrix}}{|B|}$$

Examining the above expressions of the variances of the coefficient estimates we may generalise as follows. The variances of the estimates of the model including k explanatory variables can be computed by the ratio of two determinants: the determinant appearing in the numerator is the minor formed after striking out the row and column of the terms corresponding to the coefficient whose variance is being computed; the determinant appearing in the denominator is the complete determinant of the known terms appearing on the right-hand side of the normal equations. For example the variance of $\hat{b}_k$ is given by the following expression.

$$\operatorname{var}(\hat{b}_k) = \sigma_u^2 \cdot \frac{\begin{vmatrix} \Sigma x_1^2 & \Sigma x_1 x_2 & \dots & \Sigma x_1 x_k \\ \Sigma x_1 x_2 & \Sigma x_2^2 & \dots & \Sigma x_2 x_k \\ \vdots & \vdots & & \\ \Sigma x_1 x_k & \Sigma x_2 x_k & & \Sigma x_k^2 \end{vmatrix}}{\begin{vmatrix} \Sigma x_1^2 & \Sigma x_1 x_2 & \dots & \Sigma x_1 x_k \\ \Sigma x_1 x_2 & \Sigma x_2^2 & \dots & \Sigma x_2 x_k \\ \vdots & \vdots & & \vdots \\ \Sigma x_1 x_k & \Sigma x_2 x_k & \dots & \Sigma x_k^2 \end{vmatrix}}$$

7.3. PARTIAL CORRELATION COEFFICIENTS

The meaning of a partial correlation coefficient has been briefly discussed in Chapter 3. The interpretation of a partial correlation coefficient is closely connected with multiple regression. To continue the example used in Chapter 3 of the relationship between the number of visitors in a summer resort (X_1) and the consumption of hot drinks (Y), we may postulate the following functional relationship:

where
$$Y = b_0 + b_1 X_1 + b_2 X_2 + u$$

Y = consumption of hot drinks

X_1 = number of visitors in the summer resort

X_2 = weather conditions measured by an index of temperature or rainfall.

The partial correlation coefficient measures the correlation between any two variables, when all the other variables *are held constant*, that is, when we have removed the influence of other variables. For example $r_{yx_1 . x_2}$ is the partial correlation coefficient between y and x_1 when x_2's influence has been removed so that x_2 may be considered as constant when studying the relationship between y and x_1. We saw in Chapter 3 that the formula of the partial correlation coefficient for the model including two explanatory variables is

$$r_{yx_1 . x_2} = \frac{r_{yx_1} - r_{yx_2} r_{x_1 x_2}}{\sqrt{1 - r_{yx_2}^2} \sqrt{1 - r_{x_1 x_2}^2}}$$

The partial correlation coefficient between y and x_2 when x_1 is kept constant is obtained from this expression by interchanging the position of the subscripts 1 and 2

$$r_{yx_2 . x_1} = \frac{r_{yx_2} - r_{yx_1} r_{x_1 x_2}}{\sqrt{1 - r_{yx_1}^2} \sqrt{1 - r_{x_1 x_2}^2}}$$

The rationalisation of these formulae may be propounded as follows. In order to measure the pure correlation between Y (hot drinks) and X_1 (number of visitors) we must first eliminate the influence of the third variable X_2 (weather conditions) from both Y and X_1. This is achieved by regressing Y on X_2 and X_1 on X_2

$$Y = a_0 + a_1 X_2 + v_1$$
$$X_1 = c_0 + c_1 X_2 + v_2$$

where v_1 and v_2 are random variables satisfying the usual assumptions.

From the application of least squares we obtain

$$\hat{a}_1 = \frac{\Sigma y x_2}{\Sigma x_2^2} \qquad r_{yx_2}^2 = 1 - \frac{\Sigma e_1^2}{\Sigma y^2}$$

$$\hat{c}_1 = \frac{\Sigma x_1 x_2}{\Sigma x_2^2} \qquad r_{x_1 x_2}^2 = 1 - \frac{\Sigma e_2^2}{\Sigma x_1^2}$$

The unexplained variance in each regression is

$$e_1 = y - \hat{y} = y - \hat{a}_1 x_2 = y*$$

and

$$e_2 = x_1 - \hat{x}_1 = x_1 - \hat{c}_1 x_2 = x_1*$$

These are the variations in Y and in X_1 respectively, left unexplained after removing the influence of X_2 (weather).

It can be proved that the partial correlation coefficient between Y and X_1 is defined as the simple correlation between the above two unexplained parts of the two variables

$$r_{yx_1 . x_2} = r_{y*x_1*} = \frac{\Sigma y* x_1*}{\sqrt{\Sigma y*^2}\sqrt{\Sigma x_1*^2}}$$

Proof.

(1) We have established in Chapter 5 (p. 73) the following relationship between regression coefficients and simple correlation coefficients

$$r_{yx}^2 = \hat{b}_1^2 \frac{\Sigma x^2}{\Sigma y^2} \quad \text{or} \quad \hat{b}_1 = r_{yx}\left(\frac{\sqrt{\Sigma y^2}}{\sqrt{\Sigma x^2}}\right)$$

In our example

$$\hat{a}_1 = r_{yx_2}\left(\frac{\sqrt{\Sigma y^2}}{\sqrt{\Sigma x_2^2}}\right) \text{ and } \hat{c}_1 = r_{x_1 x_2}\left(\frac{\sqrt{\Sigma x_1^2}}{\sqrt{\Sigma x_2^2}}\right)$$

(2) From the correlation coefficients of the two regressions we obtain

$$r_{yx_2}^2 = 1 - \frac{\Sigma e_1^2}{\Sigma y^2} = 1 - \frac{\Sigma y*^2}{\Sigma y^2}$$

and

$$r_{x_1 x_2}^2 = 1 - \frac{\Sigma e_2^2}{\Sigma x_1^2} = 1 - \frac{\Sigma x_1*^2}{\Sigma x_1^2}$$

Therefore

$$\Sigma y*^2 = \Sigma y^2 (1 - r_{yx_2}^2)$$

and

$$\Sigma x_1*^2 = \Sigma x_1^2 (1 - r_{x_1 x_2}^2)$$

(3) Substitute the terms with asterisks in the formula of the partial correlation coefficient

$$r_{yx_1 . x_2} = \frac{\Sigma (y - \hat{a}_1 x_2)(x_1 - \hat{c}_1 x_2)}{\sqrt{\Sigma y^2 (1 - r_{yx_2}^2)}\sqrt{\Sigma x_1^2 (1 - r_{x_1 x_2}^2)}}$$

$$= \frac{\Sigma (yx_1 - \hat{a}_1 x_1 x_2 - \hat{c}_1 yx_2 + \hat{a}_1 \hat{c}_1 x_2^2)}{\sqrt{\Sigma y^2 \Sigma x_1^2}\sqrt{(1 - r_{yx_2}^2)(1 - r_{x_1 x_2}^2)}}$$

$$= \frac{\Sigma yx_1 - \hat{a}_1 \Sigma x_1 x_2 - \hat{c}_1 \Sigma yx_2 + \hat{a}_1 \hat{c}_1 \Sigma x_2^2}{\sqrt{\Sigma y^2}\sqrt{\Sigma x_1^2}\sqrt{(1 - r_{yx_2}^2)(1 - r_{x_1 x_2}^2)}}$$

(4) Substitute the values of $\hat{a}_1$ and $\hat{c}_1$ for their expressions obtained in (1)

$$r_{yx_1 \cdot x_2} =$$

$$\frac{\Sigma yx_1 - r_{yx_2}\left(\frac{\sqrt{\Sigma y^2}}{\sqrt{\Sigma x_2^2}}\right)\Sigma x_1 x_2 - r_{x_1 x_2}\left(\frac{\sqrt{\Sigma x_1^2}}{\sqrt{\Sigma x_2^2}}\right)\Sigma yx_2 + r_{yx_2} r_{x_1 x_2}\left(\frac{\sqrt{\Sigma y^2 \Sigma x_1^2}}{\Sigma x_2^2}\right)\Sigma x_2^2}{\sqrt{\Sigma y^2}\ \sqrt{\Sigma x_1^2}\ \sqrt{(1 - r_{yx_2}^2)(1 - r_{x_1 x_2}^2)}}$$

We multiply each term of the numerator by appropriate unitary terms so as to transform them into simple correlation coefficients. For example, we multiply the first term by $[(\sqrt{\Sigma y^2}\ \sqrt{\Sigma x_1^2})/(\sqrt{\Sigma y^2}\ \sqrt{\Sigma x_1^2})] = 1$, the second term by $[\sqrt{\Sigma x_1^2}/\sqrt{\Sigma x_1^2}] = 1$ and so on.

Thus we obtain

$$r_{yx_1 \cdot x_2} =$$

$$\frac{\Sigma yx_1\left(\frac{\sqrt{\Sigma y^2 \Sigma x_1^2}}{\sqrt{\Sigma y^2 \Sigma x_1^2}}\right) - r_{yx_2}\Sigma x_1 x_2\left(\frac{\sqrt{\Sigma y^2 \Sigma x_1^2}}{\sqrt{\Sigma x_1^2 \Sigma x_2^2}}\right) - r_{x_1 x_2}\left(\frac{\Sigma yx_2 \sqrt{\Sigma x_1^2}\sqrt{\Sigma y^2}}{\sqrt{\Sigma y^2}\sqrt{\Sigma x_2^2}}\right) + r_{yx_2} r_{x_1 x_2}\sqrt{\Sigma y^2 \Sigma x_1^2}}{\sqrt{\Sigma y^2}\ \sqrt{\Sigma x_1^2}\ \sqrt{(1 - r_{yx_2}^2)(1 - r_{x_1 x_2}^2)}}$$

$$= \frac{\sqrt{\Sigma y^2}\ \sqrt{\Sigma x_1^2}\ (r_{yx_1} - r_{yx_2}r_{x_1 x_2} - r_{yx_2}r_{x_1 x_2} + r_{yx_2}r_{x_1 x_2})}{\sqrt{\Sigma y^2}\ \sqrt{\Sigma x_1^2}\ \sqrt{(1 - r_{yx_2}^2)(1 - r_{x_1 x_2}^2)}}$$

$$= \frac{r_{yx_1} - r_{yx_2}r_{x_1 x_2}}{\sqrt{1 - r_{yx_2}^2}\sqrt{1 - r_{x_1 x_2}^2}}$$

The extension of partial correlation coefficients to models including more explanatory variables is straightforward.

7.4. EXTENSION OF THE LINEAR REGRESSION MODEL TO NONLINEAR RELATIONSHIPS

The linear relationship between Y and the explanatory variables (X's) assumed in the preceding analysis may be inappropriate for many economic relationships. Indeed nonlinearities may well be expected in most economic relationships given the complexity of the real world.

Some of the most common forms of nonlinear economic relationships can be adequately presented by polynomials in the X's, for example

$$Y = b_0 + b_1 X_1 + b_2 X_1^2 + b_3 X_1^3 + \ldots + u$$

or by functions with constant elasticities, for example

$$Y = b_0 X_1^{b_1} X_2^{b_2} u$$

where b_1 = constant elasticity of Y with respect to X_1
       b_2 = constant elasticity of Y with respect to X_2

Proof. By the definition of elasticity

$$\eta_{YX_1} = \frac{dY}{dX_1} \cdot \frac{X_1}{Y}$$

The derivative of the Y function with respect to X_1 gives

$$\frac{\partial Y}{\partial X_1} = b_1 (b_0 X_1^{b_1 - 1} X_2^{b_2} u) = b_1 (b_0 X_1^{b_1} X_2^{b_2} u) X^{-1}$$
$$= b_1 \frac{Y}{X_1}.$$

Substituting $b_1 (Y/X_1)$ for $\frac{dY}{dX_1}$ in the elasticity expression we find

$$\eta_{YX_1} = b_1 \frac{Y}{X_1} \cdot \frac{X_1}{Y} = b_1.$$

Thus b_1 is the (constant) elasticity of Y with respect to X_1.

For example the traditional theory of U-shaped average cost curves may be adequately approximated by a polynomial of the third degree in output

$$C = b_0 + b_1 X - b_2 X^2 + b_3 X^3 + u$$

where C = total cost; X = output.

In this case the average total cost is

$$\frac{C}{X} = \frac{b_0}{X} + b_1 - b_2 X + b_3 X^2$$

which is a U-shaped curve.

Similarly, a demand function with constant price and income elasticities may be presented by the equation

$$Q_x = b_0 P_x^{b_1} Y^{b_2} u,$$

where Q_x = demand for commodity x
P_x = price of x
Y = consumers' disposable income
$b_1 = \eta_P = \frac{dQ}{dP} \frac{P}{Q}$ = price elasticity of demand

$b_2 = \eta_Y = \frac{dQ}{dY} \frac{Y}{Q}$ = income elasticity of demand.

Nonlinear relationships may be estimated by fitting nonlinear functions directly to the original data. However, the direct method usually involves highly complex calculations if the relationships are nonlinear in the parameters, as for example

$$Y = b_0 + b_1 X + b_2^X + u$$

However, the common forms of polynomials and of relationships with constant elasticities can be easily estimated by the method of OLS as earlier developed, by making suitable transformations of the data before the estimation of the parameters.

7.4.1. TRANSFORMATION OF PARABOLAS AND OTHER POLYNOMIALS

If the function is a polynomial in the X's

$$Y = b_0 + b_1 X + b_2 X^2 + \ldots + b_n X^n + u$$

we may set $X^2 = Z$, $X^3 = W$, etc., and proceed with the application of OLS to the linear relation

$$Y = b_0 + b_1 X + b_2 Z + \ldots + u$$

Example. Table 7.2 shows the yearly outputs of an industry and the total costs (appropriately deflated for changes in prices of the factors of production) over a 15-year period.

Table 7.3

Observations	Total cost Y (£)	Output (units) X	X^2	X^3
1	10,000	100	10,000	1,000,000
2	28,600	300	90,000	27,000,000
3	19,500	200	40,000	8,000,000
4	32,900	400	160,000	64,000,000
5	52,400	600	360,000	216,000,000
6	42,400	500	250,000	125,000,000
7	62,900	700	490,000	343,000,000
8	86,300	900	810,000	729,000,000
9	74,100	800	640,000	512,000,000
10	100,000	1,000	1,000,000	1,000,000,000
11	133,900	1,200	1,440,000	1,728,000,000
12	115,700	1,100	1,210,000	1,331,000,000
13	154,800	1,300	1,690,000	2,197,000,000
14	178,700	1,400	1,960,000	2,744,000,000
15	203,100	1,500	2,250,000	3,375,000,000

We wish to fit the total cost function

$$C = b_0 + b_1 X + b_2 X^2 + b_3 X^3 + u$$

We compute X^2 and X^3 and we apply OLS to the above function. The results are as follows

$$\hat{C} = \hat{b}_0 + \hat{b}_1 X + \hat{b}_2 X^2 + \hat{b}_3 X^3$$
$$\hat{C} = 2434 + 85 \cdot 7X - 0 \cdot 03X^2 + 0 \cdot 00004X^3 \qquad R^2 = 0 \cdot 999$$
$$s(b_i) \quad (1368) \quad (7 \cdot 17) \quad (0 \cdot 01) \qquad (0 \cdot 00000)$$

It is obvious that the total cost function is nonlinear.

7.4.3. TRANSFORMATION OF NONLINEAR FUNCTIONS INVOLVING CONSTANT ELASTICITIES

If the relationship is of the constant elasticity type

$$Y = b_0 X_1^{b_1} X_2^{b_2} u$$

the error term is multiplicative, and we cannot set $E(u) = 0$, because the function (on the average) would vanish. Instead we write the constant elasticity relationship in the convenient form

$$Y = b_0 X_1^{b_1} X_2^{b_2} e^u$$

where $e \cong 2 \cdot 718 =$ the base of the natural logarithms.

In this form we can retain our usual assumptions

$$E(u) = 0, \qquad E(u_i)^2 = \sigma_u^2, \qquad E(u_i u_j) = 0 \quad \text{for} \quad i \neq j, \qquad E(uX) = 0$$

The appropriate transformation for the estimation of the constant elasticity form is to work with the logarithms of the variables (to the base e)

$$\log_e Y = \log_e b_0 + b_1 \log_e X_1 + b_2 \log_e X_2 + u$$

Setting $Y^* = \log_e Y$, $X_1^* = \log_e X_1$, $X_2^* = \log_e X_2$ we can apply OLS to the linear transformation

$$Y^* = b_0^* + b_1 X_1^* + b_2 X_2^* + u$$

The estimates $\hat{b}_1$ and $\hat{b}_2$ are unbiased. However, although $\hat{b}_0^*$ is unbiased, the logarithmic transformation yields a biased, but consistent, estimate of the intercept b_0.[1]

Example. Table 7.4 shows the demand (Y) for commodity x and its price (X_1), measured in arbitrary units. We wish to estimate the demand function

$$Y = b_0 X_1^{b_1} e^u$$

Taking logarithms of the variables (to the base e) we may fit a regression line by the method of OLS to the linear form

$$\log_e Y = \log_e b_0 + b_1 \log_e X_1$$

The relevant data are included in table 7.4. The estimated demand function is

$$\log_e Y = 9 \cdot 121 - 0 \cdot 69 \log_e X \qquad R^2 = 0 \cdot 992$$
$$(0 \cdot 07) \quad (0 \cdot 02)$$

---

[1] Since $b_0^* = \log b_0$, we have, taking antilogs, $b_0 = e^{b_0^*}$. Thus, the suggested estimate of b_0 would be

$$\hat{b}_0 = e^{\hat{b}_0^*}$$

But $\hat{b}_0$ is not an unbiased estimator of b_0, despite the fact that $E(\hat{b}_0^*) = b_0^*$. That is

$$E(\hat{b}_0) \neq e^{E(\hat{b}_0^*)} = e^{b_0^*} = b_0$$

However, the bias and variance goes to zero as $n \to \infty$; that is, $\hat{b}_0$ is consistent.

Note that the required assumption of independence of u and X implies that $E(e^u)$ is in general different from 1, because

$$E(e^u) \neq e^{E(u)} = e^0 = 1$$

Thus in the constant elasticity form $E(Y) \neq b_0 X^{b_1} X^{b_2}$. The assumption $E(uX) = 0$ implies that $E(e^u) = C$, a constant, different in general from 1. Instead we have $E(Y) = \{b_0 E(e^u)\} X^{b_1} X^{b_2} = (b_0 C) X^{b_1} X^{b_2}$.

Table 7.4

Observations	Y	X_1	$\log_e Y$	$\log_e X_1$
1	543	61	6·2971	4·1109
2	580	54	6·3631	3·9890
3	618	50	6·4265	3·9120
4	695	43	6·5439	3·7612
5	724	38	6·5848	3·6376
6	812	36	6·6995	3·5835
7	887	28	6·7879	3·3322
8	991	23	6·8987	3·1355
9	1,186	19	7·0685	2·9445
10	1,940	10	7·5705	2·3026

or

$$\hat{Y} = A \cdot P^{-0.69}$$ (where A = antilog $9·121 = \hat{b}_0$)

The constant price elasticity is −0·69, that is the demand for commodity x is price inelastic.

EXERCISES

1. The following table shows the values of expenditure on clothing (Y), total expenditure (X_1) and the price of clothing (X_2).

	1960	1961	1962	1963	1964	1965	1966	1967	1968	1969
X_2	16	13	10	7	7	5	4	3	3·5	2
X_1	15	20	30	42	50	54	65	72	85	90
Y	3·5	4·3	5	6	7	9	8	10	12	14

(a) Find the least squares regression equation of Y on X_1 and X_2.
(b) Compute the coefficient of multiple determination and the standard errors of the estimated parameters and conduct tests of significance.
(c) Construct 95 per cent confidence intervals for the population parameters.
(d) Find the explained and unexplained variation in Y.

2. The following results were obtained from a sample of 12 firms on their output (Y), labour input (X_1) and capital input (X_2), measured in arbitrary units

$$\Sigma Y = 753 \qquad \Sigma Y^2 = 48,139 \qquad \Sigma YX_1 = 40,830$$
$$\Sigma X_1 = 643 \qquad \Sigma X_1^2 = 34,843 \qquad \Sigma YX_2 = 6,796$$
$$\Sigma X_2 = 106 \qquad \Sigma X_2^2 = 976 \qquad \Sigma X_1 X_2 = 5,779$$

(a) Find the least squares equation of Y on X_1 and X_2. What is the economic meaning of your coefficients?
(b) Given the following sample values of output (Y), compute the standard errors of the estimates and test their statistical significance.

Firms	A	B	C	D	E	F	G	H	I	J	K	L
Output	64	71	53	67	55	58	77	57	56	51	76	68

(c) Find the multiple correlation coefficient and the unexplained variation in output.

(d) Construct 99 per cent confidence intervals for the population parameters.

3. The following table shows the value of imports (Y), the level of Gross National Product (X_1) measured in arbitrary units, and the price index of imported goods (X_2), over the twelve-year period 1960–71 for a certain country.

	1960	1961	1962	1963	1964	1965	1966	1967	1968	1969	1970	1971
Y	57	43	73	37	64	48	56	50	39	43	69	60
X_1	220	215	250	241	305	258	354	321	370	375	385	385
X_2	125	147	118	160	128	149	145	150	140	115	155	152

(a) Estimate the import function $Y = b_0 + b_1 X_1 + b_2 X_2 + u$.

(b) What is the economic meaning of your estimates?

(c) Conduct tests of significance for the regression estimates at 5 per cent and 1 per cent levels of significance.

(d) Compute the coefficient of multiple determination.

4. The following table includes the output (Y), the labour input (L) and capital input (K) of 15 firms of the chemical industry.

Firms	1.	2	3	4	5	6	7	8	9	10	11	12	13	14	15
Y (1000 tons)	60	120	190	250	300	360	380	430	440	490	500	520	540	410	350
L (hours)	1100	1200	1430	1500	1520	1620	1800	1820	1800	1750	1950	1960	1830	1900	1500
K (machine hours)	300	400	420	400	510	590	600	630	610	630	850	900	980	900	800

(a) Fit a Cobb–Douglas production function to the above data

$$Y = b_0 L^{b_1} K^{b_2} e^u.$$

(b) Conduct appropriate tests of significance of the parameter estimates at the 5 per cent and 1 per cent levels of significance.

(c) What is the marginal and average productivity of the factors L and K?

(d) What do your results suggest regarding the returns to scale?

Note. Additional exercises are included in Appendix III.

8. Regression and Analysis of Variance

The analysis of variance (ANOVA) is a statistical method developed by R. A. Fisher for the analysis of experimental data. Initially it was applied to the analysis of agricultural experiments (use of various fertilisers, various seeds), but soon its application expanded to many other fields of scientific research.

With the method of analysis of variance we can break down the total variance of a variable into additive components which may be attributed to various, separate factors. These factors are the 'causes' or 'sources' of variation of the variable being analysed. The method, when applied to experimental data, assumes a certain design of the experiment, which determines the number of the relevant factors (or causes) of variation and the logical significance of each one of them. For example, assume that we have twenty plots of land on which we cultivate wheat, and we want to study the yield per unit of land. We use different seeds, different fertilisers and different systems of irrigation. Thus the variation in yields may logically be attributed to the three factors:

$$X_1 = \text{type of seed}$$
$$X_2 = \text{type of fertiliser}$$
$$X_3 = \text{type of irrigation}$$

With the method of analysis of variance we may break down the total variation in yield into three separate components: a component due to X_1, another due to X_2 and a third due to X_3.

From this definition of the analysis of variance it should be clear that this method is conceptually the same as regression analysis. In regression analysis also the aim is to determine the factors which cause the variation of the dependent variable. We saw that the total variation in the dependent variable is split into two components: the variation explained by the regression line (or regression plane), and the unexplained variation, shown by the scatter of points around the regression line. Furthermore, the multiple correlation coefficient was seen to represent the proportion of total variation explained by the regression line (or regression plane). R^2 was found to be equal to additive components, each corresponding to a relevant explanatory variable. However, there are significant differences between the two methods. The main difference is that regression analysis provides numerical values for the influence of the various explanatory factors on the dependent variable, in addition to the information concerning the breaking down of the total variance of Y into additive components, while the analysis of variance provides only the latter type of information.

Both the analysis of variance and regression analysis have as their objective the determination of the various factors which cause variations of the dependent variable. This resemblance has led to the combination of the two methods in most scientific fields. In particular, the method of analysis of variance is used in regression analysis for conducting various tests of significance, the most important being:

(1) The test of the overall significance of the regression.

(2) The test of the significance of the improvement in fit obtained by the introduction of additional explanatory variables in the function. This test is formally equivalent to the *t* test developed in Chapter 5.

(3) The test of the equality of coefficients obtained from different samples.

(4) The test of the extra-sample performance of a regression, or test of the stability of the regression coefficients.

(5) The test of restrictions imposed on coefficients of a function.

In this chapter we shall examine the use of analysis of variance ideas in regression analysis for carrying out the above tests. In order to understand them it is necessary to begin with a short description of the method of analysis of variance, as a statistical method in its own right.

8.1. THE METHOD OF ANALYSIS OF VARIANCE AS A STATISTICAL METHOD

The aim of this method is to split the total variation of a variable (around its mean) into components which may be attributed to specific (additive) causes. To simplify the analysis we will assume that there is only one systematic factor which influences the variable being studied. Any variation not accounted for by this (explanatory) factor is assumed to be random (or chance) variation, due to various random happenings. We have a series of values of a variable Y and the corresponding values of the (explanatory) variable X. The analysis of variance method concentrates on the values of Y and studies their variation. The values of X are used only for dividing the values of Y into sub-groups, sub-samples; for example one group (or sample) corresponding to large values of X and one group (or sample) corresponding to small values of X.

For each sub-sample we estimate the mean-value of Y, obtaining a set of means. If X (which is the basis of the classification of the Y's into the sub-samples) is an important cause of variation in Y (an important explanatory variable) the difference between the means of the sub-samples will be large: this would be shown by a large dispersion of the means of sub-samples Y_i's around the common mean $\overline{Y}$, that is, by a large variance of the distribution of the means. On the contrary, if X is not an important source of variation of Y, the difference between the means of the sub-samples will be small, a fact that would be reflected in a small variance of the distribution of sampling means ($\overline{Y}_i$) around the common mean $\overline{Y}$:

(a) The importance of X as a cause of variation (in Y) is judged from the difference between the means of sub-samples ($\overline{Y}_i$'s), formed on the basis of the values of X.

(b) The difference between the means is reflected in the value of the variance of the distribution of the sample means.

Hence the difference between the means may be studied and tested with two estimates of the population variance of Y. One estimate of σ_Y^2 is obtained by pooling the variances of the sub-samples, and the other is obtained from the expression of the sampling distribution (the distribution of $\overline{Y}$). Whatever the relationship of the data being studied, the method of analysis of variance reduces to the estimation of two variances, and the comparison of these variances in order to establish whether the difference between them is statistically significant, or whether it is due to chance, in which case we conclude that there is no real difference between the variance-estimates.

The comparison of any two variances is implemented by the F statistic and the F tables (reproduced on pp. 663—4). The F statistic is the ratio of any two *independent* estimates of variances, which have been obtained from sample data.[1] Each estimate involves some loss of degrees of freedom. If we have any two independent variance estimates obtained with ν_1 and ν_2 degrees of freedom respectively, their ratio has the F distribution with ν_1 and ν_2 degrees of freedom. For this reason F is called the *variance ratio*. (See Appendix I.) The letter F stands for the name of Fisher who invented this statistic.

If the two variance estimates are close to each other their ratio will approach the value of one. The greater the discrepancy (difference) between the two variances the greater is the value of the F ratio. Thus, in general, high values of F suggest that the difference between the two variances is significant, or the rejection of the null hypothesis, which assumes no significant difference between the two variances.

We will illustrate the method of analysis of variance with an example.

Test of the difference between means

Suppose three different types of petrol are used for running a car: type A rated at 90 octane, type B rated at 95 octane and type C at 100 octane. We wish to test whether these different types of petrol give the same consumption per mile, that is, we want to compare the consumption performance of the three brands of petrol. Suppose that we use each brand for ten days and we measure the miles per gallon of petrol. Thus we obtain three samples of size 10 for each brand. The observations, shown in table 8.1, report miles per gallon of petrol.

The above data may be interpreted as three random samples of size $n_1 = n_2 = n_3 = 10$, with means $\overline{Y}_1 = 33$, $\overline{Y}_2 = 38$ and $\overline{Y}_3 = 46$ miles per gallon of petrol. Our problem is to establish whether the difference between these means is significant or whether it may be attributed to chance.

We shall assume that the samples are drawn from three populations which have a normal distribution (or approximately normal) with means μ_1, μ_2 and μ_3 respectively and with equal standard deviation σ. This assumption implies

[1] See Appendix I.

Table 8.1

Sample 1 Brand A $n_1 = 10$	Sample 2 Brand B $n_2 = 10$	Sample 3 Brand C $n_3 = 10$	Total observations $N = n_1 + n_2 + n_3$
32	35	44	32
30	38	46	30
35	37	47	35
33	40	47	33
35	41	46	35
34	35	43	34
29	37	47	29
32	41	45	32
36	36	48	36
34	40	47	34
			35
			38
			37
			40
			41
			35
			37
			41
			36
			40
			44
			46
			47
			47
			46
			43
			47
			45
			48
			47
$\Sigma Y_{1i} = 330$	$\Sigma Y_{2i} = 380$	$\Sigma Y_{3i} = 460$	$\sum_j \sum_i Y_{ji} = 1170$
$\overline{Y}_1 = \dfrac{\Sigma Y_{1i}}{n_1} = 33$	$\overline{Y}_2 = \dfrac{\Sigma Y_{2i}}{n_2} = 38$	$\overline{Y}_3 = \dfrac{\Sigma Y_{3i}}{n_3} = 46$	$\overline{Y} = \dfrac{\sum \sum Y_{ji}}{N} = 39$
$S_1^2 = \dfrac{\sum\limits_i^{n_1}(Y_{1i} - \overline{Y}_1)^2}{n_1} =$ $= \dfrac{46}{10}$ $S_1^2 = 4 \cdot 6$	$S_2^2 = \dfrac{\sum\limits_i^{n_2}(Y_{2i} - \overline{Y}_2)^2}{n_2} =$ $= \dfrac{50}{10}$ $S_2^2 = 5 \cdot 0$	$S_3^2 = \dfrac{\sum\limits_i^{n_3}(Y_{3i} - \overline{Y}_3)^2}{n_3} =$ $= \dfrac{22}{10}$ $S_3^2 = 2 \cdot 2$	

that although the different octane content of the three brands of petrol may affect the average consumption of petrol, it would not affect the dispersion (variance) of the mileages around the means. In other words, if we take a large number of observations for each brand of petrol, the three distributions which we would get would be close to normal curves having the same standard deviation σ. We want to know whether there is any significant difference between the means of the populations, μ_1, μ_2 and μ_3: We want to test the null hypothesis

$$H_0: \mu_1 = \mu_2 = \mu_3$$

against the alternative hypothesis

$$H_1: \mu_j \text{ not all equal.}$$

If the three means are the same, that is if the null hypothesis is true, the three populations may be considered as one large population with mean $\mu(=\mu_1 = \mu_2 = \mu_3)$ and standard deviation σ, that is,

$$Y \sim N(\mu, \sigma)$$

and the three samples may be considered as samples drawn from this one large population.

Applying the basic sampling theorems[1] we may write the following distributions for the sample means $\overline{Y}_1, \overline{Y}_2, \overline{Y}_3$

$$\overline{Y}_1 \sim N(\mu, \sigma^2_{\overline{Y}_1}) \sim N\left(\mu, \frac{\sigma^2}{n_1}\right)$$

$$\overline{Y}_2 \sim N(\mu, \sigma^2_{\overline{Y}_2}) \sim N\left(\mu, \frac{\sigma^2}{n_2}\right)$$

$$\overline{Y}_3 \sim N(\mu, \sigma^2_{\overline{Y}_3}) \sim N\left(\mu, \frac{\sigma^2}{n_3}\right)$$

We said that under the null hypothesis ($\mu_1 = \mu_2 = \mu_3$) we may consider the three populations as forming a large population

$$Y \sim N(\mu, \sigma^2)$$

An estimate of the common mean μ may be computed from the enlarged sample $n_1 + n_2 + n_3 = N = 30$. From the data of table 8.1 we obtain

$$\hat{\mu} = \frac{\Sigma Y_i}{N} = \frac{\overset{k}{\underset{j}{\Sigma}} \overset{n_k}{\underset{i}{\Sigma}} Y_{ji}}{N} = \frac{1170}{30} = 39 = \overline{Y}$$

---

[1] See Appendix I. If a variable X is normally distributed, that is

$$X \sim N(\mu, \sigma^2)$$

then the sample means in repeating sampling will also have a normal distribution

$$\overline{X}_i \sim N(\mu, \sigma^2_{\overline{x}}) \sim N\left(\mu, \frac{\sigma^2}{n}\right)$$

An estimate of the population variance σ^2 may be obtained in two ways.

Firstly. An unbiased estimator of the population variance may be obtained from the expression

$$\hat{\sigma}^2 = \frac{\sum\limits_{j}^{k} n_j (\bar{Y}_j - \bar{Y})^2}{k-1} \tag{8.1}$$

where k is the number of samples.

Proof. This expression is derived from the relationship between the population variance σ^2 and the variance of the sampling distribution:

$$\sigma_{\bar{Y}_j}^2 = \frac{\sigma^2}{n_j} \quad \text{or} \quad \sigma^2 = \sigma_{\bar{Y}_j}^2 \cdot n_j$$

In our example we have three samples and from each one of them we may obtain a separate estimate of σ^2:

$$\hat{\sigma}_1^2 = n_1 \cdot \sigma_{\bar{Y}_1}^2 = n_1 (\bar{Y}_1 - \bar{Y})^2$$
$$\hat{\sigma}_2^2 = n_2 \cdot \sigma_{\bar{Y}_2}^2 = n_2 (\bar{Y}_2 - \bar{Y})^2$$
$$\hat{\sigma}_3^2 = n_3 \cdot \sigma_{\bar{Y}_3}^2 = n_3 (\bar{Y}_3 - \bar{Y})^2$$

where $\bar{Y}$ is the common (pooled) mean.

Taking the weighted average of these estimates we obtain

$$\hat{\sigma}^2 = \frac{1}{3} \sum\limits_{j}^{k} n_j (\bar{Y}_j - \bar{Y})^2$$

For an unbiased estimate we use the degrees of freedom $3 - 1 = 2$, or in general $k - 1$, if we have k samples. Thus the first estimate of the population variance becomes

$$\hat{\sigma}^2 = \frac{\sum\limits_{j=1}^{k} n_j (\bar{Y}_j - \bar{Y})^2}{k-1}$$

It should be clear that this estimate of the population variance is obtained from the differences between the sample means $(\bar{Y}_j)$ and the common population mean $(\bar{Y})$. Recall that the sample means are unbiased estimates of the means μ_1, μ_2, μ_3. The null hypothesis was $\mu_1 = \mu_2 = \mu_3 = \mu$. Hence if this hypothesis should be true, the sample means $\bar{Y}_1, \bar{Y}_2, \bar{Y}_3$ should not differ significantly from each other and also from the overall mean $\bar{Y}$. This implies that if the null hypothesis is not true, we should expect that the sample means, $\bar{Y}_1, \bar{Y}_2, \bar{Y}_3$ should also differ considerably from each other and from the common (pooled) mean $\bar{Y}$: the difference between these means would be larger than what may be attributed to chance. This in turn implies that the estimate $\hat{\sigma}^2$ of the population variance will be large if the null hypothesis is not true, because $\hat{\sigma}^2$ was computed from the differences $(\bar{Y}_j - \bar{Y})^2$. Thus the estimate $\hat{\sigma}^2$ is the crucial element of the test of difference between means of various samples. From the way it is estimated it reflects the variation between the sample means and it is called *'variation between'*.

To conduct our test it suffices to compare this estimate with the true population variance σ^2, and reject the null hypothesis if the divergence between $\hat{\sigma}^2$ and σ^2 is large. However, in our example, as in most actual problems of the real world, the true σ^2 is unknown, and we have to obtain another independent estimate from the sample data.

Secondly. An estimate of the population variance σ^2 may be obtained by pooling together the various sample variances. The appropriate formula is

$$\hat{\sigma}^2 = \frac{n_1 s_1^2 + n_2 s_2^2 + \ldots + n_k s_k^2}{(n_1 + n_2 + \ldots + n_k) - k}, \tag{8.2}$$

where s_j are the sample variances and n_j the sample sizes . (See Yamane, *Statistics*, p. 504.) Note that

$$\left. \begin{array}{c} n_1 s_1^2 = n_1 \; \dfrac{\Sigma(Y_{1i} - \overline{Y}_1)^2}{n_1} = \Sigma(Y_{1i} - \overline{Y}_1)^2 \\[3mm] \cdot \qquad\qquad \cdot \qquad\qquad \cdot \\ \cdot \qquad\qquad \cdot \qquad\qquad \cdot \\ \cdot \qquad\qquad \cdot \qquad\qquad \cdot \\[3mm] n_k s_k^2 = n_k \; \dfrac{\overset{n_k}{\underset{i}{\Sigma}} (Y_{ki} - \overline{Y}_k)^2}{n_k} = \Sigma(Y_{ki} - \overline{Y}_k)^2 \end{array} \right\} \tag{8.3}$$

Thus $n_1 s_1^2 + n_2 s_2^2 + \ldots + n_k s_k^2$ gives the total sum of squared deviations of all k samples, and the 'pooled-variance' expression can be considered as an operation of combining all samples into one large sample and estimating the population variance. Substituting 8.3 in 8.2 we obtain

$$\hat{\sigma}^2 = \frac{\overset{n_1}{\underset{i}{\Sigma}}(Y_{1i} - \overline{Y}_1) + \overset{n_2}{\underset{i}{\Sigma}}(Y_{2i} - \overline{Y}_2)^2 + \ldots + \overset{n_k}{\underset{i}{\Sigma}}(Y_{ki} - \overline{Y}_k)^2}{N - k},$$

where $N = n_1 + n_2 + \ldots + n_k$. Using the double summation notation (see Appendix I, p. 519), we have

$$\hat{\sigma}^2 = \frac{\overset{k}{\underset{j}{\Sigma}} \overset{n_k}{\underset{i}{\Sigma}} (Y_{ji} - \overline{Y}_j)^2}{N - k}. \tag{8.4}$$

    This estimate of the population variance is obtained from the sample variances which reflect the variation *within* each sample. The sample variances do not depend on the null hypothesis, they are not affected by differences between the sample means ($\overline{Y}_1$, $\overline{Y}_2$, $\overline{Y}_3$). In other words even if the means are significantly different, in which case we will have three populations each having its own different mean (μ_1, μ_2, μ_3), all these populations would have (by assumption) the same variance σ^2, and hence $\hat{\sigma}^2$ would be an unbiased estimate of the variance σ^2 of the 'pooled' population.

    $\hat{\sigma}^2$ is based on the variation *within* the sample values (Y_i's of each sample), and is called '*within variation*'. Now note that the variation of the values of Y_i in each sample are chance variations, so that the estimate $\hat{\sigma}^2$ may be considered as a measure of the variation in the values of Y_i's which may be attributed to chance.

We now have two unbiased estimates of the population variance σ^2:

Estimate (1) reflects the *variation between the sample means*, and depends on the validity of the null hypothesis.

Estimate (2) reflects the *variation of* Y_i's *within the samples,* and is independent of the null hypothesis.

It can be shown[1] that the two estimates are independent, so that their ratio has an F distribution with $\nu_1 = k - 1$ and $\nu_2 = N - k$ degrees of freedom:

$$F^* = \frac{\left[\sum_{j=1}^{k} n_j(\overline{Y}_j - \overline{Y})^2\right] \Big/ (k-1)}{\left[\sum_{j=1}^{k} \sum_{i=1}^{n_j} (Y_{ji} - \overline{Y}_j)^2\right] \Big/ (N-k)}$$

where: n_j = size of the jth sample

$N = \sum_{j=1}^{k} n_j$ = size of the 'pooled' (enlarged) sample

k = number of samples.

The variance ratio may be shown schematically as

$$F^* = \frac{\text{estimated variance from 'between'-the-means variation}}{\text{estimated variance from 'within'-the-samples variation}}$$

When the means (μ_1, μ_2, μ_3) are not equal the estimated variance from the 'between'-the-means differences will be large and hence the variance ratio F^* will become large. If the null hypothesis is true the observed variance ratio will approximate the value of one: the observed difference in the means $\overline{Y}_1, \overline{Y}_2, \overline{Y}_3$ in this case is not significant and may well be attributed to chance; thus the estimate appearing in the numerator of F^* will be really estimating the same unknown population variance as the denominator is also estimating.

The observed F^* variance ratio is compared with the theoretical value of F (with a chosen level of significance, e.g. the 5 per cent level), which is found from the F-table (pp. 663–4) with $\nu_1 = (k - 1)$ and $\nu_2 = (N - k)$ degrees of freedom. The theoretical (or critical) value of F is the value of F that defines the critical region of the test at the chosen level of significance.

If $F^* > F$ we reject the null hypothesis, i.e. we accept that the difference between the means is significant. From this evidence we may infer that the populations, from which the samples are drawn, do differ.

If $F^* < F$ we accept the null hypothesis, i.e. we accept that the sample means are not significantly different. In this event we may say that the sample data provide evidence that there is no significant difference between the means of the populations from which the samples are drawn.

[1] See G. Yule and M. Kendall, *An Introduction to the Theory of Statistics,* 14th edition, New York, Hefner, 1950, p. 507.

In our example we have the following results:
(1) The 'between' variance estimate is

$$\hat{\sigma}^2 = \frac{\sum\limits_{j}^{k} n_j(\overline{Y}_j - \overline{Y})^2}{k-1},$$

$$= \frac{n_1(\overline{Y}_1 - \overline{Y})^2 + n_2(\overline{Y}_2 - \overline{Y})^2 + n_3(\overline{Y}_3 - \overline{Y})^2}{3-1}$$

$$= \frac{10(33-39)^2 + 10(38-39)^2 + 10(46-39)^2}{2} = 430$$

(2) The 'within' variance estimate is

$$\hat{\hat{\sigma}}^2 = \frac{\sum\limits_{j}^{k} \sum\limits_{i}^{n_j} (Y_{ji} - \overline{Y}_j)^2}{N-k}$$

$$= \frac{\sum\limits_{1}^{10} (Y_{1j} - \overline{Y}_1)^2 + \sum\limits_{1}^{10} (Y_{2j} - \overline{Y}_2)^2 + \sum\limits_{1}^{10} (Y_{3j} - \overline{Y}_3)^2}{30-3}$$

$$= \frac{46 + 50 + 22}{27} = \frac{118}{27} \approx 4 \cdot 37$$

(3) The observed variance ratio is

$$F^* = \frac{\hat{\sigma}^2}{\hat{\hat{\sigma}}^2} = \frac{430}{4 \cdot 37} = 98 \cdot 39 \approx 98 \cdot 4.$$

(4) The theoretical value of F at the 5 per cent level of significance with $\nu_1 = k - 1 = 2$ and $\nu_2 = N - k = 27$ degrees of freedom is found from the F-tables (pp. 663–4)

$$F_{0 \cdot 05} = 3 \cdot 37$$

(5) Since $F^* > F_{0 \cdot 05}$ we reject the null hypothesis, that is, we accept that there is a significant difference in the average mileage obtained from the three types of petrol.

The above test may be examined in another way, which will systematise the analysis of variance method. We may obtain a third estimate of the population variance, σ^2, by using the enlarged sample, formed from the three sub-samples. The unbiased estimate will be

$$*\sigma^2 = \frac{\sum\limits_{i}^{N} (Y_i - \overline{Y})^2}{N-1} = \frac{\sum\limits_{j=1}^{k} \sum\limits_{n=1}^{n_j} (Y_{ji} - \overline{Y})^2}{N-1},$$

where $N - 1 = $ degrees of freedom for the estimate $*\sigma^2$. If we take the numerators of the three estimates of the population variance ($*\sigma^2, \hat{\sigma}^2, \hat{\sigma}^2$), we may establish the following relationship between these terms:

$$\sum_{j=1}^{k} \sum_{i=1}^{n_j} (Y_{ji} - \overline{Y})^2 \;=\; \sum_{j=1}^{k} n_j(\overline{Y}_j - \overline{Y})^2 \;+\; \sum_{j=1}^{k} \sum_{i=1}^{n_j} (Y_{ji} - \overline{Y}_j)^2$$

that is

$$\begin{bmatrix} \text{Total sum of} \\ \text{squared deviations} \end{bmatrix} = \begin{bmatrix} \text{Sum of squares} \\ \text{between groups} \end{bmatrix} + \begin{bmatrix} \text{Sum of squares} \\ \text{within groups} \end{bmatrix}$$

or

$$\begin{bmatrix} \text{Total variation} \\ \text{in } Y \end{bmatrix} = \begin{bmatrix} \text{Between} \\ \text{variation} \end{bmatrix} + \begin{bmatrix} \text{Within} \\ \text{variation} \end{bmatrix}$$

Proof: We start from the term on the left-hand side and we form the identity

$$(Y_{ji} - \overline{Y}) = (Y_{ji} - \overline{Y}) + \overline{Y}_j - \overline{Y}_j$$

or

$$(Y_{ji} - \overline{Y}) = (Y_{ji} - \overline{Y}_j) + (\overline{Y}_j - \overline{Y})$$

Squaring both sides, we have

$$(Y_{ji} - \overline{Y})^2 = (Y_{ji} - \overline{Y}_j)^2 + (\overline{Y}_j - \overline{Y})^2 + 2(Y_{ji} - \overline{Y}_j)(\overline{Y}_j - \overline{Y})$$

Summing over all values, we find

$$\sum_{j=1}^{k} \sum_{i=1}^{n_j} (Y_{ji} - \overline{Y})^2 = \sum_j \sum_i (Y_{ji} - \overline{Y}_j)^2 + \sum_j \sum_i (\overline{Y}_j - \overline{Y})^2 + 2 \sum_j \sum_i (Y_{ji} - \overline{Y}_j)(\overline{Y}_j - \overline{Y})$$

The last term of this expression is equal to zero, since

$$2 \sum_j \sum_i (Y_{ji} - \overline{Y}_j)(\overline{Y}_j - \overline{Y}) = 2 \sum_j [(\overline{Y}_j - \overline{Y}) \sum_i (Y_{ji} - \overline{Y}_j)]$$

and given that $\sum_i (Y_{ji} - \overline{Y}_j) = 0$, because it is the sum of the deviations within each group (sample).

Therefore

$$\sum_j^{k} \sum_i^{n_j} (Y_{ji} - \overline{Y})^2 = \sum_j^{k} \sum_i^{n_j} (Y_{ji} - \overline{Y}_j)^2 + \sum_j^{k} n_j(\overline{Y}_j - \overline{Y})^2$$

$$\text{Total} \quad = \quad \text{Within} \quad + \quad \text{Between}$$

This expression shows how the total sum of squared deviations in Y (in all the groups taken together) is partitioned into two parts: one part of the total variation of Y is due to the difference between the means (octane ratings of the three types of petrol in our example) and the other part is due to chance (for example rain, mood of the driver of the car, etc.). Note that this partitioning of the total variation into additive components holds irrespective of whether the null hypothesis ($\mu_1 = \mu_2 = \mu_3$) holds or not. In our example the total variation in Y's around the common mean ($\overline{Y} = 39$) is

$$\sum_j^{3} \sum_i^{10} (Y_{ji} - \overline{Y})^2 = 978$$

the between sum of squares is

$$\sum_{j=1}^{3} n_j(\overline{Y}_j - \overline{Y})^2 = 860$$

the within sum of squares is

$$\sum_{j}^{3} \sum_{i}^{10} (Y_{ji} - \overline{Y}_j) = 118$$

Clearly

$$978 = 860 + 118$$

Total = Between + Within

that is, the partitioning of the total variance holds despite the refutation of the null hypothesis.

We may further establish a relationship between the degrees of freedom in each of the three estimates of the population variance.

(a) The degrees of freedom for the overall variance $*\sigma^2$ is $N - 1$.
(b) The degrees of freedom for the estimate based on the 'between' (the means) difference, $\hat{\sigma}^2$, is $k - 1$.
(c) The degrees of freedom for the estimate based on the 'within' (the groups) variation, $\hat{\hat{\sigma}}^2$, is $N - k$.

It is easy to see that

$$(N-1) = (N-k) + (k-1)$$

Total   Within   Between

(For a proof of this result see Yamane, *Statistics*, p. 677.)

With the above information on the partitioning of the total sum of squares (total variation in Y) and the various degrees of freedom we may form the *Analysis of Variance Table* (table 8.2).

Table 8.2. Analysis of variance table

Source of variation (1)	Sum of squares (2)	Degrees of freedom (3)	Mean square (4) = (2) : (3)	F (5)
Between-the-means	$\sum_{j}^{k} n_j(\overline{Y}_j - \overline{Y})^2$	$\nu_1 = (k-1)$	$\dfrac{\sum_{j} n_j(\overline{Y}_j - \overline{Y})^2}{k-1}$	$F^* = \dfrac{\sum_{j} n_j(\overline{Y}_j - \overline{Y})^2/(k-1)}{\sum_{j}\sum_{i}(Y_{ji} - \overline{Y}_j)^2/(N-k)}$
Within-the-samples	$\sum_{j}^{k}\sum_{i}^{n_j}(Y_{ji} - \overline{Y}_j)^2$	$\nu_2 = (N-k)$	$\dfrac{\sum_{j}\sum_{i}(Y_{ji} - \overline{Y}_j)^2}{N-k}$	
Total variation	$\sum_{j}^{k}\sum_{i}^{n_j}(Y_{ji} - \overline{Y})^2$	$(N-1)$		F from tables with $\nu_1 = k-1$ $\nu_2 = N-k$

Note: k is the number of samples.

The F^* ratio (observed variance ratio) is formed by dividing the two 'mean-square errors' appearing in the fourth column of the Analysis of Variance Table. In our numerical example the Analysis of Variance Table is as shown in table 8.3.

Table 8.3

Source of variation	Sum of squares	Degrees of freedom	Mean square	F^*
Between	860	$(3-1) = 2$	$\dfrac{860}{2} = 430$	$F^* = \dfrac{400}{4 \cdot 37} = 98 \cdot 4$
Within	118	$(30-3) = 27$	$\dfrac{118}{27} = 4 \cdot 37$	
Total	978	$(30-1) = 29$		From F-Table $F_{0 \cdot 05} = 3 \cdot 37$ with $\nu_1 = 2$ $\nu_2 = 27$

Note: The above discussion is a simple introduction to ANOVA. This technique has been extended to examples involving two-way classification of variables and to other more complex experimental designs. The interested reader is referred to Yamane, *Statistics*, for a detailed treatment of the ANOVA.

8.2. REGRESSION ANALYSIS AND ANALYSIS OF VARIANCE

To illustrate the similarities between regression analysis and the analysis of variance method we will work out the above example with the method of least squares regression and we will subsequently compare the results.

Let us quantify the octane-rating of the three brands of petrol, by treating their octane rating as a variable rather than as a qualitative attribute. Assume that Brand A is rated at 90 octane per gallon, Brand B at 95 octane and Brand C at 100 octane. We thus obtain a sample of 30 observations on mileage per gallon and the octane rating, which are shown in table 8.4.

Using the data of table 8.4 we obtain the regression

$$\hat{Y} = -84 \cdot 5 + 1 \cdot 30 X_1$$

where Y = mileage per gallon
X_1 = octane rating.

To appraise these findings we need to find the correlation coefficient $R^2_{YX_1}$, and the standard errors of the parameters.

(a) From the regression results we obtain the estimate $\hat{\sigma}^2_u$:

$$\hat{\sigma}^2_u = \frac{\Sigma e^2}{n-K} = \frac{133}{30-2} = 4 \cdot 75$$

Table 8.4

N	Mileage per gallon Y_i	Octane rating X_{1i}	y_i $(Y_i - \overline{Y})$	x_{1i} $(X_{1i} - \overline{X}_1)$	$y_i x_{1i}$	y_i^2	x_{1i}^2
1	32	90	-7	-5	35	49	25
2	30	90	-9	-5	45	81	25
3	35	90	-4	-5	20	16	25
4	33	90	-6	-5	30	36	25
5	35	90	-4	-5	20	16	25
6	34	90	-5	-5	25	25	25
7	29	90	-10	-5	50	100	25
8	32	90	-7	-5	35	49	25
9	36	90	-3	-5	15	9	25
10	34	90	-5	-5	25	25	25
11	35	95	-4	0	0	16	0
12	38	95	-1	0	0	1	0
13	37	95	-2	0	0	4	0
14	40	95	1	0	0	1	0
15	41	95	2	0	0	4	0
16	35	95	-4	0	0	16	0
17	37	95	-2	0	0	4	0
18	41	95	2	0	0	4	0
19	36	95	-3	0	0	9	0
20	40	95	1	0	0	1	0
21	44	100	5	5	25	25	25
22	46	100	7	5	35	49	25
23	47	100	8	5	40	64	25
24	47	100	8	5	40	64	25
25	46	100	7	5	35	49	25
26	43	100	4	5	20	16	25
27	47	100	8	5	40	64	25
28	45	100	6	5	30	36	25
29	48	100	9	5	45	81	25
30	47	100	8	5	40	64	25
$N = 30$	$\overline{Y} = 39$	$\overline{X}_1 = 95$	$\Sigma y_i = 0$	$\Sigma x_{1i} = 0$	$\Sigma y_i x_{1i} = 650$	$\Sigma y_i^2 = 978$	$\Sigma x_{1i}^2 = 500$

(b) The variance of $\hat{b}_1$ is

$$\text{var}(\hat{b}_1) = \hat{\sigma}_u^2 \frac{1}{\Sigma x^2} = 4.75 \frac{1}{500} = 0.0095$$

From the variance of $\hat{b}_1$ we may compute its standard error

$$s_{(\hat{b}_1)} = \sqrt{0.0095} \approx 0.097$$

and the t statistic

$$t^* = \frac{\hat{b}_1}{s_{(\hat{b}_1)}} = \frac{1.3}{0.097} \approx 13.3$$

(c) The correlation coefficient for the regression is

$$r^2 = 1 - \frac{\Sigma e^2}{\Sigma y^2} = 1 - \frac{133}{978} = 0\cdot864$$

In summary the results of the regression are

$$\hat{Y} = -84\cdot5 + 1\cdot30 \ X_1$$
$$(0\cdot097)$$

$$r^2 = 0\cdot864 \qquad \Sigma y^2 = 978 \qquad \Sigma \hat{y}^2 = 845 \qquad \Sigma e^2 = 133$$

We established in Chapter 5 that the total variation Σy^2 is split into two additive components, one component is the variation in Y explained by the regressor X_1, and the other is the unexplained variation:

$$\Sigma y^2 \quad = \quad \Sigma \hat{y}^2 \quad + \quad \Sigma e^2$$

In our example $\quad 978 \quad = \quad 845 \quad + \quad 133$

$$\begin{bmatrix} \text{Total} \\ \text{variation} \end{bmatrix} = \begin{bmatrix} \text{Explained} \\ \text{by } X_1 \end{bmatrix} + \begin{bmatrix} \text{Unexplained} \\ \text{variation} \end{bmatrix}$$

This suggests that we can compile an analysis of variance table for the above regression, and use the F^* ratio to judge the overall significance of the results.

Table 8.5. Analysis of Variance Table for the Regression

Source of variation	Sum of squares	Degrees of freedom	MSE Mean Square Error	F^*
X_1	$\Sigma \hat{y}^2 = 845$	$K - 1 = 1$	$\frac{845}{1} = 845$	
Residual	$\Sigma e^2 = 133$	$N - K = 28$	$\frac{133}{28} = 4\cdot75$	$\frac{845}{4\cdot75} = 178$
Total	$\Sigma y^2 = 978$	$N - 1 = 29$		$F_{0\cdot05} = 4\cdot20$ with $\nu_1 = 1$ $\nu_2 = 28$

The observed F^* ratio is compared with the theoretical F value with $\nu_1 = K - 1 = 1$ and $\nu_2 = N - K = 28$ degrees of freedom (at the 95 per cent level of significance). From the F-Tables we find $F_{0\cdot05} = 4\cdot20$. Given that $F^* > F_{0\cdot05}$ we reject the null hypothesis and we accept that the regression is significant, that is X_1 is a significant explanatory factor of the variation in Y.

8.3. COMPARISON OF REGRESSION ANALYSIS AND ANALYSIS OF VARIANCE

Comparing the results of regression analysis with the results of the analysis of variance method we may draw the following conclusions.

Firstly. In both methods the total variation in Y is split into two additive components:

(a) Regression analysis

$$\Sigma y^2 = \Sigma \hat{y}^2 + \Sigma e^2$$

$$\text{Total} = \begin{bmatrix} \text{Explained by} \\ \text{regressor(s)} \end{bmatrix} + \begin{bmatrix} \text{Unexplained} \\ \text{(or Residual)} \end{bmatrix}$$

$$978 = 845 + 133$$

(b) Analysis of variance

$$\sum_j^k \sum_i^{n_j} (Y_{ji} - \overline{Y})^2 = \sum_j^k n_j (\overline{Y}_j - \overline{Y})^2 + \sum_j^k \sum_i^{n_j} (Y_{ji} - \overline{Y}_j)^2$$

Total	=	Between	+	Within
978	=	860	+	118

The total variation is the same in both methods. In regression analysis the data are not grouped in sub-groups or sub-samples. In the analysis of variance method the values of Y_i are grouped into sub-samples according to the values of the X_1 variable.

The 'explained variation' of regression analysis corresponds to the 'between means' variation of the analysis of variance method.

The unexplained or residual variation of regression analysis corresponds to the 'within variation' of the analysis of variance approach.

Secondly. The test performed in the method of analysis of variance concerns the equality between means of sub-groups or sub-samples of an enlarged population. That is, the null hypothesis being tested is

$$H_0: \mu_1 = \mu_2 = \ldots = \mu$$

and the alternative hypothesis is

$$H_1: \mu_j \text{ not all equal}$$

The test performed in regression analysis is a test concerning the overall explanatory power of the regression as measured by R^2. The F^* ratio is a test of significance of R^2, since (as we will presently show)

$$F^* = \frac{\Sigma \hat{y}^2/(K-1)}{\Sigma e^2/(N-K)} = \frac{R^2_{YX_1}/(K-1)}{(1 - R^2_{YX_1})/(N-K)}$$

If R^2 is found statistically not significant, this implies that there is no linear relationship between Y and X, that is, the true b's are zero: the null and alternative hypotheses in regression analysis are

$$H_0: b_1 = 0$$
$$H_1: b_1 \neq 0$$

Thirdly. In both methods we obtain an analysis of variance table, from which we may compute F ratios and use them for testing hypotheses related to the aim of the study.

Fourthly. It can be proved that for individual regression coefficients the t and F tests are formally equivalent, the relationship between them being

$$t^2 = F.$$

Proof. We will prove this relationship for the simple model $Y = f(X)$.

(a) Given

$$F = \frac{\Sigma \hat{y}^2/(K-1)}{\Sigma e^2/(N-K)}$$

(b) In the simple model which contains only one explanatory variable $(K-1) = 1$.

(c) We have established (in Chapter 4) that

$$\hat{y} = \hat{b}_1 x$$

Squaring through and summing over all observations we find

$$\Sigma \hat{y}^2 = \hat{b}_1^2 \Sigma x^2$$

(d) Substituting in the F ratio

$$F = \frac{\Sigma \hat{y}^2}{\Sigma e^2/(N-K)} = \frac{\hat{b}_1^2 \Sigma x^2}{\Sigma e^2/(N-K)}$$

(e) We found (in Chapter 5) that

$$t = \frac{\hat{b}_1}{s(\hat{b}_1)}$$

But

$$s(\hat{b}_1) = \sqrt{\mathrm{var}(\hat{b}_1)} = \sqrt{\sigma_u^2 \frac{1}{\Sigma x^2}} = \sqrt{\left[\frac{\Sigma e^2}{N-K}\right]\left[\frac{1}{\Sigma x^2}\right]}$$

Substituting in t and squaring we find

$$t^2 = \frac{\hat{b}_1^2}{[\Sigma e^2/(N-K)](1/\Sigma x^2)} = \frac{\hat{b}_1^2 \Sigma x^2}{\Sigma e^2/(N-K)} = F$$

Fifthly. Regression analysis is a more powerful method than the analysis of variance method when studying economic relationships from market data which are not experimental. Regression analysis gives all the information which we may obtain from the method of analysis of variance, but furthermore it provides numerical estimates for the influence of each explanatory variable. The analysis of variance approach shows only the addition to the explanation of total variation which one obtains by the introduction of an additional variable in the relationship. This is only part of the information provided by regression analysis as we will presently see.

It is often argued that the analysis of variance method is more appropriate for the study of the influence of qualitative factors on a certain variable.[1] This is so, the argument runs, because qualitative variables (for example profession, sex, religion) do not have numerical values, and hence their influence cannot be

[1] See K. Fox, *Intermediate Economic Statistics*, Wiley, New York, 1968, chapter 13.

assessed by regression analysis, while the analysis of variance technique does not require knowledge of the values of X's but it is based solely on the values of Y. This argument has lost a lot of its power with the expansion of the use of dummy variables in regression analysis. In most cases qualitative variables may be meaningfully approximated with dummy variables and their influence can be measured with regression analysis (see Chapter 12). The analysis of variance is most powerful (i) for the analysis of qualitative variables which cannot be meaningfully approximated by a dummy variable, and (ii) for the analysis of experimental data, where the design of the experiment permits the logical evaluation of the effects of each additional variable by determining the order in which each X is permitted to influence the value of Y. For the analysis of non-experimental data, like the data with which economists work, regression analysis is a more flexible and powerful technique. (See, for example, Yamane, *Statistics,* p. 805.) However, the analysis of variance technique may be incorporated into regression analysis for carrying out tests of various hypotheses (see below).

8.4. TESTING THE OVERALL SIGNIFICANCE OF A REGRESSION

This test has been explained in the preceding section for the simple regression model including one regressor. In this section we generalise the test for models including any number of explanatory variables.

The test aims at finding out whether the explanatory variables $(X_1, X_2, \ldots, X_k)$ do actually have any significant influence on the dependent variable. Formally the test of the overall significance of the regression implies testing the null hypothesis

$$H_0: b_1 = b_2 = \ldots = b_k = 0$$

against the alternative hypothesis

$$H_1: \text{not all } b_i\text{'s are zero}$$

If the null hypothesis is true, that is if all the true parameters are zero, there is no linear relationship between Y and the regressors.

The test of the overall significance may be carried out with the table of the analysis of variance. We compute the regression of Y on all the X's together and we estimate

(a) the total sum of squared deviations of the y's, Σy^2;
(b) the sum of squared deviations explained by all the regressors together, $\Sigma \hat{y}^2$;
(c) the sum of residual deviations, Σe^2.

From these terms we can evaluate the expression $\Sigma y^2 = \Sigma \hat{y}^2 + \Sigma e^2$. We next find the degrees of freedom for each of the terms of the identity. The degrees of freedom for $\Sigma \hat{y}^2$ is $K - 1$, where $K (= k + 1)$ is the total number of b's, including the constant intercept. The degrees of freedom for Σe^2 is $N - K$. where N is the sample size. Finally, the degrees of freedom of the total sum of squares is $(K - 1) + (N - K) = N - 1$. With this information we may compute the F^* ratio as

$$F^* = \frac{\Sigma \hat{y}^2/(K - 1)}{\Sigma e^2/(N - K)}$$

which is compared with the theoretical F (at the chosen level of significance) with $\nu_1 = K - 1$ and $\nu_2 = N - K$ degrees of freedom. If $F^* > F$ we reject the null hypothesis, i.e. we accept that the regression is significant: not all b_i's are zero. If $F^* < F$ we accept the null hypothesis, that is we accept that the overall regression is not significant.

The above information may be summarised in a Table of Analysis of Variance (table 8.6).

Table 8.6. Analysis of Variance Table for the General Regression Model $Y = f(X_1, X_2, \ldots, X_k)$

Source of variation	Sum of squares	Degrees of freedom	Mean Square Error	F^*
$X_1, X_2, \ldots, X_k$	$\Sigma \hat{y}^2$	$\nu_1 = K - 1$	$\dfrac{\Sigma \hat{y}^2}{K - 1}$	$\dfrac{\Sigma \hat{y}^2/(K - 1)}{\Sigma e^2/(N - K)} = \dfrac{R^2/(K - 1)}{(1 - R^2)/(N - K)}$
Residual	Σe^2	$\nu_2 = N - K$	$\dfrac{\Sigma e^2}{N - K}$	
Total	Σy^2	$N - 1$		F from tables, with $\nu_1 = K - 1$, $\nu_2 = N - K$ degrees of freedom

It can be shown that the F ratio for the overall significance of a regression reduces to

$$F = \frac{R^2/(K - 1)}{(1 - R^2)/(N - K)}$$

where K = number of b's (including the intercept b_0).
N = number of observations in the sample.

Proof. We have established that

$$F^* = \frac{\Sigma \hat{y}^2/(K - 1)}{\Sigma e^2/(N - K)}$$

We may rewrite this expression as

$$F^* = \frac{\Sigma \hat{y}^2}{\Sigma e^2} \cdot \frac{N - K}{K - 1}$$

Dividing numerator and denominator by Σy^2 we obtain

$$F^* = \frac{\Sigma \hat{y}^2/\Sigma y^2}{\Sigma e^2/\Sigma y^2} \cdot \frac{N - K}{K - 1}$$

But from Chapter 7 we know that

$$\frac{\Sigma \hat{y}^2}{\Sigma y^2} = R_Y^2 . x_1 \ldots x_k \quad \text{and} \quad \frac{\Sigma e^2}{\Sigma y^2} = 1 - R_Y^2 . x_1, x_2 \ldots x_k$$

Substituting in F^* we find

$$F^* = \frac{R_Y^2 . x_1 \ldots x_k}{1 - R_Y^2 . x_1 \ldots x_k} \cdot \frac{N - K}{K - 1} = \frac{R^2/(K - 1)}{(1 - R^2)/(N - K)}$$

(omitting the subscripts for simplicity).

By analogy to what we said about the F statistic in connection with the analysis of variance method, we may say that if the regression were meaningless, that is if the X's did not truly explain any of the variation in Y, we would expect the numerator of F^* to be very small, in other words the F^* would approach zero. The more significant the relationship denoted by the regression the higher the value of F^*. Thus, in general, high values of F^* suggest significant relationships between Y and the X's.

8.5. TESTING THE IMPROVEMENT OF FIT OBTAINED FROM ADDITIONAL EXPLANATORY VARIABLES

The significance of a new regressor was up to now judged by the standard error (or by the t statistic) of its coefficient. In this section we will examine another way of judging the significance of additional explanatory variables by using the ideas of the analysis of variance and the F statistic. The test will be illustrated by extending our earlier example of the consumption performance of three brands of petrol. We will start by a single explanatory variable X_1 (octane rating) and we will gradually introduce two additional variables in the model. One such variable is 'weather conditions' during the period of using the three types of petrol. Obviously rain, frost, snow, etc. do affect the consumption of petrol irrespective of the octane rating of the petrol: in bad weather we need more petrol than in good weather, no matter whether we use high-octane or low-octane petrol. We will measure 'weather' with an index of rainfall during the days of our experiment. Clearly we expect the sign of the coefficient of the weather variable, b_2, to be negative. As a third explanatory variable of the petrol consumption we may consider the road and traffic conditions during our experiment. If we run the car in hilly areas with bumpy roads, we will consume, in general, more petrol than if we were driving on good roads. We will measure this factor with a dummy variable, which will assume the value of one for 'good' road conditions, and the value of zero for 'bad' road conditions. We expect on *a priori* grounds the coefficient of this dummy variable, b_3, to appear with a positive value in the regression. The data for the regression are included in table 8.7.

If we fit the simple regression

$$Y = b_0 + b_1 X_1 + u$$

we obtain the following results

$$\hat{Y} = -84 \cdot 50 + 1 \cdot 30 X_1$$
$$\quad\quad (9 \cdot 27) \quad (0 \cdot 097)$$

$$R_Y^2 . x_1 = 0 \cdot 864 \qquad \Sigma \hat{y}^2 = 845 \qquad \Sigma e^2 = 133$$

Table 8.7. Data for the regression model

N	Mileage Y_i	Octane rating X_{1i}	Rain index X_{2i}	Road conditions X_{3i}	y_i $(Y_i - \bar{Y})$	x_{1i} $(X_{1i} - \bar{X}_1)$	x_{2i} $(X_{2i} - \bar{X}_2)$	x_{3i} $(X_{3i} - \bar{X}_3)$	y_i^2
1	32	90	100	0	−7	−5	4	−0·5	49
2	30	90	104	0	−9	−5	8	−0·5	81
3	35	90	102	0	−4	−5	6	−0·5	16
4	33	90	104	0	−6	−5	8	−0·5	36
5	35	90	96	0	−4	−5	0	−0·5	16
6	34	90	96	1	−5	−5	0	0·5	25
7	29	90	110	1	−10	−5	14	0·5	100
8	32	90	105	1	−7	−5	9	0·5	49
9	36	90	103	1	−3	−5	7	0·5	9
10	34	90	102	1	−5	−5	6	0·5	25
11	35	95	101	0	−4	0	5	−0·5	16
12	38	95	93	0	−1	0	−3	−0·5	1
13	37	95	91	0	−2	0	−5	−0·5	4
14	40	95	89	0	1	0	−7	−0·5	1
15	41	95	88	0	2	0	−8	−0·5	4
16	35	95	101	1	−4	0	5	0·5	16
17	37	95	97	1	−2	0	1	0·5	4
18	41	95	91	1	2	0	−5	0·5	4
19	36	95	96	1	−3	0	0	0·5	9
20	40	95	91	1	1	0	−5	0·5	1
21	44	100	91	0	5	5	−5	−0·5	25
22	46	100	93	0	7	5	−3	−0·5	49
23	47	100	96	0	8	5	0	−0·5	64
24	47	100	91	0	8	5	−5	−0·5	64
25	46	100	94	0	7	5	−2	−0·5	49
26	43	100	93	1	4	5	−3	0·5	16
27	47	100	91	1	8	5	−5	0·5	64
28	45	100	91	1	6	5	−5	0·5	36
29	48	100	89	1	9	5	−7	0·5	81
30	47	100	91	1	8	5	−5	0·5	64
$N = 30$	$\Sigma Y_i =$ 1,170	$\Sigma X_1 =$ 2,850	$\Sigma X_2 =$ 2,880	$\Sigma X_3 = 15$	$\Sigma y_i = 0$	$\Sigma x_{1i} = 0$	$\Sigma x_{2i} = 0$	$\Sigma x_{3i} = 0$	$\Sigma y^2 =$ 978

$$\bar{Y} = 39 \quad \bar{X}_1 = 95 \quad \bar{X}_2 = 96 \quad \bar{X}_3 = 0·5$$

Table 8.7 (*cont.*)

N	x_{1i}^2	x_{2i}^2	x_{3i}^2	$y_i x_{1i}$	$y_i x_{2i}$	$y_i x_{3i}$	$x_{1i} x_{2i}$	$x_{1i} x_{3i}$	$x_{2i} x_{3i}$
1	25	16	0·25	35	−28	3·5	−20	2·5	−2·0
2	25	64	0·25	45	−72	4·5	−40	2·5	−4·0
3	25	36	0·25	20	−24	2·0	−30	2·5	−3·0
4	25	64	0·25	30	−48	3·0	−40	2·5	−4·0
5	25	0	0·25	20	0	2·0	0	2·5	0
6	25	0	0·25	25	0	−2·5	0	−2·5	0
7	25	196	0·25	50	−140	−5·0	−70	−2·5	7·0
8	25	81	0·25	35	−63	−3·5	−45	−2·5	4·5
9	25	49	0·25	15	−21	−1·5	−35	−2·5	3·5
10	25	36	0·25	25	−30	−2·5	−30	−2·5	3·0
11	0	25	0·25	0	−20	2·0	0	0	−2·5
12	0	9	0·25	0	3	0·5	0	0	1·5
13	0	25	0·25	0	10	1·0	0	0	2·5
14	0	49	0·25	0	−7	−0·5	0	0	3·5
15	0	64	0·25	0	−16	−1·0	0	0	4·0
16	0	25	0·25	0	−20	−2·0	0	0	2·5
17	0	1	0·25	0	−2	−1·0	0	0	0·5
18	0	25	0·25	0	−10	1·0	0	0	−2·5
19	0	0	0·25	0	0	−1·5	0	0	0
20	0	25	0·25	0	−5	0·5	0	0	−2·5
21	25	25	0·25	25	−25	−2·5	−25	−2·5	2·5
22	25	9	0·25	35	−21	−3·5	−15	−2·5	1·5
23	25	0	0·25	40	0	−4·0	0	−2·5	0
24	25	25	0·25	40	−40	−4·0	−25	−2·5	2·5
25	25	4	0·25	35	−14	−3·5	−10	−2·5	1·0
26	25	9	0·25	20	−12	2·0	−15	2·5	−1·5
27	25	25	0·25	40	−40	4·0	−25	2·5	−2·5
28	25	25	0·25	30	−30	3·0	−25	2·5	−2·5
29	25	49	0·25	45	−63	4·5	−35	2·5	−3·5
30	25	25	0·25	40	−40	4·0	−25	2·5	−2·5
$N = 30$	$\Sigma x_1^2 =$ 500	$\Sigma x_2^2 =$ 986	$\Sigma x_3^2 =$ 7·50	$\Sigma yx_1 =$ 650	$\Sigma yx_2 =$ −778	$\Sigma yx_3 =$ −1·0	$\Sigma x_1 x_2 =$ −510	$\Sigma x_1 x_3 =$ 0	$\Sigma x_2 x_3 =$ 7·0

The simple regression of Y on X_1 explains 86 per cent of the total variation in Y, while 14 per cent remains unexplained.

If we introduce X_2 (weather) in the function, we obtain an improvement in the fit as shown by the following results.

$$\hat{Y} = -36\cdot88 + 1\cdot05\,X_1 - 0\cdot25\,X_2$$
$$(19\cdot48) \quad (0\cdot13) \quad (0\cdot09)$$

$$R^2_{Y\cdot X_1 X_2} = 0\cdot893 \qquad \Sigma\hat{y}^2 = 873 \qquad \Sigma e^2 = 105$$

The standard errors suggest that both variables are significant in explaining the variation in Y. Both coefficients have the correct sign, and the regression explains 89 per cent of the total variation in Y. By introducing X_2 we have managed to explain a higher proportion of the total variation in Y. We want to know whether this improvement in fit is statistically significant.

If we look at the overall significance of the two regressions we see that they both pass the F test, developed in the previous section. Thus the analysis of variance tables for these regressions are as shown in tables 8.8 and 8.9.

Table 8.8. Table of Analysis of Variance for the simple model $Y = f(X_1)$

Source	Sum of squares	Degrees of freedom	MSE	F^*
X_1	$\Sigma\hat{y}^2 = 845$	$K - 1 = 1$	$845/1 = 845$	$\dfrac{845}{4\cdot75} = 177\cdot8$
Residual	$\Sigma e^2 = 133$	$N - K = 28$	$133/(N-K) = 4\cdot75$	
Total	$\Sigma y^2 = 978$	$N - 1 = 29$		$\nu_1 = 1$ $\nu_2 = 28$ $F_{0.05} = 4\cdot20$

Table 8.9. Table of Analysis of Variance for the model $Y = f(X_1, X_2)$

Source	Sum of squares	Degrees of freedom	MSE	F^*
X_1, X_2	$\Sigma\hat{y}^2 = 873$	$K - 1 = 2$	$873/2 = 436$	$\dfrac{436}{3\cdot9} = 112\cdot7$
Residual	$\Sigma e^2 = 105$	$N - K = 27$	$105/27 = 3\cdot9$	
Total	$\Sigma y^2 = 978$	$N - 1 = 29$		$\nu_1 = 2$ $\nu_2 = 27$ $F_{0.05} = 3\cdot35$

Since in both cases $F^* > F_{0.05}$ we conclude that both regressions are significant. However, this test of the overall significance is not very relevant for, if the regression $Y = f(X_1)$ proves to be significant, so will any relationship including X_1 and other additional variables. What we want to know is whether the new regressor X_2 has *significantly* improved the explanation in the variation of Y, in other words whether it has significantly increased the proportion of the variation explained by the first regression. For this purpose we compile another analysis of variance table as follows.

(a) From the simple regression, $Y = f(X_1)$, we obtained

$$\Sigma \hat{y}^2 = 845 \qquad \Sigma e_1^2 = 133$$

(b) From the second regression, $Y = f(X_1, X_2)$, we found

$$\Sigma \hat{y}^2 = 873 \qquad \Sigma e_2^2 = 105$$

(c) Clearly, the additional variation accounted for by the second variable X_2 is the difference

$$\Sigma \hat{\hat{y}}^2 - \Sigma \hat{y}^2 = 873 - 845 = 28$$

With this information we proceed to form the analysis of variance table 8.10.

Table 8.10

Source of variation	Sum of squares	Degrees of freedom	MSE	F^*
X_1	$\Sigma \hat{y}^2 = 845$	$M - 1 = 2 - 1 = 1$		
X_1 and X_2	$\Sigma \hat{\hat{y}}^2 = 873$	$K - 1 = 3 - 1 = 2$		
Additional variation from X_2	$\Sigma \hat{\hat{y}}^2 - \Sigma y^2 = 28$	$K - M = 3 - 2 = 1$	$\dfrac{\Sigma \hat{\hat{y}}^2 - \Sigma \hat{y}^2}{K - M} = 28$	$\dfrac{(\Sigma \hat{\hat{y}}^2 - \Sigma \hat{y}^2)/(K - M)}{\Sigma e^2/(N - K)}$
Residual variation from $Y = f(X_1 X_2)$	$\Sigma e^2 = 105$	$N - K = 30 - 3 = 27$	$\Sigma e^2/(N-K) = \dfrac{105}{27}$ $= 3.9$	$F^* = \dfrac{28}{3.9} = 7.18$
Total variation	$\Sigma y^2 = 978$			$F_{0.05} = 4.21$ $\nu_1 = 1$ $\nu_2 = 27$

Note: M = number of all b's in the first regression (including b_0)
K = number of all b's in complete regression (including b_0).

Since F^* is greater than $F_{0.05}$ we may conclude that $b_2 \neq 0$.

It has been shown that the F test is formally equivalent to the t test which we used earlier to test the significance of b_i. On page 155 we established that $F = t^2$ for individual coefficients.

The procedure for assessing the effect of a third explanatory variable may be handled in the same way. We will present the results schematically. The results of the regression $Y = f(X_1, X_2)$ are

$$\hat{Y} = -36.88 + 1.05 X_1 - 0.25 X_2 \qquad R^2_{Y.X_1X_2} = 0.893$$
$$\phantom{\hat{Y} = -36.88 + } (19.48) \quad (0.13) \quad (0.09)$$

with

$$\Sigma \hat{y}^2 = 873 \qquad \Sigma e_1^2 = 105$$

We next compute the regression $Y = f(X_1, X_2, X_3)$:

$$\hat{Y} = -36 \cdot 64 + 1 \cdot 05\,X_1 - 0 \cdot 25\,X_2 + 0 \cdot 10\,X_3$$
$$\quad\;\;(19 \cdot 93)\quad(0 \cdot 13)\quad\;\;(0 \cdot 09)\quad\;\;(0 \cdot 74)\qquad R^2_{Y \cdot X_1 X_2 X_3} = 0 \cdot 893$$

with

$$\Sigma\hat{\hat{y}}^2 = 874 \qquad \Sigma e^2 = 104$$

Hence the effect of adding X_3 is found by

$$\Sigma\hat{\hat{y}}^2 - \Sigma\hat{y}^2 = 874 - 873 = 1$$

Table 8.11 is the analysis of variance table.

Table 8.11

Source of variation	Sum of squares	Degrees of freedom	MSE	F^*
X_1, X_2	$\Sigma\hat{y}^2 = 873$	$M - 1 = 3 - 1 = 2$		
X_1, X_2, X_3	$\Sigma\hat{\hat{y}}^2 = 874$	$K - 1 = 4 - 1 = 3$		
Additional X_3	$\Sigma\hat{\hat{y}}^2 - \Sigma\hat{y}^2 = 1$	$(K - 1) - (M - 1) = 3 - 2 = 1$	$1/1 = 1$	$F^* = 0 \cdot 25$
Residual from $Y = f(X_1 X_2 X_3)$	$\Sigma e^2 = 104$	$N - K = 30 - 4 = 26$	$\dfrac{104}{26} = 4$	
Total	$\Sigma y^2 = 978$	$N - 1 = 29$		$F_{0.05} = 4 \cdot 23$ $\nu_1 = 1$ $\nu_2 = 26$

Note: M = number of parameters in the first regression $Y = f(X_1, X_2)$
K = number of parameters in second regression $Y = f(X_1, X_2, X_3)$

The null hypothesis we are testing is $b_3 = 0$ against the alternative hypothesis: $b_3 \neq 0$.

If $F^* > F_{0.05}$ (with $\nu_1 = 1$ and $\nu_2 = 26$ degrees of freedom) we reject the null hypothesis and we accept that the third variable is an important explanatory variable. In our example $F^* < F_{0.05}$; hence we accept the null hypothesis: X_3 is not a significant variable. This is the same result as the one we reached with the standard error test.

8.5.1. GENERALISATION TO A MODEL WITH k EXPLANATORY VARIABLES

Suppose we have the model

$$Y = f(X_1, X_2 \ldots X_m, X_{m+1} \ldots X_k)$$

We first regress Y on the m variables $(X_1 \ldots X_m)$ obtaining

$$\hat{Y} = \hat{b}_0 + \hat{b}_1 X_1 + \ldots + \hat{b}_m X_m$$

with $\Sigma\hat{y}^2$ and Σe_1^2 measuring the explained and unexplained parts of the total variation in y respectively.

Next we introduce in the function the remaining explanatory variables $(X_{m+1}, X_{m+2}, \ldots, X_k)$ and we obtain

$$\hat{Y} = \hat{b}_0 + \ldots + \hat{b}_m X_m + \ldots + \hat{b}_k X_k,$$

with $\Sigma\hat{\hat{y}}^2$ and Σe^2 measuring the explained and unexplained variation.
The analysis of variance table may be formed as table 8.12.

Table 8.12. Analysis of Variance Table for the General Regression model

Source of variation	Sum of squares	Degrees of freedom	MSE	
Variation in $X_1 \ldots X_m$	$\Sigma\hat{y}^2$	$M-1$	$\Sigma\hat{y}^2/(M-1)$	(1)
Variation in all X's $X_1 \ldots X_m \ldots X_k$	$\Sigma\hat{\hat{y}}^2$	$K-1$	$\Sigma\hat{\hat{y}}^2/(K-1)$	(2)
Additional variation from $X_{m+1} \ldots X_k$	$\Sigma\hat{\hat{y}}^2 - \Sigma\hat{y}^2$	$K-M$	$(\Sigma\hat{\hat{y}}^2 - \Sigma\hat{y}^2)/(K-M)$	(3)
Residual variation from $Y = f(X_1 \ldots X_k)$	Σe^2	$N-K$	$\Sigma e^2/(N-K)$	(4)
Total variation in Y	Σy^2	$N-1$		

Note: $M = (m+1)$ = number of all parameters in first regression, including b_0.
$K = (k+1)$ = number of all parameters in second regression, including b_0.

With the information included in the analysis of variance table we may perform the following tests:

1. Test of the overall significance of the regression including all the k variables. The relevant F^* ratio is

$$F^* = \frac{\Sigma\hat{\hat{y}}^2/(K-1)}{\Sigma e^2/(N-K)} = \frac{R^2/(K-1)}{(1-R^2)/(N-K)}$$

which is compared with $F_{0.05}$ with $\nu_1 = (K-1)$ and $\nu_2 = (N-K)$ degrees of freedom (for a test conducted at the 5 per cent level).

2. Test of the improvement in fit from additional regressors $X_{m+1} \ldots X_k$. The relevant F^* ratio is

$$F^* = \frac{(\Sigma\hat{\hat{y}}^2 - \Sigma\hat{y}^2)/(K-M)}{\Sigma e^2/(N-K)}$$

which again is compared to $F_{0.05}$ with $\nu_1 = (K-M)$ and $\nu_2 = (N-K)$ degrees of freedom (for a test conducted at the 5 per cent level).

8.6. TEST OF EQUALITY BETWEEN COEFFICIENTS OBTAINED FROM DIFFERENT SAMPLES (THE CHOW TEST)

Suppose that we have two samples on the variables Y and X_1, the one containing n_1 observations and the other n_2 observations, and we use them separately for the estimation of the relationship between Y and X. We thus obtain two estimates of the same relationship for two different periods of time (or for two different cross-section samples)

$$\hat{Y}_1 = \hat{b}_0 + \hat{b}_1 X_1$$

and

$$\hat{Y}_2 = \hat{\beta}_0 + \hat{\beta}_1 X_1.$$

We want to test whether these two estimated relationships differ significantly, in which case we conclude that the relationship is changing from one sample to the other. For example suppose that we have the data on consumption and income for the period 1948–57, from which we estimate the consumption function

$$\hat{C}_1 = \hat{b}_0 + \hat{b}_1 Y$$

Subsequently we obtain a sample for the period 1958–67, from which we obtain the consumption function

$$\hat{C}_2 = \hat{\beta}_0 + \hat{\beta}_1 Y$$

Are the two estimated functions significantly different? Does the consumption function shift over time ($b_0 \neq \beta_0$)? Does the marginal propensity to consume (MPC) change over time ($b_1 \neq \beta_1$)? Or, is the difference insignificant, so that it may be attributed to chance, in which case we may conclude that the consumption function is stable over time?

To answer these questions we may perform the following F test suggested by Chow. (G. C. Chow, 'Tests of Equality Between Sets of Coefficients in Two Linear Regressions', *Econometrica,* vol. 28, 1960, pp. 591–605.)

Step. 1. We pool together the two samples, thus forming a sample of $(n_1 + n_2)$ observations. From this we compute a 'pooled' function

$$\hat{Y}_p = \hat{a}_0 + \hat{a}_1 X$$

and we estimate the unexplained variation

$$\Sigma e_p^2 = \Sigma y_p^2 - \Sigma \hat{y}_p^2$$

with $(n_1 + n_2 - K)$ degrees of freedom. (p stands for 'pooled' and K is the total number of b's, including the intercept b_0; in our example $K = 2$.)

Step 2. We perform regression analysis on each sample separately.

From the first sample we have:

$$\hat{Y}_1 = \hat{b}_0 + \hat{b}_1 X$$
$$\Sigma e_1^2 = \Sigma y_1 - \Sigma \hat{y}_1^2$$

with $(n_1 - K)$ degrees of freedom.

From the second sample we obtain

$$\hat{Y}_2 = \hat{\beta}_0 + \hat{\beta}_1 X$$
$$\Sigma e_2^2 = \Sigma y^2 - \Sigma \hat{y}_2^2$$

with $(n_2 - K)$ degrees of freedom.

Step 3. We add together the unexplained variations of the two samples and form a total unexplained variation

$$(\Sigma e_1^2 + \Sigma e_2^2)$$

with $(n_1 - K) + (n_2 - K) = (n_1 + n_2 - 2K)$ degrees of freedom.

Step 4. We subtract the above sum of residual variations from the 'pooled' residual variance of Step 1, and we obtain

$$\Sigma e_p^2 - (\Sigma e_1^2 + \Sigma e_2^2)$$

with $(n_1 + n_2 - K) - (n_1 + n_2 - 2K) = K$ degrees of freedom.

Step 5. We form the ratio

$$F^* = \frac{[\Sigma e_p^2 - (\Sigma e_1^2 + \Sigma e_2^2)]/K}{(\Sigma e_1^2 + \Sigma e_2^2)/(n_1 + n_2 - 2K)}$$

The null hypothesis is $b_i = \beta_i$, that is, there is no difference in the coefficients obtained from the two samples.

We compare the observed F^* ratio with the theoretical value of $F_{0.05}$ (or other levels of significance) with $\nu_1 = K$ and $\nu_2 = (n_1 + n_2 - 2K)$ degrees of freedom. The theoretical value of F is the value that defines the critical region of the test (at the chosen level of significance).

If $F^* > F_{0.05}$ we reject the null hypothesis, that is, we accept that the two functions differ significantly, or, the two samples give different relationships. The economic relationship being studied changes over time.

Example. Assume we have the two samples on consumption and income for the periods 1948–57 and 1958–67 which are included in table 8.13.

Table 8.13. Income and consumption data (£000 at 1958 prices)

Sample I: 1948–57			Sample II: 1958–67		
Year	Income Y_t	Consumption C_t	Year	Income Y_t	Consumption C_t
1948	17,500	12,420	1958	22,758	15,362
1949	18,253	12,690	1959	23,720	16,080
1950	18,900	13,050	1960	24,924	16,735
1951	19,126	12,863	1961	25,769	17,127
1952	19,518	12,876	1962	25,993	17,517
1953	20,413	13,450	1963	27,146	18,375
1954	21,179	13,995	1964	28,748	19,082
1955	21,911	14,559	1965	29,461	19,421
1956	22,265	14,682	1966	30,032	19,811
1957	22,706	14,985	1967	30,489	20,211

1. From the 'pooled' sample of all 20 observations we obtain

$$\hat{C} = 850 \cdot 23 + 0 \cdot 63\, Y \qquad R^2_{C \cdot Y} = 0 \cdot 992$$
$$(323 \cdot 7) \quad (0 \cdot 01)$$
$$\Sigma e_p^2 = 1{,}062{,}082 = Q_1$$

with $(n_1 + n_2 - K) = 20 - 2 = 18$ degrees of freedom.

2. From the first sample the consumption function is estimated as

$$\hat{C}_1 = 3315 \cdot 27 + 0 \cdot 51\, Y \qquad R^2_{C \cdot Y} = 0 \cdot 958$$
$$(757 \cdot 7) \quad (0 \cdot 04)$$
$$\Sigma e_1^2 = 323{,}313$$

with $n_1 - K = 10 - 2 = 8$ degrees of freedom.

3. From the second sample the consumption function is found

$$\hat{C}_2 = 1545 \cdot 57 + 0 \cdot 61\, Y \qquad R^2_{C \cdot Y} = 0 \cdot 994$$
$$(421 \cdot 7) \quad (0 \cdot 01)$$
$$\Sigma e_2^2 = 128{,}552$$

with $n_2 - K = 10 - 2 = 8$ degrees of freedom.

4. The sum of the squared residuals between the two separate regressions is

$$Q_2 = \Sigma e_1^2 + \Sigma e_2^2 = 451{,}865 \cdot 4$$

with $n_1 + n_2 - 2K = 20 - 4 = 16$ degrees of freedom.

5. The difference of the above sum and the 'pooled' residuals is:

$$Q_3 = Q_1 - Q_2 = \Sigma e_p^2 - (\Sigma e_1^2 + \Sigma e_2^2) = 610{,}217$$

with $K = 2$ degrees of freedom.

6. The F^* ratio is

$$F^* = \frac{[\Sigma e_p^2 - (\Sigma e_1^2 + \Sigma e_2^2)]/K}{[\Sigma e_1^2 + \Sigma e_2^2]/(n_1 + n_2 - 2K)} = \frac{Q_3/K}{Q_2/(n_1 + n_2 - 2K)} = \frac{610{,}217/2}{451{,}865/16} = 10 \cdot 8.$$

7. The theoretical value of F at the 95 per cent level of significance with $v_1 = 2$ and $v_2 = 16$ degrees of freedom is $3 \cdot 63$.

Thus $F^* > F_{0 \cdot 05}$ and hence we reject the null hypothesis. The two relationships do differ significantly. That is, the consumption function changed between the two periods. Note that from the Chow test we can only infer that the function has changed. This may be due to changes in either b_0 or b_1 or both. To decide which coefficient has changed we need additional information. One way is to use dummy variables, as explained in Chapter 12. If we want to test the hypothesis that the *slope* only changes over time, we may include in the function the factor tY as an additional regressor

$$C_t = b_0 + b_1 Y_t + b_2 (tY_t) + u_t$$

and test the statistical significance of $\hat{b}_2$. If $\hat{b}_2$ is found statistically significant (if $H_0 : b_2 = 0$ is rejected), we may infer that the slope b changes over time, since, in this case we may write

$$C_t = \hat{b}_0 + (\hat{b}_1 + \hat{b}_2 t)Y_t$$

(See Chapter 12).

8.7. TESTING THE STABILITY OF REGRESSION COEFFICIENTS WHEN INCREASING THE SIZE OF THE SAMPLE

The aim of this test is to investigate the stability of the coefficient estimates as the sample size increases. We want to find out whether the estimates will be different in enlarged samples and whether they will remain stable over time (or in larger cross-section samples). Working with a sample a researcher may produce a regression which is too closely tailored to his sample, by experimenting with too many formulations of his model. In this case it is not certain that the estimated function will perform equally well outside the sample of data which has been used for the estimation of the coefficients. Furthermore there may have occurred events which change the structure of the relationship, for example changes in taxation laws, introduction of birth control measures, and so on. If such changes occur, the coefficients may not be stable: they may be sensitive to changes in the sample composition.

If the additional observations are more numerous than the number of parameters in the function, one may follow the procedure outlined in the previous section; that is, use the additional observations as a separate sample and apply the Chow test by computing the ratio

$$F^* = \frac{\{\Sigma e_p^2 - (\Sigma e_1^2 + \Sigma e_2^2)\}/K}{(\Sigma e_1^2 + \Sigma e_2^2)/(n_1 + n_2 - 2K)}$$

If, however, the new observations n_2 are fewer than the number of parameters in the function we may proceed as follows:

Firstly. From the augmented sample we obtain the regression

$$\hat{Y} = \hat{\beta}_0 + \hat{\beta}_1 X_1 + \ldots + \hat{\beta}_k X_k,$$

from which we calculate the residual sum of squares

$$\Sigma e^2 = \Sigma y^2 - \Sigma \hat{y}^2$$

with $(n_1 + n_2 - K)$ degrees of freedom.

Secondly. From the original sample of size n_1 we have

$$Y = \hat{b}_0 + \hat{b}_1 X_1 + \ldots + \hat{b}_k X_k$$

from which the unexplained sum of squares is

$$\Sigma e_1^2 = \Sigma y_1^2 - \Sigma \hat{y}_1^2$$

with $n_1 - K$ degrees of freedom.

Thirdly. Subtracting the two sums of residuals we find

$$\Sigma e^2 - \Sigma e_1^2$$

with $(n_1 + n_2 - K) - (n_1 - K) = n_2$ degrees of freedom, where n_2 are the additional observations.

Fourthly. We form the F^* ratio

$$F^* = \frac{(\Sigma e^2 - \Sigma e_1^2)/n_2}{\Sigma e_1^2/(n_1 - K)}$$

The null and alternative hypotheses are

$$H_1: b_i = \beta_i \qquad (i = 0, 1, 2, \ldots, k)$$
$$H_2: b_i \neq \beta_i$$

The F^* ratio is compared with the theoretical value of F, obtained from the F-tables with $\nu_1 = n_2$ and $\nu_2 = (n_1 - K)$ degrees of freedom.

If $F^* > F$ we reject the null hypothesis, i.e. we accept that the structural coefficients are unstable, their value changing in expanded sample periods.

Example. Suppose we have the sample of imports and income of the U.K. for the period 1950–65 as shown in table 8.14.

Table 8.14. Imports and GNP of the U.K. (in £m, at 1968 prices)

Year	Imports (Z)	GNP (X)	Year	Imports (Z)	GNP (X)
1950	3,748	21,777	1958	4,753	25,886
1951	4,010	22,418	1959	5,062	26,868
1952	3,711	22,308	1960	5,669	28,134
1953	4,004	23,319	1961	5,628	29,091
1954	4,151	24,180	1962	5,736	29,450
1955	4,569	24,893	1963	5,946	30,705
1956	4,582	25,310	1964	6,501	32,372
1957	4,697	25,799	1965	6,549	33,152

The import function estimated for this period (1950–65) is

$$Z = b_0 + b_1 X + u.$$

The results of the regression are

$$\hat{Z} = -2011 \cdot 85 + 0 \cdot 26\,X$$
$$(236 \cdot 71) \quad (0 \cdot 01)$$
$$R^2 = 0 \cdot 984 \quad \Sigma e_1^2 = 208{,}581$$

Now assume that we obtain four additional observations on imports and GNP:

	Imports	GNP
1966	6,705	33,764
1967	7,104	34,411
1968	7,609	35,429
1969	8,100	36,200

We want to test whether the addition of the four observations to our original sample alters significantly the coefficients of the import function.

We compute again the import equation with the enlarged sample of the twenty yearly observations

$$Z^* = -2461 \cdot 38 + 0 \cdot 28\,X$$
$$(250 \cdot 0) \quad (0 \cdot 01)$$
$$R^2 = 0 \cdot 983 \quad \Sigma e^2 = 573{,}069$$

The observed F^* ratio is

$$F^* = \frac{(\Sigma e^2 - \Sigma e_1^2)/n_2}{\Sigma e_1^2/(n_1 - K)} = \frac{364,488/4}{208,581/14} = 6\cdot12$$

where $n_1 = 16, n_2 = 4$ and $K = 2$.

The theoretical value of $F_{0.05}$ with $\nu_1 = 4$ and $\nu_2 = 14$ degrees of freedom is 3.11.

Since $F^* > F$ we reject the null hypothesis, that is we accept that there is a significant difference between the coefficients of the two functions. The import coefficients are not stable; they are sensitive to changes in the sample size.

8.8 TEST OF A RESTRICTION IMPOSED ON THE RELATIONSHIP BETWEEN TWO (OR MORE) PARAMETERS OF A FUNCTION

We will illustrate the test by using an example from the theory of production. One of the most popular forms of production function is the Cobb–Douglas form

$$X = b_0 L^{b_1} K^{b_2}$$

where X = output, L = labour input and K = capital input.

This function is homogeneous of degree $(b_1 + b_2)$, so that if $(b_1 + b_2) = 1$ we have constant returns to scale.

Assume that by fitting a regression to a sample of 30 observations on X, L and K for a certain industry we obtain

$$\hat{Y} = \hat{b}_0 \, L^{0\cdot8223} \, K^{0\cdot2324}$$

$$R^2 = 0\cdot768 \qquad \Sigma y^2 = 180 \qquad \Sigma e_1^2 = 4\cdot64 \qquad s_{\hat{b}_1} = 0\cdot03 \qquad s_{\hat{b}_2} = 0\cdot02$$

We observe that $b_1 + b_2 = 1\cdot0547$, that is, our estimates suggest that over the sample period the industry in question experienced increasing returns to scale. We want to test the statistical reliability of this result. In other words we want to test the hypothesis

$$H_1 : (b_1 + b_2) = 1$$

against the alternative hypothesis

$$H_2 : (b_1 + b_2) \neq 1$$

This hypothesis may be tested with an F ratio as follows.

Step 1. We perform the regression with the restriction $(b_1 + b_2) = 1$. From the restriction we obtain $b_2 = 1 - b_1$, so that by substitution in the production function we find

$$Y = b_0 L^{b_1} K^{(1 - b_1)}.$$

Dividing through by K we find

$$\left(\frac{Y}{K}\right) = b_0 \left(\frac{L}{K}\right)^{b_1}$$

Fitting a regression to this expression we get $b_1^* = 0.7431$. Substituting in the restriction we find $b_2^* = 1 - b_1^* = 0.2569$. Thus the restricted production function is

$$Y^* = b^* L^{0.7431} K^{0.2569}$$

$$R^2 = 0.650 \qquad \Sigma y^2 = 180 \qquad \Sigma e_2^2 = 6.45$$

Step 2. We thus have two unexplained sum of squares:

$$\Sigma e_1^2 = \text{sum of squared residuals from the unrestricted function}$$

and

$$\Sigma e_2^2 = \text{sum of squared residuals from the restricted function.}$$

R. Tintner has suggested the following test (G. Tintner, *Econometrics*, New York, Wiley, 1952, pp. 90–1).

The statistic

$$F^* = \frac{\Sigma e_2^2 - \Sigma e_1^2}{\Sigma e_1^2} (n - K)$$

has an F distribution with $\nu_1 = 1$ and $\nu_2 = (n - K)$ degrees of freedom.

Step 3. The observed F^* value is compared with the theoretical (tabular) value of $F_{0.05}$ with $\nu_1 = 1$ and $\nu_2 = (n - K)$ degrees of freedom. If $F^* > F_{0.05}$ we reject our basic hypothesis, that is, we accept that $(b_1 + b_2) \neq 1$.

In our example

$$F^* = \frac{6.45 - 4.64}{4.64} (30 - 3) = \frac{1.81}{4.64} \cdot (27) = 10.53$$

The theoretical $F_{0.05} = 4.20$ (with $\nu_1 = 1$ and $\nu_2 = 28$ degrees of freedom). Hence $F^* > F_{0.05}$ and we conclude that $(b_1 + b_2) \neq 1$.

We may now generalise the above test to the case where we have any number c of (linear) restrictions on the parameters of a relationship.

Consider first the case of two restrictions. The general unrestricted function is

$$Y = b_0 + b_1 X_1 + b_2 X_2 + b_3 X_3 + b_4 X_4 + \ldots + b_k X_k + u$$

Assume that from other sources of information (e.g. questionnaires, other studies etc.) we know that

$$b_1 = 1 \qquad \text{and} \qquad b_2 = b_3$$

Using sample observations we want to test the null hypothesis

H_0: the two restrictions are true

against the alternative hypothesis

H_1: not all restrictions are true

We first apply OLS to the original *unrestricted* function and obtain the sum of squared residuals Σe^2 with $(n - K)$ degrees of freedom.

We next incorporate the restrictions in the model and obtain the *restricted* form

$$(Y - X_1) = b_0 + b_2(X_2 + X_3) + b_4X_4 + \ldots + b_kX_k + u$$

It should be clear that imposition of restrictions implies estimation of fewer parameters. In the above example we have to estimate $(K - 2)$ coefficients. Applying OLS to the restricted form we find the sum of squared (restricted) residuals Σe_R^2 with $(n - K + 2)$ degrees of freedom.

Finally we take the difference of the two sums of residuals $\Sigma e_R^2 - \Sigma e^2$ with $(n - K + 2) - (n - K) = 2$ degrees of freedom. (Note that the degrees of freedom of this difference is equal to the number of imposed restrictions.)

Under the null hypothesis, the test statistic

$$F^* = \frac{(\Sigma e_R^2 - \Sigma e^2)/2}{\Sigma e^2/(n - K)}$$

has an F distribution with $\nu_1 = 2$ and $\nu_2 = (n - K)$ degrees of freedom. The estimated F^* statistic is compared with the tabular value of F (at the chosen level of significance, 5 per cent or 1 per cent usually) with $\nu_1 = 2$ and $\nu_2 = (n - K)$ degrees of freedom. If $F^* > F_{\text{tabular}}$ we reject the null hypothesis and we conclude that the sample data do not provide evidence that the imposed restrictions are true. If $F^* < F_{\text{tabular}}$ we accept the null hypothesis.

In general if we have c restrictions and we want to test the null hypothesis

H_0 : all the restrictions are true

against the alternative hypothesis

H_1 : not all the restrictions are true,

we proceed as follows.

Step 1. Apply OLS to the original unrestricted relationship and obtain the sum of squared residuals Σe^2 with $(n - K)$ degrees of freedom.

Step 2. Apply OLS to the restricted relationship (i.e. the function which incorporates the restrictions) and obtain the sum of (restricted) squared residuals Σe_R^2 with $n - (K - c) = n - K + c$ degrees of freedom.

Step 3. Compute the F^* ratio

$$F^* = \frac{(\Sigma e_R^2 - \Sigma e^2)/c}{\Sigma e^2/(n - K)}$$

Step 4. Find the critical value of F at the chosen level of significance (from the F tables on pp. 663–4) with $\nu_1 = c$ and $\nu_2 = (n - K)$, where c is the number of restrictions and $(n - K)$ is the number of degrees of freedom in the *unrestricted* estimation. If $F^* > F$ we reject the null hypothesis and we conclude that the restrictions are not supported by the sample data. If $F^* < F$ we accept the null hypothesis and we conclude that the restrictions are compatible with the observed in the real-world data.[1]

EXERCISES

1. The following table shows the price index of durables, the average yearly income and expenditure on durables of a 'typical' household in country Z.

Year	1959	1960	1961	1962	1963	1964	1965	1966	1967	1968
Expenditure on durables Y (£)	115	110	115	120	140	100	105	95	135	105
Household income X_1 (£)	1855	2000	2010	2040	2275	2255	1995	1905	2355	2035
Price index X_2	100	102	95	95	94	110	110	112	115	120

(a) Fit a regression line to the function

$$Y = b_0 + b_1 X_1 + b_2 X_2 + u$$

(b) Test your results by using the Analysis of Variance table.

2. The following table shows the consumption of tobacco manufactures, consumers' income and the price of tobacco manufactures for France.

Year	Consumption (million tons) D	Income (million francs) Y	Price of tobacco (francs per kg) P
1950	59,190	76,200	23·56
1951	65,450	91,700	24·44
1952	62,360	106,700	32·07
1953	64,700	111,600	32·46
1954	67,400	119,000	31·15
1955	64,440	129,200	34·14
1956	68,000	143,400	35·30
1957	72,400	159,600	38·70
1958	75,710	180,000	39·63
1959	70,680	193,000	46·68

(a) Fit a linear regression

$$D = b_0 + b_1 P + b_2 Y + u$$

and a non-linear function of the constant elasticity type

$$D = b_0 P^{b_1} Y^{b_2} e^u$$

(b) Conduct tests of significance using the analysis of variance table.

[1] For a general treatment of linear restrictions see Chapter 17.

(c) Choose among the two alternative functions on *a priori* economic *and* on statistical criteria.

(d) Compare the price and income elasticities of the two functions. (Note that for the linear function the b's are components of the respective elasticities. For example

$$\eta_P = \hat{b}_1 \frac{\bar{P}}{\bar{D}}$$

where $\bar{D}$ is the average consumption of tobacco and $\bar{P}$ is the average price in the sample.)

3. Prove that in the constant elasticity form of the demand function $D = b_0 P^{b_1} Y^{b_2} e^u$, there is no 'money illusion' if $b_1 + b_2 = 0$, given that P and Y are measured in current prices.

Using the data of exercise 2 perform a test for the hypothesis $b_1 + b_2 = 0$.

4. The following table shows the output (in 1000 tons) and the total cost of production of commodity x over a period of 15 years.

Period	Cost (£ mn)	Output (1000 units)
1	2,150	5
2	2,370	20
3	2,570	35
4	3,400	50
5	5,350	65
6	2,250	10
7	2,420	25
8	2,740	40
9	3,850	55
10	6,440	70
11	2,310	15
12	2,490	30
13	3,060	45
14	4,500	60
15	7,150	75

(a) Estimate the total cost function.

(b) Plot the marginal cost and the average variable cost curves.

(c) Test for nonlinearities of the cost function applying the Analysis of Variance table.

(d) Perform any standard test for judging the statistical reliability of the estimated coefficients.

(e) Comment on the implications of your statistical findings for the theory of costs.

5. A sample of twenty observations on X and Y is to be used for estimating the linear function

$$Y = b_0 + b_1 X + u.$$

The first ten observations yield the following results

$$\bar{X} = 15 \cdot 30 \qquad\qquad \bar{Y} = 160 \cdot 00$$

$$\sum_{i=1}^{10} (X_i - \bar{X})^2 = 78 \cdot 00 \qquad\qquad \sum_{i=1}^{10} (Y_i - \bar{Y})^2 = 45,600$$

$$\sum_{i=1}^{10} (X_i - \bar{X})(Y_i - \bar{Y}) = -1568 \cdot 00$$

The ten subsequent pairs of values of X and Y yield

$$\bar{X} = 14 \cdot 08 \qquad\qquad \bar{Y} = 106 \cdot 00$$

$$\sum_{i=11}^{20} (X_i - \bar{X})^2 = 98 \cdot 16 \qquad\qquad \sum_{i=11}^{20} (Y_i - \bar{Y})^2 = 62,440$$

$$\sum_{i=11}^{20} (X_i - \bar{X})(Y_i - \bar{Y}) = -2308 \cdot 80$$

Has the function changed over the two decades?

Note. Additional exercises are included in Appendix III.

Econometric Problems
Second-order Tests of the Assumptions
of the Linear Regression Model

Econometric Problems
Second-order Tests of the Assumptions of the Linear Regression Model

ECONOMETRIC CRITERIA FOR THE EVALUATION OF THE LEAST SQUARES ESTIMATES

We said in Chapter 2 that the third stage in any econometric work is the assessment of the reliability of the estimates of the parameters. After the estimation of the parameters with the method of OLS (or any other econometric technique) we should establish how trustworthy these estimates are. The assessment is based on three types of criteria. Firstly, *a priori* economic criteria, which are determined by the postulates of economic theory and relate to the sign and the magnitude of the parameters. Secondly, statistical criteria (first-order tests), defined by statistical theory. Thirdly econometric criteria (second-order tests) defined by econometric theory.

The statistical criteria traditionally used in assessing the reliability of the parameter estimates have been examined in Chapters 5 and 8. They are the coefficient of multiple determination (R^2), the standard errors of the estimates and the related t and F statistics. However, these tests are valid only if the assumptions of the linear regression model stated in Chapter 4 are satisfied. If the u's do not have the assumed pattern for their behaviour the evidence provided by statistical tests is invalidated. Thus in order to attach importance to R^2 or to the standard errors (or the t and F statistics) we should first make sure that the basic assumptions of classical least squares are satisfied in any particular case. In general, if the assumptions of an econometric method are violated in any application the estimates obtained from this method do not possess some or all of their optimal properties and/or their standard errors (and related t and F statistics) become unreliable criteria.

In Part II (Chapters 9–14) we will develop the econometric criteria or second order tests, for judging the 'goodness' of the estimates. These criteria provide some evidence about the validity or the violation of the assumptions of the linear regression model. For each assumption we will adopt the following scheme of exposition. (i) We will start by discussing the plausibility of the assumption on an intuitive basis using *a priori* reasoning. (ii) We will next examine the consequences of the violation of the assumption on the parameter estimates and/or their standard errors. (iii) We will describe the tests available for each assumption. (iv) Finally we will discuss the solutions that have been suggested as 'remedies' of the situation created by the violation of the assumption.

The econometric tests of the stochastic assumptions of the linear regression model involve the examination of the regression residuals, e's, which are the estimates of the u's, in order to establish whether the u's conform to their assumed pattern of behaviour. The econometric tests of the non-stochastic assumptions (of correct aggregation, identification, correct specification, degree of collinearity of the regressors) involve the examination of the observable explanatory variables and their interrelationships. The corrective action which should be adopted if the u's or the X's violate one or more of the basic assumptions of OLS consists, as will be seen, in the respecification of the model and its re-estimation. The new specification may involve the introduction of new, or the elimination of old, explanatory variables, or the transformation of the original variables, or both. The process of respecification will continue until we arrive at a formulation in which the random term u and the X's meet as far as possible the assumptions of the linear regression model.

9. The Assumptions of Randomness, Zero Mean, Constant Variance and Normality of the Disturbance Variable u

In this chapter we shall examine four of the basic assumptions of the linear regression model, the assumption of the randomness of the disturbance variable u, the assumption of zero mean, the assumption of constant variance and the assumption of normality of this variable.

9.1. THE ASSUMPTION OF RANDOMNESS OF u

The first assumption concerning u is that it is a random variable. This means that u can assume various values in a chance way. For each value of X the term u may assume positive, negative or zero values each with a certain probability.

We said that u is introduced into the model in order to take into account the influence of various 'errors', such as errors of omitted variables, errors of the mathematical form of the model, errors of measurement of the dependent variable, and the effects of the erratic element which is inherent in human behaviour. Now, for u to be random the omitted variables should be numerous, each one individually unimportant, and they should change in different directions so that their overall effect on the dependent variable is unpredictable in any particular period. Furthermore, the errors of measurement should be random. If these errors exhibit a systematic pattern, then the assumption of randomness is violated.

In each particular econometric application the research worker should make sure that the above conditions of randomness are fulfilled, especially with respect to the omitted variables. If we have excluded some important explanatory variable it is obvious that the values of u will not show a random pattern, because they will reflect mainly the movements of this variable.

The establishment of the assumption of randomness of the u's should be attempted on *a priori* grounds, since there is no formal test for this assumption. The true u's are not observable, and their estimates, e's, are obtained with the assumption of randomness built into the estimation procedure, so that they cannot be used for testing it.

9.2. THE ASSUMPTION OF ZERO MEAN OF u

The second assumption that we made about the random variable is that each u_i (corresponding to X_i) may assume values which have a zero mean

$$E(u_i) = 0 \qquad \text{for all observations } (i = 1, 2, \ldots, n)$$

179

We assume that in each period the specific value of the random term that turns up (u_i) is drawn from a population of such values, each of which might have been observed, but in reality only the specific value u_i did happen. The population of all conceivable values of u for each period is assumed to contain positive, negative or zero values, all of which add up to zero. The essence of the zero mean assumption is that we take it as axiomatically true that the positive and negative values of u have a sum equal to zero.

This interpretation is a conceptual model that nobody can ever hope to prove or disprove. (See S. Valavanis, *Econometrics*, McGraw-Hill, New York, 1959, Chapter 1.) It is necessary, however, to make the zero mean assumption so as to be able to apply the rules of algebra to stochastic phenomena and relationships. In other words this assumption is imposed on us by the stochastic nature of economic relationships, which otherwise it would be impossible to estimate with the common rules of mathematics. By assuming that the u has·a zero mean, the expected (mean) value of Y is

$$E(Y) = (b_0 + b_1 X) + E(u) = b_0 + b_1 X$$

and can be interpreted as the linear relationship which 'on the average' holds between X and Y. The systematic part of the relationship $(b_0 + b_1 X)$ can be estimated by applying the rules of common algebra. Geometrically this assumption implies that the observations of Y and X must be scattered around the line in a random way. Only under this condition will our estimated line $(\hat{Y} = \hat{b}_0 + \hat{b}_1 X)$ be a good approximation of the true line, $E(Y) = b_0 + b_1 X$ (figure 9.1), which defines the relationship connecting Y and X 'on the average'.

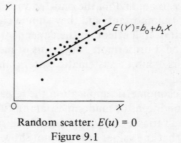

Random scatter: $E(u) = 0$

Figure 9.1

The alternative possible assumptions are either $E(u) > 0$ or $E(u) < 0$ (the mean of u is positive or negative). Let us examine the consequences for our estimates if the mean value of u is positive (similar arguments hold for the case of a negative mean value of u).

Assume that for some reason the u's had not an average value of zero, but tended most of them to be positive. This would imply that the observations of Y and X would lie above the true line (figure 9.2). It can be shown that by using these observations we would get a bad estimate of the true line. In figure 9.2 the estimated line would be $\hat{Y} = \hat{b}_0 + \hat{b}_1 X$, which obviously is not a good approximation to the true line $E(Y) = b_0 + b_1 X$. The estimate of the true

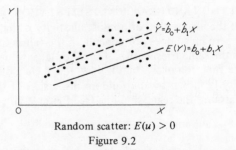

Random scatter: $E(u) > 0$

Figure 9.2

line is achieved by fitting a regression line which passes through the observations; if the true line lies below or above the observations, (which would imply that $E(u) > 0$ and $E(u) < 0$ respectively) the estimated line would be biased. This is the reason why the assumption $E(u) = 0$ is forced upon us if we are to establish the true relationship. There is no test for the verification of this assumption because we set $E(u) = 0$ at the outset of our estimation procedures. Its plausibility should be examined in each particular case on *a priori* grounds. In any econometric application we must be sure that: (a) all the important variables have been included into the function, so that the excluded ones are individually unimportant and are equally likely to have either positive or negative effects on the dependent variable which most probably would offset each other; (b) there are no systematically positive or systematically negative errors of measurement in the dependent variable.

Such considerations concerning the expected value of u are omitted from applied research, on the belief that the above two conditions are almost always satisfied in practice. This argument is not correct in general, because in most cases we are obliged, for various reasons, to omit some quite important variable or variables (for example in order to avoid multicollinearity) and furthermore, the errors of measurement in many economic variables tend to be systematic in the one or the other direction.

9.3. THE ASSUMPTION OF HOMOSCEDASTICITY

The third assumption about the random variable u is that its probability distribution remains the same over all observations of X, and in particular that the variance of each u_i is the same for all values of the explanatory variable. Symbolically we have

$$\text{var}(u) = E\{(u_i - E(u)\}^2 = E(u_i)^2 = \sigma_u^2 \qquad \text{constant}$$

This assumption is known as the assumption of homoscedasticity or the assumption of constant variance of the u's. If it is not satisfied in any particular case, we say that the u's are heteroscedastic

$$\text{var}(u_i) = \sigma_{ui}^2 \qquad \text{not constant}$$

where the subscript i signifies the fact that the individual variances may all be different.

9.3.1. INTERPRETATION AND GRAPHICAL PRESENTATION OF THE ASSUMPTION

The meaning of the assumption of homoscedasticity is that the variation of each u_i around its zero mean does not depend on the values of X. The variance of each u_i remains the same irrespective of small or large values of the explanatory variable. σ_u^2 is not a function of X_i, that is $\sigma_u^2 \neq f(X_i)$. On a diagram the case of homoscedasticity is shown by the random dispersion of the u's within a constant distance around the regression line (see figure 9.3).

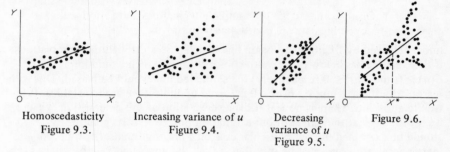

Homoscedasticity	Increasing variance of u	Decreasing	Figure 9.6.
Figure 9.3.	Figure 9.4.	variance of u	
		Figure 9.5.	

If σ_u^2 is not constant, but its values depend on the values of X, we may write $\sigma_{u_i}^2 = f(X_i)$.

The case of heteroscedasticity is shown by the increasing or decreasing dispersion of the observations from the regression line. The pattern of the observations on a scatter diagram depends on the form of heteroscedasticity, that is, on the form of the relationship between $\sigma_{u_i}^2$ and X_i. Three different forms of heteroscedasticity are shown in figures 9.4–9.6. In figure 9.4 we picture the case of (monotonically) increasing variance of the u_i's: as X increases, so does the variance of u. This is a common form of heteroscedasticity assumed in econometric applications. In figure 9.5 we show the pattern of decreasing heteroscedasticity: as X assumes higher values the deviation of the observations from the regression line decreases, that is, the variance of the random variable changes to opposite direction with the explanatory variable. Finally, in figure 9.6 we depict a more complicated form of homoscedasticity: the variance of u decreases initially as X assumes higher values, but after a certain level of X (X^* in figure 9.6) the variance of u increases with X. It should be clear that the pattern of heteroscedasticity depends on the signs and values of the coefficients of the relationship $\sigma_{u_i}^2 = f(X_i)$. Since the u_i's are not observable we do not know the true pattern of heteroscedasticity. In applied research econometricians usually make the convenient *assumption* that the heteroscedasticity is the form $\sigma_{u_i}^2 = k^2 X^2$, where k is a constant to be estimated from the model (see below).

9.3.2. PLAUSIBILITY OF THE ASSUMPTION OF HOMOSCEDASTICITY

In many econometric applications the assumption of constant variance of the random variable may well be expected not to hold. This can easily be understood if we take into account the factors whose influences are absorbed by the disturbance term. Recall that u expresses the influence on the dependent variable of errors in its measurement and of omitted variables. On both accounts there are reasons for expecting the variance of u to vary over time, or to vary systematically with the explanatory variable X, in most cases. Thus as Y increases errors of measurement tend to increase, because it becomes more difficult to collect data and check their consistency and reliability. Furthermore, the errors of measurement tend to be cumulative over time, so that their size tends to increase. In this case the variance of u_i increases with increasing values of X. On the other hand, the sampling techniques and various other methods for collecting data are continuously improving, and thus errors of measurement may decrease, in which case $\sigma_{u_i}^2$ decreases over time. Most important, many of the variables which are omitted from the function tend to change in the same direction with X, thus causing an increase of the variation of the observations from the regression line. For example, suppose we have a cross section sample of family budgets from which we want to measure the savings function

$$S_i = b_0 + b_1 Y_i + u_i$$

where S_i = savings of the ith household
Y_i = income of the ith household.

In this case the assumption of constant variance of the u's is not appropriate, because high-income families show a much greater variability in their savings behaviour than do low-income families. Families with high incomes tend to stick to a certain standard of living and when their income falls they cut down their savings rather than their consumption expenditure. On the other hand, low income families save for certain purposes (for example to pay some instalments, or to repay a debt) and thus their savings patterns are more regular. This implies that at high incomes the u_i's will be high, while at low incomes the u_i's will be small. Therefore the assumption of constant variance of the u's does not hold when estimating the savings function from a cross-section of family budgets. (See Goldberger, *Econometric Theory*, p. 231.)

As another example consider a cross-section sample of firms of a certain industry, which we use in order to estimate the Cobb—Douglas production function

$$X = b_0 . L^{b_1} . K^{b_2} . e^u$$

u in this case absorbs factors like extrepreneurship, technological differences of plants of the various firms, differences in skills or in organisation and other factors. These factors do not vary considerably in small firms, while they are expected to vary widely for large firms. Hence the u's will be heteroscedastic.

In summary we may say that on *a priori* grounds there are reasons to believe that the assumption of homoscedasticity may often be violated in practice. It is therefore important to examine what are the consequences of heteroscedasticity on the parameter estimates and on their standard errors. There is evidence[1] that the usual case of heteroscedasticity is that of increasing variance of u, and in the remainder of this section we will deal mainly with this case.

9.3.3. CONSEQUENCES OF THE VIOLATION OF THE ASSUMPTION OF HOMOSCEDASTICITY

If the assumption of homoscedastic disturbance is not fulfilled we have the following consequences:

(1) We cannot apply the formulae of the variances of the coefficients to conduct tests of significance and construct confidence intervals. The tests are inapplicable. We saw in Chapter 5 that

$$\text{var}(\hat{b}_0) = \sigma_u^2 \frac{\Sigma X^2}{n\Sigma x^2} \quad \text{and} \quad \text{var}(\hat{b}_1) = \sigma_u^2 \frac{1}{\Sigma x^2}$$

The variance σ_u^2 was taken out of the summations because it was assumed constant. With heteroscedasticity in the function the variance of u would not be a finite constant figure, but rather would tend to change with an increasing range of values of X and hence could not be taken out of the summation. Thus heteroscedasticity renders the above formulae inapplicable. One could use other expressions for computing the variance of the coefficients, but such formulae would be complicated (as they would involve the solution of a system of equations including the changing u variances, $\sigma_{u_1}^2, \sigma_{u_2}^2, \ldots, \sigma_{u_n}^2$).

(2) If u is heteroscedastic, the OLS estimates do not have the minimum variance property in the class of unbiased estimators; that is, they are inefficient in small samples. Furthermore, they are inefficient in large samples (asymptotically inefficient). (For a proof of this statement see below, p. 191.)

(3) The coefficient estimates would still be statistically unbiased; that is, even if the u's are heteroscedastic, the $\hat{b}$'s will have no statistical bias; their expected value will be equal to the true parameters, $E(\hat{b}_i) = b_i$. Recall that the property of unbiasedness of the least squares estimates does not require that the variance of the u_i's be constant. In Chapter 5 we established

$$\hat{b}_1 = b_1 + \frac{\Sigma x_i u_i}{\Sigma x_i^2}$$

and

$$E(\hat{b}_1) = b_1 + E\left[\frac{\Sigma x_i u_i}{\Sigma x_i^2}\right] = b_1$$

by Assumption 6A, that the x's are a set of fixed values in all samples. Similarly,

$$\hat{b}_0 = \overline{Y} - \hat{b}_1 \overline{X} = (b_0 + b_1 \overline{X} + \overline{u}) - \hat{b}_1 \overline{X}$$

and

$$E(\hat{b}_0) = b_0 + b_1 \overline{X} + E(\overline{u}) - E(\hat{b}_1 \overline{X}) = b_0$$

---

[1] See G. Katona *et al.*, *Contributions of Survey Methods to Econometrics*, New York: Columbia University Press, 1954, p. 203.

In establishing these results we did not make use of Assumption 3 concerning homoscedasticity.

(4) The prediction (of Y for a given value of X) based on the estimates $\hat{b}$'s from the original data, would have a high variance, that is the prediction would be inefficient. Because the variance of the prediction includes the variances of u and of the parameter estimates, which are not minimal due to the incidence of heteroscedasticity (see Chapter 20).

9.3.4. TESTS FOR HOMOSCEDASTICITY

Various tests have been suggested for establishing homoscedasticity. We will explain three such tests, which are conceptually and computationally the simplest to apply.

1. *The Spearman rank-correlation test*

This is the simplest test, which may be applied to either small or large samples, and may be outlined as follows.

1. We regress Y on X

$$Y = b_0 + b_1 X_1 + u$$

and we obtain the residuals, e's which are estimates of the u's.

2. We order the e's (ignoring their sign) and the X values in ascending or descending order and we compute the rank correlation coefficient

$$r'_{e \cdot x} = 1 - \frac{6 \, \Sigma D_i^2}{n \, (n^2 - 1)}$$

where D_i = difference between the ranks of corresponding pairs of X and e, and n = observations in the sample.[1]

A high rank correlation coefficient suggests the presence of heteroscedasticity.

If we have a relationship with more explanatory variables we may compute the rank correlation coefficient between e_i and each one of the explanatory variables separately.

2. *The Goldfeld and Quandt test*

(S. M. Goldfeld and R. E. Quandt, 'Some Tests for Homoscedasticity', *J. Am. Statist. Ass.*, vol. 60, 1965, pp. 539–47.)

This test is applicable to large samples. The observations must be at least twice as many as the parameters to be estimated. The test assumes normality and serially independent u_i's. The hypothesis to be tested is the null hypothesis

---

[1] The student might wonder why the rank correlation coefficient is chosen and not the simple correlation coefficient r_{ex}. The answer is that $r_{ex} = 0$ always if OLS has been used, since

$$r_{ex} = \frac{\Sigma ex}{\sqrt{\Sigma e^2} \, \sqrt{\Sigma x^2}} \quad \text{and} \quad \Sigma ex = 0 \qquad \text{(see Chapter 7).}$$

However, if we take the absolute value of the e's the correlation coefficient $r_{|e|x}$ can be used as a measure of heteroscedasticity. This correlation coefficient is the basis of Glejser's test. See below, pp. 186–7.

H_0 : u_i's are homoscedastic
and is tested against the alternative hypothesis

H_1 : u_i's are heteroscedastic (with increasing variances).

The steps involved in the Goldfeld and Quandt test may be outlined as follows.

Firstly. We order the observations according to the magnitude of the explanatory variable X.

Secondly. We select arbitrarily a certain number (c) of central observations which we omit from the analysis. (It has been found from some experiments by Goldfeld and Quandt that for samples larger than $n = 30$ the optimum number of central observations to be omitted from the test is approximately a quarter of the total observations, for example 8 for $n = 30$, 16 for $n = 60$.) The remaining $(n - c)$ observations are divided into two sub-samples of equal size $((n - c)/2)$, one including the small values of X and the other including the large values of X.

Thirdly. We fit separate regressions to each sub-sample, and we obtain the sum of squared residuals from each of them

Σe_1^2 = residuals from the sub-sample of low values of X, with $[(n - c)/2] - K$ degrees of freedom, where K is the total number of parameters in the model

Σe_2^2 = residuals from the sub-sample of high values of X, with the same degree of freedom, $[(n - c)/2] - K$

If each of these sums is divided by the appropriate degrees of freedom, we obtain estimates of the variances of the u's in the two sub-samples. The ratio of the two variances

$$F^* = \frac{\Sigma e_2^2 / [\{(n-c)/2\} - K]}{\Sigma e_1^2 / [\{(n-c)/2\} - K]} = \frac{\Sigma e_2^2}{\Sigma e_1^2}$$

has an F distribution (with $\nu_1 = \nu_2 = [\{n - c\}/2] - K = [\{n - c - 2K\}/2]$ degrees of freedom, where n = total number of observations, c = central observations omitted, K = number of parameters estimated from each regression).

If the two variances are the same (that is, if the u's are homoscedastic) the value of F^* will tend to 1. If the variances differ, F^* will have a large value (given that by the design of the test $\Sigma e_2^2 > \Sigma e_1^2$. The observed F^* is compared with the theoretical value of F with $\nu_1 = \nu_2 = (n - c - 2K)/2$ degrees of freedom (at a chosen level of significance). The theoretical (obtained from the F-Tables) value of F is the value of F that defines the critical region of the test. If $F^* > F$ we accept that there is heteroscedasticity (that is we reject the null hupothesis of no difference between the variances of u's in the two sub-samples). If $F^* < F$, we accept that the u's are homoscedastic (in other words we accept the null hypothesis). The higher the observed F^* ratio the stronger the heteroscedasticity of the u's.

3. *The Glejser test for homoscedasticity*

(H. Glejser, 'A New Test for Heteroscedasticity', *Journal of the American Statistical Association,* vol. 64, 1969, pp. 316–23.)

This test may be outlined as follows.

(1) We perform the regression of Y on all the explanatory variables and we compute the residuals, e's.

(2) We regress the absolute values of e's ($|e_i|$) on the explanatory variable with which $\sigma_{u_i}^2$ is thought, on *a priori* grounds, to be associated.[1]
The actual form of this regression is usually not known, so that one may experiment with various formulations, containing various powers of X, for example

$$|e| = a_0 + a_1 X_j^{\,2}$$

or

$$|e| = a_0 + a_1 X_j^{-1} = a_0 + a_1 \frac{1}{X_j}$$

or

$$|e| = a_0 + a_1 X_j^{1/2} = a_0 + a_1 \sqrt{X_j}$$

and so on.

We choose the form of regression which gives the best fit in the light of the correlation coefficient and the standard errors of the coefficients a_0 and a_1. (Note that if $a_0 = 0$, while $a_1 \neq 0$, the situation is referred to as 'pure heteroscedasticity'; if both $a_0 \neq 0$ and $a_1 \neq 0$, the case is referred to as mixed heteroscedasticity). Heteroscedasticity is judged in the light of the statistical significance of a_0 and a_1; that is we perform any standard test of significance (s_{δ_i}, t, F) for these coefficients, and if they are found significantly different from zero we accept that the u_i's are heteroscedastic. The Glejser test has the advantage that it gives also information on the form of heteroscedasticity, that is, on the particular way in which $\sigma_{u_i}^2$ is connected with X_i. This information is important, as we shall presently see, for the 'correction' of the heteroscedastic disturbance term.[2]

J. Johnston seems to accept that the Spearman rank-correlation test and the Goldfeld and Quandt test are preferable to Glejser's test for the detection of heteroscedasticity (see J. Johnston, *Econometric Methods* (1972), p. 221). Once heteroscedasticity has been established on either of these tests one may experiment with various forms of the function suggested by Glejser ($|e| = f(x)$) in order to decide what is the appropriate transformation of the original data required, to overcome the difficulties of heteroscedastic u_i's.

9.3.5. SOLUTIONS FOR HETEROSCEDASTIC DISTURBANCES

When heteroscedasticity is established on the basis of any test, the appropriate solution is to transform the original model in such a way as to obtain a form in

[1] We take the absolute values of the residuals and not their actual values since $\Sigma ex = 0$, and hence the regression $e = f(x)$ would be impossible to fit. Furthermore, in studying heteroscedasticity we are interested in the absolute value of the residuals as the X's increase, since it is this value that shows the dispersion of the original observations from the regression line.

[2] The extension of Glejser's method to models with more explanatory variables is straightforward. We regress $|e|$ on all explanatory variables and we choose the best fit. The estimated function $|\hat{e}| = f(X_1, X_2, \ldots, X_k)$ is then used for the transformation of the original variables (see below, p. 191).

which the transformed disturbance term has constant variance. (For the rationale of this corrective procedure see below, p. 189.) We then may apply the method of classical least squares to the transformed model. The transformation of the model reduces to the adjustment of the original data. The adjustment of the model depends on the particular form of homoscedasticity, that is, on the form of the relationship between the variance $\sigma^2_{u_i}$ and the values of the explanatory variable(s)

$$\sigma^2_{u_i} = f(X_i)$$

In general, the transformation of the original model consists in dividing through the original relationship by the square root of the term which is responsible for the homoscedasticity. Let us illustrate this statement with some examples. Assume that the original model is

$$Y_i = b_0 + b_1 X_i + u_i$$

where u_i is heteroscedastic, but satisfies all the other stochastic assumptions of the linear regression model.

Case (a). Suppose the heteroscedasticity is of the form $E(u_i)^2 = \sigma^2_{u_i} = k^2 X^2$ (where k is a finite constant to be estimated from the model), that is, the variance of u increases proportionately with X^2. Solving for the constant factor of proportionality, k^2, we obtain $k^2 = \sigma^2_{u_i}/X^2$. This suggests that the appropriate transformation of the original model consists of the division of the original relationship by $\sqrt{X^2} = X$, which means that the appropriate transformation version is

$$\frac{Y_i}{X_i} = \frac{b_0}{X_i} + b_1 + \frac{u_i}{X_i}$$

The new transformed random term u_i/X_i is homoscedastic, since

$$E\left(\frac{u_i}{X_i}\right)^2 = \frac{1}{X_i^2} E(u_i^2) = \frac{1}{X_i^2} \sigma^2_{u_i}$$

(given that by Assumption 6A the X's are a set of fixed values in all samples). But in our example it was assumed that $\sigma^2_{u_i} = k^2 X_i^2$

Therefore $E\left(\frac{u_i}{X_i}\right)^2 = \frac{1}{X_i^2} k^2 X^2 = k^2$

that is, the new random term has a finite constant variance (equal to k^2) and hence we may apply classical least squares to the transformed version of the model.

Case (b). Assume the form of heteroscedasticity to be

$$E(u_i)^2 = \sigma^2_{u_i} = k^2 X$$

The appropriate transformation of the original model consists of the division of the original relationship by $\sqrt{X}$

$$\frac{Y}{\sqrt{X}} = \frac{b_0}{\sqrt{X}} + b_1 \frac{X}{\sqrt{X}} + \frac{u}{\sqrt{X}}$$

$$(YX^{-\frac{1}{2}}) = b_0 X^{-\frac{1}{2}} + b_1 X^{\frac{1}{2}} + \frac{u}{\sqrt{X}}$$

The transformed random term $u/\sqrt{X}$ is homoscedastic with constant variance equal to k^2

$$E\left(\frac{u}{\sqrt{X}}\right)^2 = \frac{1}{X} E(u_i^2) = \frac{1}{X} (\sigma_{u_i}^2) = k^2$$

given that in our example it was assumed that $\sigma_{u_i}^2 = k^2 X$. Hence with the above transformation we avoid heteroscedasticity.

Case (c). Assume the form of heteroscedasticity is

$$E(u_i)^2 = \sigma_{u_i}^2 = k^2 (a_0 + a_1 X)^2$$

The appropriate transformation implies the division of the original equation by $\sqrt{(a_0 + a_1 X)^2} = (a_0 + a_1 X)$, that is

$$\frac{Y_i}{a_0 + a_1 X_i} = b_0 \frac{1}{a_0 + a_1 X_i} + b_1 \frac{X_i}{a_0 + a_1 X_i} + \frac{u_i}{a_0 + a_1 X_i}$$

The new random term is homoscedastic with constant variance equal to k^2

$$E\left[\frac{u_i}{a_0 + a_1 X_i}\right]^2 = \frac{1}{(a_0 + a_1 X_i)^2} E(u^2)$$

$$= \frac{1}{(a_0 + a_1 X_i)^2} k^2 (a_0 + a_1 X_i)^2 = k^2$$

In general if the heteroscedasticity is of the form

$$E(u_i)^2 = \sigma_{u_i}^2 = k^2 f(X_i)$$

(where k is a finite constant and $f(X_i)$ is a function of the X's), the solution is the transformation of the original function by dividing through the original model by $\sqrt{f(X_i)}$.

JUSTIFICATION FOR THE SUGGESTED TRANSFORMATION

This transformation is equivalent to the application of the method of *weighted least squares* (WLS), which is a special case of Aitken's method of generalised least squares (GLS). The latter will be examined in Chapter 19. For the present we will describe the WLS method which provides the rationalisation of the above transformation procedure.

In ordinary least squares we minimise the simple sum of squared residuals, $\Sigma e_i^2 = \Sigma(Y_i - \hat{b}_0 - \hat{b}_1 X_i)^2$, in which each residual is assigned equal weight (all weights are unity). That is, the sum Σe_i^2 is the unweighted sum of squared residuals, in which u_i, as estimated by e_i, is assumed to give an equally precise indication of where the true regression lies, due to the assumption of homoscedasticity of OLS. However, if the variance of the u_i's is not constant, but, say, increases with increasing values of X (figure 9.4), it is clear that the greater dispersion of the observations on the right (in this figure) causes them to give a less accurate indication of where the true line lies. Therefore it seems plausible to pay less attention to these observations in fitting the regression line, to assign to them less weight than to the observations on the left (in figure 9.4) which are less dispersed and hence provide a more accurate idea of the position of the true line. This can be achieved by assigning different weights to each u_i (or its estimate e_i). It is reasonable to use as weights the ratios $1/\sigma^2_{u_i}$, that is, to divide each residual by the variance of the disturbance term: when a disturbance u_i is large its variance $\sigma^2_{u_i}$ is large and the weight $1/\sigma^2_{u_i}$ will be small; hence the large disturbances are assigned smaller weights. Thus instead of minimising the simple sum of squared residuals, as in OLS, we minimise the weighted sum of squared residuals

$$\Sigma \frac{e_i^2}{\sigma^2_{u_i}} = \Sigma \frac{1}{\sigma^2_{u_i}} (Y_i - \hat{b}_0 - \hat{b}_1 X_i)^2$$

Hence the reason for naming this method *weighted least squares* (WLS). By applying calculus we may derive the partial derivatives of the weighted sum of squares and obtain formulae for $\hat{b}_0$ and $\hat{b}_1$, provided that we know $\sigma^2_{u_i}$. However, this variance is not known and the calculus may become quite complicated. It can be proved that the minimisation procedure of the weighted sum of squared residuals (that is the WLS method), yields identical formulae for the parameter estimates as the application of OLS to an appropriately transformed equation.

Proof. We will use the simple case in which the assumed form of heteroscedasticity is

$$\sigma^2_{u_i} = k^2 X_i^2$$

which results in the transformation

$$\frac{Y_i}{X_i} = b_0 \frac{1}{X_i} + b_1 + \frac{u_i}{X_i}$$

where the transformed disturbance term is homoscedastic with variance equal to k^2.
    (1) Set $v = u/X$. Now OLS on the transformed model implies choosing $\hat{b}_0$ and $\hat{b}_1$ so as to minimise the sum of squared residuals

$$\Sigma v_i^2 = \sum_i^n \left(\frac{Y_i}{X_i} - \hat{b}_0 \frac{1}{X_i} - \hat{b}_1 \right)^2 = \Sigma \frac{1}{X_i^2} (Y_i - \hat{b}_0 - \hat{b}_1 X_i)^2$$

This expression is to be minimised with respect to $\hat{b}_0$ and $\hat{b}_1$.
    (2) WLS, on the other hand, implies choosing $\hat{b}_0$ and $\hat{b}_1$ so as to minimise the weighted sum of squared residuals

$$\Sigma \frac{e_i^2}{\sigma^2_{u_i}} = \Sigma \frac{1}{\sigma^2_{u_i}} (Y_i - \hat{b}_0 - \hat{b}_1 X_i)^2 = \Sigma \frac{1}{k^2 X^2} (Y_i - \hat{b}_0 - \hat{b}_1 X_i)^2$$

which is to be minimised with respect to $\hat{b}_0$ and $\hat{b}_1$. The two sums of squared residuals differ only by the constant term $1/k^2$. Hence the values of b_0 and b_1 which minimise the first sum (of OLS as applied to the transformed model) are the same with those which also minimise the weighted sum of squares of WLS. (Recall from calculus that whatever minimises a function $f(Z)$, will also minimise $kf(Z)$, where k is any constant.) Hence WLS applied to the original equation yields identical results as OLS applied to the appropriately transformed equation.

9.3.6. ESTIMATION OF THE VARIANCE OF HETEROSCEDASTIC DISTURBANCES

It should be clear that in order to adopt the above 'corrective' procedure we must have information on the form of heteroscedasticity.

1. *Assuming known* $\dot{\sigma}^2_{u_i} = k^2 X_i^2$.

In applied research econometricians usually assume that the variance of u_i changes in proportion to the square of the explanatory variable. The main justification for this assumption is that the resulting transformation is computationally easy. It involves division of the original function by X

$$\frac{Y_i}{X_i} = b_1 + b_0 \frac{1}{X_i} + \frac{u_i}{X_i}$$

Note that in this transformation the position of the coefficients has changed: the parameter of the variable $1/X_i$ in the transformed model is the constant intercept of the original formulation, while the constant term of the transformed equation is the parameter of the explanatory variable X in the original model.

2. *Estimation of the pattern of heteroscedasticity from Glejser's test*

The test proposed by Glejser (test 3 above) does also provide information on the form of heteroscedascitity. By experimenting with various formulations of the function $|e| = f(X_i)$ we may choose the form that gives the best statistical fit. We then proceed with the transformation of the original data; that is, we divide each of the original variables (including the dependent) by the chosen function. For example, assume that $|e|$ is correlated with both X_1 and X_2. We can regress the absolute values, $|e|$'s, on X_1 and X_2 (applying OLS) and obtain $|\hat{e}|$; that is, the values estimated from this step. We then divide all the original variables by $|\hat{e}|$ to obtain the required transformed variables. We finally apply OLS to these transformed variables.

The extension of Glejser's method to any number of explanatory variables is straightforward.

It can be proved that the estimates of the transformed model have a smaller variance (are more efficient) than the estimates obtained from the application of OLS to the original model.

Let us illustrate this result in the simple heteroscedastic model in which $\sigma_{u_i}^2 = k^2 X_i^2$.

(1) The original (heteroscedastic) model is

$$Y_i = b_0 + b_1 X_i + u_i \qquad \text{with } E(u_i^2) = k^2 X_i^2$$

Applying OLS to the heteroscedastic model we find

$$\hat{b}_1 = b_1 + \frac{\Sigma x_i u_i}{\Sigma x_i^2}$$

and

$$\text{var}(\hat{b}_1) = E(\hat{b}_1 - b_1)^2 = E\left(b_1 + \frac{\Sigma x_i u_i}{\Sigma x_i^2} - b_1\right)^2 = E\left(\frac{\Sigma x_i u_i}{\Sigma x_i^2}\right)^2$$

$$= E\left(\frac{\Sigma x_i^2 u_i^2 + 2\,\Sigma x_i x_j u_i u_j}{(\Sigma x_i^2)^2}\right) = \frac{\Sigma x_i^2 E(u_i^2)}{(\Sigma x_i^2)^2} = k^2 \frac{\Sigma x_i^2 X_i^2}{(\Sigma x_i^2)^2}$$

given that in our model we assumed $E(u_i^2) = k^2 X_i^2$.

(2) The transformed version of the original model is

$$\frac{Y_i}{X_i} = b_1 + b_0 \frac{1}{X_i} + v_i$$

where $v_i = u_i/X_i$, with constant variance $\sigma_v^2 = k^2$. Applying least squares to the transformed model we obtain

$$\hat{b}_1 = \left(\overline{\frac{Y_i}{X_i}}\right) - \hat{b}_0 \left(\overline{\frac{1}{X_i}}\right)$$

and

$$\text{var}(\hat{\hat{b}}_1) = \sigma_v^2 \frac{\Sigma(1/X_i)^2}{n\Sigma\{(1/X_i)-\overline{(1/X_i)}\}^2} = k^2 \frac{\Sigma(1/X_i)^2}{n\Sigma\{(1/X_i)-\overline{(1/X_i)}\}^2}$$

Clearly $\text{var}(\hat{\hat{b}}_1) < \text{var}(\hat{b}_1)$

It should be noted that heteroscedasticity may be due to the omission of variables, that is to say the mis-specification of X's in the model, and not to mis-specification of the distribution of u. In this case the appropriate solution is the inclusion in the function of the omitted variables. The blind application of the transformation suggested above would make the random term homoscedastic, but the parameter estimates would still be wrong, due to the omission of the relevant explanatory variables. (For a formal discussion of the effects of the mis-specification of the variables see Chapter 11.)

For example, in a savings function heteroscedasticity may well be due to changes in various economic policies (monetary policy, tax reform, devaluation of the national currency). In this case the solution would be to introduce some variable in the savings function which would reflect the change in the government policy.

Example: Table 9.1 shows the personal savings and personal income of a country over a 31-year period.

Table 9.1 Personal savings and income (in £m)

Period	Savings S	Income X	Estimated savings (by OLS) $\hat{S} = \hat{b}_0 + \hat{b}_1 X$	OLS residuals $e_i = S_i - \hat{S}_i$	S/X (× 1,000)	1/X (× 10,000)
1	264	8,777	97·85	166·15	30·079	1·139
2	105	9,210	134·46	− 29·46	11·401	1·086
3	90	9,954	197·35	−107·35	9·042	1·005
4	131	10,508	244·18	−113·18	12·467	0·952
5	122	10,979	250·18	−128·18	11·112	0·911
6	107	11,912	362·87	−255·86	8·983	0·839
7	406	12,747	433·46	− 27·45	31·851	0·785
8	503	13,499	497·02	5·97	37·262	0·741
9	431	14,269	562·12	−131·12	30·205	0·701
10	588	15,522	668·04	− 80·04	37·882	0·644
11	898	16,730	770·15	127·84	53·676	0·598
12	950	17,663	849·03	100·97	53·785	0·566
13	779	18,575	926·12	−147·12	41·938	0·538
14	819	19,635	1015·73	−196·73	41·711	0·509
15	1,222	21,163	1144·90	77·10	57·742	0·473
16	1,702	22,880	1290·04	411·96	74·388	0·437
17	1,578	24,127	1395·45	182·54	65·404	0·414
18	1,654	25,604	1520·32	133·68	64·599	0·391
19	1,400	26,500	1596·06	−196·05	52·830	0·377
20	1,829	27,670,	1694·96	134·04	66·100	0·361
21	2,200	28,300	1748·22	451·78	77·739	0·353
22	2,017	27,430	1674·67	342·33	73·533	0·365
23	2,105	29,560	1854·73	250·27	71·211	0·338
24	1,600	28,150	1735·54	−135·54	56·838	0·355
25	2,250	32,100	2069·45	180·55	70·093	0·312
26	2,420	32,500	2103·26	316·74	74·462	0·308
27	2,570	35,250	2335·73	234·27	72·908	0·284
28	1,720	33,500	2187·80	−467·80	51·343	0·299
29	1,900	36,000	2399·14	−499·14	52·778	0·278
30	2,100	36,200	2416·04	−316·04	58·011	0·276
31	2,300	38,200	2585·11	−285·11	60·209	0·262

Applying OLS to the data of table 9.1 we obtain

$$\hat{S}_t = -644 \cdot 1 + 0 \cdot 085\, X_t$$

$$(117 \cdot 6)\ (0 \cdot 005) \qquad R^2 = 0 \cdot 903$$

Plotting the observations on a scatter diagram (figure 9.7) we observe a pattern of increasing dispersion of the savings at higher levels of income, which suggests that the u_i's are heteroscedastic

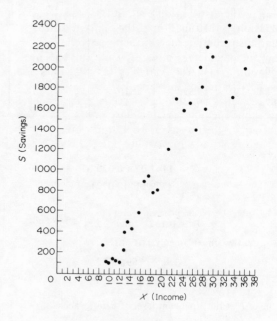

Figure 9.7

Test 1. The Goldfeld and Quandt test

The Goldfeld and Quandt test yields the following results..

We order the observation in ascending order of the X's, and omitting the nine central observations, we are left with two subsets of data, one with the lower values of X and one with the higher values of X. (Table 9.2)

Applying OLS to each subset we obtain
(a) For subset 1

$$\hat{S}_1 = -738 \cdot 84 + 0 \cdot 088\, X$$

$$(189 \cdot 4)\quad (0 \cdot 015)$$

with

$$R^2 = 0 \cdot 787 \quad \text{and} \quad \Sigma e_1^2 = 144{,}771 \cdot 5$$

Table 9.2

	Subset 1			Subset 2	
n_1	S	X_L	n_2	S_1	X_H
1	264	8,777	1	1,829	27,670
2	105	9,210	2	1,600	28,150
3	90	9,954	3	2,200	28,300
4	131	10,508	4	2,105	29,560
5	122	10,979	5	2,250	32,100
6	107	11,912	6	2,420	32,500
7	406	12,747	7	1,720	33,500
8	503	13,499	8	2,570	35,250
9	431	14,269	9	1,900	36,000
10	588	15,522	10	2,100	36,200
11	898	16,730	11	2,300	38.200

(b) For subset 2

$$\hat{S}_2 = 1141 \cdot 07 + 0 \cdot 029 \, X$$

$$(709 \cdot 8) \quad (0 \cdot 022)$$

with

$$R^2 = 0 \cdot 152 \quad \text{and} \quad \Sigma e_2^2 = 769{,}899 \cdot 2$$

We form the ratio of the two unexplained variations

$$F^* = \frac{\Sigma e_2^2}{\Sigma e_1^2} = \frac{769{,}899 \cdot 2}{144{,}771 \cdot 6} \approx 5$$

The theoretical value of F at the 5 per cent level of significance with

$$\nu_1 = \nu_2 = \frac{n - c - 2K}{2} = \frac{31 - 9 - (2)(2)}{2} = 9$$

degrees of freedom is $3 \cdot 18$. Given that $F^* > F_{0 \cdot 0 5}$ we reject the assumption of homoscedasticity.

Test 2. Spearman's rank correlation test

To apply this test we rank the X's and e's in ascending order. The rankings are shown in table 9.3.

The rank correlation coefficient estimated from the data of table 9.3 is

$$r' = 1 - \frac{6 \Sigma D^2}{n(n^2 - 1)} = 1 - \frac{(6)(1{,}474)}{(31)(31^2 - 1)} \cong 0 \cdot 703$$

The standard error of r' is $\dfrac{1}{\sqrt{n - 1}} = \dfrac{1}{\sqrt{30}} \cong 0 \cdot 14$, showing that the rank correlation is

statistically significant (see pp. 96–7).

Thus both tests suggest the existence of heteroscedasticity in the savings function.

Table 9.3

Rank of X	Rank of e	D	D^2
1	16	−15	225
2	3	− 1	1
3	7	− 4	16
4	8	− 4	16
5	10	− 5	25
6	23	−17	289
7	2	5	25
8	1	7	49
9	11	− 2	4
10	5	− 5	25
11	9	− 2	4
12	6	6	36
13	15	− 2	4
14	20	− 6	36
15	4	11	121
16	28	−12	144
17	18	− 1	1
18	12	6	36
19	19	0	0
21	13	8	64
23	29	− 6	36
20	27	− 7	49
24	22	2	4
22	14	8	64
25	17	8	64
26	26	0	0
28	21	7	49
27	30	− 3	9
29	31	− 2	4
30	25	5	25
31	24	7	49
			$D^2 = 1,474$

We assume that the pattern of heteroscedasticity is

$$\sigma_{u_i}^2 = k^2 X_i^2$$

so that the appropriate transformation of the original model is

$$\frac{S_t}{X_t} = b_0 \frac{1}{X_t} + \frac{u_t}{X_t}$$

The transformed variables (S_t/X_t and $1/X_t$) are shown in the last two columns on table 9.1. Applying OLS to the new variables we obtain

$$\frac{S_t}{X_t} = \hat{b}_0 \frac{1}{X_t} + \hat{b}_1 = -718 \cdot 88 \frac{1}{X_t} + 0 \cdot 088$$
$$(71 \cdot 27) \qquad (0 \cdot 004)$$

$$R^2 = 0 \cdot 770$$

The value of the Spearman correlation coefficient of the transformed equation is $r' = -0.22$. Its standard error of ≈ 0.14 shows that the transformation has eliminated heteroscedasticity.

Thus the new savings function is

$$S_t^* = -718.88 + 0.088\, X_t \quad R^2 = 0.770$$
$$(71.27)\ (0.004)$$

as compared with the old equation

$$S_t = -644.1 + 0.085\, X_t \quad R^2 = 0.903$$
$$(117.6)\ (0.005)$$

Note that the R^2 of the transformed model is lower than R^2 in the original model. This is due to the way in which weights are assigned to the individual observations in the transformation process.

9.4. THE ASSUMPTION OF NORMALITY OF u

The random variable u is assumed to have a normal distribution. Symbolically we may write

$$u \sim N(0, \sigma_u^2)$$

which reads: u is normally distributed around zero mean and constant (finite) variance σ_u^2. For each u_i there is a distribution of the above type. Thus we may depict the assumptions concerning the distribution of u on a diagram as shown in Figure 9.8.

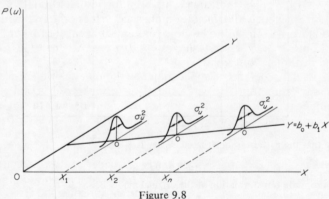

Figure 9.8

The meaning of the normality assumption is that small values of u have a higher probability to be observed than large values: extreme values of u are more and more unlikely the more extreme they get.[1]

---

[1] Recall that probabilities are areas under a curve. From figure 9.9, which depicts a normal distribution of a variable (u) whose mean value is zero, we see that the probability of u assuming the values between 1 and 2 is greater than the probability of u assuming the values between 4 and 5: obviously the area $[abcd] = P(1 < u < 2)$ is larger than the area $[efgh] = P(4 < u < 5)$.

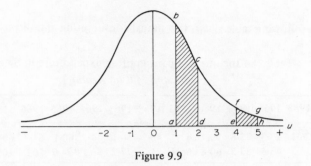

Figure 9.9

The assumption of normality is necessary for conducting the statistical tests of significance of the parameter estimates and for constructing confidence intervals. If this assumption is violated, the estimates $\hat{b}_0$ and $\hat{b}_1$ are still unbiased and best, but we cannot assess their statistical reliability by the classical tests of significance (t, F, etc.) because the latter are based on normal distributions.

However, even when the distribution is not normal, we can make use of the Central Limit Theorem (see Appendix I). According to this theorem even if the population is not normal, the sampling distribution of the mean tends to the normal distribution as the sample size n tends to ∞. At first sight even the Central Limit Theorem might seem not very helpful, since in practice n is not large. However, from applied research it has been found that a good approximation is generally obtained for quite small values of n. In practice the approximation has been found to be close for samples as small as 10 or 20. (See J. Thomas, *Notes on the Theory of Regression Analysis*, Athens 1964, Center of Planning and Economic Research.)

In any particular econometric application one should establish the plausibility of the normality assumption. However, the u's are not observable, and examination of the residuals e's, does not necessarily help, since the e's may be affected by mis-specification of the model and hence do not always reflect the true distribution of the u's. Thus econometricians tend, in general, either to ignore the implications of the normality assumption by implicitly assuming that the Central Limit Theorem applies in any particular case, or they attempt to rationalise the normality assumption on the following *a priori* grounds: u absorbs mainly influences of numerous unimportant variables and erratic elements in the human behaviour. Thus small values of u are more likely to appear in any particular period than large values, since it is more likely that the econometrician will make minor rather than major 'mistakes' when deciding which are the most important variables to be included in the function. This 'rationalisation' of course assumes that the important explanatory variables are included in the function. If some important variable is omitted due to mis-specification, or in order to avoid some other econometric implications (for example multi-collinearity), the values of u may not show the required normal distribution.

EXERCISES

1. The following table shows the annual consumption and disposal income of Sweden.

Table 9.4 Income and consumption expenditure in Sweden
(*Thousand Million Kronor*)

	1953	1955	1958	1960	1961	1962	1963	1964	1965	1966	1967	1968
$C_{(t)}$	26·1	29·3	35·6	39·4	42·7	46·3	50·1	54·5	60·1	64·9	69·2	73·1
$Y_{d(t)}$	38·3	43·5	53·5	60·8	66·4	71·2	77·2	86·1	94·6	102·4	109·9	115·6

(a) Estimate the savings function $S_t = f(Y_{d(t)})$.
(b) Test for heteroscedasticity using Spearman's rank correlation coefficient.
(c) Estimate from the sample data the form of heteroscedasticity.
(d) Re-estimate the savings function with an appropriately transformed model.

2. Suppose that $Y_t = b_0 + b_1 X_t + u_t$ describes the savings behaviour of a cross section of families and that low-income families have very similar and fairly stable spending habits, while high-income families have very different and versatile spending habits.

(a) Is the above equation appropriate for the estimation of the savings function?
(b) Discuss briefly alternative formulations of the savings function which would describe adequately the savings patterns of the families in the cross-section sample.

3. Summarise and compare critically the several tests for and corrective procedures associated with heteroscedasticity.

4. The data shown in table 9.5 show the rentals of flats in an area of London.
(a) Estimate the function for rentals

$$R = b_0 + b_1 X_1 + b_2 X_2 + u$$

(b) Test for heteroscedasticity with the Glejser test and with the Spearman's r'.
(c) Estimate from the sample data the form of heteroscedasticity and re-estimate the 'rentals' function with an appropriately transformed model.*

*Explore in particular the following schemes

(a) $|e| = a_0 + a_1 X_1 + v$
(b) $|e| = a_0 + a_1 X_1 + a_2 X_2 + v$
(c) $|e| = a_0 + a_1 X_1^2 + a_2 X_2^2 + v$
(d) $|e| = a_0 + a_1 X_2 + v$
(e) $|e| = a_0 + a_1 X_1^2 + v$

Table 9.5

n	Rent of flat = R (£)	Number of rooms per flat X_1	Central Heating X_2 H_i = 1 with central heating H_i = 0 without central heating
1	21·2	5	0
2	11·4	2	0
3	14·8	4	0
4	15·0	3	0
5	12·2	1	1
6	14·0	2	1
7	16·2	5	0
8	14·8	2	1
9	21·2	5	0
10	15·8	3	1
11	12·0	1	1
12	9·6	1	0
13	14·8	2	1
14	17·4	4	1
15	9·6	1	0
16	13·2	3	0
17	18·8	5	1
18	21·2	5	0
19	15·8	3	1
20	18·0	4	0

5. Using the data of table 9.1 test for heteroscedasticity using Glejser's test.

Note. Additional exercises are included in Appendix III.

10. Autocorrelation

10.1. THE MEANING OF THE ASSUMPTION OF SERIAL INDEPENDENCE

The fourth assumption of ordinary least squares is that the successive values of the random variable u are temporally independent, that is, that the value which u assumes in any one period is independent from the value which it assumed in any previous period. This assumption implies that the covariance of u_i and u_j is equal to zero

$$\text{cov}(u_i u_j) = E\{[u_i - E(u_i)]\,[u_j - E(u_j)]\}$$
$$= E(u_i u_j) = 0 \quad (\text{for } i \neq j)$$

given that by Assumption 2 $E(u_i) = E(u_j) = 0$.

If this assumption is not satisfied, that is, if the value of u in any particular period is correlated with its own preceding value (or values) we say that there is *autocorrelation* or *serial correlation* of the random variable.

It is convenient to change the subscripts of the u's and use $t, t-1, t-2$, etc. as subscripts, so as to show clearly the fact that we are at present concerned with the temporal dependence of the u's, their dependence through time. Thus we will write u_t for the value that u assumes in period t, u_{t-1} for the value of u in period $(t-1)$ and so on.

Autocorrelation is a special case of correlation. Autocorrelation refers to the relationship, not between two (or more) different variables, but between the successive values of the same variable. In this section we are particularly interested in the autocorrelation of the u's. However, autocorrelation may exist, and indeed it is a common phenomenon, in most economic variables. Thus we will treat autocorrelation of the u's in the same way as correlation in general.

Most of the standard econometric textbooks deal with the simple case of *linear* relationship between any two successive values of u

$$u_t = \rho u_{t-1} + v_t$$

This is known as a first-order autoregressive relationship (see below). We will begin our analysis with this form of simple relationship of the u's. In particular we will deal with the simple autocorrelation coefficient $\rho_{u_t u_{t-1}}$ (as a special form of the simple correlation coefficient ρ_{YX} developed in Chapter 3). Obviously $\rho_{u_t u_{t-1}}$ is subject to all the criticisms of the simple correlation coefficient cited in Chapter 3, for example $\rho_{u_t u_{t-1}}$ is not appropriate for non-linear relationships between u_t and u_{t-1}. Furthermore the simple $\rho_{u_t u_{t-1}}$ is not appropriate if the u's are related with more complex forms, with higher order autoregressive schemes. In a subsequent section we shall examine some solutions for such complex autoregressive structures.

We may obtain a rough idea of the existence or absence of autocorrelation in the u's by plotting the values of the regression residuals, e's, on a two-dimensional diagram, as we did in simple correlation theory for the variables X and Y. The e's are estimates of the true values of u; thus if the e's are correlated this suggests autocorrelation of the true u's. Drawing the scatter diagram of the e's we should bear in mind the following:

(1) The 'variables' whose correlation we attempt to detect in this case are e_t and e_{t-1} (or some other lagged value of e, for example e_{t-2}).

Variable I: e_t			Variable II: e_{t-1}		
e_{t+1}	or	(e_2)	e_t	or	(e_1)
e_{t+2}		(e_3)	e_{t+1}		(e_2)
e_{t+3}		(e_4)	e_{t+2}		(e_3)
.		.	.		.
.		.	.		.
.		.	.		.
$e_{t+(n-1)}$		(e_{n-1})	$e_{t+(n-2)}$		(e_{n-2})
e_{t+n}		(e_n)	$e_{t+(n-1)}$		(e_{n-1})

The observational points to be plotted are $e_t e_{t-1}$, or $(e_1, e_2), (e_2, e_3)$, $(e_3, e_4) \ldots (e_n, e_{n-1})$.

The mean of both 'variables' is zero $(\bar{e} = 0)$ by definition. Hence the perpendiculars which pass through the 'means' are actually the two orthogonal axes. By analogy to what we said in Chapter 3, it is clear that if most of the points (e_t, e_{t-1}) fall in quadrants I and III (figure 10.1), the autocorrelation will be positive, since the products $(e_t)(e_{t-1})$ are positive. If most of the points (e_t, e_{t-1}) fall in quadrants II and IV (figure 10.2), the autocorrelation will be negative, because the products $(e_t)(e_{t-1})$ are negative.

It is obvious that autocorrelation, as indeed the simple correlation between any two variables, may be positive or negative in theory. However, *in practice autocorrelation is in most cases positive*. The main reasons for this are economic growth and cyclical movements of the economy. Most economic variables tend to grow in periods of growth, or they tend to show cyclical patterns. (See Fox, *Economic Statistics*, p. 199.)

Another method commonly used in applied econometric research for the detection of autocorrelation is to plot the regression residuals, e's, against time. If the e's in successive periods show a regular time pattern (for example a sawtooth pattern, or a cyclical pattern) we conclude that there is autocorrelation in the function. In figures 10.3 and 10.4 we show hypothetical e's which are autocorrelated. In general if the successive (in subsequent time periods) values of the e's change sign frequently (figure 10.3) autocorrelation is negative. If the e's do not change sign frequently so that several positive e's are followed by several negative values of e (figure 10.4) autocorrelation is positive.

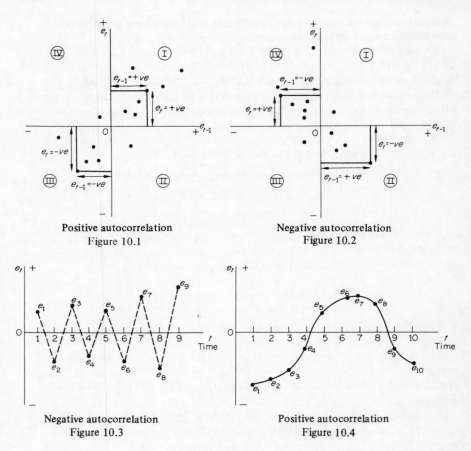

Positive autocorrelation
Figure 10.1

Negative autocorrelation
Figure 10.2

Negative autocorrelation
Figure 10.3

Positive autocorrelation
Figure 10.4

A measure of the first-order linear autocorrelation is provided by the auto-correlation coefficient

$$r_{e_t e_{t-1}} = \frac{\Sigma e_t e_{t-1}}{\sqrt{\Sigma e_t^2}\,\sqrt{\Sigma e_{t-1}^2}} = \hat{\rho}_{u_t u_{t-1}}$$

$r_{e_t e_{t-1}}$ is an estimate of the true autocorrelation coefficient $\rho_{u_t u_{t-1}}$ which measures the correlation of the true population of u's.

We will presently see that the test suggested by Durbin and Watson for auto-correlation reduces to the test of the statistical significance of the estimated autocorrelation coefficient ρ, that is we test whether $\rho = 0$ (see below).

Some definitions are appropriate at this stage. If the value of u in any particular period depends on its own value in the preceding period alone, we say that the u's follow a *first-order autoregressive scheme* (or *first-order Markov process*). The relationship between the u's is then of the form

$$u_t = f(u_{t-1})$$

If u depends on the values of the two previous periods, that is $u_t = f(u_{t-1}, u_{t-2})$, the form of autocorrelation is called a *second-order autoregressive scheme*, and so on. In most applied research it is assumed that, when autocorrelation is present, it is of the simple first-order form $u_t = f(u_{t-1})$ and more particularly

$$u_t = a_1 u_{t-1} + v_t$$

where a_1 = the coefficient of the autocorrelation relationship

v = a random variable satisfying all the usual assumptions

$$E(v) = 0 \qquad E(v^2) = \sigma_v^2 \qquad E(v_i v_j) = 0$$

Clearly this is the simplest possible form of autocorrelation: a linear relationship between u_t and u_{t-1} (with suppressed constant intercept). If we apply ordinary least squares to this relationship we obtain

$$\hat{a}_1 = \frac{\displaystyle\sum_{t=2}^{n} u_t u_{t-1}}{\displaystyle\sum_{t=2}^{n} u_{t-1}^2}$$

On the other hand the autocorrelation coefficient $\rho_{u_t u_{t-1}}$ is given by the formula

$$\rho_{u_t u_{t-1}} = \frac{\Sigma u_t u_{t-1}}{\sqrt{\Sigma u_t^2}\sqrt{\Sigma u_{t-1}^2}}$$

Given that for large samples $\Sigma u_t^2 \approx \Sigma u_{t-1}^2$, we may write

$$\rho \approx \frac{\Sigma u_t u_{t-1}}{\sqrt{(\Sigma u_{t-1}^2)^2}} = \frac{\Sigma u_t u_{t-1}}{\Sigma u_{t-1}^2}$$

Clearly $\rho \simeq \hat{a}_1$ for large samples. (See Kane, *Economic Statistics and Econometrics*, p. 366.) This is the reason why in most textbooks the simple first-order autoregressive model is given in the form

$$u_t = \rho u_{t-1} + v_t$$

where ρ = the first-order autocorrelation coefficient. Clearly if $\rho = 0$, $u_t = v_t$, that is u_t is not autocorrelated (given that by assumption v_t is not auto-correlated).

10.2. SOURCES OF AUTOCORRELATION

Autocorrelated values of the disturbance term u may be observed for many reasons.

1. *Omitted explanatory variables.* It is known that most economic variables tend to be autocorrelated. If an autocorrelated variable has been excluded from the set of explanatory variables, obviously its influence will be reflected in the random variable u, whose values will be autocorrelated. This case may be called 'quasi-autocorrelation' since it is due to the autocorrelated pattern of omitted explanatory variables (X's) and not to the behavioural pattern of the values of the true u. Of course, if several autocorrelated X's are omitted, u may not be autocorrelated, since the autocorrelation patterns of the omitted regressors may be such as to offset each other.

2. *Mis-specification of the mathematical form of the model.* If we have adopted a mathematical form which differs from the true form of the relationship, the u's may show serial correlation. For example if we have chosen a linear function while the true relationship between Y and the X's is of a cyclical form, the values of u will be temporally dependent.

3. *Interpolations in the statistical observations.* Most of the published time series data involve some interpolation and 'smoothing' processes which do average the true disturbances over successive time periods. As a consequence the successive values of the u are interrelated and exhibit autocorrelation patterns.

4. *Mis-specification of the true random term u.* It may well be expected in many cases for the successive values of the true u to be correlated. Thus even the purely random factors (wars, droughts, storms, strikes, etc.) exert influences that are spread over more than one period of time. For example a strike will have disruptive effects on the production process which will persist through several future periods. An exceptionally low cropping period in the agricultural sector, caused by abnormal weather conditions, will influence the performance of almost all other economic variables in several time periods; and so on. Such causes result in serially (temporally) dependent values of the disturbance term u, so that if we assume $E(u_i u_j) = 0$ we really mis-specify the true pattern of values of u. This case of autocorrelation may be called 'true autocorrelation' because its root lies in the u term itself.

It should be noted that the source of autocorrelation has a strong bearing on the solution which must be adopted for the 'correction' of the incidence of serial correlation. In other words the type of corrective action in each particular econometric application depends on the cause or source of autocorrelation. We will discuss this topic in a subsequent section.

10.3. PLAUSIBILITY OF THE ASSUMPTION OF NON-AUTOCORRELATED u's

From the discussion of the preceding paragraph it should be obvious that the assumption of temporal independence of the values of u can be easily violated in practice. Thus:

(a) Taking into account that in most applied econometric research only the most important (three or four) explanatory variables are included explicitly in the function, it is natural to expect that omitted variables are a frequent cause of 'quasi-autocorrelation'. In particular, if we use time series it is almost certain that some at least of these omitted variables will be serially correlated, since in economic life it is usual for the value of any variable in one particular period to be partly determined by its own value in the preceding period (or periods). For example output in period t depends on output in period $t - 1$; current income depends on past levels of income; investment decisions depend on past levels of investment; and so on. One can hardly think of any significant economic magnitude which is not somehow determined by the values which the same magnitude assumed in the past. Furthermore, in actual life, as we said, autocorrelation tends to be positive. If a disturbance (or an omitted variable) causes a positive u in period t, it is most probable that the u_{t+1} will also be positive. Similarly, if u assumes a negative value in t, the chances are that its value will be also negative in period $(t + 1)$.

(b) Interpolations and, in general, the customary data-collecting and processing techniques impart serial correlation in many aggregative time series.

(c) Random factors tend to persist in several time periods.

10.4. THE FIRST-ORDER AUTOREGRESSIVE SCHEME

In this section we will limit our analysis of the autocorrelation problem to the simple first-order autoregressive scheme, since most classical textbooks refer to this model as the most frequently assumed in applied econometric research. (In section 10.6 we will suggest a simple method for dealing with higher order autocorrelation structures.) We will first establish the mean, variance and covariance of u when its values are correlated with the simple Markov process. In this case the autoregressive structure is

$$u_t = \rho u_{t-1} + v_t \qquad \text{with } |\rho| < 1$$

where ρ = the coefficient of the autocorrelation relationship. [1]

v_t = a random term which fulfills all the usual assumptions of a random variable, that is,

$$E(v) = 0$$

$$E(v^2) = \sigma_v^2$$

$$E(v_i v_j) = 0 \qquad \text{(for } i \neq j)$$

The complete form of the first-order Markov process (the pattern of autocorrelation for all the values of u), is

$$u_t = f(u_{t-1}) = \rho u_{t-1} + v_t$$

$$u_{t-1} = f(u_{t-2}) = \rho u_{t-2} + v_{t-1}$$

$$u_{t-2} = f(u_{t-3}) = \rho u_{t-3} + v_{t-2}$$

$$\cdot \qquad \cdot \qquad \cdot \qquad \cdot$$

$$\cdot \qquad \cdot \qquad \cdot \qquad \cdot$$

$$\cdot \qquad \cdot \qquad \cdot \qquad \cdot$$

$$u_{t-r} = f(u_{t-(r+1)}) = \rho u_{t-(r+1)} + v_{t-r}$$

[1] ρ is also approximately equal to the first-order autocorrelation coefficient $\rho_{u_t u_{t-1}}$. See page 203.

In order to define the error term in any particular period t we work as follows. We start from the autocorrelation relationship in period t

$$u_t = \rho u_{t-1} + v_t$$

and we perform continuous substitutions of the lagged values of u, as follows. Substitute u_{t-1} and obtain

$$u_t = \rho\left[\rho u_{t-2} + v_{t-1}\right] + v_t = \rho^2 u_{t-2} + (\rho v_{t-1} + v_t)$$

Substitute u_{t-2} and obtain

$$u_t = \rho^2\left[\rho u_{t-3} + v_{t-2}\right] + (\rho v_{t-1} + v_t)$$
$$= \rho^3 u_{t-3} + (\rho^2 v_{t-2} + \rho v_{t-1} + v_t)$$

Substitute u_{t-3} and obtain

$$u_t = \rho^3\left[\rho u_{t-4} + v_{t-3}\right] + (\rho^2 v_{t-2} + \rho v_{t-1} + v_t)$$
$$= \rho^4 u_{t-4} + (\rho^3 v_{t-3} + \rho^2 v_{t-2} + \rho v_{t-1} + v_t)$$

If we continue the substitution process for r periods (where r is large) we find

$$u_t = v_t + \rho v_{t-1} + \rho^2 v_{t-2} + \rho^3 v_{t-3} + \ldots$$

(given that as the power of ρ increases to infinity the term with the lagged u, $\rho^r u_{t-r}$, tends to zero, since $|\rho| < 1$).

Thus

$$u_t = \sum_{r=0}^{\infty} \rho^r v_{t-r}$$

This is the value of the error term when it is autocorrelated with a first-order autoregressive scheme.

We will next establish the mean, variance and covariance of this autocorrelated disturbance variable.

1. *Mean of the autocorrelated* u's

$$E(u_t) = E \sum_{r=0}^{\infty} \rho^r v_{t-r} = \sum_{r=0}^{\infty} \rho^r \cdot E(v_{t-r})$$

But by the assumptions of the distribution of v we have

$$E(v_{t-r}) = 0$$

Therefore $E(u_t) = 0 \qquad (t = 1, 2, \ldots, n)$

2. *Variance of the autocorrelated u's*

By the definition of the variance we have

$$E(u_t^2) = E\left[\sum_{r=0}^{\infty} \rho^r v_{t-r}\right]^2$$

$$= \Sigma(\rho^r)^2 E(v_{t-r})^2$$

$$= \Sigma(\rho^r)^2 \ \text{var}(v_{t-r})$$

$$= \Sigma\rho^{2r}\sigma_v^2$$

$$= \sigma_v^2(1 + \rho^2 + \rho^4 + \rho^6 + \ldots)$$

The expression in brackets is the sum of a geometric progression of infinite terms, whose first term is unity and the common ratio is ρ^2. The progression converges since $|\rho| < 1$. Thus, taking the sum of the geometric progression,[1] we have

$$E(u_t^2) = \sigma_v^2\left[\frac{1}{1 - \rho^2}\right] \qquad (\text{for } |\rho| < 1)$$

or

$$\text{var}_{(u_t)} = \frac{\sigma_v^2}{1 - \rho^2}$$

3. *The covariance of the autocorrelated u's*

Given that

$$u_t = v_t + \rho v_{t-2} + \rho^2 v_{t-2} + \ldots$$

and

$$u_{t-1} = v_{t-1} + \rho v_{t-2} + \rho^2 v_{t-3} + \ldots$$

we obtain:

$$\text{cov}(u_t u_{t-1}) = E\{[u_t - E(u_t)]\ [u_{t-1} - E(u_{t-1})]\} = E[u_t u_{t-1}]$$

$$= E[(v_t + \rho v_{t-1} + \rho^2 v_{t-2} + \ldots)(v_{t-1} + \rho v_{t-2} + \rho^2 v_{t-3} + \ldots)]$$

$$= E[\{v_t + \rho(v_{t-1} + \rho v_{t-2} + \ldots)\}\ (v_{t-1} + \rho v_{t-2} + \rho^2 v_{t-3} + \ldots)]$$

$$= E[(v_t)(v_{t-1} + \rho v_{t-2} + \rho^2 v_{t-3} + \ldots)] + E[\rho(v_{t-1} + \rho v_{t-2} + \ldots)^2]$$

$$= 0 + \rho E(v_{t-1} + \rho v_{t-2} + \ldots)^2$$

$$= \rho E(v_{t-1}^2 + \rho^2 v_{t-2}^2 + \ldots + \text{cross products})$$

[1] The sum of n terms of a geometric progression is given by the formula

$$S = \frac{a(1 - \lambda^n)}{1 - \lambda}$$

where: a = the first term of the geometric progression

λ = the common ratio.

For infinite series ($n \to \infty$), where $|\lambda| < 1$, the formula reduces to $S = \frac{a}{1 - \lambda}$.

$$= \rho(\sigma_v^2 + \rho^2 \sigma_v^2 + \ldots + 0)$$

$$= \rho[\sigma_v^2(1 + \rho^2 + \rho^4 + \rho^6 + \ldots)] = \rho\sigma_v^2 \frac{1}{1 - \rho^2} \qquad (\text{for } |\rho| < 1)$$

$$= \rho\sigma_u^2$$

Similarly, $\text{cov}(u_t u_{t-2}) = E(u_t u_{t-2}) = \rho^2 \sigma_u^2$ and in general

$$\text{cov}(u_t u_{t-s}) = \rho^s \cdot \sigma_u^2 \qquad (\text{for } s \neq t)$$

Summarising the above discussion we conclude that when there is auto-correlation of the simple form of first-order autoregressive scheme, the auto-correlated disturbance term has the following characteristics

$$u_t = \sum_{r=0}^{\infty} \rho^r v_{t-r}$$

$$E(u_t) = 0$$

$$\text{var}(u_t) = \sigma_v^2 \frac{1}{1 - \rho^2} = \sigma_u^2$$

$$\text{cov}(u_t u_{t-s}) = \rho^s \cdot \sigma_u^2 \neq 0$$

where v is the random term and ρ is the autocorrelation coefficient in the first-order autoregressive scheme

$$u_t = \rho u_{t-1} + v_t$$

The above properties will be used presently in establishing the consequences of autocorrelation.

10.5. CONSEQUENCES OF AUTOCORRELATION

When the disturbance term exhibits serial correlation the value as well as the standard errors of the parameter estimates are affected. In particular:

(1) The estimates of the parameters do not have the statistical bias defined in Chapter 6. In other words, even when the residuals are serially correlated the parameter estimates of OLS are statistically unbiased, in the sense that their expected value is equal to the true parameters.

In Chapter 5 we established that

$$\hat{b}_1 = b_1 + \frac{\Sigma x_i u_i}{\Sigma x^2}$$

Taking expected values we obtain

$$E(\hat{b}_1) = b_1 + \Sigma x_i E(u_i)/\Sigma x_i^2$$

Recalling that the statistical bias was defined (in Chapter 6) as the difference between the expected value of the estimate and the true parameter, we have

$$\text{bias in } \hat{b}_1 = E(\hat{b}_1) - b_1 = \frac{\Sigma x_i E(u_i)}{\Sigma x_i^2}$$

But we found that the expected value of the random term u, even when autocorrelated, is zero:

$$E(u_t) = 0$$

Hence

$$\text{bias in } \hat{b}_1 = 0$$

Thus, irrespective of whether the residuals are serially independent or not, the estimates of the parameters have no statistical bias, so long as the u's and X's are uncorrelated.

(2) With autocorrelated values of the disturbance term *the OLS variances of the parameter estimates are likely to be larger than those of other econometric methods.*

We will prove that the OLS variance of the estimate $\hat{b}_1$ is larger when the u's are positively autocorrelated, and the values of X are also positively autocorrelated. These conditions are often met in the real economic world.

It can be shown that the variance of the least squares estimate $\hat{b}_1$ is given by the formula

$$\text{var}(\hat{b}_1) = \Sigma \left[\frac{x_i}{\Sigma x_i^2}\right]^2 E(u_i^2) + 2\Sigma \frac{x_i x_j}{(\Sigma x^2)^2} E(u_i u_j)$$

When the u's are serially independent $E(u_i u_j) = 0$ and the last term disappears, so that the variance of $\hat{b}_1$ becomes

$$\text{var}(\hat{b}_1) = \frac{\sigma_u^2}{\Sigma x^2}$$

However, with u's related with a first-order autoregressive scheme we have

$$E(u_t^2) = \sigma_u^2$$

and

$$E(u_t u_{t-s}) = \rho^s \sigma_u^2$$

Therefore

$$\text{var}(\hat{b}_1) = \sigma_u^2 \frac{1}{\Sigma x_i^2} + 2\sigma_u^2 \Sigma \frac{x_i x_j}{(\Sigma x_i^2)^2} \rho^s$$

Expanding the second term we obtain the following result for the variance of $\hat{b}_1$ when there is autocorrelation in the function

$$\text{var}(\hat{b}_1) = \frac{\sigma_u^2}{\Sigma x^2} + 2\sigma_u^2 \left[\rho \frac{\sum\limits^{n-1} x_i x_{i+1}}{\left(\sum\limits_{i}^{n} x^2\right)^2} + \rho^2 \frac{\sum\limits^{n-2} x_i x_{i+2}}{\left(\sum\limits_{i}^{n} x^2\right)^2} + \ldots\right]$$

$$= \frac{\sigma_u^2}{\Sigma x^2} \left[1 + 2\rho \cdot \frac{\sum\limits^{n-1} x_i x_{i+1}}{\sum\limits_{i}^{n} x^2} + 2\rho^2 \frac{\sum\limits^{n-2} x_i x_{i+2}}{\sum\limits_{i}^{n} x^2} + \ldots + 2\rho^{n-1} \frac{x_i x_n}{\sum\limits_{i}^{n} x_i^2}\right]$$

If we compare the two variances of $\hat{b}_1$ (for non-autocorrelation and for serially dependent u's) we see that the simple least squares variance does not take into account the terms in parentheses.

If ρ is positive and if the successive values of X (in consecutive time periods) are positively autocorrelated, the expression in parentheses is almost certainly greater than unity, and hence the true variance of $\hat{b}_1$ will be larger than the simple formula $\text{var}(\hat{b}_1) = \sigma_u^2/\Sigma x_i^2$ implies. In other words we are in a situation whence autocorrelation causes the *actual* (*true*) variance of $\hat{b}_1$ to increase, while the *estimate* of this variance (from the application of the above simple formula) will be smaller: the simple OLS formula will underestimate the true variance of $\hat{b}_1$. Furthermore, as we will see in the next paragraph, the OLS residuals will underestimate the variance of the error term (i.e. σ_u^2 will be underestimated from the OLS expression $\Sigma e^2/(n-2)$) and this will be an additional source of underestimation of the true variance of the parameter estimate $\hat{b}_1$.

(3) *The variance of the random term u* may be seriously underestimated if the u's are autocorrelated. In particular, the underestimation of the variance of u will be more serious in the case of positive autocorrelation of the error term (u_t) and of positively autocorrelated values of X (in successive time periods). To see how the underestimation of $\text{var}(u)$ occurs, recall that (p. 79) we established that if there is no autocorrelation

$$E(\Sigma e^2) = (n-2)\sigma_u^2 \qquad \text{or} \qquad \hat{\sigma}_u^2 = \Sigma e^2/(n-2)$$

If we assume a first-order autoregressive scheme, it can be shown that

$$E(\Sigma e^2) = \sigma_u^2 \left\{ n - 2 - \left(2\rho \cdot \frac{\sum\limits_{i=1}^{n-1} x_i x_{i+1}}{\sum\limits_{i=1}^{n} x_i^2} + 2\rho^2 \cdot \frac{\sum\limits_{i=1}^{n-2} x_i x_{i+2}}{\sum\limits_{i=1}^{n} x_i^2} + \ldots + 2\rho^{n-1} \cdot \frac{x_i x_n}{\sum\limits_{i=1}^{n} x_i^2} \right) \right\}$$

(See J. Johnston, *Econometric Methods*, 2nd edition, McGraw-Hill, 1972, p. 248.) If both u and X are positively autocorrelated, then the OLS formula $(\Sigma e^2/(n-2))$ will most likely underestimate σ_u^2, because it would ignore the expression in parentheses which is almost certainly positive.

Note that if X is not autocorrelated, but is approximately random, then, even if u is autocorrelated $(\rho \neq 0)$, the bias in $\text{var}(u)$ and in $\text{var}(\hat{b}_i)$ is not likely to be serious. In the real world, however, the successive values of most explanatory variables $(X$'s) are positively autocorrelated, and this would tend to underestimation (sometimes substantial) of the variance of u and of the variance of the estimates of the b's if OLS were applied. The underestimation of σ_u^2 is shown in figures 10.5 and 10.6.

In both figures we show hypothetical sample observations, a true relationship, $E(Y) = b_0 + b_1 X$, and an OLS regression line $\hat{Y} = \hat{b}_0 + \hat{b}_1 X$. In both diagrams we assumed that the explanatory variable is positively autocorrelated (X_t and X_{t-1} are presumed to be positively related). In figure 10.5 we see that the fact that the first value, u_1, of the true positively autocorrelated error term u happened to be large and positive resulted in the cluster of the sample observations above

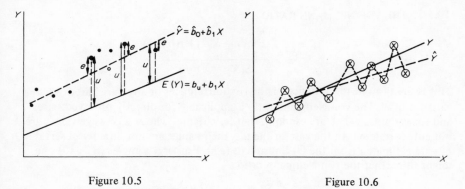

Figure 10.5   Figure 10.6

the true relation. (If the first disturbance term had been negative, the sample observations would tend to lie below the true relation.) By fitting the OLS regression line to these observations, the variance of u would be underestimated: in figure 10.5 the e's are closer to the regression line than are the u's to the true line, and thus we would have a serious underestimation of σ_u^2. In figure 10.6 the sawtooth pattern of the residuals suggests the presence of negative autocorrelation. In this case the alternation of positive and negative values of e's (and u's) makes it less likely to underestimate σ_u^2. (See E. Kane, *Economic Statistics and Econometrics*, p. 369.)

In summary. Autocorrelated errors can be much higher in the series of u's than for e's. This is important in small single samples, with which we are dealing in applied econometric research. In repeated sampling or in very large samples, deviations caused by signs and magnitudes of the initial values of the random term should cancel out, so that $E(b_i) = \hat{b}_i$ despite the presence of autocorrelation.

(4) Finally, if the values of u are autocorrelated, the predictions based on ordinary least squares estimates will be inefficient, in the sense that they will have a larger variance as compared with predictions based on estimates obtained from other econometric techniques. The variance of the forecast will be developed in Chapter 20. We will see that this variance depends on the variances of the coefficient estimates and the variance of u. Since these variances are not minimal as compared with other techniques (for example GLS), the standard error of the forecast (from OLS) will not have the least value, due to autocorrelated u's.

10.6. TESTS FOR AUTOCORRELATION

We said that some rough idea of the existence and the pattern of autocorrelation may be gained by plotting the regression residuals either against their own lagged value(s), or against time.

However, there are more accurate tests for the incidence of autocorrelation. The traditionally applied tests are the von Neumann ratio and the Durbin—Watson test.

10.6.1. THE VON NEUMANN RATIO

$$\frac{\delta^2}{s_x^2} = \frac{\sum\limits_{t=2}^{n}(X_t - X_{t-1})^2/(n-1)}{\Sigma(X_t - \bar{X})^2/n}$$

This is the ratio of the variance of the first differences of any variable X over the variance of X. The von Neumann ratio is applicable for directly observed series and for variables which are random, that is, variables whose successive values are not autocorrelated. In the case of the u's, their values are not directly observable but are estimated from the OLS residuals (e's). For large samples ($n > 30$) one might think that the von Neumann ratio

$$\frac{\delta^2}{s_e^2} = \frac{\sum\limits_{i=2}^{n}(e_t - e_{t-1})^2/(n-1)}{\sum\limits_{i=1}^{n}(e_t - \bar{e})^2/n}$$

could be applied approximately (with $\bar{e} = 0$ by definition). However, this is not possible because the values of the OLS residuals (e's) are not independently distributed, even if the population u_t's are independently distributed. Hence this test is not applicable for testing the autocorrelation of the u's, especially if the sample is small ($n < 30$). Thus we will not develop this test further. The interested reader is referred to K. A. Fox, *Intermediate Economic Statistics,* Chapter 6, pp. 193–199.

10.6.2. THE DURBIN–WATSON TEST

(J. Durbin and G. S. Watson, 'Testing for Serial Correlation in Least-squares Regression', two articles in *Biometrica* 1950 and 1951.)

Durbin and Watson have suggested a test which is applicable to small samples. However the test is appropriate only for the first-order autoregressive scheme ($u_t = \rho u_{t-1} + v_t$). The test may be outlined as follows.

The null hypothesis is

$$H_0 : \rho = 0$$

or H_0 : the u's are not autocorrelated with a first-order scheme.
This hypothesis is tested against the alternative hypothesis

$$H_1 : \rho \neq 0$$

or H_1 : the u's are autocorrelated with a first-order scheme.

To test the null hypothesis we use the Durbin–Watson statistic

$$d = \frac{\sum\limits_{t=2}^{n}(e_t - e_{t-1})^2}{\sum\limits_{t=1}^{n}e_t^2}$$

It can be shown that the values of d lie between 0 and 4, and that when $d = 2$ then $\rho = 0$. Thus, testing $H_0: \rho = 0$ is equivalent to testing $H_0: d = 2$.
Expanding the d statistic we obtain

$$d = \frac{\sum\limits_{t=2}^{n} (e_t - e_{t-1})^2}{\sum\limits_{t=1}^{n} e_t^2} = \frac{\sum\limits_{t=2}^{n} (e_t^2 + e_{t-1}^2 - 2e_t e_{t-1})}{\sum\limits_{t=1}^{n} e_t^2}$$

$$d = \frac{\sum\limits_{t=2}^{n} e_t^2 + \sum\limits_{t=2}^{n} e_{t-1}^2 - 2\sum\limits_{t=2}^{n} e_t e_{t-1}}{\sum\limits_{t=1}^{n} e_t^2}.$$

But for large samples the terms

$$\sum\limits_{t=2}^{n} e_t^2 \quad \sum\limits_{t=2}^{n} e_{t-1}^2 \quad \text{and} \quad \sum\limits_{t=1}^{n} e_t^2$$

are approximately equal. Therefore we may write

$$d \approx \frac{2\Sigma e_{t-1}^2}{\Sigma e_{t-1}^2} - \frac{2\Sigma e_t e_{t-1}}{\Sigma e_{t-1}^2}$$

$$d \approx 2\left(1 - \frac{\Sigma e_t e_{t-1}}{\Sigma e_{t-1}^2}\right)$$

But

$$\frac{\Sigma e_t e_{t-1}}{\Sigma e_{t-1}^2} = \hat{\rho}$$

Therefore

$$d \approx 2(1 - \hat{\rho})$$

From this expression it is obvious that the values of d lie between 0 and 4.

Firstly. If there is no autocorrelation $\hat{\rho} = 0$ and $d = 2$. Thus if from the sample data we find $d^* \approx 2$ we accept that there is no autocorrelation in the function.

Secondly. If $\hat{\rho} = +1$, $d = 0$ and we have perfect positive autocorrelation. Therefore if $0 < d^* < 2$ there is some degree of positive autocorrelation, which is stronger the closer d^* is to zero.

Thirdly. If $\hat{\rho} = -1, d = 4$ and we have perfect negative autocorrelation. Therefore if $2 < d^* < 4$ there is some degree of negative autocorrelation, which is
stronger the higher the value of d^*.

It should be clear that in the Durbin–Watson test the null hypothesis of zero
autocorrelation ($\rho = 0$) is carried out indirectly, by testing the equivalent
hypothesis $d = 2$.

The next step is to use the sample residuals (e_t's) and compute the empirical
value of the Durbin–Watson statistic, d^*. Finally, the empirical d^* must be
compared with the theoretical values of d; that is, the values of d which define
the critical region of the test. The problem with this test is that the exact
distribution of d is not known. However, Durbin and Watson have established
upper (d_u) and lower (d_L) limits for the significance levels of d which are
appropriate to test the hypothesis of zero first-order autocorrelation against the
alternative hypothesis of *positive* first-order autocorrelation. Durbin and Watson
have tabulated these upper and lower values at the 5 per cent and the 1 per cent
level of significance. The Durbin–Watson tables are reproduced on pp. 665–6
of Appendix IV.[1] The tables assume that the u's are normal, homoscedastic, and
not autocorrelated, and that the X's are truly exogenous. As usual n is the sample
size, while k' is the number of exogenous explanatory variables in the equation
being estimated.

The test itself compares the empirical d^* value, calculated from the regression
residuals, with the d_L and d_u in the Durbin–Watson tables, and with their transforms $(4 - d_L)$ and $(4 - d_u)$. The comparison using d_L and d_u investigates the
possibility of *positive* autocorrelation, which comparison with $(4 - d_L)$ and
$(4 - d_u)$ investigates the possibility of *negative* autocorrelation:

1. If $d^* < d_L$ we reject the null hypothesis of no autocorrelation and accept
   that there is positive autocorrelation of the first order.
2. If $d^* > (4 - d_L)$ we reject the null hypothesis of no autocorrelation and
   accept that there is *negative* autocorrelation of the first order.
3. If $d_u < d^* < (4 - d_u)$ we accept the null hypothesis of no autocorrelation.
4. If $d_L < d^* < d_u$ or if $(4 - d_u) < d^* < (4 - d_L)$ the test is inconclusive.

---

[1] The Durbin–Watson d statistic is related to the von Neumann ratio by the relationship

$$d = \left(\frac{\delta^2}{s^2}\right)\left(\frac{n-1}{n}\right).$$

Because from the von Neumann ratio we obtain

$$\frac{\delta^2}{s^2}\frac{n-1}{n} = \sum_{t=2}^{n}(e_t - e_{t-1})^2 \Big/ \sum_{t=1}^{n} e_t^2 = d.$$

For large n we have $n \approx n - 1$, and thus d tends to the von Neumann ratio asymptotically.

The critical regions of the d test are shown in figure 10.7.

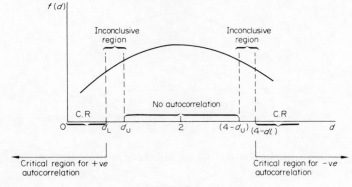

Figure 10.7

The Durbin–Watson test has several shortcomings. Firstly, the d statistic is not an appropriate measure of autocorrelation if among the explanatory variables there are lagged values of the endogenous variable. This problem will be discussed in Chapter 14, in connection with the lagged-variable models. Secondly, the range of values of d over which the Durbin–Watson test is inconclusive $(d_L < d^* < d_U$ and $(4 - d_U) < d^* < (4 - d_L))$ has been a drawback to its application. Various writers,[1] including Durbin himself,[2] have suggested alternative tests for serial correlation, which are more accurate and more power-ful than the Durbin–Watson test. However, these tests are invariably more complicated and costly in computations. Furthermore, some of them are based on stronger assumptions. Given the shortcomings of the alternative tests several econometricians have followed the practice of applying the Durbin–Watson test in the following amended form:

Reject the null hypothesis $(H_0: \rho = 0)$ if $d^* < d_U$ or $d^* > (4 - d_U)$
Accept the null hypothesis if $d_U < d^* < (4 - d_U)$

In the amended test the rejection (critical) region includes not only the values of $d < d_L$ and $d > (4 - d_L)$ but also the inconclusive values in the original Durbin–Watson test (figure 10.8). The above amendment of the original Durbin–Watson test is inaccurate, because the levels of significance of the original test are certainly affected by extending the rejection region over the range of the inconclusive d values. The amendment, however, may be justified

[1] See H. Theil and A. L. Nagar, 'Testing the Independence of Regression Disturbances', *J. Am. Statist. Ass.*, vol. 56, 1961, pp. 793–806. See also R. C. Henshaw, Jr., 'Testing Single-equation Least-squares Regression Models for Autocorrelated Disturbances', *Econometrica*, vol. 34, 1966, pp. 646–60.
[2] J. Durbin, 'An Alternative to the Bounds Test for Testing for Serial Correlation in Least-squares Regression', *Econometrica*, vol. 38, 1970, pp. 422–9.

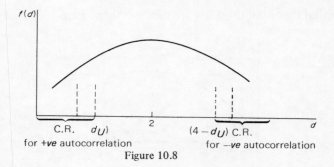

Figure 10.8

on the grounds of the seriousness of the effects of autocorrelation. To quote
Professor J. Johnston[1]

Amending the Durbin–Watson test to reject the null hypothesis if $d < d_U$ is only a rough
and ready procedure, which is not to be recommended in general since the exact significance
level of the test will almost certainly differ from the nominal 5 per cent or 1 per cent being
used. However, since the consequences of incorrectly accepting the null hypothesis in this
case are so much more serious than those of incorrectly rejecting it, one might have a
preference for rejecting the null hypothesis in cases of doubt.

Thirdly, the Durbin–Watson test is inappropriate for testing for higher order
serial correlation or for other forms of autocorrelation (e.g. nonlinear forms of
serial dependence of the values u_t).

10.6.3. *An Alternative Test for Autocorrelation*

The use of the following test is suggested for testing for autocorrelation. It has
the advantage that it is applicable to any form of autocorrelation and it provides
estimates of the coefficients of the autocorrelation relationship, which are
required for the remedial transformations of the original observations (see below).
We first apply OLS to the sample observations and obtain the values of the
regression residuals, e_t's. Since we cannot be *a priori* certain about the existence
of autocorrelation or about its pattern, we may experiment with various forms
of autoregressive structures, for example

$$e_t = \rho e_{t-1} + v_t$$

or

$$e_t = \rho e_{t-1}^2 + v_t$$

or

$$e_t = \rho_1 e_{t-1} + \rho_2 e_{t-2} + v_t$$

or

$$e_t = \rho \sqrt{e_{t-1}} + v_t$$

and so on.

Autocorrelation is judged in the light of the statistical significance of the $\hat{\rho}(s)$
and the overall fit of the above regression. That is, we may carry out any one of

[1] See J. Johnston, *Econometric Methods,* 2nd edn., p. 258.

the standard tests of statistical significance for the estimates ($\hat{\rho}$'s) of the auto-correlation relationship (e.g. $t = \hat{\rho}_i/s_{(\hat{\rho}_i)}$) as well as an F test for the overall signi-cance of the regression. If the $\hat{\rho}$'s are found statistically significant we accept that the u's are autocorrelated, provided that the overall correlation coefficient (for the autoregressive relationship) is statistically significant and reasonably large.

This test does not have the power properties of the Durbin—Watson test in finite samples, but is asymptotically equivalent.

10.7. SOLUTIONS FOR THE CASE OF AUTOCORRELATION

The solution to be adopted in each particular case depends on the source of autocorrelation. Thus if the source is omitted variables, the appropriate procedure is to include these variables in the set of explanatory variables. We may illustrate the occurrence of quasi-autocorrelation with the 'ratchet effect' in a consumption function. Consumption in period t depends not only on current income (X_t), but also on the level of income in previous periods. In its simplest form this type of consumption function may be written as follows

$$C_t = b_0 + b_1 X_t + b_2 X_{t-1} + u_t$$

If lagged income is omitted, its influence will be reflected in the random term u_t (and probably in the coefficient of current income, which will be biased). Since the successive values of income are usually positively autocorrelated, omission of X_{t-1} will result in a pattern of quasi-autocorrelated u's. Autocorrelation would be eliminated in this case by introducing into the function explicitly lagged income as an explanatory variable of current consumption.

The simplest way to detect whether autocorrelation is due to omitted variables is to regress the residuals, e's, against variables which on *a priori* grounds might be relevant explanatory variables of the phenomenon being studied.

Similarly, if the source of autocorrelation is the mis-specification of the mathematical form of the relationship the relevant approach is to change the initial (linear) form. This can be investigated by regressing the residuals against higher powers of the explanatory variable(s), or by computing a 'linear in logs' form and re-examining the resulting new residuals, etc.

Only when the above sources of autocorrelation have been ruled out should we accept that the true u's are temporally dependent. For this case (of true auto-correlation) the appropriate procedure is the transformation of the original data so as to produce a model whose random variable satisfies the assumptions of classical least squares, and consequently the parameters can be optimally estimated with this method. We will illustrate the procedure starting from the simple first-order autoregressive scheme.

Once autocorrelation is detected by applying any relevant test, the appropriate corrective procedure is to obtain an estimate of the ρ's and apply OLS to a set of transformed data. The transformation of the original data depends on the pattern of the autoregressive structure.

First-order autoregressive scheme

If autocorrelation is of the first-order scheme

$$u_t = \rho u_{t-1} + v_t$$

the appropriate transformation is to subtract from the original observations of each period the product of $\hat{\rho}$ times the value of the variables in the previous period.[1] That is we apply OLS to the model

$$Y_t^* = b_0 + b_1 X_{1t}^* + \ldots + b_k X_{kt}^* + v_t$$

where

$$Y_t^* = Y_t - \hat{\rho} Y_{t-1}$$

$$X_{jt}^* = X_{jt} - \hat{\rho} X_{j(t-1)} \qquad (j = 1, 2, \ldots, k)$$

$$v_t = u_t - \rho u_{t-1}$$

Rationalisation of the transformation procedure

The above transformation is obtained as follows.
The original model is

$$Y_t = b_0 + b_1 X_{1t} + b_2 X_{2t} + \ldots + b_k X_{kt} + u_t$$

where

$$u_t = \rho u_{t-1} + v_t$$

with v_t satisfying all the assumptions of a random variable.
The relationship for the period $t - 1$ is

$$Y_{t-1} = b_0 + b_1 X_{1(t-1)} + b_2 X_{2(t-1)} + \ldots + b_k X_{k(t-1)} + u_{t-1}$$

Premultiplying this equation by ρ we get

$$\rho Y_{t-1} = \rho b_0 + b_1 \rho X_{1(t-1)} + b_2 \rho X_{2(t-1)} + \ldots + b_k \rho X_{k(t-1)} + \rho u_{t-1}$$

Subtracting from the original relationship we obtain

$$[Y_t - \rho Y_{t-1}] = b_0(1 - \rho) + b_1[X_{1(t)} - \rho X_{1(t-1)}] + $$
$$ + \ldots + b_k[X_{k(t)} - \rho X_{k(t-1)}] + (u_t - \rho u_{t-1}).$$

The new error term $u_t - \rho u_{t-1}$ is equal to v_t and hence is *ex hypothesi* a random

[1] This procedure is equivalent to the application of an econometric technique which is known as Aitken's Generalised Least Squares. This method has been briefly discussed on pp. 183–4 and is further developed in Chapter 19.

uncorrelated variable. Consequently, if we know ρ we can apply ordinary least squares to the transformed relationship.

$$Y^* = b_0 + b_1 X_1^* + b_2 X_2^* + \ldots + b_k X_k^* + u_t^*$$

where

$$Y^* = Y_t - \rho Y_{t-1}$$
$$X_1^* = X_{1(t)} - \rho X_{1(t-1)}$$
$$X_2^* = X_{2(t)} - \rho X_{2(t-1)}$$

$$\begin{matrix} \cdot & \cdot & \cdot \\ \cdot & \cdot & \cdot \\ \cdot & \cdot & \cdot \end{matrix}$$

$$X_k^* = X_{k(t)} - \rho X_{k(t-1)}$$
$$u_t^* = u_t - \rho u_{t-1} = v_t.$$

Note that with the above transformation we are able to retain in our analysis only $n - 1$ observations since we loose one observation in the process. To avoid this loss, K. R. Kadiyala[1] has suggested the following transformation of the first observation

$$Y_1^* = Y_1 \sqrt{1 - \rho^2}$$
$$X_{j1}^* = X_{j1} \sqrt{1 - \rho^2} \quad (j = 1, 2, \ldots, k)$$

Higher order autoregressive schemes

The Durbin and Watson test is not intended to be used for testing for higher order lag structures of the disturbance term. However, such structures can be tested by the procedure developed in section 10.6.3, that is by conducting the traditional (t, standard error, F) tests of significance for the ρ's of the higher-order autoregressive model(s)

$$e_t = \rho_1 e_{t-1} + \rho_2 e_{t-2} + \rho_3 e_{t-3} + \ldots$$

Once a higher order autoregressive structure has been found to exist in the function, we proceed in the transformation of the original data and the original relationship in exactly the same way as before. For example assume that a second-order autoregressive scheme has been detected in the function. The original model is

$$Y_t = b_0 + b_1 X_{1(t)} + b_2 X_{2(t)} + \ldots + b_k X_{k(t)} + u_t$$

where

$$u_t = \rho_1 u_{t-1} + \rho_2 u_{t-2} + w_t$$

[1] See K. R. Kadiyala. 'A Transformation Used to Circumvent the Problem of Autocorrelation', *Econometrica*, vol. 36, 1968, pp. 93–6.

with w_t meeting all the assumptions of a random variable (homoscedastic, non-autocorrelated, etc.).

The relationships for the periods $(t - 1)$ and $(t - 2)$ are

$$Y_{t-1} = b_0 + b_1 X_{1(t-1)} + \ldots + b_k X_{k(t-1)} + u_{t-1}$$

$$Y_{t-2} = b_0 + b_1 X_{1(t-2)} + \ldots + b_k X_{k(t-2)} + u_{t-2}$$

Premultiplying these equations with ρ_1 and ρ_2 respectively we have

$$\rho_1 Y_{t-1} = \rho_1 b_0 + b_1 \rho_1 X_{1(t-1)} + b_2 \rho_1 X_{2(t-1)} + \ldots + b_k \rho_1 X_{k(t-1)} + \rho_1 u_{t-1}$$

$$\rho_2 Y_{t-2} = \rho_2 b_0 + b_1 \rho_2 X_{1(t-2)} + b_2 \rho_2 X_{2(t-2)} + \ldots + b_k \rho_2 X_{k(t-2)} + \rho_2 u_{t-2}$$

Subtracting these equations from the original model we find

$$[Y_t - \rho_1 Y_{t-1} - \rho_2 Y_{t-2}] = b_0 (1 - \rho_1 - \rho_2) +$$
$$+ b_1 [X_{1t} - \rho_1 X_{1(t-1)} - \rho_2 X_{1(t-2)}] +$$
$$+ \ldots + [u_t - \rho_1 u_{t-1} - \rho_2 u_{t-2}]$$

The new disturbance term $(u_t - \rho_1 u_{t-1} - \rho_2 u_{t-2})$ is equal to w_t and hence is by assumption serially independent. Therefore if we know ρ_1 and ρ_2 (the coefficients of the second-order scheme) we can apply ordinary least squares to the transformed relationship:

$$Y_t^* = b_0^* + b_1^* X_{1t}^* + \ldots + b_k^* X_k^* + u_t^*$$

where $Y_t^* = Y_t - \rho_1 Y_{t-1} - \rho_2 Y_{t-2}$

$X_{1t}^* = X_{1t} - \rho_1 X_{1(t-1)} - \rho_2 X_{1(t-2)}$

$$\begin{matrix} \cdot & & \cdot & & \cdot & & \cdot \\ \cdot & & \cdot & & \cdot & & \cdot \\ \cdot & & \cdot & & \cdot & & \cdot \end{matrix}$$

$X_{kt}^* = X_{kt} - \rho_1 X_{k(t-1)} - \rho_2 X_{k(t-2)}$

$u_t^* = u_t - \rho_1 u_{t-1} - \rho_2 u_{t-2} = w_t$ (serially independent)

The extension of this procedure to higher-order lag structures of the u term is straightforward.

We see that if we know the values of ρ's we can proceed with the above transformation of the original data and then apply ordinary least squares to the transformed relationship. However, ρ is unknown and we must estimate its value in some way or another. In the next section we will examine various methods for obtaining an estimate $\hat{\rho}$ of the autocorrelation coefficient(s).

10.8. METHODS FOR ESTIMATING THE AUTOCORRELATION PARAMETERS

10.8.1. METHOD I. *A priori information on ρ (or ρ's)*

In most applied econometric research, when autocorrelation is suspected or established on the basis of a formal test, the investigator makes some 'reasonable' guess about the value of the autoregressive coefficient(s) ρ, using his knowledge and intuition about the relationship being studied.

A usual case is to assume that $\rho = 1$. Under this assumption the appropriate transformation is to take the first differences of the original data and apply ordinary least squares to the transformed model

$$(Y_t - Y_{t-1}) = b_1(X_t - X_{t-1}) + v_t$$

where $v_t = u_t - u_{t-1}$.

The original relationship is

$$Y_t = b_0 + b_1 X_t + u_t$$

where $u_t = \rho u_{t-1} + v_t$
with v_t satisfying all the usual assumptions of a random variable. Assuming $\rho = 1$

$$u_t = u_{t-1} + v_t$$

or
$$u_t - u_{t-1} = v_t$$

Now, lagging the original equation by one period and premultiplying by ρ we obtain

$$\rho Y_{t-1} = \rho b_0 + b_1 \rho X_{t-1} + \rho u_{t-1}$$

or
$$Y_{t-1} = b_0 + b_1 X_{t-1} + u_{t-1} \qquad \text{(given that } \rho = 1\text{)}$$

Subtracting from the original equation we have

$$(Y_t - Y_{t-1}) = b_1(X_t - X_{t-1}) + (u_t - u_{t-1})$$

where $u_t - u_{t-1} = v_t$, serially independent by assumption.

Note that for the computation of this function we must suppress the constant intercept. Otherwise the constant intercept that will appear in the function would imply that time is implicitly introduced in the function as an explanatory variable. (For a proof of this statement see Chapter 12.) Of course there is nothing *a priori* wrong in incorporating time in the function; a time factor has the meaning that there is an autonomous growth of the dependent variable over time. If this hypothesis is justified in the particular phenomenon being studied, working with first differences is the appropriate procedure to adopt. On the other hand, if the relationship being studied is incompatible with the hypothesis of an autonomous growth, the first-differences transformation is not appropriate.

It is obvious that when one assumes $\rho = 1$ and then takes the first differences of the variables as the appropriate transformation, the computational procedure is greatly simplified. This is the reason why first differences are popular in applied research whenever autocorrelation is present in the original model. (See for example R. Stone, *Measurement of Consumers' Expenditure in the United*

Kingdom, 1954 and 1967, Cambridge University Press.) However, the assumption $\rho = 1$ is the extreme opposite of Assumption 5 ($\rho = 0$) of the linear regression model, and the true ρ may actually lie somewhere between these two extreme values ($0 < \rho < 1$).

10.8.2. METHOD II. *Estimation of ρ from the d statistic*

Another crude method for the estimation of the coefficient of the auto-regressive scheme is to solve for ρ the expression (derived on page 213).

$$d \simeq 2(1 - \rho)$$

From the application of the Durbin–Watson test we obtain d^* which we may substitute in the above expression and get

$$\hat{\rho} = 1 - \frac{1}{2} d^*$$

If the sample is small the estimate $\hat{\rho}$ will not be accurate, since the relationship

$$d \simeq 2(1 + \rho)$$

holds asymptotically (for large samples).

10.8.3. METHOD III: *The Cochrane–Orcutt Iterative Method*[1]

This method involves a gradual approximation (convergence) to the estimate of the autocorrelation coefficient, ρ. It may be outlined as follows:

Step 1. Apply OLS to the original data and obtain estimates of the coefficients $\hat{b}_0$ and $\hat{b}_1$:

$$\hat{Y}_t = \hat{b}_0 + \hat{b}_1 X_t$$

Compute the 'first-round' residuals

$$e_t = Y_t - \hat{b}_0 - \hat{b}_1 X_t \quad (t = 1, 2, \ldots, n)$$

and from these estimate the 'first-round' estimate of ρ by using the earlier developed formula

$$\hat{\rho} = \frac{\Sigma e_t e_{t-1}}{\Sigma e_{t-1}^2} \qquad (t = 2, 3, \ldots, n)$$

Step 2. Use $\hat{\rho}$ to transform the original data and apply OLS to the model

$$[Y_t - \hat{\rho} Y_{t-1}] = b_0(1 - \hat{\rho}) + b_1[X_t - \hat{\rho} X_{t-1}] + u_t^*$$

Denote the estimates of this 'second-round' by $\hat{\hat{b}}_0$ and $\hat{\hat{b}}_1$ (where $\hat{\hat{b}}_0$ is an estimate of the intercept $b_0(1 - \hat{\rho})$).

---

[1] See C. Cochrane and G. H. Orcutt, 'Application of Least-squares Regressions to Relationships Containing Autocorrelated Error Terms', *J. Am. Statis. Ass.*, vol. 44, 1949, pp. 32–61.

Using $\hat{\hat{b}}_0$ and $\hat{\hat{b}}_1$ compute the 'second-round' residuals

$$\hat{\hat{e}}_t = Y_t - \hat{\hat{b}}_0 - \hat{\hat{b}}_1 X_t \quad (t = 1, 2, 3, \ldots, n)$$

and from these obtain the 'second-round' estimate of ρ

$$\hat{\hat{\rho}} = \frac{\Sigma \hat{\hat{e}}_t \hat{\hat{e}}_{t-1}}{\Sigma \hat{\hat{e}}_{t-1}^2} \quad (t = 2, 3, \ldots, n)$$

Step 3. Use $\hat{\hat{\rho}}$ to transform the original variables and apply OLS to the model

$$[Y_t - \hat{\hat{\rho}} Y_{t-1}] = b_0 (1 - \hat{\hat{\rho}}) + b_1 [X_t - \hat{\hat{\rho}} X_{t-1}] + u_t^{**}$$

We obtain the 'third-round' estimates, $\hat{\hat{\hat{b}}}_0$ and $\hat{\hat{\hat{b}}}_1$, which yield the 'third-round' residuals

$$\hat{\hat{\hat{e}}}_t = Y_t - \hat{\hat{\hat{b}}}_0 - \hat{\hat{\hat{b}}}_1 X_t \quad (t = 1, 2, \ldots, n)$$

From these residuals we obtain the 'third-round' estimate of ρ

$$\hat{\hat{\hat{\rho}}} = \frac{\Sigma \hat{\hat{\hat{e}}}_t \hat{\hat{\hat{e}}}_{t-1}}{\Sigma \hat{\hat{\hat{e}}}_{t-1}^2} \quad (t = 2, 3, \ldots, n)$$

This iterative procedure is repeated until the value of the estimate of ρ converges.

Sometimes researchers stop at the 'second-round' estimates, $\hat{\hat{b}}_0$ and $\hat{\hat{b}}_1$. This is then called a *two-stage Cochrane–Orcutt method.*

An alternative approach is to use at each step of the iteration (for the first-order autoregressive scheme) the Durbin–Watson d statistic to test the residuals for autocorrelation. If they pass the test of zero autocorrelation, the iterations stop. If not, the iterations proceed until the hypothesis of zero autocorrelation is accepted. Tests of significance of the $\hat{b}$'s are conducted only at the final iteration.

The estimate of the ρ's is more cumbersome if the autoregressive scheme is more complicated (for example if we have a second-order or third-order scheme); however, the procedure is the same as the one described above for the simple first-order autoregressive structure. For example assume a second-order autoregressive scheme

$$u_t = \rho_1 u_{t-1} + \rho_2 u_{t-2} + v_t$$

From the OLS residuals of the original observations we obtain the 'first-round' estimates of the ρ's by using least squares on the function

$$e_t = \hat{\rho}_1 e_{t-1} + \hat{\rho}_2 e_{t-2}$$

The estimates $\hat{\rho}_1$ and $\hat{\rho}_2$ are used to obtain the transformations

$$Y_t^* = (Y_t - \hat{\rho}_1 Y_{t-1} - \hat{\rho}_2 Y_{t-2})$$

$$X_{jt}^* = (X_{jt} - \hat{\rho}_1 X_{j(t-1)} - \hat{\rho}_2 X_{j(t-2)}) \quad (j = 1, 2, \ldots, k)$$

We apply OLS to the function

$$Y_t^* = b_0^* + b_1^* X_{1t}^* + \ldots + b_k^* X_{kt}^* + u_t^*$$

We use the new residuals $\hat{\hat{e}}_t$ to obtain the 'second-round' estimates of the ρ's, by applying OLS to the function

$$\hat{\hat{e}}_t = \hat{\hat{\rho}}_1 \hat{\hat{e}}_{t-1} + \hat{\hat{\rho}}_2 \hat{\hat{e}}_{t-2}$$

and so on. The iterations cease when the estimates of the ρ's converge.

An alternative procedure is to apply the third test for autocorrelation (page 216), and use the ρ's which are found statistically significant in order to transform the original observations.

10.8.4. METHOD IV. *Durbin's "two-step" method of estimation of ρ*

(J. Durbin, 'Estimation of Parameters in Time-Series Regression Models', *J. of R. Statist. Soc.*, vol. 22, 1960, Series B, pp. 139–53.)

Durbin has suggested the following two-step method for estimating ρ which is applicable for any order of autoregressive scheme.

Assume the original function is

$$Y_t = b_0 + b_1 X_{1t} + b_2 X_{2t} + \ldots + b_k X_{kt} + u_t$$

where $u_t = f(u_{t-1}, u_{t-2}, \ldots)$. For simplicity let $u_t = \rho u_{t-1} + v_t$.

Stage 1. We start from the transformed model

$$(Y_t - \rho Y_{t-1}) = b_0(1 - \rho) + b_1(X_{1t} - \rho X_{1(t-1)}) +$$
$$+ \ldots + b_k(X_{kt} - \rho X_{k(t-1)}) + (u_t - \rho u_{t-1})$$

We re-write this equation as follows

$$Y_t = b_0(1 - \rho) + \rho Y_{t-1} + b_1 X_{1t} - b_1 \rho X_{1(t-1)} + \ldots + b_k X_{kt} - b_{k\rho} X_{k(t-1)} + v_t$$

Setting
$$b_0(1 - \rho) = a_0$$
$$b_1 = a_1$$
$$b_1 \rho = a_2, \text{ etc.}$$

we may write the equation in the following form

$$Y_t = a_0 + \rho Y_{t-1} + a_1 X_{1t} + a_2 X_{1(t-1)} + \ldots + v_t$$

Applying least squares to this equation we obtain an estimate of ρ, $\hat{\rho}$, which is the coefficient of the lagged variable Y_{t-1}.

Stage 2. We use the estimate $\hat{\rho}$ to obtain the transformed variables

$$(Y_t - \hat{\rho}Y_{t-1}) = Y^*$$

$$(X_{1t} - \hat{\rho}X_{1(t-1)}) = X_1^*$$

$$\cdot \qquad \cdot \qquad \cdot$$

$$\cdot \qquad \cdot \qquad \cdot$$

$$(X_{kt} - \hat{\rho}X_{k(t-1)}) = X_k^*$$

which we use in order to estimate the parameters of the original relationship

$$Y_t^* = b_0 + b_1 X_1^* + \ldots + b_k X_k^* + v_t$$

Durbin's method provides estimates which have optimal asymptotic properties and are more efficient for samples of all sizes.

The extension of Durbin's two-step method to higher order autoregressive schemes is straightforward. For example assume a second-order autoregressive scheme, which yields the transformed equation

$$[Y_t - \rho_1 Y_{t-1} - \rho_2 Y_{t-2}] = b_0(1 - \rho_1 - \rho_2) + b_1[X_{1t} - \rho_1 X_{1(t-1)} - \rho_2 X_{1(t-2)}] +$$
$$+ \ldots + b_k[X_{kt} - \rho_1 X_{k(t-1)} - \rho_2 X_{k(t-2)}] + v_t$$

where $v_t = u_t - \rho_1 u_{t-1} - \rho_2 u_{t-2}$. The above equation may be rewritten as follows

$$\overset{\circ}{Y}_t = b_0(1 - \rho_1 - \rho_2) + \rho_1 Y_{t-1} + \rho_2 Y_{t-2} + b_1[X_{1t} - \rho_1 X_{1(t-1)} - \rho_2 X_{1(t-2)}] + \ldots$$

In the first stage we apply OLS to this equation and obtain estimates $\hat{\rho}_1$ and $\hat{\rho}_2$, which are the coefficients of the lagged variables Y_{t-1} and Y_{t-2}.

In the second stage $\hat{\rho}_1$ and $\hat{\rho}_2$ are used to transform the original observations

$$Y_t^* = Y_t - \hat{\rho}_1 Y_{t-1} - \hat{\rho}_2 Y_{t-2}$$

$$X_{jt}^* = X_{jt} - \hat{\rho}_1 X_{j(t-1)} - \hat{\rho}_2 X_{j(t-2)}$$

We next apply OLS to the function

$$Y_t^* = b_0 + b_1 X_{1t}^* + \ldots + b_k X_{kt}^* + u_t^*$$

10.9. SUMMARY AND CONCLUSIONS

1. Autocorrelation or serial correlation is the temporal dependence of successive values of the disturbance term u.

2. Autocorrelation is measured by the autocorrelation coefficient

$$\rho_{u_t \, . \, u_{t-1} u_{t-2} \, . \, . \, . \, .}$$

For the simple case of the first-order autoregressive scheme

$$u_t = \rho u_{t-1} + v_t$$

the autocorrelation coefficient is

$$\rho_{u_t u_{t-1}} = \frac{\Sigma u_t u_{t-1}}{\sqrt{\Sigma u_t^2}\sqrt{\Sigma u_{t-1}^2}}$$

For more complicated autoregressive patterns the autocorrelation coefficient may be computed by analogy to the multiple correlation coefficient $(R^2_{Y \cdot X_1 X_2 \cdots})$.

3. For the simple first-order autoregressive scheme the most efficient test is the Durbin—Watson d statistic defined by

$$d = \frac{\sum\limits_{t=2}^{n}(e_t - e_{t-1})^2}{\sum\limits_{t=1}^{n} e_t^2}$$

A more general test for autocorrelation is provided by the classical (t, F) tests applied on the coefficients $(\hat{\rho}\text{'s})$ of the autoregresive structure having been estimated by using the regression residuals e's; for example by testing the ρ's appearing in the function

$$e_t = \rho_1 e_{t-1} + \rho_2 e_{t-2} + \ldots + v_t$$

4. Autocorrelation is a problem specific to time series data. Due to economic growth and business cycles autocorrelation is positive in most economic relationships.

Autocorrelation does not arise in cross-section data (unless the sample is not random). Such data refer to a given 'point' of time; hence temporal dependence is ruled out by the nature itself of cross-section random samples.

5. The most common sources of autocorrelation are: (a) omission of some important variable; (b) error in the mathematical form of the equation; (c) errors in the macrovariables (e.g. smoothing processes of seasonal variations); (d) mis-specification of the behaviour of u.

6. The consequences of autocorrelation are serious for the values and the standard errors of the parameter estimates. When the u's are temporally dependent we have the following consequences:

(i) The values of the parameter estimates are statistically unbiased despite the presence of autocorrelation.

(ii) The variance of u may be underestimated. The underestimation is serious in the case of positive autocorrelation of the u's and of positively autocorrelated X_t's, which is the usual case in the real economic world.

(iii) The variances of the parameter estimates are likely to be seriously underestimated when both the u's and the X's are positively autocorrelated. Thus we run the danger of accepting as significant variables which in reality are not significant explanatory variables.

(iv) The estimates $\hat{b}$'s are not best (they do not possess the minimum variance property) as compared with estimates from other econometric techniques.

(v) The predictions based on estimates obtained from OLS applied to a model with autocorrelated u's are not efficient.

7. If autocorrelation is due to one of the three first causes mentioned above, the appropriate solution is clear: (1) inclusion of the missing important variable(s); (2) 'correction' of the mathematical form; (3) improvement of the accuracy of the data, respectively.

8. If autocorrelation is due to mis-specification of u, the appropriate solution is to obtain an estimate of ρ (or ρ's) by some method, transform the original data

$$Y^* = Y_t - \hat{\rho}_1 Y_{t-1} - \hat{\rho}_2 Y_{t-2} \ldots$$
$$X_1^* = X_{1t} - \hat{\rho}_1 X_{1(t-1)} - \hat{\rho}_2 X_{1(t-2)} \ldots$$

$$X_k^* = X_{kt} - \hat{\rho}_1 X_{k(t-1)} - \hat{\rho}_2 X_{k(t-2)} \ldots$$

and apply least squares to the transformed function

$$Y_t^* = b_0 + b_1 X_1^* + \ldots + b_k X_k^* + v_t$$

This method is equivalent to Aitken's Generalised Least Squares (see p. 189 and Chapter 19). There are various methods for estimating $\hat{\rho}(s)$. The more efficient and more general in its applicability is Durbin's two-step method.

In many cases research workers find it convenient to assume $\rho = 1$ (perfect positive autocorrelation of the first order) and proceed in the estimation of the relationship expressed in *the first differences of the variables*. In this case one should suppress the constant intercept, if one does not wish to incorporate an autonomous growth factor in the relationship.

9. If autocorrelation and heteroscedasticity occur simultaneously, one may apply the appropriate transformations of the variables in tandem.

Example. Table 10.1 includes data on imports and the gross national product of the U.K. Applying OLS to these observations we obtain the following imports function

$$\hat{Z}_t = -2{,}461 + 0{\cdot}28 X_t \qquad r^2 = 0{\cdot}983$$
$$S_{\hat{b}_i} \quad (250) \quad (0{\cdot}01)$$

It is found that $\qquad \Sigma e_t^2 = 573{,}069$

$$\Sigma(e_t - e_{t-1})^2 = 537{,}192$$

The Durbin–Watson d statistic from the above sample is

$$d^* = \frac{\Sigma(e_t - e_{t-1})^2}{\Sigma e_t^2} = \frac{537{,}192}{573{,}069} = 0{\cdot}937$$

Table 10.1 Imports and gross national product of the U.K. (£m, 1968 prices)

Year t	Imports Z_t	GNP X_t	Estimated imports $\hat{Z}_t$	Error $e_t = Z_t - \hat{Z}_t$	$e_t - e_{t-1}$
1950	3,748	21,777	3,626	122	
1951	4,010	22,418	3,805	205	83
1952	3,711	22,308	3,774	−63	−268
1953	4,004	23,319	4,057	−53	10
1954	4,151	24,180	4,298	−147	−94
1955	4,569	24,893	4,497	72	219
1956	4,582	25,310	4,613	−31	−103
1957	4,697	25,799	4,750	−53	−22
1958	4,753	25,886	4,774	−21	32
1959	5,062	26,868	5,049	13	34
1960	5,669	28,134	5,403	266	253
1961	5,628	29,091	5,670	−42	−308
1962	5,736	29,450	5,771	−35	7
1963	5,946	30,705	6,121	−175	−140
1964	6,501	32,372	6,587	−86	89
1965	6,549	33,152	6,805	−256	−170
1966	6,705	33,764	6,976	−271	15
1967	7,104	34,411	7,157	−53	218
1968	7,609	35,429	7,442	167	220
1969	8,100	36,200	7,657	443	276

From the Durbin–Watson table, with 5 per cent level of significance, $n = 20$ observations, and $k' = 1$ independent variable, the significance points of d_L and d_U are:

$$d_L = 1 \cdot 20 \qquad d_U = 1 \cdot 41$$

Since $d^* < d_L$, we conclude there is positive autocorrelation in the imports function. We will use two of the previously developed corrective procedures, namely the method discussed in section 10.6.3, and Durbin's two-step method.

A. We regress e_t on e_{t-1}, and e_{t-2}, and obtain the following results

$$\hat{e}_t = 0 \cdot 53\, e_{t-1}$$
$$(0 \cdot 26)$$

$$\hat{e}_t = 0 \cdot 55\, e_{t-1} - 0 \cdot 21\, e_{t-2}$$
$$(0 \cdot 29) \qquad\quad (0 \cdot 29)$$

One could experiment with other forms of autocorrelation, but we limit our example to the first-order and second-order autoregressive schemes.

The above regressions indicate a first-order autoregression, since $\hat{\rho}_1$ is just significant but $\hat{\rho}_2$ not significant at the 5 per cent level.

Using the estimate $\hat{\rho} = 0 \cdot 53$ we obtain the transformed variables

$$Y_t^* = Y_t - 0 \cdot 53\, Y_{t-1}$$
$$X_t^* = X_t - 0 \cdot 53\, X_{t-1}$$

Applying OLS to the above transformed data we obtain

$$\hat{Y}_t^* = -1394\cdot36 + 0\cdot296 X_t^* \qquad R^2 = 0\cdot949$$
$$(235\cdot35) \quad (0\cdot02) \qquad d = 1\cdot87$$

B. Using Durbin's two-step method we find

$$Y_t = a_0 + \rho Y_{t-1} + a_1 X_t + a_2 X_{t-1} + v_t$$

$$Y_t^* = -1107\cdot67 + 0\cdot6475\, Y_{t-1} + 0\cdot3403 X_t - 0\cdot2345\, X_{t-1}$$
$$(692\cdot8) \qquad (0\cdot29) \qquad\quad (0\cdot10) \qquad\quad (0\cdot13)$$

From $\rho^* = 0\cdot6475$ we obtain the transformed data

$$Y_t^* = (Y_t - \rho^* Y_{t-1}) = Y_t - 0\cdot6475\, Y_{t-1}$$

$$X_t^* = (X_t - \rho^* X_{t-1}) = X_t - 0\cdot6475\, X_{t-1}$$

Applying OLS to the above transformed data we find

$$\hat{\hat{Y}}_t^* = -372\cdot18 + 0\cdot228 X_t^* \qquad R^2 = 0\cdot872$$
$$(223\cdot0) \quad (0\cdot02) \qquad d = 2\cdot11$$

We observe that with the appropriate transformations the value of d comes close to the 'crucial' value of 2 (which corresponds to zero autocorrelation).

10.10. PREDICTION FROM AUTOCORRELATED FUNCTIONS

Assume that we have obtained estimates of the parameters of a function whose error term is autocorrelated. Applying any of the above developed methods we estimate the parameters from the transformed data

$$Y_t^* = b_0 + b_1 X_{1t}^* + \ldots + b_k X_{kt}^*$$

where $Y_t^*, X_{1t}^*, \ldots, X_{kt}^*$ are the appropriately transformed variables.

We are given the values of the X's in period $n + 1$ (where n is the last observation of our sample) and we want to estimate the value Y in period $n + 1$. It can be proved that the most efficient prediction is obtained from the expression[1]

$$\hat{Y}_{(n+1)} = b_0^* + b_1^* X_{1(n+1)} + b_2^* X_{2(n+1)} + \ldots + b_k^* X_{k(n+1)} + \rho^* e_n$$

where e_n = the residual of the nth observation in the final model.

ρ^* = estimate of ρ from the final iteration (see pp. 222–3).

b^*'s = estimates of the b's from the transformed variables in the final iteration.

[1] For a further discussion of this topic see J. Johnston, *Econometric Methods,* 2nd edn., pp. 265–6.

EXERCISES

1. The following table shows the annual consumption and disposable income for a certain country (in $ million).

Year	C	Y_d	Year	C	Y_d
1957	11,378	11,617	1963	20,074	21,512
1958	13,012	13,297	1964	21,439	23,124
1959	15,263	15,790	1965	22,833	24,724
1960	16,873	18,017	1966	24,205	26,175
1961	17,764	19,314	1967	25,307	27,219
1962	18,857	20,198	1968	27,020	28,915

Application of OLS yields the following results

$$\hat{C} = 8{,}526 + 0{\cdot}65\, Y_d \qquad r^2 = 0{\cdot}953$$

(a) Find the residuals and test for autocorrelation.
(b) Estimate the value of ρ (or ρ's if autocorrelation is of a higher order) with any two of the methods of section 10.6.
Use your estimates of ρ to transform your original data

$$Y_t^* = (Y_t - \hat{\rho}_1 Y_{t-1})$$

$$X_t^* = (X_t - \hat{\rho}_1 X_{t-1})$$

Apply OLS to the transformed data and compare your results with the OLS estimates obtained from the original sample observations.

2. Assuming that $\rho = 1$, compute the OLS estimate of the consumption function of exercise 1 with the appropriately transformed data. Compare your results with those obtained in the previous exercise.

3. Given the structural true model

$$Y_t = 20 + 2X_t + u_t$$

$$u_t = u_{t-2} + v_t$$

$$u_{t-2} = 5 \qquad u_{t-1} = -6$$

$$v_t = 0 \qquad \text{in all observations}$$

X_t takes the values from 1 to 20.

(a) Generate a sample of 20 observations.
(b) Use the generated sample to estimates $\hat{b}_0$ and $\hat{b}_1$. Compute d and test for first-order autocorrelation.
(c) Estimate ρ and apply OLS to the transformed data (Y_t^* and X_t^*). Are your new estimates b_0^* and b_1^* improved by the applied transformation?

4. The data of the following table are the OLS residuals of a certain relationship ($Y = b_0 + b_1 X + u$). Calculate d and estimate ρ with any two of the methods explained in section 10.6. Do your results support the use of first differences for the estimation of b_0 and b_1?

Year	Residual (e_i)	Year	Residual (e_i)	Year	Residual (e_i)	Year	Residual (e_i)
1950	1	1955	−0·3	1960	−4·6	1965	−2·6
1951	−1·5	1956	−3·1	1961	−4·3	1966	−2·3
1952	−0·7	1957	−5·5	1962	1·9	1967	0·9
1953	−1·3	1958	−4·7	1963	1·9	1968	1·4
1954	−4·6	1959	−1·3	1964	2·9	1969	3·7

5. Assume that a firm's production decision is described by the function

$$S_t = b_0 + b_1 P_t + u_t$$

where S_t = quantity produced, P_t = price, u_t = random disturbance. It is known that, whenever anything causes the firm to 'overproduce' in period $t - 1$, the managers will cut production in period t.

Given the above information, what would be the consequences if we attempted to estimate b_0 and b_1 by the method of OLS?

6. Prove that working with a model expressed in the first differences of the variables

$$(Y_t - Y_{t-1}) = b_0 + b_1 (X_t - X_{t-1}) + u_t$$

is equivalent to a model in which the variables assume their current values and a trend appears as a separate regressor

$$Y_t = a_0 + a_1 X_t + a_2 t + v_t$$

Establish the relationship between the coefficients of the above forms.

7. A researcher used OLS to estimate the following demand for money function for the U.S.A. over the 39-year period 1919−57.

$$\log \frac{M}{P} = 2\cdot310 - 0\cdot761 \log(i) + 0\cdot008 \log \frac{Y}{P} + 0\cdot012 \frac{L}{P}$$
$$\text{s.e. } (0\cdot11) \quad (0\cdot44) \quad\quad (0\cdot001) \quad\quad (0\cdot006)$$

where M = quantity of nominal money demanded, i = interest rate, L = nominal amount of liquid assets, P = price index (to deflate nominal values, so as to eliminate changes in purchasing power). The residuals (e_t) showed that

$$\sum_{t=1}^{39} e_t^2 = 1\cdot0567 \qquad\qquad \sum_{t=2}^{39} (e_t - e_{t-1})^2 = 0\cdot2240$$

On the basis of this information the researcher decided to re-estimate the demand for money function, using the first differences of the original variables.

   i. Calculate the Durbin—Watson d statistic.
  ii. Does the value of d justify the 'first-differences' solution, adopted by the researcher?

Note. Additional exercises are included in Appendix III.

11. Multicollinearity

11.1. THE MEANING OF MULTICOLLINEARITY

A crucial condition for the application of least squares is that the explanatory variables are not perfectly linearly correlated ($r_{x_i x_j} \neq 1$). The term multicollinearity is used to denote the presence of linear relationships (or near linear relationships) among explanatory variables. If the explanatory variables are perfectly linearly correlated, that is, if the correlation coefficient for these variables is equal to unity, the parameters become indeterminate: it is impossible to obtain numerical values for each parameter separately and the method of least squares breaks down. At the other extreme if the explanatory variables are not intercorrelated at all (that is if the correlation coefficient for these variables is equal to zero), the variables are called orthogonal[1] and there are no problems concerning the estimates of the coefficients, at least so far as multicollinearity is concerned. Actually, in the case of orthogonal X's, there is no need to perform a multiple regression analysis: each parameter, b_i, can be estimated by a *simple* regression of Y on the corresponding regressor: $Y = f(X_i)$. (See A. Goldberger, *Econometric Theory*, p. 201.)

In practice neither of the above extreme cases (of orthogonal X's or perfect collinear X's) is often met. In most cases there is some degree of intercorrelation among the explanatory variables, due to the interdependence of many economic magnitudes over time. In this event the simple correlation coefficient for each pair of explanatory variables will have a value between zero and unity, and the multicollinearity problems *may* impair the accuracy and stability of the parameter estimates, but the exact effects of collinearity have not as yet been theoretically established.

Multicollinearity is not a condition that either exists or does not exist in economic functions, but rather a phenomenon inherent in most relationships due to the nature of economic magnitudes. There is no conclusive evidence concerning the degree of collinearity which, if present, will affect seriously the parameter estimates. Intuitively, when any two explanatory variables are changing in nearly the same way, it becomes extremely difficult to establish the influence of each one regressor on Y separately. For example assume that the consumption expenditure of an individual depends on his income and liquid assets. If over a period of time income and the liquid assets change by the same proportion, the influence on consumption of one of these variables may be erroneously attributed to the other. The effects of these variables on consumption cannot be sensibly investigated, due to their high intercorrelation.

---

[1] Orthogonal variables are the variables whose covariance is zero: $\Sigma x_i x_j / n = 0$.

11.2. PLAUSIBILITY OF THE ASSUMPTION

Strictly speaking the assumption concerning multicollinearity, that is that the variables be not perfectly linearly correlated, is easily met in practice, because it is very rare for any two variables to be exactly intercorrelated in a linear form. However, the estimates of least squares may be seriously affected with a less than perfect intercorrelation between the explanatory variables (see below).

Multicollinearity may arise for various reasons. *Firstly*, there is a tendency of economic variables to move together over time. Economic magnitudes are influenced by the same factors and in consequence once these determining factors become operative the economic variables show the same broad pattern of behaviour over time. For example in periods of booms or rapid economic growth the basic economic magnitudes grow, although some tend to lag behind others. Thus income, consumption, savings, investment, prices, employment, tend to rise in periods of economic expansion and decrease in periods of recession. Growth and trend factors in time series are the most serious cause of multicollinearity. *Secondly*, the use of lagged values of some explanatory variables as separate independent factors in the relationship. Models with distributed lags have given satisfactory results in many fields of applied econometrics, and their use is expanding fast. For example in consumption functions it has become customary to include among the explanatory variables past as well as the present levels of income. Similarly, in investment functions distributed lags concerning past levels of economic activity are introduced as separate explanatory variables. Naturally the successive values of a certain variable are intercorrelated, for example income in the current period is partly determined by its own value in the previous period, and so on. Thus multicollinearity is almost certain to exist in distributed lag models. (Distributed lag models are discussed in Chapter 13.)

Taking the above considerations into account it is clear that some degree of collinearity is expected to appear in most economic relationships.

It should be noted that although multicollinearity is usually connected with time series, it is quite frequent in cross-section data as well. For example in a cross-section sample of manufacturing firms labour and capital inputs are almost always highly intercorrelated, because large firms tend to have large quantities of both factors while small firms usually have smaller quantities of both labour and capital. However, multicollinearity tends to be more common and more serious a problem in time series.

11.3. CONSEQUENCES OF MULTICOLLINEARITY

If the intercorrelation between the explanatory variables is perfect ($r_{x_i x_j} = 1$), then (a) the estimates of the coefficients are indeterminate, and (b) the standard errors of these estimates become infinitely large.

Proof (a). Suppose that the relation to be estimated is

$$Y = b_0 + b_1 X_1 + b_2 X_2 + u$$

and that X_1 and X_2 are related with the exact relation $X_2 = kX_1$, where k is any arbitrary constant number.

The formulae for the estimation of the coefficients $\hat{b}_1$ and $\hat{b}_2$ are

$$\hat{b}_1 = \frac{(\Sigma x_1 y)(\Sigma x_2^2) - (\Sigma x_2 y)(\Sigma x_1 x_2)}{(\Sigma x_1^2)(\Sigma x_2^2) - (\Sigma x_1 x_2)^2}$$

$$\hat{b}_2 = \frac{(\Sigma x_2 y)(\Sigma x_1^2) - (\Sigma x_1 y)(\Sigma x_1 x_2)}{(\Sigma x_1^2)(\Sigma x_2^2) - (\Sigma x_1 x_2)^2}$$

Substituting kX_1 for X_2 we obtain

$$\hat{b}_1 = \frac{k^2(\Sigma x_1 y)(\Sigma x_1^2) - k^2(\Sigma x_1 y)(\Sigma x_1^2)}{k^2(\Sigma x_1^2)^2 - k^2(\Sigma x_1^2)^2} = \frac{0}{0}$$

$$\hat{b}_2 = \frac{k(\Sigma x_1 y)(\Sigma x_1^2) - k(\Sigma x_1 y)(\Sigma x_1^2)}{k^2(\Sigma x_1^2)^2 - k^2(\Sigma x_1^2)^2} = \frac{0}{0}$$

Therefore the parameters are indeterminate: there is no way of finding separate values of each coefficient.

Proof (b). If $r_{x_i x_j} = 1$ the standard errors of the estimates become infinitely large. In the two-variable model

$$Y = b_0 + b_1 X_1 + b_2 X_2 + u$$

if X_1 and X_2 are perfectly correlated ($X_2 = kX_1$) the variances of $\hat{b}_1$ and $\hat{b}_2$ will be

$$\text{var}(\hat{b}_1) = \sigma_u^2 \frac{\Sigma x_2^2}{\Sigma x_1^2 \Sigma x_2^2 - (\Sigma x_1 x_2)^2}$$

and

$$\text{var}(\hat{b}_2) = \sigma_u^2 \frac{\Sigma x_1^2}{\Sigma x_1^2 \Sigma x_2^2 - (\Sigma x_1 x_2)^2}$$

Substituting kX_1 for X_2 we obtain

$$\text{var}(\hat{b}_1) = \sigma_u^2 \frac{k^2 \Sigma x_1^2}{k^2 \Sigma x_1^2 \Sigma x_1^2 - k^2(\Sigma x_1^2)^2} = \frac{\sigma_u^2 \Sigma x_1^2}{0} = \infty$$

Thus the variances of the estimates become infinite unless $\sigma_u^2 = 0$. However, there is no *a priori* reason why σ_u^2 should tend to zero when intercorrelation of the explanatory variables increases. Haavelmo has suggested that 'the estimate of σ_u^2 is not impaired by the fact that the independent variables are highly intercorrelated'. (See 'Remarks on Frisch's Confluence Analysis and its Use in Econometrics', chapter 5 in T. Koopmans (ed.), *Statistical Inference in Dynamic Economic Models*, Wiley 1950, p. 260.)

To illustrate the problem let us take the following example of a relationship including three explanatory variables. Suppose that the true consumption function for a certain country is

$$Y = b_0 + b_1 X_1 + b_2 X_2 + b_3 X_3 + u$$

where Y = total consumption

X_1 = income of rural areas

X_2 = income of urban areas

X_3 = tax on income

On *a priori* grounds one should expect $b_1 < b_2$, since the marginal propensity to consume in urban areas is in general higher than the MPC in rural areas. We wish to obtain estimates of the individual propensities and of the other parameters. Assume that over the sample period X_1 and X_2 happened to be equal (that is, income is equally distributed between urban and rural areas so that $X_1 = X_2$). Under these circumstances it would be impossible to obtain a separate estimate of b_1 or b_2, because X_1 and X_2 change together. We may substitute X_1 for X_2 and obtain

$$Y = b_0 + b_1 X_1 + b_2 X_1 + b_3 X_3 + u$$

or

$$Y = b_0 + (b_1 + b_2)X_1 + b_3 X_3 + u$$

Thus by dropping one of the two (equal) variables we can obtain an estimate of the sum of their coefficient, but not individual values for b_1 and b_2. That is, the sum $(b_1 + b_2)$ will be identified, but neither b_1 nor b_2 is identified separately. (There is a close relation between multicollinearity and identification which will be discussed in Chapter 15.)

If the X's are not perfectly collinear, but are to a certain degree correlated $(0 < r_{x_i x_j} < 1)$, the effects of collinearity are uncertain. The evidence from the theoretical econometric studies (with controlled data) as well as from applied research is controversial and by no means conclusive. In some studies the values of the coefficients become unstable as additional collinear variables are introduced into the function, or as the size of the sample increases; in other studies the values of the estimates are not significantly affected. The same holds for the standard errors of the estimates: in some studies the standard errors of the estimates are considerably increased when collinear variables are present in the function, while in other instances the standard errors have not been affected by the incidence of multicollinearity.

Two points should be stressed. Firstly, the estimates of the coefficients are statistically unbiased $(E(\hat{b}_i) = b_i)$ even when multicollinearity is strong. The statistical property of unbiasedness of the OLS estimates does not require that the X's be uncorrelated. On the other hand, samples with multicollinear X's may render the values of the estimates seriously imprecise and unstable. Unfortunately no firm rules have been established for assessing the seriousness of such errors. Yet the instability of the estimates may be so serious as to even cause a change in the sign of the parameter estimates as the degree of collinearity increases. There is some evidence[1] that increasing multicollinearity produces various changes in the values of the parameters, depending on the importance of each explanatory variable,

[1] See K. A. Fox, *Intermediate Economic Statistics*, pp. 259–265. See also Farrar and Glauber: 'However real the dependency relationship between *y* and each member of a relatively large explanatory variable set *X* may be, the growth of interdependence within *X* as its size increases, rapidly decreases the stability of each independent variable's contribution to explained variance.' D. E. Farrar and R. R. Glauber, 'Multicollinearity in Regression Analysis: The Problem Re-visited', *Review of Economics and Statistics*, vol. 49, 1967, pp. 92–107.

'importance' being usually measured by the simple correlation coefficient of Y and each of the X's (r_{yx_i}). Such evidence has led many econometricians to argue that the effects of multicollinearity on the parameter estimates depend on the *severity* of interdependence as well as on the *importance* of the variables which happen to be collinear. In any particular study certain explanatory variables are more important than others. (For example in a demand function the price of the commodity, consumers' income and the price of close substitutes are on *a priori* grounds more important than prices of distant substitutes of the commodity being studied.) If these strategically crucial explanatory variables happen to be strongly intercorrelated, the seriousness of the problem is greater than in the case of secondary factors being multicollinear, because the latter may be dropped from the analysis without seriously impairing the results. Secondly, many writers seem to accept that when multicollinearity is present in a function the standard errors of the estimates will, in general, be large. This is not always so, because both the numerator and the denominator of the formulae of the variances will usually be affected by terms involving sums of cross products of the X's so that the final size of the variance of the b's may not be large.

L. R. Klein seems to accept that multicollinearity is not necessarily a problem unless it is high relative to the overall degree of multiple correlation among all variables simultaneously. That is Klein argues that collinearity is harmful if

$$r_{x_i x_j}^2 \geqslant R_{y \, . \, x_1, \, x_2, \, \ldots, \, x_k}^2$$

where $r_{x_i x_j}^2$ is the simple correlation between any two explanatory variables $(X_i$ and $X_j)$ and R^2 is the overall (multiple) correlation of the relationship. (L. R. Klein, *Introduction to Econometrics*, Prentice-Hall International, London, pp. 64 and 101. Klein's approach has been attacked by Farrar and Glauber 'Multicollinearity in Regression Analysis', *Rev. Econ. & Statist.*, 1967.)

On the other hand Theil argues that in a model with more than two X's even small intercorrelations between variables may lead to non-significance due to the increase of the standard errors. (See H. Theil, 'Specification Errors and the Estimation of Economic Relationships', *Rev. Int. Statist. Inst.*, vol. 25, 1957.) Finally Frisch (in *Statistical Confluence Analysis by means of Complete Regression Systems*, University Economics Institute, Oslo 1934) showed that the standard errors are not always large when multicollinearity is present. Thus we may obtain very inaccurate estimates of the coefficients due to multicollinearity, and yet the standard errors of these 'wrong' estimates may not show it. (See C. Leser, *Econometric Techniques and Problems*, p. 27.)

Summing up the above arguments we may say that although there may be exceptions, in general, increasing standard errors appear when we include intercorrelated variables as explanatory in the function. Thus with multicollinearity in a function we run the danger of mis-specification, because we may reject a variable whose standard error appears high, although this variable is an important determinant of the variations of the dependent variable. This danger is very serious due to the traditional procedure followed in applied econometric research. In particular, in most cases the whole set of explanatory variables is not known and it has become a common practice to approximate it by experimentation, that is, by gradually including additional variables in the relationship and judging their importance by using, among others, as criterion their standard errors. For example suppose that the true relationship is

$$Y = b_0 + b_1 X_1 + b_2 X_2 + u$$

Since the true specification is not known, the researcher usually starts his study with the simpler tentative formulation

$$Y = a_0 + a_1 X_1 + v$$

This model will most probably yield significant results, although a_1 will have a specification error due to the omission of X_2. The addition of X_2 in the relationship should normally improve the fit, since the model is in this case correctly specified. However, if X_1 and X_2 are highly correlated and their standard errors are large, the researcher will usually reject X_2, being misguided by its large standard error. In this case multicollinearity results in the wrong decision and hence in the wrong specification of the model, since X_2 is by assumption (that is in the postulated model) an important explanatory variable in the relationship. (See Theil, *Economic Forecasts and Policy*, p. 217. See also Farrar and Glauber, *op. cit.*, p. 94.)

However, large standard errors do not always appear even in functions in which the regressors are strongly multicollinear. For example production functions with overall correlations much in excess of 0·950 have been well-estimated with intercorrelations between labour and capital as high as 0·800 to 0·900. If these functions were not well estimated, we would tend to find high sampling errors of the estimates coefficients. By conventional criteria the estimated parameters of most Cobb—Douglas production functions are large relative to their standard error. The coefficients are generally high multiples of their standard errors. (See L. R. Klein, *Introduction to Econometrics*, p. 101.) Recently S. D. Silvey has published a study on the problem of multicollinearity. (See S. Silvey, 'Multicollinearity and Imprecise Estimation', *Royal Statistical Society*, 1969.) We will not examine Silvey's approach here, since it is not substantially superior to Farrar's and Glauber's test, which will be developed in the next section.

11.4. TESTS FOR DETECTING MULTICOLLINEARITY

11.4.1. A METHOD BASED ON FRISCH'S CONFLUENCE ANALYSIS

The seriousness of the effects of multicollinearity seems to depend on the degree of intercorrelation $(r_{x_i x_j})$ as well as on the overall correlation coefficient $(R_{Y.x_1 x_2 \ldots x_k})$. Thus one might suggest that the standard errors, the partial correlation coefficients $(r_{x_i x_j}$'s) and the total R^2 may be used for testing for multicollinearity. Yet none of these criteria *by itself* is a satisfactory indicator of multicollinearity, because:

(a) Large standard errors do not always appear with multicollinearity (see evidence of Cobb–Douglas production functions). Furthermore large standard errors may arise for various reasons and not only because of the presence of linear relationships among the explanatory variables.

(b) The intercorrelations of the explanatory variables need not be high for the values of the b's and their standard errors to be affected badly, that is $r_{x_i x_j}$ is not an adequate criterion by itself.

(c) The overall R^2 may be high (relative to the $r_{x_i x_j}$'s) and yet the results may be highly imprecise and insignificant (with wrong signs and/or large standard errors).

However, a combination of all these criteria may help the detection of multicollinearity. In order to gain as much knowledge as possible as to the seriousness of multicollinearity we suggest the adoption of the following method which is in its essence a revised version of Frisch's 'Confluence Analysis' (or 'Bunch-Map Analysis').

The procedure is to regress the dependent variable on each one of the explanatory variables separately. Thus we obtain all the elementary regressions, and we examine their results on the basis of *a priori* and statistical criteria.

We choose the elementary regression which appears to give the most plausible results, on both *a priori* and statistical criteria. Then we gradually insert additional variables and we examine their effects on the individual coefficients, on their standard errors, and on the overall R^2. A new variable is classified as *useful, superfluous* or *detrimental,* as follows:

(1) If the new variable improves R^2 without rendering the individual coefficients unacceptable ('wrong') on *a priori* considerations, the variable is considered useful and is retained as an explanatory variable.

(2) If the new variable does not improve R^2 and does not affect to any considerable extent the values of the individual coefficients, it is considered as superfluous and is rejected (i.e. is not included among the explanatory variables).

(3) If the new variable affects considerably the signs or the values of the coefficients, it is considered as detrimental. If the individual coefficients are affected in such a way as to become unacceptable on theoretical, *a priori*, considerations, then we may say that this is a warning that multicollinearity is a serious problem. The new variable is important, but because of intercorrelations with the other explanatory variables its influence cannot be assessed statistically by ordinary least-squares. This does not mean that we must reject the detrimental variable. If we did so, we would ignore information valuable to our attempts of approaching as best we can the 'true' specification of the relationship. In order to avoid the complications of multicollinearity and take into account the influence of the detrimental variable we have to follow one of the solutions developed in the following section. If we omit the detrimental variable completely in an attempt to avoid its detrimental influence on the other coefficients, we must bear in mind that in so doing we simply leave its influence to be absorbed by the other coefficients (whose values thus become mixed), and by the random term which may become correlated with the variables left

in the function, with the consequence of violation of Assumption 6, since in this case $E(u_i X_j \neq 0)$.

The method described above for establishing multicollinearity differs from Frisch's Confluence Analysis in that the latter estimates all possible regressions between the variables which are present in a relationship, taking each variable successively as the dependent variable and considering all possible regressions of each variable on all others which are gradually introduced into the analysis. It is thus obvious that Confluence Analysis requires many more computations, so that comparisons of the results become more complicated as compared with the proposed 'experimental technique'.

Example. Table 11.1. includes time-series data for the period 1951—68 on clothing expenditure, disposable income, liquid assets, a price index for clothing items and a general price index for a certain country.

Table 11.1. Data for the estimation of the demand function for clothing

Year	Expenditure on clothing (£ m)	Disposable income (£ m)	Liquid assets (£ m)	Price index for clothing 1963 = 100	General price index 1963 = 100
1959	8·4	82·9	17·1	92	94
1960	9·6	88·0	21·3	93	96
1961	10·4	99·9	25·1	96	97
1962	11·4	105·3	29·0	94	97
1963	12·2	117·7	34·0	100	100
1964	14·2	131·0	40·0	101	101
1965	15·8	148·2	44·0	105	104
1966	17·9	161·8	49·0	112	109
1967	19·3	174·2	51·0	112	111
1968	20·8	184·7	53·0	112	111

On *a priori* grounds consumers' expenditure on clothing is influenced by all the factors included in the above table, so that the demand function for clothing should be

$$C = b_0 + b_1 Y + b_2 L + b_3 P_c + b_4 P_o + u$$

where C = expenditure on clothing

Y = income

L = liquid assets

P_c = price of clothing

P_o = price of other commodities.

Applying least squares to this function we obtain the following estimates:

$$C = -13.53 + 0.097\,Y + 0.015\,L - 0.199\,P_c + 0.34\,P_o$$
$$S_{(b_i)} \qquad (7.5) \quad (0.03) \quad (0.05) \quad (0.09) \quad (0.15)$$

$$R^2 = 0.998 \qquad \Sigma \hat{y}^2 = 28.15 \qquad \Sigma e^2 = 0.33 \qquad d = 3.4$$

Applying analysis of variance to test the overall significance of the fit we find

$$F^* = \frac{\Sigma \hat{y}^2/(K-1)}{\Sigma e^2/(n-K)} = \frac{28.15/4}{0.33/5} = 15.6$$

Since the theoretical $F_{0.05}$ value with $v_1 = K - 1 = 4$ and $v_2 = n - K = 5$ degrees of freedom is 5·19, we reject the null hypothesis, accepting the alternative that there is a significant relationship between clothing expenditure and the explanatory variables.

However, all the explanatory variables are seriously multicollinear as can be seen by the simple correlation coefficients

$$r_{YL} = 0.993$$
$$r_{YP_c} = 0.980$$
$$r_{YP_o} = 0.987$$
$$r_{LP_c} = 0.964$$
$$r_{LP_o} = 0.973$$
$$r_{P_c P_o} = 0.991$$

To explore the effects of multicollinearity we compute the elementary regressions

(1) $\hat{C} = \hat{a}_0 + \hat{a}_1 Y = -1.24 + 0.118 Y$ $R^2 = 0.995$ $d = 2.6$
             (0·37)   (0·002)

(2) $\hat{C} = \hat{b}_0 + \hat{b}_1 P_c = -38.51 + 0.516 P_c$ $R^2 = 0.951$ $d = 2.4$
             (4·20)   (0·04)

(3) $\hat{C} = \hat{c}_0 + \hat{c}_1 L = 2.11 + 0.327 L$ $R^2 = 0.967$ $d = 0.4$
             (0·81) (0·02)

(4) $\hat{C} = \hat{d}_0 + \hat{d}_1 P_o = -53.65 + 0.663 P_o$ $R^2 = 0.977$ $d = 2.1$
             (3·63)   (0·03)

We choose the first elementary regression ($C = f(Y)$) as the first step in our analysis, since income (Y) seems on *a priori* grounds to be the most important explanatory variable during the period under consideration. We then introduce the remaining explanatory variables gradually into the function. The results are shown in table 11.2.

Table 11.2

	b_0 Constant	$\hat{b}_1$ (Y)	$\hat{b}_2$ (P_c)	$\hat{b}_3$ (L)	$\hat{b}_4$ (P_o)	R^2	d
$C = f(Y)$	−1·24 (0·37)	0·118 (0·002)	−	−	−	0·995	2·6
$C = f(Y, P_c)$	1·40 (4·92)	0·126 (0·01)	−0·036 (0·07)	−	−	0·996	2·5
$C = f(Y, P_c, L)$	0·94 (5·17)	0·138 (0·02)	−0·034 (0·06)	−0·037 (0·05)	−	0·996	3·1
$C = f(Y, P_c, P_o)$	−12·76 (6·52)	0·104 (0·01)	−0·188 (0·07)	−	0·319 (0·12)	0·997	3·5
$C = f(Y, P_c, L, P_o)$	−13·53 (7·5)	0·097 ((0·03)	−0·199 (0·09)	0·015 (0·05)	0·34 (0·15)	0·998	3·4

Note. The numbers in brackets are the standard errors of the estimates.

Changes in income seems to be important in explaining the variation in clothing expenditure.

The introduction of P_c improves slightly the overall R^2. The signs of the $\hat{b}$'s are correct but the standard errors show that $\hat{b}_2$ is not statistically significant. The high intercorrelation of Y and P_c does not affect the stability or the significance of $\hat{b}_1$.

The introduction of liquid assets does not give a satisfactory estimate for either b_2 or b_3. Clearly the high intercorrelation of P_c and L makes it impossible to obtain separate meaningful estimates of b_2 and b_3. However, the estimate $\hat{b}_1$ is not affected, despite the serious intercorrelation of Y, P_c and L. Thus L may be considered as a superfluous variable.

Dropping L and introducing P_0 in the function we obtain a better overall fit. R^2 is slightly increased, and all the parameter estimates have the correct sign and are statistically significant. Despite the high degree of collinearity of all regressors the standard errors are not large.

The regression with all four explanatory variables shows that the effect of multicollinearity is not serious for $\hat{b}_1$ and $\hat{b}_2$. The coefficient of L, $\hat{b}_3$, is not significant, so that L is clearly a superfluous variable.

Thus the best fit is obtained from the function

$$C = f(Y, P_c P_0)$$

11.4.2. THE FARRAR–GLAUBER TEST FOR MULTICOLLINEARITY

(D. E. Farrar and R. R. Glauber, 'Multicollinearity in Regression Analysis', *Rev. Econ. & Statist.*, vol. **49**, 1967, pp. 92–107.)

A statistical test for multicollinearity has been recently developed by Farrar and Glauber. It is really a set of three tests, that is the authors use three statistics for testing for multicollinearity. The first test is a Chi-Square test for the detection of the existence and the severity of multicollinearity in a function including several explanatory variables. The second test is an F test for locating which variables are multicollinear. The third test is a t test for finding out the pattern of multicollinearity, that is for determining which variables are responsible for the appearance of multicollinear variables.

Farrar and Glauber consider multicollinearity in a sample as a departure of the observed X's from orthogonality.[1] Their approach emerged from the general ideas developed in the preceding paragraphs, namely that if multicollinearity is perfect then the coefficients become indeterminate, and that the intercorrelations among the various explanatory variables can be measured by multiple correlation coefficients and partial correlation coefficients. The Farrar–Glauber tests may be outlined as follows.

Firstly. A chi-square (χ^2) test for the presence and severity of multicollinearity in a function with several explanatory variables.

The hypothesis being tested at this stage is that the sample X's are orthogonal ($r_{x_i x_i} = 1$ and $r_{x_i x_j} = 0$). For this, it is convenient to standardise the variables for sample size and for standard deviation. Standardisation is implemented through division of all observations of each X, expressed in deviations from its mean, by $\sqrt{n}$ times the standard deviation of X; that is the standardised value of the tth

---

[1] Strictly speaking the Farrar–Glauber statistics are descriptive of the correlations among the X's of the *sample*, and not test statistics of correlation features of the population of X's.

observation of the jth variable is

$$\frac{(X_{jt} - \bar{X}_j)}{\sqrt{n}\ (s_{x_j})}$$

This operation is equivalent to division of each element of the determinant of the sums of squares and sums of products of the X's (expressed in deviation form) by the square roots of the sums of squared deviations of the variables appearing in this element. For example the determinant of the X's (in deviation form) in the three-variable model is

$$\begin{vmatrix} \Sigma x_1^2 & \Sigma x_1 x_2 & \Sigma x_1 x_3 \\ \Sigma x_1 x_2 & \Sigma x_2^2 & \Sigma x_2 x_3 \\ \Sigma x_1 x_3 & \Sigma x_2 x_3 & \Sigma x_3^2 \end{vmatrix}$$

To obtain the standardised form of this determinant we divide the first element by $(\sqrt{\Sigma x_1^2}\sqrt{\Sigma x_1^2}) = (\sqrt{\Sigma x_1^2})^2$, the second element by $(\sqrt{\Sigma x_1^2}\ \sqrt{\Sigma x_2^2})$ and so on. In general, the element $\Sigma x_i x_j$ is divided by $(\sqrt{\Sigma x_i^2}\ \sqrt{\Sigma x_j^2})$ to give the corresponding element of the standardised determinant. For the three-variable model the standardised determinant is

$$\begin{vmatrix} \dfrac{\Sigma x_1^2}{(\sqrt{\Sigma x_1^2})^2} & \dfrac{\Sigma x_1 x_2}{\sqrt{\Sigma x_1^2}\sqrt{\Sigma x_2^2}} & \dfrac{\Sigma x_1 x_3}{\sqrt{\Sigma x_1^2}\sqrt{\Sigma x_3^2}} \\[3ex] \dfrac{\Sigma x_1 x_2}{\sqrt{\Sigma x_1^2}\sqrt{\Sigma x_2^2}} & \dfrac{\Sigma x_2^2}{(\sqrt{\Sigma x_2^2})^2} & \dfrac{\Sigma x_2 x_3}{\sqrt{\Sigma x_2^2}\sqrt{\Sigma x_3^2}} \\[3ex] \dfrac{\Sigma x_1 x_3}{\sqrt{\Sigma x_1^2}\sqrt{\Sigma x_3^2}} & \dfrac{\Sigma x_2 x_3}{\sqrt{\Sigma x_2^2}\sqrt{\Sigma x_3^2}} & \dfrac{\Sigma x_3^2}{(\sqrt{\Sigma x_3^2})^2} \end{vmatrix}$$

(c) The standardised determinants of the denominators of the least squares estimates may be rewritten in a slightly different form bearing in mind that the main diagonal elements are equal to unity and the off-diagonal elements are the simple correlation coefficients among the explanatory variables. Thus the standardised determinants are called *correlation determinants*. In the three-variable case the standardised determinant is

$$\begin{vmatrix} 1 & r_{x_1 x_2} & r_{x_1 x_3} \\ r_{x_1 x_2} & 1 & r_{x_2 x_3} \\ r_{x_1 x_3} & r_{x_2 x_3} & 1 \end{vmatrix}$$

From these forms we can easily examine the two extreme cases of orthogonality and of perfect multicollinearity.

In the case of perfect multicollinearity the simple correlation coefficients $r_{x_1 x_2}$, $r_{x_2 x_3}$, etc. are equal to unity and hence the value of the standardised (correlation) determinant is equal to zero. For the two-variable model we have

$$\begin{vmatrix} 1 & r_{x_1 x_2} \\ r_{x_1 x_2} & 1 \end{vmatrix} = \begin{vmatrix} 1 & 1 \\ 1 & 1 \end{vmatrix} = 0$$

In the case of orthogonality of the X's the simple correlation coefficient for each pair of X's is equal to zero and hence the value of the standardised determinant is equal to unity. In the two-variable model we have

$$\begin{vmatrix} 1 & r_{x_1 x_2} \\ r_{x_1 x_2} & 1 \end{vmatrix} = \begin{vmatrix} 1 & 0 \\ 0 & 1 \end{vmatrix} = 1$$

It follows that if the value of the standardised determinant lies between zero and unity, there is some degree of multicollinearity in the function.

The above analysis suggests that multicollinearity may be considered as a departure from orthogonality. The stronger the departure from orthogonality, that is the closer the value of the determinant to zero, the stronger the degree of multicollinearity, and *vice versa*. Starting from this fact Glauber and Farrar suggested the following χ^2 test for detecting the strength of multicollinearity over the whole set of explanatory variables. The basic hypothesis here is

$$H_0 : \text{the } X\text{'s are orthogonal}$$

and it is tested against the alternative hypothesis

$$H_1 : \text{the } X\text{'s are not orthogonal}$$

Glauber and Farrar have found that the quantity

$$*\chi^2 = -[n - 1 - \tfrac{1}{6}(2k + 5)] \cdot \log_e \begin{bmatrix} \text{value of the} \\ \text{standardised} \\ \text{determinant} \end{bmatrix}$$

(where $*\chi^2$ = observed (computed from the sample) value of χ^2, n = size of the sample, and k = number of explanatory variables) has a χ^2 distribution with $\nu = \tfrac{1}{2} k(k - 1)$ degrees of freedom.

From the sample data we obtain the empirical value $*\chi^2$ which we compare with the theoretical value of χ^2 at the chosen level of significance (which may be obtained from the χ^2 table on page 661) with $\nu = \tfrac{1}{2} k(k - 1)$ degrees of freedom. It should be clear that the theoretical value of χ^2 is the value that defines the critical region of the test at the chosen level of significance and with the appropriate degrees of freedom.

If the observed $*\chi^2$ is greater than the theoretical value of χ^2 with $\tfrac{1}{2} k(k - 1)$ degrees of freedom, we reject the assumption of orthogonality, that is, we accept that there is multicollinearity in the function. The higher the observed $*\chi^2$ the more severe the multicollinearity.

If the observed $*\chi^2 < \chi^2$ we accept the assumption of orthogonality, that is we accept that there is *no significant* multicollinearity in the function.

Secondly. An F test for the location of multicollinearity

To locate the factors which are multicollinear Glauber and Farrar compute the multiple correlation coefficients among the explanatory variables $(R^2_{x_1 . x_2 x_3 \ldots x_k}, R^2_{x_2 . x_1 x_3 \ldots x_k}$, and in general $R^2_{x_i . x_1 x_2 \ldots x_k})$ and they test the statistical significance of these multiple correlation coefficients with an F test as follows. For each multiple correlation coefficient we compute the observed F^*

$$F^* = \frac{(R^2_{x_i . x_1 x_2 \ldots x_k})/(k-1)}{(1 - R^2_{x_i . x_1 x_2 \ldots x_k})/(n-k)}$$

where n = size of the sample
      k = number of explanatory variables.

The hypothesis being tested at this stage is

$$H_0 : R^2_{x_i . x_1 x_2 \ldots x_k} = 0$$

and the altervative hypothesis is

$$H_1 : R^2_{x_i . x_1 x_2 \ldots x_k} \neq 0$$

The observed value F^* is compared with the theoretical value F (from the F tables on pp. 663–4) with $\nu_1 = (k-1)$ and $\nu_2 = (n-k)$ degrees of freedom (at the chosen level of significance). The theoretical F value is the value of F that defines the critical region of the test. (a) If $F^* > F$, we accept that the variable X_i is multicollinear, that is we reject the null hypothesis. (b) If $F^* < F$ we accept that the variable X_i is not multicollinear.

Thirdly. A t test for the pattern of multicollinearity

This is a t test which aims at the detection of the variables which cause multicollinearity.

To find which variables are responsible for the multicollinearity we compute the partial correlation coefficients among the explanatory variables and test their statistical significance with the t statistic. The meaning and formulae of the partial correlation coefficients have been developed in Chapter 7. Recall that the partial correlation coefficient between any two variables, X_i and X_j, shows the degree of correlation between these two variables, all others being kept constant. For the two-variable model the partial correlation coefficient is the same as the simple correlation coefficient. For the three-variable model the partial correlation coefficients are given by the formulae

$$r^2_{x_1 x_2 . x_3} = \frac{(r_{12} - r_{13} r_{23})^2}{(1 - r^2_{23})(1 - r^2_{13})}$$

$$r^2_{x_1 x_3 . x_2} = \frac{(r_{13} - r_{12} r_{23})^2}{(1 - r^2_{23})(1 - r^2_{12})}$$

$$r^2_{x_2 x_3 . x_1} = \frac{(r_{23} - r_{12} r_{13})^2}{(1 - r^2_{13})(1 - r^2_{12})}$$

For models involving more than three explanatory variables similar formulae can be developed.

The basic hypothesis here is

$$H_0 : r_{x_i x_j . x_1 x_2 \ldots x_k} = 0$$

and is tested against the alternative hypothesis

$$H_1 : r_{x_i x_j . x_1 x_2 \ldots x_k} \neq 0$$

Having estimated the partial correlation coefficients, we test their significance by computing for each of them the statistic

$$t^* = \frac{(r_{x_i x_j . x_1 x_2 \ldots x_k}) \sqrt{n-k}}{\sqrt{1 - r^2_{x_i x_j . x_1 x_2 \ldots x_k}}}$$

where $r_{x_i x_j . x_1 x_2 \ldots x_k}$ denotes the partial correlation coefficient between x_i and x_j. (Tests of significance for the correlation coefficient were discussed in Chapter 5.)

The observed value t^* is compared with the theoretical t value (from the Student's t-Table on page 660) with $\nu = (n-k)$ degrees of freedom (at the chosen level of significance).

If $t^* > t$ we accept that the partial correlation coefficient between the variables X_i and X_j is significant, that is, the variables X_i and X_j are responsible for the multicollinearity in the function.

If $t^* < t$ we accept that X_i and X_j are not the cause of multicollinearity, since their partial correlation coefficient is not statistically significant.

With the above three statistics we find the severity, the location and the pattern of multicollinearity.

Example. As an application of the above tests of multicollinearity we give the results of a cost function computed by Farrar and Glauber for the maintenance of ships. The function fitted on a cross-section sample of 96 ships is of the form

$$\log Y = b_0 + b_1 \log X_1 + b_2 \log X_2 + \ldots + b_7 \log X_7 + \log u$$

where: Y = maintenance cost of ship per year (000 dollars per year)
X_1 = age of ship (years)
X_2 = size of ship (displacement, thousands of tons)
X_3 = time between successive overhauls (overhaul cycle, in years)

X_4 = fuel consumption
X_5 = dummy variable for 'propulsion mode' (e.g. diesel, steam, nuclear, etc.)
$\quad X_5$ = 1 if the ship is diesel propelled
$\quad X_5$ = 0 if the ship is not diesel propelled
X_6 = dummy variable for 'complexity of ship structure'
$\quad X_6$ = 1 if radar picket
$\quad X_6$ = 0 if not
X_7 = dummy variable for describing whether the ship has been converted under the FRAM program (the capitals stand for Fleet Rehabilitation And Modernisation)
$\quad X_7$ = 1 if FRAM
$\quad X_7$ = 0 if not FRAM.

The results obtained from the classical least squares are $R^2_{Y \cdot X_1 \ldots X_7} = 0.80$ with an F value = 56 (with $\nu_1 = k - 1 = 7$ and $\nu_2 = 96 - 8 = 88$ degrees of freedom)

	$\hat{b}_1$	$\hat{b}_2$	$\hat{b}_3$	$\hat{b}_4$	$\hat{b}_5$	$\hat{b}_6$	$\hat{b}_7$
	0·34	0·40	−0·79	0·05	−0·03	0·11	−0·16
$s(\hat{b}_i)$	(0·03)	(0·08)	(0·09)	(0·10)	(0·09)	(0·04)	(0·06)

The overall F test as well as the small standard errors for most of the estimates suggest that the regression is meaningful in the sense that Y does actually depend on the set of $X_1 \ldots X_7$ variables.

To test for the overall degree of multicollinearity the $*\chi^2$ was computed and found equal to 261. The theoretical $\chi^2_{0 \cdot 0 5}$ (with $\frac{1}{2} k(k-1) = 21$ degrees of freedom) is equal to 32·7. Since $*\chi^2$ is much higher than $\chi^2_{0 \cdot 0 5}$ we conclude that there is a substantial degree of multicollinearity in the function.

To find which are the multicollinear variables we compute the multiple correlation coefficients and their associated F-statistics within the set of explanatory variables.

$$R^2_{x_1 \cdot x_2 x_3 \ldots x_7} = 0.30 \qquad F_{x_1} = 6.3$$
$$R^2_{x_2 \cdot x_1 x_3 \ldots x_7} = 0.57 \qquad F_{x_2} = 19.9$$
$$R^2_{x_3 \cdot x_1 x_2 \ldots x_7} = 0.30 \qquad F_{x_3} = 6.3$$
$$R^2_{x_4 \cdot x_1 x_2 \ldots x_7} = 0.76 \qquad F_{x_4} = 47.5$$
$$R^2_{x_5 \cdot x_1 x_2 \ldots x_7} = 0.76 \qquad F_{x_5} = 47.1$$
$$R^2_{x_6 \cdot x_1 x_2 \ldots x_7} = 0.46 \qquad F_{x_6} = 12.7$$
$$R^2_{x_7 \cdot x_1 x_2 \ldots x_6} = 0.24 \qquad F_{x_7} = 4.8$$

From the above results it follows that the factors which are mostly affected by multicollinearity are X_4 (fuel consumption) and X_5 (diesel propulsion).

Finally, in order to find out which factors are responsible for the multicollinearity in the variables X_4 and X_5 we compute the partial correlation coefficients for the explanatory variables as well as the corresponding t-statistic for each partial correlation coefficient.

The computations shown in table 11.3 reveal that the cause of multicollinearity lies mainly in intercorrelation between (a) X_4 and X_5, and (b) X_5 and X_6.

To sum up: from the above tests we established:
(1) that there is a high degree of intercorrelation in the cost function (severity);
(2) that multicollinearity is present in variables X_4 and X_5 (location);
(3) that multicollinearity is due to intercorrelation between X_4 and X_5 on the one hand, and between X_5 and X_6 on the other (pattern).

Table 11.3

		X_1	X_2	X_3	X_4	X_5	X_6	X_7
Age	X_1	—						
Size	X_2	$r_{12\cdot} = 0\cdot13$ (1·27)	—					
Cycle	X_3	$r_{13\cdot} = 0\cdot21$ (2·01)	$r_{23\cdot} = 0\cdot27$ (2·60)	—				
Fuel	X_4	$r_{14\cdot} = -0\cdot35$ (-3·57)	$r_{24\cdot} = 0\cdot34$ (3·44)	$r_{34\cdot} = 0\cdot09$ (0·82)	—			
Diesel	X_5	$r_{15\cdot} = -0\cdot27$ (1·27)	$r_{25\cdot} = -0\cdot21$ (-2·03)	$r_{35\cdot} = 0\cdot12$ (1·15)	$r_{45\cdot} = -0\cdot68$ (-8·77)	—		
Radar	X_6	$r_{16\cdot} = 0\cdot45$ (4·72)	$r_{26\cdot} = 0\cdot08$ (0·78)	$r_{36\cdot} = -0\cdot35$ (-3·51)	$r_{46\cdot} = 0\cdot31$ (3·13)	$r_{56\cdot} = 0\cdot50$ (5·51)	—	
FRAM	X_7	$r_{17\cdot} = 0\cdot34$ (3·38)	$r_{27\cdot} = -0\cdot13$ (-1·27)	$r_{37\cdot} = -0\cdot06$ (0·59)	$r_{47\cdot} = 0\cdot40$ (4·06)	$r_{57\cdot} = 0\cdot27$ (2·68)	$r_{67\cdot} = -0\cdot26$ (-2·55)	—

Note: The numbers in parentheses are the t^* values for the corresponding partial correlation coefficients.

This test enables the researcher to consider the whole extent and pattern of multicollinearity and hence helps him to make up his mind as to what he thinks should be the appropriate procedure for dealing with the problem. He may decide to follow one of the approaches developed in the following section. Or he may decide to drop the factor(s) which causes multicollinearity on the grounds that it is unimportant in the particular study. Or he may decide to accept the estimates of the original model (despite multicollinearity), because he may be interested in forecasting. (We will see at the end of this section that forecasting with a multicollinear function assumes that the pattern of multicollinearity will not change in the period of the forecast.) Or he may decide that those b's which are rather stable (and with small standard errors) are reliable as analytical values of the true parameters and hence use them for policy decisions, while not accepting the b's which are unstable.

It should be noted that the Farrar–Glauber method for testing multicollinearity is based only on the correlation coefficients (simple or partial) of the explanatory variables. It does not make use of the overall $R^2_{Y . x_1 \ldots x_k}$, which measures the strength of dependence of Y on the X's. Yet, it is a fact (and the authors recognise it at the end of their article) that the effects of multicollinearity (large standard errors and mis-specification, that is rejection of relevant factors) depend partly on the overall $R^2_{Y . x_1 \ldots x_k}$. Thus it seems that the Frisch type approach for detecting multicollinearity is superior to the Farrar–Glauber approach in two respects: (a) we take $R^2_{Y . x_1 \ldots x_k}$ into account; (b) we can study the effects of new variables on the values and standard errors of the estimates of the parameters of the strategically important variables which are introduced first in the function at the initial stages of the exploration of the relationship.

Another method for detecting multicollinearity is the method of Principal Components, which will be developed in Chapter 16.

11.5. SOLUTIONS FOR THE INCIDENCE OF MULTICOLLINEARITY

The solutions which may be adopted if multicollinearity exists in a function vary, depending on the severity of multicollinearity, on availability of other sources of data (larger samples, or cross-section samples, etc.), on the importance of factors which are multicollinear, on the purpose for which the function is being estimated and other considerations.

(1) Some writers have suggested that if multicollinearity does not seriously affect the estimates of the coefficients, one may tolerate its presence in the function, although the integrity of the least squares estimates is to a certain extent impaired.

(2) Others have suggested that if multicollinearity affects some of the unimportant factors one may exclude these factors from the function. Again specification error may well be expected to undermine the BLU character of the ordinary least-squares.

(3) Multicollinearity may affect only a part of the $\hat{b}$'s, while other estimates may remain fairly stable and reliable. In this case: (a) the reliable $\hat{b}$'s may be

used for any purpose, forecast or policy formulation (which requires reliable information about structural coefficients); (b) all the estimates may be used for forecasts, provided that the same multicollinearity pattern will continue to exist in the forecast period.

If, however, multicollinearity has serious effects on the coefficient estimates of important factors one should adopt one of the following *corrective* solutions.

11.5.1. *Application of Methods Incorporating Extraneous Quantitative Information*

The most important of these methods are: (a) the method of restricted least squares; (b) the method of pooling cross-section and time series data (which is actually a special case of restricted least squares); (c) Durbin's version of generalised least squares; (d) the mixed estimation technique, proposed by Theil and Goldberger. These methods are examined in Chapter 17, since they are general econometric methods which may be applied in any particular research, irrespective of the presence of linear relationships among the explanatory variables.

11.5.2. *Increase of the Size of the Sample*

It has been suggested that multicollinearity may be avoided or reduced if we increase the size of the sample by gathering more observations. Thus Christ says that by increasing the sample, high covariances among estimated parameters resulting from multicollinearity in an equation can be reduced, because these covariances are inversely proportional to sample size. (See C. F. Christ, *Econometric Models and Methods*, p. 389.) This is true only if multicollinearity is due to errors of measurement, as well as when intercorrelation happens to exist only in our original sample but not in the population of the X's. (See Stone, *Consumers' Expenditure in the U.K.*, p. 302.) If the populations of the variables are multicollinear, obviously an increase in the size of the sample will not help in the reduction of multicollinear relations among the variables.

11.5.3. *Substitution of Lagged Variables for Other Explanatory Variables in Distributed-lag Models*

In recent years a lot of research in econometrics has been directed towards the use of lagged values of explanatory variables (distributed lags). This means that researchers have eventually recognised the fact that a certain pattern of behaviour is determined not only by the current values of the explanatory variables, but also by past values of these variables. The influence is smaller the more remote the value becomes. For example the consumption patterns of individuals depend on current incomes as well as on past incomes; however, more recent income levels exert a higher influence on consumption decisions than remoter past levels of earnings.

Thus the original function may be written as

$$Y_t = b_0 + b_1 X_t + b_2 X_{(t-1)} + b_3 X_{(t-2)} + \ldots + u_t$$

For obvious reasons the successive values (X_t, X_{t-1}, X_{t-2}, etc.) of any explanatory variable X_i are often highly correlated. Multicollinearity may be avoided in this case by adopting Koyck's suggestion of substitution of the lagged values of X for a single lagged value of the dependent variable

$$Y_t = b_0 + b_1 X_t + \rho Y_{t-1} + (u_t - \rho u_{t-1})$$

In this model instead of having all the lagged values of X in the function we have only X_t and Y_{t-1}, which in general are expected to be less correlated than the lagged values of X. (For the derivation of this model see Chapter 13.)

11.5.4. *Introduction of Additional Equations in the Model*

Multicollinearity may be overcome if we introduce additional equations into our model to express *meaningfully* the relationships between the multicollinear X's. When looking at the set of explanatory variables one is able, in most cases, to find relationships between the X's (and other new variables) which make economic sense. By explicitly formulating these relationships one can form a simultaneous-equation model, which, if identified, can be estimated with a simultaneous-equation technique (see Chapter 14). The reduced form method will bypass the problem of multicollinearity in the original equation provided that the new model is exactly identified (see Chapter 15). If the new model is over-identified one may use extraneous information for some parameters in order to obtain unique values of the remaining parameters from the reduced form model. (See E. J. Kane, *Economic Statistics and Econometrics,* Harper International Edition, p. 279.)

11.5.5. *Application of the Principal Components Method*

The method of principal components will be developed in Chapter 17. For the present we note that its application for avoiding the effects of multicollinearity has been questioned by various writers on the grounds that it uses less information from the sample than the OLS method. (See Glauber and Farrar, pp. 92–107.) Econometricians are unanimous in accepting the fact that multicollinearity impairs the estimates due to lack of sufficient independent variation in the sample. The information of the sample is not sufficient for reliable estimation of all the coefficients of the model. The greater the degree of multicollinearity, the more arbitrarily and unreliably does OLS allocate the variation in Y among the individual explanatory variables. The corrective solutions suggested earlier involve the use of more information, acquired from extraneous estimation, from increased samples, from subjective imposition of restrictions on the values of some coefficients or on the relations among the explanatory variables. With the principal components method we construct some artificial orthogonal variables (from linear combinations of the X's). We thus transform the multicollinear X's in orthogonal variables. If these artificial variables can be given any specific economic meaning, then they can be used as variables in their own right, and the transformation provides a defensible solution to the multicollinearity problem, because in this case we achieve a *meaningful* reduction in the number of the parameters of the original model. However, in most cases the constructed variables cannot be interpreted directly as economic variables, and their use implies utilisation of only a part of all the information of the sample (the part incorporated into the principal components), that is, a reduction of information instead of application of the required increase in the information of the sample.

11.6. MULTICOLLINEARITY AND PREDICTION

It has been suggested that the inclusion or not of intercorrelated variables in the function depends on the purpose of the estimation. In general, the purpose of estimating a model, is *either* the verification of theory (or rather non-refutation of theory) via an accurate estimation of the value of individual coefficients, since these are the elasticities and propensities of economic theory, *or* the prediction of the value of the dependent variable in a future period.

If the purpose is the estimation of individual coefficients, either the inclusion or the exclusion of intercorrelated variables will not help, because the estimates in both cases will most probably be imprecise. In this case the only real improvement in the estimate is to use additional information, for example extraneous estimates, larger samples, and so on.

If the purpose of the estimation is to *forecast* the values of the dependent variable, then we may include the intercorrelated variables and ignore the problems of multicollinearity, provided that we are certain that the same pattern of intercorrelation of the explanatory variables will continue in the period of prediction. We may get good forecasts even without being able to disentangle the separate influences of the explanatory variables, provided the latter continue to change in the same way as in the sample period. But if the relationship between the explanatory variables is expected to change in the period of the forecast, then accurate forecasting requires accurate knowledge of the separate coefficients, that is, of the separate influences of the explanatory variables on the dependent variable. (See for example Christ, *Econometric Models and Methods*, pp. 389–90.)

11.7. MULTICOLLINEARITY AND IDENTIFICATION

Multicollinearity has a strong connection with under-identification, although the former refers to the values of the X's in the *particular sample* with which we attempt to estimate our model, while identification refers to the *structure* of the model irrespective of sample size or sample quality and content. This connection will be formally discussed in Chapter 15. For the present we note the following.

In both cases there are too many relationships among the variables which prevent the determination of the parameters of the relationship. The incidence of multicollinearity, like under-identification, creates estimating difficulties for the structural parameters. It does not however, impair the theoretical validity of the model. In other words the specification of the model may be correct, and yet the estimation of the structural parameters may be impaired by the presence of multicollinearity in the particular sample with which we work, or by the fact that the model is not identified.

For example from economic theory we may specify the consumption function as

$$C = b_0 + b_1 Y_1 + b_2 Y_2 + u$$

where Y_1 = farmer's income
  Y_2 = other income
  b_1 = MPC of the agricultural sector
  b_2 = MPC of the urban districts.

The specification is correct on *a priori* grounds since $b_1 \neq b_2$ and in particular $b_1 < b_2$ (the MPC is lower in agricultural districts). However if Y_1 and Y_2 happen to show the same variability over time (for example if $Y_1 = \frac{1}{2} Y_2$ over the period of the sample), the above function cannot be estimated due to multicollinearity.

In general, when two (or more) variables show the same pattern of variation, they act truly as one, and from the point of view of statistical procedure the variables *are* one. Such data do not show sufficient independent variability to enable us to disentangle the separate effects of the variables in question. Multicollinearity is a 'disease' of the sample data and not of the construction (specification) of the model, although the latter may be affected in practice because of the collinearity of the explanatory variables and because of the uncertainty of the researcher about the correctness of his maintained hypothesis.

11.8. MULTICOLLINEARITY AND MIS-SPECIFICATION IN VARIABLES: SPECIFICATION BIAS

Multicollinearity is often a serious source of error in the individual coefficients. Model builders tend to omit variables from various functions in order to avoid the consequences of multicollinearity, for rendering the model identified, for simplification, because of data limitations or from sheer ignorance of all the factors that determine the phenomenon being studied. This procedure introduces a specification error in the model, since the omission of variables will affect the values of the parameters of the remaining variables. By omitting (or adding) variables one may avoid multicollinearity (or the consequences of underidentification) but one is bound to have a specification error in the parameters. Which source of error (the one arising from multicollinearity or the one due to mis-specification of variables) is more serious, is not as yet established in econometric theory. Let us examine the consequences of specification error in the simple case of a function from which a variable is wrongly excluded.

Assume that the true function explaining the variation in y is

$$y = b_1 x_1 + b_2 x_2 + u$$

However, either due to ignorance of the true relation or because x_1 and x_2 are strongly multicollinear, we exclude x_2 from the function and instead we apply least squares to the equation

$$y = b_1^* x_1 + u^*$$

Clearly b_1^* will be different than b_1. The actual difference may be found as follows.

(a) Applying OLS to the mis-specified function we obtain

$$b_1^* = \frac{\Sigma y x_1}{\Sigma x_1^2}$$

(b) The normal equations for the correctly specified model are

$$\Sigma y x_1 = b_1 \Sigma x_1^2 + b_2 \Sigma x_1 x_2$$
$$\Sigma y x_2 = b_1 \Sigma x_1 x_2 + b_2 \Sigma x_2^2$$

Dividing the first equation through by Σx_1^2 we obtain

$$\frac{\Sigma y x_1}{\Sigma x_1^2} = b_1 + b_2 \frac{\Sigma x_1 x_2}{\Sigma x_1^2}$$

We observe that

$$\frac{\Sigma y x_1}{\Sigma x_1^2} = b_1^*$$

and $\Sigma x_1 x_2 / \Sigma x_1^2$ is the slope of the regression of x_2 on x_1, that is, the coefficient in the function $x_2 = a_1 x_1$

$$a_1 = \frac{\Sigma x_1 x_2}{\Sigma x_1^2}$$

Hence we may write

$$E(b_1^*) = b_1 + b_2 \cdot a_1$$

In other words we see that the coefficient b_1^* in the incorrect specification is different from b_1, the coefficient of the correct specification. The specification error is

[specification bias] $= [E(b_1^*) - b_1] = (b_2)(a_1)$

By the definition of the correct model we know that $b_2 \neq 0$. Therefore b_1^* would be equal to b_1 only if $a_1 = 0$, that is, if x_1 and x_2 are not correlated at all (if they are orthogonal). In real life we cannot expect to have orthogonal variables in an econometric model, since most economic magnitudes are interdependent. Thus omission of variables from the function will yield biased estimates of the parameters of the included variables.

The above analysis may easily be extended to functions with more explanatory variables. For example assume that the correct specification is

$$y = b_1 x_1 + b_2 x_2 + b_3 x_3 + u$$

If we omit x_2 and x_3 from the function, incorrectly, we will obtain an estimate b_1^*

$$b_1^* = \frac{\Sigma y x_1}{\Sigma x_1^2}$$

which would be biased (specification bias). This bias is given by the expression

$$\text{bias} = [E(b_1^*) - b_1] = b_2 \frac{\Sigma x_1 x_2}{\Sigma x_1^2} + b_3 \frac{\Sigma x_1 x_3}{\Sigma x_1^2}$$

or

$$[E(b_1^*) - b_1] = (b_2)(a_1) + (b_3)(a_2)$$

where a_1 = the coefficient of the 'regression' of x_2 on x_1
a_2 = the coefficient of the 'regression' of x_3 on x_1

In general the bias imparted in any one parameter estimate $\hat{b}_i$ through the omission of some explanatory variables depends on the parameters (b's) of the omitted variables and the relationships between the included and excluded variables. For example assume that the correct specification of the model includes k explanatory variables

$$y = b_1 x_1 + b_2 x_2 + \ldots + b_r x_r + b_{(r+1)} x_{(r+1)} + \ldots + b_k x_k + u$$

but we incorrectly specify our equation to include, say, r explanatory variables

$$y = b_1 x_1 + b_2 x_2 + \ldots + b_r x_r + v$$

Each one of the estimates $\hat{b}_1, \hat{b}_2, \ldots, \hat{b}_r$ will be biased. To define the bias we 'regress' each one of the excluded $(k - r)$ variables on the included variables

$$x_{(r+1)} = a_{1,\,(r+1)} x_1 + a_{2,\,(r+1)} x_2 + a_{3,\,(r+1)} x_3 + \ldots + a_{r,\,(r+1)} x_r$$
$$x_{(r+2)} = a_{1,\,(r+2)} x_1 + a_{2,\,(r+2)} x_2 + a_{3,\,(r+1)} x_3 + \ldots + a_{r,\,(r+2)} x_r$$

$$x_{(k)} = a_{1,\,(k)} x_1 + a_{2,\,(k)} x_2 + a_{3,\,(k)} x_3 + \ldots + a_{r,\,(k)} x_r$$

We may arrange the coefficients of the above relationships which connect the excluded with the included explanatory variables in a table

$a_{1,\,(r+1)}$	$a_{2,\,(r+1)}$	$a_{3,\,(r+1)}$	$\cdots \cdots$	$a_{r,\,(r+1)}$
$a_{1,\,(r+2)}$	$a_{2,\,(r+2)}$	$a_{3,\,(r+2)}$	$\cdots \cdots$	$a_{r,\,(r+2)}$
$a_{1,\,(k)}$	$a_{2,\,(k)}$	$a_{3,\,(k)}$	$\cdots \cdots$	$a_{r,\,(k)}$

Using this table we may generalise the procedure of determination of the specification bias in any one on the parameter estimates of the included variables. Thus the bias in $\hat{b}_1$ is the sum of products of the coefficients of the first column of the table multiplied by the b's of the excluded variables

$$E(\hat{b}_1) = b_1 + \underbrace{[a_{1,(r+1)}b_{(r+1)} + a_{1,(r+2)}b_{(r+2)} + \ldots + a_{1,(k)}b_k]}_{\text{specification bias in } b_1}$$

Similarly, the specification bias in $\hat{b}_2$ is the sum of the products of the second column of the table multiplied by the b's of the excluded variables

$$E(\hat{b}_2) = b_2 + \underbrace{[a_{2,(r+1)}b_{(r+1)} + a_{2,(r+2)}b_{(r+2)} + \ldots + a_{2,(k)}b_k]}_{\text{specification bias in } \hat{b}_2}$$

and so on.

The omission of relevant X's from the function has an additional effect: it causes an overestimation of the residual variance (that is $\Sigma e^2/(n-k)$ will be larger when relevant X's are omitted), with the consequence that the standard errors of the estimates will be overestimated. Hence inferences about the b's of the included variables will be inaccurate.

The above discussion refers to the omission of relevant variables from the model. It can be shown that the inclusion of irrelevant variables in a function does not introduce statistical bias in the parameter estimates. Thus, if the researcher is in doubt about the relevance of a regressor, it is preferable to include it in the function, provided that the sample is large (so that there are adequate degrees of freedom), and provided that data are available on the variable whose relevance is not sure on *a priori* considerations. (See J. Johnston, *Econometric Methods*, 1972, p. 169.)

EXERCISES

1. The following table shows time series on five variables Y_1, X_1, X_2, X_3, X_4, in arbitrary units.

Y	6·0	6·0	6·5	7·1	7·2	7·6	8·0	9·0	9·0	9·3
X_1	40·1	40·3	47·5	49·2	52·3	58·0	61·3	62·5	64·7	66·8
X_2	5·5	4·7	5·2	6·8	7·3	8·7	10·2	14·1	17·1	21·3
X_3	108	94	108	100	99	99	101	97	93	102
X_4	63	72	86	100	107	111	114	116	119	121

(a) Test for multicollinearity with any appropriate method.
(b) How does multicollinearity affect the parameter estimates?

2. The following table shows the value of output (X_i) the labour input (L_i) and the capital input (K_i) of 20 firms.

X_i	82	73	58	68	98	83	100	110	120	95
L_i	15	39	99	12	42	95	45	36	40	65
K_i	90	40	20	60	60	30	60	80	80	40

X_i	115	64	140	85	56	150	65	36	57	50
L_i	30	60	100	95	75	90	25	80	12	65
K_i	80	30	60	40	20	90	30	10	40	20

(a) Obtain estimates of a Cobb–Douglas production function using the observations 1–15.

(b) Explore the pattern of multicollinearity and its effects on the estimates.

(c) Test the hypothesis that the estimates are sensitive to sample size, utilising the additional information of observations 16–20.

(d) Comment on your results.

3. Consider the following linear production function of an economy

$$X_t = b_0 + b_1 L_t + b_2 K_t + u_t$$

where X_t = quantity of output in period t
L_t = labour input (in man-hours)
K_t = capital input (in machine-hours)

(a) If it is known that technical progress is taking place, discuss the nature and effects of the mis-specification bias imparted in the $\hat{b}$'s.

(b) Suppose that K is omitted from the function. Explore the bias imparted in $\hat{b}_1$.

4. Consider the model

$$Y_t = b_0 + b_1 X_{1t} + b_2 X_{2t} + u_t$$

where the X's are orthogonal. Show that

(a) the $\hat{b}$'s from multiple regression are identical to the coefficient estimates obtained by a *simple* regression of Y on the corresponding X;

(b) the total sum of squared residuals is just the sum of the sum of squared residuals of all the *simple* regressions.

Note. Additional exercises are included in Appendix III.

12. Errors in Variables
   Time as a Variable
   Dummy Variables
   Estimation from Grouped Data

12.1. ERRORS IN VARIABLES

The random variable u, in a correctly specified model, absorbs primarily stochastic variations in the dependent variable (Y) produced by omitted from the equation variables and possibly errors of measurement in the Y_i's. If the ordinary least squares (OLS) estimates are to possess the optimal properties of unbiasedness and consistency the u's and the X's should be independent. Accordingly the sixth assumption in connection with the random variable u is that the values of the disturbance variable are independent of the values of the regressors $(X$'s)

$$\text{cov}(u_i X_j) = 0 \qquad \text{for } i = 1, 2, \ldots, n$$
$$j = 1, 2, \ldots, k$$

This assumption implies that the value of u in any one period does not depend on the values of the X's in any period. For this assumption to be fulfilled one of the following conditions should hold.

(1) The X's should be exogenous to the particular relationship; there should be one-way causation between Y and the X's.

The relationship being studied should not belong to a model of simultaneous equations, because in this case it is almost certain that some of the regressors in any particular equation will be endogenous to the system and hence will determine and be determined by other variables in the model.

(2) The omitted variables from any particular relationship whose influence is absorbed by the error term u should not be related to the regressors of that relationship. Otherwise their omission would cause u and the explicit X's to be correlated.

(3) The X's should be non-stochastic, and they should be measured without error.

If the X's are stochastic, then their distribution should be independent of the distribution of the Y's.

(i) If the X's are stochastic but are distributed independently of the error term u, then the OLS estimates are unbiased (and, hence, also consistent).

(ii) If the X's are lagged values of Y, then these X's and u are not fully independent. Y_{t-s} will be dependent on u_{t-s}, but if the u_t's are not autocorrelated then Y_{t-s} will be independent of u_t. For example, assume that the model is

$$Y_t = b_0 + b_1 X_t + b_2 Y_{t-1} + u_t$$

Then

$$Y_{t-1} = b_0 + b_1 X_{t-1} + b_2 Y_{t-2} + u_{t-1}$$

Clearly u_{t-1} influences Y_{t-1}; and since Y_{t-1} is an explicit regressor in the equation and affects Y_t, apparently u_{t-1} influences Y_t even if the u's are not autocorrelated. However, if the u's are serially independent then u_t and Y_{t-1} are not correlated and therefore $E(u_t Y_{t-1}) = 0$, and the OLS estimates will be consistent.

(iii) If the X's are stochastic and are not independently distributed of the u's, then OLS yields biased and inconsistent estimates.

If u and the X's are not independent, the estimates ($\hat{b}$'s) obtained from OLS will be biased. Furthermore, the bias will not tend to zero as we increase the size of the sample, so that the distribution of the $\hat{b}$'s will not collapse (in the limit) on the true value of the structural parameters. That is if $E(u_i X_i) \neq 0$ the OLS estimates will be both biased and inconsistent.

The assumption of the independence of the u's and the X's is easily violated in practice. The most common causes of dependence between the u's and the explanatory variables occur: Firstly, when the relationship being studied belongs to a system of simultaneous equations, because in this case it is almost certain that there will be a two-way causation between the regressors and the regressand in any particular equation. Secondly, when the X's are stochastic and/or include errors of measurement.

In the previous analysis of the linear regression model we were concerned with single equation models, *assuming* that the phenomenon being studied could be represented adequately with a single equation. Furthermore, we were assuming that the X's were a fixed set of values (in the hypothetical repeating sampling process underlying the application of OLS) and that they were measured without error. These assumptions are clearly unrealistic given the interdependence of economic variables and the nature of statistical data which are used for the measurement of economic relationships.

In this chapter we will examine only the case of errors of measurement in the X's. We will continue to assume that the X's are non-stochastic and that the relationship being studied is a single-equation model and does not belong to a system of simultaneous equations. In summary, we will examine the effects of errors of measurement in the X's in a single-equation model. The case of simultaneous relationships (multi-equation models) will be discussed in Chapter 14.

12.1.1. PLAUSIBILITY OF THE ASSUMPTION OF NO MEASUREMENT ERRORS IN THE X's

The assumption of absence of errors of measurement in the explanatory variables does not seem plausible in most cases. The X's, like the Y's, may well be expected to include errors of measurement.

(a) No matter how reliable the source of data, there will always be some error in the observations used for the estimation of the coefficients. This is due to the fact that most aggregate published series are obtained from samples which are 'blown up' to cover the aggregate macro-variables. Errors in sampling and errors in the extrapolation of the samples are certain to occur, and therefore errors in observations are common in the X's as well as in the Y's.

(b) In some cases the published data refer to some variables different in content than the variables required by economic theory. For example, the theory of the consumption function requires the disposable income to be used as an explanatory variable, while official statistics give figures of the GNP. If we use these figures in the consumption function we are bound to have an error of measurement in the explanatory variable.

(c) Usually the variables included in the relationships are expressed in current values, while economic theory requires 'quantity' variables. In this case it is common practice to use price indexes and deflate the value figures. The deflating procedure may lead to errors of measurement if the index of prices is not appropriate or if it contains errors.

(d) It is common to use dummy variables in a function as an approximation to some explanatory variables. Dummy variables are by their nature subject to 'errors of measurement', since they are proxies for the variables they represent.

(e) Similarly, the use of indexes (of prices, wages, etc.) as explanatory variables may contain errors which are bound to be connected with the random term u.

For all these reasons it seems that the assumption of no errors in the explanatory variables should be questioned in all econometric applications. Yet, the presence of such errors does not matter if the economic agents, producers, consumers or government agencies, take their decisions on the basis of the published data rather than on the probably unknown error-free true variables. Most government policy is based on the results of estimates obtained from published series, and decisions are made by extrapolating the observed values of the variables. This holds *a fortiori* for the decisions of firms, which are even less likely to know the true, error-free values of the variables, and thus are bound to use the available published series. If the behaviour of individuals is based on the observed values of the variables, then the error of measurement does not affect their decision-making process and the OLS method, as previously developed, is valid. The subsequent analysis, then, is relevant only in the cases where we know that the decision makers react to the true values of the variables, and not to their measured values.

12.1.2. CONSEQUENCES OF THE VIOLATION OF THE ASSUMPTION OF NO ERRORS OF MEASUREMENT

The presence of errors of measurement in the variables renders the estimates of the coefficients both *biased* and *inconsistent*.

In particular, when there are errors of measurement (or errors of observation) in the X's superimposed on the errors of measurement in Y and of omitted variables we have the following consequences on a linear function. *Firstly,* the value of the slope b_1 of the regression line is underestimated, that is the estimate $\hat{b}_1$ has a downward bias, while the value of the constant intercept $\hat{b}_0$ is overestimated, in other words the estimate $\hat{b}_0$ has an upward bias. *Secondly*, the bias in the parameter estimates does not tend to decrease as we increase the size of the sample, that is, the estimates of the parameters are asymptotically biased and therefore inconsistent.

Recall that for an estimator $\hat{b}$ to be a consistent estimator of the true parameter b two conditions should be satisfied: (1) the estimator should be asymptotically unbiased, its bias tending to zero as we increase the size of the sample infinitely (bias $\rightarrow 0$ as $n \rightarrow \infty$); and (2) the asymptotic variance must go to zero so that the distribution of the values of the estimator (in hypothetical repeated sampling) collapses on the true b as $n \rightarrow \infty$ (plim $\hat{b} = b$). In the case of errors of measurement in the variables the estimate $\hat{b}$ is biased not only for small samples but for large samples as well. Therefore the first condition of consistency is violated and $\hat{b}$ is inconsistent.

Proof of the consequences of errors in the explanatory variables

Assume that errors of measurement are superimposed on errors of omission. Thus the relationship between the true variables is

$$\psi = b_0 + b_1 \chi + u$$

where ψ = true (but unobservable) value of the dependent variable
   χ = true (but unobservable) value of the explanatory variable
   u = errors of omission.

Let us further assume that in our sample we observe the values Y and X which are related to the true values by the following relationships

$$X_i = \chi_i + v_x$$
$$Y_i = \psi_i + v_y$$

where v_x and v_y are random variables representing the errors of measurement in X and Y. To simplify our analysis and notation we may include in u both errors of omitted explanatory variables and errors of measurement in the dependent variable Y, but not errors in the explanatory variables.

We assume that both u and v satisfy the usual set of assumptions of random variables, that is
   (1) $E(u) = 0$ and $E(v) = 0$, the error terms have zero means.
   (2) $E(u^2) = \sigma_u^2$ and $E(v^2) = \sigma_v^2$, the error terms have constant variances.
   (3) $E(u_i u_j) = 0$ and $E(v_i v_j) = 0$, the error terms are serially independent.
   (4) The error in measuring the variables is independent from the true values of these variables

$$E(v\chi) = 0 \qquad E(v_y \psi) = 0$$

Furthermore, we make the following assumptions concerning the connection between the two error terms:
   (5) The error in measuring χ is independent from the true value of ψ, and similarly the error u is independent of the true value of χ

$$E(v\psi) = 0 \quad \text{and} \quad E(u\chi) = 0$$

(6) The two error terms are not connected in any way

$$E(uv) = 0$$

Substituting the observed values Y and X into the true relationship we find

$$Y = b_0 + b_1(X - v) + u$$

or

$$Y = b_0 + b_1 X + (u - b_1 v)$$

The error term in the function which we actually measure is $(u - b_1 v)$. Denoting it by w we may write the equation

$$Y = b_0 + b_1 X + w$$

Thus in practice we have a set of observed values X and Y which include errors. Y includes stochastic errors as well as measurement errors, while X includes only errors of measurement. From the observed values of Y and X we want to get estimates $\hat{b}_0$ and $\hat{b}_1$ of the true parameters (b_0 and b_1) by the method of classical least squares.

We will prove that the straightforward application of the method of least squares is not appropriate because w is not independent of the explanatory variable X with the consequence of rendering the estimates $\hat{b}_0$ and $\hat{b}_1$ both biased and inconsistent. In particular, we will prove that
  (1) The error term w is not independent of X, $\text{cov}(wX) \neq 0$.
  (2) The estimate of the slope, $\hat{b}_1$, has a downward bias: $E(\hat{b}_1) < b_1$
  (3) The estimates $\hat{b}_1$ and $\hat{b}_0$ are inconsistent.

Proof 1. If there are errors of measurement in the variables, the error term w is not independent from X.

The equation with the actual observations is

$$Y = b_0 + b_1 X_1 + w$$

where $w = (u - b_1 v)$.

Let us derive the characteristics of the distribution of w.
  (1) w has zero mean $E(w) = 0$, because $E(w) = E(u) - b_1 E(v) = 0$ (by assumption 1)
  (2) w has constant variance $E(w^2) = \sigma_w^2$, because u and v have constant variances.
  (3) We can prove that w is not autocorrelated, since the u's and the v's are serially independent

$$E(w_i w_j) = 0 \qquad i \neq j$$

Thus

$$
\begin{aligned}
E(w_i w_j) &= E[(u_i - b_1 v_i)(u_j - b_1 v_j)] \\
&= E[u_i u_j - b_1 v_i u_j - b_1 u_i v_j + b_1^2 v_i v_j] \\
&= E(u_i u_j) - b_1 E(v_i u_j) - b_1 E(u_i v_j) + b_1^2 E(v_i v_j) \\
&= 0
\end{aligned}
$$

by assumptions set above.

However, the w's and X's are dependent as can be seen from their covariance

$$\text{cov}(wX) = E\left\{[w - E(w)] \cdot [X - E(X)]\right\}$$

Now
  (a) $w = u - b_1 v \quad \text{and} \quad E(w) = 0$

  (b) $X = \chi + v \quad \text{and} \quad E(X) = E(\chi) + E(v) = \chi$

because $E(v) = 0$ by assumption 1, and the true values of the variable χ are constant in repeated sampling.

Substituting we obtain

$$\text{cov}(wX) = E[(u - b_1 v)(\chi + v - \chi)]$$
$$= E[uv - b_1 v^2]$$
$$= E(uv) - b_1 E(v^2)$$

But, by assumption, $E(v^2) = \sigma_v^2$ and $E(uv) = 0$. Therefore

$$\text{cov}(wX) = b_1 \cdot \sigma_v^2 \neq 0$$

Since neither b_1 can be zero (because in this event there would be no functional relationship between the variables) nor σ_v^2 can be zero (it is a square), it is obvious that the covariance of w and X is not zero. This implies that w and X change together (co-vary), therefore they are not independent. As a consequence the least squares estimator of b_1 and b_0 is inconsistent (see below).

Proof 2. If there are errors of measurement the estimate of the slope $\hat{b}_1$, has a downward bias.

The proof consists in finding $\hat{b}_1$ from OLS and then examining its expected value.
Applying least squares to the relation $Y = b_0 + b_1 X + w$ we obtain

$$\hat{b}_1 = \frac{\Sigma xy}{\Sigma x^2} = \frac{\Sigma(X - \overline{X})(Y - \overline{Y})}{\Sigma(X - \overline{X})^2}$$

Substitute

$$X = \chi + v \qquad \overline{X} = \overline{\chi} + \overline{v}$$
$$Y = \psi + v_y \qquad \overline{Y} = \overline{\psi} + \overline{v}_y$$

and obtain

$$\hat{b}_1 = \frac{\Sigma(\chi - \overline{\chi})(\psi - \overline{\psi}) + \Sigma(\psi - \overline{\psi})(v - \overline{v}) + \Sigma(\chi - \overline{\chi})(v - \overline{v}) + \Sigma(v - \overline{v})(v_y - \overline{v}_y)}{\Sigma(\chi - \overline{\chi})^2 + 2\Sigma(\chi - \overline{\chi})(v - \overline{v}) + \Sigma(v - \overline{v})^2]}$$

Taking into account that the errors of measurement are independent from each other as well as from the true values of the variables (assumptions 5 and 6), the three last terms of the numerator and the middle term of the denominator are zero asymptotically (as $n \to \infty$). Therefore in the limit

$$\text{plim}(\hat{b}_1) = \frac{\left\{\Sigma(\chi - \overline{\chi})(\psi - \overline{\psi})\right\}/\left\{\Sigma(\chi - \overline{\chi})^2\right\}}{1 + [(n\sigma_v^2)/\left\{\Sigma(\chi - \overline{\chi})^2\right\}]} = \frac{b}{1 + [\left\{(n)(\sigma_v^2/n)\right\}/\left\{\Sigma(\chi - \overline{\chi})/n\right\}]}$$

or

$$\text{plim}(\hat{b}_1) = b\left[\frac{1}{1 + (\sigma_v^2/\sigma_\chi^2)}\right] \neq b$$

Since $\sigma_v^2/\sigma_\chi^2 > 0$ (being the ratio of squares),

$$\text{plim}\,\hat{b}_1 < b_1$$

i.e. $\hat{b}_1$ is biased asymptotically: the OLS $\hat{b}_1$ underestimates the true slope b_1.

Proof 3. If there are errors of measurement in the explanatory variables the estimates $\hat{b}_0$ and $\hat{b}_1$ are inconsistent, because their bias does not tend to zero as we increase the size of the sample and thus the first condition for consistency is violated. We found that

$$\text{plim}(\hat{b}_1) = b_1\left[\frac{1}{1 + \sigma_v^2/\sigma_\chi^2}\right]$$

$\hat{b}_1$ is asymptotically biased and hence inconsistent

12.1.3. TESTING FOR ERRORS IN THE REGRESSORS

There is no formal test for assessing the validity or the violation of Assumption 6. However, taking into account the sources of errors of measurement, one hardly needs to conduct any test, since such errors, as said, are almost certain to be present in all applications.

One could get some rough idea about the correlation between the u's and the X's by ordering the observations in terms of the size of the explanatory variable X (rather than in time). For example in figure 12.1 we plot hypothetical sample values of X and the related to them e_j's. Note that the e's do *not* correspond to Y_1, Y_2, etc., but to increasing values of X (that is, $X_1 < X_2 < X_3 \ldots$).

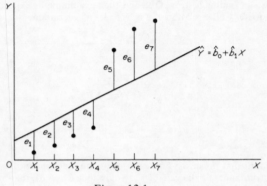

Figure 12.1

The observed pattern shows that the e_j's and X_j's are positively nonlinearly correlated; to small values of X correspond small values of e's, and vice versa. If the distribution of u is independent of the distribution of X we should not observe any strong *nonlinear* patterns between e_j and X_j. (Linear correlations between e_j and X_j are, of course, ruled out by assumption in the normal equations, where it is assumed $\Sigma ex = 0$.) The above figure suggests strongly that u depends on higher powers of X; that is, a nonlinear relationship. (See E. Kane, *Economic Statistics and Econometrics*, p. 362.)

From the above discussion it should be clear that when there are errors of measurement in the observed values of the X's the estimates of the parameters are more seriously affected than by heteroscedasticity of the random term u. In the case of errors of observation OLS yields biased and inconsistent estimates, while when the u's are heteroscedastic the estimates are unbiased and it is only their variance that loses its power as a criterion for assessing the reliability of the estimates.

12.1.4. SOLUTIONS FOR THE CASE OF ERRORS IN VARIABLES

Various solutions have been suggested for the problem of errors in variables. We will discuss the most important, starting from the simpler ones.

Solution I: Inverse Least Squares

This method may be applied when X only is subject to error, but not Y. Y is assumed to be nonstochastic and error-free. Then u (the error associated with Y) is zero and the relationship to be measured from the observed values Y and X becomes

$$Y = b_0 + b_1(X - v)$$

Solving for X we obtain

$$X = -\frac{b_0}{b_1} + \frac{1}{b_1}Y + v$$

Set $-(b_0/b_1) = \beta_0$ and $1/b_1 = \beta_1$, so that the relationship may be written

$$X = \beta_0 + \beta_1 Y + v$$

We may apply OLS to this relationship and obtain unbiased estimates of β_0 and β_1 since in this case Y and v are independent. The OLS estimates are

$$\hat{\beta}_1 = \frac{\Sigma xy}{\Sigma y^2} \quad \text{and} \quad \hat{\beta}_0 = \overline{X} - \hat{\beta}_1 \overline{Y}$$

Substituting $\hat{\beta}_0$ and $\hat{\beta}_1$ in the expressions

$$\beta_0 = -\frac{b_0}{b_1} \quad \text{and} \quad \beta_1 = \frac{1}{b_1}$$

we can obtain biased but consistent estimates of the structural coefficients b_1 and b_0

$$\hat{b}_1 = \frac{1}{\hat{\beta}_1} \quad \text{and} \quad \hat{b}_0 = -\hat{\beta}_0 \hat{b}_1$$

Clearly $\hat{b}_1$ is the inverse of $\hat{\beta}_1$. Hence the name of the method as inverse least squares.

Solution II: The two-group method

(A. Wald, 'The Fitting of Straight Lines if both Variables are Subject to Error', *Ann. Math. Statist.*, vol. 11, 1940, pp. 284–300.)

The two-group method may be outlined as follows.

1. We rank the observations in ascending order on the basis of the values of X, and we divide them in two equal sub-samples. If the total number of observations is odd we omit the central observation.

2. We compute the arithmetic means $(\overline{X}_1, \overline{Y}_1)$ for the lowest group of observations and $(\overline{X}_2, \overline{Y}_2)$ for the highest group.

3. We obtain an estimate of the slope parameter, b_1, by the formula

$$\tilde{b}_1 = \frac{(\overline{Y}_2 - \overline{Y}_1)}{(\overline{X}_2 - \overline{X}_1)}$$

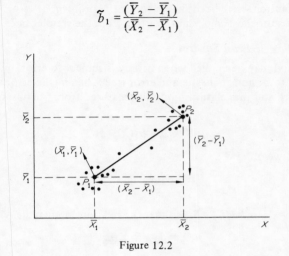

Figure 12.2

If we draw a diagram we can easily see that the two-group method for obtaining $\tilde{b}_1$ amounts to drawing a straight line through the two points P_1 and P_2 defined by the respective means of the two sub-sets of the observations. In figure 12.2 we see that the slope of the line $P_1 P_2$ is

$$\frac{\overline{Y}_2 - \overline{Y}_1}{\overline{X}_2 - \overline{X}_1} = \tilde{b}_1$$

Thus the regression line is taken to be the line through the means of the sub-samples. The constant intercept is obtained in the usual way from the expression

$$\tilde{b}_0 = \overline{Y} - \tilde{b}_1 \overline{X}$$

where $\overline{Y}$ and $\overline{X}$ are the means of all the sample observations.[1]

The two-group method yields consistent estimates. However, their variance is not the smallest possible and therefore the estimates are not best. Thus by adopting the two-group method we assign to the property of asymptotic unbiasedness a higher weight than to the minimum-variance property.

Solution III: The three-group method

(Bartlett, 'Fitting a Straight Line if Both Variables are Subject to Error', *Biometrica*, vol. **5**, 1949, pp. 207–42.)

---

[1] The two-group and three-group methods may be viewed alternatively as a special case of the application of the method of instrumental variables; see below, p. 261 and Chapter 16. See also J. Johnston, *Econometric Methods*, 2nd edn., pp. 283–6.

The three-group method is based on the same idea as the two-group method of fitting a straight line to the data, passing through the means of sub-samples. However, the observations in Bartlett's approach are divided into three sub-groups. The method may be outlined as follows.

1. We arrange the observations in ascending order on the basis of the X values and we divide them into *three equal groups* (or approximately equal if the number of observations is not exactly divisible by 3). The middle group is ignored from the analysis.

2. We compute the arithmetic means $(\bar{X}_1, \bar{Y}_1)$ for the lowest group and $(\bar{X}_3, \bar{Y}_3)$ for the highest group.

3. We obtain the estimate of the slope parameter, $\tilde{b}_1$, by the formula

$$\tilde{b}_1 = \frac{(\bar{Y}_3 - \bar{Y}_1)}{(\bar{X}_3 - \bar{X}_1)}$$

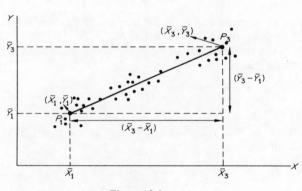

Figure 12.3

If we draw a diagram we can easily see that the three-group method for obtaining $\tilde{b}_1$, amounts to drawing a straight line through the two points $P_1(\bar{X}_1, \bar{Y}_1)$ and $P_3(\bar{X}_3, \bar{Y}_3)$ defined by the respective means of the lowest and highest groups of observations: the slope of the line $P_1 P_3$ is

$$\frac{(\bar{Y}_3 - \bar{Y}_1)}{(\bar{X}_3 - \bar{X}_1)} = \tilde{b}_1$$

$\tilde{b}_0$ is obtained from the expression $\tilde{b}_0 = \bar{Y} - \tilde{b}_1 \bar{X}$, where $\bar{Y}$ and $\bar{X}$ are the means of all the observations of the sample.

The three-group method gives in general consistent estimates[1] of the

[1] For a proof see C. Leser, *Econometric Techniques and Problems*, Griffin, London, 1966, p. 7.

coefficients b_1 and b_0. Furthermore, the estimates are more efficient, that is, they have a smaller asymptotic variance than the two-group method.

The three-group and two-group methods have been extended to apply to models with more than one explanatory variables. However, the extension is complicated and will not be examined here. The interested reader is referred to J. W. Hooper and H. Theil, 'The Extension of Wald's Method of Fitting Straight Lines to Multiple Regression', *Rev. Int. Statist. Inst.*, vol. 26, 1958, pp. 37–47.

Solution IV: Weighted regression

This is a common approach in applied econometric research. It may be outlined as follows.

(a) Obtain an estimate of b from the regression $Y = f(X)$, that is,

$$\hat{Y} = \hat{b}_0 + \hat{b}_1 X.$$

(b) Obtain an estimate of b from the inverse regression $X = f(Y)$, or $\hat{X} = \hat{\beta}_0 + \hat{\beta}_1 Y$, from which we derive $\hat{b}_1 = 1/\hat{\beta}_1$.

(c) Take as the final estimate of b the geometric mean of the above two estimates, that is

$$\hat{\hat{b}}_1 = \pm \sqrt{\hat{b}_1 \cdot \frac{1}{\hat{\beta}_1}}$$

Given that $\hat{b}_1 = \Sigma xy/\Sigma x^2$ and $\hat{\beta}_1 = \Sigma xy/\Sigma y^2$ so that $1/\hat{\beta}_1 = \Sigma y^2/\Sigma xy$, we obtain

$$\hat{\hat{b}}_1 = \sqrt{\frac{\Sigma xy}{\Sigma x^2} \cdot \frac{\Sigma y^2}{\Sigma xy}}$$

and

$$\hat{\hat{b}}_1 = \pm \sqrt{\frac{\Sigma y^2}{\Sigma x^2}} = \pm \sqrt{\frac{\Sigma y^2/n}{\Sigma x^2/n}} = \pm \sqrt{\frac{\sigma_y^2}{\sigma_x^2}}$$

The sign of $\hat{\hat{b}}_1$ is chosen on the basis of the sign of the covariance of X and Y, that is, on the sign of the term Σxy.

The estimate of the constant intercept $\hat{\hat{b}}_0$ may be obtained from the formula

$$\hat{\hat{b}}_0 = \bar{Y} - \hat{\hat{b}}_1 \bar{X}$$

The weighted regression method is based on the implicit assumption that the ratio of the variances of the errors is equal to the ratio of the variances of the observed variables, that is

$$\frac{\sigma_u^2}{\sigma_v^2} = \frac{\sigma_y^2}{\sigma_x^2} = \frac{\Sigma y^2}{\Sigma x^2}$$

(See C. Lesser, *Econometric Techniques and Problems,* p. 19.) This assumption is necessary in order to make $\hat{b}_1$ a consistent estimate.

The weighted regression is a special case of the maximum likelihood method which we shall examine in a subsequent paragraph.

Solution V: Durbin's 'ranking' method

(Durbin, 'Errors in Variables', *Rev. Int. Statist. Inst.,* vol. 22, 1954, pp. 23–32.) Durbin has suggested the following solution for the case of errors of measurement.

1. The *deviations* of the observations are ranked in ascending order on the basis of the X values.[1] These rankings are considered as the values of a new variable Z_i. ($i = 1, 2, 3, \ldots, n.$)

2. We multiply through the original equation (expressed in deviation form $y = b_1 x_1 + u$) by the values of Z_i, and we sum over all ranked observations, thus obtaining the equation

$$\sum_{i=1}^{n} Z_i y_i = b_1 \sum_{i=1}^{n} Z_i x_i + \sum_{i=1}^{n} Z_i u_i$$

(Note that the x's and y's are ranked in ascending order, on the basis of the X values.)

Setting the last term equal to its zero-expected value and applying classical least squares we obtain

$$\tilde{b}_1 = \frac{\displaystyle\sum_{i=1}^{n} (Z_i y_i)}{\displaystyle\sum_{i=1}^{n} (Z_i x_i)}$$

which is consistent.

The constant intercept is obtained as usual by the expression

$$\tilde{b}_0 = \overline{Y} - \tilde{b}_1 \overline{X}$$

Durbin has proved that the variance of $\tilde{b}_1$ obtained from this method has a smaller variance than the two-group and three-group methods.

The extension of this method to models with more than two variables has not yet been explored.

Durbin's method may be viewed as a special case of the method of instrumental variables, where the instrumental variable is the dummy variable Z_i taking the values of the ranking of x's (1, 2, 3 ... n). See next paragraph and Chapter 16.

---

[1] This is necessary for the estimation of the constant intercept, which would be impossible if we ranked the actual values of the X's. See Johnston, *Econometric Methods,* 2nd ed., p. 285.

Solution VI: Instrumental variables

This method has been developed by Reiersøl and Geary.[1]

The method of instrumental variables will be examined in detail in Chapter 16. For the present it suffices to outline the method.

The basic idea behind the method of instrumental variables is to replace the term Σxu from the normal equations of ordinary least squares when u and the X's are dependent.

In classical least squares the structural equation is

$$Y = b_0 + b_1 X + u$$

or, in deviation form

$$y = b_1 x + u$$

The normal equation in this simple model is obtained by multiplying the structural equation through by x and summing over all observations

$$\Sigma xy = b_1 \Sigma x^2 + \Sigma xu$$

If the u's and X's are independent

$$E(\Sigma xu) = \Sigma E(xu) = 0$$

and hence we may ignore the term Σxu in the normal equation and proceed with the solution for b_1.

However, with errors in the explanatory variables the independence of X and u does not hold, $E(ux) \neq 0$ and the OLS breaks down.

If instead of pre-multiplying the function with X we can find another variable Z uncorrelated with u, we may follow the above process; that is, multiply the original function by z

$$\Sigma zy = b_1 \Sigma zx + \Sigma zu$$

and ignore the term Σzu, since z is independent of u so that

$$E(\Sigma zu) = \Sigma E(zu) = 0$$

Therefore using Z as 'instrument' we may obtain an estimate for b_1, applying least squares to the above equation

$$\hat{b}_1 = \frac{\Sigma zy}{\Sigma zx}$$

$\hat{b}_0$ is then obtained by the formula $\hat{b}_0 = \bar{Y} - \hat{b}_1 \bar{X}$.

The instrumental variable Z must fulfil the following conditions: (a) Z must be an economically meaningful variable, strongly correlated with X so that it

[1] Reiersøl, O., *Confluence Analysis by means of Instrumental Sets of Variables,* Stockholm: Almquist and Wiksell, 1945; Geary, G., 'Determination of Linear Relations between Systematic Parts of Variables with Errors of Observations, the Variances of which are Unknown', *Econometrica,* vol. 17, 1949, pp. 30–58.

can substitute X and reflect the relationship between X and Y adequately. If X and Z are not strongly correlated their covariance $\Sigma zx/n$ will be low and hence the denominator of the above expression will be small, thus rendering the estimate $\hat{b}_1$ unstable. (b) Z must be independent of the errors u and v. (See Chapter 16.)

The method of instrumental variables yields consistent estimates. However, the variance of the estimators depends on how closely correlated the instrumental variable is with X. We cannot be sure that the estimates have minimum asymptotic variance.

In order to facilitate the computations we usually measure the instrumental variable in such a way that the mean of Z (in the units with which it will be used in the regression) is equal to $\bar{X}$. This is attained by multiplying each observation of Z by the factor $\bar{X}/\bar{Y}$, where $\bar{Z}$ is the average of the sample observations of the instrumental variable. This procedure does not affect the correlations between Z and u, and between Z and X.

The asymptotic variance of $\hat{b}_1$ and $\hat{b}_0$ is

$$\text{var}(\hat{b}_1) = \sigma_{u*}^2 * \frac{\Sigma z_i^2}{(\Sigma x_i z_i)^2} \quad \text{and} \quad \text{var}(\hat{b}_0) = \sigma_{u*}^2 * \left[\frac{1}{n} + \frac{\bar{X}\Sigma z_i^2}{(\Sigma x_i z_i)^2} \right]$$

where $\sigma_{u*}^2 = \sigma_u^2 + \sigma_v^2$.

If x and z are not closely correlated their covariance will be small (i.e. Σxz will be small), hence the variance of $\hat{b}_1$ will be large. In the extreme case of zero correlation of z and x, $\Sigma xz = 0$ and $\text{var}(\hat{b}_1) = \infty$.

The method of instrumental variables can easily be extended to models with two or more explanatory variables. Let us consider the extension of the method to a model with two explanatory variables. *Firstly*, we must find as many instrumental variables as there are explanatory variables (unless some explanatory variable is not correlated with u, in which case this variable may be used as its own 'instrument'). Assume that Z_1 and Z_2 are appropriate instrumental variables. *Secondly*, we express the original equation in deviation form: $y = b_1 x_1 + b_2 x_2 + u$. *Thirdly*, we multiply this equation in turn by z_1 and z_2. The equations obtained in this way are the required 'normal equations' which may be solved for b_1 and b_2 by setting $\Sigma z_1 u$ and $\Sigma z_2 u$ equal to their zero (asymptotic) mean value

$$\Sigma z_1 y = b_1 \Sigma z_1 x_1 + b_2 \Sigma z_1 x_2 + \Sigma z_1 u$$
$$\Sigma z_2 y = b_1 \Sigma z_2 x_1 + b_2 \Sigma z_2 x_2 + \Sigma z_2 u$$

The instrumental variables estimates are obtained from the solution of this system. Using the method of determinants (see Appendix II) we find

$$\hat{b}_1 = \frac{(\Sigma z_1 y)(\Sigma z_2 x_2) - (\Sigma z_2 y)(\Sigma z_1 x_2)}{(\Sigma z_1 x_1)(\Sigma z_2 x_2) - (\Sigma z_2 x_1)(\Sigma z_1 x_2)}$$

$$\hat{b}_2 = \frac{(\Sigma z_2 y)(\Sigma z_1 x_1) - (\Sigma z_1 y)(\Sigma z_2 x_1)}{(\Sigma z_1 x_1)(\Sigma z_2 x_2) - (\Sigma z_2 x_1)(\Sigma z_1 x_2)}$$

The variances of these estimates are

$$\text{var}(\hat{b}_1) = s_u^2 \frac{\Sigma z_1^2 (\Sigma z_2 x_2)^2 + \Sigma z_2^2 (\Sigma z_1 x_2)^2 - 2\Sigma z_1 x_2 \Sigma z_2 x_2 \Sigma z_1 z_2}{\{(\Sigma z_1 x_1)(\Sigma z_2 x_2) - (\Sigma z_2 x_1)(\Sigma z_1 x_1)\}^2}$$

$$\text{var}(\hat{b}_2) = s_u^2 \frac{\Sigma z_1^2 (\Sigma z_2 x_1)^2 + \Sigma z_2^2 (\Sigma z_1 x_1)^2 - 2\Sigma z_1 x_1 \Sigma z_2 x_1 \Sigma z_1 z_2}{\{(\Sigma z_1 x_1)(\Sigma z_2 x_2) - (\Sigma z_2 x_1)(\Sigma z_1 x_2)\}^2}$$

where $s_u^2 = \dfrac{\Sigma(y - \hat{b}_1 x_1 - \hat{b}_2 x_2)^2}{n - K}$.

The extension of the method of instrumental variables to models with three or more explanatory variables is straightforward.

Although the method of instrumental variables appears simpler than the previously examined ones, in practice it is very difficult to apply, because it is difficult to find appropriate instrumental variables. In general, the instrumental variables technique has serious disadvantages: *Firstly*. In choosing Z, there is always a degree of arbitrariness which affects the estimates. Usually there are many variables which can be used as instrumental, and the choice of one of them will yield different results than the choice of another. *Secondly*. It is difficult to find Z such that it is strongly correlated to X. *Thirdly*. It is almost impossible to check the assumption that Z is independent of all errors (v_x, v_y and u). *Fourthly*. We cannot be sure that our arbitrarily chosen instrumental variable will yield estimates with the minimum asymptotic variance. Thus the instrumental variables method gives priority to consistency, and pays less attention to the possibility of high standard errors which Z may produce.

Solution VII: The maximum likelihood approach

The method of maximum likelihood as a general statistical estimation technique is explained in detail in Chapter 18. In this section we will give the *modified system of normal equations* which is derived from the application of the maximum likelihood technique, and is appropriate for obtaining consistent estimates of the b's when the X's involve errors of measurement.

The assumptions of the maximum likelihood method as applied to a model involving variables with measurement errors are the same as in the previous methods, except that in the maximum likelihood technique we make the additional assumptions that the distributions of the variables and their errors are normal and that the variances of the errors of measurement in the X's are known from the statistical sources. Thus in applying the ML method we make the following assumptions.

1. The X's are normally distributed, independently of the errors in their observed values, that is independently of the v_k's).

2. The error term u related to Y (which absorbs errors of omission and any measurement error in Y) is normally distributed with zero mean and constant variance, independently of the distributions of the errors of measurement in the X_k's (in other words the u's are distributed independently of the v_k's).

3. The errors of measurement in the X's are normally distributed with zero means and constant variances, independently of each other and of the error term u.

Under these assumptions our model of k explanatory variables may be formally stated as follows.

The model

$$Y = b_0 + b_1 \chi_1 + b_2 \chi_2 + \ldots + b_k \chi_k + u$$
$$X_1 = \chi_1 + v_1$$
$$\ldots\ldots\ldots\ldots$$
$$X_k = \chi_k + v_k$$

The assumptions:

1. $\chi_1 = N(\overline{\chi}_1, \sigma_{\chi_1}^2), \ldots, \chi_k = N(\overline{\chi}_k, \sigma_{\chi_k}^2)$
2. $u = N(0, \sigma_u^2), \quad v_1 = N(0, \sigma_{v_1}^2), \quad v_2 = N(0, \sigma_{v_2}^2), \ldots, \quad v_k = N(0, \sigma_{v_k}^2)$
3. Independence of the χ's and the errors (u and v's)

$$E(u\chi) = 0, \qquad E(\chi_1 v_1) = 0, \qquad E(\chi_2 v_2) = 0, \ldots, E(\chi_k v_k) = 0$$

4. Independence of Y and the errors v_j

$$E(v_j Y) = 0 \qquad (j = 1, 2, \ldots, k) .$$

5. Independence of the errors (u and the v's)

$$E(uv) = 0$$
$$E(v_i v_j) = 0 \qquad \text{(where } i \text{ and } j \text{ refer to any two } X\text{'s)}$$

6. The variance of the error of measurement in the X's is known (σ_v^2 is known or can be reasonably guessed from *a priori* information).

Under the above set of assumptions the following transformed normal equations are appropriate for obtaining consistent estimates. (The derivation of these equations is explained in the Appendix to this section.)

Model with one explanatory variable
$$\Sigma x_1 y = b_1 [\Sigma x_1^2 - \sigma_{v_1}^2]$$

Model with two explanatory variables
$$\Sigma x_1 y = b_1 [\Sigma x_1^2 - n\sigma_{v_1}^2] + b_2 \Sigma x_1 x_2$$
$$\Sigma x_2 y = b_1 \Sigma x_1 x_2 + b_2 [\Sigma x_2^2 - n\sigma_{v_2}^2]$$

Model with three explanatory variables
$$\Sigma x_1 y = b_1 [\Sigma x_1^2 - n\sigma_{v_1}^2] + b_2 \Sigma x_1 x_2 + b_3 \Sigma x_1 x_3$$
$$\Sigma x_2 y = b_1 \Sigma x_1 x_2 + b_2 [\Sigma x_2^2 - n\sigma_{v_2}^2] + b_3 \Sigma x_2 x_3$$
$$\Sigma x_3 y = b_1 \Sigma x_1 x_3 + b_2 \Sigma x_2 x_3 + b_3 [\Sigma x_3^2 - n\sigma_{v_3}^2]$$

Model with k explanatory variables

$$\Sigma x_1 y = b_1 [\Sigma x_1^2 - n\sigma_{v_1}^2] + b_2 \Sigma x_1 x_2 + \ldots + b_k \Sigma x_1 x_k$$

$$\Sigma x_2 y = b_1 \Sigma x_1 x_2 + b_2 [\Sigma x_2^2 - n\sigma_{v_2}^2] + \ldots + b_k \Sigma x_2 x_k$$

$$\vdots \qquad \vdots \qquad \qquad \vdots \qquad \qquad \vdots$$

$$\Sigma x_k y = b_1 \Sigma x_1 x_k + b_2 \Sigma x_2 x_k \ldots\ldots\ldots + b_k [\Sigma x_k^2 - n\sigma_{v_k}^2]$$

where $\sigma_{v_k}^2$ is the variance of the measurement error in the variable X_k. All $\sigma_{v_i}^2$ are assumed known from the source of sample data.

The variances of the estimates can be obtained by the general formulae developed in Chapter 7.

It should be noted that the above transformed systems of normal equations differ from the ordinary least squares normal equations only in that from the elements of the main diagonal of the right-hand side (that is from the terms including the sum of squares of the deviations of the explanatory variables) we subtract the variance of the error of the respective variable multiplied by the size of the sample (n). In other words the only difference between the above system of equations and the respective one of OLS is that the terms $\Sigma x_1^2, \Sigma x_2^2, \ldots, \Sigma x_k^2$, have been 'corrected' by subtracting n times the variances of the errors of measurement in $X_1, X_2, \ldots, X_k$ respectively.

The variances of the errors in the X's are often given in the statistical sources of the data being used, or they can be reasonably estimated from the information of these sources. For example suppose that from a cross section sample we obtain the information that the average family income is £600 and that the maximum error of this measurement is very unlikely to exceed 5 per cent, or £30. Using the concept of a confidence interval we may interpret this piece of information as meaning that the interval $600 \pm 2\sigma_v$ contains 95 per cent of all incomes or the interval $600 \pm 3\sigma_v$ contains 99 per cent of all incomes. Assume that we adopt the second level of significance. We may then say

$$3\sigma_v = (0.05)(600) = 30$$

$$\sigma_v = 10 \text{ and } \sigma_v^2 = 100$$

which is the variance of the measurement error in the variable X, income.

The estimates of the maximum likelihood method are consistent and hence asymptotically unbiased; however, they are biased for small samples and they do not have the minimum variance (see also Chapter 18).

APPENDIX TO SECTION 12.1

We will examine the mechanism by which we arrived at the transformed normal equations of the maximum likelihood method. We will begin with a simple model involving one explanatory variable. We will then extend the analysis to more complex models.

1. Model with one explanatory variable

The model

$$Y = b_0 + b_1\chi + u$$
$$X = \chi + v$$

The assumptions

$$\chi = N(\overline{\chi}, \sigma_\chi^2)$$
$$u = N(0, \sigma_u^2)$$
$$v = N(0, \sigma_v^2)$$
$$E(\chi u) = 0 \qquad E(\chi v) = 0 \qquad E(uv) = 0$$

that is the errors are normally and independently distributed of χ and of each other, with zero means and constant variances.

Under these assumptions we derive that X and Y have a bivariate normal distribution. The simple distributions of X and Y are

$$X = N[\mu, (\sigma_\chi^2 + \sigma_v^2)]$$

$$Y = N[(b_0 + b_1\overline{\chi}), (b_1^2\sigma_\chi^2 + \sigma_u^2)]$$

The covariance of X and Y which will also appear in the bivariate distribution is

$$\text{cov}_{xy} = b_1\sigma_\chi^2.$$

Let us derive formally the mean and variance of the distributions of X and Y.

(a) Mean X $\qquad\qquad\qquad E(X) = \mu$ $\qquad\qquad\qquad\qquad\qquad$ (1)

Because $\qquad\qquad\qquad X = \chi + v$
$$E(X) = E(\chi) + E(v) = \mu$$

(b) Variance X $\qquad\qquad \sigma_X^2 = \sigma_\chi^2 + \sigma_v^2$ $\qquad\qquad\qquad\qquad$ (2)

Because $\quad E(X - \overline{\chi})^2 = E(\chi + v - \overline{\chi})^2$
$$= E[\chi^2 + v^2 + \overline{\chi}^2 + 2\chi v - 2v\overline{\chi} - 2\chi\overline{\chi}]$$
$$= E[\chi^2 + v^2 + \overline{\chi}^2 - 2\chi\overline{\chi}]$$
$$= E[(\chi^2 + \overline{\chi}^2 - 2\chi\overline{\chi}) + v^2]$$
$$= E(\chi^2) - \overline{\chi}^2 + E(v^2)$$
$$= \sigma_\chi^2 + \sigma_v^2$$

(c) Mean Y $\qquad\qquad\qquad E(Y) = b_0 + b_1\overline{\chi}$ $\qquad\qquad\qquad\qquad$ (3)

Because $\qquad\qquad Y = b_0 + b_1\chi + u$
$$E(Y) = E(b_0) + b_1 E(\chi) + E(u)$$
$$E(Y) = b_0 + b_1\overline{\chi}$$

(d) Variance Y $\qquad\qquad \sigma_Y^2 = b_1^2\sigma_\chi^2 + \sigma_u^2$ $\qquad\qquad\qquad\qquad$ (4)

Because

$$E[Y - E(Y)]^2 = E(Y - b_0 - b_1 \bar{\chi})^2$$
$$= E(b_0 + b_1 \chi + u - b_0 - b_1 \bar{\chi})^2$$
$$= E[b_1(\chi - \bar{\chi}) + u]^2$$
$$= E[b_1^2(\chi - \bar{\chi})^2 + u^2 + 2b_1(\chi - \bar{\chi})u]$$
$$= b_1^2 E(\chi - \bar{\chi})^2 + E(u^2)$$
$$= b_1^2 \sigma_\chi^2 + \sigma_u^2$$

(e) Covariance YX $\qquad\qquad \sigma_{XY} = b_1 \sigma_\chi^2$ $\qquad\qquad\qquad\qquad$ (5)

Because:

$$E\{[Y - E(Y)] [X - E(X)]\}$$
$$= E[(b_0 + b_1 \chi + u - b_0 - b_1 \bar{\chi})(X - \bar{\chi})]$$
$$= E[b_1(\chi - \bar{\chi}) + u](X - \bar{\chi})]$$
$$= E[b_1(\chi - \bar{\chi})^2 + u(\chi + v - \bar{\chi})]$$
$$= E[b_1(\chi - \bar{\chi})^2 + u(\chi - \bar{\chi}) + uv]$$
$$= E[b_1(\chi - \bar{\chi})^2] + Eu(\chi - \bar{\chi}) + E(uv)$$
$$= b_1 E(\chi - \bar{\chi})^2 = b_1 \sigma_\chi^2$$

Since X and Y have a bivariate normal distribution with parameters $E(Y)$, $E(X)$, σ_X^2, σ_Y^2, σ_{XY}, the sample estimates of the above parameters will be maximum likelihood estimates. So we can use the sample to obtain estimates of parameters. However, we have five relationships, (1 to 5 above), which contain six unknowns: b_0, b_1, $\bar{\chi}$, σ_χ^2, σ_u^2, σ_v^2. The system may be solved only if we put some restriction either on the value of one of these unknowns or on the relationship between any two of them. The most plausible (and the easiest) approach is to assume that the variance of the error of measurement is known; most statistical sources usually give some information about the probable size of the errors of measurement of published data.[1] Under this assumption, using the maximum likelihood method, we obtain the relations

sample mean $\qquad\qquad\qquad \bar{X} = \hat{\bar{\chi}}$ $\qquad\qquad\qquad\qquad\qquad$ (6)

sample mean $\qquad\qquad\qquad \bar{Y} = \hat{b}_0 + \hat{b}_1 \hat{\bar{\chi}}$ $\qquad\qquad\qquad\qquad$ (7)

sample variance $\qquad\qquad \dfrac{\Sigma x^2}{n} = \hat{\sigma}_\chi^2 + \sigma_v^2$ $\qquad\qquad\qquad\qquad$ (8)

---

[1] Some writers make the assumption that the ratio of the variance of the errors is known, that is σ_u^2/σ_v^2, is known. This is a formidable assumption for the model of errors of omission and errors of measurement, since σ_u^2 in this case includes both influences and is one of the parameters of the model which must be estimated and indeed cannot be plausibly assumed to be known: we may know something about the variances of the errors of measurement, but not about the errors of omissions. See Johnston, *Econometric Methods*, 2nd ed., p. 286.

sample variance $\qquad \dfrac{\Sigma y^2}{n} = \hat{b}_1^2 \hat{\sigma}_X^2 + \hat{\sigma}_u^2$ $\qquad\qquad$ (9)

sample co-variance $\qquad \dfrac{\Sigma xy}{n} = \hat{b}_1 \hat{\sigma}_X^2$ $\qquad\qquad$ (10)

From the solution of this system we obtain the estimates $\hat{b}_0$, $\hat{b}_1$, $\hat{\sigma}_u^2$, $\hat{\bar{\chi}}$ as follows. From (8), solving for $\hat{\sigma}_X^2$ we find

$$\hat{\sigma}_X^2 = (\Sigma x^2/n) - \sigma_v^2 \qquad \text{(since } \sigma_v^2 \text{ is assumed known)}$$

Substituting in (10) we obtain

$$\hat{b}_1 = \frac{\Sigma xy/n}{\hat{\sigma}_X^2} = \frac{\Sigma xy/n}{\Sigma x^2/n - \sigma_v^2} = \frac{\Sigma xy}{\Sigma x^2 - n\sigma_v^2}$$

Then $\hat{b}_0 = \bar{Y} - \hat{b}_1 \bar{X}$ (from 7).
Finally, substituting $\hat{b}_1$ and $\hat{\sigma}_X^2$ into (9) we obtain

$$\hat{\sigma}_u^2 = \frac{\Sigma y^2}{n} - \hat{b}_1 \frac{\Sigma xy}{n}$$

2. Extension of the above method to a model with two explanatory variables

The model is

$$Y = b_0 + b_1 \chi_1 + b_2 \chi_2 + u$$
$$X_1 = \chi_1 + v_1$$
$$X_2 = \chi_2 + v_2$$

Under the assumptions that $\chi_1, \chi_2, u, v_1, v_2$ are normally and independently distributed with parameters

$$\chi_1 = N(\bar{\chi}_1, \sigma_1^2)$$
$$\chi_2 = N(\bar{\chi}_2, \sigma_2^2)$$
$$u = N(0, \sigma_u^2)$$
$$v_1 = N(0, \sigma_{v_1}^2)$$
$$v_2 = N(0, \sigma_{v_2}^2)$$

it can be proved that the observed variables Y, X_1, X_2 will have a multivariate normal distribution, whose parameters will be the parameters of the single distributions of Y, X_1 and X_2, and their covariances. The single distributions are as follows

$$X_1 = N[\bar{\chi}_1, (\sigma_{\chi_1}^2 + \sigma_{v_1}^2)]$$
$$X_2 = N[\bar{\chi}_2, (\sigma_{\chi_2}^2 + \sigma_{v_2}^2)]$$
$$Y = N\{(b_0 + b_1\bar{\chi}_1 + b_2\bar{\chi}_2), (b_1^2 \sigma_{\chi_1}^2 + b_2^2 \sigma_{\chi_2}^2 + 2b_1 b_2 \, \text{cov}(\chi_1 \chi_2) + \sigma_u^2)\}$$

The covariances of Y, X_1 and X_2 are

$$\text{cov}(YX_1) = b_1 \sigma_{\chi_1}^2 + b_2 \text{ cov}(\chi_1 \chi_2)$$
$$\text{cov}(YX_2) = b_1 \text{ cov}(\chi_1 \chi_2) + b_2 \sigma_{\chi_2}^2$$
$$\text{cov}(X_1 X_2) = \text{cov}(\chi_1 \chi_2)$$

From the above parameters we obtain the following expressions for the populations of X_1, X_2, Y

$$E(X_1) = \overline{\chi}_1 \tag{11}$$
$$E(X_2) = \overline{\chi}_2 \tag{12}$$
$$E(Y) = b_0 + b_1 \overline{\chi}_1 + b_2 \overline{\chi}_2 \tag{13}$$
$$\sigma_Y^2 = E(Y - E(Y))^2$$
$$= b_1^2 \sigma_{\chi_1}^2 + b_2^2 \sigma_{\chi_2}^2 + 2 b_1 b_2 \text{ cov}(\chi_1 \chi_2) + \sigma_u^2 \tag{14}$$
$$\sigma_{X_1}^2 = E(X_1 - \overline{\chi}_1)^2 = \sigma_{\chi_1}^2 + \sigma_{v_1}^2 \tag{15}$$
$$\sigma_{X_2}^2 = E(X_2 - \overline{\chi}_2)^2 = \sigma_{\chi_2}^2 + \sigma_{v_2}^2 \tag{16}$$
$$\sigma_{YX_1} = b_1 \sigma_{\chi_1}^2 + b_2 \text{ cov}(\chi_1 \chi_2) \tag{17}$$
$$\sigma_{YX_2} = b_1 \text{ cov}(\chi_1 \chi_2) + b_2 \sigma_{\chi_2}^2 \tag{18}$$
$$\sigma_{X_1 X_2} = \text{cov}(\chi_1 \chi_2) \tag{19}$$

This is a system of nine equations in eleven unknowns. Assuming the variances of the measurement errors in X_1 and X_2 known the above system can be solved.

The sample estimates will give maximum likelihood estimates of the parameters under the above assumptions about the distributions of χ_1, χ_2 and of the three error terms.

From the above relations we obtain

$$\hat{b}_1 = \frac{(\Sigma x_1 y)(\Sigma x_2^2 - n\sigma_{v_2}^2) - (\Sigma x_2 y)(\Sigma x_1 x_2)}{(\Sigma x_1^2 - n\sigma_{v_1}^2)(\Sigma x_2^2 - n\sigma_{v_2}^2) - (\Sigma x_1 x_2)^2}$$

$$\hat{b}_2 = \frac{(\Sigma x_2 y)(\Sigma x_1^2 - n\sigma_{v_1}^2) - (\Sigma x_1 y)(\Sigma x_1 x_2)}{(\Sigma x_1^2 - n\sigma_{v_1}^2)(\Sigma x_2^2 - n\sigma_{v_2}^2) - (\Sigma x_1 x_2)^2}$$

$$\hat{b}_0 = \overline{Y} - \hat{b}_1 \overline{X}_1 - \hat{b}_2 \overline{X}_2$$

3. Extension to models with more than two explanatory variables

The extension of the above method to models with any number of explanatory variables is straightforward.

Thus we may observe that the estimates of the coefficients of the model with one explanatory variable have been obtained from the solution of the equation

$$\Sigma x_1 y = b_1 (\Sigma x_1^2 - n\sigma_{v_1}^2)$$

The estimates of the model with two explanatory variables has been obtained from the system

$$\Sigma x_1 y = b_1 (\Sigma x_1^2 - n\sigma_{v_1}^2) + b_2 \Sigma x_1 x_2$$
$$\Sigma x_2 y = b_1 \Sigma x_1 x_2 + b_2 (\Sigma x_2^2 - n\sigma_{v_2}^2)$$

This system differs from the normal equations of OLS only in that from the elements of the main diagonal of the right-hand side (that is, from the terms including the sum of squares of the deviations of the explanatory variables) we subtract the variance of the error of the respective variable multiplied by the size of sample (n). In other words, the only difference between the above normal equations and the respective ones of ordinary least squares is that the terms Σx_1^2 and Σx_2^2 have been 'corrected' by subtracting n times the variances of the errors of measurement in X_1 and X_2.

With this point in mind, it is easy to form the normal equations for models including any number of explanatory variables, applying the rules of thumb developed in Chapter 7 and noting that from each term Σx_i^2 we subtract $n\sigma_{v_i}^2$. For example the normal equations of a model with four explanatory variables which are measured with errors, are:

$$\Sigma x_1 y = b_1 [\Sigma x_1^2 - n\sigma_{v_1}^2] + b_2 \Sigma x_1 x_2 + b_3 \Sigma x_1 x_3 + b_4 \Sigma x_1 x_4$$
$$\Sigma x_2 y = b_1 \Sigma x_1 x_2 + b_2 (\Sigma x_2^2 - n\sigma_{v_2}^2) + b_3 \Sigma x_2 x_3 + b_4 \Sigma x_2 x_4$$
$$\Sigma x_3 y = b_1 \Sigma x_1 x_3 + b_2 \Sigma x_2 x_3 + b_3 [\Sigma x_3^2 - n\sigma_{v_3}^2] + b_4 \Sigma x_3 x_4$$
$$\Sigma x_4 y = b_1 \Sigma x_1 x_4 + b_2 \Sigma x_2 x_4 + b_3 \Sigma x_3 x_4 + b_4 (\Sigma x_4^2 - n\sigma_{v_4}^2)$$

12.2. TIME AS A VARIABLE

It is possible to take into account the influence of time on the dependent variable in various ways: 1) by introducing explicitly a variable t in the function, measured in time periods from the first given year onwards; 2) by a dummy variable; 3) by removing the trend from the variables before performing the regression; 4) by working with the first differences of the variables; 5) by introducing lagged variables in the function; 6) by derivatives of the function with respect to time.

1. In many cases researchers introduce time, measured by the number of observation periods from a starting year onwards, as an explanatory variable in the model. The meaning of such a time variable is that there is an autonomous trend experienced by the dependent variable. The coefficient of time is interpreted as a measure of autonomous growth; that is, one is making the assumption implicitly that the constant term in the equation increases or decreases steadily, but that the coefficients of the explanatory variables remain constant. If in addition there is *a priori* information that the coefficients of the explanatory variables change autonomously over time, a term 'tX' (where t stands for the time factor) may be introduced into the equation as an explicit variable in addition to the simple variable X. From the test of significance of the regression coefficient of the variable 'tX' we will decide whether the hypothesis of autonomously changing coefficient of X over time is plausible or not.

2. It can be shown that the introduction of time as an explicit variable is equivalent to regressing each explanatory variable on time, obtaining the residual deviations

$$X_k^* = X_k - \hat{X}_k$$

(where $\hat{X}_k = b_{0k}^* + b_{1k}^* t$) and then performing the regression of Y on the X^*'s, that is

$$Y = b_0 + b_1 X_1^* + b_2 X_2^* + \ldots + b_k X_k^*$$

3. Time is introduced implicitly into the function if we formulate our model in the first differences of the variables. For example if the original function is

$$Y_t = b_0 + b_1 X_t + b_2 t + u_t$$

it is also true that

$$Y_{t-1} = b_0 + b_1 X_{t-1} + b_2 (t-1) + u_{t-1}.$$

Subtracting we obtain

$$(Y_t - Y_{t-1}) = b_1 (X_t - X_{t-1}) + b_2 (t - t + 1) + (u_t - u_{t-1})$$

$$= b_2 + b_1 (X_t - X_{t-1}) + (u_t - u_{t-1}).$$

The term containing time drops out of the function because the variable t is eliminated and the coefficient of the time (b_2) becomes the constant term of the new function expressed in the first differences of the variables. The coefficient of X is the same in both formulations, but the disturbance term is different.[1] The estimates of the parameters from first differences are in general different as compared with the estimates from the original variables.

The introduction of time as an explicit variable or implicitly through the constant term in first differences has the meaning that there is an autonomous growth in the dependent variable. The interpretation of the coefficient of time as a growth factor may be plausible in some cases, but not in others. In many applications the coefficient of time represents in reality not any autonomous growth in Y but the joint effect of the factors which have been omitted from the function; trends are usually the expression of our ignorance of the true forces that determine the growth of the dependent variable.

4. The influence of time on the dependent variable may be taken into account by introducing lagged values of the endogenous or the explanatory variables. The problems of lagged variables are discussed in Chapter 13.

5. Finally short term influences of time, e.g. seasonal variations, may be taken into account by using dummy variables (see below).

---

[1] If in the first-difference approach the disturbance term $(u_t - u_{t-1})$ is to be non-autocorrelated, then u in the original formulation must be autocorrelated with $\rho = 1$, i.e. with a first order autoregressive scheme $u_t = u_{t-1} + w_t$. See Chapter 10.

12.3. DUMMY VARIABLES (or BINARY VARIABLES)

A dummy variable is a variable which we construct to describe the development or variation of the variable under consideration. We assign to it arbitrary units in such a way as to approximate as best we can the variations in the factor which we want to express quantitatively.

Dummy variables are constructed by econometricians to be mainly used as proxies for other variables which cannot be measured in any particular case for various reasons (see Chapter 2). In this section we will examine some of the uses of dummy variables in applied econometric research.

12.3.1. DUMMY VARIABLES AS PROXIES TO QUALITATIVE (CATEGORICAL) FACTORS

Dummy variables are commonly used as proxies for qualitative factors such as profession, religion, sex, region. For example suppose we have a sample of family budgets from all regions of the country, rural and urban, and we want to estimate the demand for tobacco manufactures as a function of income. It is known that town dwellers are heavier smokers than farmers. Thus 'region' is an important explanatory factor in this case. We may represent this factor by a dummy variable to which we might assign arbitrarily the value 1 for a town dweller and zero for a person living in a rural area. The demand function is

$$D_i = b_0 + b_1 X_{1i} + b_2 X_{2i} + u_i$$

where X_1 = income and X_2 = dummy variable for 'region', $(b_2 > 0)$.

12.3.2. DUMMY VARIABLES AS PROXIES TO NUMERICAL FACTORS

Dummy variables may be used as proxies for quantitative factors, when no observations on these factors are available or when it is convenient to do so. For example suppose we want to measure the savings function $(S = f(Y))$ from a cross section sample of consumers. Obviously 'age' is an important explanatory factor of the consumption and savings patterns of a community, since people become more thrifty with age. Although 'age' is a quantitative factor, we may approximate it by a dummy variable as follows. We may divide the consumers in three age groups, each group containing persons with more or less similar consumption and savings patterns:

group A = people of 20–35 years of age
group B = people of 35 and over

On the assumption that people become more thrifty as they grow old, the dummy variable for 'age' may be assigned the value of zero, if the person belongs to the first age group, and the value 1 if the person belongs to the second group. The savings function assumes the form

$$S_i = b_0 + b_1 X_i + b_2 Z_i + u_i$$

where Y_i = income and Z_i = dummy variable for 'age', $(b_2 > 0)$.

12.3.3. USE OF DUMMY VARIABLES FOR MEASURING THE SHIFT OF A FUNCTION OVER TIME

A shift of a function implies that the constant intercept changes in different periods, while the other coefficients remain constant. Such shifts may be taken into account by the introduction of a dummy variable in the function.

For example suppose that we have data on the consumption for the period 1900–1968. During this period we had two world wars (1914–1918 and 1940–1945) and a deep depression (1929–1933). The abnormal conditions prevailing in these years have caused a shift of the consumption function downwards, due to rationing, various controls and other factors. To capture this shift we may use a dummy variable, Z, which would assume the value 0 during the above 'abnormal' years and 1 in the other years. The consumption function assumes the form

$$C_t = b_0 + b_1 Y + b_2 Z + u \qquad\qquad b_2 > 0$$

where Y = income

Z = dummy variable for the shift in the function.

For a normal year the function would be

$$\hat{C}_t = \hat{b}_0 + \hat{b}_1 Y + \hat{b}_2$$
$$= (\hat{b}_0 + \hat{b}_2) + \hat{b}_1 Y$$

and for an abnormal period

$$\hat{C}_t = \hat{b}_0 + \hat{b}_1 Y$$

If we plot these two functions we can clearly see the shift of the consumption function during the abnormal (war or depression) years (figure 12.4).

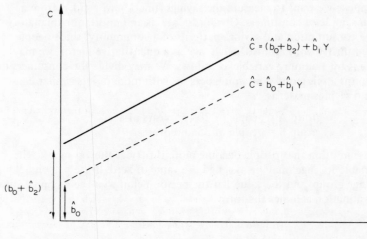

Figure 12.4

The slope of the consumption function (the MPC) is assumed to be the same both in normal and abnormal periods; hence the two regression lines are parallel.[1]

12.3.4. USE OF DUMMY VARIABLES FOR MEASURING THE CHANGE OF PARAMETERS (SLOPES) OVER TIME

It is known that over long periods of time, or in abnormal (war) years not only do the functions shift (their constant intercept changes) but also their slope(s) may well be expected to change: elasticities and propensities change over time. The change in the parameters of a function may be captured by introducing appropriate dummy variables in the function.[2] In the above example of the consumption function if the MPC changes as well as b_0, we may introduce a second dummy variable Z_2 which would be equal to the product of Y and Z_1, i.e. $Z_2 = YZ_1$. Given that $Z_1 = 0$ for abnormal years and $Z_1 = 1$ for normal years, it is obvious that $Z_2 = 0$ for periods of war and depression and $Z_2 = Y$ for normal periods. The general consumption function would assume the form:

$$C_t = b_0 + b_1 Y + b_2 Z_1 + b_3 Z_2 + u$$

Consequently for a peace period the consumption function would be given by

$$C_t = (\hat{b}_0 + \hat{b}_2) + (\hat{b}_1 + \hat{b}_3) Y$$

while for an abnormal year the function would be

$$C_t = \hat{b}_0 + \hat{b}_1 Y$$

12.3.5. USE OF DUMMY VARIABLES AS PROXIES FOR THE DEPENDENT VARIABLE

The dependent variable of a function may be a dummy variable. For example suppose that we want to measure the determinants of car-ownership from a cross-section sample. Some people will have cars while others will not. Assume that the determinants of the ownership function are income and profession:

$$C = b_0 + b_1 Y + b_2 A + u$$

where C = car owners or non-owners
Y = income
A = a dummy variable for 'profession'.

[1] The alternative method would be to fit two regression lines, one for the normal periods and another for the abnormal years. The model would be

$$C = b_0 + b_1 Y + u \quad \text{for normal years}$$

$$C = c_0 + c_1 Y + w \quad \text{for abnormal years.}$$

The slopes (marginal propensities to consume) would not in general be the same. Thus following this approach we avoid imposing the restriction that the MPC be the same in all periods. But the number of abnormal observations may be small in which case the estimates of the coefficients would be unreliable. See Wonnacott & Wonnacott, *Econometrics*, page 71.

[2] We saw in section 12.2 that if b changes over time an alternative way to capture this change is to introduce (apart from X) the variable 'Xt' in the function as a separate explanatory variable, where t stands for 'time'.

Obviously the dependent variable, C, will be a dummy variable which may be assigned the value 1 for a person who owns a car, and zero for a person who does not. In this case we say that the dependent variable is *dichotomous*. In such functions the disturbance term will be heteroscedastic,[1] so that the method of ordinary least squares is not appropriate.[2]

Extensive application of dummy variables is being used by various econometricians in the study of socio-economic relationships, in an attempt to measure the interrelationships between pure economic variables and sociological factors.

12.3.6. USE OF DUMMY VARIABLES FOR SEASONAL ADJUSTMENT OF TIME SERIES

One of the most common applications of dummy variables is in removing seasonal variations in time series. For example if we have quarterly data on retail sales, we should adjust for bulk purchases at Christmas and Easter before attempting to measure the influence of other factors on demand. The seasonal adjustment in this case can be estimated by including among the explanatory variables three dummy variables, Q_1, Q_2 and Q_3. The quarterly regression model is

$$Y_t = b_0 + b_1 X_{1t} + \ldots + b_k X_{kt} + a_1 Q_{1t} + a_2 Q_{2t} + a_3 Q_{3t} + u_t$$

where

$$Q_{1t} = \begin{cases} 1 \text{ in the first quarter} \\ 0 \text{ in all other quarters} \end{cases}$$

$$Q_{2t} = \begin{cases} 1 \text{ in the second quarter} \\ 0 \text{ in all other quarters} \end{cases}$$

$$Q_{3t} = \begin{cases} 1 \text{ in the third quarter} \\ 0 \text{ in all other quarters} \end{cases}$$

A Note on the 'Dummy Variable Trap'

It should be noted that we cannot introduce a fourth dummy variable (with values 1 for the fourth quarter and zero for all other quarters) because the determinant of the terms of sums of squares and sums of products of the explanatory variables (including the quarterly dummies) would be zero. This is due to the dummy variable X_0 which is introduced with values equal to 1 in all periods and is associated with the constant intercept b_0. If we apply OLS to the above quarterly model the parameter estimates for the Q's will give the seasonal effect for each of the three quarters. In the fourth quarter all the Q's are zero and the seasonal effect for the fourth quarter is given by the constant intercept b_0.[3]

---

[1] See J. Johnston, *Econometric Methods*, 1962, pp. 224–228.

[2] See Chapter 9 for the appropriate corrective action when the u's are heteroscedastic.

[3] See J. Thomas, *Notes on the Theory of Multiple Regression*, Athens, 1963, Center of Planning and Economic Research.

12.4. GROUPING OF OBSERVATIONS

In many cases the available data are published in the form of groupings of observations of individuals, consumers or producers. The most common case is the published information on family budgets. Such information is often given for groups of households, the grouping being done on the basis of one or more variables. For example a cross section sample of several thousand households may be divided in ten groups on the basis of their income. For each income group the published data give the average expenditure $(\bar{Y}_1, \bar{Y}_2, \ldots, \bar{Y}_{10})$, the average income $(\bar{X}_1, \ldots, \bar{X}_{10})$ and the number of households $(n_1, n_2, \ldots, n_{10})$ in the group. We may use the group-observations (the mean incomes and mean expenditures of the groups) to obtain an estimate of the marginal propensity to consume.

In this section we shall examine the 'correct' way for using the grouped observations in regression analysis. We shall begin with a model with a single explanatory variable and we shall next extend the analysis to models with more explanatory variables i.e. models involving classifications of the individual observations based on more explanatory variables.

12.4.1. GROUPED OBSERVATIONS IN A MODEL WITH A SINGLE EXPLANATORY VARIABLE

Assumptions. It is assumed that the populations of the variables from which the groups of observations are drawn are related with the linear regression model

$$Y_{ij} = b_0 + b_1 X_{ij} + u_{ij} \qquad \begin{array}{l} (i = 1, 2, \ldots, n_j) \\ (j = 1, 2, \ldots, m) \end{array}$$

where i refers to the individual and j to the group that the individual belongs. This implies that we have m groups of individuals, and we want from the observations of these groups to estimate the relationship between Y and X.

The u_i's satisfy the usual set of assumptions, that is

$$u_{ij} \sim N(0, \sigma_u^2)$$

i.e.

$$E(u_{i1}) = E(u_{i2}) = \ldots = E(u_{im}) = 0$$

and

$$E(u_{i1})^2 = E(u_{i2}) = \ldots = E(u_{im})^2 = \sigma_u^2 \text{ constant}$$

Furthermore the u_i's have zero covariances, and the X's are non-stochastic variables (a set of constant values).

If the observations of all groups were individually known we could apply OLS to these observations and obtain

$$\hat{b}_1 = \frac{\sum\limits_{i}^{N} (Y_i - \bar{Y})(X_i - \bar{X})}{\sum\limits_{i}^{N}(X_i - \bar{X})^2}$$

and

$$\hat{b}_0 = \bar{Y} - \hat{b}_1 \bar{X}$$

where $i = 1, 2, 3, \ldots, N = n_1 + n_2 + \ldots + n_k = \sum_{j=1}^{k} n_k = N$

N = total individuals in all groups

The estimates $\hat{b}_0$ and $\hat{b}_1$ would be best, linear, unbiased. The variance of $\hat{b}_1$ is

$$\text{var}(\hat{b}_1) = \sigma_u^2 \frac{1}{\sum_{i}^{N}(X_i - \bar{X})^2} \qquad (i = 1, 2, \ldots, N)$$

However, the individual observations of the groups are not known, but for each group we have the mean values of Y and X and the group frequency (n_j).

Number of group-observations	n_j	$\bar{Y}_j$	$\bar{X}_j$
1	n_1	$\bar{Y}_1$	$\bar{X}_1$
2	n_2	$\bar{Y}_2$	$\bar{X}_2$
⋮	⋮	⋮	⋮
m	n_k	$\bar{Y}_m$	$\bar{X}_m$

where $\bar{Y}_j = \dfrac{\sum_{i=1}^{n_j} Y_{ij}}{n_j}$ and $\bar{X}_j = \dfrac{\sum_{i=1}^{n_j} X_{ij}}{n_j}$ $\qquad (j = 1, 2, \ldots, m)$

Thus we have m *'group-observations'* consisting of the means of the variables Y and X in each group. The regression model with the group-observations is

$$\bar{Y}_j = b_0 + b_1 \bar{X}_j + \bar{u}_j \qquad (j = 1, 2, \ldots, m)$$

where $\bar{u}_j = \sum_{i=1}^{n_j} u_{ij}/n_j$.

If the number of observations in each group is the same $(n_1 = n_2 = \ldots = n_m)$ then all the assumptions of the linear regression model would be satisfied for the 'grouped' model (or 'condensed' model) and hence we could apply OLS to the group-means and obtain best, linear, unbiased estimates of the b's.

Let us establish the mean, variance and covariance of the 'grouped' random term $\bar{u}_j$.

1. Mean $\bar{u}_j$:

$$E(\bar{u}_j) = E\frac{1}{n_j}(u_{1j} + u_{2j} + \ldots + u_{mj})$$

$$= \frac{1}{n_j}[E(u_{1j}) + E(u_{2j}) + \ldots + E(u_{mj})] = 0$$

2. Covariance of $\bar{u}_j$'s:

$$E(\bar{u}_j\bar{u}_s) = E\left[\frac{1}{n_j}(u_{1j} + u_{2j} + \ldots + u_{mj})\right]\left[\frac{1}{n_s}(u_{1s} + u_{2s} + \ldots + u_{ms})\right] = 0$$

3. Variance $\bar{u}_j$:

$$\text{var}(\bar{u}_j) = \frac{1}{n_j^2}(\sigma_u^2 + \sigma_u^2 + \ldots + \sigma_u^2) = \frac{n_j\sigma_u^2}{n_j^2} = \frac{\sigma_u^2}{n_j}$$

If $n_1 = n_2 = \ldots = n_m$ then $\text{var}(\bar{u}_j) = \sigma_u^2/n_j = $ constant, that is the $\bar{u}_j$'s are homoscedastic. However, if the number of observations in the various groups is not the same, the error term of the 'grouped function' is heteroscedastic and OLS is not the appropriate method of estimation. The form of heteroscedasticity is actually

$$\text{var}(\bar{u}_j) = \sigma_u^2\frac{1}{n_j}$$

The corrective action in this case is the transformation of the original grouped observations (group-means). The transformation consists in the division of $\bar{Y}_j$ and $\bar{X}_j$ by $\sqrt{1/n_j}$ (see Chapter 9)

$$\bar{Y}_j/\sqrt{1/n_j} = b_0/\sqrt{1/n_j} + b_1\bar{X}_j/\sqrt{1/n_j} + \bar{u}_j/\sqrt{1/n_j}$$

$$\text{or } (\bar{Y}_j\sqrt{n_j}) = b_0(\sqrt{n_j}) + b_1(\sqrt{n_j}\bar{X}_j) + \bar{u}_j(\sqrt{n_j}) \tag{12.4.1}$$

The new error term is homoscedastic, because:

$$\text{var}(\bar{u}_j\sqrt{n_j}) = E(\bar{u}_j\sqrt{n_j})^2 = n_jE(\bar{u}_j)^2 = n_j\,\text{var}(\bar{u}_j) = n_j\cdot\sigma_u^2\cdot\frac{1}{n_j} = \sigma_u^2 \text{ constant.}$$

This procedure amounts to the application of Weighted Least Squares (WLS) where we use the group frequencies as weights for the group means (see Chapter 9).

The normal equations of the transformed model are obtained by applying the rules of thumb developed in Chapter 7. That is, we multiply the 'transformed equation' (12.4.1) first by $\sqrt{n_j}$ and next by $(X_j\sqrt{n_j})$, and sum over all (m)

observations:

$$\sum_j^m \bar{Y}_j n_j = \tilde{b}_0 \sum_j^m n_j + \tilde{b}_1 \sum_j^m \bar{X}_j n_j$$

$$\sum_j^m \bar{Y}_j \bar{X}_j n_j = \tilde{b}_0 \sum_j^m \bar{X}_j n_j + \tilde{b}_1 \sum_j^m \bar{X}_j^2 n_j$$

Solving for $\tilde{b}_1$ we find

$$\tilde{b}_1 = \frac{(\sum_j^m n_j)(\sum_j^m \bar{Y}_j n_j) - (\sum_j^m \bar{X}_j n_j)(\sum_j^m \bar{Y}_j \bar{X}_j n_j)}{(\sum_j^m n_j)(\sum_j^m \bar{X}_j^2 n_j) - (\sum_j^m \bar{X}_j n_j)^2}$$

and $\tilde{b}_0 = \bar{Y} - \tilde{b}_1 \bar{X}$.

The variance of $\tilde{b}_1$ from WLS is

$$\text{var}(\tilde{b}_1) = \sigma_u^2 \frac{\sum_j^m n_j}{(\sum_j^m n_j)(\sum_j^m \bar{X}_j^2 n_j) - (\sum_j^m \bar{X}_j n_j)^2} = \sigma_u^2 \frac{1}{\sum_j^m n_j(\bar{X}_j - \bar{X})^2}$$

Proof:

(a) $\Sigma n_j = N$

(b) $\Sigma \bar{X}_j n_j = \sum_i \sum_j X_{ij} = N\bar{X} \quad \left(\text{given } \bar{X} = \dfrac{\sum_i \sum_j X_{ij}}{N} \right)$

Therefore

$$\text{var}(\tilde{b}_1) = \sigma_u^2 \frac{N}{N(\Sigma \bar{X}_j^2 n_j) - N^2 X^2} = \sigma_u^2 \frac{1}{\Sigma n_j(\bar{X}_j - \bar{X})^2}$$

Because

$$\Sigma n_j(\bar{X}_j - \bar{X})^2 = \Sigma n_j \bar{X}_j^2 + \Sigma n_j \bar{X}^2 - 2\Sigma n_j \bar{X}_j \bar{X}$$

$$= \Sigma n_j \bar{X}_j^2 + \bar{X}^2 \Sigma n_j - 2\bar{X}(\Sigma n_j \bar{X}_j)$$

$$= \Sigma n_j \bar{X}_j^2 + N\bar{X}^2 - 2X(N\bar{X})$$

$$= \Sigma n_j \bar{X}_j^2 - N\bar{X}^2$$

The variances of the WLS $\tilde{b}$'s involve the true variance σ_u^2 which of course is unknown. An estimate of this variance may be obtained by using the formula

$$\hat{\sigma}_u^2 = \frac{\Sigma e_j^2}{m - K} = \frac{\Sigma n_j(\bar{Y}_j - \tilde{b}_0 - \tilde{b} \bar{X}_j)^2}{m - 2}$$

where m = number of groups (= number of grouped observations)

K = number of parameters in the model.

Two points are important in applying regression analysis to grouped observations.

First. The variance of the estimates $(\widetilde{b}$'s$)$ obtained from the grouped data is larger than the variance of the estimates $(\widehat{b}$'s$)$ obtained from the application of OLS to the ungrouped observations

$$\operatorname{var}(\widetilde{b}_i) > \operatorname{var}(\widehat{b}_i)$$

Proof:

$$\frac{\operatorname{var}(\widetilde{b}_1)}{\operatorname{var}(\widehat{b}_1)} = \frac{\sigma_u^2 \Big/ \sum_j^m n_j(\bar{X}_j - \bar{X})^2}{\sigma_u^2 \Big/ \sum_i^n (X_i - \bar{X})^2}$$

But in Chapter 8 we established that

$$\sum_i^n (X_i - \bar{X})^2 = \sum_i^{n_j} \sum_j^m (X_{ij} - \bar{X})^2 + \sum_j^m n_j(\bar{X}_j - \bar{X})^2$$

[Total variation] = [Within variation] + [Between variation]

Therefore

$$\frac{\operatorname{var}(\widetilde{b}_1)}{\operatorname{var}(\widehat{b}_1)} = \frac{\sigma_u^2 \Big/ [\Sigma n_j(\bar{X}_j - \bar{X})^2]}{\sigma_u^2 \Big/ [\sum_i \sum_j (X_{ij} - \bar{X}_j)^2 + \Sigma n_j(\bar{X}_j - \bar{X})^2]}$$

$$= \frac{\sum_i \sum_j (X_{ij} - \bar{X}_j)^2 + \Sigma n_j(\bar{X}_j - \bar{X})^2}{\Sigma n_j(\bar{X}_j - \bar{X})^2}$$

$$= 1 + \frac{\sum_i \sum_j (X_{ij} - \bar{X}_j)^2}{\sum_j n_j(\bar{X}_j - \bar{X})^2} = 1 + \frac{\text{Within variation}}{\text{Between variation}}$$

The ratio, as shown in Chapter 8, is greater than unit (or the most equal to unity). Hence

$$\operatorname{var}(\widetilde{b}_1) > \operatorname{var}(\widehat{b}_1)$$

This is due to the loss of information included in the variation of the observations within each sample, which is unknown if the data are given in grouped form.

Second. It has been shown by Cramer[1] that the overall correlation coefficient in the 'grouped' model is higher than in the ungrouped regression. Since the basic sample is the same in both the 'grouped' and the ungrouped regression, the

[1] See J. S. Cramer, 'Efficient Grouping, Regression and Correlation in Engel Curve Analysis', *Journal of the American Statistical Association*, vol. 59, 1964, pp. 233–250.

higher R^2 obtained from the grouped model is misleading. The higher the degree of aggregation the stronger the correlation will deceptively appear to be. This reflects the fact that the group means tend to cluster closer around the regression line than the individual observations.

Example. Table 12.1 shows the mean incomes $(\bar{X}_j)$ and mean expenditures $(\bar{Y}_j)$ of 100 families which are classified in 10 groups on the basis of their income. We wish to obtain an estimate of the MPC of these families.

Table 12.1. Grouped data for 100 families

Number of grouped observations	Group frequency n_j	Mean Expenditure $\bar{Y}_j$	Mean Income $\bar{X}_j$	$n_j\bar{Y}_j$	$n_j\bar{X}_j$	$n_j\bar{X}_j^2$	$n_j\bar{Y}_j\bar{X}_j$
1	$n_1 = 5$	14	16	70	80	1,280	1,120
2	$n_2 = 10$	15	20	150	200	4,000	3,000
3	$n_3 = 20$	17	22	340	440	9,680	7,480
4	$n_4 = 15$	22	25	330	375	9,375	8,250
5	$n_5 = 5$	25	30	125	150	4,500	3,750
6	$n_6 = 10$	28	33	280	330	10,890	9,240
7	$n_7 = 6$	30	36	180	216	7,776	6,480
8	$n_8 = 9$	35	43	315	387	16,641	13,545
9	$n_9 = 6$	39	48	234	288	13,824	11,232
10	$n_{10} = 14$	45	55	630	770	42,350	34,650
$m = 10$	$\Sigma n_j = 100$			2,654	3,236	120,316	98,747

The grouped model is heteroscedastic since the number of observations in the groups is not the same. Hence the estimate of the MPC will be obtained from the transformed normal equations

$$\Sigma(n_j\bar{Y}_j) = \tilde{b}_0(\Sigma n_j) + \tilde{b}_1(\Sigma n_j\bar{X}_j)$$

$$\Sigma(n_j\bar{Y}_j\bar{X}_j) = \tilde{b}_0(\Sigma n_j\bar{X}_j) + \tilde{b}_1(\Sigma n_j\bar{X}_j^2)$$

The relevant data are shown in table 12.1. Solving the above system we obtain

$$\bar{Y}_j = 0{\cdot}02 + 0{\cdot}82\,\bar{X}_j.$$

12.4.2. EXTENSION OF THE 'GROUPED' MODEL TO TWO (OR MORE) EXPLANATORY VARIABLES

The extension of the simple model is straightforward if the classification of the observations is complete, that is, it is done on the basis of all the explanatory variables. Suppose that the observations are grouped on the basis of two explanatory variables, e.g. consumers are classified according to their income (X_1) and wealth (X_2). In this case we speak of a two-way complete classification. For each group we have the means of the relevant variables $(\bar{Y}_j, \bar{X}_{1j}, \bar{X}_{2j})$ and the group frequency.

Group frequency n_j	$\bar{Y}_j$	$\bar{X}_{1j}$	$\bar{X}_{2j}$
n_1	$\bar{Y}_1$	$\bar{X}_{11}$	$\bar{X}_{21}$
n_2	$\bar{Y}_2$	$\bar{X}_{12}$	$\bar{X}_{22}$
$\vdots$	$\vdots$	$\vdots$	$\vdots$
n_{10}	$\bar{Y}_{10}$	$\bar{X}_{1, 10}$	$\bar{X}_{2, 10}$

Note: The number of grouped observations is $m = 10$.

The grouped model is

$$\bar{Y}_j = b_0 + b_1 \bar{X}_{1j} + b_2 \bar{X}_{2j} + \bar{u}_j \qquad (j = 1, 2, \ldots, 10)$$

In most cases the group frequencies are different; hence the model is heteroscedastic. It can be shown that the appropriate transformation of the group means is to use the group frequencies as weights. The system of the required three normal equations is obtained by multiplying the expression

$$Y_j\sqrt{n_j} = (b_0\sqrt{n_j}) + b_1 \bar{X}_{1j}\sqrt{n_j} + b_2 \bar{X}_{2j}\sqrt{n_j}$$

firstly, by $\sqrt{n_j}$ and sum over all sample observations;

secondly, by $(X_{1j}\sqrt{n_j})$ and sum over all sample observations;

thirdly, by $(X_{2j}\sqrt{n_j})$ and sum over all sample observations.

Thus the system of 'normal equations' in this case is

$$\sum_j^m \bar{Y}_j n_j = \tilde{b}_0(\sum_j^m n_j) + \tilde{b}_1 \sum_j^m \bar{X}_{1j} n_j + \tilde{b}_2 \sum_j^m \bar{X}_{2j} n_j$$

$$\sum_j^m \bar{Y}\bar{X}_{1j} n_j = \tilde{b}_0 \sum_j^m \bar{X}_{1j} n_j + \tilde{b}_1 \sum_j^m \bar{X}_{1j}^2 n_j + \tilde{b}_2 \sum_j^m \bar{X}_{1j}\bar{X}_{2j} n_j$$

$$\sum_j^m \bar{Y}_j \bar{X}_{2j} n_j = \tilde{b}_0 \sum_j^m \bar{X}_{2j} n_j + \tilde{b}_1 \sum_j^m \bar{X}_{1j}\bar{X}_{2j} n_j + \tilde{b}_2 \sum_j^m \bar{X}_{2j}^2 n_j$$

If there are two (or more) explanatory variables, but the grouping is not complete, that is, the classification is done only on one variable, there are several methods for the estimation of the 'grouped' model. The interested reader is referred to Y. Haitovsky's articles, 'Unbiased Multiple Regression Coefficients

Estimated from One-way Classification Tables when the Cross Classifications are Unknown', *Journal of the American Statistical Association*, vol. **61**, pp. 720–728, 1966, and 'Regression Estimation from Grouped Observations', National Bureau of Economic Research, New York, October 1967.

The extension of the 'grouped' model to higher order *complete* classifications (i.e. classifications of observations on the basis of three or more explanatory variables) is straightforward.

EXERCISES

1. Consider the models

(a) $\psi_i = b_0 + b_1 \chi_i + v$ (b) $\psi_i = b_0 + b_1 \chi_i + u$

     $Y_i = \psi_i$ $Y_i = \psi_i + v_1$

     $X_i = \chi_i + v$ $X_i = \chi_i + v_2$

where ψ_i and χ_i are the true values and Y_i and X_i are the observed values of the variables. The errors v_i are independent from one another and from u, and they satisfy the usual stochastic assumptions.

(i) Establish for each model the properties of the OLS estimates obtained from the equation

$$Y_i = \hat{b}_0 + \hat{b}_1 X_i$$

(ii) Discuss alternative methods for rectifying the effects of the errors of measurement in the above models. Indicate the difference in underlying assumptions in each method and discuss their plausibility in real situations.

2. Given the function

$$Y = b_0 + b_1 X + b_2 t + u$$

Show that b_1 is identical to the value that would be obtained from regressing Y on X^*, where $X^* =$ value of X free from trend.

3. Prove that the constant intercept of a function expressed in the first differences of the variables is equivalent to the assumption that the dependent variable Y has an autonomous rate of growth, measured by t.

4. The following table contains information on the consumption function of a certain country over two different periods. (Variables are measured in arbitrary units.)

	Year	C_t	Y_t	$\hat{C}_t$	e_t	e_t^2
Regression for	1961	297·0	331·4	300·35	−3·35	11·22
sample 1	1962	303·8	333·2	301·91	1·89	3·57
$\hat{C} = 6·21 + 0·87\,Y$	1963	308·1	338·1	306·16	1·94	3·76
s.e. (2·49) (0·06)	1964	325·2	360·7	325·50	−0·30	0·09
	1965	338·6	375·7	338·77	−0·17	0·03
					$\Sigma e_t^2 = 18·67$	

	Year	C_t	Y_t	$\hat{C}_t$	e_t	e_t^2
Regression for	1966	358·0	410·2	363·72	−5·72	32·72
sample 2	1967	378·7	417·7	370·50	8·20	67·24
$\hat{C} = -6.93 + 0.90\ Y$	1968	391·7	445·9	395·98	−4·28	18·32
s.e. (44·84) (0·10)	1969	413·1	462·7	411·16	1·94	3·76
	1970	432·8	486·8	432·94	−0·14	0·02
						$\Sigma e_t^2 = 122·06$

(i) Test the hypothesis that the consumption function is stable over time, using the Chow test outlined in Chapter 8.

(ii) Does this test give you any information regarding the changes of either the slope or the intercept separately?

(iii) Outline the procedure which you would adopt if you wanted to test the hypothesis that both the slope and the intercept change over time.

(iv) Outline the procedure which you would adopt if you wanted to test the hypothesis that *only* the MPC changes over time?

Note. Additional exercises are included in Appendix III.

13. Lagged Variables Distributed-lag Models

Distributed-lag models are models which include lagged values of the exogenous variables and/or lagged values of the dependent variables among the set of explanatory variables.

The general form of a distributed-lag model with only lagged exogenous variables is

$$Y_t = a + b_0 X_t + b_1 X_{t-1} + b_2 X_{t-2} + \ldots + b_s X_{t-s} + \ldots + u_t$$

They are called distributed lag models because the influence of the explanatory variable on the dependent variable is distributed over a number of past values of X. The number of lags, s, may be either finite or infinite. However, in order to avoid explosive values of Y_t, we assume that the b's have a finite sum

$$\sum_{i=0}^{s} b_i < \infty$$

The average lag is defined as the weighted average of all the lags involved, with weights being the relative size of the respective b coefficients

$$\text{Average lag} = \frac{\sum_{i=0}^{s} i b_i}{\sum_{i=0}^{s} b_i} = \sum_{i=0}^{s} i \frac{b_i}{\sum_{i=0}^{s} b_i}$$

Lagged values of the variables are important explanatory variables in most economic relationships, because economic behaviour in any one period is to a great extent determined by past experience and past patterns of behaviour. Some examples will illustrate the importance of lagged variables.

Example 1. The consumption function

Recent versions of the consumption function postulate that the current level of consumption depends on past levels of consumption, due to 'habit persistence', on current income and past levels of income and other factors

$$C_t = f(C_{t-1}, C_{t-2}, \ldots, Y_t, Y_{t-1}, Y_{t-2}, \ldots, X_{1t}, X_{2t} \ldots)$$

Example 2. The demand for durables

The demand for durables (D_d) depends, among others, on present income (Y_t), past levels of income (Y_{t-s}) which determine the amount saved for the acquisition of the durables, on the stocks of durables or, equivalently, on past acquisitions of durables ($S_{d,\,t-1}$), prices (P_t), and so on

$$D_d = f(Y_t, Y_{t-1}, \ldots, S_{d,\,t-1}, P_t \ldots)$$

Example 3. The demand for inventory investment

The firms usually define their inventories on the basis of the actual sales of the three past periods (and other factors)

$$I_t = f(X_{t-1}, X_{t-2}, X_{t-3} \ldots)$$

Example 4. The investment function

Investment projects depend on past outputs, on expectations about future profits, on capital stock and other factors

$$I_t = f(X_t, X_{t-1}, X_{t-2}, \ldots, \Pi_t, K_{t-1}, r_{t-4} \ldots)$$

where $\quad X$ = level of output
Π = profit
K = capital stock
r = interest rate

Example 5. Demand for nondurables (e.g. tobacco)

The habit-persistence is a characteristic of human behaviour. The quantity demanded for food, tobacco and other nondurables depends, among others, on the past levels of consumption of these commodities

$$Q_t = f(Q_{t-1}, Y_t, P_t, \ldots)$$

Indeed lags are involved in all economic behaviour. We live in a dynamic world of continuous adjustment. Clearly an adjustment process takes time, the length of the time period depending on the nature of the particular phenomenon. Yet economic theory is mostly static. In comparative statics where different equilibria are compared, adjustments are assumed instantaneous. The process of adjustment and the lags involved are scarcely discussed. Yet these lags are of paramount importance for decision making. It is crucial for the government official to know how fast, after how many time periods will the economic units react to changes of various policy variables (instruments). How fast will consumers react to the imposition of a sales tax or a credit squeeze? How fast will firms react to tax concessions and other incentives for investment and innovation? How fast will be the effects of a devaluation? How fast will investors react to changes in the interest rates?

Similarly the lags involved in the demand for consumers goods following a change in the 'policy instruments' (price, quality, style, advertising) of a firm are of crucial importance for managerial decisions. Again the micro-economic theory of the firm is mostly static. The lag patterns in the adjustment of buyers to changes in various variables are scarcely mentioned.

In view of the nature of economic behaviour any realistic formulation of economic models should involve some lagged variables among the set of explanatory variables. Lagged variables are one way for taking into account the length of time in the adjustment processes of economic behaviour and perhaps the most efficient way for rendering them dynamic. Lagged models have become increasingly popular in applied econometric research. Their refinement has made possible the handling of expectations about future events, if only in a rigid and not very satisfactory way. In short, lagged models offer much flexibility to the formulation of models of economic behaviour.

Distributed lag models involve a high degree of empiricism, which is due to the unsatisfactory state of economic theory with regard to the length of the adjustment processes of economic phenomena. Economic theory, even where it recognises the importance of time lags, never suggests the precise number of lags that should be included in a function. Rather the pattern of lags is explored and determined from the available sample observations, by adopting an experimental approach involving various lag patterns and then choosing among them the one that gives the best statistical fit. The researcher experiments with models including different lag patterns (geometric lags, arbitrary lags, polynomial lags, compound geometric lags) and chooses among them the one that gives the most satisfactory fit on the basis of statistical (mainly) criteria.

We shall start with the examination of models including lagged values of exogenous variables only. We shall next extend the analysis by examining models including lagged values of the endogenous variable (Y_{t-1}, Y_{t-2} etc.) among the set of explanatory variables. In a last section we shall discuss methods of estimation of the parameters of distributed lag models.

13.1. EXOGENOUS LAGGED VARIABLES

Assume that Y depends on the values of X over s periods. This is a finite lag structure of the form

$$Y_t = a + b_0 X_t + b_1 X_{t-1} + \ldots + b_s X_{t-s} + u_t$$

13.1.1. ESTIMATION OF LAGS BY APPLYING OLS

If the model includes only lagged values of the exogenous variable(s) in the set of explanatory variables we can, in principle, make the usual assumptions about the error term u

$$u \sim N(0, \sigma_u^2)$$
$$E(u_i u_j) = 0 \qquad (i \neq j)$$
$$E(u_i X_j) = 0 \qquad (j = 1, 2 \ldots k)$$

and proceed with the application of OLS to the sample observations.

However, two difficulties are almost certain to arise in attempting to apply OLS to this type of model. *Firstly*, if the number of lags is large and the sample is small (which is usually the case with time series data), we may be unable to estimate the parameters, because there will be no adequate degrees of freedom to carry out the traditional statistical tests of significance. *Secondly,* it is almost certain that we will have multicollinearity problems, since one might expect a strong correlation between successive values of the same variable. With strong collinearity the values of the estimates will be imprecise and their standard errors will be large so that we may be led to mis-specification of the model by dropping variables which may in fact be important.

To avoid these difficulties various methods have been suggested, all of which have as their basic aim a 'meaningful' reduction of the number of lagged variables. This is achieved by imposing restrictions on the b's and constructing new variables (we shall call them W_i) from a linear combination of the lagged variables. The methods differ in the weights which are used in constructing these new variables, i.e. in the way the restrictions on the b's are imposed.

13.1.2. ESTIMATION BY ASSIGNING ARBITRARY VALUES TO THE WEIGHTS OF THE LAGGED VARIABLES

Our concern is mainly to find ways for economising degrees of freedom, that is reduce meaningfully the number of parameters to be directly estimated from the given sample. The simplest method is to construct new variables (W's) from a linear combination of the lagged X's, assigning arbitrary numerical values as weights for the individual lagged variables.

There are various versions in this approach.

(a) *The declining lag-scheme*

In this scheme it is *assumed* that the weights are declining, i.e. the more recent values of X have a greater influence on Y than more remote values. For example assume $s = 4$. Then

$$W_{1t} = w_0 X_t + w_1 X_{t-1} + w_2 X_{t-2} + w_3 X_{t-3} + w_4 X_{t-4}$$

where

$$w_0 > w_1 > w_2 > w_3 > w_4$$

For example

$$W_{1t} = \tfrac{1}{3} X_t + \tfrac{1}{5} X_{t-1} + \tfrac{1}{6} X_{t-2} + \tfrac{1}{8} X_{t-3} + \tfrac{1}{10} X_{t-4}$$

(b) *The rectangular lag-scheme*

In this scheme all lagged values are given equal weights, i.e. it is *assumed* that each past value of X has the same influence on Y.

For example

$$W_{2t} = \tfrac{1}{3} X_t + \tfrac{1}{3} X_{t-1} + \tfrac{1}{3} X_{t-2} + \tfrac{1}{3} X_{t-3} + \tfrac{1}{3} X_{t-4}$$

(c) *The 'inverted V' lag pattern*

Here it is assumed that the weights are initially increasing, and subsequently declining.

For example

$$W_{3t} = \tfrac{1}{10} X_t + \tfrac{1}{4} X_{t-1} + \tfrac{1}{5} X_{t-2} + \tfrac{1}{7} X_{t-3} + \tfrac{1}{9} X_{t-4}$$

These general shapes of weights are shown in figure 13.1.

In many applications economic considerations may suggest which is the most probable pattern of lag structure. For example in a consumption function the

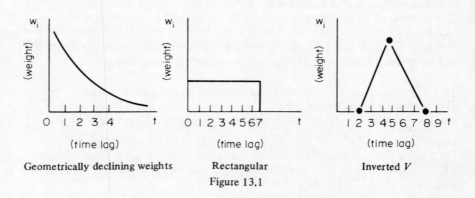

Geometrically declining weights   Rectangular   Inverted V

Figure 13.1

declining weights for past levels of income seem more plausible, while in an investment function, where the lagged X's are past capital appropriations, it may be more reasonable to assume an 'inverted V' lag scheme.

In general, the method of arbitrary weights is an extremely arbitrary method of dealing with the lags. The researcher specifies not only the general form of the weights (declining, rectangular, 'inverted V'), but he also assigns actual values to the weights (w's) of the lagged variables. Having constructed various W_i's the researcher experiments with functions including each W_i in turn as a *single* explanatory variable. For example one may apply OLS to the models

(1) $Y_t = c_0 + c_1 W_{1t} + u_t$

(2) $Y_t = a_0 + a_1 W_{2t} + u_t$

(3) $Y_t = d_0 + d_1 W_{3t} + u_t$

(4) $Y_t = b_0 + b_1 X_t + b_2 W_t + u_t$

where

$$W_t = \tfrac{1}{6} X_{t-1} + \tfrac{1}{5} X_{t-2} + \tfrac{1}{5} X_{t-3} + \tfrac{1}{10} X_{t-4}$$

and so on. The choice among these alternative models is based mainly on statistical criteria, that is on the goodness of fit as measured by R^2 and on the size of the standard errors of the estimates. Sometimes rationalisation of the choice is attempted on *a priori* economic considerations as well.

A good example of the arbitrary-weights lag scheme is provided by De Leeuw's study of investment, based on quarterly data.[1] He experimented with the following three types of distributed lag functions:

(1) $I_t = b_1(X_t + \lambda X_{t-1} + \lambda^2 X_{t-2} + \ldots + \lambda^s X_{t-s}) + u_t$ $0 < \lambda < 1$

This is a standard distributed lag function with declining weights. (The weights are geometrically declining; this form has been suggested by Koyck and will be discussed in detail in section 13.2 below.)

(2) $I_t = b_2(wX_t + wX_{t-1} + wX_{t-2} + \ldots + wX_{t-s}) + u_t$

This is a lag scheme with constant weights (rectangular distribution of weights), in which all output levels are assigned an equal weight of w for all s past periods.

(3) $I_t = b_3[X_t + 2X_{t-1} + 3X_{t-2} + \ldots + kX_{t-k+1} + (k-1)X_{t-k} +$
$+ (k-2)X_{t-k-1} + (k-3)X_{t-k-2} + \ldots + X_{t-2k+2}] + u_t$

This is a function with an 'inverted V' lag pattern, where the weights increase initially and then fall. In particular DeLeeuw assumed that for a total lag of s periods the first half of the weights are proportional to the increasing series $1, 2, 3 \ldots, s/2$ (for even values of s), and the other half of the weights are proportional to the declining series $(s/2) - 1, (s/2) - 2, \ldots, 3, 2, 1$. DeLeeuw, after numerous experimentations with various lag periods, concluded that the best fit was obtained by a function of the third type (with an 'inverted V' lag scheme) and with a twelve-quarters lag period (i.e. $s = 12$ quarters). His preferred function, chosen on the basis of highest R^2, was of the form

$$I_t = b_3(X_t + 2X_{t-1} + 3X_{t-2} + 4X_{t-3} + 5X_{t-4} + 6X_{t-5} + 7X_{t-6} + 6X_{t-7} +$$
$$+ 5X_{t-8} + 4X_{t-9} + 3X_{t-10} + 2X_{t-11} + X_{t-12})$$

13.1.3. THE ALMON SCHEME OF POLYNOMIAL LAG

(S. Almon, 'The Distributed Lag Between Capital Appropriations and Expenditures', *Econometrica*, vol. 33, 1965, 178–96.)

Almon proposed the following method for estimating the parameters of the lagged exogenous variables.

The lagged model is finite and includes only exogenous lagged variables

$$Y_t = b_0 X_t + b_1 X_{t-1} + \ldots + b_s X_{t-s} + u_t \tag{13.1}$$

Instead of attempting to estimate directly all the b's (which are $s + 1$ in number)

[1] F. DeLeeuw, 'The Demand for Capital goods by Manufacturers: A Study of Quarterly Time Series', *Econometrica*, vol. 30, July 1962, pp. 407–23. A similar arbitrary-weight approach has been applied by P. J. Lund and K. Holden, 'An Econometric Study of Private Sector Gross Fixed Capital Formation in the United Kingdom, 1923–1938', *Oxford Economic Papers*, vol. 20, 1968, pp. 56–73.

by applying OLS to the above function, we may obtain estimates of all the b's indirectly as follows.

Assume that the b's in the lagged model can be approximated by some function $b \simeq f(z)$. The function $f(z)$ is unknown if we do not make any prior assumptions about its form. The usual assumption is that the function $f(z)$ may be approximated by a polynomial in z of the rth degree

$$f(z) \simeq a_0 + a_1 z + a_2 z^2 + a_3 z^3 + \ldots + a_r z^r$$

This is called 'the approximation polynomial', because of its role. That is $f(z)$ yields the values of the b's (approximately) if we know the a's and the degree (r) of the polynomial. Almon develops a general method for estimating $f(z)$ which is highly complex and has several disadvantages.[1] In most cases the following simpler approach is adopted.

Step 1. We specify the degree of the approximating polynomial, r, and the number of lags, s. Usually the degree of the polynomial is assumed low ($r = 3$ or 4). If the degree of the polynomial is high we do not achieve the intended reduction in the number of the parameters which we will estimate from our sample. (In a later stage we will examine how one may increase the degree r and test whether the higher-degree polynomial yields a better fit. See below.)

Step 2. We express the b's in terms of the a's of the approximation polynomial, by assigning to z the successive integer values $z = 0$, $z = 1$, $z = 2, \ldots, z = s$. Thus we obtain the following system.

$$\left. \begin{aligned}
b_0 &= f(0) = (a_0) \\
b_1 &= f(1) = (a_0 + a_1 + a_2 + a_3 + \ldots + a_r \\
b_2 &= f(2) = (a_0 + 2a_1 + 2^2 a_2 + 2^3 a_3 + \ldots + 2^r a_r \\
b_3 &= f(3) = (a_0 + 3a_1 + 3^2 a_2 + 3^3 a_3 + \ldots + 3^r a_r \\
&\ \cdot \quad \cdot \quad \cdot \quad \cdot \quad \cdot \quad \cdot \quad \cdot \quad \cdot \\
b_s &= f(s) = (a_0 + sa_1 + s^2 a_2 + s^3 a_3 + \ldots + s^r a_r
\end{aligned} \right\} \qquad (13.2)$$

In this system the b's are expressed as linear functions of the a's. We shall call this system "*the b-system*". If we knew the a's, we could obtain the b's by substitution in the above system.

Before we show how to obtain the estimates of the a's it is useful to rewrite the coefficients of the "b-system" in a table, so as to show clearly the numerical pattern of these coefficients. This is done in table 13.1.

---

[1] Note that the general Almon scheme is computationally cumbersome and has several disadvantages in applied research (see J. Johnston, *Econometric Methods*, 2nd Edition, McGraw-Hill, 1972, pp. 296—7). The method presented in this section is a simplified version of the general Almon scheme, which is most often used in practice because of its simplicity and its computational advantages.

Table 13.1 Numerical Coefficients of the 'b-system'

b_i	a_j			$(j = 0, 1, 2, \ldots, r)$
$(i = 0, 1, 2, \ldots, s)$	a_0	a_1	a_2	$a_3 \ldots a_r$
b_0	1	0	0	$0 \ldots 0$
b_1	1	1	1	$1 \ldots 1$
b_2	1	2	2^2	$2^3 \ldots 2^r$
.	.	.	.	.
.	.	.	.	.
.	.	.	.	.
b_s	1	s	s^2	$s^3 \ldots s^r$

In general

$$b_s = \sum_{j=0}^{r} s^{(j)} a_j \qquad (j = 0, 1, \ldots, r)$$

Step 3. We obtain estimates of the a's by applying OLS to the transformed model

$$Y_t = a_0 W_0 + a_1 W_1 + a_2 W_2 + \ldots + a_r W_r + u_t \qquad (13.3)$$

where the W's are linear combinations of the lagged X's, with the weights shown in table 13.2.

Table 13.2. Weights in an Almon Lag Scheme

W \ X	X_t	X_{t-1}	X_{t-2}	X_{t-3}	X_{t-4}	X_{t-5}	$\ldots$	X_{t-s}
W_0	1	1	1	1	1	1	$\ldots$	1
W_1	0	1	2	3	4	5	$\ldots$	s
W_2	0	1	2^2	3^2	4^2	5^2	$\ldots$	s^2
W_3	0	1	2^3	3^3	4^3	5^3	$\ldots$	s^3
W_4	0	1	2^4	3^4	4^4	5^4	$\ldots$	s^4
.	.	.	.	.	.	.		.
.	.	.	.	.	.	.		.
.	.	.	.	.	.	.		.
W_r	0	1	2^r	3^r	4^r	5^r	$\ldots$	s^r

Looking at the pattern of the weights we may derive the following generalisations.

1. There will be as many constructed W's as the arbitrarily chosen degree of the polynomial plus one (that is the number of the W's is $r + 1$).
2. The W's are linear combinations of all the X values (current and lagged).
   (a) The weights used in the first constructed variable (W_0) are all equal to unity

$$W_0 = X_t + X_{t-1} + X_{t-2} + \ldots + X_{t-s}$$

(b) The weights of W_1 will be the simple increasing series of integers

$$0, 1, 2, 3, \ldots, s$$

that is

$$W_1 = X_{t-1} + 2X_{t-2} + 3X_{t-3} + \ldots + sX_{t-s}$$

(c) The weights of the third constructed variable, W_2, will be the squares of the weights of W_1, that is

$$W_2 = X_{t-1} + 2^2 X_{t-2} + 3^2 X_{t-3} + \ldots + s^2 X_{t-s}$$

(d) The weights used in the construction of W_3 are the weights of W_1 raised to the third power, that is

$$W_3 = X_{t-1} + 2^3 X_{t-2} + 3^3 X_{t-3} + \ldots + s^3 X_{t-s}$$

(e) In general the weights of W_r are the weights used in constructing W_1 raised to the r th power

$$W_r = X_{t-1} + 2^r X_{t-2} + 3^r X_{t-3} + \ldots + s^r X_{t-s}$$

Formal Derivation of the W's

The procedure for the derivation of the W's is the following. We substitute the b's for the a's in the original function 13.1, and obtain

$$
\begin{aligned}
Y_t = a_0 X_t \quad &+ \quad (a_0 + a_1 + a_2 + \ldots + a_r) X_{t-1} \\
&+ \quad (a_0 + 2a_1 + 2^2 a_2 + \ldots + 2^r a_r) X_{t-2} \\
&+ \quad (a_0 + 3a_1 + 3^2 a_2 + \ldots + 3^r a_r) X_{t-3} \\
&\quad \cdots \cdots \cdots \cdots \\
&+ \quad (a_0 + s a_1 + s^2 a_2 + \ldots + s^r a_r) X_{t-s} + u_t
\end{aligned}
\tag{13.4}
$$

Rearranging we obtain

$$
\begin{aligned}
Y_t = a_0 (X_t + X_{t-1} &+ X_{t-2} + X_{t-3} + \ldots + X_{t-s}) \\
+ a_1 (X_{t-1} &+ 2X_{t-2} + 3X_{t-3} + \ldots + sX_{t-s}) \\
+ a_2 (X_{t-1} &+ 2^2 X_{t-2} + 3^2 X_{t-3} + \ldots + s^2 X_{t-s}) \\
\cdots &\cdots \cdots \cdots \\
+ a_r (X_{t-1} &+ 2^r X_{t-2} + 3^r X_{t-3} + \ldots + s^r X_{t-s}) + u_t
\end{aligned}
\tag{13.5}
$$

Clearly the expressions in brackets are the W's appearing in 13.3.

Step 4. We substitute the OLS estimates of the a's obtained from 13.3 into the "b-system" (13.2) and we find the estimates of the parameters of the lagged model, $\hat{b}_0, \hat{b}_1, \hat{b}_2, \ldots, \hat{b}_s$.

Example

1. Assume that the number of lags is 7 (i.e. $s = 1, 2, \ldots, 7$), and the degree of the polynomial is 3 (that is, $r = 3$). Thus our original model is

$$Y_t = b_0 X_t + b_1 X_{t-1} + b_2 X_{t-2} + \ldots + b_7 X_{t-7} + u_t$$

2. We express the b's in terms of the a's of the approximation polynomial, by assigning to z the values $z = 0, z = 1, \ldots, z = 7$. The "$b$-system" is

$$b_0 = a_0$$
$$b_1 = a_0 + a_1 + a_2 + a_3$$
$$b_2 = a_0 + 2a_1 + 2^2 a_2 + 2^3 a_3$$
$$b_3 = a_0 + 3a_1 + 3^2 a_2 + 3^3 a_3$$
$$b_4 = a_0 + 4a_1 + 4^2 a_2 + 4^3 a_3$$
$$b_5 = a_0 + 5a_1 + 5^2 a_2 + 5^3 a_3$$
$$b_6 = a_0 + 6a_1 + 6^2 a_2 + 6^3 a_3$$
$$b_7 = a_0 + 7a_1 + 7^2 a_2 + 7^3 a_3$$

3. The required number of W's is $4(= r + 1)$. They are

$$W_0 = X_t + X_{t-1} + X_{t-2} + \ldots + X_{t-7}$$
$$W_1 = X_{t-1} + 2X_{t-2} + 3X_{t-3} + \ldots + 7X_{t-7}$$
$$W_2 = X_{t-1} + 2^2 X_{t-2} + 3^2 X_{t-3} + \ldots + 7^2 X_{t-7}$$
$$W_3 = X_{t-1} + 2^3 X_{t-2} + 3^3 X_{t-3} + \ldots + 7^3 X_{t-7}$$

Thus the transformed model is

$$Y_t = a_0 W_0 + a_1 W_1 + a_2 W_2 + a_3 W_3 + u_t$$

Applying OLS we obtain the estimates $\hat{a}_0, \hat{a}_1, \hat{a}_2, \hat{a}_3$.

4. We substitue the OLS estimates, $\hat{a}$'s, in the "b-system", and we obtain the estimates of the b's of the original model, $\hat{b}_0, \hat{b}_1, \hat{b}_2, \ldots, \hat{b}_7$. With the application of the Almon scheme we managed to obtain four estimates $(\hat{a}_0, \hat{a}_1, \hat{a}_2, \hat{a}_3)$ from our sample, instead of the eight $(b_0, b_1, \ldots, b_7)$ which we would have to compute if we applied OLS to the original model directly.

In summary, the steps involved in the simplified Almon polynomial lag scheme are the following.

1. We choose an arbitrary degree for the approximation polynomial. Usually a low degree, say $r = 2$, or $r = 3$.

2. We assign the values $0, 1, 2, \ldots, s$ to the z's of the approximation polynomial and we find the system of b's in terms of the a's of this polynomial. We call this the 'b-system'. It is of the form (13.2).

3. The coefficients of the 'b-system' are used to construct $r + 1$ composite W variables. The weights in the W's are given in table 13.2.

4. We estimate the a's by applying OLS to the equation

$$Y_t = a_0 W_0 + a_1 W_1 + a_2 W_2 + a_3 W_3 + \ldots + a_r W_r + u_t$$

5. We use the OLS $\hat{a}$ to substitute into the 'b-system' and obtain the $\hat{b}$'s.

This simplified scheme has the following advantages over the general Almon scheme. (See J. Johnston, *Econometric Methods*, 2nd edition, p. 297.)

Firstly, it is computationally simpler.

Secondly, it yields a direct test of the degree of the approximation polynomial. In our example a third degree polynomial was specified and a_3 denotes the coefficient of the third degree term; and it is clear that a test of significance for a_3 is provided by the standard error of a_3 from OLS in step 4.

Thirdly, changing the degree of the polynomial involves adding extra W explanatory variables, leaving the previous variables unchanged.

The above simplified Almon scheme can easily be extended to many explanatory lagged variables, each having a different length of lag. For example assume that we have k variables with their lagged values

$$X_{1t} \quad X_{1(t-1)} \quad X_{1(t-2)} \ldots X_{1(t-s_1)}$$
$$X_{2t} \quad X_{2(t-1)} \quad X_{2(t-2)} \ldots X_{2(t-s_2)}$$

$$\phantom{X_{kt}}$$

$$X_{kt} \quad X_{k(t-1)} \quad X_{k(t-2)} \ldots X_{k(t-s_k)}$$

Clearly the lags $s_1, s_2 \ldots s_k$ need not be the same. To estimate such a model we must specify the degree of the polynomial r and the length of the lag period s for *each* explanatory variable and repeat the Almon scheme for all X's.

Tinsley has extended the model of lagged variables to allow for changes in the lag coefficients (b's) over time. (P. A. Tinsley, 'An Application of Variable Weight Distributed Lags', *J. Am. Statist. Assoc.*, vol. **62**, 1967, pp. 1277–89.)

It is assumed that the effect of X_{t-i} on Y_t depends not only on the length of the time period of the lag and on the value of X_{t-i}, but also on the value of some other variable, ψ, which causes the value of the lag coefficient b_i to change. Thus we may write

$$b_i = c_i + \gamma \psi_{t-i} \qquad (i = 0, 1, 2, \ldots, s)$$

Substituting in the lagged model

$$Y_t = b_0 X_t + b_1 X_{t-1} + \ldots + b_s X_{t-s} + u_t$$

we obtain

$$Y_t = c_0 X_t + c_1 X_{t-1} + \ldots + c_s X_{t-s} + \gamma_0 (W_t X_t) + \gamma_1 (W_{t-1} X_{t-1}) + \ldots + \\ + \gamma_s (W_{t-s} X_{t-s}) + u_t$$

This form includes lagged values of two explanatory variables, X and WX, and takes into account changes in the lag coefficients of the original model. For the estimation of this transformed model we need a twofold application of the Almon scheme.

13.2. ENDOGENOUS LAGGED VARIABLES

Up to now we have examined lagged models including lagged values of exogenous variables only. In this section we will discuss models with lagged values of endogenous variables among the set of regressors.

13.2.1. KOYCK'S GEOMETRIC LAG SCHEME

This is one of the most popular distributed lag models in applied research.[1]

---

[1] See L. M. Koyck, *Distributed Lags and Investment Analysis*, North-Holland, 1954.

Koyck's distributed lag model assumes that the weights (lag coefficients) are declining continuously following the pattern of a geometric progression.

The original model includes only exogenous lagged variables

$$Y_t = a_0 + b_0 X_t + b_1 X_{t-1} + b_2 X_{t-2} + \ldots + u_t$$

where

$$u \sim N(0, \sigma_u^2)$$
$$E(u_i u_j) = 0 \qquad (i \neq j)$$
$$E(u_i X_j) = 0 \qquad (j = 1, 2, \ldots, k)$$

Koyck's geometric lag-scheme implies that more recent values of X exert a greater influence on Y than remoter values of X. In particular the lag coefficients of this model decline in the form of a geometric progression

$$b_1 = \lambda b_0$$
$$b_2 = \lambda^2 b_0$$

and in general

$$b_i = \lambda^i b_0 \qquad 0 < \lambda < 1$$

Substituting in the original model we obtain

$$Y_t = a_0 + b_0 X_t + (\lambda b_0) X_{t-1} + (\lambda^2 b_0) X_{t-2} + \ldots + u_t$$

Lagging by one period

$$Y_{t-1} = a_0 + b_0 X_{t-1} + (\lambda b_0) X_{t-2} + (\lambda^2 b_0) X_{t-3} + \ldots + u_{t-1}$$

Multiplying through by λ and subtracting from the first we obtain

$$Y_t - \lambda Y_{t-1} = a_0(1 - \lambda) + b_0 X_t + (u_t - \lambda u_{t-1})$$

or

$$Y_t = a_0(1 - \lambda) + b_0 X_t + \lambda Y_{t-1} + v_t \tag{13.6}$$

where

$$v_t = u_t - \lambda u_{t-1}$$

A note on 'Koyck's transformation'.

Ignoring the constant intercept (for simplicity) we may write Koyck's model as follows:

The original model is

$$Y_t = b_0 X_t + b_1 X_{t-1} + b_2 X_{t-2} + \ldots + u_t$$

Given Koyck's assumption of the geometrically declining lag form

$$b_i = b_0 \lambda^i \qquad 0 < \lambda < 1$$

we may rewrite the lagged model in the form

$$Y_t = b_0 \sum_{i=0}^{\infty} \lambda^i X_{t-i} + u_t \tag{13.7}$$

which may be transformed to

$$Y_t = b_0 X_t + \lambda Y_{t-1} + v_t \tag{13.8}$$

In general the transformation of an equation of form (13.7) into an equation of form (13.8) is called *Koyck's transformation*.

A *modified Koyck transformation* is a lag scheme in which one or more of the initial lags are determined directly from the original function and the remaining lags are allowed to decline geometrically. For example if we want the first two lags to be determined freely from the model and the remaining to decline geometrically, our original model is of the form

$$Y_t = b_0 X_t + b_1 X_{t-1} + [b_2 X_{t-2} + (b_2 \lambda) X_{t-3} + (b_2 \lambda^2) X_{t-4} + \dots] + u_t$$

or

$$Y_t = b_0 X_t + b_1 X_{t-1} + b_2 \sum_{i=0}^{\infty} \lambda^i X_{t-i-2} + u_t$$

and the *modified Koyck transformation* is

$$Y_t = b_0 X_t + (b_1 - \lambda b_0) X_{t-1} + (b_2 - \lambda b_1) X_{t-2} + \lambda Y_{t-1} + [u_t - \lambda u_{t-1}]$$

The final version of Koyck's model includes the lagged value Y_{t-1} of the endogenous variable in the set of regressors. With Koyck's geometric lag structure we avoid the two basic defects of the distributed lag models, that is we achieve the maximum economy of degrees of freedom (since all the lagged X's have been meaningfully substituted for a single variable, Y_{t-1}), and we avoid multicollinearity to a certain extent, since Y_{t-1} will in general be less correlated with X_t than the successive values of the latter. However, the appearance of the lagged dependent variable among the explanatory variables has other undesirable consequences.

Firstly, in the new formulation the error term, $v_t = u_t - \lambda u_{t-1}$, is auto-correlated, despite the fact that the error term of the original model (u) is serially independent.

Proof: Let us examine the expected value of two successive values of the error term of Koyck's transformation.

$$\begin{aligned} E(v_t v_{t+1}) &= E(u_t - \lambda u_{t-1})(u_{t+1} - \lambda u_t) \\ &= E(u_t u_{t+1} - \lambda u_{t-1} u_{t+1} - \lambda u^2{}_t + \lambda^2 u_{t-1} u_t) \\ &= -\lambda E(u_t^2) = -\lambda \sigma_u^2 \neq 0 \end{aligned}$$

given

$$E(u_t u_{t+1}) = \lambda E(u_{t-1} u_{t+1}) = \lambda^2 E(u_{t-1} u_t) = 0$$

by the assumption of serially independent u's. Clearly $-\lambda\sigma_u^2 \neq 0$ since $\sigma_u^2 \neq 0$ and $\lambda \neq 0$ by the specification of the model. (If λ were zero, there would be no lag in the model.)

Secondly, the lagged variable Y_{t-1} is not independent of the error term v, because clearly

$$E(v_t Y_t) \neq 0$$

and so

$$E(v_t Y_{t+s}) \neq 0$$

for $s \geq 0$ and all t.

As a consequence of the violation of Assumption 6 of the linear regression model the OLS estimates will be biased in small samples.

Thirdly, autocorrelation of v_t, superimposed on values of Y_{t-1}, which are interdependent with the error term v, renders the OLS estimates not only biased, but also inconsistent in large samples. The OLS estimates are asymptotically biased, that is the bias in small samples, due to $E(Y_{t-1}, v_t) \neq 0$, does not vanish as $n \to \infty$, hence the estimates are inconsistent.

Proof: We will prove these results for the simple model

$$Y_t = b Y_{t-1} + v_t \tag{13.9}$$
$$v_t = \lambda v_{t-1} + \epsilon_t$$

where ϵ_t satisfies the usual stochastic assumptions.

(a) *The small sample bias in b*

Applying OLS to (13.9) we obtain

$$\hat{b} = \frac{\sum\limits_{t=2}^{n} Y_t Y_{t-1}}{\sum\limits_{t=2}^{n} Y_{t-1}^2}$$

Lagging (13.9) by one period and multiplying by λ we find

$$\lambda Y_{t-1} = \lambda b Y_{t-2} + \lambda v_{t-1} \tag{13.10}$$

Subtracting (13.10) from (13.9) we find

$$Y_t = (b + \lambda) Y_{t-1} - b\lambda Y_{t-2} + \epsilon_t \tag{13.11}$$

Multiplying through by Y_{t-1}, and summing over all sample observations we have

$$\sum Y_t Y_{t-1} = (b + \lambda) \sum Y_{t-1}^2 - b\lambda \sum Y_{t-1} Y_{t-2} + \sum \epsilon_t Y_{t-1} \tag{13.12}$$

Divide by $\sum Y_{t-1}^2$ and obtain

$$\frac{\sum\limits_{t=2}^{n} Y_t Y_{t-1}}{\sum\limits_{t=2}^{n} Y_{t-1}^2} = (b + \lambda) - b\lambda \frac{\sum Y_{t-1} Y_{t-2}}{\sum Y_{t-1}^2} + \frac{\sum \epsilon_t Y_{t-1}}{\sum Y_{t-1}^2} = \hat{b} \tag{13.13}$$

By rearranging we obtain

$$\hat{b} = b \left[1 - \lambda \frac{\Sigma Y_{t-1} Y_{t-2}}{\Sigma Y_{t-1}^2} \right] + \lambda + \frac{\Sigma \epsilon_t Y_{t-1}}{\Sigma Y_{t-1}^2}$$

Taking expected values we have

$$E(\hat{b}) = b \left[1 - \lambda \frac{E(\Sigma Y_{t-1} Y_{t-2})}{E(\Sigma Y_{t-1}^2)} \right] + \lambda \neq b$$

so that

$$(\text{bias}) = E(\hat{b}) - b \neq 0$$

(b) *The asymptotic bias in* $\hat{b}$

We established in (13.13) that

$$\hat{b} = (b + \lambda) - b\lambda \frac{\Sigma Y_{t-1} Y_{t-2}}{\Sigma Y_{t-1}^2} + \frac{\Sigma \epsilon_t Y_{t-1}}{\Sigma Y_{t-1}^2}$$

Taking probability limits

$$(\text{plim } \hat{b}) = (b + \lambda) - b\lambda (\text{plim } \hat{b})$$

(since, as $n \to \infty$, $\Sigma Y_{t-1} Y_{t-2} \simeq \Sigma Y_t Y_{t-1}$, and hence asymptotically $\dfrac{\Sigma Y_{t-1} Y_{t-2}}{\Sigma Y_{t-1}^2} = \hat{b}$).

Rearranging we find

$$(\text{plim } \hat{b}) = \frac{b + \lambda}{1 + b\lambda}$$

and

$$[\text{asymptotic bias}] = (\text{plim } \hat{b}) - b = \frac{\lambda(1 - b^2)}{1 + b\lambda} \neq 0 \qquad (13.14)$$

Fourthly, the combined violation of two assumptions of the OLS method impairs the power of the d statistic in detecting autocorrelation.

We established that the asymptotic bias is equal to

$$\frac{\lambda(1 - b^2)}{1 + b\lambda}$$

It is obvious that the asymptotic bias depends on λ (the autocorrelation coefficient). In the usual case of positive autocorrelation ($\lambda > 0$) the bias will be positive. In other words contemporaneous violation of Assumptions 5 and 6 leads to overestimation of the $\hat{b}$, and the bias does not vanish as n increases. Monte Carlo type studies[1] have provided evidence that the bias can be very large especially for low b's and large λ's. Thus in the Koyck type distributed lag models where lagged Y's appear in the set of explanatory variables detection of autocorrelation is crucial. Nerlove and Wallis found[2] that the classical Durbin–Watson

---

[1] See Z. Griliches, 'A note on the Serial Correlation Bias in Estimates of Distributed Lags', *Econometrica*, vol. 29, 1961, pp. 65–73.

[2] See M. Nerlove and K. Wallis, 'Use of the Durbin–Watson Statistic in Inappropriate Situations', *Econometrica*, vol. 34, 1966, pp. 235–8.

d statistic is biased towards 2 (its asymptotic value in the absence of auto-correlation) if Y_{t-1} appears as an explanatory variable in the right-hand side of the equation. This finding has alarmed econometricians unduly, because the bias of d (towards 2) is serious for models containing only Y_{t-1}. Malinvaud[1] has shown that the bias in d tends to decrease if apart from Y_{t-1} there are exo-genous X's in the model. Taylor and Wilson[2] have explored the power of d in detecting autocorrelation in various models which included various values of $\hat{\lambda}$ (i.e. $\hat{\rho}$), various values of R^2, and various autoregressive schemes, namely first order and second order schemes, stable and explosive. They adopted the 'amended' form of the Durbin—Watson test (see Chapter 10), namely they adopted the procedure of rejecting the null hypothesis (H_0: zero autocorrelation) if $d < d_u$ and accepting it if $d > d_u$. They found that the d test performs well (a) the larger the size of the sample, (b) the larger R^2, (c) the larger the absolute value of $\hat{\lambda}$ (or $\hat{\rho}$), (d) in stable second order autoregressive schemes. But d was found to perform badly in small samples, in models with low R^2, when $|\hat{\lambda}|$ (or $|\hat{\rho}|$) was small, and in cases of unstable explosive first order and second order schemes.

In view of the defects of the d statistic, Durbin[3] has suggested the following test for models involving lagged Y's and for large samples ($n > 30$). *Firstly*, apply OLS to the original model and estimate the residuals, e's. *Secondly*, regress e_t on e_{t-1} and all the other variables of the original model and conduct the classical tests of significance for the coefficient of e_{t-1}. For example assume the model

$$Y_t = b_0 + b_1 Y_{t-1} + b_2 X_t + b_3 X_{t-1} + \ldots + u_t$$

Applying OLS we obtain the residuals e_t's. We next apply OLS to the function

$$e_t = c_0 + c_1 e_{t-1} + c_2 Y_{t-1} + c_3 X_t + c_4 X_{t-1} + \ldots$$

If the standard error of $\hat{c}_1$ is small ($s_{(\hat{c})} < \hat{c}/2$) we accept that there is auto-correlation in the function. Of course this is a large sample test and nothing is as yet known about its power in small samples.

In summary, if the model is

$$Y_t = b_0 + b_1 Y_{t-1} + b_2 X_t + \ldots + v_t$$

where $v_t = u_t - \lambda u_{t-1}$ $0 < \lambda < 1$
(with $u \sim N(0, \sigma_u^2)$, $E(u_i u_j) = 0$)

we have violation of two Assumptions (5 and 6) of the linear regression model simultaneously and under these circumstances OLS is not an appropriate estimation technique. A method for estimating the parameters of Koyck's model has been suggested by Zellner and Geisel (see section 13.3 below).

[1] See Malinvaud, *Statistical Methods of Econometrics*, 1966, pp. 460–5.
[2] See Taylor and Wilson, 'Three-Pass Least Squares: A Method for Estimating Models with a Lagged Dependent Variable', *Rev. Econ. Statist.*, vol. 46, 1964, pp. 329–46.
[3] See J. Durbin, 'Testing for Serial Correlation in Least-Squares Regression when Some of the Regressors are Lagged Dependent Variables', *Econometrica*, vol. 38, 1970, pp. 410–21.

A similar form to Koyck's transformation ($Y_t = f(X_t, Y_{t-1})$) may be established by applying other behavioural assumptions, different from Koyck's. Two such models are discussed below. They are Nerlove's *'partial adjustment'* model and Cagan's *'adaptive expectations'* model. The use of these models has been rapidly expanded in the last few years. It should be noted, however, that the latter model (of 'adaptive expectations') creates the same estimation difficulties as Koyck's model. It is only the 'partial adjustment' model that does not lead to a rigid autocorrelation scheme such as the one implied in Koyck's and in the 'adaptive expectations' model, and hence its estimation procedure is more straightforward (see section 13.3 below).

13.2.2. NERLOVE'S PARTIAL ADJUSTMENT MODEL[1]

Nerlove (and others) in an attempt to avoid the estimation difficulties which arise with Koyck's assumption, postulated the following model, which is based on a different behavioural hypothesis. There is a *desired* level of Y in period t, say Y_t^*, which depends on the value of X in period t, X_t, that is

$$Y_t^* = b_0 + b_1 X_t + u_t \tag{13.15}$$

For example, recent formulations of the theory of investment in fixed capital are based on what is known as the *'stock adjustment principle'*, which postulates the following behaviour of the firm. It is assumed that there is a *desired* level of capital stock, Y_t^*, which the entrepreneur thinks is right for a smooth production process, without excess capacity or overworking of the existing machinery. The desired level of capital stock is determined by the level of output X_t.

The model

$$Y_t^* = b_0 + b_1 X_t + u_t$$

cannot be measured because the desired quantity Y_t^* is not observable. To replace it we must postulate some behavioural principle. i.e. some specific rule for decision-making by the investing firm. The 'stock adjustment principle' implies the following behavioural pattern. Because of the gestation period involved in all investment projects and the administrative and financial problems associated with investment, the actually *realised change* in the capital stock in any one period is only a fraction of the *desired change*. In other words the adjustment of capital to the desired level is only gradual due to technological, financial or administrative managerial constraints. This gradual adjustment process may be expressed in the so-called 'adjustment equation'

$$Y_t - Y_{t-1} = \delta(Y_t^* - Y_{t-1}) + v_t \tag{13.16}$$
$$0 < \delta \leqslant 1$$

[1] See M. Nerlove, 'Estimates of the Elasticities of Supply of Selected Agricultural Commodities', *Journal of Farm Economics*, vol. 38, 1956. Also, M. Nerlove, *Distributed Lags and Demand Analysis*, USDA, Agriculture Handbook No. 141, Washington, 1958.

where $Y_t - Y_{t-1}$ = actual change in capital stock (i.e. realised investment in period t)

$Y_t^* - Y_{t-1}$ = desired change in capital stock (desired investment)

δ = adjustment coefficient

This behavioural rule reads: the achieved (realised) by the firm in any one period change $(Y_t - Y_{t-1})$ in the capital stock is only a fraction of the desired change $(Y_t^* - Y_{t-1})$.

Substituting $Y_t^* = b_0 + b_1 X_t + u_t$ into the adjustment equation (13.16) we obtain

$$Y_t - Y_{t-1} = \delta \left[(b_0 + b_1 X_t + u_t) - Y_{t-1} \right] + v_t$$

Rearranging we find

$$Y_t = (\delta b_0) + (\delta b_1) X_t + (1 - \delta) Y_{t-1} + (v_t + \delta u_t) \qquad (13.17)$$

which reads as follows: the capital stock in any one period t depends partly on the level of output in that period and partly on the existing capital stock at the beginning of the period.

Note that this is a total capital function (gross investment). A net investment function may be obtained by noting that $Y_t - Y_{t-1} = \Delta K = I_t$, so that

$$I_t = (\delta b_0) + (\delta b_1) X_t - \delta Y_{t-1} + (v_t + \delta u_t)$$

The similarity of this model with Koyck's formulation is obvious. Both models include the same variables (Y_t, X_t, Y_{t-1}), but the error term of the 'partial adjustment model' does not involve any autoregressive scheme in the u's, as does Koyck's. In the present model the disturbance term has no direct connection *with its own* previous values, so that we may assume that the new error term $(v_t + \delta u_t)$ is not autocorrelated, and let this assumption be tested by the d statistic or other tests that have been devised for measuring the degree of autocorrelation in lagged models. If such tests show that the term $(v_t + \delta u_t)$ is in fact serially correlated, special estimation methods have to be applied, since the OLS collapses completely. These methods, however, are less complicated than those developed for the Koyck formulation. Furthermore, in the 'partial adjustment model' the coefficient $(1 - \delta)$ of the lagged Y_{t-1} has a clear economic meaning, since it involves δ, the adjustment coefficient. Information about the value of δ (i.e. the length of the adjustment period) may be obtained from firms, and hence we may apply a mixed estimation procedure (see Chapter 17). In other words we may substitute δ^* (extraneously estimated) and proceed with the model

$$[Y_t - (1 - \delta^*) Y_{t-1}] = (\delta b_0) + (\delta b_1) X_t + (v_t + \delta u_t)$$

where δ^* = value of the adjustment coefficient obtained from firms (or other sources).

The 'stock adjustment principle' has become the most popular behavioural hypothesis for the explanation of the behaviour of economic units. Houthakker and Taylor[1] have extended this principle to the behaviour of consumers regarding the demand for non-durables. They argue that the quantity demanded in any one period depends, among others, on the quantity demanded in previous periods due to a habit formation process which is characteristic of human behaviour. They termed this behavioural hypothesis 'the habit-formation principle'. Due to habit persistence the demand for non-durables (e.g. tobacco) may be written as

$$Q_t = c_0 + c_1 X_t + c_2 Q_{t-1} + c_3 P_t + v_t$$

where Q_t = demand for tobacco
X_t = income
P_t = price for tobacco
Q_{t-1} = lagged demand, i.e. quantity of tobacco consumed in period $t-1$.

The same form of demand function would hold for durables. In the Houthakker–Taylor model the coefficient of Q_{t-1} would be positive for non-durables, while it would be negative, on *a priori* grounds, for durables.

The reason for the popularity of this particular formulation of lagged models is that it is very flexible. It allows the dynamisation of economic relationships and allows the estimation of long-run and short-run elasticities (and other parameters of economic theory). For example assume that the long-run demand function is

$$D_{tL} = b_0 P_t^{b_1} Y_t^{b_2} u_t$$

However, the available data show the short-run quantities demanded. To estimate the long-run elasticities from short-run data we may postulate the following principle. The ration (D_{tL}/D_{tS}) will be closer to unity than will the ratio $(D_{tL}/D_{t-1, s})$ because there will tend to be greater coincidence between short- and long-run in year t than between short- and long-run demand in successive years.[2] This implies that

$$\frac{D_{tL}}{D_{tS}} = \left(\frac{D_{tL}}{D_{t-1, s}^\lambda}\right)^\lambda   \qquad 0 < \lambda < 1$$

By substitution into the demand function, we obtain

$$D_{tL} = \left(\frac{D_{tS}}{D_{t-1, s}^\lambda}\right)^{1/(1-\lambda)} = b_0 P_t^{b_1} Y_t^{b_2} u_t$$

so that

$$D_{tS} = b_0^{(1-\lambda)} P_t^{b_1 (1-\lambda)} Y_t^{b_2 (1-\lambda)} D_{t-1, s}^\lambda u_t$$

---

[1] H. S. Houthakker and L. D. Taylor, *Consumer Demand in the United States 1929–1970, Analysis and Projections*, Harvard University Press, Massachusetts, 1966.

[2] See M. Nerlove and William Addison, 'Statistical Estimation of Long-run Elasticities of Supply and Demand', *Journal of Farm Economics*, XL4, 1958, pp. 861–80. Also, Ira Horowitz, 'An Econometric Analysis of Supply and Demand in the Synthetic Rubber Industry', *International Economic Review*, vol. 4, 1963, pp. 325–45.

or

$$D_{ts} = b_0^* P_t^{b_1^*} Y_t^{b_2^*} D_{t-1}^{b_3^*}, s u_t$$

This is the short-run demand curve, from which we can estimate both the short and long-run elasticities. Thus from

$$b_1(1 - \lambda) = b_1^*$$
$$b_2(1 - \lambda) = b_2^*$$
$$\lambda = b_3^*$$

we obtain

$$b_1 = \frac{b_1^*}{1 - b_3^*}$$

$$b_2 = \frac{b_2^*}{1 - b_3^*}$$

where the b^*'s are the short-run, and the b's are the long-run elasticities of demand.

13.2.3. CAGAN'S ADAPTIVE EXPECTATION MODEL

This model is based on the following behavioural hypothesis.[1] The value of Y in any one period t depends not on the actual value of X_t but on the 'expected' or 'permanent' level of X at time t, say X_t^*.

This model has become popular because it can deal somehow with 'expectations' (about future factors) whose importance in economic behaviour is being increasingly recognised. Some examples will illustrate the nature of the 'adaptive expectations' model.

Suppose that the quantity demanded (as in a period of rapid inflation) is determined by the expected price P_t^* rather than the actual price

$$Q_t = b_0 + b_1 P_t^* + u_t$$

Similarly, according to Friedman's 'permanent income hypothesis', the level of consumption C_t is determined by the 'expected' income or by the 'permanent' income Y_t^*

$$C_t = c_1 Y_t^* + u_t$$

Now the 'expected' variables are *ex ante* variables which are not observable. To measure such expectational models we must find some way to substitute 'expected' variables. This is done by postulating a specific rule for the formulation of expectations.

Let us first write the 'adaptive expectation' model in the general form

$$Y_t = b_0 + b_1 X_t^* + u_t \tag{13.18}$$

[1] See P. Cagan, 'The Monetary Dynamics of Hyper Inflations', in Friedman, ed., *Studies in the Quantity Theory of Money*, Chicago University Press, 1956.

Since X_t^* is not directly observable, we postulate that expectations concerning its value are formed on the 'adaptive' rule

$$X_t^* - X_{t-1}^* = \gamma(X_t - X_{t-1}^*) \qquad 0 < \gamma \leqslant 1 \tag{13.19}$$

where γ = expectation coefficient, implying that the 'elasticity of expectations' is less than one.

This rule implies that *expectations are adaptive*. That is, current expectations are formed by modifying (adapting) previous expectations in the light of the actual achievements, the current experience. Expectations are reformulated in each period; $X_t^* - X_{t-1}^*$ is the change in current expectations. The change is only a fraction of the difference between the currently achieved (observed, realised) value of the variable X_t and the previous expectations X_{t-1}^*. We may put this in another way. Expectations are seldom fully realised; there is usually a gap between actual and expected levels of output, between actual and expected prices, between actual and expected incomes. Thus the current expectations, X_t^*, are partly determined by past expectations, X_{t-1}^*, and partly by the fact that economic agents want to close the above gap, by adapting their expectations in the light of current experience, that is

$$X_t^* = X_{t-1}^* + \gamma(X_t - X_{t-1}^*)$$

where $0 < \gamma \leqslant 1$, since adaptation can only be gradual. This, of course, reduces to the previous 'rule'

$$X_t^* - X_{t-1}^* = \gamma(X_t - X_{t-1}^*)$$

We next proceed with the following transformations, leading to the substitution of the unobservable variable X_t^* in the original model

$$Y_t = b_0 + b_1 X_t^* + u_t$$

Solving for X_t^* we obtain

$$X_t^* = -\frac{b_0}{b_1} + \frac{1}{b_1} Y_t - \frac{1}{b_1} u_t \tag{13.20}$$

Lagging one period

$$X_{t-1}^* = -\frac{b_0}{b_1} + \frac{1}{b_1} Y_{t-1} - \frac{1}{b_1} u_{t-1}$$

Substituting X_t^* and X_{t-1}^* in the "adaptive expectations" equation (13.19) we obtain

$$\left(-\frac{b_0}{b_1} + \frac{1}{b_1} Y_t - \frac{1}{b_1} u_t \right) - \left(-\frac{b_0}{b_1} + \frac{1}{b_1} Y_{t-1} - \frac{1}{b_1} u_{t-1} \right) =$$

$$= \gamma \left[X_t - \left(-\frac{b_0}{b_1} + \frac{1}{b_1} Y_{t-1} - \frac{1}{b_1} u_{t-1} \right) \right]$$

Collecting terms we find

$$Y_t = (\gamma b_0) + (\gamma b_1)X_t + (1 - \gamma)Y_{t-1} + [u_t - (1 - \gamma)u_{t-1}] \qquad (13.21)$$

Thus we arrive again at an expression which contains the same variables as Koyck's model and the 'partial adjustment' model. The similarity in all three models is due to the fact that all three assume the same lag-scheme, that is a declining geometric pattern for the lag-coefficients.

The 'expectational' model is intuitively appealing since it can deal with expectation formation (although in a rigid pattern). However, its error term suffers from the same defect as the error term of Koyck's model: it is auto-correlated in the u's of the original model. Hence we have the same estimation difficulties as in Koyck's model.

A variant of the 'adaptive expectations' model is often used in practice, including X_{t-1} instead of X_t. This replacement is done because when expectations are formed in period t, the current level of X, X_t, is usually unknown, so we may replace it by X_{t-1}, the most recent available information on X. This replacement implies the behavioural (expectation formation) rule

$$(X_t^* - X_{t-1}^*) = \gamma(X_{t-1} - X_{t-1}^*)$$

that is expectations in t are modified in the light of the most recent experience, reflected in X_{t-1}. Thus the 'expectations' model in fact becomes

$$Y_t = f(X_{t-1}, Y_{t-1})$$

13.2.4. A COMPOUND GEOMETRIC LAG MODEL

This is formed by a combination of the two previous models, the 'adaptive expectations' and the 'partial adjustment' models.

The combination of the underlying two behavioural rules seems intuitively attractive and may be considered *a priori* plausible when seen in the following lines. Note first, that the two models are versions of the general linear regression model

$$Y_t = b_0 + b_1 X_t + u_t$$

(a) In the 'partial adjustment' model Y_t is replaced by its 'desired' level Y_t^*

$$Y_t^* = a_0 + a_1 X_t + u_t^*$$

(b) In the 'adaptive expectations' model X_t is replaced by its 'expected' value X_t^*

$$Y_t = c_0 + c_1 X_t^* + u_t^*$$

In both versions considerations about future levels of X and Y are involved. Thus combining 'desires' and 'expectations' we may obtain

$$Y_t^* = b_0^* + b_1^* X_t^* \qquad (13.22)$$

which implies the behavioural rule: the 'desired' level of Y depends on the 'expected' level of X. We now postulate the two behavioural rules

$$Y_t - Y_{t-1} = \delta(Y_t^* - Y_{t-1}) + u_t \qquad 0 < \delta \leqslant 1 \qquad (13.23)$$

$$X_t^* - X_{t-1}^* = \gamma(X_t - X_{t-1}^*) \qquad 0 < \gamma \leqslant 1 \qquad (13.24)$$

and we proceed as follows.

Firstly, we solve (13.23) for Y_t^*

$$\delta Y_t^* = Y_t - Y_{t-1} + \delta Y_{t-1} - u_t$$

or

$$Y_t^* = \left(\frac{1}{\delta}\right) Y_t + \left(\frac{\delta - 1}{\delta}\right) Y_{t-1} - \left(\frac{1}{\delta}\right) u_t \qquad (13.25)$$

Secondly, we substitute Y_t^*, as given in (13.25), in (13.22)

$$\frac{1}{\delta} Y_t + \frac{\delta - 1}{\delta} Y_{t-1} - \frac{1}{\delta} u_t = b_0^* + b_1^* X_t^*$$

Solving for X_t^* we find

$$X_t^* = \frac{1}{b_1^* \delta} Y_t + \frac{\delta - 1}{b_1^* \delta} Y_{t-1} - \frac{1}{b_1^* \delta} u_t - \frac{b_0^*}{b_1^*} \qquad (13.26)$$

Lagging by one period

$$X_{t-1}^* = -\frac{b_0^*}{b_1^*} + \frac{1}{b_1^* \delta} Y_{t-1} + \frac{\delta - 1}{b_1^* \delta} Y_{t-2} - \frac{1}{b_1^* \delta} u_{t-1} \qquad (13.27)$$

Thirdly, we substitute (13.26) and (13.27) into (13.24) and obtain

$$Y_t = (b_0^* \gamma \delta) + (b_1^* \gamma \delta) X_t + [(1-\gamma) + (1-\delta)] Y_{t-1} - [(1-\gamma)(1-\delta)] Y_{t-2} + \\ + [u_t - (1-\gamma) u_{t-1}]$$

Compared with the 'partial adjustment' and the 'adaptive expectation' models, this formulation contains the additional variable Y_{t-2}, but the γ and δ parameters appear symmetrically so that it is impossible to obtain separate estimates of each one of them. However, we may obtain estimates for $(\gamma + \delta)$, $(\gamma\delta)$ and hence for b_0^* and b_1^*. (See J. Johnston, *Econometric Methods,* 2nd edition, McGraw-Hill 1972, p. 303.)

13.2.5. THE PASCAL LAG-SCHEME

Solow[1] suggested the following lag scheme. The form of lag pattern is specified to be of the 'inverted V' type. The values of the weights are not arbitrarily specified, but are defined on the basis of the so-called *Pascal lag distribution.*

[1] R. M. Solow, 'On a Family of Lag Distributions', *Econometrica*, vol. **28**, 1960, pp. 393–406.

We rewrite the lagged function

$$Y_t = a + b_0 X_t + b_1 X_{t-1} + \ldots + b_s X_{t-s} + u_t$$

in the form

$$Y_t = a + b[w_0 X_t + w_1 X_{t-1} + w_2 X_{t-2} + \ldots + w_s X_{t-s}] + u_t \qquad (13.28)$$

where $u \sim N(0, \sigma_u^2)$. The weights $w_0, w_1 \ldots w_s$ are defined on the basis of the Pascal lag model:[1]

$$w_i = \binom{i+r-1}{i} (1-\lambda)^r \lambda^i = {}_{i+r-1}C_i(1-\lambda)^r \lambda^i = \frac{(i+r-1)!}{i!(r-1)!}(1-\lambda)^r \lambda^i$$

where i = the period of the lag (i = 0, 1, 2, . . ., s)
  r = some positive integer arbitrarily chosen *a priori*[2]
  λ = a parameter which will be estimated from the regression model.

The regression equation (13.28) then becomes

$$Y_t = a + b(1-\lambda)^r \left[X_t + r\lambda X_{t-1} + \frac{r(r+1)}{2!} \lambda^2 X_{t-2} + \ldots \right] + u_t \qquad (13.29)$$

Note that when r = 1 we get

$$w_i = (1-\lambda)\lambda^i$$

that is the Pascal distribution reduces to a geometric lag distribution when r = 1.

For values $r > 1$ we get 'inverted-V' lag distributions. Figure 13.2 shows the distribution of weights for λ = 0·6 and for different values of r.

The estimation of a Pascal lag model is much more complicated than the arbitrary-weights method or the geometric lag models.

For example assume (arbitrarily) that r = 2.

The Pascal lag model is

$$Y_t = a + b(1-\lambda)^2 [X_t + 2\lambda X_{t-1} + 3^2 \lambda X_{t-2} + 4^3 \lambda X_{t-3} + \ldots] + u_t \qquad (13.30)$$

By lagging (13.30) by one period and multiplying through by -2λ we obtain

$$-2\lambda Y_{t-1} = -2a\lambda + b(1-\lambda)^2 [-2\lambda X_{t-1} - 4^2 \lambda X_{t-2} - 6^2 \lambda X_{t-3} - \ldots] - 2\lambda u_{t-1} \qquad (13.31)$$

---

[1] This model is based on the application of the combinatorial formula

$$_nC_r = \frac{n!}{r!(n-r)!}$$

which gives the number of different combinations of r objects drawn from n objects. Sometimes instead of the symbol $_nC_r$ we use the alternative notation $\binom{n}{r}$. See J. Parry Lewis, *An Introduction to Mathematics for Students of Economics*, Macmillan London 1966, p. 43.

[2] The value of r may also be estimated by maximum likelihood procedures. See J. Kmenta, *Elements of Econometrics*, Macmillan, New York 1971, pp. 489–91.

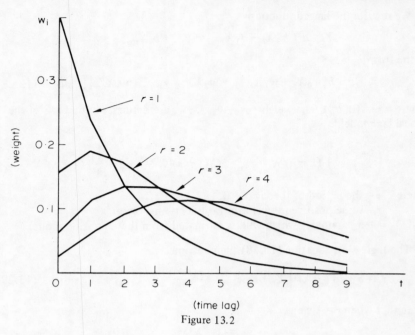

Figure 13.2

By lagging (13.30) by two periods and multiplying through by λ^2 we obtain

$$\lambda^2 Y_{t-2} = a^2\lambda + b(1-\lambda)^2 [\lambda^2 X_{t-2} + 2^3\lambda X_{t-3} + 3^4\lambda X_{t-4} + \dots] + \lambda^2 u_{t-2}$$

(13.32)

Now adding (13.30), (13.31) and (13.32) we find

$$Y_t = a(1-\lambda)^2 + b(1-\lambda)^2 X_t + 2\lambda Y_{t-1} - \lambda^2 Y_{t-2} + [u_t - 2\lambda u_{t-1} + \lambda^2 u_{t-2}]$$

(13.33)

This equation involves lagged values of Y; furthermore the new error term is autocorrelated. The estimation procedures of models involving lagged Y's and autocorrelated errors are explained in section 13.3 below.

It should be clear that the problem of estimating the parameters of a Pascal lag model becomes increasingly complex for increasing values of r. Solow has worked out some formulations which might be statistically estimated, but in practice this method has not yielded successful results.

13.2.6. JORGENSON'S 'RATIONAL DISTRIBUTED LAG MODEL'

(D. Jorgenson, 'Rational Distributed Lag Functions', *Econometrica*, vol. **34**, 1966, pp. 135–49.)

Equation (13.33) of the Pascal lag model (for $r = 2$) can be extended to any non-negative integer value of r as follows:

$$Y_t + \binom{r}{1}(-\lambda)^1 Y_{t-1} + \binom{r}{2}(-\lambda)^2 Y_{t-2} + \ldots + \binom{r}{r}(-\lambda)^r Y_{t-r} =$$

$$= a(1-\lambda)^r + b(1-\lambda)^r X_t + \left[u_t + \binom{r}{1}(-\lambda)^{-1} u_{t-1} + \ldots + \binom{r}{r}(-\lambda)^r u_{t-r} \right]$$

$$(13.34)$$

Note that in (13.34) the coefficients of the current and lagged Y's (and u's) are all constrained to be equal to specific functions of λ, i.e.

the coefficient of Y_{t-1} is $\binom{r}{1}(-\lambda)^1 = {}_rC_1 (-\lambda)^1$

the coefficient of Y_{t-2} is $\binom{r}{2}(-\lambda)^2 = {}_rC_2 (-\lambda)^2$

$$. \qquad . \qquad . \qquad . \qquad . \qquad . \qquad .$$

$$. \qquad . \qquad . \qquad . \qquad . \qquad . \qquad .$$

the coefficient of Y_{t-r} is $\binom{r}{r}(-\lambda)^r = {}_rC_r (-\lambda)^r$

If we generalise the form of (13.34) by removing these constraints, we obtain the so-called *rational distributed lag model* introduced by Jorgenson

$$Y_t + \delta_1 Y_{t-1} + \delta_2 Y_{t-2} + \ldots + \delta_r Y_{t-r} = a_0 + b_0 X_t + [u_t + \delta_1 u_{t-1} + \ldots]$$

$$(13.35)$$

This is a general model involving lagged values of Y, and methods for its estimation are discussed in section 13.3 below.

13.3. METHODS OF ESTIMATION OF THE b's OF MODELS INVOLVING LAGGED VALUES OF ENDOGENOUS VARIABLES (Y_{t-i})

If the lagged model includes only exogenous lagged variables no special estimation problems arise. One may apply *either* OLS directly to the original model, *or* assign arbitrary weights to the lagged variables, thus reducing the coefficients to be estimated directly from the model, *or* adopt the more sophisticated technique of an Almon lag scheme, from which all the lagged coefficients b's are estimated indirectly.

However, if the model involves lagged values of the dependent variable(s) estimation difficulties do arise. One obvious difficulty is that Y_{t-i} is not independent from v_t; Assumption 6 of the linear regression model is violated and OLS will yield biased estimates. Whether or not additional defects in the parameters occur depends on whether v_t is autocorrelated or not. We will examine estimation methods for the simple model

$$Y_t = b_0 + b_1 Y_{t-1} + b_2 X_t + v_t$$

and for the following cases:

Case 1. The v's are not autocorrelated

$$v \sim N(0, \sigma_v^2)$$
$$E(v_i v_j) = 0$$

Case 2. The v's are autocorrelated in a specific form of autoregressive scheme

$$v_t = u_t - \rho u_{t-1}$$

This form of autoregressive scheme appears in Koyck's model, in Cagan's 'adaptive expectations' model, in Solow's and in Jorgenson's models.

Case 3. The v's are autocorrelated in the general form

$$v_t = \rho v_{t-1} + \epsilon_t$$

where $\epsilon \sim N(0, \sigma_\epsilon^2)$ and $E(\epsilon_i \epsilon_j) = 0$.

13.3.1. CASE 1. THE v's ARE NOT AUTOCORRELATED

The model is $Y_t = b_0 + b_1 Y_{t-1} + b_2 X_t + v_t$

$$v \sim N(0, \sigma_v^2)$$
$$E(v_i v_j) = 0$$

In this model Y_{t-1} and v_t are independent, $E(v_t Y_{t-1}) = 0$, but Y_{t-1} is dependent on the past values of v, that is

$$E(v_{t-s} Y_{t-1}) \neq 0 \qquad \text{for } s > 0.$$

Method (i). OLS

Application of OLS to this model will yield biased estimates for small samples. However, the OLS estimates will be consistent and asymptotically efficient for large samples. (See J. Johnston, *Econometric Methods,* 2nd edn, pp. 305–307.) Various 'corrective' suggestions have been put forward for the elimination of the bias, but they have not worked well in practice. (See J. B. Copas, 'Monte Carlo Results for Estimation in a Stable Markov Time Series', *J. Royal Statist. Soc., Series A,* vol. **129**, 1966, pp. 110–16.)

Method (ii). Instrumental variables

This method has been discussed in Chapter 12 and will be examined again in detail in Chapter 16.

We want to find an appropriate instrumental variable in order to replace Y_{t-1}, which causes the trouble in the lagged model. For this:

1. We regress Y_t on lagged values oɪ X only and obtain

$$\hat{Y}_t = \hat{a}_0 + \hat{a}_1 X_{t-1} + \hat{a}_2 X_{t-2} + \ldots$$

The number of lags is decided on the basis of the improvement in the fit as additional lagged values of X are introduced. If X is highly autocorrelated a good fit will be achieved with two or three lagged X's.

2. We lag $\hat{Y}_t$ by one period to obtain $\hat{Y}_{t-1}$, which we then use as an instrumental variable to replace Y_{t-1} in the original model, and apply OLS to the model

$$Y_t = b_0 + b_1 \hat{Y}_{t-1} + b_2 X_t + v_t^*$$ (13.37)

The estimates from the instrumental variables method will still be biased for small samples, but will be asymptotically consistent and efficient (for large samples).

13.3.2. CASE 2. THE v TERM IS AUTOCORRELATED WITH THE SCHEME $v_t = u_t - \rho u_{t-1}$

The transformed distributed lag model is

$$Y_t = b_0 + b_1 Y_{t-1} + b_2 X_t + v_t$$
$$v_t = u_t - \rho u_{t-1}$$

where

$$u \sim N(0, \sigma_u^2)$$
$$E(u_i u_j) = 0$$

This form of autocorrelation appears when the model is derived from Koyck's geometric lag model, from the 'adaptive expectations' model, from Solow's model and from Jorgenson's model. u is the error term of the original model

$$Y_t = f(X_t, X_{t-1}, X_{t-2}, \ldots, X_{t-s}, u_t).$$

In the transformed distributed lag model we have violation of two assumptions of OLS: $E(Y_{t-1}, v_t) \neq 0$, and v_t is aurocorrelated. As a consequence the application of OLS breaks down completely, since its estimates will be biased (in small samples), and inconsistent, since in large samples the bias will not tend to disappear. (For a proof of these results see page 307.) Thus other methods of estimation must be applied.

If ρ is known or can be assigned a plausible value on *a priori* considerations, then we may apply generalised least squares (GLS), which in this particular case reduces to the application of OLS to the transformed original data as follows

$$(Y_t - \rho Y_{t-1}) = b_0 + b_2 X_t + v_t$$

since in Koyck's model and the 'adaptive expectation' model ρ is the coefficient of the lagged Y_{t-1}.

However, if ρ is unknown Zellner and Geisel[1] have suggested the following

[1] A. Zellner and M. S. Geisel, 'Analysis of Distributed Lag Models with Applications to Consumption Function Estimation', Paper presented to European Meeting of the Econometric Society, 1968.

'search' procedure. They have shown that the model can be reduced to the following form

$$Y_t = a_0 \rho^t + b_0(1 + \rho + \rho^2 + \ldots + \rho^{t-1}) + b_2(X_t + \rho X_{t-1} + \rho^2 X_{t-2} + \ldots + \\ + \rho^{t-1} X_1) + u_t \qquad (13.38)$$

Derivation:
The model is

$$Y_t = b_0 + \rho Y_{t-1} + b_2 X_t + v_t$$

We substitute

$$v_t = u_t - \rho u_{t-1}$$
$$Y_t = b_0 + \rho Y_{t-1} + b_2 X_t + u_t - \rho u_{t-1}$$

Set

$$a_t = Y_t - u_t$$

and

$$a_{t-1} = Y_{t-1} - u_{t-1}$$

Therefore

$$a_t - \rho a_{t-1} = Y_t - \rho Y_{t-1} - (u_t - \rho u_{t-1}) = b_0 + b_2 X_t$$

or

$$a_t = \rho a_{t-1} + b_0 + b_2 X_t$$

By continuous substitution of a in the right-hand side we obtain

$$a_t = a_0 \rho^t + b_0(1 + \rho + \rho^2 + \ldots + \rho^{t-1}) + b_2(X_t + \rho X_{t-1} + \rho^2 X_{t-2} + \ldots + \rho^{t-1} X_1)$$

In this expression we may substitute $a_t = Y_t - u_t$ so that we may write

$$Y_t = a_0 \rho^t + b_0(1 + \rho + \rho^2 + \ldots + \rho^{t-1}) + b_2(X_t + \rho X_{t-1} + \rho^2 X_{t-2} + \ldots + \rho^{t-1} X_1) + u_t$$

Thus we have a new model with unknowns a_0, b_0, b_2 and ρ.

Zellner and Geisel have suggested the application of OLS to this model *with various values of ρ ($0 < \rho < 1$)*. Among those OLS models they say that one should choose the model whose estimates of b's yield the minimum sum of squares.

13.3.3. CASE 3. THE v's OF THE DISTRIBUTED LAG MODEL ARE AUTOCORRELATED WITH A FIRST ORDER AUTOREGRESSIVE SCHEME $v_t = \rho v_{t-1} + \epsilon_t$

The complete distributed lag model is

$$Y_t = b_0 + b_1 Y_{t-1} + b_2 X_t + v_t \qquad (13.39)$$
$$v_t = \rho v_{t-1} + \epsilon_t$$

where ϵ_t satisfies all the usual stochastic assumptions

$$\epsilon \sim N(0, \sigma_\epsilon^2)$$
$$E(\epsilon_i \epsilon_j) = 0 \qquad (i \neq j)$$

This is a general model, which may be derived from different basic theoretical assumptions concerning the behaviour of the economic agents to which the model refers. It need not necessarily be a Koyck transformation, or a 'partial adjustment' model or an 'adaptive expectation' model. It is a general formulation which states that the current value of Y is partly determined by its own value in the previous period and partly by the exogenous variable X_t. In this model the random variable v_t is serially correlated with a first order autoregressive scheme. Furthermore the lagged explanatory variable Y_{t-1} is related to the error term v and hence OLS yields both biased and inconsistent estimates.

Two methods have been proposed for the estimation of the general model.

Method (i). The instrumental variables method

This is identical to the one suggested for Case 1, of non-autocorrelated v's. That is we replace Y_{t-1} by $\hat{Y}_{t-1}$, obtained as follows:

(a) Regress Y_t on lagged X's

$$\hat{Y}_t = \hat{a}_0 + \hat{a}_1 X_{t-1} + \hat{a}_2 X_{t-2} + \dots$$

(b) Lag $\hat{Y}_t$ by one period to obtain $\hat{Y}_{t-1}$, which is then included in the original model as a replacement of $\hat{Y}_{t-1}$:

$$Y_t = b_0 + b_1 \hat{Y}_{t-1} + b_2 X_t + v_t \qquad (13.40)$$

The application of OLS on this instrumental-variable transformation yields biased estimates for small samples; but the bias tends to disappear for very large samples, and thus the instrumental variables method yields consistent estimates. However, since autocorrelation has not been 'cured', the estimates are asymptotically inefficient. In other words the method of instrumental variables provides a 'cure' for the presence of the lagged Y_{t-1}, but does not deal with autocorrelation.

Method (ii). The Generalised Least Squares

We said in Chapter 10 that if the error term of a linear regression model is autocorrelated with a first order autoregressive scheme, the appropriate estimation method is the generalised least squares method (GLS), which is equivalent to the application of OLS to the transformed original variables

$$(Y_t - \rho Y_{t-1}) = b_0(1 - \rho) + b_1(Y_{t-1} - \rho Y_{t-2}) + b_2(X_t - \rho X_{t-1}) + \epsilon_t$$
$$(13.41)$$

where ρ is the autoregressive coefficient. If ρ is known we can apply OLS to the transformed variables and obtain estimates, which, although biased for small samples, are consistent and asymptotically efficient. (The bias is due to the presence of the lagged variable Y_{t-1}, because autocorrelation alone does not lead to biased estimates of OLS.)

However, ρ is unknown in most cases. Of course (13.41) can be estimated by OLS since ϵ_t satisfies, *ex-hypothesi*, all the stochastic assumptions of the linear regression model. However, if we attempt to obtain values for the b's and ρ in one go by OLS we are faced with new estimation difficulties, because equation (13.41) is non-linear in the parameters, as can be seen if we rewrite it in the form

$$Y_t = b_0(1 - \rho) + (b_1 + \rho)Y_{t-1} - (b_1\rho)Y_{t-2} + b_2X_t - (b_2\rho)X_{t-1} + \epsilon_t$$

$$(13.42)$$

This difficulty can be avoided if we can obtain an estimate of ρ, which we can then substitute in (13.41) and obtain estimates of the b's. Various methods for estimating ρ have been suggested. We shall examine three of them.

(a) *Estimation of ρ by iteration.* This method has been developed in Chapter 10. We may summarise it as follows.

1. Choose an arbitrary value of ρ within the range zero and unity ($0 < \rho < 1$), say ρ^*.

2. Substitute ρ^* in (13.41) and obtain the transformed model

$$(Y_t - \rho^*Y_{t-1}) = b_0(1 - \rho^*) + b_1(Y_{t-1} - \rho^*Y_{t-2}) + b_2(X_t - \rho^*X_{t-1}) + \epsilon_t$$

$$(13.43)$$

3. Apply next OLS to (13.43) and obtain the estimates $\hat{b}_i$ and the residuals $\hat{e}_t$'s. Regress $\hat{e}_t$ on its own lagged value $\hat{e}_{t-1}$

$$\hat{e}_t = \rho\hat{e}_{t-1} + \omega_t$$

and obtain an estimate, $\hat{\rho}$, for the autoregressive parameter.

4. Using the new $\hat{\rho}$, we re-estimate 13.41, substituting in it the new estimate of ρ. From the regression

$$(Y_t - \hat{\rho}Y_{t-1}) = b_0(1 - \hat{\rho}) + b_1(Y_{t-1} - \hat{\rho}Y_{t-2}) + b_2(X_t - \hat{\rho}X_{t-1}) + \epsilon_t$$

$$(13.44)$$

we obtain a new set of parameter estimates, $\hat{\hat{b}}_i$, and of new residuals, $\hat{\hat{e}}_t$.

5. We·regress $\hat{\hat{e}}_t$ on $\hat{\hat{e}}_{t-1}$ and we repeat the process until the values of the b's converge to any specified degree of accuracy (e.g. when the b's do not change further in their third decimal figure).

(b) *Estimation of ρ directly from the transformed model.* We saw that the difficulty in estimating 13.42

$$Y_t = b_0(1 - \rho) + (b_1 + \rho)Y_{t-1} - (b_1\rho)Y_{t-2} + b_2X_t - (b_2\rho)X_{t-1} + \epsilon_t$$

arises from the nonlinear nature of the parameters. However we may set

$$\left. \begin{aligned} c_0 &= b_0(1 - \rho) \\ c_1 &= (b_1 + \rho) \\ c_2 &= (-b_1\rho) \\ c_3 &= b_2 \\ c_4 &= (-b_2\rho) \end{aligned} \right\} \qquad (13.45)$$

and rewrite the above model as

$$Y_t = c_0 + c_1 Y_{t-1} + c_2 Y_{t-2} + c_3 X_t + c_4 X_{t-1} + \epsilon_t \qquad (13.46)$$

We apply OLS to this model without any restriction on the value of ρ, and we obtain estimates $\hat{c}_0, \hat{c}_1, \hat{c}_2, \hat{c}_3, \hat{c}_4$.

Using these estimates in (13.45) we find

$$\hat{c}_3 = \hat{b}_2$$

and hence

$$\hat{c}_4 = -\hat{b}_2 \rho = -\hat{c}_3 \rho$$

or

$$\hat{\rho} = -\frac{\hat{c}_4}{\hat{c}_3} = -\frac{\text{coefficient of } X_{t-1}}{\text{coefficient of } X_t}$$

This estimate of ρ may not be very reliable due to the collinearity of the lagged Y's and the lagged X's.

(c) *Estimation of ρ by the Wallis' Method.* This method involves the following practical stages.

1. We use X_{t-1} as an instrument for Y_{t-1}, and apply OLS to the form

$$Y_t = b_0 + b_1 X_{t-1} + b_2 X_t + \epsilon_t$$

2. We obtain the residuals $\hat{\epsilon}_t$ which we use to estimate the simple correlation coefficient between successive values of $\hat{\epsilon}_t$'s by applying the formula

$$r_{\hat{\epsilon}_t \hat{\epsilon}_{t-1}} = \frac{\sum\limits_{t=2}^{n} \hat{\epsilon}_t \hat{\epsilon}_{t-1} \Big/ (n-1)}{\sum\limits_{t=1}^{n} \hat{\epsilon}_t^2 \Big/ n} + \frac{K}{n}$$

where K is the number of parameters in the model ($K = 3$ in our example). The term $\dfrac{K}{n}$ is used to correct for bias.

3. We use $r_{\hat{\epsilon}_t \hat{\epsilon}_{t-1}}$ as an estimate for $\tilde{\rho}$, say ρ, and we apply OLS to the transformed model

$$(Y_t - \tilde{\rho} Y_{t-1}) = b_0^* + b_1^*(Y_{t-1} - \tilde{\rho} Y_{t-2}) + b_2^*(X_t - \tilde{\rho} X_{t-1}) + \epsilon_t$$

It should be noted that the estimates of the b's (obtained from all three ways of estimating ρ) will be biased, but consistent and asymptotically efficient.

EXERCISES

1. Formulate a model of the consumption function incorporating in it the 'permanent income hypothesis'.

Using the data of the following table estimate your model (a) by OLS, (b) by an appropriate transformation which would 'correct' the model for autocorrelation. Compare critically the estimates of the two methods.

Table. Consumption expenditure and disposable income (in billions of $)

Period	1954	1955	1956	1957	1958	1959	1960	1961	1962	1963	1964	1965
Consumption	236	254	267	281	290	311	325	335	355	375	401	431
Disposable Income	257	275	293	309	319	337	350	364	385	405	437	469

2. Extend the Wallis method to a model including two lagged values of Y among the set of explanatory variables.

3. Consider the 'stock adjustment' model

$$Y_t = (b_0 \delta) + (b_1 \delta) X_t + (1 - \delta) Y_{t-1} + \epsilon_t$$

(a) What is the economic meaning of the coefficients if Y is a durable commodity?

(b) Would this model be plausible for a non-durable commodity? What would be the meaning of the coefficients in this case? How would they differ from the coefficients of the model for a durable commodity?

4. The following table shows data on the expenditure on durables and total expenditure in the U.S.A. (in thousand million $).

Year	Expenditure on durables (Y)	Total consumption expenditure (X_1)	Price index for durables $(1963 = 100)$ (X_2)
1955	33·5	255·2	90·8
1956	33·5	267·5	95·2
1957	33·6	282·3	98·0
1958	30·4	291·1	99·7
1959	36·0	312·3	99·5
1960	36·7	326·5	101·1
1961	35·3	336·6	100·9
1962	40·0	356·6	100·5
1963	43·7	376·6	100·0
1964	47·8	402·9	99·8
1965	54·1	434·7	98·9
1966	56·7	468·3	99·5
1967	58·0	494·3	99·7
1968	66·8	538·9	99·4
1969	76·5	587·0	99·3

Construct and estimate

(a) a constant elasticity demand model for durables. (Use OLS.)

(b) a distributed-lag model for the demand for durables. (Use both OLS and the Wallis-method for estimation.)

Compare critically the results from the various models and estimation methods.

5. Consider the distributed-lag model

$$Y_t = b_0 + b_1 X_{1t} + b_2 X_{2t} + b_3 Y_{t-1} + u_t$$

where $u_t = \rho u_{t-1} + \epsilon_t$, and ϵ_t satisfies the usual stochastic assumptions

$$\epsilon \sim N(0, \sigma_\epsilon^2)$$
$$E(\epsilon_t \epsilon_s) = 0 \qquad \text{(for } t \neq s)$$

(a) What would be the properties of the estimates if OLS were applied?
(b) Discuss methods of estimating the model which give estimates 'better' than those of OLS.
(c) Could you obtain unbiased estimates with any econometric method? Why?

Note. Additional exercises are included in Appendix III.

PART THREE

Models of Simultaneous Relationships

14. Simultaneous-equation Models

14.1. SIMULTANEOUS DEPENDENCE OF ECONOMIC VARIABLES

The application of least squares to a single equation assumes, among others, that the explanatory variables are truly exogenous, that there is one-way causation between the dependent variable Y and the explanatory X's. If this is not true, that is if the X's are at the same time determined by Y, Assumption 6 of OLS is violated ($E(Xu) \neq 0$), and the application of this method yields biased and inconsistent estimates. (For a proof see below, page 334.)

If we have a two-way causation in a function this implies that the function cannot be treated in isolation as a single equation model, but belongs to a wider system of equations which describes the relationships among all the relevant variables. If $Y = f(X)$, but also $X = f(Y)$ we are not allowed to use a single-equation model for the description of the relationship between Y and X. We must use a multi-equation model, which would include separate equations in which Y and X would appear as endogenous variables, although they might appear as explanatory in other equations of the model. A system describing the joint dependence of variables is called a *system of simultaneous equations*.

Given the nature of economic phenomena it is almost certain that any equation will belong to a wider system of simultaneous equations. Some examples will illustrate the meaning of simultaneous relationships and the violation of Assumption 6 of ordinary least squares, which creates what is known as *simultaneous equations bias*.

Example 1. Suppose we want to estimate the demand for food. We know from economic theory that the demand for any particular commodity depends on its price, P, on other prices, P_0, and on income, Y. Thus we may write the demand function for food as

$$Q = b_0 + b_1 P + b_2 P_0 + b_3 Y + u$$

where Q = quantity demanded
         P = price of food
         P_0 = price of other commodities
         Y = income
         u = random variable.

If we apply least squares to this equation we will obtain biased estimates of b_0 and b_1, because P and u are not independent. The demand for any commodity is a function of its price (*inter alia*), but at the same time the price in the market is influenced by the quantity demanded of that commodity. Consequently the above single equation cannot be treated as a complete (single-equation) model. There should be at least one more equation in the model giving the relationship between P and Q, for example

$$P = c_0 + c_1 Q + c_2 W + v$$

331

where W = index of weather conditions.

Substituting Q in this equation with its equal, we obtain

$$P = c_0 + c_1 (b_0 + b_1 P + b_2 P_0 + b_3 Y + u) + c_2 W + v$$

Obviously P is dependent on u and hence we have violation of Assumption 6 of the method of least squares. P is not an exogenous variable in the demand function.

Example 2. Suppose we want to estimate the supply of money. This of course is regulated by the government in an attempt to avoid inflation. Thus we may say that the main determinant of the decision of the government about the supply of money is the real level of income. Hence we may write the supply function of money as

$$M = b_0 + b_1 Y + u$$

where M = money supply
         Y = level of real income.

However, the level of real income is in turn influenced by the supply of money as well as by other real forces, like the investment decisions of businessmen, the welfare policies of the government, and so on. Consequently the supply of money cannot be treated as a single-equation model. Y is not truly exogenous. There is a joint dependence between M and Y and hence we must construct a model with simultaneous equations, one of which would be

$$Y = a_0 + a_1 M + a_2 I_t + \ldots + v$$

Substituting M, we obtain

$$Y = a_0 + a_1 (b_0 + b_1 Y + u) + a_2 I_t + \ldots + v$$

Obviously $Y = f(u)$ and hence in the function of the supply of money the explanatory variable Y is not independent of the random variable u.

The bias arising from the application of classical least squares to an equation belonging to a system of simultaneous relations is called *simultaneous equations bias*. It originates from the violation of Assumption 6 of OLS, that is it arises from the dependence of the explanatory variables and u, $[E(uX) \neq 0]$.

This creates several problems. Firstly, there arises the problem of identification of the parameters of individual relationships. Secondly, there arise problems of estimation. The application of OLS yields biased and inconsistent estimates. One should therefore choose other estimation methods.

14.2. CONSEQUENCES OF SIMULTANEOUS RELATIONS

We said that when there is a joint dependence between Y and X, their relationship cannot be described with a single equation, but with a system of simultaneous equations. In each relation there are explanatory variables which are endogeneous to the system, that is, they appear as dependent in other equations of the system. Thus for any particular equation the random variable is not independent of the explanatory variable(s). Assumption 6 of OLS is not fulfilled ($E(uX) \neq 0$) and as a consequence the estimates are both biased and inconsistent.

Assume we have the simple model

$$Y = b_0 + b_1 X + u \qquad\qquad E(u) = 0 \qquad\qquad E(v) = 0$$

$$X = a_0 + a_1 Y + a_2 Z + v \qquad\qquad E(u^2) = \sigma_u^2 \qquad\qquad E(v^2) = \sigma_v^2$$

$$E(u_i u_j) = 0 \qquad\qquad E(v_i v_j) = 0$$

$$E(uv) = 0$$

The model is mathematically complete: it contains two equations in two endogenous variables, X and Y. Z is assumed to be exogenously determined (for example by the government). Substituting X in the second equation we obtain

$$X = a_0 + a_1(b_0 + b_1 X + u) + a_2 Z + v$$

or

$$X = \frac{a_0 + b_0 a_1}{1 - b_1 a_1} + \frac{a_2}{1 - b_1 a_1} Z + \left(\frac{a_1 u + v}{1 - b_1 a_1} \right)$$

X and the disturbance term u are related. X is not a truly exogenous variable in the first equation.

It can be proved that the covariance of X and u is not zero.

$$\text{cov}(Xu) \neq 0$$

Proof. By definition the covariance of u and X is

$$\text{cov}(uX) = E\left\{ [u - E(u)] [X - E(X)] \right\}$$

But $E(u) = 0$. Therefore

$$\text{cov}(uX) = E\left\{ u[X - E(X)] \right\}$$

Given that

$$X = \frac{a_0 + b_0 a_1}{1 - b_1 a_1} + \frac{a_2}{1 - b_1 a_1} Z + \left(\frac{a_1 u + v}{1 - b_1 a_1} \right)$$

and Z is exogenously determined we have

$$E(X) = \frac{a_0 + b_0 a_1}{1 - b_1 a_1} + \frac{a_2}{1 - b_1 a_1} Z$$

Therefore

$$\text{cov}(uX) = E\left[\frac{u}{1 - b_1 a_1} \left\{ a_0 + a_1 b_0 + a_2 Z + a_1 u + v - (a_0 + a_1 b_0 + a_2 Z) \right\} \right]$$

$$= E\left[\frac{u}{1 - b_1 a_1} (a_1 u + v) \right]$$

$$= \frac{1}{1 - b_1 a_1} E(a_1 u^2 + uv) = \frac{a_1}{1 - b_1 a_1} E(u^2) \neq 0$$

As a consequence, if we apply the method of least squares to the first function the estimates of the coefficients will be biased and inconsistent.

Proof. We established in Chapter 7 that the first normal equation is obtained by multiplying the structural equation through by x and summing over all sample observations. In deviation form we have

$$y = b_1 x + u$$
$$\Sigma xy = b_1 \Sigma x^2 + \Sigma xu \tag{14.1}$$

The last term which expresses the covariance of x and the random term u could be ignored by either of the following assumptions:

(a) If the X's are a set of fixed values in (hypothetical) repeating sampling, it is clear that the covariance of the X's and the u's is zero

$$E(\Sigma xu) = 0$$

(b) Even if the X's are stochastic (not fixed), the covariance of u's and the X's will still be zero so long as the X's are independent of the error term u.

With either of these conditions satisfied $E(\Sigma xu) = 0$ and we can obtain an unbiased estimate of b_1 by dividing (14.1) through by Σx^2

$$\frac{\Sigma xy}{\Sigma x^2} = b_1 + \frac{\Sigma xu}{\Sigma x^2} \tag{14.2}$$

Setting $\hat{b}_1 = \Sigma xy / \Sigma x^2$ and taking expected values we obtain

$$E(\hat{b}_1) = b_1$$

However, if the X's and the u's are not independent, their covariance is different from zero, so that

$$E\left\{ \Sigma(xu) \right\} \neq 0$$

The bias in $\hat{b}_1$ can be established by taking expected values of (14.2)

$$E\left(\frac{\Sigma xy}{\Sigma x^2}\right) = E(b_1) + E\left(\frac{\Sigma xu}{\Sigma x^2}\right)$$

or

$$E(\hat{b}_1) = b_1 + E\left(\frac{\Sigma xu}{\Sigma x^2}\right)$$

The bias is measured by the second term on the right-hand side and depends on the model being studied and the particular form of the dependence between X and u

$$\text{bias} = \left\{ E(\hat{b}_1) - b_1 \right\} = E\left(\frac{\Sigma xu}{\Sigma x^2}\right) \neq 0 \tag{14.3}$$

In our example of the consumption function it can be proved that

$$\hat{b}_1 = \frac{b_1 \Sigma z^2 + (1 + b_1) \Sigma zu + \Sigma u^2}{\Sigma z^2 + 2 \Sigma zu + \Sigma u^2}$$

(See J. Johnston, *Econometric Methods*, 1972, p. 344.) Letting $n \to \infty$ and noting that investment (I) is exogenous, the middle terms in the numerator and denominator will tend to zero. Hence the limiting value of the estimate b_1 is

$$\text{plim } \hat{b}_1 = \frac{b_1 \sigma_z^2 + \sigma_u^2}{\sigma_z^2 + \sigma_u^2}$$

or

$$\text{plim } \hat{b}_1 = b_1 + \frac{(1 - b_1) \sigma_u^2}{\sigma_z^2 + \sigma_u^2}$$

If $0 < b_1 < 1$ then the second additive term will be positive and the OLS estimate $\hat{b}_1$ will overestimate the true b_1.

If the first equation is a consumption function, b_1 is the MPC which on *a priori* grounds is positive but less than unity $(0 < b_1 < 1)$; hence the estimate $\hat{b}_1$ will have an upward bias, while $\hat{b}_0$ will have a downward bias. For the particular example of the consumption function the consequences of the violation of the assumption of the independence of the explanatory variable Y and u may be shown diagrammatically as in figure 14.1.

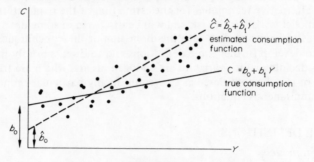

Figure 14.1

An intuitive explanation of the bias may be formulated on the following lines. In applying OLS for explaining the variation in Y we give as little emphasis as possible to the error term u and as much as possible to the explanatory variables. But u is unobservable and will not appear in the estimated equation. If u and the X's are correlated this specification bias (omission of u) will cause an error in the b's, because some of the effect of u will be wrongly absorbed by the coefficients of the X's.

It is clear from (14.3) that the bias is independent of the sample size; as n increases the terms that we sum increase in both the numerator and the denominator. Hence the bias cannot be eliminated by increasing the number of observations in the sample. Thus the first condition for consistency (the condition of asymptotic unbiasedness) does not hold and the estimates obtained from OLS will be inconsistent.

14.3. SOLUTION TO THE SIMULTANEOUS-EQUATION BIAS

Since the application of ordinary least squares to an equation belonging to a system of simultaneous equations yields biased and inconsistent estimates, the obvious solution is to apply other methods of estimation which give better estimates of the parameters. There are several methods for this purpose. The most common are:

(1) The reduced form method, or indirect least squares (ILS).
(2) The method of instrumental variables (IV).
(3) Two-stage least squares (2SLS).
(4) Limited information maximum likelihood (LIML).

(5) The mixed estimation method.
(6) Three-stage least squares (3SLS).
(7) Full information maximum likelihood (FIML).

The first five methods are called *single-equation methods,* because they are applied to one equation of the system at a time. The three-stage least squares and the full information maximum likelihood are called *systems methods,* because they are applied to all the equations of the system simultaneously. The above methods will be developed in chapters 16–19 of this book. The choice among the alternative techniques for the estimation of the parameters of a particular model is a difficult task and will be discussed in some detail in Chapter 21. Before proceeding with the discussion of these techniques, it is necessary to develop further some definitions and to discuss briefly the problem of deciding which variables are endogenous and which are truly exogenous or may be considered as exogenous in any particular econometric model of simultaneous equations.

14.4. SOME DEFINITIONS

1. Structural models

A structural model is a complete system of equations which describe the structure of the relationships of the economic variables. Structural equations express the endogenous variables as functions of other endogenous variables, predetermined variables and disturbances (random variables).

As an illustration we will use the following simple model for a closed economy.

$$C_t = a_0 + a_1 Y_t + u_1$$
$$I_t = b_0 + b_1 Y_t + b_2 Y_{t-1} + u_2$$
$$Y_t = C_t + I_t + G_t$$

The first equation is a consumption function, the second is an investment function, the third is a definitional equation. The system is complete in that it contains three equations in three endogenous variables, C_t, I_t, Y_t. The model contains two predetermined variables, government expenditure, G, and lagged income, Y_{t-1}.

In the remainder of this chapter, for the sake of simplicity, we will ignore the constant intercepts of the structural equations. (If one wants to retain the intercepts in the analysis, one should introduce a dummy variable, X_0, in the set of explanatory variables, which would always assume the value of 1.)

The structural parameters are, in general, propensities, elasticities or other parameters of economic theory. A structural parameter expresses the *direct effect* of each explanatory variable on the dependent variable. Indirect effects can be computed only by the solution of the structural system, but not by the individual structural parameters. Factors not appearing in any function explicitly may have an indirect influence on the dependent variable of that function. For example a change in consumption will affect investment indirectly, through the increase that the consumption, C, will produce on income, Y, which is a determinant of investment. The effect of C on I cannot be measured directly by any of the structural parameters, but it will be taken into account by the simultaneous solution of the system.

Traditionally the structural parameters are represented by β's when they refer to endogenous variables, and by γ's when they are attached to a pre-determined variable. Similarly endogenous variables are denoted by y's while exogenous variables are represented by x's. Using the conventional notation (and ignoring the constant intercepts) the structural system above becomes

$$y_1 = \beta_{13} y_3 + u_1$$
$$y_2 = \beta_{23} y_3 + \gamma_{21} x_1 + u_2$$
$$y_3 = y_1 + y_2 + x_2$$

where

$$y_1 = C \qquad y_2 = I \qquad y_3 = Y$$
$$x_1 = Y_{t-1} \qquad x_2 = G$$

Transferring all the observable variables to the left-hand side we may obtain the complete table of structural parameters as follows

$$y_1 + 0y_2 - \beta_{13} y_3 + 0x_1 + 0x_2 = u_1$$
$$0y_1 + y_2 - \beta_{23} y_3 - \gamma_{21} x_1 + 0x_2 = u_2$$
$$-y_1 - y_2 + y_3 + 0x_1 - x_2 = 0$$

Table of structural coefficients				
1	0	$-a_1$	0	0
0	1	$-b_1$	$-b_2$	0
-1	-1	1	0	-1

Table of structural coefficients in standard notation				
1	0	$-\beta_{13}$	0	0
0	1	$-\beta_{23}$	γ_{21}	0
-1	-1	1	0	-1

Values of the structural parameters may be obtained by using sample observations on the variables of the model and applying an appropriate econometric method. (See Chapters 16–21.)

2. Reduced form models

The reduced form of a structural model is the model in which the endogenous variables are expressed as a function of the predetermined variables only. The reduced form is obtained in two ways. The first is to express the endogenous variables directly as functions of the predetermined variables

$$y_i = \pi_{i1} x_1 + \pi_{i2} x_2 + \ldots + \pi_{ik} x_k + v_i \quad (i = 1, 2, \ldots, G)$$

and proceed with the estimation of the π's by applying some appropriate technique to this expression (see below). In our example of the simple three-equation model the reduced form would be

$$C_t = \pi_{11} Y_{t-1} + \pi_{12} G_t + v_1$$
$$I_t = \pi_{21} Y_{t-1} + \pi_{22} G_t + v_2$$
$$Y_t = \pi_{31} Y_{t-1} + \pi_{32} G_t + v_3$$

The second method for obtaining the reduced form of a model is to solve the structural system of endogenous variables in terms of the predetermined variables, the structural parameters and the disturbances. The structural system of our example gives the following reduced form model:

$$C_t = \frac{a_1 b_2}{1 - a_1 - b_1} Y_{t-1} + \frac{a_1}{1 - a_1 - b_1} G_t + \frac{u_1 + a_1 u_2 - b_1 u_1}{1 - a_1 - b_1}$$

$$I_t = \frac{b_2(1 - a_1)}{1 - a_1 - b_1} Y_{t-1} + \frac{b_1}{1 - a_1 - b_1} G_t + \frac{u_2 + b_1 u_1 - a_1 u_2}{1 - a_1 - b_1}$$

$$Y_t = \frac{b_2}{1 - a_1 - b_1} Y_{t-1} + \frac{1}{1 - a_1 - b_1} G_t + \frac{u_1 + u_2}{1 - a_1 - b_1}$$

Clearly for the two reduced forms to be consistent the following relationships between the π's and the structural parameters must hold

$$\pi_{11} = \frac{a_1 b_2}{1 - a_1 - b_1} \qquad \pi_{12} = \frac{a_1}{1 - a_1 - b_1}$$

$$\pi_{21} = \frac{b_2(1 - a_1)}{1 - a_1 - b_1} \qquad \pi_{22} = \frac{b_1}{1 - a_1 - b_1}$$

$$\pi_{31} = \frac{b_2}{1 - a_1 - b_1} \qquad \pi_{32} = \frac{1}{1 - a_1 - b_1}$$

It should be clear that there is a definite relationship between the reduced-form parameters and the structural parameters: the π's are functions of the structural parameters.

Derivation of the reduced form parameters.
(a) Substitute C_t and I_t in the third structural equation

$$Y_t = (a_1 Y_t + u_1) + (b_1 Y_t + b_2 Y_{t-1} + u_2) + G_t$$

By rearranging we obtain

$$Y_t = \frac{b_2}{1 - a_1 - b_1} Y_{t-1} + \frac{1}{1 - a_1 - b_1} G_t + \frac{u_1 + u_2}{1 - a_1 - b_1}$$

This is the reduced form of the third structural equation.
(b) Substitute Y_t into the consumption function

$$C_t = a_1 \left[\frac{b_2}{1 - a_1 - b_1} Y_{t-1} + \frac{1}{1 - a_1 - b_1} G_t + \frac{u_1 + u_2}{1 - a_1 - b_1} \right] + u_1$$

or

$$C_t = \frac{a_1 b_2}{1 - a_1 - b_1} Y_{t-1} + \frac{a_1}{1 - a_1 - b_1} G_t + \frac{u_1 + a_1 u_2 - b_1 u_1}{1 - a_1 - b_1}$$

This is the reduced form of the consumption function.

(c) Substitute Y_t into the investment function

$$I_t = b_1 \left[\frac{b_2}{1 - a_1 - b_1} Y_{t-1} + \frac{1}{1 - a_1 - b_1} G_t + \frac{u_1 + u_2}{1 - a_1 - b_1} \right] + b_2 Y_{t-1} + u_2$$

or

$$I_t = \frac{b_2(1 - a_1)}{1 - a_1 - b_1} Y_{t-1} + \frac{b_1}{1 - a_1 - b_1} G_t + \left(\frac{u_2 + b_1 u_1 - a_1 u_2}{1 - a_1 - b_1} \right)$$

This is the reduced form of the investment function.

The reduced-form parameters measure the *total effect*, direct and indirect, of a change in the predetermined variable on the endogenous variables, after taking account of the interdependences among the jointly dependent endogenous variables, while a structural parameter indicates only the direct effect within a single sector of the economy.[1] For example π_{21} measures the effect of a unit increase in Y_{t-1} on the value of investment. This effect consists of two parts: firstly, there is the direct effect on I through the coefficient b_2 as set out in the structural equation of investment; secondly there is the additional effect due to the fact that an increase in Y_{t-1} affects $I_t \rightarrow$ and I_t influences $Y_t \rightarrow$ which in turn affects I_t; finally Y_t affects $C_t \rightarrow$ which in turn affects Y_t and hence I_t. Thus the total effect (measured by π_{21}) of Y_{t-1} on I_t may be split into the following components

$$\pi_{21} = \frac{b_2(1 - a_1)}{1 - a_1 - b_1} = b_2 \left(1 + \frac{b_1}{1 - a_1 - b_1} \right)$$

or

$$\pi_{21} \quad = \quad b_2 \quad + \quad \frac{b_2 b_1}{1 - a_1 - b_1}$$

$$\begin{bmatrix} \text{total} \\ \text{effect} \end{bmatrix} = \begin{bmatrix} \text{direct} \\ \text{effect} \end{bmatrix} + \begin{bmatrix} \text{indirect} \\ \text{effect} \end{bmatrix}$$

The reduced form coefficients are used for forecasting and policy analysis, since it is the total effect of a change in the exogenous variables on the dependent variable(s) that is of interest to the policy maker.

The above two ways of defining the reduced-form model suggest that estimates of the reduced-form coefficients may be obtained in two ways.

Firstly. Direct estimation of the reduced-form coefficients. The reduced-form π's may be estimated by the method of least-squares-no-restrictions

[1] See A. Walters, *An Introduction to Econometrics*, Macmillan, London 1968, p. 181–4.

(LSNR). We express all the endogenous variables as functions of all the pre-determined variables of the system and we apply ordinary least squares to these reduced-form functions. This method of obtaining the π's is called least-squares-no-restrictions (LSNR), because it does not take into account any information on the structural parameters, that is, it does not use any restrictions imposed by the form of the structural system. For example the structural equations define that some coefficients are zero if the respective variables are not included in a function; this information is not taken into account by the method of LSNR. This method does not require complete knowledge of the structural system. What is required is knowledge of the predetermined variables appearing in the whole system.

Secondly. Indirect estimation of the reduced-form coefficients. We saw that there is a definite relationship between the reduced-form coefficients and the structural parameters. It is thus possible first to obtain estimates of the structural parameters by any appropriate econometric technique and then sub-stitute these estimates into the *system of parameters' relationships* to obtain (indirectly) values for the π's. This indirect method involves three steps: (1) Solve the system of endogenous variables so that each equation contains only predetermined explanatory variables. This, as we saw, may be done by continuous substitutions of variables, until we arrive at the reduced-form of all the equations. In this way we obtain *the system of parameters' relations*, that is to say the system which defines the relations between the π's and the β's and γ's. (2) Obtain estimates of the structural parameters by any appropriate econometric method. (3) Substitute the estimates β's and γ's into the system of parameters' relations to find the estimates of the reduced-form coefficients.

This method is more complicated, but it has several advantages over the direct estimation of π's from LSNR. (a) The derivation of reduced-form π's from the structural β's and γ's is more efficient because in this way we take into account all the information (that is all the *a priori* restrictions imposed by the structure on the parameters) incorporated into the structural model. (b) Structural changes occur continuously over time. If we know these changes in the β's and γ's we may easily recompute the π's. While if the π's are computed with the LSNR method it will not, in general, be possible to take this informa-tion into account, because each π is a function of several structural parameters, and if the exact relationship between π's, β's and γ's has not been established, we cannot incorporate into the former the changes that may have occurred to the latter. (c) Extraneous information on some structural parameters may become available from other studies; such information again will be useless if we have not estimated the π's from previous estimates of β's and γ's. (See Goldberger, *Econometric Theory*, pp. 379–80.)

3. Recursive models

A model is called recursive if its structural equations can be ordered in such a way that the first includes only predetermined variables in the right-hand side;

the second equation contains predetermined variables and the first endogenous variable (of the first equation) in the right-hand side; and so on. For example

$$y_1 = f(x_1, x_2 \ldots x_k; u_1)$$
$$y_2 = f(x_1, x_2 \ldots x_k; y_1; u_2)$$
$$y_3 = f(x_1, x_2 \ldots x_k; y_1, y_2; u_3)$$

and so on.

The random variables are assumed to be independent.

The special feature of a recursive model is that its equations may be estimated, one at a time, by OLS without simultaneous-equations bias. To understand this, let us write the above recursive model in its complete form. Assume that there are G endogenous variables k exogenous variables in the model

$$y_1 = \gamma_{11}x_1 + \gamma_{12}x_2 + \ldots + \gamma_{1k}x_k + u_1$$
$$y_2 = \gamma_{21}x_1 + \gamma_{22}x_2 + \ldots + \gamma_{2k}x_k + \beta_{21}y_1 + u_2$$
$$y_3 = \gamma_{31}x_1 + \gamma_{32}x_2 + \ldots + \gamma_{3k}x_k + \beta_{31}y_1 + \beta_{32}y_2 + u_3$$

$$\cdot \qquad \cdot \qquad \qquad \cdot$$
$$\cdot \qquad \cdot \qquad \qquad \cdot$$
$$\cdot \qquad \cdot \qquad \qquad \cdot$$

$$y_G = \gamma_{G1}x_1 + \gamma_{G2}x_2 + \ldots + \gamma_{Gk}x_k + \beta_{G1}y_1 + \beta_{G2}y_2 + \ldots + u_G$$

Given values of the exogenous variables (x_i) we may apply OLS to each equation individually, because by assumption the distribution variables u_i and u_j are independent, and hence the y's appearing in the right-hand side of each equation are independent of this equation's error term. For example, in the second equation y_1 is independent of u_2, given u_1 and u_2 are *ex hypothesi* independent.

Recursive systems are also called *triangular systems* because the coefficients of the endogenous variables (the β's) form a triangular array: the main diagonal of the array of β's contains units, and no coefficients appear above the main diagonal. For example assume that we have a model with four endogenous and five predetermined variables

$$y_1 = \gamma_{11}x_1 + \gamma_{12}x_2 + u_1$$
$$y_2 = \beta_{21}y_1 + \gamma_{21}x_1 + \gamma_{22}x_2 + \gamma_{23}x_3 + u_2$$
$$y_3 = \beta_{31}y_1 + \beta_{32}y_2 + \gamma_{31}x_1 + \gamma_{34}x_4 + u_3$$
$$y_4 = \beta_{41}y_1 + \beta_{42}y_2 + \beta_{43}y_3 + \gamma_{44}x_4 + \gamma_{45}x_5 + u_4$$

To see whether this model is recursive it suffices to examine the form of the array of the β's. If it is triangular the system is recursive. The system may be rewritten in the slightly different form

$$y_1 - \gamma_{11}x_1 - \gamma_{12}x_2 = u_1$$
$$y_2 - \beta_{21}y_1 - \gamma_{21}x_1 - \gamma_{22}x_2 - \gamma_{23}x_3 = u_2$$
$$y_3 - \beta_{31}y_1 - \beta_{32}y_2 - \gamma_{31}x_1 - \gamma_{34}x_4 = u_3$$
$$y_4 - \beta_{41}y_1 - \beta_{42}y_2 - \beta_{43}y_3 - \gamma_{44}x_4 - \gamma_{45}x_5 = u_4$$

The array of structural parameters is shown below.

β's of endogenous variables				γ's of exogenous variables				
y_1	y_2	y_3	y_4	x_1	x_2	x_3	x_4	x_5
1	0	0	0	$-\gamma_{11}$	$-\gamma_{12}$	0	0	0
$-\beta_{21}$	1	0	0	$-\gamma_{21}$	$-\gamma_{22}$	$-\gamma_{23}$	0	0
$-\beta_{31}$	$-\beta_{32}$	1	0	$-\gamma_{31}$	0	0	$-\gamma_{34}$	0
$-\beta_{41}$	$-\beta_{42}$	$-\beta_{43}$	1	0	0	0	$-\gamma_{44}$	$-\gamma_{45}$

Obviously the array of β's is triangular: the main diagonal contains units and all the coefficients above it are zero. Hence the system is recursive, and its equations can be estimated by OLS, which will yield unbiased and consistent estimates.

14.5. LEVEL OF AGGREGATION – NUMBER OF EQUATIONS – NUMBER OF VARIABLES

The level of aggregation depends on the purpose of the model. For the exploration of the growth pattern of income and of a few other basic economic magnitudes highly aggregative models have been used successfully in economic planning. For forecasting and policy analysis the level of aggregation must be chosen carefully. The usefulness of a model for appraising economic policies depends primarily upon the number of equations and the variables included.

Economic reality is very complex, so that the number of mathematical relationships which would be required for a complete description of an economic phenomenon would be large. Systems with large numbers of equations are difficult to handle. So, if we are to construct an operational econometric model we must simplify the relationships of the actual world. Simplification is done in several ways:

(1) *Aggregation of individual consumers.* The equations of an econometric model describe group behaviour rather than individual behaviour. Equations of this type are called market demand functions.

(2) *Aggregation of firms into an industry,* or even aggregation of industries into a few sectors. For example the production function of the chemical industries, or of the manufacturing sector as a whole.

(3) *Aggregation over commodities.* Large groups of commodities are considered as a single product, for example 'food', 'household equipment', etc.

(4) *Selection of the most important explanatory variables.* Many of the variables in the system are removed from each equation (we impose on their coefficients 'zero' restrictions) and their influence is left to be absorbed by the random component of the function, *u*.

(5) *Simplification of the mathematical form of the functions.* The complexity of the real world often requires the functions to include nonlinearities, discontinuities, etc. However, in econometric models we usually employ functions with simple mathematical properties. Functions are assumed to be linear in the original variables or in their logs, with continuous partial derivatives, linear in the parameters, and so on.

What is the optimal number of equations that should be included in a model? There is no firm rule to indicate how many equations should be included in a model. This depends on various considerations: (a) the purpose of the model, (b) data availability, (c) importance of various sectors and/or various variables, (d) the level of detailed information in which we are interested, and so on.

The optimal level of simplification cannot be determined on *a priori* grounds, because it depends on several factors which must be weighted in any particular case. However, the main determinant of the level of aggregation is the purpose for which the model is being estimated.

With respect to the number of variables we note the following.

The number of endogenous variables is the same as the number of equations of the model. However, the number of exogenous variables may be as large as we choose. There is no restriction on the number of exogenous variables as there is for the endogenous variables. Yet the model builder must be careful with the use of exogenous variables. The more variables we introduce in a model the more complicated it becomes and the heavier the data requirements and computational difficulties grow. If the model is intended for policy analysis it should include as many as possible policy instruments (that is, variables under the direct control of the government, like taxes of various items, subsidies of different forms, tariffs and so on) so that it may be effectively used for the evaluation of the effects of alternative economic policies. A policy model should provide the appropriate coefficients (equations and variables) for the appraisal of any set of economic policies.

Which variables will be endogenous and which will be considered as exogenous in any particular model depends on the purpose of the model as well as on the nature of the variables. The same variable (for example exports, government taxation revenues) may be treated as exogenous in some models and as endogenous in others.

For example take the following simple Keynesian model

$$C = a_0 + a_1 Y$$
$$I = \bar{I}$$
$$Y = C + I + G$$

In this model consumption and income are endogenous variables which are interdependent (jointly dependent). In the first equation income (Y) determines consumption, while in the third equation income is determined by consumption. The other two variables, investment (I) and government expenditure (G) are exogenous variables, whose values are given outside this particular model. However, one would be wrong to think that the exogenous variables are absolutely independent from other factors. In most cases exogenous variables can in principle be explained by other variables in some other model. But for the particular model which is studied their value is taken as autonomously given. In this particular model the exogenous variable determines the value of some endogenous variable(s), but its own value is not determined by other variables in the model. For example in the previous Keynesian model of income determination investment was assumed exogenous, that is the level of investment was determined by forces outside this model. It determines other variables in the model but it is not determined by them. However, we may express investment as a function of the interest rate and the past level of income

$$C = a_0 + a_1 Y$$
$$I = b_0 + b_1 r + b_2 Y_{t-1}$$
$$Y = C + I + G$$

This formulation differs from the first only in the investment function. Investment is endogenously determined by the rate of interest and the past level of income. The latter variable is known (lagged variables are predetermined and known). The interest rate may be taken as an exogenous variable, for example determined by the government. If, however, we assume that r is not exogenous, we must introduce an additional equation to explain its determination. Thus we may say that the rate of interest is determined by the level of past investment and by the money supply. The money supply is an additional variable which may be assumed exogenous. If not, we must introduce another variable (or variables) to explain it, and so on.

Of course we cannot continue in this way indefinitely. We must stop somewhere, otherwise the system becomes impossible to handle. If we continue to introduce new equations and new variables in order to explain the 'explanatory' variables of some other equation, we eventually come to factors which are non-economic, that is, we eventually arrive at functions which include non-economic explanatory variables. Exogenous variables are ultimately determined by technological, political, physical, or institutional factors. However, in most applied research we take a lot of economic variables as exogenous, because we are not able or we are not interested in having separate equations for all the variables of a system.

EXERCISES

1. Construct a simultaneous equation model describing the market mechanism of an agricultural commodity. Derive the reduced form parameters in terms of the structural parameters of your model. What is the economic meaning of the structural and of the reduced form parameters?

2. What is the economic meaning of the imposition of 'zero restrictions' on the parameters of a model? How would you proceed if you wanted to test whether the *a priori* imposition of a 'zero restriction' on the parameter of a certain variable is valid?

3. Given the simple Keynesian model of income determination

$$C_t = a_0 + a_1 Y_t + u_1$$
$$I_t = b_0 + b_1 Y_t + b_2 Y_{t-1} + u_2$$
$$Y_t = C_t + I_t + G_t$$

(i)   Derive the reduced form coefficients of the behavioural equations.
(ii) Show that the reduced-form parameters measure the *total effect*, direct and indirect, of a change in the exogenous variable on the endogenous variables. Use as an example the reduced form of the above investment function.

4. Consider the following simultaneous equation model

$$Y = b_0 + b_1 X_1 + b_2 X_2 + u_1$$
$$X_2 = c_0 + c_1 Y + u_2$$

(i)   Show that, under the usual assumptions (regarding each one of the random terms u_1 and u_2), X_2 and u_1 are not independent, that is

$$E[X_{2t} u_1] = \frac{c_1 \cdot \sigma_{u1}^2}{1 - c_1 b_2} + \frac{\text{cov}(u_1, u_2)}{1 - c_1 b_2} \neq 0$$

(ii) What are the implications of this finding?
(iii) What is the appropriate procedure for estimating the coefficients of the model, given $E(X_2 u_1) \neq 0$?

Note. Additional exercises are included in Appendix III.

15. Identification

15.1. THE PROBLEM OF IDENTIFICATION STATED

Identification is a problem of model formulation, rather than of model estimation or apprasial. We say a model is identified if it is in a unique statistical form, enabling unique estimates of its parameters to be subsequently made from sample data. If a model is not identified then estimates of parameters of relationships between variables measured in samples may relate to the model in question, or to another model, or to a mixture of models.

An econometric model is frequently in the form of a system of simultaneous equations. The model may be said to be complete if it contains at least as many independent equations as endogenous variables. For identification of the entire model, it is necessary for the model to be complete and for each equation in it to be identified. Tests of identification are examined later in this chapter.

To illustrate the meaning of the identification problem let us take an example from the theory of market equilibrium. Assume that the market mechanism for a certain commodity is given by the following simple model

$$D = b_0 + b_1 P + u$$
$$S = a_0 + a_1 P + v$$
$$D = S$$

where D = quantity demanded, S = quantity supplied, P = price.

The first equation is the demand function, the second expresses the supply function and the third is the equilibrium condition of the market (or clearance equation). The model is complete in that there are three equations and three endogenous variables (S, D, P). But is each equation identified?

Assume we are interested in the measurement of the coefficients of the demand equation. To obtain estimates of b_0 and b_1 we normally use published time series reporting the quantity bought of the commodity. However, the quantity bought is identical with the quantity sold at any particular price. Market data register points of equilibrium of supply and demand at the price prevailing in the market at a certain point of time. A sample of time-series observations shows simultaneously the quantity demanded, D, and the quantity supplied, S, at the prevailing market price, P. If we use these data for estimation, we actually measure the coefficients of a function of the form $Q = f(P)$. This equation may be either the demand function or the supply function (or even a 'bogus' equation, as we will presently see). How can we be sure which function we do really measure? If two econometricians use these data and one claims that he has estimated a demand function, while the other claims that he has estimated a supply function, how are we to decide who is right? Clearly, we need some criteria which will enable us to verify that the estimated coefficients belong to the one or the other relationship. Such criteria are known as 'identification conditions' of a function and will be developed in a subsequent section. For the time being let us return to our example. One might think that a scatter diagram of the sample observations might help. This is not always so. Suppose we plot the sample data on a diagram. The scatter of points may reveal one of the patterns shown in figures 15.1, 15.2, 15.3.

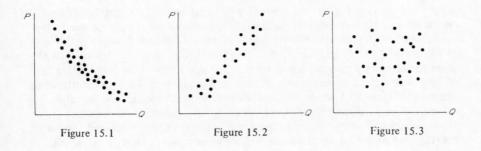

Figure 15.1   Figure 15.2   Figure 15.3

One might be tempted to conclude that the scatter of data in figure 15.1 identities the demand curve, the scatter of figure 15.2 identifies the supply curve, while the data of figure 15.3 identify neither relationship. This assertion is not necessarily true. In order to be able to say that the data identify the demand or the supply function we need to know the changes in the other factors which determine the supply and demand. Any model (like the one presented above) in which each equation contains the same explanatory variables, is statistically impossible to measure. Demand and supply are determined by many factors other than price. Changes in these factors cause shifts of the curves. We must have information on the shifts of the demand and the supply curves in order to be able to identify the coefficients of these relationships. It can be easily seen that the scatter of figure 15.1 will not identify the demand function, despite the apparent (spurious) high correlation between Q and P, if the observations have been generated by the intersection of shifting demand and supply curves. On figure 15.4 we plot imaginary sample points which represent the intersection of shifting demand and supply curves

Such sample data show a spurious high negative correlation, which is misleading: if we use the sample for estimating the relationship between Q and P that is $Q = f(P)$ we will obtain a high R^2 and a negative b_1, and we will be pretending that we measure the demand function, which obviously is not true. We are

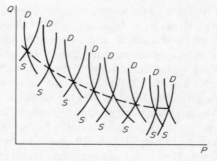

Figure 15.4

measuring a 'mongrel' function, that is, a function which is a mixture of
supply and demand forces, and whose coefficients are really a mixture of the
coefficients of both functions (see below). These spurious results are due to the
omission of 'shift factors', in other words of variables which caused the shift
of the demand and supply functions. If we have information on the shifts of the
demand and supply curves (that is, on the changes of the other determining
factors of demand and supply) we can say which function the data identify. For
example in figure 15.5 we depict observations which show that the demand
curve has remained fairly stable over the sample period, because the other
factors which affect it — income, tastes, other prices — have remained almost
constant, while the supply has been shifting widely due to changes in its other
determinants (for example weather conditions). Such conditions, of fairly stable
demand and widely shifting supply, give rise to observations which identify the
demand function. This is the case with most agricultural products, whose supply
is heavily influenced by weather conditions, while their demand does not shift
much over time (they have low income elasticity of demand and the tastes of
consumers for agricultural products do not change appreciably).

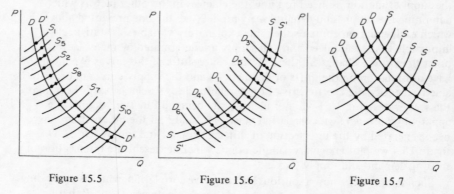

Figure 15.5   Figure 15.6   Figure 15.7

In figure 15.6 the supply is fairly stable while demand shifts within a wide
range, because, say, of changes in tastes, incomes, war conditions. Under such

circumstances the observations generated by the interaction of demand and supply forces trace (identify) the supply function.

Finally, in figure 15.7, both supply and demand are shifting widely so that their interaction gives observations scattered all over the $Q-P$ plane. However, if we know the factors that cause the shifts we may be able to identify both functions, or one of them. For example if D shifts due to income changes and S shifts due to weather conditions we will have the model $D = f(P, Y)$ and $S = f(P, W)$ and both functions can be identified despite the scatter of observations all over the $Q-P$ plane (see below).

The above discussion may be summarised as follows. If we want to measure a given function belonging to a simultaneous-equations model, the function must be fairly stable over the sample period, that is, it must shift within a smaller range as compared with other relationships of the same model: we can measure the demand function if it is fairly stable while the supply function shows adequate variability. This condition is fulfilled if some factors *not included* in the demand function change considerably, causing a shift in the supply (or in other relevant equations). In other words, in order to identify the demand function, some factors *absent* from it but included in the supply function (or in other relations of the system) must be changing over the period of the sample.

Similarly, we can trace the supply function if it is fairly stable while demand shows enough variability. This implies that if the supply function is to be identified, some variables *absent* from it but affecting the demand function must be changing.

This may be called the *paradox of identification*: the identification of a function depends on variables *absent* from it, while at the same time being operative in the other function(s) of the model. We are able to identify a function by what variables *it does not include*.

The above was a diagrammatic presentation of the problem of identification of an econometric model. We may now examine the identification problem regarding a particular function in a more formal way.

A function belonging to a system of simultaneous equations is identified if it has a *unique statistical form*, that is if there is no other equation in the system, or formed by algebraic manipulation of the other equations of the system, which contains the same variables as the function in question. To illustrate this definition let us return to our earlier example of the model of the market mechanism of a certain product

$$D = b_0 + b_1 P + u \qquad (15.1)$$

$$S = a_0 + a_1 P + v \qquad (15.2)$$

$$D = S \qquad (15.3)$$

We want to find out whether the estimates, which we may obtain by using sample data on demand and price can be identified as estimates of the true demand parameters b_0 and b_1. We may substitute S in equation (15.3) and obtain

$$D = a_0 + a_1 P + v \qquad (15.4)$$

We thus have two equations (15.1) and (15.4) of the same statistical form, that is containing the same variables (D and P). However, the first contains the demand parameters (b_0, b_1), while the second contains the supply parameters (a_0, a_1). Regressing D on P with sample data we cannot be sure that the estimates which we will obtain are really the b's or the a's. The demand equation has not a unique statistical form, hence its parameters cannot be statistically identified.

Let us proceed further. By algebraic manipulations we may form an infinite number of equations which have the same statistical form with the demand function. For example multiplying equations (15.1) and (15.4) by k and c (arbitrary constants) respectively we obtain

$$kD = kb_0 + kb_1P + ku$$

$$cD = ca_0 + ca_1P + cv$$

Adding these expressions we obtain

$$(k + c)D = (kb_0 + ca_0) + (kb_1 + ca_1)P + (ku + cv)$$

or
$$D = \left(\frac{kb_0 + ca_0}{k + c}\right) + \left(\frac{kb_1 + ca_1}{k + c}\right) P + \left(\frac{ku + cv}{k + c}\right)$$

Setting

$$A_0 = \frac{kb_0 + ca_0}{k + c} \qquad A_1 = \frac{kb_1 + ca_1}{k + c} \qquad u^* = \frac{ku + cv}{k + c}$$

we may write the above expression in the form

$$D = A_0 + A_1P + u^*$$

This equation contains the same variables as the first equation of the structural model, but its parameters are a mixture (linear combination) of the parameters of the demand function, of the supply function and of the arbitrary constants (k, c). Thus by manipulating the relations of the structural model we obtained a 'bogus' equation, an equation which is neither the supply nor the demand function, but a mixture of both, which, however, has the same statistical form as the demand function. Consequently the demand function is not identified (or, more precisely, the parameters of the demand function are not identified). Under the above circumstances, if we use a sample of actual observations and perform the regression $D = f(P)$ we cannot be sure whether we obtain estimates of the b's, the a's, or of the mixed coefficients A_0 and A_1.

The conclusion from the above discussion is that (a) the identification of a system boils down to the identification of each one of its equations; (b) identification of the parameters of any equation is established if we can prove that its statistical form is unique. There are two formal rules with which we can establish the identification of a relationship. These rules set conditions for the identifiability of a relationship. They are (i) the *order condition* and (ii) the *rank condition* for identification. Before examining formally these conditions we must give some traditional definitions referring to identification.

In econometric theory two possible situations of identifiability are traditionally distinguished:

1. Equation underidentified.
2. Equation identified
   (a) Exactly identified.
   (b) Overidentified.

An equation is underidentified if its statistical form is not unique. *A system* is underidentified when one or more of its equations are underidentified.

If an *equation* has a unique statistical form we say that it is identified. It may be exactly identified or overidentified. But in both cases it is identified. A *system* is identified if *all* its equations are identified.

It should be noted that identification problems arise only for those equations which contain coefficients which must be estimated statistically (from sample data). Identification difficulties do not arise for definitional equations, identities, or statements of equilibrium conditions, because such relationships do not require measurement.

15.2. IMPLICATIONS OF THE IDENTIFICATION STATE OF A MODEL

Identification is closely related to the estimation of the model.

(1) If an equation (or a model) is underidentified it is impossible to estimate all its parameters with any econometric technique.

(2) If an equation is identified, its coefficient can, in general, be statistically estimated. In particular: (a) If the equation is exactly identified, the appropriate method to be used for its estimation is the method of indirect least squares (ILS, see Chapter 16). (b) If the equation is overidentified, indirect least squares cannot be applied, because it will not yield unique estimates of the structural parameters. There are various other methods which can be used in this case, for example two-stage least squares (2SLS), or maximum likelihood methods. These methods will be developed in subsequent chapters.

15.3. FORMAL RULES (CONDITIONS) FOR IDENTIFICATION

Identification may be established either by the examination of the specification of the structural model, or by the examination of the reduced form of the model (see below).

Traditionally identification has been approached via the reduced form. Actually the term 'identification' was originally used to denote the possibility (or impossibility) of deducing the values of the parameters of the structural relations from a knowledge of the reduced-form parameters. (See Johnston, *Econometric Methods,* 2nd ed., pp. 334—75.) In this section we will examine both approaches. However, we think that the reduced form approach is conceptually confusing and computationally more difficult than the structural model approach, because it requires the derivation of the reduced form first and then examination of the values of the determinant formed from some of the reduced form coefficients. The structural form approach is simpler and more useful.

In applying the identification rules we should either ignore the constant term, or, if we want to retain it, we must include in the set of variables a dummy variable (say X_0) which would always take on the value 1. Either convention leads to the same results as far as identification is concerned. In this chapter we will ignore the constant intercept.

15.3.1. ESTABLISHING IDENTIFICATION FROM THE STRUCTURAL FORM OF THE MODEL

We mentioned earlier that there are two conditions which must be fulfilled for an equation to be identified.

1. *The Order Condition for Identification*

This condition is based on a counting rule of the variables included and excluded from the particular equation. It is a necessary but not sufficient condition for the identification of an equation. The order condition may be stated as follows.

For an equation to be identified the total number of variables (endogenous and exogenous) excluded from it must be equal to or greater than the number of endogenous variables in the model less one. Given that in a complete model the number of endogenous variables is equal to the number of equations of the model, the order condition for identification is sometimes stated in the following equivalent form.

For an equation to be identified the total number of variables excluded from it but included in other equations must be at least as great as the number of equations of the system less one.

Let G = total number of equations (= total number of endogenous variables)

K = number of total variables in the model (endogenous and predetermined)

M = number of variables, endogenous and exogenous, included *in a particular equation.*

Then the order condition for identification may be symbolically expressed as

$$
\begin{array}{rcl}
(K - M) & \geqslant & (G - 1) \\
\begin{bmatrix} \text{excluded} \\ \text{variables} \end{bmatrix} & \geqslant & [\text{total number of equations} - 1]
\end{array}
$$

For example, if a system contains 10 equations with 15 variables, ten endogenous and five exogenous, an equation containing 11 variables is not identified, while another containing 5 variables is identified.

(a) For the first equation we have

$$G = 10 \qquad K = 15 \qquad M = 11$$

Order condition:

$$(K - M) \geqslant (G - 1)$$

$$(15 - 11) < (10 - 1)$$

that is, the order condition is not satisfied and the equation is underidentified.

(b) For the second equation we have

$$G = 10 \qquad K = 15 \qquad M = 5$$

Order condition:

$$(K - M) \geqslant (G - 1)$$

$$(15 - 5) > (10 - 1)$$

that is, the order condition is satisfied.

The order condition for identification is necessary for a relation to be identified, but it is not sufficient, that is, it may be fulfilled in any particular equation and yet the relation may not be identified.

2. *The Rank Condition for Identification*

The rank condition states that: *in a system of G equations any particular equation is identified if and only if it is possible to construct at least one non-zero determinant of order* $(G - 1)$ *from the coefficients of the variables excluded from that particular equation but contained in the other equations of the model.*[1]

The practical steps for tracing the identifiability of an equation of a structural model may be outlined as follows.

Firstly. Write the parameters of all the equations of the model in a separate table, noting that the parameter of a variable excluded from an equation is equal to zero.

For example let a structural model be

$$y_1 = 3y_2 - 2x_1 + x_2 + u_1$$

$$y_2 = y_3 + x_3 + u_2$$

$$y_3 = y_1 - y_2 - 2x_3 + u_3$$

where the y's are the endogenous variables and the x's are the predetermined variables.

---

[1] This condition is called rank condition because it refers to the rank of the matrix of parameters of excluded variables. The rank of a matrix is the order of the largest non-zero determinant which can be formed from the matrix. In our case the relevant matrix is the submatrix of coefficients of the absent variables. Hence the rank condition may be also stated as follows: a sufficient condition for identification of a relationship is that the rank of the matrix of parameters of all the excluded variables (endogenous and predetermined) from that equation be equal to $(G - 1)$.

This model may be rewritten in the form

$$-y_1 + 3y_2 + 0y_3 - 2x_1 + x_2 + 0x_3 + u_1 = 0$$

$$0y_1 - y_2 + y_3 + 0x_1 + 0x_2 + x_3 + u_2 = 0$$

$$y_1 - y_2 - y_3 + 0x_1 + 0x_2 - 2x_3 + u_3 = 0$$

Ignoring the random disturbances the table of the parameters of the model is as follows.

Equations	Variables					
	y_1	y_2	y_3	x_1	x_2	x_3
1st equation	−1	3	0	−2	1	0
2nd equation	0	−1	1	0	0	1
3rd equation	1	−1	−1	0	0	−2

Secondly. Strike out the row of coefficients of the equation which is being examined for identification.

For example if we want to examine the identifiability of the second equation of the model we strike out the second row of the table of coefficients.

Thirdly. Strike out the columns in which a non-zero coefficient of the equation being examined appears. By deleting the relevant row and columns we are left with the coefficients of variables *not included* in the particular equation, but contained in the other equations of the model.

For example if we are examining for identification the second equation of the system, we will strike out the second, third and the sixth columns of the above table, thus obtaining the following tables.

Table of structural parameters

	y_1	y_2	y_3	x_1	x_2	x_3
1st	−1	3	0	−2	1	0
2nd	0	−1	1	0	0	1
3rd	1	−1	−1	0	0	−2

Table of parameters of excluded variables

	y_1	x_1	x_2
	−1	−2	1
	1	0	0

Fourthly. Form the determinant(s) of order $(G - 1)$ and examine their value. If at least one of these determinants is non-zero, the equation is identified. If all the determinants of order $(G - 1)$ are zero, the equation is underidentified.

In the above example of exploration of the identifiability of the second structural equation we have three determinants of order $(G - 1) = 3 - 1 = 2$. They are

$$\Delta_1 = \begin{vmatrix} -1 & -2 \\ 1 & 0 \end{vmatrix} \neq 0 \qquad \Delta_2 = \begin{vmatrix} -2 & 1 \\ 0 & 0 \end{vmatrix} = 0 \qquad \Delta_3 = \begin{vmatrix} -1 & 1 \\ 1 & 0 \end{vmatrix} \neq 0$$

(the symbol Δ stands for 'determinant'; see Appendix II) We see that we can form two non-zero determinants of order $G - 1 = 3 - 1 = 2$; hence the second equation of our system is identified.

Fifthly. To see whether the equation is exactly identified or overidentified we use the order condition $(K - M) \geqslant (G - 1)$. With this criterion, if the equality sign is satisfied, that is if $(K - M) = (G - 1)$, the equation is exactly identified. If the inequality sign holds, that is, if $(K - M) > (G - 1)$, the equation is overidentified.

In the case of the second equation we have

$$G = 3 \qquad K = 6 \qquad M = 3$$

and the counting rule $(K - M) \geqslant (G - 1)$ gives

$$(6 - 3) > (3 - 1)$$

Therefore the second equation of the model is overidentified.

The identification of a function is achieved by assuming that some variables of the model have a zero coefficient in this equation, that is, we assume that some variables do not directly affect the dependent variable in this equation. This, however, is an *assumption* which can be tested with the sample data. We will examine some *tests of identifying restrictions* in a subsequent section.

Some examples will illustrate the application of the two formal conditions for identification.

Example 1. Assume that we have a model describing the market of an agricultural product. From the theory of partial equilibrium we know that the price in a market is determined by the forces of demand and supply. The main determinants of the demand are the price of the commodity, the prices of other commodities, incomes and tastes of consumers. Similarly, the most important determinants of the supply are the price of the commodity, other prices, technology, the prices of factors of production, and weather conditions. The equilibrium condition is that demand be equal to supply. The above theoretical information may be expressed in the form of the following mathematical model

$$D = a_0 + a_1 P_1 + a_2 P_2 + a_3 Y + a_4 t + u$$
$$S = b_0 + b_1 P_1 + b_2 P_2 + b_3 C + b_4 t + w$$
$$D = S$$

where
D = quantity demanded
S = quantity supplied
P_1 = price of the given commodity
P_2 = prices of other commodities
Y = income
C = costs (index of prices of factors of production)
t = time trend. In the demand function it stands for 'tastes'; in the supply function it stands for 'technology'.

The above model is mathematically complete in the sense that it contains three equations in three endogenous variables, D, S and P_1. The remaining variables, Y, P_2, C, t are exogenous. Suppose we want to identify the supply function. We apply the two criteria for identification:

1. *Order condition:* $(K - M) \geqslant (G - 1)$
In our example we have

$$K = 7 \qquad M = 5 \qquad G - 3$$

Therefore
$$(K - M) = (G - 1)$$
or
$$(7 - 5) = (3 - 1) = 2$$

Consequently the second equation satisfies the first condition for identification.
2. *Rank condition*
The table of the coefficients of the structural model is as follows.

	Variables						
Equations	D	P_1	P_2	Y	t	S	C
1st equation	-1	a_1	a_2	a_3	a_4	0	0
2nd equation	0	b_1	b_2	0	b_4	-1	b_3
3rd equation	-1	0	0	0	0	1	0

Following the procedure explained earlier we strike out the second row and the second, third, fifth, sixth and seventh columns. Thus we are left with the table of the coefficients of excluded variables:

Complete table of structural   *Table of parameters of variables excluded*
parameters   *from the second equation*

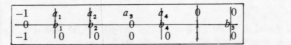

From this table we can form only one non-zero determinant of order $(G - 1) = (3 - 1) = 2$

$$\Delta = \begin{vmatrix} -1 & a_3 \\ -1 & 0 \end{vmatrix} = (0)(-1) - (-1)(a_3) = a_3 .$$

The value of the determinant is non-zero, provided that $a_3 \neq 0$.
We see that both the order and rank conditions are satisfied. Hence the second equation of the model is identified. Furthermore, we see that in the order condition the equality holds: $(7 - 5) = (3 - 1) = 2$. Consequently the second structural equation is *exactly* identified.

Example 2. Assume the following simple version of the Keynesian model of income determination.

Consumption function: $C_t = a_0 + a_1 Y_t - a_2 T_t + u$

Investment function: $I_t = b_0 + b_1 Y_{t-1} + v$

Taxation function: $T_t = c_0 + c_1 Y_t + w$

Definition: $Y_t = C_t + I_t + G_t$

This model is mathematically complete in the sense that it contains as many equations as endogenous variables. There are four endogenous variables, C, I, T, Y, and two predetermined variables, lagged income (Y_{t-1}) and government expenditure (G).

A. *The first equation (consumption function) is not identified*

1. *Order condition:* $(K - M) \geqslant (G - 1)$.

There are six variables in the model ($K = 6$) and four equations ($G = 4$). The consumption function contains three variables ($M = 3$).

$$(K - M) = 3 \qquad \text{and} \qquad (G - 1) = 3$$

Thus $(K - M) = (G - 1)$, which shows that the order condition for identification is satisfied.

2. *Rank condition*

The table of structural coefficients is as follows.

Equations	Variables					
	C	Y	T	I	Y_{t-1}	G
1st equation	-1	a_1	a_2	0	0	0
2nd equation	0	0	0	-1	b_1	0
3rd equation	0	c_1	-1	0	0	0
4th equation	1	-1	0	1	0	1

We strike out the first row and the three first columns of the table and thus obtain the table of coefficients of excluded variables:

Complete table of structural parameters

$$\begin{array}{|cccccc|}
-1 & a_1 & a_2 & 0 & 0 & 0 \\
0 & 0 & 0 & -1 & b_1 & 0 \\
0 & c_1 & -1 & 0 & 0 & 0 \\
1 & -1 & 0 & 1 & 0 & 1
\end{array}$$

Table of coefficients of excluded variables

$$\begin{array}{|ccc|}
-1 & b_1 & 0 \\
0 & 0 & 0 \\
1 & 0 & 1
\end{array}$$

We evaluate the determinant of this table. Clearly the value of this determinant is zero, since the second row contains only zeros (see Appendix II). Consequently we cannot form any nonzero determinant of order $3(= G - 1)$. The rank condition is violated. Hence we conclude that the consumption function is not identified, despite the satisfaction of the order criterion.

B. *The investment function is overidentified*

1. *Order condition*

The investment function includes two variables. Hence

$$K - M = 6 - 2$$

Clearly $(K - M) > (G - 1)$, given that $G - 1 = 3$. The order condition is fulfilled.

2. *Rank condition*

Deleting the second row and the fourth and fifth columns of the structural-coefficients table we obtain

Complete table of structural parameters

$$\begin{array}{|cccccc|}
-1 & a_1 & a_2 & 0 & 0 & 0 \\
0 & 0 & 0 & b_1 & 0 \\
0 & c_1 & -1 & 0 & 0 & 0 \\
1 & -1 & 0 & 1 & 0 & 1
\end{array}$$

Table of coefficients of excluded variables

$$\begin{array}{|cccc|}
-1 & a_1 & a_2 & 0 \\
0 & c_1 & -1 & 0 \\
1 & -1 & 0 & 1
\end{array}$$

The value of the first 3×3 determinant of the parameters of excluded variables is

$$\Delta_1 = -1 \begin{vmatrix} c_1 & -1 \\ -1 & 0 \end{vmatrix} -a_1 \begin{vmatrix} 0 & -1 \\ 1 & 0 \end{vmatrix} +a_2 \begin{vmatrix} 0 & c_1 \\ 1 & -1 \end{vmatrix} = 1 + a_1 - a_2 c_1 \neq 0$$

(provided $a_1 - a_2 c_1 \neq -1$)

The rank condition is satisfied since we can construct at least one non-zero determinant of order $3 = (G - 1)$.

Applying the counting rule $(K - M) \geqslant (G - 1)$ we see that the inequality sign holds: $4 > 3$; hence the investment function is overidentified.

The detection of the identifiability of the tax equation is left to the student as an exercise.

15.3.2 ESTABLISHING IDENTIFICATION FROM THE REDUCED FORM

There are two conditions for identification based on the reduced form of the model, an order condition and a rank condition. The order condition is the same as in the structural model. The rank condition here refers to the value of the determinant formed from some of the reduced form parameters, π's.

1. Order condition (necessary condition), as applied to the reduced form.

An equation belonging to a system of simultaneous equations is identified if

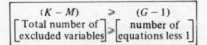

$$(K - M) \geqslant (G - 1)$$
$$\begin{bmatrix} \text{Total number of} \\ \text{excluded variables} \end{bmatrix} \geqslant \begin{bmatrix} \text{number of} \\ \text{equations less 1} \end{bmatrix}$$

where K, M and G have the same meaning as before:

K = total number of variables, endogenous and exogenous, in the entire model

M = number of variables, endogenous and exogenous, in any particular equation

G = number of structural equations = number of all endogenous variables in the model.

If $(K - M) = (G - 1)$, the equation is exactly identified, provided that the rank condition set out below is also satisfied. If $(K - M) > (G - 1)$, the equation is overidentified, while if $(K - M) < (G - 1)$, the equation is underidentified, under the same proviso.

2. Rank condition as applied to the reduced form.

Let G^* stand for the number of endogenous variables contained in a particular equation. The rank condition as applied to the reduced form may be stated as follows.

An equation containing G^* endogenous variables is identified if and only if it is possible to construct at least one non-zero determinant of order $G^* - 1$ from the reduced form coefficients of *the exogenous* (predetermined) *variables excluded* from that particular equation.

The practical steps involved in this method of identification may be outlined as follows.

Firstly. Obtain the reduced form of structural model. For example assume that the original model is

$$y_1 = b_{12} y_2 + \gamma_{11} x_1 + \gamma_{12} x_2 + u_1$$

$$y_2 = b_{23} y_3 + \gamma_{23} x_3 + u_2$$

$$y_3 = b_{31} y_1 + b_{32} y_3 + \gamma_{33} x_3 + u_3$$

This model is complete in the sense that it contains three equations in three endogenous variables. The model contains altogether six variables, three endogenous (y_1, y_2, y_3) and three exogenous (x_1, x_2, x_3).

The reduced form of the model is obtained by solving the original equations for the exogenous variables. The reduced form in the above example is

$$y_1 = \pi_{11}x_1 + \pi_{12}x_2 + \pi_{13}x_3 + v_1$$

$$y_2 = \pi_{21}x_1 + \pi_{22}x_2 + \pi_{23}x_3 + v_2$$

$$y_3 = \pi_{31}x_1 + \pi_{32}x_2 + \pi_{33}x_3 + v_3$$

where the π's are functions of the structural parameters.

Secondly. Form the complete table of the reduced form coefficients.

	Exogenous variables		
Equations	x_1	x_2	x_3
1st equation: y_1	π_{11}	π_{12}	π_{13}
2nd equation: y_2	π_{21}	π_{22}	π_{23}
3rd equation: y_3	π_{31}	π_{32}	π_{33}

Strike out the *rows* corresponding to *endogenous variables excluded* from the particular equation being examined for identifiability.

Also strike out all the *columns* referring to *exogenous variables included* in the structural form of the particular equation.

After these deletions we are left with the reduced form coefficients of exogenous variables excluded (absent) from the structural equation.

For example assume that we are investigating the identifiability of the second equation. The reduced form coefficients relevant to the identification procedure are found by striking out the first row (since y_1 does not appear in the second equation) and the third column (since x_3 is included in this equation).

Complete table of reduced-form coefficients

π_{11}	π_{12}	π_{13}
π_{21}	π_{22}	π_{23}
π_{31}	π_{32}	π_{33}

Table of reduced form coefficients of excluded *exogenous variables*

π_{21}	π_{22}
π_{31}	π_{32}

Thirdly. Examine the order of the determinants of the π's of excluded exogenous variables and evaluate them. If the order of the largest non-zero determinant is $G^* - 1$, the equation is identified. Otherwise the equation is not identified.

Numerical example. Assume that a structural model is of the form

$$y_1 = 3y_2 - 2x_1 + x_2 + u_1$$

$$y_2 = y_3 + x_3 + u_2$$

$$y_3 = y_1 - y_2 - 2x_3 + u_3$$

We will examine the identification of each structural equation using the reduced-form approach.

The reduced form of the structural model is

$$y_1 = \pi_{11}x_1 + \pi_{12}x_2 + \pi_{13}x_3 = 4x_1 - 2x_2 + 3x_3$$

$$y_2 = \pi_{21}x_1 + \pi_{22}x_2 + \pi_{23}x_3 = 2x_1 - x_2 + x_3$$

$$y_3 = \pi_{31}x_1 + \pi_{32}x_2 + \pi_{33}x_3 = 2x_1 - x_2$$

First equation: $y_1 = 3y_2 - 2x_1 + x_2 + u_1$

1. *Order condition:* $(K - M) \geqslant (G - 1)$

                                         $K = 6$ $M = 4$ $G = 3$

so that $(K - M) = (G - 1)$

or $(6 - 4) = (3 - 1)$

Thus the equation satisfies the necessary condition for identification.

2. *Rank condition*
Excluded endogenous variables: y_3
Included exogenous variables: x_1, x_2

<table>
<tr><td>Table of all reduced
form coefficients</td><td></td><td></td><td></td><td>Table of π's of excluded
exogenous variables</td></tr>
</table>

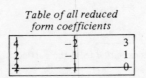

4	−2	3
2	−1	1
2	−1	0

3
1

From the table of π's of excluded exogenous variables we can form two non-zero determinants of order 1×1.

Now $G^* = 2$, since the first equation contains two endogenous variables. Thus the order of the determinant of π's relating to excluded X's is one:

$$(G^* - 1) = 1$$

The rank condition is satisfied and the equation is identified. Furthermore, by virtue of the order condition we see that the first equation is exactly identified since the equality sign holds for this condition (that is $K - M = G - 1$).

Second equation: $\ddot{y}_2 = y_3 + x_3 + u_2$

1. *Order condition*

                                         $K = 6$ $M = 3$ $G = 3$

Thus $(K - M) > (G - 1)$

or $(6 - 3) > (3 - 1)$

Thus the order condition is satisfied.

2. *Rank condition*
Excluded endogenous variables: y_1
Included exogenous variables: x_3

Table of all π's			*Table of π's of excluded exogenous variables*	
4	−2	3		
2	−1	1	2	−1
2	−1	0	2	−1

The order of the determinant of π's of the excluded exogenous variables is 2×2; however its value is zero:

$$\Delta = \begin{vmatrix} 2 & -1 \\ 2 & -1 \end{vmatrix} = 0$$

Hence the highest non-zero determinant which we may form from the π's is 1×1.
The second equation contains two endogenous variables, that is $G^* = 2$.
Therefore the order of highest non-zero determinant is $G^* - 1 = 1$.
Consequently the second equation is identified. Furthermore, using the order condition $(6 - 3) > (3 - 1)$ we conclude that the second structural equation is overidentified.

Third equation: $y_3 = y_1 - y_2 - 2x_3 + u_3$.

1. Order condition

$$K = 6 \qquad M = 4 \qquad G = 3$$

so that
$$(K - M) = (G - 1)$$

or
$$(6 - 4) = (3 - 1)$$

The order condition is satisfied
2. Rank condition
Excluded endogenous variables: none
Included exogenous variables: x_3

Table of all π's

$$\begin{vmatrix} 4 & -2 & 3 \\ 2 & -1 & 1 \\ 2 & -1 & 0 \end{vmatrix}$$

Table of π's of excluded exogenous variables

$$\begin{vmatrix} 4 & -2 \\ 2 & -1 \\ 2 & -1 \end{vmatrix}$$

The highest non-zero determinant is of order 1×1, since,

$$\Delta = \begin{vmatrix} 4 & -2 \\ 2 & -1 \end{vmatrix} = 0 \qquad \text{and} \qquad \Delta = \begin{vmatrix} 2 & -1 \\ 2 & -1 \end{vmatrix} = 0$$

The equation contains three endogenous variables, that is $G^* = 3$.
Hence (order of largest non-zero determinant) $< (G^* - 1)$.
The rank condition is not satisfied and therefore the third equation is not identified, despite the fulfilment of the first condition for identification.

15.4. IDENTIFYING RESTRICTIONS

In many cases an investigator is interested in only one (or a few) of the equations of the model and attempts to measure its parameters statistically without a complete knowledge of the entire model. Under these circumstances identification of the relationship cannot be established by the application of the above formal rules, because the structure of the model is not known. Customarily then identification is established by making one of the following assumptions, or identifying restrictions.

A. Imposition of restrictions on the values of the parameters of some variables.

Such restrictions may be of the form of:
   (1) Zero restrictions.
   (2) Equality restrictions, or other linear relationships between some of the
       parameters.
   (3) Extraneous estimates of some parameters.
   B. Imposition of restrictions concerning the relative variances of the random
variables of the various equations of the model.
   Of the above identifying restrictions the most important and most widely
used are the restrictions on the values of the structural parameters.

15.4.1. CONSTRAINTS ON THE VALUES OF THE STRUCTURAL PARAMETERS

1. *Zero restrictions*
   Imposing a zero restriction on the value of a parameter in a particular function
means that the variable to which the parameter refers does not appear in this
function.
   A priori knowledge usually enables the investigator to decide that some
coefficients must be zero in the particular function, while they assume non-
zero values in other equations of the system. We said that identification of a
statistical function is based on variables not included (not appearing) in it. To be
identifiable a function must be independent of one or more *important* variables
which are included in other equations of the system. Such excluded variables, if
operative during the sample period, will generate shifts in the other equations of
the model which will identify the particular function from which they are absent
(i.e. in which they appear with zero coefficient).
   On the basis of *a priori* information the investigator should make a list,
which should be as complete as possible, of the factors which are relevant to the
phenomenon being studied and decide which of these factors would normally
appear in each relationship. For example assume we want to study the demand
of an agricultural product. The demand function belongs to a system of equations
describing the market mechanism. The factors relevant to this model and their
appearance or exclusion from the demand and supply functions are shown in
table 15.1.
   From this *a priori* information it is clear that there are several 'shift' factors in
the supply function which do not affect (do not appear in) the demand function.
This suggests that the demand function, in which we are interested is identified.
Imposition of the restriction of some coefficients being equal to zero in the
demand function assists in the investigation of the identifiability of this function.
   One might argue that one can always 'render' an equation identified by
imposing zero restrictions: one can always *think* of some factors which do not
appear in a particular function while they are, at the same time, included in other
equations of the model. However, there are tests for the identifying restrictions
(explained in a subsequent section) which restrict the freedom of the investigator
and prevent the abuse of unjustified restrictions on the values of the parameters.

Table 15.1. *A priori* information on the demand for commodity x.

Variables		Determinants of demand	Determinants of supply
Price of x	P	P	P
Lagged price	P_{t-1}	–	P_{t-1}
Other prices	P_o	P_o	–
Income	Y	Y	–
Weather	W	–	W
Stocks	S	–	S
Tastes	t	t	–
Income distribution	V	V	–
Population	N	N	–
Technology	T	–	T
Factor prices	C	–	C

Identification should not be cheaply achieved by assuming that some unimportant variables are included in other equations. The researcher must be sure that the identifying variables contribute substantially to the explanation of the variation of other endogenous variables: one must be able to defend identification of a function by 'adding' to another function(s) significant factors which were previously mistakenly ignored.

2. *Restrictions on the relative values (or on the relationship) of two or more parameters*

If an equation is underidentified it is not possible to uniquely estimate all its parameters. However, *a priori* information may again provide assistance. From such information the researcher is usually able to define the relationship among some of the parameters. For example it may be possible to establish *a priori:*

(a) The sum of some parameters; for example $b_1 + b_2 = c$, where c is a constant. For example in their original formulation of the production function Cobb and Douglas assumed constant returns to scale which enabled them to set $b_1 + b_2 = 1$ in their model: $X = b_0 L^{b_1} K^{b_2}$. With this restriction the function may be written as $(X/K) = b_0 (L/K)^{b_1}$.

(b) The equality of some parameters; for example in a model containing two consumption functions (one for the agricultural sector and one for the urban areas), one may impose the restriction that the coefficients of income are different while the coefficients of liquid assets are equal in the two functions. Similarly, in our example on page 356, the consumption function will be identified if we impose the restriction $a_1 = a_2$, in which case the function could be written as $C = a_0 + a_1(Y - T) + u$.

(c) The ratio of some parameters; $b_1/b_2 = k$, where k is a constant, and so on.

3. *Extraneous estimates*

If some parameters are identified, while others are not and there exists information on their value from other (extraneous) sources, the researcher may proceed with the estimation of the identified coefficients and use the extraneously known value for the non-identified ones.

15.4.2. RESTRICTIONS ON THE RELATIVE VARIANCES OF THE RANDOM VARIABLES OF THE EQUATIONS

In some cases the investigator may be able on *a priori* information to specify which one of the equations of the model is likely to show wider random variation as compared with other equations. For example in the case of many agricultural products the supply is subject to wide random fluctuations due to weather conditions, while their demand is fairly stable over time. The market data on quantity and price would, under such conditions, identify the demand function. The model would be

$$D = a_0 + a_1 P + u$$
$$S = b_0 + b_1 P + v$$
$$D = S$$
$$\text{var}(u) < \text{var}(v)$$

This situation would portray the data as having been generated by the supply curve shifting along the demand curve which would have remained roughly stable (figure 15.5).

In general, knowledge of the conditions of the particular phenomenon may provide *a priori* information which would enable the researcher to impose restrictions on the relative size of the variances of the random variables of the equations of the system. However, the error terms are defined by so many unknown and complex forces, that assumptions concerning their variances would usually be highly arbitrary

15.4.3. NOTE ON THE APPLICABILITY OF THE RANK AND ORDER CONDITIONS

It should be stressed that the above theory of identification is applicable to models which are linear in variables and parameters. However, in the real economic world many models may well be expected to be nonlinear in variables and/or *a priori* restrictions. In general the rank and order conditions as stated earlier are *not* applicable to such nonlinear models.

The theory of identification of nonlinear models is not as yet satisfactorily developed, and it will not be presented here. The interested reader is referred to F. M. Fisher's systematic treatise *The Identification Problem in Econometrics*, McGraw-Hill, 1966. An elementary discussion of some simple cases is included in C. F. Christ's *Econometric Models and Methods*, chap. 8, Wiley, 1966.

15.5. TESTS FOR IDENTIFYING RESTRICTIONS

In applied econometric work researchers usually impose zero restrictions on the parameters of some variables, that is, they exclude such variables from the function whose identification they want to 'establish'. This procedure does not necessarily secure identifiability. Identification is established if (a) the coefficients of some variables are zero in the particular equation, and (b) the coefficients of the same variables are non-zero in other equations of the system.

One might think that condition (a) could be tested by applying the test of significance of additional regressors described in Chapter 8 (pp. 158–64). However, the simultaneous interdependence of the various equations of the model renders this procedure invalid.

Systematic tests for identifying restrictions have been developed by Hood and Koopmans[1] and by Basmann.[2] These tests are cumbersome and of limited applicability. Certainly their examination goes beyond the scope of an introductory textbook.

15.6. IDENTIFICATION AND MULTICOLLINEARITY

Identification and multicollinearity have several common features.

1. Both multicollinearity and identification create estimation problems. Identifiability and absence of strong multicollinearity are necessary prerequisites for the estimation of a model, but not for the theoretical validity of the model, which is judged by the ability of the model to describe adequately the economic relationships to which it refers. Theoretical plausibility is a matter of correct specification of the model: specification of its variables and its mathematical form. It does not depend on identifiability or on the collinearity of the explanatory variables. A model may be theoretically plausible despite any difficulties in obtaining numerical values for its parameters from sample data. Or, to put the matter another way, estimation difficulties do not render a model implausible. For example the theoretical model of income determination includes a consumption function of the form

$$C = f(Y, L)$$

where Y = income and L = liquid assets.

If Y and L are strongly correlated, the structural coefficients cannot be correctly estimated (see Chapter 11). Similarly, if over the sample period Y has remained fairly constant, we cannot measure from the sample data the MPC. Such estimation difficulties do not impair the theoretical validity of the consumption function. Actually adoption of some of the corrective actions (suggested above for identifiability and in Chapter 11 for multicollinearity) in order to by-pass the estimation difficulties created by strong collinearity of the explanatory variables or by underidentification, may result in a model which is theoretically less plausible than its original form.

2. In both cases, of underidentification and of multicollinearity, there are too many relationships between the variables of the model which do not permit

[1] Hood and T. C. Koopmans, editors, *Studies in Econometric Method,* Wiley, New York, 1953, pp. 178–83.
[2] R. L. Basmann, 'On Finite Sample Distributions of Generalized Classical Linear Identifiability Tests Statistics', *J. Am. Statist. Ass.,* vol. 55, 1960.

adequate independent variation of the variables, with the result that their separate influence on the endogenous variables cannot be disentangled and statistically assessed.

3. Multicollinearity may be viewed as a special case of underidentification or of weak identifiability. If some variables are strongly multicollinear they are practically the same from the statistical point of view: either variable can be used as a proxy for the other. Such multicollinear variables cannot serve as two distinctly separate variables. If identification is established on the basis of excluded variables which are multicollinear, identifiability should be viewed with some suspicion: we might have a case of spurious identification.

4. The conditions for identification are strictly algebraic and apply to the parameters in the structural system. These conditions must be satisfied by the structural model. However, not all identified systems can be statistically estimated, due to data deficiencies. For example, the sample may be small relative to the number of parameters which one wants to estimate.

Clearly identification and multicollinearity are closely related.

15.7. IDENTIFICATION AND CHOICE OF ECONOMETRIC METHOD

Identification determines basically the choice of the technique by which the model will be statistically estimated.

(a) If a relationship is underidentified its parameters cannot be statistically estimated by any econometric technique.

(b) If a relationship is exactly identified the most appropriate method of estimation is the indirect least squares (ILS) method (see Chapter 16).

(c) If an equation is overidentified the method of ILS cannot be applied because it does not give unique estimates of the structural parameters. There are various econometric techniques which may be applied for the estimation of overidentified relationships. These methods and the problem of choosing among them will be examined in later chapters.

In most applied research the estimated relationships are assumed to be overidentified. Exact identification is rather a rare situation. Under such conditions one has to choose among the alternative estimation methods available for overidentified functions (see Chapter 21).

However, some writers have taken the opposite view, namely that economic relationships are in almost all cases underidentified: too many variables are excluded from each function for various reasons (lack of data, incomplete information, etc.). The excluded variables should really be present in the function for correct specification. Thus, the argument runs, identification is spurious in most cases, established on wrong specification of variables included and excluded from the relationships. Under these conditions one should not attempt to obtain accurate and correct values of individual structural coefficients. The most one could do is to obtain the reduced form coefficients and use them for prediction.

This latter view has been adopted by Liu.[1] We will examine again the various views about the identifiability of economic relationships in Chapter 21.

EXERCISES

1. Examine the identification state of the following models of income determination.

(a) $C = a_0 + a_1 Y_d + u_1$

$I = b_0 + b_1 r + b_2 Y_{t-1} + u_2$

$Y_d = Y - T$

$T = \bar{T}$

$Y = C + I + \bar{G}$

(endogenous variables: C, I, Y)

(b) $C = a_0 + a_1 Y + a_2 T + u_1$

$I = b_0 + b_1 r + b_2 Y_{t-1} + u_2$

$M_D = c_0 + c_1 r + c_2 Y + c_3 L + u_3$

$M_D = \bar{M}_S$

$Y = C + I + \bar{G}$

(endogenous variables: C, I, r, Y)

where r = interest rate, L = liquid assets, M_D = demand for money, M_S = supply of money.

2. Establish the identification state of the following market models

(a) $Q_d = b_0 + b_1 P + u_1$

$Q_s = a_0 + a_1 P + a_2 P_{t-1} + u_2$

$Q_d = Q_s$

(b) $Q_d = b_0 + b_1 P + b_2 Y + u_1$

$Q_s = a_0 + a_1 P + a_2 P_{t-1} + u_2$

$Q_d = Q_s$

3. Derive the reduced form of the models 1(a) and 2(a) and establish the identification state by applying the relevant rules on the reduced forms.

4. Suggest ways for rendering any unidentified model exactly identified.

5. (a) What do you understand by an identification problem? Illustrate your answer with examples of your own.

(b) State the formal identifiability rules, with reference to your examples.

(c) What are the implications of the state of identification of a model for choice of estimation method?

[1] T. C. Liu, 'Underidentification, Structural Estimation and Forecasting', *Econometrica*, vol. 28, 1960, pp. 855–65.

6. Let a model consist of the following equations

$$y_1 = 4y_2 - 3x_1 + u_1$$
$$y_2 = 2y_3 + 2x_3 + u_2$$
$$y_3 = 2y_1 - 3y_2 - x_2 - x_3 + u_3$$

Establish for each equation whether it is exactly identified, overidentified or underidentified.

7. Are economic relationships likely on *a priori* grounds to be generally over-identified or underidentified?

8. Discuss critically Liu's view that economic models are in general under-identified. What are the implications of this view?

9. Given the simple Keynesian model of income determination

$$C_t = a_0 + a_1 Y_t + u_1$$

$$I_t = b_0 + b_1 Y_t + b_2 Y_{t-1} + u_2$$

$$Y_t = C_t + I_t + G_t$$

(a)   Derive the reduced form coefficients of the behavioural equations.
(b)   Show that the reduced-form parameters measure the *total effect*, direct and indirect, of a change in the exogenous variable on the endogenous variables. Use as an example the reduced form of the above investment function.
(c)   Establish the identification state of each of the behavioural equations, using the order and rank conditions.
(d)   What is the identification state of the entire model?
(e)   What estimation method is appropriate for each of the behavioural equations?
(f)   Show under what conditions could the system become exactly identified.

Note. Additional exercises are included in Appendix III.

16. Simultaneous-equation Methods

16.1. THE REDUCED-FORM METHOD OR INDIRECT LEAST SQUARES

16.1.1. THE METHOD

The reduced form method is a single-equation method in that it is applied to one equation of a system at a time. It is appropriate when the equations of the structural system contain both predetermined and endogenous variables among the set of explanatory variables, *provided that the equations of the system are exactly identified.*

The reduced-form method, which is also known as indirect least squares method (ILS) may be outlined as follows.

Step I. We first obtain the reduced form of the structural model by rewriting the equations in such a way that the endogenous variables are expressed as a function of the predetermined variables only. Thus in the reduced form the explanatory variables are truly exogenous or lagged values of the endogenous variables, and hence the situation of joint determination (two-way causation) of the variables appearing in a single equation is avoided.

Step II. Provided that the other usual assumptions about the disturbance term of the reduced-form equations are satisfied, we apply ordinary least squares to each equation of the reduced-form system and we obtain estimates of the reduced form coefficients. These coefficients are conventionally denoted by the Greek letter π, and are a mixture of the coefficients of the structural model (see Chapter 14). The relationships between the π's and the structural parameters, β's and γ's, form a system of equations in which the reduced-form coefficients are expressed as functions of the structural parameters. The system of relationships between the structural β's and γ's and the reduced-form π's may be called *system of coefficients' relationships.*

Step III. The final step of the indirect least squares method consists of using the estimates of the reduced form coefficients, π's, obtained in the previous stage, and solving the 'system of coefficients' relationships' for the structural parameters. These estimates will be unique, if the structural model is exactly identified.

To illustrate the application of the indirect least squares we will take an example from the theory of price determination. Assume that the market mechanism of a given commodity is described by the following system of simultaneous equations

$$D = a_0 + a_1 P + a_2 Y + u_1 \tag{16.1}$$

$$S = b_0 + b_1 P + b_2 W + u_2 \tag{16.2}$$

$$D = S \tag{16.3}$$

369

where D = quantity demanded, S = quantity supplied, P = price, Y = income, W = index of weather conditions.

This is the structural model which is mathematically complete in the sense that it contains three equations in three endogenous variables (D, S, P). The system contains two exogenous variables, income Y, and weather conditions W. The system is exactly identified since it can be shown that each behavioural equation is exactly identified (see Chapter 15).

The reduced-form model, in which the endogenous variables are expressed as a function of the exogenous variables only, may be obtained by continuous substitutions (see Chapter 14). It is

$$D = \frac{a_0 b_1 - a_1 b_0}{b_1 - a_1} + \frac{a_2 b_1}{b_1 - a_1} Y + \frac{-a_1 b_2}{b_1 - a_1} W + v_1 \qquad \left(\text{where } v_1 = \frac{u_1 b_1 - v_2 a_1}{b_1 - a_1}\right)$$

$$P = \frac{a_0 - b_0}{b_1 - a_1} + \frac{a_2}{b_1 - a_1} Y + \frac{-b_2}{b_1 - a_1} W + v_2 \qquad \left(\text{where } v_2 = \frac{u_1 - u_2}{b_1 - a_1}\right)$$

Using the conventional notation of π's for the reduced-form coefficients, we have

$$D = \pi_{10} + \pi_{11} Y + \pi_{12} W + v_1$$

$$P = \pi_{20} + \pi_{21} Y + \pi_{22} W + v_2$$

where it can be shown that

$$\pi_{10} = \frac{a_0 b_1 - a_1 b_0}{b_1 - a_1} \qquad \pi_{11} = \frac{a_2 b_1}{b_1 - a_1} \qquad \pi_{12} = \frac{-a_1 b_2}{b_1 - a_1}$$

$$\pi_{20} = \frac{a_0 - b_0}{b_1 - a_1} \qquad \pi_{21} = \frac{a_2}{b_1 - a_1} \qquad \pi_{22} = \frac{-b_2}{b_1 - a_1}$$

Using sample data on D, P, Y, W we may apply OLS to the reduced-form equations (taking one at a time) and obtain estimates of the π's.

We next substitute the $\hat{\pi}$'s into the system of coefficients' relationships and obtain

$$a_0 = \pi_{20}\left(\frac{\pi_{10}}{\pi_{20}} - \frac{\pi_{12}}{\pi_{22}}\right) \qquad b_0 = \pi_{20}\left(\frac{\pi_{10}}{\pi_{20}} - \frac{\pi_{11}}{\pi_{21}}\right)$$

$$a_1 = \frac{\pi_{12}}{\pi_{22}} \qquad b_1 = \frac{\pi_{11}}{\pi_{21}}$$

$$a_2 = \pi_{21}\left(\frac{\pi_{11}}{\pi_{21}} - \frac{\pi_{12}}{\pi_{22}}\right) \qquad b_2 = \pi_{22}\left(\frac{\pi_{12}}{\pi_{22}} - \frac{\pi_{11}}{\pi_{21}}\right)$$

Since the structural equations are exactly identified the equations describing the relations between the b's and the π's will give unique values for the b's. In our example the 'system of coefficients' relationships' contains six equations in six unknowns, which are the structural coefficients $a_0, a_1, a_2, b_0, b_1, b_2$. Solving the system we obtain estimates of the structural parameters.

The asymptotic variances and covariances of the structural estimates may be derived from that of the reduced-form estimates by use of the general formulae for asymptotic variances and covariances of functions of random variables. (See A. Goldberger, *Econometric Theory*, pp. 327–34.)

Numerical example. The data relevant for the estimation of the structural coefficients of the model describing the market mechanism of commodity x are given in table 16.1.

Table 16.1. Data for the estimation of the market model

Observations	Y_1 Demand = Supply (Q in tons)	Y_2 Price (P) £ per ton	X_1 Income (Y) £m	X_2 Weather (index of rainfall) (W)
1	12,917	2,260	1,089	100
2	17,920	2,150	1,169	110
3	18,475	1,970	1,281	110
4	28,180	1,620	1,335	112
5	26,330	1,380	1,388	105
6	31,029	1,200	1,452	107
7	41,430	1,310	1,516	110
8	48,924	1,080	1,536	100
9	52,739	1,180	1,558	105
10	55,009	1,390	1,587	105
11	50,100	1,340	1,625	98
12	67,559	1,350	1,693	105
13	61,986	1,360	1,774	95
14	55,986	1,250	1,826	88
15	60,311	1,210	1,899	95

We apply ordinary least squares to the first of the reduced-form equations

$$D = \pi_{10} + \pi_{11} Y + \pi_{12} W + v_1$$

and obtain

$$\hat{\pi}_{10} = -108,849 \cdot 81 \qquad \hat{\pi}_{11} = 77 \cdot 47 \qquad \hat{\pi}_{12} = 325 \cdot 15 \qquad R^2 = 0 \cdot 875$$

We next apply ordinary least squares to the second of the reduced-form equations

$$P = \pi_{20} + \pi_{21} Y + \pi_{22} W + v_2$$

and obtain the estimates

$$\hat{\pi}_{20} = 5,491 \cdot 09 \qquad \hat{\pi}_{21} = -1 \cdot 54 \qquad \hat{\pi}_{22} = -16 \cdot 38 \qquad R^2 = 0 \cdot 676$$

We substitute these estimates into the 'system of coefficients' relationships' and obtain the estimates of the structural parameters

$$\hat{a}_0 = 5{,}491 \left(\frac{-108{,}849}{5{,}491} - \frac{325 \cdot 15}{-16 \cdot 38} \right) \approx 149 \cdot 19$$

$$\hat{a}_1 = \frac{325 \cdot 15}{-16.38} = -19 \cdot 85$$

$$\hat{a}_2 = -1 \cdot 54 \left(\frac{77 \cdot 47}{-1 \cdot 54} - \frac{325 \cdot 15}{-16 \cdot 38} \right) \approx 46 \cdot 90$$

$$\hat{b}_0 = 5{,}491 \left(\frac{-108{,}849}{5{,}491} - \frac{77 \cdot 47}{-1 \cdot 54} \right) \approx 167{,}376$$

$$\hat{b}_1 = \frac{77 \cdot 47}{-1 \cdot 54} = -50 \cdot 31$$

$$\hat{b}_2 = -16 \cdot 38 \left(\frac{325 \cdot 15}{-16 \cdot 38} - \frac{17 \cdot 47}{-1 \cdot 54} \right) = 498 \cdot 9$$

16.1.2. THE ASSUMPTIONS OF THE REDUCED-FORM METHOD

The method of indirect least squares is based on the following assumptions.

Firstly. The structural equations must be exactly identified. We said in Chapter 15 that if the equations of the structural system are not identified it is impossible to obtain estimates for all its parameters. One can still estimate the reduced form of an underidentified system and use the $\hat{\pi}$'s for forecasting and policy formulation, but one cannot obtain estimates of the structural parameters: the 'system of coefficients' relationships' will contain less equations than the number of unknown structural parameters; hence the system has no solution. If the structural system is overidentified the application of the reduced-form method will not give unique estimates of the coefficients: the 'system of coefficients' relationships' will contain more equations than the number of the unknown structural parameters.

Secondly. The random variable of the reduced-form equation must satisfy the six stochastic assumptions of ordinary least squares. This is so because this method is applied to the reduced-form equations in order to obtain estimates of the π's. The random variable v of the reduced-form equations, which is a linear combination of the random variables of the structural model (u's) and the structural parameters, must have the following properties:

(1) v is random
(2) v has zero mean, $E(v_i) = 0$
(3) v has constant variance, $E(v_i^2) = \sigma_v^2$
(4) v is serially independent, $E(v_i v_j) = 0$ (for $i \neq j$)
(5) v is normally distributed, $v \sim N(0, \sigma_v^2)$
(6) v is independent of the exogenous variables of the model, $E(v_i X_j) = 0$.

If the above stochastic assumptions are satisfied, the estimates of the reduced-form parameters ($\hat{\pi}$'s) are best, linear, unbiased. If these assumptions are not fulfilled, the $\hat{\pi}$'s will have some error which will be transmitted to the estimates of the structural parameters, $\hat{b}$'s, or to their standard errors.

Thirdly. The exogenous variables of the model must not be perfectly collinear.

Fourthly. The macro-variables must be properly aggregated.

From the above it should be clear that the ILS method is based on all the assumptions of OLS and on the additional one that the model be exactly identified.

16.1.3. PROPERTIES OF THE ESTIMATES ($\hat{b}$'s) OBTAINED FROM THE METHOD OF INDIRECT LEAST SQUARES

We said that if the assumptions of ILS are fulfilled the estimates of the reduced-form coefficients ($\hat{\pi}$'s will) be best, linear, unbiased. However, the estimates of the structural parameters, ($\hat{b}$'s) obtained from these optimal $\hat{\pi}$'s, are biased for small samples but they are consistent, that is their bias tends to zero as the size of the sample increases and their distribution collapses on the true parameter b, while the OLS estimates are inconsistent.

Proof. Assume the following simple Keynesian model:

$$C = b_0 + b_1 Y + u$$
$$Y = C + Z$$

where Z is exogenous (e.g. autonomous investment and government expenditure).

The reduced form of this model is

$$C = \frac{b_0}{1 - b_1} + \frac{b_1}{1 - b_1} Z + \frac{u}{1 - b_1}$$

$$Y = \frac{b_0}{1 - b_1} + \frac{1}{1 - b_1} Z + \frac{u}{1 - b_1}$$

The equations of the means are

$$\bar{C} = \frac{b_0}{1 - b_1} + \frac{b_1}{1 - b_1} \bar{Z} + \frac{\bar{u}}{1 - b_1}$$

and

$$\bar{Y} = \frac{b_0}{1 - b_1} + \frac{1}{1 - b_1} \bar{Z} + \frac{\bar{u}}{1 - b_1}$$

Subtracting the mean expressions from the original ones we obtain the reduced-form model in deviations from the means

$$(C - \bar{C}) = \frac{b_1}{1 - b_1} (Z - \bar{Z}) + \frac{1}{1 - b_1} (u - \bar{u})$$

$$(Y - \bar{Y}) = \frac{1}{1 - b_1} (Z - \bar{Z}) + \frac{1}{1 - b_1} (u - \bar{u})$$

or, using lower case letters for the deviations

$$c = \frac{b_1}{1 - b_1} \, z + \frac{1}{1 - b_1} \, (u - \bar{u})$$

$$y = \frac{1}{1 - b_1} \, z + \frac{1}{1 - b_1} \, (u - \bar{u})$$

Hence
$$c = \pi_{11} z + v.$$

where
$$\pi_{11} = \frac{b_1}{1 - b_1} \quad \text{and} \quad v = \frac{1}{1 - b_1} \, (u - \bar{u})$$

Applying least squares to the reduced form of the consumption function we have

$$\hat{\pi}_{11} = \frac{\Sigma cz}{\Sigma z^2}$$

where

$$z = Z - \bar{Z} \quad \text{and} \quad c = C - \bar{C}$$

Given that $\pi_{11} = b_1/(1 - b_1)$, we obtain, by substituting

$$\frac{\Sigma zc}{\Sigma z^2} = \frac{b_1^*}{1 - b_1^*}$$

(where b_1^* = the ILS estimate of the true b_1)

or
$$b_1^* = \frac{\Sigma cz}{\Sigma z^2 + \Sigma cz}$$

But from the definitional equation of income we have

$$Y = C + Z$$

and
$$y = c + z$$

Multiplying through by z and summing over all sample observations we obtain

$$\Sigma yz = \Sigma cz + \Sigma z^2$$

Thus, substituting in the formula for b_1^*, we find

$$b_1^* = \frac{\Sigma cz}{\Sigma yz}$$

Substituting

$$c = C - \bar{C} = \frac{b_1}{1 - b_1} \, (Z - \bar{Z}) + \frac{1}{1 - b_1} \, (u - \bar{u})$$

and

$$y = Y - \bar{Y} = \frac{1}{1 - b_1} \, (Z - \bar{Z}) + \frac{1}{1 - b_1} \, (u - \bar{u})$$

we obtain

$$b_1^* = \frac{\Sigma\{[b_1/(1-b_1)](Z-\bar{Z})^2 + [1/(1-b_1)]/(Z-\bar{Z})(u-\bar{u})\}}{\Sigma\{[1/(1-b_1)](Z-\bar{Z})^2 + [1/(1-b_1)]/(Z-\bar{Z})(u-\bar{u})\}}$$

$$= \frac{[1/(1-b_1)][b_1\Sigma(Z-\bar{Z})^2 + \Sigma(Z-\bar{Z})(u-\bar{u})]}{[1/(1-b_1)][\Sigma(Z-\bar{Z})^2 + \Sigma(Z-\bar{Z})(u-\bar{u})]}$$

$$= \frac{b_1\Sigma z^2 + \Sigma zu}{\Sigma z^2 + \Sigma zu} = \frac{b_1\dfrac{\Sigma z^2}{n} + \dfrac{\Sigma zu}{n}}{\dfrac{\Sigma z^2}{n} + \dfrac{\Sigma zu}{n}}$$

Taking limits we find

$$\lim_{n\to\infty} b_1^* = \lim_{n\to\infty}\left[\frac{b_1(\Sigma z^2/n) + (\Sigma zu)/n}{(\Sigma z^2/n) + (\Sigma zu)/n}\right]$$

Since $(\Sigma zu/n) \to 0$ as $n \to \infty$ the second terms in the numerator and denominator vanish (in the limit) and we have

$$\lim_{n\to\infty} b_1^* = b_1$$

In other words the ILS estimates are asymptotically unbiased . Furthermore, it can be proved that the variance of the ILS estimates (b^*'s) is of the form $n^{-1}k$, where k is a constant. Hence the ILS estimates are consistent.

However, for small (finite) samples the ILS estimates are biased. The bias is found by taking expected values of b_1^*:

$$E(b_1^*) = E\left[\frac{b_1\Sigma z^2 + \Sigma zu}{\Sigma z^2 + \Sigma zu}\right]$$

By definition z and u are independent, hence $E(\Sigma zu) = 0$ for any given sample, but this is not sufficient to make b_1^* an unbiased estimator. For example assume that the true b_1 is $0·8$ and the sample contains values of u and z which yield $\Sigma z_i^2 = 1$ and the following values of Σzu with their respective probabilities.

Σzu	*Probability*	$b_1^* = \dfrac{b_1\Sigma z^2 + \Sigma zu}{\Sigma z^2 + \Sigma zu}$
−0·3	1/6	0·71
−0·2	1/6	0·75
−0·1	1/6	0·77
0·1	1/6	0·82
0·2	1/6	0·83
0·3	1/6	0·85
$\Sigma zu = 0$	$\Sigma p_i = 1$	$E(b_1^*) = 0·78$

In this example $E(\Sigma zu) = 0$, but $E(b_1^*) \neq b_1$.

To sum up. Indirect least squares yields:

(a) unbiased (and consistent) estimates of the reduced-form parameters ($\hat{\pi}$'s);

(b) biased but consistent estimates for the structural parameters, $\hat{b}$'s;

(c) in general not fully efficient estimates of the structural parameters, that is the $\hat{b}$'s in general have not the minimum sampling variance. (See C. Leser, *Econometric Techniques and Problems,* pp. 44 and 57.)

Yet ILS is generally preferred to OLS because of the consistency property of its estimates and because of its simplicity as compared with other methods which give consistent estimates.

16.2. THE METHOD OF INSTRUMENTAL VARIABLES

16.2.1. THE METHOD

The instrumental variables method is a single-equation method, being applied to one equation of the system at a time. It has been developed as a solution to the simultaneous equation bias and is appropriate for overidentified models. The instrumental variables method attains the reduction of the dependence of u and the explanatory variables, by using appropriate exogenous variables (as instruments). The estimates obtained from this method are consistent for large samples, although biased for small samples.

The method of instrumental variables is not often used in applied econometric research due to the disadvantages it involves, which will be discussed at the end of this section. However, it is convenient to develop this method at this stage because it will facilitate the understanding of other, more important, econometric methods like two-stage least squares (2SLS) and limited information maximum likelihood (LIML).

The method of instrumental variables may be outlined as follows.

Step I. Choose the appropriate instrumental variables which will replace the endogenous variables appearing as explanatory in the right-hand side of the structural equation.

An instrumental variable is an exogenous variable located somewhere in the system of simultaneous equations which satisfies the following conditions.

(a) It must be strongly correlated with the endogenous variable which it will replace in the structural equation.

(b) It must be truly exogenous and hence uncorrelated with the random term u of the structural equation.

(c) It must be least correlated with the exogenous variables already appearing in the set of explanatory variables of the particular structural equation. These variables will be the 'instruments' for themselves, so that in order to avoid the complications of multicollinearity the instrumental variables must not be highly collinear with the exogenous variables already present in the particular function.

(d) If more than one instrumental variable is to be used in the same structural equation, they must be the least correlated with each other for the same reason, that is for avoiding the difficulties arising from multicollinear explanatory variables.

It should be noted that we must choose as many instrumental variables as there are endogenous variables in the set of explanatory variables of the particular structural equation. If the structural equation contains exogenous variables, these will be used as instrumental for themselves.

Step II. Multiply the structural equation through by each one of the instrumental variables (as well as by the exogenous variables already present in it, since these predetermined variables are their own instruments) and sum the equation over all sample observations. This procedure will provide as many linear equations as there are unknown parameters. From the solutions of these equations we obtain estimates of the structural parameters.

To illustrate the method of instrumental variables we will examine its procedure in two simple models.

(1) *Model with one explanatory variable*

Suppose that the structural equation contains only one explanatory variable, X_1, which is correlated with u, because X_1 is endogenous to the system. Application of ordinary least squares to the equation

$$Y = b_0 + b_1 X_1 + u$$

will yield biased and inconsistent estimates. To avoid this difficulty it suffices to know that in some other part (equation) of the system, to which the above relation belongs, there is an exogenous variable, Z_1, which fulfils the above conditions, that is, it is strongly correlated with X_1, but not with u. Hence we may use Z_1 as an instrument for replacing X_1 in our function. Before proceeding to the next step it is convenient to express the structural equation in deviation form, so as to eliminate the constant intercept b_0. Thus we have

$$y = b_1 x_1 + u$$

where $y = (Y - \bar{Y})$ and $x_1 = (X_1 - \bar{X}_1)$.

The next step is to multiply the structural equation through by the instrumental variable, and sum over all sample observations:

$$\Sigma(zy) = b_1 \Sigma(zx_1) + \Sigma(zu)$$

But z and u are, by assumption, not correlated, so that their expected value is zero, $E(\Sigma zu) = 0$. Hence we may drop the last term of this equation setting it equal to its zero expected value. We thus obtain

$$\Sigma(zy) = b_1^* \Sigma(zx_1)$$

or

$$b_1^* = \frac{\Sigma zy}{\Sigma zx_1}$$

(2) *Model with two explanatory variables*

Suppose that the structural equation contains two explanatory variables, X_1 and X_2, which are endogenous to the system of simultaneous equations and hence are correlated with the disturbance term u. The original model is

$$Y = b_0 + b_1 X_1 + b_2 X_2 + u$$

or, in deviation form

$$y = b_1 x_1 + b_2 x_2 + u$$

where $E(X_1 u) \neq 0$ and $E(X_2 u) \neq 0$. To avoid least squares bias it suffices to know that this equation is part of a larger system of simultaneous equations in which the exogenous variables Z_1 and Z_2 appear and satisfy the conditions of instrumental variables. Hence we may multiply all the variables of the structural equation by each of the instrumental variables and sum over all sample observations to obtain two equations (in deviation form)

$$\Sigma z_1 y = b_1 \Sigma z_1 x_1 + b_2 \Sigma z_1 x_2 + \Sigma z_1 u$$

$$\Sigma z_2 y = b_1 \Sigma z_2 x_1 + b_2 \Sigma z_2 x_2 + \Sigma z_2 u$$

The last terms can be substituted by their zero expected value and hence dropped from the equations. Thus we have two linear equations in two unknowns (b_1^* and b_2^*) which may be solved for the estimates of the parameters

$$\Sigma z_1 y = b_1^* \Sigma z_1 x_1 + b_2^* \Sigma z_1 x_2$$

$$\Sigma z_2 y = b_1^* \Sigma z_2 x_1 + b_2^* \Sigma z_2 x_2$$

Note that if one of the explanatory variables, say X_1, is exogenous we use it as an instrument for itself, that is we set $z_1 = x_1$, and follow the same procedure.

The above transformation (of the structural equation) may easily be extended to equations containing any number of explanatory variables.

The instrumental variables estimates are obtained by solving the above system. Using the method of determinants (see Appendix II) we find

$$b_1^* = \frac{(\Sigma z_1 y)(\Sigma z_2 x_2) - (\Sigma z_2 y)(\Sigma z_1 x_2)}{(\Sigma z_1 x_1)(\Sigma z_2 x_2) - (\Sigma z_2 x_1)(\Sigma z_1 x_2)}$$

$$b_2^* = \frac{(\Sigma z_2 y)(\Sigma z_1 x_1) - (\Sigma z_1 y)(\Sigma z_2 x_1)}{(\Sigma z_1 x_1)(\Sigma z_2 x_2) - (\Sigma z_2 x_1)(\Sigma z_1 x_2)}$$

The variances of these estimates are

$$\text{var}(b_1^*) = s_u^2 \frac{\Sigma z_1^2 (\Sigma z_2 x_2)^2 + \Sigma z_2^2 (\Sigma z_1 x_2)^2 - 2\Sigma z_1 x_2 \Sigma z_1 x_2 \Sigma z_1 z_2}{\{(\Sigma z_1 x_1)(\Sigma z_2 x_2) - (\Sigma z_2 x_1)(\Sigma z_1 x_2)\}^2}$$

$$\text{var}(b_2^*) = s_u^2 \frac{\Sigma z_1^2 (\Sigma z_2 x_1)^2 - \Sigma z_2^2 (\Sigma z_1 x_1)^2 - 2\Sigma z_1 x_1 \Sigma z_2 x_1 \Sigma z_1 z_2}{\{(\Sigma z_1 x_1)(\Sigma z_2 x_2) - (\Sigma z_2 x_1)(\Sigma z_1 x_2)\}^2}$$

where $s_u^2 = \dfrac{\Sigma(y_i - b_i^* x_{1i} - b_2^* x_{2i})^2}{n - K}$

Note that s_u^2 is computed from the IV estimates b_s^*, multiplied by the original observations, y_i, x_{1i} and x_{2i}.

Table 16.2. Data for the estimation of the consumption function (in Billions of dollars)

Quarterly periods	Y_t Consumption Expenditure	X_t Income	L_t Liquid Assets
1955 I	248·7	263·0	207·6
II	253·7	271·5	209·4
III	259·9	276·5	211·1
IV	261·8	281·4	213·2
1956 I	263·2	282·0	214·1
II	263·7	286·2	216·5
III	263·4	287·7	217·3
IV	266·9	291·0	217·3
1957 I	268·9	291·1	218·2
II	270·4	294·6	218·5
III	273·4	296·1	219·8
IV	272·1	293·3	219·5
1958 I	268·9	291·3	220·5
II	270·9	292·6	222·7
III	274·4	299·9	225·0
IV	278·7	302·1	229·4
1959 I	283·8	305·9	232·2
II	289·7	312·5	235·2
III	290·8	311·3	237·2
IV	292·8	313·2	237·7
1960 I	295·4	315·4	238·0
II	299·5	320·3	238·4
III	298·6	321·0	240·1
IV	299·6	320·1	243·3
1961 I	297·0	318·4	246·1
II	301·6	324·8	250·0

Source: Z. Griliches *et al.*, 'Notes on Estimated Aggregate Quarterly Consumption Functions', *Econometrica*, 1962, p. 500.

Example. We will illustrate the instrumental variables method by applying it for the estimation of a simple consumption function. The data used are shown in table 16.2.

The structural relationship to be estimated is

$$Y_t = b_0 + b_1 X_t + u_t$$

where Y = consumption expenditure in year t

X = income in period t

X (income) is known on *a priori* grounds to be correlated with u. We know that in the system there is some equation which contains Z (= liquid assets) as an explanatory variable. Liquid assets may well be expected, on theoretical grounds, to be an exogenous variable highly correlated with income (X_1). Hence liquid assets may be used as an instrumental variable for replacing income in the structural equation. The system of transformed equations will be

$$\Sigma Y = nb_0 + b_1 \Sigma X_1$$

$$\Sigma ZY = b_0 \Sigma Z + b_1 \Sigma X_1 Z$$

From the solution of these equations we obtain

$$Y = 7 \cdot 54 + 0 \cdot 95 X_1 \qquad\qquad R^2 = 0 \cdot 979$$

$$(1 \cdot 59) \ (0 \cdot 02)$$

For the sake of comparison we have computed the estimates $\hat{b}_0$ and $\hat{b}_1$ by applying ordinary least squares to the original structural function

$$Y = -1 \cdot 75 + 0 \cdot 93 \ X_1 \qquad\qquad R^2 = 0 \cdot 980$$

$$(8 \cdot 2) \ (0 \cdot 03)$$

The rationalisation of the use of instrumental variables is fairly simple to understand. This method seeks to cure the defect of the dependence of the explanatory variable(s) X and u, which violates one of the basic assumptions of the method of ordinary least squares (Assumption 6). If we can transform the structural equation in such a way as to eliminate as far as possible the dependence between X and u, the application of least squares becomes more appropriate.

In the instrumental variables method the transformation consists of multiplying the structural equation through by the appropriate instrumental variable(s) z_i. The transformed equation is

$$\Sigma zy = b_1 \Sigma zx + \Sigma zu$$

In this transformation the new explanatory variable (zx) contains X_1 and hence it is still correlated with the new disturbance term (zu). As a result the coefficient estimates will be biased for small samples. Nevertheless the correlation between the transformed variable and the transformed random term is *sufficiently weak*; and as the size of the sample increases the last term of the above equation decreases, becoming, in the limit, equal to zero (plim $\Sigma zu \to 0$, as $n \to \infty$).[1] Thus we may set this term equal to its zero asymptotic mean value and proceed with the application of least squares to the transformed data. The estimates obtained from this procedure will be consistent for large samples (although biased for small samples). (For the proof of this statement see below.)

16.2.2. ASSUMPTIONS OF THE METHOD OF INSTRUMENTAL VARIABLES

The instrumental variables method involves the solution of the transformed normal equations of OLS: each of the normal equations is multiplied through by an instrumental variable. The assumptions of this method are the following.

Firstly. Knowledge of some exogenous variables in other equations of the complete system, which may be used as instruments.

Secondly. The new random term zu must satisfy the usual assumptions of ordinary least squares (asymptotically).

[1] plim $\Sigma zu = 0$ is the value (in probability) of Σzu in the limit, that is to say as n reaches infinity.

Thirdly. The exogenous variables (instrumental variables) must not be perfectly multicollinear.

Fourthly. The structural function must be identified.

Fifthly. The variables must be properly aggregated.

In summary the instrumental variables method is based on all the usual assumptions of the method of least squares and on the additional assumption of the existence (in the system) of the appropriate instrumental variables.

16.2.3. PROPERTIES OF THE INSTRUMENTAL VARIABLES' ESTIMATES

Provided that the above assumptions are fulfilled in any particular application, the estimates of the structural parameters have the following properties.

Firstly. For small samples the estimates are biased. We saw that in the transformed equation the 'new' explanatory variable is (zx), which contains x, while the new disturbance term (zu) contains z. Hence, despite the transformation, there is some dependence between the explanatory variable and the random term which renders the estimates of the coefficients statistically biased in small samples.

Secondly. For large samples the estimates are consistent. We saw that for an estimate to be (asymptotically) consistent two conditions must be fulfilled: (a) the estimate must be asymptotically unbiased and (b) the distribution of the values of the estimate must collapse on the true b, that is they must be centred on the true structural parameter. It can be proved (see Goldberger, *Econometric Theory*, p. 128) that if the variance of an estimate, b^*, is of the form

$$\text{var}(b^*) = n^{-1} k$$

(where k is a constant) the estimate is consistent.

We will prove that the instrumental-variables estimates satisfy the above conditions, and hence are consistent.

(a) The estimates are asymptotically unbiased: $\lim_{n \to \infty} b_1^* = b_1$. We have established that

$$b_1^* = \frac{\Sigma yz}{\Sigma zx_1}$$

But
$$y = b_1 x_1 + u$$

Hence
$$b_1^* = \frac{\Sigma(b_1 x_1 + u)z}{\Sigma zx_1} = \frac{b_1 \Sigma zx_1 + \Sigma zu}{\Sigma zx_1} = b_1 + \frac{(\Sigma zu/n)}{(\Sigma zx_1/n)}$$

The asymptotic expectation (mean) of the estimate b_1^* is

$$\lim_{n \to \infty} b_1^* = \lim_{n \to \infty} b_1 + \lim_{n \to \infty} \left[\frac{(\Sigma zu/n)}{(\Sigma zx_i/n)} \right]$$

But $\lim_{n \to \infty} b_1 = b_1$, and $\lim_{n \to \infty} (\Sigma zu)/n = 0$ given than z and u are by assumption independent.

Hence

$$\lim_{n \to \infty} b_1^* = b_1$$

that is, b_1^* is asymptotically unbiased.

(b) The asymptotic variance of the estimates is of the form

$$\mathrm{var}(b^*) = n^{-1} k \qquad \text{(where } k \text{ is a constant)}$$

Proof

For the simple model with one explanatory variable the sample variance is

$$\mathrm{var}(b_1^*) = E\{(b_1^* - E(b_1^*)\}^2 = E(b_1^* - b_1)^2$$

We established in the previous paragraph that

$$b_1^* = b_1 + \frac{\Sigma zu}{\Sigma xz}$$

Thus

$$\mathrm{var}(b_1^*) = E \left(b_1 + \frac{\Sigma zu}{\Sigma xz} - b_1 \right)^2 = E \left(\frac{\Sigma zu}{\Sigma xz} \right)^2 = \frac{1}{(\Sigma xz)^2} E(\Sigma zu)^2$$

$$= \frac{1}{(\Sigma xz)^2} E(\Sigma z^2 u^2 + 2\Sigma_i z_i z_j u_i u_j)$$

$$= \frac{1}{(\Sigma xz)^2} \Sigma z^2 E(u^2) + 2\Sigma z_i z_j E(u_i u_j)$$

$$= \left\{ \frac{1}{(\Sigma xz)^2} \Sigma z^2 \sigma_u^2 \right\} = \sigma_u^2 \frac{\Sigma z^2}{(\Sigma xz)^2} \qquad \text{(given } E(u^2) = \sigma_u^2 \quad \text{and} \quad E(u_i u_j) = 0)$$

Multiplying numerator and denominator by Σx^2

$$\mathrm{var}(b_1^*) = \sigma_u^2 \frac{\Sigma z^2 \, \Sigma x^2}{(\Sigma xz)^2 \, \Sigma x^2} = \sigma_u^2 \left(\frac{1}{r_{xz}^2} \right) \left(\frac{1}{\Sigma x^2} \right)$$

Now, the asymptotic variance is

$$[\text{Asym var}(b_1^*)] = n^{-1} \lim_{n \to \infty} E[\sqrt{n}(b_1^* - b_1)]^2$$

$$= n^{-1} \lim_{n \to \infty} [nE(b_1^* - b_1)^2] = n^{-1} \lim_{n \to \infty} \left[n \cdot \sigma_u^2 \left(\frac{1}{r_{xz}^2} \right) \left(\frac{1}{\Sigma x^2} \right) \right]$$

$$= n^{-1} \sigma_u^2 \lim_{n \to \infty} \left[\left(\frac{1}{r_{xz}^2} \right) \left(\frac{1}{\Sigma x^2/n} \right) \right]$$

$$= n^{-1} \sigma_u^2 \lim_{n \to \infty} \left[\left(\frac{1}{r_{xz}^2} \right) \left(\frac{1}{s_x^2} \right) \right]$$

But, as $n \to \infty$, r_{xz}^2 converges to the population correlation coefficient, ρ_{xz}^2, and s_x^2 converges to the population variance of X, σ_x^2.

Thus, clearly the asymptotic variance of b_1^* is of the form $n^{-1} k$, where k is a constant, involving σ_u^2 and the inverse of the limiting values of r_{xz}^2 and s_x^2. Hence the asymptotic variance tends to zero as $n \to \infty$.

Thirdly. The instrumental variables estimates, although consistent are not asymptotically efficient; that is, they do not possess the minimum variance as compared with other consistent estimates obtained from alternative econometric techniques.[1]

The variance of the instrumental variables estimates depends inversely on the correlation of x and its instrument z:

$$\text{var}(b_1^*) = \frac{\sigma_u^2}{\Sigma x^2} \cdot \frac{1}{r^2_{xz}}$$

If x and z are not strongly correlated the denominator will be small, hence the variance will be large. In this event the consistency property of the estimates is achieved at the cost of large variances, that is, the estimates become inefficient.

16.2.4. SOME NOTES ON THE INSTRUMENTAL VARIABLES METHOD

The instrumental variables method has various disadvantages.

Firstly. In each equation we use as many instrumental variables as there are endogenous variables appearing in the set of explanatory variables. However, in most cases there are more exogenous (predetermined) variables in the entire model, and among them we choose some to use as instrumental. The selection is to a certain extent arbitrary. It is clear that the value of the estimates will differ according to the set of instrumental variables chosen: to each choice of instrumental variables corresponds a different set of parameter estimates. The set of instrumental variables which we may choose is not unique. Our choice, and hence the estimates, are arbitrary, a fact that renders this method not particularly desirable.

Secondly. As a consequence of the inclusion of only certain exogenous variables and the omission of others, the method of instrumental variables takes into account only part of the influence of the exogenous variables on the dependent variable. Yet it is known that a complete causal chain is inherent in any simultaneous equations model: every endogenous variable affects and is affected by all the other endogenous variables of the system.[2] Furthermore *every* exogenous variable, regardless of the equation in which it appears, affects *all* the endogenous variables of the system either directly (if it is present in the equation) or indirectly (by influencing other endogenous variables in the equation in which it does not appear explicitly). Yet with the method of instrumental variables we ignore the influence of the exogenous variables omitted from the equation for the mere reason that we did not (arbitrarily) choose them as instrumental.

Thirdly. In practice each endogenous variable is related to more than one predetermined variable. The choice of a particular one as instrumental is difficult. Furthermore the exogenous variables are usually intercorrelated, so that the problem of finding the 'appropriate' instrumental variables is not easy.

---

[1] See Leser, *Econometric Techniques*. p. 20.

[2] See Brennan, *Preface to Econometrics,* South-Western Publishing Company, Cincinnati, Ohio 1965, p. 406.

(See J. D. Sargan, 'The Estimation of Economic Relationships using Instrumental Variables', *Econometrica*, vol. 26, 1958, pp. 393–405.)

Fourthly. Since *u* is unobservable, it is difficult to say with certainty whether *u* is independent from the instrumental variables. The method has the advantage of simplicity of computation. Because of that it can be used fairly easily for estimation with various sets of instrumental variables, when one is doubtful as to which set is the appropriate one. In this 'experimental' approach we may be helped in the choice among various alternative solutions, each of which may be based on acceptable *a priori* assumptions. (See L. R. Klein, *A Textbook of Econometrics*, p. 125.).

It should be noted that the defect of the arbitrariness in choosing the appropriate instrumental variables may be eliminated to some extent by using linear combinations of instrumental variables instead of single variables. (Such combinations can be found by the method of Principal Components, the Factor Analysis technique, or by 2SLS, see below.) In this way we use more predetermined variables of the entire system and hence our estimates will be more accurate.

Finally we note that although there exists usually more than one set of instrumental variables which will yield consistent estimates of the structural parameters, we can choose among such estimates the ones that have the least variance property (asymptotic efficiency) for large samples, that is those estimates whose variance tends to zero (as *n* increases) faster than the variance of other estimates. (See A. Goldberger, *Econometric Theory*, p. 286, and J. D. Sargan, 'The Estimation of Economic Relationships using Instrumental Variables', *Econometrica*, 1958.)

16.3. TWO-STAGE LEAST SQUARES (2SLS)

16.3.1. THE METHOD

This method has been developed by Theil[1] and independently by Basmann.[2] It is a single-equation method, being applied to one equation of the system at a time. It has provided satisfactory results for the estimates of the structural parameters and has been accepted as the most important of the single-equation techniques for the estimation of overidentified models.

Theoretically two-stage least squares may be considered as an extension of indirect least squares (ILS) and of the instrumental variables (IV) method. We will prove below that 2SLS is identical to the instrumental variables method using the regressed values ($\hat{y}_i$) of the endogenous variables as instruments for the corresponding observed values (y_i), and with the predetermined variables included in the function serving as their own instruments (see below).

Two-stage least squares, like other simultaneous-equations techniques, aims at the elimination as far as possible of the simultaneous-equation bias. We saw

[1] H. Theil, *Estimation and Simultaneous Correlation in Complete Equation Systems*, The Hague: Central Planning Bureau (mimeographed), 1953.

[2] R. L. Basmann, 'A Generalized Classical Method of Linear Estimation of Coefficients in a Structural Equation', *Econometrica*, vol. 25, 1957, pp. 77–83.

that the source of this bias is the existence of endogenous variables in the set of explanatory variables of the function. Such endogenous variables have a systematic component, determined by the predetermined (exogenous) variables of the model, and a random component. And it is the latter that creates the dependence of the relative variable with the random term u of the structural equation. In general, if we examine the reduced form equations of the model, we see that each endogenous variable is a function of all the predetermined variables (X's) of the model, and of a random element (v). The reduced form of the ith endogenous variable is of the form

$$y_1 = \underbrace{\pi_{i1}x_1 + \pi_{i2}x_2 + \ldots + \pi_{ik}x_k}_{\text{[exact component]}} + \underbrace{v_1}_{+ \ \text{[random component]}}$$

The exact (non-stochastic) component is formed from the terms including the exogenous variables, x's, and the associated reduced-form coefficients, π's, and the random component is v_i, which is a function of the random variables of the structural equations (u's) and the structural parameters, b's, that is

$$v_1 = f(u_1, \ldots u_G; b_1 \ldots b_G)$$

where G = number of endogenous variables of the model and k = number of predetermined variables (see pp. 336–7). It is clear that the random component v_1 causes the appearance of the simultaneous-equation bias in the least squares estimates, because it is correlated with the u's of the structural equations. If we knew v_i we could subtract the random element from y_i and use only its exact component in the structural equation. However, v_i is unobservable, and hence the exact component of y_i is not known. We may obtain an estimate of this component by regressing y_i on *all the predetermined variables of the model*, find the estimate, $\hat{y}_i$, and use this computed value ($\hat{y}_i$) as an explanatory variable in the original equation instead of y_i.

It should be noted that $\hat{y}$ does contain some random variation: it is made up of *estimated* reduced-form coefficients. Indeed $\hat{y}$ is even correlated with the structural u's; what happens in 2SLS is that this correlation vanishes as $n \to \infty$.

From the above discussion we see that the two-stage least squares method boils down to the application of ordinary least squares in two stages:

In the first stage we apply least squares to the reduced-form equations in order to obtain an estimate of the exact and the random components of the endogenous variables

$$y_i = \hat{y}_i + v_i$$

where $\hat{y}_i = \hat{\pi}_{i1}x_1 + \hat{\pi}_{i2}x_2 + \ldots + \hat{\pi}_{ik}x_k$.

In the second stage we replace the endogenous variables appearing in the right-hand side of the equation with their estimated value $\hat{y}_i = y_i - v_i$, and we apply ordinary least squares to the transformed original equation to obtain estimates of the structural parameters.

To introduce formally the 2SLS method we will use the following notation:

y_i's will denote endogenous variables $(i = 1, 2, \ldots, G)$
x_i's will denote predetermined variables $(i = 1, 2, \ldots, k)$
b's will represent the coefficients of endogenous variables
γ's will represent the coefficients of predetermined variables.
Thus the ith structural equation is of the general form

$$y_i = b_{i1}y_1 + b_{i2}y_2 + \ldots + b_{iG}y_G + \gamma_{i1}x_1 + \ldots + \gamma_{ik}x_k + u_i$$

In the first stage we apply ordinary least squares to the reduced-form equations to obtain estimates of the π's

$$y_1 = \pi_{11}x_1 + \pi_{12}x_2 + \ldots + \pi_{1k}x_k + v_1$$
$$y_2 = \pi_{21}x_1 + \pi_{22}x_2 + \ldots + \pi_{2k}x_k + v_2$$

.   .   .   .   .

.   .   .   .   .

$$y_G = \pi_{G1}x_1 + \pi_{G2}x_2 + \ldots + \pi_{Gk}x_k + v_G$$

Using the reduced-form coefficients, $\hat{\pi}$'s, we obtain a set of estimated (computed) values for the endogenous variables: $\hat{y}_1, \hat{y}_2, \ldots \hat{y}_G$.

It should be noted that we need not perform all the usual substitutions in order to obtain the reduced form model. We simply express the y's as functions of all the x's, and, applying OLS, obtain values of the π's. We need not know the exact relationships between the π's and the structural parameters (b's and γ's), because we are not going to estimate the latter from the former (as in the ILS method). We will only use the $\hat{\pi}$'s to obtain the estimated values, $\hat{y}$'s. What is required is the knowledge of *all* the predetermined variables appearing everywhere (in all the structural equations) in the model. This knowledge enables us to write directly the reduced-form model in its general form (as above) without bothering to derive it by successive substitutions.

In the second stage we substitute the $\hat{y}$'s into the structural equation and obtain the transformed functions

$$y_i = b_{i1}\hat{y}_1 + b_{i2}\hat{y}_2 + \ldots b_{iG}\hat{y}_G + \gamma_{i1}x_1 + \ldots + \gamma_{ik}x_k + u_i^*$$

where $u_i^* = u_i + b_{i1}v_1 + b_{i2}v_2 + \ldots + b_{iG}v_G$.

The original function is

$$y_i = b_{i1}y_1 + \ldots + b_{iG}y_G + \gamma_{i1}x_1 + \ldots + \gamma_{ik}x_k + u_i$$

Substitute $y_i = \hat{y}_1 + v_1, y_2 = \hat{y}_2 + v_2, \ldots, y_G = \hat{y}_G + v_G$

to obtain $y_i = b_{i1}(\hat{y}_1 + v_1) + \ldots + b_{iG}(\hat{y}_G + v_G) + \gamma_{i1}x_1 + \ldots + \gamma_{ik}x_k + u_i$

Rearranging we obtain

$$y_i = b_{i1}\hat{y}_1 + \ldots + b_{iG}\hat{y}_G + \gamma_{i1}x_1 + \ldots + \gamma_{ik}x_k + (u_i + b_{i1}v_1 + \ldots + b_{iG}v_G)$$

Applying OLS to the transformed structural equation we obtain the 2SLS estimates of the structural parameters.

The formulae for the two-stage least squares estimates are the same as those of ordinary least squares, with explanatory variables the estimated values ($\hat{y}$'s) of the endogenous variables appearing in the right-hand side and the predetermined variables of the function. Thus for the simple structural equation with two explanatory variables

$$y_1 = b_2 y_2 + \gamma_1 x_1 + u$$

the transformed equation is

$$y_1 = b_2 \hat{y}_2 + \gamma_1 x_1 + (u + b_2 v_2)$$

and the normal equations are

$$\left. \begin{array}{l} \Sigma y_1 \hat{y}_2 = b_2^* \Sigma \hat{y}_2^2 + \gamma_1^* \Sigma x_1 \hat{y}_2 \\ \Sigma y_1 x_1 = b_2^* \Sigma x_1 \hat{y}_2 + \gamma_1^* \Sigma x_1^2 \end{array} \right\} \tag{16.4}$$

The formulae for the 2SLS estimates are

$$b_2^* = \frac{\begin{vmatrix} \Sigma y_1 \hat{y}_2 & \Sigma x_1 \hat{y}_2 \\ \Sigma y_1 x_1 & \Sigma x_1^2 \end{vmatrix}}{\begin{vmatrix} \Sigma \hat{y}_2^2 & \Sigma x_1 \hat{y}_2 \\ \Sigma x_1 \hat{y}_2 & \Sigma x_1^2 \end{vmatrix}} \quad \text{and} \quad \gamma_1^* = \frac{\begin{vmatrix} \Sigma \hat{y}_2^2 & \Sigma y_1 \hat{y}_2 \\ \Sigma x_1 \hat{y}_2 & \Sigma y_1 x_1 \end{vmatrix}}{\begin{vmatrix} \Sigma \hat{y}_2^2 & \Sigma x_1 \hat{y}_2 \\ \Sigma x_1 \hat{y}_2 & \Sigma x_1^2 \end{vmatrix}}$$

or

$$b_2^* = \frac{(\Sigma y_1 \hat{y}_2)(\Sigma x_1^2)}{(\Sigma \hat{y}_2^2)(\Sigma x_1^2) - (\Sigma x_1 \hat{y}_2)^2}$$

$$\gamma_1^* = \frac{(\Sigma \hat{y}_2^2)(\Sigma y_1 x_1)}{(\Sigma \hat{y}_2^2)(\Sigma x_1^2) - (\Sigma x_1 \hat{y}_2)^2}$$

The variances of the 2SLS estimates are computed from the following expressions

$$\text{var}(b_2^*) = s_u^2 \cdot \frac{\Sigma x_1^2}{(\Sigma \hat{y}_2^2)(\Sigma x_1^2) - (\Sigma x_1 \hat{y}_2)^2}$$

$$\text{var}(\gamma_1^*) = s_u^2 \cdot \frac{\Sigma \hat{y}_2^2}{(\Sigma \hat{y}_2^2)(\Sigma x_1^2) - (\Sigma x_1 \hat{y}_2)^2}$$

where

$$s_u^2 = \frac{\Sigma(y_1 - b_2^* y_2 - \gamma_1^* x_1)^2}{n - K}$$

Note that s_u^2 is estimated by using the estimates b_2^* and γ_1^* obtained from the second stage, multiplied by the *original* observations of *all* the variables.

We will prove that the 2SLS estimates are identical with the instrumental variables method, provided that we use as instruments the estimated values $(\hat{y}_i)$ of the right-hand side endogenous variables to replace the original y's, and the predetermined variables included in the function as their own instruments. This proof will allow us to draw on the consistency property of the instrumental variables method, which we established in the previous section. In other words the proof of the 2SLS estimates being identical to the instrumental variables estimates establishes the consistency of the former automatically, without requiring to prove anew this property.

Let us start from the original equation of a model containing two explanatory variables, one endogenous (y_2) and one predetermined (x_1):

$$y_1 = b_2 y_2 + \gamma_1 x_1 + u_1$$

We will use $\hat{y}_2$ as an instrumental variable to replace y_2, and x_1 as an instrument for itself.

Applying the method of instrumental variables we obtain the normal equations

$$\Sigma y_1 \hat{y}_2 = b_2^* \Sigma y_2 \hat{y}_2 + \gamma_1^* \Sigma x_1 \hat{y}_2$$

$$\Sigma y_1 x_1 = b_2^* \Sigma y_2 x_1 + \gamma_1^* \Sigma x_1^2$$

The solution of these equations yields the instrumental variables estimates of the structural parameters.

Comparing the instrumental variables' expressions with the 2SLS equations (16.4) we see that they differ only by the terms related to the parameter b_2 in the normal equations

2SLS	*Instrumental Variables*
$\Sigma \hat{y}_2^2$	$\Sigma y_2 \hat{y}_2$
$\Sigma x_1 \hat{y}_2$	$\Sigma y_2 x_1$

However, it can be proved that $\Sigma \hat{y}_2^2 = \Sigma y_2 \hat{y}_2$ and $\Sigma x_1 \hat{y}_2 = \Sigma x_1 y_2$, so that the two sets of equations (and hence the parameter estimates) are identical for 2SLS and for the IV methods.

Proof (i). We want to prove that $\Sigma \hat{y}_2^2 = \Sigma y_2 \hat{y}_2$

(a) $\Sigma \hat{y}_2^2 = \Sigma (\hat{\pi}_{21} x_1)^2$

$\quad = \hat{\pi}_{21}^2 \Sigma x_1^2$

$\quad = \left(\dfrac{\Sigma y_2 x_1}{\Sigma x_1^2} \right)^2 (\Sigma x_1^2), \qquad$ because $\hat{\pi}_{21} = \dfrac{\Sigma y_2 x_1}{\Sigma x_1^2}$

$\quad = \dfrac{(\Sigma y_2 x_1)^2}{\Sigma x_1^2}$

(b) $\Sigma y_2 \hat{y}_2 = \Sigma y_2 (\hat{\pi}_{21} x_1)$

$\qquad = \hat{\pi}_{21} \Sigma y_2 x_1$

$\qquad = \dfrac{\Sigma y_2 x_1}{\Sigma x_1^2} \cdot \Sigma y_2 x_1$

$\qquad = \dfrac{(\Sigma y_2 x_1)^2}{\Sigma x_1^2}.$

Hence $\qquad\qquad\qquad\qquad \Sigma \hat{y}_2^2 = \Sigma y_2 \hat{y}_2.$

Proof (ii). We will prove that $\Sigma x_1 \hat{y}_2 = \Sigma x_1 y_2$.

Substituting $\hat{y}_2 = \hat{\pi}_{21} x_1$, we find

$$\Sigma x_1 \hat{y}_2 = \hat{\pi}_{21} (\Sigma x_1^2).$$

But

$$\hat{\pi}_{21} = \frac{\Sigma y_2 x_1}{\Sigma x_1^2}$$

Therefore

$$\Sigma x_1 \hat{y}_2 = \frac{\Sigma y_2 x_1}{\Sigma x_1^2} (\Sigma x_1^2) = \Sigma y_2 x_1$$

We thus have established the identity of 2SLS estimates and instrumental variables' estimates when we use the calculated $\hat{y}$'s as instruments for the y_i's in the right-hand side of the equation, and the exogenous x_i's as their own instrument.

An Example. To illustrate the application of the method of 2SLS we will use it for the estimation of an overidentified function. Suppose we have the simple Keynesian model of income determination

$$C_t = b_0 + b_1 Y_t + b_2 C_{t-1} + u$$

$$I_t = a_0 + a_1 Y_{t-1} + a_2 Y_t + v$$

$$Y_t = C_t + I_t + G_t$$

where lagged income (Y_{t-1}), lagged consumption (C_{t-1}), and government expenditure (G_t) are exogenous. In this model the consumption function is overidentified, because:

(a) Order condition for identification: $K - M \geqslant G - 1$. In our example

$$K = 6 \qquad M = 3 \qquad G = 3$$

Therefore $\qquad\qquad K - M = 3 \quad$ and $\quad G - 1 = 2$

Obviously $(K - M) > (G - 1)$, so that the necessary condition for identification is satisfied for the first equation.

(b) The rank condition for identification is also satisfied for the consumption function:

Complete table of structural parameters

Table of parameters of excluded variables

Equations	Variables					
	C_t	C_{t-1}	Y	Y_{t-1}	I	G_t
1st equation	1	1	b	0	0	0
2nd equation	0	0	-1	$-a_1$	1	0
3rd equation	-1	0	1	0	-1	-1

$$\begin{matrix} -a_1 & 1 & 0 \\ 0 & -1 & -1 \end{matrix}$$

From the table of coefficients of 'absent' variables we may form three determinants of order $(G - 1) = 2$. Hence the consumption function is overidentified. We may estimate its parameters by the 2SLS method. The relevant data are given in table 16.3.

Table 16.3 Data of National Income Accounts of the U.K. (£m at 1963 prices)

Year	C_t	GNP_t (Y_t)	I_t	G_t	Y_{t-1}	C_{t-1}
1948	13,844	20,431	2,285	3,890	20,015	13,205
1949	14,098	20,999	2,498	4,112	20,431	13,844
1950	14,493	21,777	2,632	4,103	20,999	14,098
1951	14,300	22,418	2,643	4,410	21,777	14,493
1952	14,219	22,308	2,654	4,845	22,418	14,300
1953	14,862	23,319	2,942	4,972	22,308	14,219
1954	15,472	24,180	3,192	4,952	23,319	14,862
1955	16,102	24,893	3,372	4,801	24,180	15,472
1956	16,236	25,310	3,526	4,761	24,893	16,102
1957	16,581	25,799	3,714	4,687	25,310	16,236
1958	17,008	25,886	3,737	4,572	25,799	16,581
1959	17,736	26,868	4,025	4,668	25,886	17,008
1960	18,418	28,134	4,418	4,770	26,868	17,736
1961	18,846	29,091	4,847	4,945	28,134	18,418
1962	19,258	29,450	4,829	5,100	29,091	18,846
1963	20,125	30,705	4,916	5,184	29,450	19,258
1964	20,819	32,372	5,717	5,272	30,705	20,125
1965	21,169	33,152	5,949	5,420	32,372	20,819
1966	21,617	33,764	6,102	5,561	33,152	21,169
1967	22,039	34,411	6,525	5,825	33,764	21,617
1968	22,562	35,429	6,791	5,851	34,411	22,039

We first obtain the reduced-form value of the endogenous variable (GNP):

$$Y_t = \pi_0 + \pi_1 G_t + \pi_2 Y_{t-1} + \pi_3 C_{t-1} + v$$

$$\hat{Y}_t = -3251 \cdot 9 + 1 \cdot 027\, G_t + 0 \cdot 087\, Y_{t-1} + 1 \cdot 346\, C_{t-1}$$

We next substitute the calculated value of income for the original Y variable, and perform the regression

$$C_t^* = b_0^* + b_1^* \hat{Y}_t + b_2^* C_{t-1} + u^*$$

The results are as follows

$$C_t = -75 \cdot 93 + 0 \cdot 0846\, \hat{Y}_t + 1 \cdot 1643\, C_{t-1}$$
$$\qquad (436 \cdot 9) \quad (0 \cdot 21) \qquad (0 \cdot 34)$$

$$R^2 = 0 \cdot 992 \qquad\qquad d = 1 \cdot 63$$

For comparison we have computed the consumption function with the method of OLS. The results are

$$\hat{C}_t = 380 \cdot 90 + 0 \cdot 3018\, Y_t + 0 \cdot 5259\, C_{t-1}$$

$$(351 \cdot 0) \quad (0 \cdot 12) \qquad (0 \cdot 21)$$

$$R^2 = 0 \cdot 994 \qquad d = 1 \cdot 10$$

16.3.2. ASSUMPTIONS OF TWO-STAGE LEAST SQUARES

We saw that 2SLS involves the application of the classical least squares to two types of functions: to the reduced-form equations and to the transformed structural function, the transformation consisting of the replacement of the endogenous variables by their estimated values ($\hat{y}$'s) obtained from the reduced-form equations. The assumptions of this method may be outlined as follows.

Firstly. The disturbance term u of the original structural equations must satisfy the usual stochastic assumptions of zero mean, constant variance and zero covariance. Otherwise the reduced-form error terms v_i's will not possess these characteristics and hence the whole method breaks down.

Secondly. The error term of the reduced form equations v_i must satisfy the usual stochastic assumptions, that is (a) v has zero mean, constant variance, zero covariance, and (b) v must be independent of the exogenous variables of the whole structural model $(x_1, x_2, \ldots, x_k)$. The assumptions of zero mean, constant variance and zero covariance for v_i are fulfilled as soon as the random terms of all structural equations (u's) satisfy these conditions, because v_i is an exact linear function of the structural u's. (See H. Theil, *Economic Forecasting and Policy*, p. 230.)

Thirdly. The explanatory variables are not perfectly multicollinear, and all macro-variables are properly aggregated.

Fourthly. It is assumed that the specification of the model is correct so far as the exogenous variables are concerned. That is we assume knowledge of *all* the exogenous (predetermined) variables of the system, irrespective of the equations in which they appear. It is not necessary to know the mathematical formulation of the whole system in all its details, but we must know correctly all the exogenous variables of the system.

Fifthly. It is assumed that the sample is large enough, and in particular that the number of observations is greater than the number of predetermined variables in the structural system. If the sample size is small in relation to the total number of exogenous variables, it may not be possible to obtain significant estimates of the reduced-form coefficients (π's) when applying ordinary least squares at the first stage. (See K. Fox *et al., The Theory of Quantitative Economic Policy*, North-Holland, 1966, p. 92.) If the sample size is small, one might try to reduce the number of exogenous variables by applying the method of Principal Components (see below).

16.3.3. PROPERTIES OF THE 2SLS ESTIMATES

Provided that the above assumptions are satisfied the estimates obtained from the 2SLS have the following properties.

Firstly. From small samples the estimates are biased. It has been established that in the simple two-variable model

$$y_1 = b_2 y_2 + u$$

the transformed function becomes

$$y_1 = b_2 \hat{y}_2 + (u + b_2 v)$$

where $\hat{y}_2 = \pi_i x_1$. Now $\hat{y}_2$ is an exact function of x_1, which is uncorrelated with u. Furthermore x_1 is by assumption uncorrelated with v. Thus $\hat{y}_2$ is uncorrelated with the composite random term $(u + b_2 v)$. However,

$$\hat{y}_2 = y_2 - v$$

so that

$$y_1 = b_2(y_2 - v) + (u + b_2 v)$$

It is thus clear that, despite the transformation, the simultaneous-equation bias is not eliminated in small samples. This may be formally proved by deriving an explicit formula for the bias. We will not pursue this proof here. (See A. Goldberger, *Econometric Theory*, p. 332.)

Secondly. However, in large samples (as $n \to \infty$) the bias tends to zero, that is, the 2SLS estimates are asymptotically unbiased. Again this property can be established by deriving an explicit formula for the bias and examining the size of the bias as $n \to \infty$. Alternatively we may draw on the proof of the asymptotic unbiasedness of the instrumental variables method, since we have established that 2SLS is identical to an instrumental variable estimation if in 2SLS we use the estimated $\hat{y}_i$'s as instrumental variables for their corresponding original values.

Thirdly. The 2SLS estimates are consistent, that is their distribution collapses on the true parameter b as $n \to \infty$. For the proof of the consistency property similar considerations (to the proof of asymptotic unbiasedness) hold. In other words one may either proceed with a formal proof of $var_{(b*)} = n^{-1} k$ (where k is an expression constant for any particular sample), *or* one may draw on the proof of the consistency property of the instrumental variables' estimates. Thus we may say that the identity (earlier established) of the two-stage least squares with an instrumental-variables estimation establishes its consistency. (See A. Goldberger, *Econometric Theory*, p. 332.)

Fourthly. The two-stage least squares estimates are asymptotically efficient under certain assumptions about the distribution of the disturbances. (See H. Theil, *Economic Forecasting and Policy*, p. 232.)

16.3.4. SOME REMARKS ON TWO-STAGE LEAST SQUARES

1. The method of 2SLS is appropriate for the estimation of overidentified equations. When the equation is exactly identified it can be proved that the 2SLS estimates are identical with the estimates of ILS method. Two-stage least squares also does not have any advantage over ordinary least squares in the estimation of recursive models.

2. The method of two-stage least squares yields consistent estimates under conditions in which the classical least squares method fails (that is in over-identified relations).

3. The method of 2SLS is more general than the instrumental variables method, because it takes into account the influence on the dependent variable of all the predetermined variables of the system, while the method of instrumental variables, as we saw, chooses only a certain subset of the predetermined variables (as instruments), and ignores the effects of the other exogenous variables.

4. The method of two-stage least squares assumes knowledge of *all* the predetermined variables of the complete system of simultaneous equations. If the specification of these variables is not correct, the estimates of the parameters will not have the optimal properties mentioned above. In other words 2SLS, as indeed any other econometric technique, is sensitive to specification errors. Taking into account the complexity of economic phenomena, it seems that errors in the specification of the predetermined variables may well be expected in any particular application. Hence some source of error in the estimates may not be avoided.

5. The method of 2SLS requires rather a large number of observations, especially if the model includes many predetermined variables, which will be used in the first stage for obtaining the estimated values ($\hat{y}$'s) of the endogenous variables.

6. The method is fairly simple in conception and in computations. It has yielded more satisfactory results than any of the other econometric methods and has become the most important technique for the estimation of overidentified functions. (See Chapter 21.)

16.4. '*k*-CLASS' ESTIMATORS

The k-class estimators may be obtained by a generalisation of the 2SLS method. Assume we have the model

$$y_1 = \beta_2 y_2 + \beta_3 y_3 + \ldots + \beta_G y_G + \gamma_1 x_1 + \ldots + \gamma_k x_k + u_1$$

This equation includes endogenous variables ($y_2, y_3, \ldots, y_G$) in the set of explanatory variables.

(a) If we apply OLS, we use the original observations on the variables $y_2, y_3, \ldots, y_G$, and we obtain biased and inconsistent estimates.

(b) To avoid this situation we may apply 2SLS, in which we use the estimated values $\hat{y}_2, \hat{y}_3, \ldots, \hat{y}_G$, obtained by applying OLS to the unrestricted reduced-form equations

$$\hat{y}_i = \hat{\pi}_{i1} x_1 + \hat{\pi}_{i2} x_2 + \ldots + \hat{\pi}_{ik} x_k \quad (i = 2, 3, \ldots, G)$$

We may generalise our estimation procedure, by taking a weighted average of these two methods, with weights $(1 - k)$ and k. In other words we take the weighted average of the original y's and the estimated reduced-form $\hat{y}$'s and use these new 'k-class' variables as instrumental to replace the original y's

$$(1 - k)y_i + k\hat{y}_i = y_i + k(\hat{y}_i - y_i) \quad (i = 1, 2, \ldots, G)$$

while retaining the exogenous x's (as their own instruments) in the function.

It is obvious that: (i) when $k = 0$, we get OLS estimators (ii) when $k = 1$, we get 2SLS estimators.

Thus OLS and 2SLS estimators may be viewed as special cases of the general 'k-class' estimators. The scalar k can be set *a priori* equal to some constant number, or its value can be determined from the observations of the sample according to some rule. (See J. Kmenta, *Elements of Econometrics*, pp. 565–7.) It should be noted, however, that the k-class estimators change considerably if the value of k exceeds 1 greatly. If k does not greatly exceed unity, the estimators do not vary appreciably. For a further discussion of the 'k-class' estimators the reader is referred to A. S. Goldberger, *Econometric Theory*, pp. 341–4.

EXERCISES

1. The following system represents the market of a given agricultural product

$$D_t = b_0 + b_1 P_t + b_2 Y_t + u_1$$
$$S_t = a_0 + a_1 P_t + a_2 P_{f,t-1} + a_3 t + u_2$$
$$D_t = S_t$$

where Y = consumers' income, P_f = farmers' price, t = trend

Given the data of table 16.4 estimate the parameters of the market model applying 2SLS. Compare your results with the estimates obtained from OLS. (The variables are measured in arbitrary units.)

2. Consider the wage–price model

$$\dot{W}_t = a_0 + a_1 \dot{P}_t + a_2 (\text{UN})_t + u_{1t}$$
$$\dot{P}_t = b_0 + b_1 \dot{W}_t + u_{2t}$$

where $\dot{W}$ = the percentage change in money wages
$\dot{P}$ = the percentage changes in prices
UN = the rate of unemployment
u_{1t} and u_{2t} satisfy the usual assumptions

(i) Show that 2SLS breaks down if we attempt to apply it in estimating the first equation.
(ii) Does the 2LSL method also break down if we attempt to estimate with it the coefficients of the second equation?
Explain why, by deriving the two normal equations of the second stage.

3. Assume the following aggregate econometric model

$$C_t = a_0 + a_1 (Y_t - T_t) + u_1$$
$$I_t = b_0 + b_1 Y_t + b_2 Y_{t-1} + u_2$$
$$T_t = c_1 Y_t$$
$$Y_t = C_t + I_t + \bar{G}_t$$

where T = direct taxes

Table 16.4

	$D_t = S_t$	P_t	Y_t	$P_{f,t-1}$
1	98·5	100·3	87·4	98·0
2	99·2	104·3	97·6	99·1
3	102·2	103·4	96·7	99·1
4	101·5	104·5	98·2	98·1
5	104·2	98·0	99·8	110·8
6	103·2	99·5	100·5	108·2
7	104·0	101·1	103·2	105·6
8	100·0	104·8	107·8	109·8
9	100·3	96·4	96·6	108·7
10	102·8	91·2	88·9	100·6
11	95·4	93·1	75·1	81·0
12	92·4	98·8	76·9	68·6
13	94·5	102·9	84·6	70·9
14	98·8	98·8	90·6	81·4
·15	105·8	95·1	103·1	102·3
16	100·2	98·5	105·1	105·0
17	100·5	86·5	96·4	110·5
18	99·9	104·0	104·4	92·5
19	105·2	105·8	110·7	89·3
20	106·2	113·5	127·1	93·0

(a) Examine the identification condition of the equations of the model.
(b) Obtain OLS, ILS or 2SLS estimates (wherever appropriate) of the parameters of the model using the data of table 16.5.

Table 16.5

Period	C_t	I_t	Y_t	T_t	Y_{t-1}	G_t
1953	230·7	60·9	306·6	43·7	293·2	73·4
1954	245·1	65·8	304·9	44·2	306·6	70·2
1955	255·2	71·3	333·0	45·9	304·9	68·3
1956	265·5	73·8	352·8	51·6	333·0	72·9
1957	280·3	76·9	368·2	56·2	352·8	80·2
1958	291·1	77·0	370·0	56·2	368·2	84·8
1959	308·2	80·5	402·4	63·3	370·0	88·3
1960	326·5	85·9	417·1	70·3	402·4	91·2
1961	336·6	85·7	430·1	72·4	417·1	99·0
1962	356·6	94·0	460·6	79·8	430·6	107·2
1963	376·6	99·5	485·3	86·2	460·6	112·2
1964	402·9	108·0	521·7	85·6	485·3	118·6
1965	434·7	120·0	568·4	93·4	521·7	126·2
1966	468·3	130·3	625·1	111·4	568·4	146·9
1967	494·3	133·9	659·0	123·2	625·1	168·3
1968	538·9	146·2	719·8	142·6	659·0	184·6

Note. Additional exercises are included in Appendix III.

17. Mixed Estimation Methods
The Method of Principal Components

17.1. MIXED ESTIMATION METHODS: GENERAL NOTES

The mixed estimation methods are methods which combine sample information with prior (extraneous) information available on some or all the values of the parameters.

Extraneous (or prior) information is information obtained from any other source outside the sample which is used for the estimation of a relationship. Extraneous information may be available from economic theory (theoretical prior information); from law or other institutional or empirical source (institutional or empirical prior information); from other econometric studies (statistical prior information).

Some examples will illustrate the variety of extraneous information which may be available to the econometrician in any particular application.

Firstly. We may have information on the *exact* value of some parameter from institutional information. For example assume that the tax law on cigarette consumption defines that the taxation is 70 per cent of the retail price of tobacco manufactures. This is a piece of extraneous information which may be used in any model including functions of government revenues and expenditures. For example if we want to include in a model a function for government revenues from excise taxes, we might express it in the form

$$T = b_0 + b_1 E_f + b_2 E_c + b_3 E_t + \ldots + u$$

where E_f = consumers' expenditure on food
E_c = consumers' expenditure on clothing
E_t = consumers' expenditure on tobacco manufactures.

The information from the tax law, expressed in mathematical form, yields $b_3 = 0.70$. With this information we may eliminate the influence of E_t on the total tax-revenue function. Intuitively we may express the tax function as

$$T - 0.7 E_t = b_0 + b_1 E_f + b_2 E_c + \ldots + u^*$$

The rationalisation of this procedure will be formally examined in one of the subsequent paragraphs.

Secondly. We may have information on the exact (linear) relationship between the parameters: we may know the sum of the parameters or their ratio ($b_1 + b_2 = c$, or $b_1/b_2 = c$, where c is a constant). For example suppose that from engineering information we know that the technology of a firm yields constant returns to scale. This prior information implies that in a production function of the Cobb–Douglas form

$$X = b_0 . L^{b_1} . K^{b_2} . e^u$$

(where X = output, L = labour input and K = capital input) the sum of the coefficients must be equal to one: $b_1 + b_2 = 1$.

Recall that returns to scale are defined as the proportionate change in output induced by an increase in all factor inputs by the same proportion. Thus if we change L and K by λ per cent, the new output will be

$$X^* = b_0 . (\lambda L)^{b_1} . (\lambda K)^{b_2} . e^u$$

or

$$X^* = (b_0 L^{b_1} . K^{b_2} . e^u) . \lambda^{(b_1 + b_2)}$$

$$X^* = X . \lambda^{(b_1 + b_2)}$$

The new output is equal to the initial level X multiplied by the factor $\lambda^{(b_1 + b_2)}$. Thus the sum $(b_1 + b_2)$ measures the returns to scale. If $(b_1 + b_2) = 1$, $X^* = \lambda X$, that is, we have constant returns to scale, since output changes by the same percentage as the factor inputs. If $(b_1 + b_2) > 1$, we have increasing returns to scale. Finally if $(b_1 + b_2) < 1$ we have decreasing returns to scale.

We may utilise this information as follows:

(a) Use the above relationship (restriction on the coefficients) and eliminate some of the coefficients (for example set $b_2 = 1 - b_1$).

(b) Apply classical least squares to the transformed equation, that is the equation in which we substitute $b_2 = 1 - b_1$. The transformed equation in the case of a Cobb–Douglas function is $(X/K) = b_0(L/K)^{b_1} e^u$

(c) Use the restriction again, inserting in it the least squares estimate $(\hat{b}_1)$ obtained in the previous stage, and estimate the other coefficient, that is, the coefficient which was eliminated in the first stage.

Another example may be drawn from the theory of the behaviour of the consumer. It is suggested by economic theory that the rational consumer does not suffer from 'money illusion', in other words he will not change his pattern of purchases when income and prices change by the same percentage rate. This *a priori* information implies that if the demand for a certain commodity is expressed as a function of its price and income in the (linear in the logs) form

$$D = a_0 P^{a_1} . Y^{a_2} . e^{a_3} . u$$

(where D = demand, P = price, Y = income, e^{a_3} = rate of autonomous growth) the sum of the coefficients of the variables Y and P must be equal to zero. Thus we have the restriction on the values of the elasticities $a_1 + a_2 = 0$. We may utilise this piece of extraneous information as in the previous example of the production function.

As a final example of information on the exact relationship of coefficients we may refer to the theory of the consumption function. This theory suggests that wage earners have a higher MPC than the rentier class. We may know from experience of the developed countries that the MPC of the rentier class is equal to two-thirds of the MPC of the wage earners. In the consumption function

$$C = b_0 + b_1 W + b_2 R + u$$

(where C = consumption expenditure, W = wages and salaries, R = rents and profits) we may impose the restriction $b_2 = \frac{2}{3} b_1$, that is $(b_2/b_1) = \frac{2}{3}$ and proceed in the estimation of this function as in the previous examples. The transformed equation will be

$$C = b_0 + b_1 (W + \frac{2}{3} R) + u$$

Applying OLS we obtain the estimate $\hat{b}_1$, which is subsequently inserted into the prior restriction to yield an estimate of b_2:

$$\hat{b}_2 = \frac{2}{3} \hat{b}_1$$

Thirdly. We may have extraneous information of a statistical nature, that is we may have an *unbiased estimate* of some parameter from other econometric studies already conducted in the particular field in which we are interested. Or we may have a cross-section sample, apart from our main sample of time series. In this case we may obtain unbiased estimates of some parameters from the cross-section sample and then incorporate these prior statistical estimates into the function, whose (remaining) coefficients will be subsequently estimated from the main time series sample. This technique is known as the technique of pooling together cross-section and time series data, and will be examined in some detail below.

Fourthly. Finally we may have *the range of values* of some coefficient(s). For example economic theory postulates that goods classified as necessities with no substitutes have low price and income elasticities, their demand is inelastic. This information, translated into mathematical form, implies

$$0 < |\eta_P| < 1$$
$$0 < \eta_Y < 1$$

where η_P = price elasticity of demand
            η_Y = income elasticity of demand.

Similarly from economic theory we know that any increase in income will lead to some increase in consumption. In the extreme case all the increase in income will either be consumed or saved. This bit of prior information implies that the MPC will lie between 0 and 1, that is,

$$0 < \text{MPC} < 1$$

This sort of information may be incorporated into the model by using some of the methods which will be developed in this chapter.

Various econometric methods have been suggested for the incorporation of the above type of prior information into the estimation procedure of economic models. We will examine four of these methods, namely

(1) The method of Restricted Least Squares.
(2) The method of 'Pooling Cross-section and Time Series' data. This is a special case of Restricted Least Squares. However, we examine it in some detail because of its wide use in applied research.
(3) Durbin's version of Generalised Least Squares.
(4) Theil and Goldberger's Linear Mixed Estimation method.

17.2. RESTRICTED LEAST SQUARES

This method is appropriate when we have information on the *exact* value of one or more parameters or of the *exact (linear) relationship* between them. Of course it can be applied in cases in which we have other types of information (for example estimates from other samples, or knowledge of the range of values of parameters), but in these cases there are other superior methods of estimation (for example Durbin's version of generalised least squares or the linear mixed estimation technique) as we will see in subsequent sections.

Assume we have the function

$$Y = b_0 + b_1 X_1 + b_2 X_2 + u$$

or in deviation form

$$y = b_1 x_1 + b_2 x_2 + u$$

and we have information on the value of b_1, namely $b_1 \doteq b_1^*$. This information may be taken into account by substituting b_1^* for b_1 in the function and applying least squares to the transformed equation, that is

$$(y - b_1^* x_1) = b_2 x_2 + u$$

In the transformed equation set $y^* = y - b_1^* x_1$ and apply least squares to obtain

$$b_2^* = \frac{\Sigma y^* x_2}{\Sigma x_2^2} = \frac{\Sigma (y - b_1^* x_1) x_2}{\Sigma x_2^2}$$

or

$$b_2^* = \frac{\Sigma y x_2 - b_1^* \Sigma x_1 x_2}{\Sigma x_2^2}$$

The variance of the parameter estimate b_2^* is

$$\text{var}(b_2^*) = \sigma_u^2 \frac{1}{\Sigma x_2^2}$$

The estimate b_2^* is clearly unbiased. It can be easily shown that it is more efficient than the estimate which would be obtained from the application of classical least squares directly to the original relation.

If we apply least squares to $y = b_1 x_1 + b_2 x_2 + u$, the variance of b_2 is

$$\text{var}(\hat{b}_2) = \frac{\sigma_u^2 \Sigma x_1^2}{\Sigma x_1^2 \Sigma x_2^2 - (\Sigma x_1 x_2)^2}$$

This may be written as

$$\text{var}(\hat{b}_2) = \sigma_u^2 \frac{1}{\Sigma x_2^2 - (\Sigma x_1 x_2)^2 / \Sigma x_1^2}$$

Comparing $\text{var}(b_2^*)$ with $\text{var}(\hat{b}_2)$ we see that the two expressions differ by the term $(\Sigma x_1 x_2)^2 / \Sigma x_1^2$ which appears in the denominator of the variance of the OLS estimate. This ratio is positive. Therefore the denominators of the variances are

$$\Sigma x_2^2 > \left\{ \Sigma x_2^2 - \frac{(\Sigma x_1 x_2)^2}{\Sigma x_1^2} \right\}$$

and so $\text{var}(b_2^*) < \text{var}(\hat{b}_2)$.

The method is called *restricted least squares* because it boils down to the application of least squares to a constrained relation. In other words in restricted least squares we minimise the sum of squared residuals (Σe^2) of the structural relation subject to the restriction $b_1 = b_1^*$, where b_1^* is an extraneously known value of b_1.

Proof. Assume that the model is $y = b_1 x_1 + b_2 x_2 + u$ and yields the sum of squared residuals

$$\Sigma e^2 = \Sigma(y - \hat{y})^2 = \Sigma(y - \hat{b}_1 x_1 - \hat{b}_2 x_2)^2$$

We want to minimise this expression subject to the restriction $b_1 = b_1^*$ or $\hat{b}_1 = b_1^*$.

This is a constrained minimisation problem, which may be solved by using Lagrange multipliers. Thus, using λ for the multiplier, we form the function

$$\phi = \Sigma e^2 - \lambda(\hat{b}_1 - b_1^*)$$

which is to be minimised with respect to $\hat{b}_1$, $\hat{b}_2$ and λ. We take the partial derivatives and equate to zero

$$\frac{\partial \phi}{\partial \hat{b}_1} = -2\Sigma(y - \hat{b}_1 x_1 - \hat{b}_2 x_2)(x_1) - \lambda = 0 \qquad (17.1)$$

$$\frac{\partial \phi}{\partial \hat{b}_2} = -2\Sigma(y - \hat{b}_1 x_1 - \hat{b}_2 x_2)(x_2) = 0 \qquad (17.2)$$

$$\frac{\partial \phi}{\partial \lambda} = \hat{b}_1 - b_1^* = 0 \qquad (17.3)$$

From (17.1) we obtain

$$2(\Sigma y x_1 - \hat{b}_1 \Sigma x_1^2 - \hat{b}_2 \Sigma x_1 x_2) = -\lambda$$

From (17.2)

$$-2(\Sigma y x_2 - \hat{b}_1 \Sigma x_1 x_2 - \hat{b}_2 \Sigma x_2^2) = 0$$

From (17.3) we get $\hat{b}_1 = b_1^*$. Substituting $\hat{b}_1$ in 17.2 and rearranging we obtain

$$\Sigma y x_2 - b_1^* \Sigma x_1 x_2 = \hat{b}_2 \Sigma x_2^2$$

or

$$\hat{b}_2 = \frac{\Sigma y x_2 - b_1^* \Sigma x_1 x_2}{\Sigma x_2^2}$$

This formula is identical with the one obtained earlier from the direct substitution of b_1^* into the original function.

Example. Suppose we want to estimate the consumption function of the United Kingdom from time series data of the period 1950–68. Assume that the mathematical form of the function is

$$C_t = b_0 + b_1 W_t + b_2 R_t + u$$

where C_t = consumption
  W_t = income of employees
  R_t = property income

The relevant data are shown in table 17.1. Applying OLS we obtain

$$\hat{C}_t = 2202 \cdot 97 + 0 \cdot 77\ W_t + 0 \cdot 36\ R_t \qquad R^2 = 0 \cdot 998$$
$$\phantom{\hat{C}_t = } (188 \cdot 9) \quad (0 \cdot 05) \quad (0 \cdot 21)$$

Due to the high degree of collinearity between W and R we also fitted the consumption function with the restriction

$$b_2 = \tfrac{2}{3} b_1$$

The restricted model is

$$C_t = b_0 + b_1 (W + \tfrac{2}{3}R) + v_t$$

The OLS estimates of this model are

$$C_t^* = 2120 \cdot 13 + 0 \cdot 74\ (W_t + \tfrac{2}{3}R_t) \qquad R^2 = 0 \cdot 998$$
$$ (130 \cdot 7) \quad (0 \cdot 01)$$

Finally we estimated the simple model

$$C_t = c_0 + c_1 Y_t + v_t$$

where $Y_t = W_t + R_t$. This model implies $b_1 = b_2 = c_1$. The OLS results are shown below

$$C_t^{**} = 1994 \cdot 9 + 0 \cdot 697\ Y_t \qquad R^2 = 0 \cdot 998$$
$$\phantom{C_t^{**} = } (139 \cdot 1) \quad (0 \cdot 01)$$

It is obvious that the restricted model yields more satisfactory estimates.

In this way we may impose a considerable variety of *a priori* restrictions upon the relation in which we are interested. However, the researcher must be aware that the quality of the estimates depends on the accuracy of the restrictions. In particular, the statistically estimated coefficients are a linear function of the pre-assigned values to the other coefficients. This may be seen from the following expression. We saw that in the simple case of two explanatory variables ($Y = b_0 + b_1 X_1 + b_2 X_2 + u$) if we impose the restriction $b_1 = b_1^*$, the statistical (least squares) estimate of b_2 will be

$$b_2^* = \frac{\Sigma(y - b_1^* x_1)x_2}{\Sigma x_2^2}$$

This expression may be written as

$$b_2^* = \left(\frac{\Sigma y x_2}{\Sigma x_2^2}\right) - \left(\frac{\Sigma x_1 x_2}{\Sigma x_2^2}\right) b_1^*$$

The terms in parentheses are known constants from the sample observations. Thus the least squares estimate of b_2 depends on the value which we preassign on the basis of our prior information to the parameter b_1. If our information is accurate, b_2 will not suffer from the pre-assigned value to b_1. If on the other hand there are errors in the assigned value b_1^*, the estimate of b_2 will also have some error. (See K. Fox, *Economic Statistics*, pp. 490–1 for further discussion on the sensitivity of estimated coefficients to alternative values pre-assigned to some coefficients.)

Table 17.1. Data for the estimation of the consumption function of the U.K. (in £m)

	C_t	Wages-salaries W_t	Property income R_t	Total personal income Y_t	$(W + \frac{2}{3}R)$
1948	8,552	7,433	2,522	9,955	9,114
1949	8,907	7,929	2,579	10,508	9,648
1950	9,400	8,322	2,657	10,979	10,093
1951	10,150	9,221	2,705	11,926	11,024
1952	10,691	9,943	2,775	12,718	11,793
1953	11,402	10,560	2,932	13,492	12,515
1954	12,091	11,237	3,025	14,262	13,254
1955	13,038	12,288	3,195	15,483	14,418
1956	13,744	13,384	3,261	16,645	15,558
1957	14,509	14,144	3,407	17,551	16,415
1958	15,296	14,890	3,642	18,532	17,318
1959	16,117	15,677	3,958	19,635	18,316
1960	16,933	16,310	4,853	21,163	19,545
1961	17,830	18,138	4,742	22,880	21,299
1962	18,910	19,212	4,915	24,127	22,489
1963	20,087	20,347	5,257	25,604	23,852
1964	21,459	21,985	5,685	27,670	25,775
1965	22,885	23,893	6,197	30,090	28,024
1966	24,232	25,610	6,482	32,092	29,931
1967	25,362	26,857	6,796	33,653	31,388
1968	27,113	29,058	7,174	36,232	33,841
1969	28,618	31,362	7,209	38,571	36,169

17.3. THE METHOD OF POOLING TOGETHER CROSS-SECTION AND TIME-SERIES DATA

This method is a special case of the method of restricted least squares. We examine it here in some detail because of its wide use and in order to draw the attention of the reader to the problems involved in this technique.

Suppose we want to estimate the coefficients of the demand function for food, which is of the form

$$D_t = b_0 . P_t^{b_1} . Y_t^{b_2} . e^u$$

where D = demand for food (some index of all food items)
   P = price of food (some price index of food items)
   Y = consumers' income.

Suppose further that we have a time series sample for the period 1950–68 and a cross-section sample of family budgets taken in May 1967.

On theoretical grounds time series data are more appropriate for the estimation of economic relationships. However, in practice we find that there are many problems associated with time series, the most important being the problem of intercorrelation of the explanatory variables which tend to change contemporaneously over time. In this case we cannot assess the accuracy of our estimates, because there is a tendency towards indeterminacy and instability of the coefficients of the relationship. On the other hand from the cross-section sample we cannot obtain an estimate of the price coefficient, because the price structure is the same for all the consumers at any particular point of time. Under such conditions we may use the pooling technique which avoids to a certain extent the problems associated with either time series or cross-section if each is used as the only source of information.

The fact that all the consumers are faced with the same price structure does not mean that all the households in the cross-section sample do actually pay the same price for the various commodities. Individuals pay different prices because they buy different qualities of a certain commodity. In general consumers in higher income brackets pay a higher price because they buy better quality products. This fact creates various problems which will be discussed at the end of this section.

The basic idea of the pooling technique is to obtain estimates of one or more coefficients from the cross-section data, insert them in the original function, subtract from the dependent variable the terms involving the estimated parameters, and then regress the residual value of the dependent variable on the remaining explanatory variables, obtaining estimates of the remaining coefficients from the time series sample.

In our example of the demand function for food the pooling technique may be outlined as follows.

In the first stage we use the cross-section sample to obtain an estimate of the income coefficient, b_2^*. Using this coefficient we eliminate the influence of changes in income (Y) on the dependent variable (D) by subtracting from the latter the term $b_2^* Y$. Thus we form a new variable

$$Z_t = \log D_t - b_2^* \log Y_t$$

which is the residual demand, in other words the variation of the demand which is not accounted for by changes in income.

In the second stage of the pooling technique we perform the regression

$$Z_t = \log b_0 + b_1 \log P_t + u_t$$

using the time series sample.

The combined estimated relationship becomes

$$D_t = b_0 . P_t^{\hat{b}_1} . Y_t^{b_2^*}$$

where $\hat{b}_1$ has been derived from the time series sample, while b_2^* has been obtained from the cross-section sample.

Advantages of the pooling technique

The justification of combining time series and cross-section data in estimating the parameters of economic relationships is that *under certain conditions* our estimates will be more reliable than those obtained from the application of classical least squares to the original function using only the time series sample. In particular, using cross-section data in combination with time series in the estimation of demand functions we may avoid to a certain extent the problems of multicollinearity, identification, simultaneous equation bias, and the effects of changes in income distribution (aggregation bias in the income macro-coefficient).[1]

We will discuss these issues with particular reference to the demand functions, where pooling techniques have been widely used.[2]

Firstly. Multicollinearity. From the preceding example it is clear how the pooling technique helps in avoiding the multicollinearity complications which are almost certain to appear in a time series sample, given that prices and incomes as well as most other economic magnitudes tend to move together over time. Using the pooling technique we avoid the contemporaneous presence of multicollinear variables in the relationship.

Secondly. Identification. We said that time series report equilibrium points of supply and demand ($S \equiv D$) at the ruling market price (see Chapter 15). Thus using time series data we cannot be sure that we actually estimate the coefficients of the demand function, of the supply function or of a 'bogus' function, containing elements of both supply and demand conditions. On the other hand in cross-section samples we know that the information reported about households' expenditures refers clearly to consumers' behaviour, and cannot be confused with supply conditions. Thus the income elasticity obtained from a cross-section sample is identifiable as belonging to a demand relationship.

Thirdly. Least squares simultaneous-equation bias. We said that the simultaneous-equation bias is due to the fact that some of the explanatory variables appearing in the function are not truly exogenous but are jointly determined with the dependent variable. In our example income may not be exogenous, since 'food expenditure' is an important component of total income (Y) and hence we may well expect to have the two-way causation $D = f(Y)$ and $Y = f(D)$. This joint relationship should be presented with a system of simultaneous equations, estimated with some appropriate technique, since application of classical least squares to the demand function in isolation will yield biased estimates. This source of bias, however, may be avoided to a

---

[1] The case may be different with the estimation of other functions. For example using cross-section for the estimation of production functions does not always help in identifying the relationship (see A. A. Walters, *An Introduction to Econometrics,* Macmillan, London, 1968, pp. 181–4), or in avoiding the high intercorrelation between the explanatory variables (usually labour and capital) because large firms tend to use large quantities of factor inputs while small firms tend to use small quantities of factors.

[2] See R. Stone, *Consumers' Demand in the U.K.,* 1954 and 1967.

certain extent with the pooling technique, because of the elimination of the variable Y in the second stage of the pooling procedure.

Fourthly. Aggregation bias due to changes in the distribution of income. In a demand function estimated from time series the income coefficient (and perhaps other coefficients as well) will have an aggregation bias if the distribution of income has been changing over time. However, in obtaining an estimate of the income coefficient from a cross-section sample this source of bias is avoided, because the distribution of income is given in the sample and thus the estimate of the income elasticity will be free from aggregation bias.

Yet, if income distribution changes over time we must either introduce special variables in the demand function in the second stage of the pooling technique or follow some other corrective procedure (see L. R. Klein, *An Introduction to Econometrics,* Prentice-Hall International, London, 1962, pp. 64–6, 86–7, 104–5).

Problems in pooling time series and cross-section samples

There are various snags in pooling cross-section and time series samples, which must be carefully watched if the values of the coefficients are to be properly estimated.

Firstly. Problems of interpretation of the function estimated from the application of the pooling technique. The cross-section estimates are long-run elasticities while the time series estimates are short-run elasticities. This difference in the meaning of the estimates is due to the implicit assumptions underlying the two types of estimates. Recall that in estimating the income coefficient from a cross-section sample we make the assumption that all *consumers are homogeneous* except for differences arising from income or other factors explicitly introduced in the cross-section function. Under this assumption we infer that if A acquires the higher income of B, he will also acquire B's expenditure pattern of behaviour, and since such adjustment of expenditure behaviour requires time, cross-section estimates must be interpreted as long-run elasticities. On the other hand, in time series regression analysis, we make the implicit assumption that the various *time periods are homogeneous* except for factors explicitly appearing in the function. Since the underlying conditions of an explicit relationship change through time, estimates obtained from time series are considered as short-term elasticities.

Another problem of interpretation may arise from the fact that in the cross-section sample we assume that all consumers have the same micro-elasticities (see R. G. D. Allen, *Mathematical Economics,* Macmillan, London 1956, chapter 20).

If we take the above difference in the meaning of the two types of estimates as valid, the problem arises of what is the nature of the estimated demand function, since some of its coefficients are short-run while others are long-run elasticities. Is it a long-run demand function or a short-run relationship that we estimate from the application of the pooling technique? Such considerations have induced various writers to argue that functions estimated from pooling techniques are not efficient for prediction. (See for example Shupack, 'The Predictive Accuracy of Empirical Demand Analysis', *Econ. J.,* 1962.)

Secondly. Problems of accuracy of the cross-section estimates. In a cross-section sample there are many inter-individual differences which account for the differences in the consumption expenditures of the various households. Thus, apart from income, the size of the household, the age and sex distribution of its members, profession, education, location and religion, are responsible for the observed patterns of expenditures. Such 'nuisance' variables should be taken into account when estimating the income—expenditure relationship, if the income coefficient is to be meaningful. Some factors may be accounted for before estimating the cross-section relationship. For example the number, age, and sex of members of the households can be taken into account by some measure of 'per capita' or 'per equivalent adult' expenditure. Other factors may be adequately presented with dummy variables (for example location, profession). But the computational burden may become cumbersome if the investigator wants to combine the two types of samples properly.

Thirdly. Problems arising from the reference of the cross-section estimate to a single 'point' of time. It is clear that from a cross-section sample we obtain estimates in a particular 'point' of time. We then use these estimates in order to eliminate the influence of the respective variables on the dependent variable in *all the periods* of the time series sample. This procedure implies that we consider the cross-section coefficients as remaining constant over the whole period of the time series sample, an assumption which may well be expected to be unrealistic. (Income elasticities vary considerably over time.) Thus the use of the single cross-section estimate in various time periods may involve serious bias. One way to avoid this difficulty is to use various cross-section samples referring to different 'points' of time and compare the various estimates of the same coefficient over time, interpolating for the intervening (between the various cross-section samples) years.

Fourthly. Problems of adjustment of the cross-section elasticities. Cross-section samples contain information on the expenditures of consumers on various items as well as the total expenditures of each household. Incomes are not correctly reported in the questionnaires by consumers for various reasons, and there is no way of forcing them to make accurate income statements. Thus from the cross-section sample we obtain *expenditure elasticities* from the regression of expenditure on commodity i on total expenditure

$$E_{ij} = a_0 \cdot E_j^{a_1} \cdot u_i$$

where E_{ij} = expenditure on commodity i by the jth household
E_j = total expenditure of the jth household (on all items).

In this formulation a_1 is the constant elasticity of expenditure on commodity i with respect to total expenditure

$$\eta_{E_i \cdot E} = \frac{dE_i/E_i}{dE/E} = a_1$$

However, in demand functions we want to have income elasticities

$$\eta_{Q_i \cdot Y} = \frac{dQ_i/Q_i}{dY/Y}$$

Thus when we use the pooling technique we must transform the expenditure elasticities obtained from the cross-section data into income elasticities of demand.

Expenditure elasticities obtained from a cross-section sample are higher than income elasticities for various reasons.

(a) Expenditures of households belonging to higher income brackets are larger than those of households of lower income brackets, not only because the former buy a larger quantity of i, but also because they buy a better quality of i: when income increases, expenditure on various commodities increases because we buy a greater quantity and possibly because we buy a better quality paying a higher price. Thus expenditure elasticities tend to be much greater than quantity (income) elasticities.

(b) Total expenditure, which is used as an explanatory variable in the cross-section function, is generally smaller than the income of the consumers (part of the income is saved). As income increases by a certain proportion, expenditure tends to increase at a decreasing rate. Thus the denominator of the expenditure elasticity (dE/E) tends to be smaller than the denominator of the income elasticity of demand (dY/Y). Hence expenditure elasticities tend to be higher than income elasticities for this additional reason.

The transformation of expenditure elasticities into income elasticities may be obtained by the formula

$$(\eta_{E_i \cdot E}) \cdot (\eta_{E \cdot Y}) - (\eta_{P_i \cdot Y}) = (\eta_{Q_i \cdot Y})$$

where $\eta_{E_i \cdot Y}$ = elasticity of expenditure on commodity i with respect to total E.

$\eta_{E \cdot Y}$ = elasticity of total expenditure (E) with respect to total income.

$\eta_{P_i \cdot Y}$ = elasticity of price with respect to total income. This measures the change in 'quality' bought as income increases.

$\eta_{Q_i \cdot Y}$ = elasticity of demand (quantity demanded) with respect to income.

Proof. The relationship between expenditure elasticity and income elasticity of demand may be established as follows.

$$(\eta_{E_i \cdot E} \eta_{E \cdot Y}) - \eta_{P_i \cdot Y} = \frac{dE_i}{dE} \frac{E}{E_i} \cdot \frac{dE}{dY} \frac{Y}{E} - \frac{dP_i}{dY} \frac{Y}{P}$$

$$= \frac{dE_i}{dY} \frac{Y}{E_i} - \frac{dP_i}{dY} \frac{Y}{P}$$

Now $E_i = P_i Q_i$, where $P_i = f(Y)$ and $Q_i = f(Y)$. Therefore, applying the rule of the derivative of 'function of a function' we obtain

$$\frac{dE_i}{dY} = Q_i \frac{dP_i}{dY} + P_i \frac{dQ_i}{dY}$$

Substituting we find

$$
(\eta_{E_i.E}.\eta_{E.Y}) - \eta_{P_i.Y} = \left(Q_i \frac{dP_i}{dY} + P_i \frac{dQ_i}{dY} \right) \frac{Y}{P_i Q_i} - \frac{dP_i}{dY} \frac{Y}{P_i}
$$

$$
= \frac{dP_i}{dY} \frac{Y}{P_i} + \frac{dQ_i}{dY} \frac{Y}{Q_i} - \frac{dP_i}{dY} \frac{Y}{P_i}
$$

$$
= \frac{dQ_i}{dY} \frac{Y}{Q_i} = \eta_{Q_i.Y}
$$

For the transformation of expenditure elasticities obtained from a cross-section sample we need some measure of $\eta_{E.Y}$ and of $\eta_{P_i.Y}$. An estimate of $\eta_{E.Y}$ may be obtained from a straightforward regression of total private expenditure on total income ($E = f(Y)$), both time series obtainable from the National Accounts statistics.

The calculation of 'quality' elasticities presents enormous difficulties. Some researchers use an arbitrary coefficient of adjustment (for example they reduce the expenditure elasticity by 10 per cent), a procedure which is subject to criticism because of its arbitrariness.

Note that if the demand function is measured in expenditure terms one need not adjust for $\eta_{E.Y}$; however, one should still adjust the expenditure elasticity for quality changes ($\eta_{P_i.Y}$).

17.4. DURBIN'S GENERALISED LEAST SQUARES

The restricted least squares method has the defect that it does not use the main sample of observations to improve on the prior estimates known from other statistical measurements. Durbin has suggested the following method which allows the use of the main sample to improve on prior statistical estimates of coefficients.

Assume that from a cross-section sample (or from other published research) we have an unbiased estimate of some coefficient. For example for the function

$$
y = b_1 x_1 + b_2 x_2 + u
$$

we have the statistical information

$$
b_1^* = b_1 + v
$$

where v is a random variable such that

$$
E(v) = 0
$$
$$
E(v^2) = \sigma_v^2
$$
$$
E(vu) = 0
$$

In our simple example $\sigma_v^2 = \sigma_{b_1^*}^2$.

We can incorporate this information in the function and, using our (main) sample, we may obtain a new, more efficient estimate for b_1 as well as obtaining an estimate for b_2. This is achieved by the following procedure.[1]

Firstly. Apply ordinary least squares to the original relationship and obtain an estimate of the variance of the disturbance term

$$\hat{\sigma}_u^2 = \frac{\Sigma e^2}{n - K}$$

(where $K = k + 1 = 3$ in our example).

Secondly. Given the value b_1^* and its variance $\sigma_{b_1^*}^2$, we solve the following system of equations

$$\Sigma x_1 y + b_1^* \frac{\hat{\sigma}_u^2}{\sigma_{b_1}^2} = b_1 \left[\Sigma x_1^2 + \frac{\hat{\sigma}_u^2}{\sigma_{b_1}^2} \right] + b_2 \Sigma x_1 x_2$$

$$\Sigma x_2 y = b_1 \Sigma x_1 x_2 + b_2 \Sigma x_2^2$$

The difference between these equations and the normal equations of classical least squares is in the first equation only. This is due to the assumption of having information only on one coefficient, b_1^* and its variance, $\text{var}(b_1^*)$. If we have information on more coefficients the transformation of the normal equations becomes more complicated. Suppose we have prior information on both b_1^* and b_2^* and on their variances and covariance

$$b_1^* = b_1 + v_1$$
$$b_2^* = b_2 + v_2$$
$$\text{var}(b_1^*) \qquad \text{var}(b_2^*) \qquad \text{cov}(b_1^* b_2^*)$$

If the covariances of the estimates are zero, the transformation of the original normal equations is similar to the one described above, that is

$$\Sigma x_i y + b_1^* \frac{\hat{\sigma}_u^2}{\text{var}(b_1^*)} = b_1 \left[\Sigma x_1^2 + \frac{\hat{\sigma}_u^2}{\text{var}(b_1^*)} \right] + b_2 \Sigma x_1 x_2$$

$$\Sigma x_2 y + b_2^* \frac{\hat{\sigma}_u^2}{\text{var}(b_2^*)} = b_1 \Sigma x_1 x_2 + b_2 \left[\Sigma x_2^2 + \frac{\hat{\sigma}_u^2}{\text{var}(b_2^*)} \right]$$

In general if we have information on various coefficients *whose covariances are zero,* the transformation consists of adding the term $\left(b_i^* \dfrac{\hat{\sigma}_u^2}{\text{var}(b_i^*)} \right)$ to the left-hand side of the relevant (*i*th) normal equation and the ratio $\hat{\sigma}_u^2 / \text{var}(b_i^*)$ to the term (of the same equation) which contains the sum of squares of the *i*th explanatory variable.

---

[1] The justification of this procedure lies in that if we incorporate the information $b_1^* = b_1 + v$ into our original equation, the new disturbance term is heteroscedastic, and hence the appropriate solution is to apply the method of generalised least squares, that is we apply ordinary least squares to transformed original data. The type of transformation is found from the form of the variance of the new (composite) disturbance term. See A. Goldberger, *Econometric Theory,* p. 259. See also Chapter 9 of this book.

For example suppose we have the structural relation

$$y = b_1 x_1 + b_2 x_2 + b_3 x_3 + b_4 x_4 + u$$

together with the information

$$b_1^* = b_1 + v_1 \qquad E(v_1) = 0$$
$$b_2^* = b_2 + v_2 \qquad E(v_2) = 0$$
$$b_3^* = b_3 + v_3 \qquad E(v_3) = 0$$
$$\text{var}(b_1^*) \qquad\qquad \text{var}(b_2^*) \qquad\qquad \text{var}(b_3^*)$$

$$\text{cov}(b_1^* b_2^*) = \text{cov}(b_1^* b_3^*) = \text{cov}(b_2^* b_3^*) = 0.$$

The system of transformed normal equations is then

$$\Sigma x_1 y + [b_1^* \{\hat{\sigma}_u^2 / \text{var}(b_1^*)\}] = \tilde{b}_1 [\Sigma x_1^2 + \hat{\sigma}_u^2 / \text{var}(b_1^*)] + \tilde{b}_2 \Sigma x_1 x_2 + \tilde{b}_3 \Sigma x_1 x_3 + \\ + \tilde{b}_4 \Sigma x_1 x_4$$

$$\Sigma x_2 y + [b_2^* \{\hat{\sigma}_u^2 / \text{var}(b_2^*)\}] = \tilde{b}_1 \Sigma x_1 x_2 + \tilde{b}_2 [\Sigma x_2^2 + \hat{\sigma}_u^2 / \text{var}(b_2^*)] + \tilde{b}_3 \Sigma x_2 x_3 + \\ + \tilde{b}_4 \Sigma x_2 x_4$$

$$\Sigma x_3 y + [b_3^* \{\hat{\sigma}_u^2 / \text{var}(b_3^*)\}] = \tilde{b}_1 \Sigma x_1 x_3 + \tilde{b}_2 \Sigma x_2 x_3 + \tilde{b}_3 [\Sigma x_3^2 + \hat{\sigma}_u^2 / \text{var}(b_3^*)] + \\ + \tilde{b}_4 \Sigma x_3 x_4$$

$$\Sigma x_4 y = \tilde{b}_1 \Sigma x_1 x_4 + \tilde{b}_2 \Sigma x_2 x_4 + \tilde{b}_3 \Sigma x_3 x_4 + \tilde{b}_4 \Sigma x_4^2.$$

However, in most applications the covariances of the prior b^*'s are not zero. Hence we must examine the transformation of the normal equations required when $\text{cov}(b_i^* b_j^*) \neq 0$. We shall begin with a model in which two of the b's are known together with their variances and covariances from other statistical studies or other sources of extraneous information.

The model in deviation form is

$$y = b_1 x_1 + b_2 x_2 + \ldots + b_k x_k + u$$
$$b_1^* = b_1 + v_1 \qquad E(u) = 0$$
$$b_2^* = b_2 + v_2 \qquad E(v_1) = E(v_2) = 0$$
$$E(u v_i) = 0$$

The variances and covariances of the prior b^*'s may be written in the form of a determinant

$$\begin{vmatrix} \text{var}(b_1^*) & \text{cov}(b_1^* b_2^*) \\ \text{cov}(b_1^* b_2^*) & \text{var}(b_2^*) \end{vmatrix} = \begin{vmatrix} s_1^2 & s_{12} \\ s_{21} & s_2^2 \end{vmatrix} = |\Delta_2| \text{ known}$$

(The subscript of Δ indicates the number of known prior b^*'s.)

The system of normal equations in this case is

$$\Sigma yx_1 + \hat{\sigma}_u^2 \cdot \frac{\begin{vmatrix} b_1^* & s_{12} \\ b_2^* & s_2^2 \end{vmatrix}}{|\Delta_2|} = \tilde{b}_1\left[\Sigma x_1^2 + \hat{\sigma}_u^2 \cdot \frac{(+1)\begin{vmatrix} s_1^2 & s_{12} \\ s_{12} & s_2^2 \end{vmatrix}}{|\Delta_2|}\right] + \tilde{b}_2\left[\Sigma x_1 x_2 + \right.$$

$$\left. + \hat{\sigma}_u^2 \frac{(-1)\begin{vmatrix} s_1^2 & s_{12} \\ s_{12} & s_2^2 \end{vmatrix}}{|\Delta_2|}\right] + \tilde{b}_3 \Sigma x_1 x_3 + \ldots + \tilde{b}_k \Sigma x_1 x_k$$

$$\Sigma yx_2 + \hat{\sigma}_u^2 \cdot \frac{\begin{vmatrix} s_1^2 & b_1^* \\ s_{12} & b_2^* \end{vmatrix}}{|\Delta_2|} = \tilde{b}_1\left[\Sigma x_1 x_2 + \hat{\sigma}_u^2 \cdot \frac{(-1)\begin{vmatrix} s_1^2 & s_{12} \\ s_{12} & s_2^2 \end{vmatrix}}{|\Delta_2|}\right] + \tilde{b}_2\left[\Sigma x_2^2 + \right.$$

$$\left. + \hat{\sigma}_u^2 \cdot \frac{(+1)\begin{vmatrix} s_1^2 & s_{12} \\ s_{12} & s_2^2 \end{vmatrix}}{|\Delta_2|}\right] + \tilde{b}_3 \Sigma x_2 x_3 + \ldots + \tilde{b}_k \Sigma x_2 x_k$$

$$\Sigma yx_3 = \tilde{b}_1 \Sigma x_1 x_3 + \tilde{b}_2 \Sigma x_2 x_3 + \tilde{b}_3 \Sigma x_3^2 + \ldots + \tilde{b}_k \Sigma x_3 x_k$$

$$\cdot \qquad \cdot \qquad \cdot \qquad \cdot$$
$$\cdot \qquad \cdot \qquad \cdot \qquad \cdot$$
$$\cdot \qquad \cdot \qquad \cdot \qquad \cdot$$

$$\Sigma yx_k = \tilde{b}_1 \Sigma x_1 x_k + \tilde{b}_2 \Sigma x_2 x_k + \tilde{b}_3 \Sigma x_3 x_k \ldots + \tilde{b}_k \Sigma x_k^2$$

A careful inspection of the transformed model will help in the generalisation of the procedure to models for which we have prior (theoretical or statistical) information on any number of parameters. Looking at the above transformed model we observe the following.

Firstly. In the transformed system of normal equations, only the equations associated to the b's on which we have prior information will be 'corrected' by appropriate terms. The remaining equations associated with b's on which no prior information is available will be the same as in the OLS method.

Secondly. The 'correction' consists of adding some terms involving the prior b^*'s and their variances and covariances as well as an estimate of the σ_u^2, obtained from OLS applied to the sample observations. Thus:

(i) To the *left-hand side* of the jth equation (corresponding to the jth parameter on which we have prior information) we add the product of the estimate $\hat{\sigma}_u^2$ multiplied by the ratio of two determinants: In the denominator we set the determinant of the variances and covariances of the prior b^*'s, and in the numerator the same determinant with the column corresponding to b_j substituted for the column of prior b^*'s.

(ii) To the *right-hand side* we 'correct' the terms that correspond to the b's on which we have prior information. To *each* such term in the right-hand side we add the product of $\hat{\sigma}_u^2$ (obtained from OLS applied to the sample observations) multiplied by the ratio of two determinants: the determinant in the denominator is the variance—covariance determinant of the prior b^*'s, $|\Delta|$, while the determinant in the numerator is the pre-signed minor determinant left after we strike out the row and column of $|\Delta|$ which contains the variance or the covariance element (s_i^2 or s_{ij}) corresponding to the variables appearing in the term which we transform. (Note that the variance—covariance determinant is symmetric: the variances of the prior b^*'s appear once only in the main diagonal of $|\Delta|$, but the covariances s_{ij} of b_i^* and b_j^*'s ($i \neq j$) appear twice, above and below the main diagonal symmetrically, that is, each s_{ij} appears in two rows and in two columns of $|\Delta|$. In transforming the relevant $\Sigma x_i x_j$ term of any normal equation we strike out of $|\Delta|$ only one of the columns (and the corresponding row) in which s_{ij} appears, and not both columns.

As an illustration of the above transformation rules let us form the normal equations for a k-variable model for which we have the following prior information:

The model is

$$y = b_1 x_1 + b_2 x_2 + \ldots + b_k x_k + u$$

and the available prior information

$$b_1^* = b_1 + v_1$$
$$b_2^* = b_2 + v_2$$
$$b_3^* = b_3 + v_3$$

where the b_i^*'s are unbiased with variances and covariances known

$$|\Delta_3| = \begin{vmatrix} \operatorname{var}(b_1^*) & \operatorname{cov}(b_1^* b_2^*) & \operatorname{cov}(b_1^* b_3^*) \\ \operatorname{cov}(b_1^* b_2^*) & \operatorname{var}(b_2^*) & \operatorname{cov}(b_2^* b_3^*) \\ \operatorname{cov}(b_1^* b_3^*) & \operatorname{cov}(b_2^* b_3^*) & \operatorname{var}(b_3^*) \end{vmatrix} = \begin{vmatrix} s_1^2 & s_{12} & s_{13} \\ s_{12} & s_2^2 & s_{23} \\ s_{13} & s_{23} & s_3^2 \end{vmatrix}$$

We wish to obtain the set of mixed estimates $\tilde{b}_i$ ($i = 1, 2, \ldots, k$).

Step 1. We apply OLS to the sample and we obtain the variance estimate $\hat{\sigma}_u^2 = \Sigma e^2/(n - K)$.

Step 2. We form the system of transformed normal equations. In our example only the three first equations will differ from the corresponding OLS equations, as follows.

1st Equation

$$\Sigma y x_1 + \hat{\sigma}_u^2 \cdot \frac{\begin{vmatrix} b_1^* & s_{12} & s_{13} \\ b_2^* & s_2^2 & s_{23} \\ b_3^* & s_{23} & s_3^2 \end{vmatrix}}{|\Delta_3|} = \tilde{b}_1 \left[\Sigma x_1^2 + \hat{\sigma}_u^2 \cdot \frac{(+1)\begin{vmatrix} s_1^2 & s_{12} & s_{13} \\ s_{12} & s_2^2 & s_{23} \\ s_{13} & s_{23} & s_3^2 \end{vmatrix}}{|\Delta_3|} \right] +$$

$$+ \tilde{b}_2 \left[\Sigma x_1 x_2 + \hat{\sigma}_u^2 \cdot \frac{(-1)\begin{vmatrix} s_1^2 & s_{12} & s_{13} \\ s_{12} & s_2^2 & s_{23} \\ s_{13} & s_{23} & s_3^2 \end{vmatrix}}{|\Delta_3|} \right] +$$

$$+ \tilde{b}_3 \left[\Sigma x_1 x_3 + \hat{\sigma}_u^2 \cdot \frac{(+1) \begin{vmatrix} s_1^2 & s_{12} & s_{13} \\ s_{12} & s_2^2 & s_{23} \\ s_{13} & s_{23} & s_3^2 \end{vmatrix}}{|\Delta_3|} \right] +$$

$$+ \tilde{b}_4 \Sigma x_1 x_4 + \ldots + \tilde{b}_k \Sigma x_1 x_k$$

2nd Equation

$$\Sigma y x_2 + \hat{\sigma}_u^2 \cdot \frac{\begin{vmatrix} s_1^2 & b_1^* & s_{13} \\ s_{12} & b_2^* & s_{23} \\ s_{13} & b_3^* & s_3^2 \end{vmatrix}}{|\Delta_3|} = \tilde{b}_1 \left[\Sigma x_1 x_2 + \hat{\sigma}_u^2 \cdot \frac{(+1) \begin{vmatrix} s_1^2 & s_{12} & s_{13} \\ s_{12} & s_2^2 & s_{23} \\ s_{13} & s_{23} & s_3^2 \end{vmatrix}}{|\Delta_3|} \right] +$$

$$+ \tilde{b}_2 \left[\Sigma x_2^2 + \hat{\sigma}_u^2 \cdot \frac{(-1) \begin{vmatrix} s_1^2 & s_{12} & s_{13} \\ s_{12} & s_2^2 & s_{23} \\ s_{13} & s_{23} & s_3^2 \end{vmatrix}}{|\Delta_3|} \right] +$$

$$+ \tilde{b}_3 \left[\Sigma x_2 x_3 + \hat{\sigma}_u^2 \cdot \frac{(-1) \begin{vmatrix} s_1^2 & s_{12} & s_{13} \\ s_{12} & s_2^2 & s_{23} \\ s_{13} & s_{23} & s_3^2 \end{vmatrix}}{|\Delta_3|} \right] +$$

$$+ \tilde{b}_4 \Sigma x_2 x_4 + \ldots + \tilde{b}_k \Sigma x_2 x_k$$

3rd Equation

$$\Sigma y x_3 + \hat{\sigma}_u^2 \cdot \frac{\begin{vmatrix} s_1^2 & s_{12} & b_1^* \\ s_{12} & s_2^2 & b_2^* \\ s_{13} & s_{23} & b_3^* \end{vmatrix}}{|\Delta_3|} = \tilde{b}_1 \left[\Sigma x_1 x_3 + \hat{\sigma}_u^2 \cdot \frac{(+1) \begin{vmatrix} s_1 & s_{12} & s_{13} \\ s_{12} & s_2^2 & s_{23} \\ s_{13} & s_{23} & s_3^2 \end{vmatrix}}{|\Delta_3|} \right] +$$

$$+ \tilde{b}_2 \left[\Sigma x_2 x_3 + \hat{\sigma}_u^2 \cdot \frac{(-1) \begin{vmatrix} s_1^2 & s_{12} & s_{13} \\ s_{12} & s_2^2 & s_{23} \\ s_{13} & s_{23} & s_3^2 \end{vmatrix}}{|\Delta_3|} \right] +$$

$$+ \tilde{b}_3 \left[\Sigma x_3^2 + \hat{\sigma}_u^2 \cdot \frac{(+1) \begin{vmatrix} s_1^2 & s_{12} & s_{13} \\ s_{12} & s_2^2 & s_{23} \\ s_{13} & s_{23} & s_3^2 \end{vmatrix}}{|\Delta_3|} \right] +$$

$$+ \tilde{b}_4 \Sigma x_3 x_4 + \ldots + \tilde{b}_k \Sigma x_3 x_k$$

The remaining equations of the system do not invovle any 'correction': they are identical to the OLS normal equations.

The extension to cases in which we have prior information on more b^*'s is straight-forward.

17.5. THEIL AND GOLDBERGER'S MIXED LINEAR ESTIMATION

(See Theil and Goldberger, 'On Pure and Mixed Statistical Estimation in Economics', *Int. Econ. Rev.,* vol. 2, No. 1, January 1961.)

This method has been called mixed estimation by its inventors because it combines sample information with prior information on some or all the structural parameters. It is distinct from pure estimation methods which use only information from a particular sample.

The method is suggested as a better alternative to what we called 'experimental approach' in Chapter 2. Recall that the experimental approach involves the following procedure: the econometrician formulates a model using his *a priori* knowledge about the relationship to be measured. Such prior information is derived from the economic theory and experience and is usually of a qualitative type; that is, it concerns: (a) the variables which are to be included in the model, (b) the sign of the coefficients, (c) some order of magnitude of the coefficients which seems plausible (for example the income elasticity of demand for food is expected to be positive but less than unity, which implies $0 < \eta_Y < 1$), (d) some idea of the mathematical form (linear, linear in logarithms) of the model. The model formulated on the basis of such qualitative information is called *the maintained hypothesis.* The econometrician uses then sample observations to measure this model, that is, to test his maintained hypothesis. Given that he cannot be absolutely certain about the exact specification of the true model, he experiments with various sets of explanatory variables and alternative mathematical forms, and then he *chooses* among these alternative models the one *he thinks* is best in the light of his *a priori* (qualitative) knowledge as well as on the basis of statistical and econometric criteria (see Chapter 2). This procedure has been criticised on the grounds that it involves frequent change of the maintained hypothesis, that it involves subjective judgement of the researcher, that it disregards the loss of degrees of freedom caused by the 'experiments' and that it does not incorporate into the model the *a priori* quantitative knowledge of the probable magnitude and sign of the coefficient. This information is only used as a criterion for the acceptance or rejection of the results; that is, if the estimates violate the *a priori* information not included in the model (in the maintained hypothesis), the model is rejected with the justification that 'wrong' information was erroneously incorporated in its formulation, and then a new model, excluding some variable(s) and including some other(s) is tried again.

Theil and Goldberger's mixed estimation method is designed especially for the incorporation of *a priori* information into the model *before its estimation.* The basic characteristic of the method is that the research worker has prior knowledge on *the range of values* within which the value of the true parameter will 'most probably' fall. From this knowledge the research worker obtains a 'point estimate' as well as its 'sampling variance'. This information is subsequently used in the same way as in Durbin's version of generalised least squares examined in the previous section. The inventors furthermore adopt an iterative procedure involving the use of new estimates of the variance of the u term, obtained in previous iterations. The *a priori* information must be quantitative, that is we must have knowledge of the range within which the value of the coefficient is expected to lie. Usually such knowledge is provided by the general economic theory. For example suppose that we want to estimate the demand for food as a function of price and consumers' income

$$\log D = \log b_0 + b_1 \log P + b_2 \log Y + u.$$

In this formulation b_1 and b_2 are straightforward price and income elasticities respectively. Suppose we know that the income elasticity of demand is almost certain to lie between 0·4 and 0·8. With the mixed linear estimation method we can incorporate this information into the model because it provides the lower and upper limits of the value of the true income parameter in the sense that the researcher considers it very implausible that the coefficient may lie outside the interval. If we have knowledge of the signs of the coefficients only, this information is useless for mixed estimation methods, because the range of values which this information implies is very wide. For example we know from economic theory that the income elasticity of demand is positive (except for inferior goods). If we have no further information, the above *a priori* knowledge of the sign of the income elasticity does not help, because the income elasticity may assume any value between 0 and ∞ without violation of our prior information about the positive sign. The narrower the range within which we know that the coefficient must lie, the more useful our information becomes for mixed estimation techniques.

The mixed estimation method may be outlined as follows.

We assume that (1) the random variable of the structural model satisfies the usual assumptions of zero mean, constant variance and zero covariance; (2) we have *a priori* information on the range of plausible values of some or all the parameters.

Step I. We use the range of plausible values in order to obtain a point estimate of the respective coefficient as well as of its variance. (Alternatively we may have some information on the average value of the coefficient and its variance from previous studies.) This is achieved by interpreting the known *a priori* range of values as the 95 per cent confidence interval of the coefficient in question. Thus we take the mid-value of the range as the point estimate of the coefficient, b_i. We then assume, with a 95 per cent probability, that the true value b_i will lie between the lower and upper values of the range. From the confidence interval formula (developed in Chapter 5) we may write that the interval

$$b_i^* \pm 2 s_{(b_i^*)}$$

(where $b_i^* =$ the mid value of the boundary values) contains 95 per cent of the values of the true parameter. We may obtain the standard error of b_i^* as follows

$$s_{(b_i^*)} = (b_i^* \pm \text{boundary value})/2.$$

To return to our earlier example of the income coefficient, assume we know that the range of plausible values of the income elasticity is between 0·4 and 0·8. The point estimate will be the mid-value 0·6. Thus the boundary values for the income elasticity are

$$0\cdot4 = 0\cdot6 - 2s_{(b_i^*)}$$
$$0\cdot8 = 0\cdot6 + 2s_{(b_i^*)}$$

From either of these expressions we obtain

$$s_{(b_i^*)} = 0\cdot1$$

and therefore

$$s^2_{(b_i^*)} = 0\cdot01$$

Step II. Having this information we may use the sample observations in order to obtain an improved estimate of the coefficient(s) on whom we have prior knowledge as well as of the remaining coefficients of the model. This is achieved by applying Durbin's version of generalised least squares, which we examined in the preceding section. For this we require, apart from $s^2_{(b_i^*)}$, knowledge of the variance of the disturbance term, σ_u^2. In the initial stage we use the sample data, apply least squares (or, depending on the identification condition of the function, another suitable method, for example 2 SLS) and obtain $\hat{\sigma}_u^2$.

Step III. Having $\hat{\sigma}_u^2$ and $s^2_{(b_i^*)}$ we apply least squares to the transformed normal equations developed in the previous section. Thus in the general case in which we have prior information on all the structural parameters of the function $y = b_1 x_1 + b_2 x_2 + \ldots + b_k x_k + u$ (and provided that the covariances of the prior b^*'s are zero) the system of transformed equations is identical to that on page 412, that is

$$\Sigma x_1 y + \left[b_1^* \frac{\hat{\sigma}_u^2}{s_{b_1^*}^2} \right] = b_1 \left[\Sigma x_1^2 + \frac{\hat{\sigma}_u^2}{s_{b_1^*}^2} \right] + b_2 \Sigma x_1 x_2 + \ldots + b_k \Sigma x_1 x_k$$

$$\Sigma x_2 y + \left[b_2^* \frac{\hat{\sigma}_u^2}{s_{b_2^*}^2} \right] = b_1 \Sigma x_1 x_2 + b_2 \left[\Sigma x_2^2 + \frac{\hat{\sigma}_u^2}{s_{b_2^*}^2} \right] + \ldots + b_k \Sigma x_2 x_k$$

$$\cdot \qquad \cdot \qquad \cdot \qquad \cdot$$

$$\cdot \qquad \cdot \qquad \cdot \qquad \cdot$$

$$\Sigma x_k y + \left[b_k^* \frac{\hat{\sigma}_u^2}{s_{b_k^*}^2} \right] = b_1 \Sigma x_1 x_k + b_2 \Sigma x_2 x_k + \ldots + b_k \left[\Sigma x_k^2 + \frac{\hat{\sigma}_u^2}{s_{b_k^*}^2} \right]$$

To illustrate the application of the mixed estimation technique we will use the example of Theil and Goldberger. They start with a model of the market mechanism for meat in the USA:

$$y_1 = \gamma y_2 + \beta_1 x_1 + \beta_2 x_2 + u \qquad \text{(supply)}$$
$$y_1 = \gamma' y_2 + \beta_3 x_3 + u' \qquad \text{(demand)}$$

where
y_1 = per capita consumption of meat (pounds per year)
y_2 = retail price (index, 1935–9 = 100)
x_1 = cost of processing meat (index, 1935–9 = 100)
x_2 = cost of producing agricultural products (index, 1935–9 = 100)
x_3 = per capita real disposable income (dollars per year).

Theil and Goldberger set out to estimate the coefficients of the supply function using a sample of 23 annual observations (covering the period 1919–41). All variables are measured in deviation form. The sums of squares and products are included in table 17.2.

Table 17.2. Sums of squares and products of deviations from the means

	Supply y_1	Price y_2	Cost of meat x_1	Cost of agricul. products x_2	Per capita income x_3
y_1	1369·54	−352·55	−536·48	983·86	3671·91
y_2		1581·49	850·33	1235·76	8354·59
x_1			2534·80	730·78	3611·72
x_2				2626·99	12204·77
x_3					83433·65
Means	$\bar{y}_1$ = 166·19	$\bar{y}_2$ = 92·34	$\bar{x}_1$ = 88·42	$\bar{x}_2$ = 102·22	

On *a priori* grounds γ is expected to have a positive sign, while β_1 and β_2 are expected to have a negative sign.

Theil and Goldberger's example involves some experimentation: initially they assume *a priori* knowledge of only one coefficient (γ, the price coefficient), while in the end they incorporate in their model prior information on all three structural parameters. We will examine only the last part which is more general.

Step I. Assume that we have the following information on the average elasticities and their standard deviations

$$\text{price elasticity:} \quad \eta_{(y_1 y_2)} = 0.5 \qquad s_{\eta_{(y_1 y_2)}} = 0.2$$
$$\text{cost elasticity 1:} \quad \eta_{(y_1 x_1)} = -0.5 \qquad s_{\eta_{(y_1 x_1)}} = 0.2$$
$$\text{cost elasticity 2:} \quad \eta_{(y_1 x_2)} = -0.5 \qquad s_{\eta_{(y_1 x_2)}} = 0.2$$

Since the supply function is assumed linear the above elasticities must be converted into slopes and from the standard deviations of the elasticities we must derive the standard deviations of the slopes. The conversion is achieved by using the classical formula

$$\eta_{(yx_i)} = b_i \frac{\overline{X}_i}{\overline{Y}}$$

The means are computed from the sample observations and are given in the last row of table 17.2. Substituting in the above formula the values of the elasticities and the relevant means we obtain:

Slopes	Standard errors	Variances
$\gamma^* = (0.5)\left(\dfrac{166.19}{92.34}\right) = 0.9$	$s(\gamma^*) = (0.2)\left(\dfrac{166.19}{92.34}\right) = 0.36$	$\sigma_{\gamma*}^2 = 0.1296$
$\beta_1^* = (-0.5)\left(\dfrac{166.19}{88.42}\right) = -0.94$	$s(\beta_1^*) = (0.2)\left(\dfrac{166.19}{88.42}\right) = 0.376$	$\sigma_{\beta_1*}^2 = 0.1414$
$\beta_2^* = (-0.5)\left(\dfrac{166.19}{102.22}\right) = -0.81$	$s(\beta_2^*) = (0.2)\left(\dfrac{166.19}{102.22}\right) = 0.324$	$\sigma_{\beta_2*}^2 = 0.1050$

Step II. The initial estimate of the variance of the random disturbance u is obtained by applying 2SLS to the original function. This method is chosen because the supply equation contains the endogenous variable y_2 (price of meat) among the set of explanatory variables. The results of this method are included in the third column of table 17.3. We see that $\hat{\sigma}_u^2 = 21.13$. The sign of γ is 'wrong' on *a priori* grounds and its value statistically insignificant.

We substitute the values of the variance of u and the variances of the coefficients in the system of transformed equations and we obtain the initial solution, included in the fourth column of table 17.3. The set of equations is as follows: (note that $\text{cov}(\gamma\beta_1) = \text{cov}(\gamma\beta_2) = \text{cov}(\beta_1\beta_2) = 0$)

$$\Sigma y_1 y_2 + \gamma^* \frac{\hat{\sigma}_u^2}{\sigma_{\gamma*}^2} = \hat{\gamma}\left(\Sigma y_2^2 + \frac{\hat{\sigma}_u^2}{\sigma_\gamma^2}\right) + \hat{\beta}_1 \Sigma y_2 x_1 + \hat{\beta}_2 \Sigma y_2 x_2$$

$$\Sigma y_1 x_1 + \beta_1^* \frac{\hat{\sigma}_u^2}{\hat{\sigma}_{\beta_1^*}^2} = \hat{\gamma}\Sigma y_2 x_1 + \hat{\beta}_1\left(\Sigma x_1^2 + \frac{\hat{\sigma}_u^2}{\hat{\sigma}_{\beta_1^*}^2}\right) + \hat{\beta}_2 \Sigma x_1 x_2$$

$$\Sigma y_1 x_2 + \beta_2^* \frac{\hat{\sigma}_u^2}{\hat{\sigma}_{\beta_2^*}^2} = \hat{\gamma}\Sigma y_2 x_2 + \hat{\beta}_1 \Sigma x_1 x_2 + \hat{\beta}_2\left(\Sigma x_2^2 + \frac{\hat{\sigma}_u^2}{\hat{\sigma}_{\beta_2^*}^2}\right)$$

Using the estimates of the variances and the sums of squares and products included in table 17.2 we have

$$-352.55 + (0.9)\frac{21.13}{0.1296} = \hat{\gamma}\left(1581.49 + \frac{21.13}{0.1296}\right) + \hat{\beta}_1(850.33) + \hat{\beta}_2(1235.76)$$

$$-536.48 + (-0.94)\frac{21.13}{0.1414} = \hat{\gamma}(850.33) + \hat{\beta}_1\left(2534.80 + \frac{21.13}{0.1414}\right) + \hat{\beta}_2(730.78)$$

$$983.86 + (-0.81)\frac{21.13}{0.1056} = \hat{\gamma}(1235.76) + \hat{\beta}_1(730.78) + \hat{\beta}_2\left(2626.99 + \frac{21.13}{0.1056}\right)$$

From the above initial solution we obtain a new estimate of the variance of u, $\hat{\hat{\sigma}}_u^2 = 74.39$. This value we use in the next iteration, which involves the solution of the following system of equations:

$$-352.55 + (0.9)\frac{74.39}{0.1296} = \hat{\hat{\gamma}}\left(1581.49 + \frac{74.39}{0.1296}\right) + \hat{\hat{\beta}}_1(850.33) + \hat{\hat{\beta}}_2(1235.76)$$

$$-536.48 + (-0.94)\frac{74.39}{0.1414} = \hat{\hat{\gamma}}(850.33) + \hat{\hat{\beta}}_1\left(2534.80 + \frac{74.39}{0.1414}\right) + \hat{\hat{\beta}}_2(730.78)$$

$$983.86 + (-0.81)\frac{74.39}{0.1056} = \hat{\hat{\gamma}}(1235.76) + \hat{\hat{\beta}}_1(730.78) + \hat{\hat{\beta}}_2\left(2626.99 + \frac{74.39}{0.1056}\right)$$

This system differs from the previous one only in the value of the variance of the u term: in the first system $\hat{\sigma}_u^2 = 21.13$, in the second $\hat{\hat{\sigma}}_u^2 = 74.39$.

The iterative process continues until the values of the coefficients converge (to any desired decimal place). Theil and Goldberger choose to stop the iterative process at the fifth iteration, at which the coefficients are stable to two decimal places. The results are shown in table 17.3.

Table 17.3. Estimate of the meat supply equation using *a priori* information on all coefficients.

Coef-ficients	Prior informa-tion	2SLS estimates (Pure sample estimates)	Mixed estimation					
			Initial solution	Itera-tion I	Itera-tion II	Itera-tion III	Itera-tion IV	Itera-tion V
γ	0.90 (0.36)	−0.321 (0.29)	0.412 (0.41)	0.849 (0.38)	0.965 (0.33)	0.987 (0.31)	0.991 (0.31)	0.992 (0.31)
β_1	−0.94 (0.375)	−0.278 (0.11)	−0.444 (0.19)	−0.556 (0.23)	−0.603 (0.23)	−0.616 (0.22)	−0.619 (0.22)	−0.620 (0.22)
β_2	−0.81 (0.326)	0.603 (0.15)	0.225 (0.23)	−0.068 (0.24)	−0.205 (0.23)	−0.243 (0.22)	−0.251 (0.22)	−0.253 (0.22)
σ_u^2		21.13	74.39	134.11	158.58	164.77	166.14	166.44

Note: The figures in parentheses are the standard errors of the coefficients.

CRITIQUE OF THE MIXED ESTIMATION METHODS

The method of mixed estimation has a sound basis. Instead of omitting information from the maintained hypothesis (original model) and rejecting it after the estimation if the results do not agree with the prior information, it is better to incorporate this information into the model from the beginning, before the estimation is attempted.

However, with this method we do not avoid the disadvantages of the 'experimental approach'. *Firstly.* Some experimentation is unavoidable and necessary at the initial stages of the formulation of the maintained hypothesis. *Secondly.* The selection of the extraneous values to be used in mixed estimation involve considerable subjective judgement. *Thirdly.* The problem of 'data mining' takes a different form in mixed estimation as compared with the 'experimental approach', but is not avoided. There is too much discussion about the loss of degrees of freedom from the experimentation with alternative formulations of a relationship. However, it is not clear how the use of iterative procedures does avoid 'data mining'. In each iteration we use the same sample and yet we do not adjust our estimates for losing degrees of freedom. In general however, we do not attach much importance to 'data mining'. The problem arises from purely statistical considerations, which should not be allowed to restrict the econometrician in his work. Econometrics has been developed in a way which tends to ascribe the greatest importance to statistical rules rather than to economic aspects of the relationships being measured. In particular the arguments underlying the 'data mining' problem seem to be irrelevant generally for the measurement of economic relationships. The proponents of 'data mining' argue that statistical theory, on which econometrics draws heavily, assumes that the research worker forms his model and sticks to it without any experimentation with alternative theoretically plausible structures. The form of each relationship is chosen before the data have been used, so that the data have no chance to influence the choice. Only if this assumption is met are the estimated standard error tests accurate and can be used for testing the significance of the parameters. If some sort of experimentation has been done, however, and the finally adopted model has been chosen in the light of such experimental approach, then one is more likely to get a good fit simply as a matter of chance than if one had only one's initial equation-form, because one has several opportunities to choose from instead of just one. Hence, the argument runs, the standard deviations should be adjusted for the loss of degrees of freedom during the experimentations, otherwise they will be deceptively small and would affect the tests of significance and the choice of parameters based on such tests. However, let us consider the following situation. Suppose that two research workers use the same sample independently from each other for the measurement of the same relationship, for example the consumption function of the United Kingdom. The first researcher, either because he has a deep knowledge of the factors which affect consumption or from sheer luck, formulates 'the' correct model before estimating it, for example

$$C_t = b_1 Y_t + b_2 C_{t-1} + b_3 L_t + u$$

(where L = liquid assets).

   The second researcher is less qualified (or less lucky!) and starts experimenting with various formulations of the consumption function, for example

$$C_t = b_1 Y_t + u$$
$$C_t = b_1 Y_t + b_2 Y_{t-1} + u$$
$$C_t = b_1 Y_t + b_2 C_{t-1} + b_3 C_{t-2} + u_t$$

and so on. After certain experiments he hits upon the correct model

$$C_t = b_1 Y_t + b_2 C_{t-1} + b_3 L_t + u$$

Both econometricians will obviously find the same values for the coefficients (b_1, b_2, b_3) since they adopt the same model and use the same sample. Yet the proponents of the 'data mining' argument would insist that the estimates of the second research worker are 'inferior', although they are identical to those obtained by the first researcher!

The mixed estimation methods have been criticised on the following grounds.

Firstly. The mixed estimates are a weighted average of the pure estimates, that is an average of the estimates obtained from the sample and the prior information values of the parameters.[1] It has been argued that pooling together sample information and prior information is not always the appropriate solution in the case of unsatisfactory pure estimates. If the pure estimates of the parameters obtained from the sample are widely different from the prior information values, the two sources of information may well be incompatible. This may be due to several reasons. (a) The period of the sample is usually different from the period of the prior information, and it is quite possible that the structure of the relationship being studied has changed between the two periods. (b) The discrepancy between the values of the coefficients may be due to poor prior information. (c) The difference may have arisen from a poor specification of the relationship when estimated with the sample data.

In all these cases the application of the mixed estimation methods gives imprecise weighted average coefficients which clearly are not desirable. In order to apply mixed estimation techniques one must be sure that the structure of the function is stable in the two different periods, that the source of the prior information is reliable and that the specification of the relationship is correct. Under these circumstances the discrepancy in the prior information and the sample information should be attributed to other causes, such as multicollinearity or other sample deficiencies.

Of course, one should have some yardstick in order to decide when the sample and prior information are incompatible. Theil[2] has suggested the following χ^2 test for testing the null hypothesis

H_0: the two sources of information are compatible

against the alternative hypothesis

H_1: the two sources of information are not compatible.

(a) Assume that we have prior information on r parameters and on their variances and covariances

$$b_1^* = b_1 + v_1$$
$$b_2^* = b_2 + v_2$$
$$\cdot \qquad \cdot \qquad \cdot$$
$$\cdot \qquad \cdot \qquad \cdot$$
$$b_r^* = b_r + v_r$$

---

[1] For a proof see J. Johnston, *Econometric Methods,* 1972, pp. 221–7.

[2] H. Theil, 'On the use of Incomplete Prior Information in Regression Analysis', *J. Am. Statist. Ass.,* vol. 58, 1963, pp. 401–14.

$$E(v_1) = E(v_2) = \ldots = 0$$

$$|S^*| = \begin{vmatrix} s_1^{*2} & s_{12}^* & s_{13}^* & \ldots & s_{1r}^* \\ s_{12}^* & s_2^{*2} & s_{23}^* & \ldots & s_{2r}^* \\ \cdot & \cdot & \cdot & & \cdot \\ \cdot & \cdot & \cdot & & \cdot \\ \cdot & \cdot & \cdot & & \cdot \\ s_{1r}^* & s_{2r}^* & s_{3r}^* & \ldots & s_r^{*2} \end{vmatrix}$$

The b^*'s are unbiased

$$E(b_i^*) = b_i$$

and their variances and covariances are shown in the determinant $|S^*|$.

(b) Apply OLS to the sample observations (assuming $u \sim N(0, \sigma_u^2)$) and obtain estimates of *all* b's ($\hat{b}_1, \hat{b}_2, \ldots, \hat{b}_r, \hat{b}_{r+1}, \ldots, \hat{b}_k$). Take the OLS estimates of the r parameters and their variances and covariances

$$\hat{b}_1, \hat{b}_2, \ldots, \hat{b}_r$$

and

$$|\hat{S}| = \begin{vmatrix} \hat{s}_1^2 & \hat{s}_{12} & \ldots & \hat{s}_{1r} \\ \hat{s}_{12} & \hat{s}_2^2 & \ldots & \hat{s}_{2r} \\ \cdot & & & \\ \cdot & & & \\ \cdot & & & \\ \hat{s}_{1r} & \hat{s}_{2r} & \ldots & \hat{s}_r^2 \end{vmatrix}$$

(c) It is assumed that the prior b^*'s are independent of the OLS estimates, $\hat{b}$'s.

(d) Theil has established that the differences between the prior b^*'s and their OLS estimates, $\hat{b}$'s,

$$(b_1^* - \hat{b}_1), (b_2^* - \hat{b}_2), \ldots, (b_k^* - \hat{b}_k)$$

will be normally distributed with zero mean and with variances and covariances equal to the sum of the variances and covariances of the prior b^*'s and the OLS $\hat{b}$'s:

$$|S_r| = |S_r^* + \hat{S}_r| = \begin{vmatrix} (s_1^{*2} + \hat{s}_1^2) & (s_{12}^* + \hat{s}_{12}) & \ldots & (s_{1r}^* + \hat{s}_{1r}) \\ (s_{12}^* + \hat{s}_{12}) & (s_2^{*2} + \hat{s}_2^2) & \ldots & (s_{2r}^* + \hat{s}_{2r}) \\ \cdot & \cdot & & \cdot \\ \cdot & \cdot & & \cdot \\ \cdot & \cdot & & \cdot \\ (s_{1r}^* + \hat{s}_{1r}) & (s_{2r}^* + \hat{s}_{2r}) & \ldots & (s_r^{*2} + \hat{s}_r^2) \end{vmatrix}$$

(e) The statistic

$$*\chi^2 = \sum_{i=1}^{r} (b_i^* - \hat{b}_i)^2 \cdot \frac{\begin{vmatrix} \vdots & \vdots & \vdots \\ \hline (\hat{s}_i^{*2} & \hat{s}_i^2) \\ \hline \vdots & \vdots & \vdots \end{vmatrix}}{|S_r|} + 2 \sum_{i \neq j}^{r} (b_i^* - \hat{b}_i)(b_j^* - \hat{b}_j) \cdot \frac{(-1)^{i+j} \begin{vmatrix} \vdots & \vdots \\ \hline (s_{ij}^* & \hat{s}_{ij}) \end{vmatrix}}{|S_r|}$$

has a χ^2 distribution with r (= number of known prior estimates) degrees of freedom.

The expression

$$\begin{vmatrix} \vdots & \vdots & \vdots \\ \hline (\hat{s}_i^{*2} & \hat{s}_i^2) \\ \hline \vdots & \vdots & \vdots \end{vmatrix}$$

denotes the minor determinant formed from (S_r) by deleting the row and column in which the term $(s_i^{*2} + \hat{s}_i^2)$ appears. Similarly the expression

$$\begin{vmatrix} \vdots & \vdots & \vdots \\ \hline (s_{ij}^* & \hat{s}_{ij}) \end{vmatrix}$$

denotes the minor determinant formed from $| S_r |$ by deleting one of the columns (and the row crossing it) in which the sum of covariances $(s_{ij}^* + \hat{s}_{ij})$ appears.

(f) From the two sources of data we compute the observed value $*\chi^2$ which we next compare with the tabular value of χ^2 (at the chosen level of significance) with r degrees of freedom. If $*\chi^2 > \chi^2$ we reject H_0, that is we accept that the two sources of information are not compatible, and hence mixed estimation should not be applied.

Example

(a) Assume we have prior information on two parameters b_1^* and b_2^*, and on their variances and covariances

$$\begin{vmatrix} s_1^{*2} & s_{12}^* \\ s_{12}^* & s_2^{*2} \end{vmatrix}$$

(b) From OLS applied to the sample data we obtain $\hat{b}_1$ and $\hat{b}_2$ and their variances and covariances

$$\begin{vmatrix} \hat{s}_1^2 & \hat{s}_{12} \\ \hat{s}_{12} & \hat{s}_2^2 \end{vmatrix}$$

(c) The relevant $| S_2 |$ is then

$$\begin{vmatrix} (s_1^{*2} + \hat{s}_1^2) & (s_{12}^* + \hat{s}_{12}) \\ (s_{12}^* + \hat{s}_{12}) & (s_2^{*2} + \hat{s}_2^2) \end{vmatrix}$$

(d) The test statistic is

$$\chi^2 = (b_1^* - \hat{b}_1)^2 \cdot \frac{\begin{vmatrix} (\hat{s}_1^{*2} & \hat{s}_1^2) & (s_{12}^* + \hat{s}_{12}) \\ (s_{12}^* & \hat{s}_{12}) & (s_2^{*2} + \hat{s}_2^2) \end{vmatrix}}{|S_2|} + (b_2^* - \hat{b}_2)^2 \cdot \frac{\begin{vmatrix} (s_1^{*2} + \hat{s}_1^2) & (s_{12}^* + \hat{s}_{12}) \\ (s_{12}^* + \hat{s}_{12}) & (\hat{s}_2^{*2} & \hat{s}_2^2) \end{vmatrix}}{|S_2|} +$$

$$+ 2(b_1^* - \hat{b}_1)(b_2^* - \hat{b}_2) \cdot \frac{(-1)^{(1+2)} \begin{vmatrix} (\hat{s}_1^{*2} + \hat{s}_1^2) & (s_{12}^* + \hat{s}_{12}) \\ (s_{12}^* + \hat{s}_{12}) & (\hat{s}_2^{*2} + \hat{s}_2^2) \end{vmatrix}}{|S_2|}$$

or

$$\chi^2 = (b_1^* - \hat{b}_2)^2 \cdot \frac{(\hat{s}_2^{*2} + \hat{s}_2^2)}{|S_2|} + (b_2^* - \hat{b}_2)^2 \cdot \frac{(\hat{s}_1^{*2} + \hat{s}_1^2)}{|S_2|} - 2(b_1^* - \hat{b}_1)(b_2^* - \hat{b}_2) \cdot \frac{(\hat{s}_1^{*2} + \hat{s}_1^2)}{|S_2|}$$

This value is compared with the tabular (theoretical) value of χ^2 with $r = 2$ degrees of freedom. If $^*\chi^2 > \chi^2$ we reject the null hypothesis, that is, we accept that the prior information is not compatible with the sample, hence the two sources of information should not be combined in mixed estimation.

Secondly. The iterative procedure adopted by Theil and Goldberger leads to an increase in the residual variance in the sample as the number of iterations increases. Theil seems to accept that one should stop with the first iteration, on the grounds that it is impossible to gain in asymptotic efficiency by iteration on σ_u^2 and the $\hat{b}$'s, as the $\hat{b}$'s in all iterations will have the same asymptotic distribution. (H. Theil, 'On the use of Incomplete Prior Information in Regression Analysis', *J. Am. Statist. Ass.*, 1963, pp. 401–14.)

17.6. THE METHOD OF PRINCIPAL COMPONENTS

The method of principal components is a special case of the more general method of Factor Analysis.[1]

The aim of the method of principal components is the construction out of a set of variables, X_j's ($j = 1, 2, \ldots, k$) of new variables (P_i) called *principal components*, which are linear combinations of the X's:

$$P_1 = a_{11}X_1 + a_{12}X_2 + \ldots + a_{1k}X_k$$
$$P_2 = a_{21}X_1 + a_{22}X_2 + \ldots + a_{2k}X_k$$
$$\cdot \qquad \cdot \qquad \cdot$$
$$\cdot \qquad \cdot \qquad \cdot$$
$$\cdot \qquad \cdot \qquad \cdot$$
$$P_k = a_{k1}X_1 + a_{k2}X_2 + \ldots + a_{kk}X_k$$

It should be noted at the outset that the method of principal components can be applied by using the original values of the X_j's, or their deviations from their means $x_j = X_j - \bar{X}_j$, or the standardised variables (measured as the deviations of the X_j's from the means and subsequently divided by the standard deviations)

[1] For an introductory exposition see D. Child, *The Essentials of Factor Analysis*, 1970. For a more advanced treatment see R. B. Cattell, *Factor Analysis*, New York: Harper, 1952. Also H. H. Harmann, *Modern Factor Analysis*, University of Chicago Press, 1967.

$Z_j = x_j/s_{x_j}$. We will adopt the latter procedure of standardised variables, because it is more general, in that it can be applied to variables measured in different units. Note, however, that the values of the principal components will be different, depending on the way in which the variables are used (original values, deviations, or standardised values).

The a's, called *loadings*, are chosen so that the constructed principal components satisfy two conditions: (a) the principal components are uncorrelated (orthogonal), and (b) the first principal component P_1 absorbs and accounts for the maximum possible proportion of the total variation in the set of all X's, the second principal component absorbs the maximum of the remaining variation in the X's (after allowing for the variation accounted for by the first principal component) and so on.

The method of principal components has wide applications in the social and biological sciences. In econometrics it has been suggested that this method is appropriate in two cases: Firstly, when the number of explanatory variables which should, on *a priori* grounds, be included in a function, is very large relative to the size of sample. If the number of variables is larger than the number of observations the coefficients of the functions cannot be mathematically estimated. But even with a large sample, if the number of explanatory variables is great the computations become difficult, and the reliability of the estimates may not be possible to assess sensibly due to the loss of degrees of freedom and of intercorrelation of the X's. Secondly, the method of principal components has been suggested as a solution to the problem of multicollinearity (see Chapter 11).

The method is also being used in the field of index numbers in order to assess the reliability of such indexes. Tintner has suggested that with the application of Principal Components one may tentatively answer questions such as: how good is the representation of all the various prices by a general price index? What proportion of the total variation of the various quantities produced in the different industries is accounted for by an index of industrial output? We will not discuss the application of principal components in relation to index numbers. The interested student is referred to the extensive bibliography on index numbers. (See G. Tintner, *Econometrics*, 1965, Chapter 6.)

17.6.1. THE METHOD OUTLINED

Stage I. The problem is to obtain estimates of the a's (loadings) with which we will be able to transform the X's into orthogonal artificial variables, the principal components. In the first place, we have to estimate these coefficients. Next we have to conduct some test of significance to decide whether the estimates, $\hat{a}$'s, are statistically significant. Finally, we must establish some rule of decision, some criterion, on the basis of which to decide how many of the principal components (how many of all the possible P's) to retain into the analysis.

The maximum number of principal components is equal to the number of the X's. However, only a small number of P's is usually retained in the analysis.

Stage II. Having found the $\hat{a}$'s, computed the P's (principal components) and having decided how many principal components to retain in our analysis, we proceed with the regression of Y on these principal components

$$Y = \hat{\gamma}_1 P_1 + \hat{\gamma}_2 P_2 + \ldots + \hat{\gamma}_m P_m \qquad (m < k)$$

Stage III. From the $\hat{a}$'s and the $\hat{\gamma}$'s we may find the $\hat{b}$'s of the original model, transferring back from the P's into the standardised X's.

Let us examine each of these stages in detail.

17.6.2. A SIMPLE SUMMATION METHOD FOR THE ESTIMATION OF THE a's, LOADINGS, OF THE PRINCIPAL COMPONENTS

The method developed in this section for finding factor loadings has been devised by C. Burt. (See D. Child, *Essentials of Factor Analysis*, p. 89.)

The method may be outlined as follows:

1. We start by the simple correlation coefficients between the k explanatory variables. These correlation coefficients may be arranged in a table which we shall call the *correlation table* (table 17.4). The main diagonal includes units since the elements of this diagonal are the *self-correlations*, that is the correlations of each X_i with itself ($r_{x_i x_i} = 1$ for all i's). The correlation matrix is symmetrical, that is, the elements of each row are identical to the elements of the corresponding columns, since

$$r_{x_i x_j} = r_{x_j x_i}$$

Table 17.4. Correlation table of the set of k variables (X's)

	X_1	X_2		X_k	$\sum\limits_{i}^{k} r_{x_i x_j}$
X_1	$r_{x_1 x_1}$	$r_{x_1 x_2}$	......	$r_{x_1 x_k}$	$\sum\limits_{i}^{k} r_{x_1 x_i}$
X_2	$r_{x_1 x_2}$	$r_{x_2 x_2}$	......	$r_{x_2 x_k}$	.
.	.	.	.	.	.
.	.	.	.	.	.
.	.	.	......	.	.
X_k	$r_{x_1 x_k}$	$r_{x_2 x_k}$	......	$r_{x_k x_k}$	.
$\sum\limits_{j}^{k} r_{x_i x_j}$	$\sum\limits_{j}^{k} r_{x_1 x_j}$	$\sum\limits_{j}^{k} x_2 x_j$	......	$\sum x_k x_j$	$\sum\limits_{i}^{k}\sum\limits_{j}^{k} r_{x_i x_j}$

.2. We next sum each column (or row) of the correlation table, obtaining k sums of simple correlation coefficients

$$\sum_{j}^{k} r_{x_i x_j} = \sum_{i}^{k} r_{x_i x_j}.$$

3. We compute the sum total of the column (or row) sums

$$\sum_{i}^{k} \sum_{j}^{k} r_{x_i x_j}$$

and we take its square root.

4. Finally we obtain the loadings ($\hat{a}_{ij}$'s) for the first principal component P_1 by dividing each column (row) sum by the square root of the grand total

$$a_{1j} = \left(\sum_{j}^{k} r_{x_i x_j} \right) \bigg/ \sqrt{\sum_{i}^{k} \sum_{j}^{k} r_{x_i x_j}}$$

where i refers to the ith variable X.

It should be clear that the loadings, which we will denote from now on with the letter l_i, are in effect a form of correlation coefficient.

5. The sum of the squares of the loadings of each principal component is called the *latent root* (or eigen value, or characteristic root) of this component and will be denoted by the Greek letter λ with the subscript of the principal component to which it refers. For example the latent root of the first principal component P_1 is

$$\lambda_1 = \begin{bmatrix} \text{latent root} \\ \text{of } P_1 \end{bmatrix} = \sum_{i}^{k} l_i^2 = l_1^2 + l_2^2 + \ldots + l_k^2$$

$$= \sum_{i}^{k} a_{1i}^2 = a_{11}^2 + a_{12}^2 + \ldots + a_{1k}^2$$

In general

$$\lambda_m = \sum_{i}^{k} l_{mi}^2 = \begin{bmatrix} \text{latent root of the } m^{\text{th}} \\ \text{principal component} \end{bmatrix}$$

m refers to the order of construction of the principal component.

Example. Assume we have thirty observations on eight explanatory variables, $X_1, X_2, \ldots, X_8$, which give the simple correlation (first-order correlation) coefficients shown in table 17.5.

The grand total of the simple correlations is

$$\sum_{i=1}^{8} \sum_{j=1}^{8} r_{x_i x_j} = 21{\cdot}40$$

and its square root

$$\sqrt{21{\cdot}46} \approx 4{\cdot}63$$

The loadings for the first principal component P_1 are

$$\hat{a}_{11} = \frac{2{\cdot}28}{4{\cdot}63} = 0{\cdot}49 = l_{11} \qquad \hat{a}_{15} = \frac{3{\cdot}31}{4{\cdot}63} = 0{\cdot}71 = l_{15}$$

$$\hat{a}_{12} = \frac{1{\cdot}71}{4{\cdot}63} = 0{\cdot}38 = l_{12} \qquad \hat{a}_{16} = \frac{2{\cdot}53}{4{\cdot}63} = 0{\cdot}55 = l_{16}$$

$$\hat{a}_{13} = \frac{3{\cdot}12}{4{\cdot}63} = 0{\cdot}68 = l_{13} \qquad \hat{a}_{17} = \frac{2{\cdot}93}{4{\cdot}63} = 0{\cdot}63 = l_{17}$$

$$\hat{a}_{14} = \frac{3{\cdot}16}{4{\cdot}63} = 0{\cdot}69 = l_{14} \qquad \hat{a}_{18} = \frac{2{\cdot}36}{4{\cdot}63} = 0{\cdot}52 = l_{18}$$

Table 17.5. Table of simple correlations of the X's

	X_1	X_2	X_3	X_4	X_5	X_6	X_7	X_8	$\sum\limits_{i}^{k} r_{x_i x_j}$
X_1	1·00	0·54	0·08	0·18	0·20	0·13	0·10	0·05	
X_2	0·54	1·00	0·01	0·05	0·07	−0·01	0·08	0·03	
X_3	0·08	0·01	1·00	0·58	0·51	0·26	0·46	0·22	
X_4	0·18	0·05	0·58	1·00	0·46	0·40	0·27	0·22	
X_5	0·20	0·07	0·51	0·46	1·00	0·46	0·40	0·21	
X_6	0·13	−0·01	0·26	0·40	0·46	1·00	0·11	0·18	
X_7	0·10	0·08	0·46	0·27	0·40	0·11	1·00	0·51	
X_8	0·05	−0·03	0·22	0·22	0·21	0·18	0·51	1·00	
$\sum\limits_{j}^{k} r_{x_i x_j}$	2·28	1·71	3·12	3·16	3·31	2·53	2·93	2·36	21·40
Loadings for Z_1 l_{1i}	l_{11} $=\dfrac{2\cdot28}{4\cdot63}$ $=0\cdot49$	l_{12} $=\dfrac{1\cdot71}{4\cdot63}$ $=0\cdot38$	l_{13} $=\dfrac{3\cdot12}{4\cdot63}$ $=0\cdot68$	l_{14} $=\dfrac{3\cdot16}{4\cdot63}$ $=0\cdot69$	l_{15} $=\dfrac{3\cdot31}{4\cdot63}$ $=0\cdot71$	l_{16} $=\dfrac{2\cdot53}{4\cdot63}$ $=0\cdot55$	l_{17} $=\dfrac{2\cdot93}{4\cdot63}$ $=0\cdot63$	l_{18} $=\dfrac{2\cdot36}{4\cdot63}$ $=0\cdot52$	$\sqrt{21\cdot40}\approx$ $4\cdot63$
Latent root of Z_1	$\lambda_1 = \sum\limits_{i}^{k} l_{1i}^2 = l_{11}^2 + l_{12}^2 + \ldots + l_{1k}^2 = 2\cdot797$								

Thus the first principal component P_1 is

$P_1 = l_{11}Z_1 + l_{12}Z_2 + \ldots + l_{18}Z_8$

$P_1 = 0\cdot49Z_1 + 0\cdot38Z_2 + 0\cdot68Z_3 + 0\cdot69Z_4 + 0\cdot71Z_5 + 0\cdot55Z_6 + 0\cdot63Z_7 + 0\cdot52Z_8$

(where the Z_j's denote the standardised values of X_j's.)

The latent root of P_1 is

$$\lambda_1 = \sum\limits_{i}^{k} l_{1i}^2 = (0\cdot49)^2 + (0\cdot38)^2 + \ldots + (0\cdot52)^2 = 2\cdot797$$

The sum of the latent roots of all the principal components is equal to the number of X's

$$\sum\limits_{i}^{k} \lambda_i = k.$$

In our example $\Sigma\lambda_i = 8$. It is thus intuitively clear that the latent-root of any Z_i provides an indication of the 'importance' of Z_i, of the amount of the total variation that the particular Z_i has extracted from the set of the X's. In effect the latent root is the actual variation extracted (accounted for) by the Z_i^{th} principal component. A convenient way of presenting the latent roots is to express them as a percentage of the total variation in the set of X's. When we use the correlation table the percentage contribution of P_i in the total variance in the standardised X's is defined by the expression

$$\begin{bmatrix} \text{percentage variance} \\ \text{accounted by } P_m \end{bmatrix} = \frac{\lambda_m}{k} 100 = \frac{\overset{k}{\underset{i}{\Sigma}} l_{mi}^2}{k} \cdot 100$$

In our example the first principal component accounts for (extracts) 35 per cent of the total variance in the set of standardised X's:

$$\frac{\lambda_1}{k} = \frac{2 \cdot 797}{8} \, 100 \approx 35 \text{ per cent.}$$

Note that, by the design of the method, the first principal component P_1 has a higher latent root than the second; the second principal component P_2 has a higher latent root than the third, and so on. That is the values of the latent roots become smaller and smaller for subsequent P's because the principal component procedure extracts the maximum possible variance for each P in turn.

The second principal component P_2 is computed as follows.

We form a new *'residual correlation table'*, from the original one, by removing the part of the total variation which has been absorbed by P_1. This is achieved by subtracting from each element the product $l_i l_j (i = 1, \ldots, k; j = 1, \ldots, k)$. This is justified, intuitively, as follows. The first element of the original correlation table is unity and is the self-correlation for X_1. Out of this correlation l_1^2 is accounted for by the first principal component, P_1; hence the remaining self-correlation is $(1 - l_1^2)$ and forms the first element of the new 'residual-correlation' table. For our numerical example the first new element is $1 - (0 \cdot 49^2) = 0 \cdot 760$. Clearly this figure is the *residual correlation*, after accounting for the part of variation in the standardised X_1 'absorbed' by P_1. The remaining residual correlations are found in a similar way, that is from each simple correlation coefficient we subtract the product $l_i l_j$. For example, the second element in the first row (or the first column) is

$$r_{x_2 x_1} - l_2 l_1 = 0 \cdot 54 - (0 \cdot 49)(0 \cdot 38) = 0 \cdot 540 - 0 \cdot 186 = 0 \cdot 354$$

Continuing in this way by subtracting the part of the variation explained by the first principal component (P_1) from the corresponding correlation coefficient of the original correlation table, a new table of residual correlations can be found, from which we compute the loadings, $(a_{2i}$'s or l_{2i}'s) of the second principal component Z_2 (table 17.6).

The new table of residual-correlations will be the starting point for the *extraction* of the second principal component; that is for the estimation of the loading appearing in the second principal component P_2

$$P_2 = a_{21} Z_1 + a_{22} Z_2 + a_{23} Z_3 + \ldots + a_{2k} Z_k$$

or
$$P_2 = l_{21} Z_1 + l_{22} Z_2 + l_{23} Z_3 + \ldots + l_{2k} Z_k$$

Table 17.6. Residual correlation table for the extraction of the second principal component P_2

	X_1		X_2			X_k	
X_1	$r^*_{x_1 x_1} = (1 - l_1^2)$		$r^*_{x_1 x_2} = (r_{x_1 x_2} - l_1 l_2)$	$\ldots$		$r^*_{x_1 x_k} = (r_{x_1 x_k} - l_1 l_k)$	
X_2	$r^*_{x_1 x_2} = (r_{x_1 x_2} - l_1 l_2)$		$r^*_{x_2 x_2} = (1 - l_2^2)$	$\ldots$		$r^*_{x_2 x_k} = (r_{x_2 x_k} - l_2 l_k)$	
.	.		.			.	
.	.	.	.			.	
.	.		.			.	
X_k	$r^*_{x_1 x_k} = (r_{x_1 x_2} - l_1 l_k)$						
$\sum\limits_j^k r^*_{x_i x_j}$	$\sum\limits_j^k r^*_{x_1 x_j}$		$\sum\limits_j^k r^*_{x_2 x_j}$	$\ldots$			$\sum\limits_i^k \sum\limits_j^k r^*_{x_i x_j}$

Note: r^* stands for the residual correlation after removing the part of the correlation (covariance) allowed for into the first principal component P_1.

In our example the residual correlation table for the loadings of the second principal component is shown below (table 17.7)

Table 17.7.

	X_1	X_2	X_3	X_4	X_5	X_6	X_7	X_8	$\sum r^*_{x_i x_j}$
X_1	0·76	0·35	−0·25	−0·16	−0·15	0·14	0·21	−0·20	
X_2	0·35	0·86	−0·25	−0·21	−0·20	0·20	−0·16	0·17	
X_3	−0·25	−0·25	0·54	0·11	0·03	−0·11	0·03	−0·13	
X_4	−0·16	−0·21	0·11	0·52	−0·03	0·02	−0·16	−0·14	
X_5	−0·15	−0·20	0·03	−0·03	0·50	0·07	−0·05	−0·16	
X_6	0·14	0·20	−0·11	0·02	0·07	0·70	−0·24	−0·11	
X_7	0·21	−0·16	0·03	−0·16	−0·05	−0·24	0·60	0·18	
X_8	−0·20	0·17	−0·13	−0·14	−0·16	−0·11	0·18	0·73	
$\sum r^*_{x_i x_j}$	0·70	0·76	−0·03	−0·05	0·02	0·67	0·61	0·34	3·02
Loadings for P_2 l_{2i}	0·41	0·44	−0·02	−0·03	0·01	0·40	0·36	0·20	$\sqrt{3·02} = 1·7$

Thus the second principal component is

$$P_2 = (0·41)Z_1 + (0·44)Z_2 + (−0·02)Z_3 + (−0·03)Z_4 + (0·01)Z_5 + \\ + (0·40)Z_6 + (0·36)Z_7 + (0·20)Z_8.$$

The latent root of the second principal component is

$$\lambda_2 = \sum_i^k l_{2i}^2 = l_{21}^2 + \ldots + l_{2k}^2 = 0·56$$

Thus the second principal component P_2, accounts for 7 per cent of the total variation in the standardised X's

$$\frac{\lambda_2}{k} \cdot 100 = \frac{0 \cdot 56}{8} \cdot 100 = 7 \text{ per cent.}$$

The third and subsequent principal components are extracted by repeating the above process. We stress that the maximum number of principal components is the number of the X's. Usually however, a small number of principal components is retained in the analysis. (If all the P's are retained the principal components method yields identical results to OLS.) The decision on the number of P's to be extracted and retained in the analysis is discussed below.

17.6.3. TESTS FOR THE SIGNIFICANCE OF THE LOADINGS

Several tests have been suggested for assessing the significance of the loadings, l_{ij}'s, appearing in the principal components. The most frequently used are the following three.

1. *An 'empirical' test*

A very crude rule-of-thumb is to consider as significant only those loadings which have a value greater than $\pm 0 \cdot 30$, provided that the sample contains at least 50 observations.

2. *A test based on the levels of significance (standard errors) of the Pearson correlation coefficients*

We said that the loadings are in effect similar to correlation coefficients. On these grounds various writers have suggested that loadings may be tested for significance in the same way as the Pearson correlation coefficients.

Table 17.8 (reproduced from D. Child's book *Essentials of Factor Analysis,* 1970) includes critical values for the significance of the Pearson product-moment correlation coefficients for different sample sizes.

It should be clear that the critical values appearing in table 17.8 are the standard errors for the Pearson product-moment correlation coefficients. We use the same values as standard errors for the loadings. For example if $n = 30$ a loading is significant at the 5 per cent level if its value is greater than $\pm 0 \cdot 338$, and at the 1 per cent level if its value is greater than $\pm 0 \cdot 440$. In our earlier example all the loadings of the first principal component are statistically significant at the 1 per cent level, all of them being greater than $0 \cdot 44$ with the exception of $l_{12} (= 0 \cdot 38)$ which is significant at the 5 per cent level (but not at the 1 per cent level of significance).

It is obvious from table 17.8 that the smaller the sample the greater the value of the loading required for it to be statistically significant. For $n > 50$ a loading is significant at the 1 per cent level if its value is greater than $\pm 0 \cdot 346$. This fact provided the justification of the rule of thumb developed above, namely the rule that l_i is considered significant if its value is greater than $\pm 0 \cdot 30$.

Table 17.8. Critical values for the significance of Pearson correlation coefficients

Sample size	Critical values of correlations required for significance	
	at 5% level	*at 1% level*
5	0·755	0·875
10	0·576	0·714
15	0·483	0·605
20	0·425	0·538
25	0·380	0·488
30	0·338	0·440
35	0·320	0·417
40	0·300	0·394
45	0·280	0·370
50	0·262	0·346
60	0·248	0·328
70	0·233	0·308
80	0·220	0·290
90	0·206	0·272
100	0·194	0·255
150	0·158	0·209
200	0·137	0·182
250	0·125	0·163
500	0·088	0·115

Source: D. Child, *Essentials of Factor Analysis*, 1970, p. 95.

3. *The Burt–Banks test*

C. Burt and C. Banks, 'A Factor Analysis of Body Measurements for British Adult Males', *Ann. Eugen.*, vol. **13**, 1947, pp. 238–56.

The previous tests do not take into account the number of variables, X's, in the set, and the order of extraction of the principal components. Burt and Banks have suggested the following adjustment to the standard error of the correlation coefficients (obtained from table 17.8) in order to obtain the standard error of the loadings

$$s_{(l_{mj})} = \left\{ s_{(r_{x_i x_j})} \right\} \cdot \sqrt{\frac{k}{k + 1 - m}}$$

where k = number of X's in the set
m = subscript of P, that is, the order of its extraction (the position of P in the extraction process).

The Burt–Banks test-formula, clearly takes into account both the number of X's and the order of extraction of the P's.

Example. Assume that we have a set of 200 observations on thirty variables. We want to find the standard error of the loadings of the twentieth principal component.

(a) We have

$$n = 200 \qquad k = 30 \qquad m = 20$$

(b) The standard error of $r_{x_i x_j}$ is found from table 17.8 equal to 0·182 (for $n = 200$) at the 1 per cent level).

What magnitude should an l_i have in order to reach significance in the twentieth P? Substituting in the Burt—Banks formula we find

$$s_{(l_i)} = 0·182 \sqrt{\frac{30}{30 + 1 - 20}} = 0·182 \sqrt{\frac{30}{11}} \approx 0·3$$

That is for any l_i to satisfy the 1 per cent level of significance in P_{20} its value must be at least equal to ±0·3.

17.6.4. CRITERIA FOR THE NUMBER OF PRINCIPAL COMPONENTS, P's TO BE EXTRACTED

We said that usually the number of principal components which are extracted from the X's is smaller than the number of the X's. How can we decide how many principal components to retain in any particular study? There are various criteria which have been suggested for this decision. Three of the most commonly used are stated below.

1. *Kaiser's criterion*

This decision rule has been suggested by Guttman and adapted by Kaiser. Its application is simple: only principal components (P's) having latent root greater than one are considered as essential and should be retained in the analysis. In other words we retain P_m if

$$\lambda_m > 1.$$

Recall that by the design of the method of extraction the first principal component has a higher latent root than the second; the second P_2 has a higher latent root than the third, and so on. Thus according to Kaiser's criterion the process of extraction of P's should stop when we encounter a principal component with a latent root smaller than unity, since all the remaining P's will have an even smaller latent root.

It has been suggested by Cattell that Kaiser's criterion is most reliable when the number of variables is between 20 and 50 ($20 < k < 50$). When $k < 20$ there is some tendency for this criterion to extract a conservative number of P's. When $k > 50$, this decision rule tends to allow too many P's to remain in the analysis.

2. *Cattell's 'Scree test'*[1]

We plot the latent roots against the order of extraction of the P's and we use the shape of the resulting curve to judge how many P's to retain in the analysis. The decision rule is to retain the P's up to the point where the resulting curve has some curvature and reject the P's for which the curve becomes a straight line. In other words the point at which the curve straightens out

[1] See *Handbook of Measurement and Assessment in the Behavioural Sciences* (ed. D. K. Whitla), Addison-Wesley, Reading, Mass., 1968. 'Scree' is a geological term which is used for the debris which collects on the lower part of rocky slopes.

(develops into a linear relationship between the order of P's and their latent roots) determines the maximum number of P's to be extracted. Beyond that point the P's are unreliable because they are heavily affected by factors which are not common to all X's.

In a recent study D. Child has found the following pattern (Figure 17.1) for Cattell's test. Cattell's criterion selected eleven principal components while Kaiser's criterion selected only nine components (P's) in this particular study. (See D. Child, *Essentials of Factor Analysis*, pp. 44–5.)

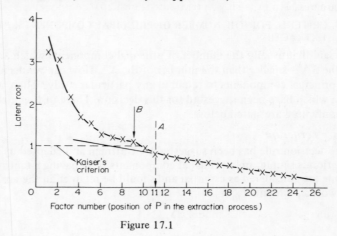

Figure 17.1

3. Bartlett's criterion

Assume the latent roots are computed for k variables, $\lambda_1, \lambda_2, \ldots, \lambda_k$, and that the first r roots, $\lambda_1, \lambda_2, \ldots, \lambda_r$ (for $r < k$) seem both sufficiently large and sufficiently different to be retained. The question then is whether the remaining $(k - r)$ roots are sufficiently alike for one to conclude that the associated P's should be retained in the analysis. Bartlett has suggested that the quantity

$$\chi^{*2} = n \log_e \left\{ (\lambda_{r+1} \lambda_{r+2} \ldots \lambda_k)^{-1} \left(\frac{\lambda_{r+1} + \lambda_{r+2} + \ldots + \lambda_k}{k - r} \right)^{k+r} \right\}$$

has a χ^2 distribution (approximately) with $\frac{1}{2}(k - r - 1)(k - r + 2)$ degrees of freedom. This observed value of χ^{*2} is compared with the tabular value of χ^2 with the above degrees of freedom. The theoretical $\chi^2_{0.05}$ (or $\chi^2_{0.025}$ etc.) is the value of χ^2 that defines the critical region of the test. (The null hypothesis here assumes equality of the excluded latent roots, that is H_0: $\lambda_{r+1} = \lambda_{r+2} \ldots = \lambda_k$).

If $\chi^{*2} > \chi^2_{0.05}$ we reject the null hypothesis, that is we accept that the excluded latent roots are not equal; hence we should include additional P's in our analysis. (See M. G. Kendall and A. Stuart, *The Advanced Theory of Statistics*, vol. 3, London, Griffin, 1966, pp. 292–3.)

17.6.5. ESTIMATION OF THE PRINCIPAL COMPONENTS MODEL

Assume that with the above procedure we have retained r (where $r < k$) out of all the principal components. For simplicity let $r = 2$ and $k = 4$, so that

$$P_1 = l_{11}Z_1 + l_{12}Z_2 + l_{13}Z_3 + l_{14}Z_4$$

$$P_2 = l_{21}Z_1 + l_{22}Z_2 + l_{23}Z_3 + l_{24}Z_4$$

(where the Z's are the standardised values of the original X's).

We regress Y on the chosen (extracted) principal components

$$Y = \gamma_1 P_1 + \gamma_2 P_2 + v$$

(where v is a random variable satisfying the usual assumptions) from which we obtain the OLS estimates $\hat{\gamma}_1$ and $\hat{\gamma}_2$.

17.6.6. ESTIMATION OF THE STRUCTURAL PARAMETERS, b's

Given the $\hat{a}$'s (or $\hat{l}$'s) and the $\hat{\gamma}$'s we can transform back from the $\hat{\gamma}$'s to obtain estimates of the b's, the coefficients of the standardised X's in the original model.

The original model is

$$Y = b_1 X_1 + b_2 X_2 + b_3 X_3 + b_4 X_4 + u$$

The principal components model is

$$Y = \gamma_1 P_1 + \gamma_2 P_2 + v$$

Substitute
$$P_1 = \hat{a}_{11}Z_1 + \ldots + \hat{a}_{41}Z_4 = \hat{l}_{11}Z_1 + \ldots + \hat{l}_{14}Z_4$$

$$P_2 = \hat{a}_{12}Z_1 + \ldots + \hat{a}_{42}Z_4 = \hat{l}_{12}Z_1 + \ldots + \hat{l}_{24}Z_4$$

into the principal components model and obtain

$$Y = \hat{\gamma}_1(\hat{a}_{11}Z_1 + \hat{a}_{21}Z_2 + \hat{a}_{31}Z_3 + \hat{a}_{41}Z_4) + \hat{\gamma}_2(\hat{a}_{12}Z_1 + \ldots + \hat{a}_{42}Z_4).$$

Rearranging we obtain

$$Y = (\hat{\gamma}_1\hat{a}_{11} + \hat{\gamma}_2\hat{a}_{12})Z_1 + (\hat{\gamma}_1\hat{a}_{21} + \hat{\gamma}_2\hat{a}_{22})Z_2 + (\hat{\gamma}_1\hat{a}_{31} + \hat{\gamma}_2\hat{a}_{32})Z_3$$
$$+ (\hat{\gamma}_1\hat{a}_{41} + \hat{\gamma}_2\hat{a}_{42})Z_4.$$

Setting

$$\hat{\gamma}_1\hat{a}_{11} + \hat{\gamma}_2\hat{a}_{12} = \hat{b}_1$$

$$\hat{\gamma}_1\hat{a}_{21} + \hat{\gamma}_2\hat{a}_{22} = \hat{b}_2$$

$$\hat{\gamma}_1\hat{a}_{31} + \hat{\gamma}_2\hat{a}_{32} = \hat{b}_3$$

$$\hat{\gamma}_1\hat{a}_{41} + \hat{\gamma}_2\hat{a}_{42} = \hat{b}_4$$

we have the principal components estimates of the original variables, $\hat{b}$'s. If we retain all $k (= 4)$ principal components the coefficients of the standardised X's would be identical with those obtained by the straightforward application of OLS of Y on the standardised X's.

17.6.7. SOME COMMENTS ON THE METHOD OF PRINCIPAL COMPONENTS

1. The method assumes that the X's are linearly related. If the relationship between the X's is non-linear (a fact which can be roughly judged by the scattergram of X_i and X_j) the component analysis is not appropriate.

2. One cannot easily assign any specific economic meaning to the new variables. The principal components are linear combinations of the explanatory variables. They are artifical orthogonal variables not directly identifiable with a particular economic magnitude.

3. There is some doubt as to the appropriate rule of decision concerning the number of P's to be finally retained in the analysis.

4. There is some doubt regarding the tests of significance of the loadings of the principal components.

5. The method uses less of the information contained in the sample since the number of P's retained is smaller than the number of X's. This is the reason why this method is considered inappropriate as a solution to multicollinearity (see Chapter 11).

However, if one can attribute to the P's a clear economic meaning justifiable from the common force (which causes the common variance in the set of X's) this loss of information does not really matter: with the transformation of X's into P's we can say in this case that we have achieved a 'meaningful' reduction of the parameters of the model. However, this is rarely the case. The P's are artificial variables to which no specific economic meaning can be assigned.

By selecting a number of P's smaller than the number of X's we cannot be sure that the principal components' estimates are in general better than the estimates of OLS applied to the original X's. It is only when the number of X's is too large relative to the small size of the sample that one should adopt the principal components techniques. Such considerations have led to the following combination of the two techniques. (a) Divide the X's into subsets according to their *a priori* importance; (b) use the important X's as they stand and extract principal components from the remaining less important set. This approach has been adopted by G. B. Pidot Jr., in his study 'A Principal Components Analysis of the Determinants of Local Government Fiscal Patterns', *The Review of Economics and Statistics*, vol. 51, 1969.

6. As we said at the beginning of this section, the method of principal components can be applied either on the original X_j's, or on their deviations from the means (x_j's), or on the standardised values of the original variables ($z_j = x_j/s_{x_j}$). However, the values of the principal components will be different in each case. This dependence on the unit of measurement is obviously a serious weakness of the principal components technique. (See H. Theil, *Principles of Econometrics*, John Wiley, 1971, pp. 46–55.)

18. Maximum Likelihood Methods

In this chapter we will examine two methods of estimation: the limited information maximum likelihood (LIML) and the full information maximum likelihood (FIML). The former is a single equation method, being applied to one equation at a time, while the latter is a system-method, that is a method which is applied to all the equations of the model contemporaneously and provides estimates of all the structural parameters at the same time.

Both methods are quite complicated, especially the FIML which requires complete specification of the model and a large amount of data. The LIML was used frequently before the development of two-stage least squares. In recent years the latter method is preferred because of its simplicity and also because there has been evidence that it yields better estimates than LIML for small samples (see Chapter 21). We will return to these points later. Before the examination of these methods we will give an outline of the general method of maximum likelihood of which FIML and LIML are special cases.

18.1. INTRODUCTION TO THE METHOD OF MAXIMUM LIKELIHOOD

The maximum likelihood method is another method for obtaining estimates of the parameters of a population from a random sample.

Assume we take a sample of n values of X drawn randomly from the population of (all possible values of) X. Each observation of the sample has a certain probability of occurring in any random drawing. This probability may be computed from the frequency function of the variable X if we know its parameters, that is, if we know the mean, the variance or other constants which define the distribution. The reader is reminded that the frequency function of a variable is a function which gives the probability of the variable assuming a specific value. (See Appendix I.) For example assume that the variable X is normally distributed with mean $\mu = 4$ and variance $\sigma_x^2 = 9$, and we want to find what is the probability of X assuming a certain value within a given range. We know that the equation normal curve is

$$y = f(x) = \frac{1}{\sqrt{2\pi\sigma^2}} \exp\left\{-\frac{1}{2}\left(\frac{X_i - \mu}{\sigma_x}\right)^2\right\}$$

The probability of observing any given value (within a range) may be evaluated given that we know the mean and variance of the population and that π and e are constants ($\pi = 3 \cdot 14$, $e = 2 \cdot 718$).

Assume now that the population has a normal distribution, but we do not know its parameters: μ and σ_x^2 are unknown. We take a random sample (of

437

independent drawings) of X's and use it to obtain estimates of the unknown population parameters.

One estimation method would be to compute the arithmetic mean $\bar{X} = \Sigma X_i/n$ and the sample variance $s_x^2 = \{\Sigma(X - \bar{X})^2\}/n$ and use them as estimates of the population mean and variance respectively.

Another estimating method is the maximum likelihood method, which may be outlined as follows. We take a fixed random sample (of independent observations). This sample might have been generated by many different normal populations, each having its own parameters, μ and σ_x^2. Which of these possible alternative populations is most probable to have given rise to the observed n sample values $(X_1, X_2, \ldots; X_n)$? To answer this question we must estimate the joint probability of obtaining all the n values for each possible normal population (that is for each set of μ and σ_x^2) and then choose the population whose parameters (μ and σ_x^2) maximise the joint probability of the observed sample values.

Looking at the frequency function of any variable X, it is easy to see that the probability of observing any particular value X_i (in a sample) will be different for various values of the parameters of the frequency function. For example the parameters of the normal distribution of a single variable X are μ and σ_x^2. The probability of X assuming any particular value X_i will differ according to the values of μ and σ_x^2: for each set of these parameters we will have various probabilities for the sample observations. Among all possible values of μ and σ_x^2 we choose as our estimates those which maximise the joint probability of observing all sample observations. In other words, from the individual probability of each sample observation we evaluate the joint probability of observing all the sample values $X_1, X_2, \ldots, X_n$. The maximum likelihood method chooses among all possible estimates of the parameters those values which make the probability of obtaining the observed sample as large as possible. (See L. R. Klein, *A Textbook of Econometrics*, Row-Peterson, Evanston, Ill., 1953, p. 53.) The function which defines the joint (total) probability of any sample being observed is called the *likelihood function* of the variable X. The general expression of the likelihood function is

$$L(X_1, X_2, \ldots, X_n; \theta_1, \theta_2, \ldots, \theta_k)$$

where $\theta_1, \theta_2, \ldots, \theta_k$ denote the parameters of the function which we want to estimate. In the case of a normal distribution of X the likelihood function in its general form is

$$L(X_1, X_2, \ldots, X_n; \mu, \sigma_x^2).$$

Thus if we draw a random sample of n observations from the population of a variable $X \sim N(\mu, \sigma_x^2)$, the likelihood function is

$$\begin{bmatrix} \text{Joint probability} \\ \text{of observing the} \\ \text{particular sample} \\ X_1, X_2, \ldots, X_n \end{bmatrix} = P(X_1, X_2, \ldots, X_n) = L(X_1, X_2, \ldots, X_n; \mu, \sigma_x^2)$$

The maximum likelihood method consists of the maximisation of the likelihood function. From the general conditions of maximisation we know that the maximum value of a function is that value where the first derivatives of the function with respect to its parameters are equal to zero. Thus we take the partial derivatives of the likelihood function with respect to μ and σ_x^2, we equate them to zero and solve for the unknown parameters. The estimated values of the parameters are the *maximum likelihood estimates* of the population parameters.

The various stages of the maximum likelihood method may be outlined as follows.

Firstly. Form the likelihood function, which gives the total probability of the particular sample values being observed.

Secondly. Take the partial derivatives of the likelihood function with respect to the parameters which we want to estimate and equate to zero.

Thirdly. Solve the equations of the partial derivatives for the unknown parameters, to obtain their maximum likelihood estimates.

Example. Assume that the variable $X \sim N(\mu, \sigma_x^2)$. Its probability function is the equation of the normal curve

$$f(X_i) = \frac{1}{\sqrt{2\pi\sigma_x^2}} \cdot \exp\left\{-\frac{1}{2}\left(\frac{X_i - \mu}{\sigma_x}\right)^2\right\}$$

We want to obtain maximum likelihood estimates of the parameters μ and σ_x^2 from a sample of n independent observations of X. We form the likelihood function $L(X_1, X_2, \ldots, X_n; \mu, \sigma_x^2)$, starting from the individual probabilities of the sample values.

$$f(X_1) = \frac{1}{\sqrt{2\pi\sigma_x^2}} \cdot \exp\left\{-\frac{1}{2}\left(\frac{X_1 - \mu}{\sigma_x}\right)^2\right\}$$

$$f(X_2) = \frac{1}{\sqrt{2\pi\sigma_x^2}} \cdot \exp\left\{-\frac{1}{2}\left(\frac{X_2 - \mu}{\sigma_x}\right)^2\right\}$$

. . . .

$$f(X_n) = \frac{1}{\sqrt{2\pi\sigma_x^2}} \cdot \exp\left\{-\frac{1}{2}\left(\frac{X_n - \mu}{\sigma_x}\right)^2\right\}$$

The total probability of obtaining all the values in the sample is the product of the individual probabilities given that each observation is independent of the others. (This is the multiplication rule of probabilities of independent events; see Appendix I.) The joint probability of the n sample values is given by the likelihood function

$$L = f(X_1, X_2, \ldots, X_n; \mu, \sigma_x^2)$$

$$= \prod_{i=1}^{n} \frac{1}{\sqrt{2\pi\sigma_x^2}} \cdot \exp\left\{-\frac{1}{2}\left(\frac{X_i - \mu}{\sigma_x}\right)^2\right\}$$

where $\prod\limits_{i=1}^{n}$ denotes the product of n terms. Expanding this expression we obtain

$$L = \left[\frac{1}{\sqrt{2\pi\sigma_x^2}} \cdot \exp\left\{-\frac{1}{2}\left(\frac{X_1 - \mu}{\sigma_x}\right)^2\right\}\right] \cdot \left[\frac{1}{\sqrt{2\pi\sigma_x^2}} \cdot \exp\left\{-\frac{1}{2}\left(\frac{X_2 - \mu}{\sigma_x}\right)^2\right\}\right] \cdots$$

$$\cdots \left[\frac{1}{\sqrt{2\pi\sigma_x^2}} \cdot \exp\left\{-\frac{1}{2}\left(\frac{X_n - \mu}{\sigma_x}\right)^2\right\}\right]$$

Applying the rule of exponentials (according to which $x^a.x^b = x^{a+b}$), we can express this product in the following form, which involves the sum of the exponents

$$L = \left\{\frac{1}{\sqrt{2\pi\sigma_x^2}}\right\}^n \cdot \exp\left\{-\frac{1}{2}\sum_{}^{n}\left(\frac{X_i - \mu}{\sigma_x}\right)^2\right\}$$

or
$$L = \left\{\sigma_x\sqrt{2\pi}\right\}^{-n} \cdot \exp\left\{-\frac{1}{2}\sum\left(\frac{X_i - \mu}{\sigma_x}\right)^2\right\}$$

Next we take the partial derivatives of the likelihood function with respect to μ and σ_x, and equate to zero. To simplify the partial differentiation we express the likelihood function in the logarithms of the variables,

$$\log_e L = -n \log_e \sigma_x - n \log_e \sqrt{2\pi} + \left\{-\frac{1}{2}\sum\left(\frac{X_i - \mu}{\sigma_x}\right)^2 \log_e e\right\}$$

$$= -n \log_e \sigma_x - n \log_e \sqrt{2\pi} - \frac{1}{2\sigma_x^2}\Sigma(X_i - \mu)^2$$

$$= -n \log_e \sigma_x - n \log_e \sqrt{2\pi} - \frac{1}{2}\sigma_x^{-2}\Sigma(X_i - \mu)^2$$

Since $\log_e L$ is a monotonic function of L, the values of the parameters that maximise $\log L$ will also maximise L. Thus we maximise the logarithmic expression of the likelihood function by setting its partial derivatives with respect to μ and σ_x equal to zero

$$\frac{\partial \log L}{\partial \sigma_x} = -n\frac{1}{\sigma_x} + \sigma_x^{-3}\,\Sigma(X_i - \mu)^2 = 0$$

$$\frac{\partial \log L}{\partial \mu} - \frac{1}{2}\sigma_x^{-2}\Sigma 2(X_i - \mu) = 0$$

We solve these equations for σ_x^2 and μ. From the second equation we get

$$\Sigma X_i - n\mu = 0$$

and
$$\hat{\mu} = \frac{\Sigma X_i}{n} = \text{sample arithmetic mean}$$

From the first equation we obtain

$$-\frac{n}{\hat{\sigma}_x} + \frac{\Sigma(X_i - \mu)^2}{\hat{\sigma}_x^3} = 0$$

$$\frac{1}{\hat{\sigma}_x}\left[-n + \frac{\Sigma(X_i - \mu)^2}{\hat{\sigma}_x^2}\right] = 0$$

$$\frac{\Sigma(X_i - \mu)^2}{\hat{\sigma}_x^2} = n$$

and $$\hat{\sigma}_x^2 = \frac{\Sigma(X_i - \mu)^2}{n} = \text{sample variance}$$

This result shows that the maximum likelihood estimates of the parameters of a normal population are the sample mean and the sample variance.

18.1.1. SOME COMMENTS ON THE MAXIMUM LIKELIHOOD CONCEPT

It should be intuitively clear that, irrespective of the adopted method of estimation, the more representative of the population is the sample, the closer will the sample estimates be to the true population parameters. However, in most cases we do not know the parent population; hence we cannot directly judge how representative our particular sample is. The maximum likelihood principle is an attempt to deal with the problem of the representativeness of a random sample. The maximum likelihood principle turns, essentially, the concept of statistical inference inside out.

(i) In the classical statistical inference we assume that a single population may generate a large number of random samples. The sample observed is assumed to be random and from it we draw inferences about the single population, that is, about its fixed coefficients. In a sampling distribution *the samples are assumed to be variable* (the process is a hypothetical repeating sampling, yielding a large number of random samples and hence a large number of sample estimates of the population parameters), but the parameters of the population are assumed to be fixed.

(ii) When applying the maximum likelihood principle, we assume that *the sample is fixed*; but this sample can be generated by various different parent populations, each having its own parameters. In the maximum likelihood approach the sample is fixed, but the parameters are assumed variable, since they belong to different alternative parent populations. Among all possible sets of parameters we choose the one that gives the maximum probability (maximum likelihood) that its population would generate the sample actually observed.

18.2. THE MAXIMUM LIKELIHOOD PRINCIPLE AS APPLIED TO A SIMPLE LINEAR REGRESSION MODEL

The estimation of parameters (b's) from a given sample of values of Y's and X's is a case of the general process of statistical inference. Having a set of observations we attempt to find sample estimates ($\hat{b}$'s) from which to make guesses about the unknown population parameters. Our model is

$$Y = \quad b_0 + b_1 X \quad + \quad u$$

$$\begin{bmatrix} \text{non-stochastic} \\ \text{component} \end{bmatrix} + \begin{bmatrix} \text{stochastic} \\ \text{component} \end{bmatrix}$$

where $u \sim N(0, \sigma_u^2)$ and $E(u_i u_j) = 0$. The regressor is also non-stochastic.

We take a random sample of X and Y values and we want to obtain maximum likelihood estimates of b_0 and b_1.

Given
$$u \sim N(0, \sigma_u^2),$$

it can be shown (see Chapter 4) that

$$Y_i = N\{(b_0 + b_1 X_i), \sigma_u^2\}$$

that is Y_i is normally distributed with mean

$$E(Y_i) = E(b_0 + b_1 X_i) + E(u) = b_0 + b_1 X_i$$

and variance equal to the variance of the random component σ_u^2. Thus the assumptions of the maximum likelihood method are:

(i) The form of the distribution of the parent population of Y's is assumed known. In particular we assume that the distribution of Y_i is normal.

(ii) The sample is random, and each u_i is independent of any other value u_j (or, equivalently, Y_i is independent of Y_j).

(iii) The random sampling always yields the single most probable result: any sample is representative of the underlying population. This is a strong assumption, especially for small samples.

The assumption of normality is crucial for the estimation procedure in ML, while in OLS the assumption of normality is only necessary for the tests of significance, but not for the estimation procedure of the b's.

The likelihood function of Y, that is, the joint probability of all Y_i sample observations, is

$$L = f(Y_1, Y_2, \ldots, Y_n; b_0, b_1, \sigma_u^2) = f(Y_1) \cdot f(Y_2) \ldots f(Y_n).$$

In our simple model the regressor is assumed non-stochastic. If the X's are stochastic the basic procedure of ML is the same, provided that the distribution of the X's is independent of the distribution of u.

For any particular sample value Y_i the individual probability is

$$f(Y_i) = \frac{1}{\sqrt{2\sigma_u^2}} \cdot \exp\left[-\frac{1}{2\sigma_u^2} \left\{ Y_i - (b_0 + b_1 X_i) \right\}^2 \right]$$

that is the probability of observing the particular value Y_i in any random drawing from the normal population of Y is evaluated by substituting into the general expression of the normal function the value Y_i with its mean $(b_0 + b_1 X_i)$ and variance σ_u^2. The joint probability (likelihood function) of all n sample values is the product of the individual probabilities, since, by assumption, the Y values are independent of one another

$$L = f(Y_1, Y_2, \ldots, Y_n) = \prod_{i=1}^{n} \frac{1}{\sqrt{2\pi\sigma_u^2}} \cdot \exp\left[-\frac{1}{2\sigma_u^2}\left\{Y_i - (b_0 + b_1 X_i)\right\}^2\right]$$

or, applying the rule of exponentials,

$$L = \left\{\frac{1}{\sqrt{2\pi\sigma_u^2}}\right\}^n \cdot \exp\left[\sum^{n}\left(-\frac{1}{2\sigma_u^2}\right)\{Y_i - (b_0 + b_1 X_i)\}^2\right]$$

Given that σ_u^2 is constant[1] we may take the relevant term out of the summation

$$L = \left\{\frac{1}{\sqrt{2\pi\sigma_u^2}}\right\}^n \cdot \exp\left\{-\frac{1}{2\sigma_u^2}\sum^{n}(Y_i - \widetilde{b}_0 - \widetilde{b}_1 X_i)^2\right\}$$

To minimise L we take the partial derivatives with respect to $\widetilde{b}_0$ and $\widetilde{b}_1$ and equate to zero

$$\frac{\partial L}{\partial \widetilde{b}_0} = 0 \quad \text{and} \quad \frac{\partial L}{\partial \widetilde{b}_1} = 0$$

The computations can be greatly facilitated by noting that maximising a function with a negative exponent is equivalent to minimising the value of the exponent. Thus our problem of maximisation of the likelihood function reduces to the minimisation of the exponent, ignoring the term outside the summation which is constant and hence does not affect the derivatives; thus we minimise

$$\Sigma(Y_i - \widetilde{b}_0 - \widetilde{b}_1 X_i)^2$$

The necessary condition for a minimum is that the partial derivatives with respect to $\widetilde{b}_0$ and $\widetilde{b}_1$ be zero

$$\frac{\partial \Sigma(Y_i - \widetilde{b}_0 - \widetilde{b}_1 X_i)^2}{\partial \widetilde{b}_0} = 0$$

$$\frac{\partial \Sigma(Y_i - \widetilde{b}_0 - \widetilde{b}_1 X_i)^2}{\partial \widetilde{b}_1} = 0$$

Working out the partial derivatives we obtain the equations

$$\Sigma Y_i = n\widetilde{b}_0 + \widetilde{b}_1 \Sigma X_i$$

$$\Sigma Y_i X_i = \widetilde{b}_0 \Sigma X_i + \widetilde{b}_1 \Sigma X_i^2$$

These equations are identical with the normal equations of OLS. Thus the maximum likelihood estimates ($\widetilde{b}_0$ and $\widetilde{b}_1$) are identical to the OLS estimates.

---

[1] In the case of heteroscedastic or autocorrelated u's the variance σ_u^2 is not constant and hence cannot be taken out of the summation. See Chapters 9 and 10.

The maximum likelihood principle involves choice among various possible alternative populations. How likely is each of these populations to give rise to the sample we observed? We can think that we move repeatedly the regression line to all possible positions: clearly each position implies a different set of values of the b's. In each position (that is for each set of b's) we evaluate the probability of observing the particular sample observations (Y's). Then among all the possible regression lines we choose the one whose coefficients (b's) maximise the joint probability (likelihood) of observing the n sample values.

Maximum likelihood estimates are biased for small samples but have the desired properties of consistency and efficiency.

In econometrics maximum likelihood estimation makes use of normal distributions of the variables, because for other distributions the computational difficulties are severe.

The assumption of normality and the assumption of any random sample being representative of the parent population are strong, especially in small samples. This is the reason why OLS is preferred to ML for single equation models.

Before proceeding with the examination of methods involving the application of the ML principle to models of simultaneous relationships we will develop some calculus rules, through which we can simplify the computations of maximum likelihood methods of estimation.

18.3. TRANSFORMATION OF VARIABLES AND MAXIMUM LIKELIHOOD ESTIMATION

In many cases we may find it convenient to work not with the frequency function of the original variable (Y), but with the frequency function of some other random variable (say u) with which Y is related, provided that we know the exact relationship between these variables. This relationship is used to transform Y into u (and vice versa) and is called the transformation function. In other words the transformation function tells us how to replace Y by u (or vice versa) so as to facilitate the calculation of probabilities.

18.3.1. TRANSFORMATIONS

The transformation procedure may be outlined as follows.

(1) *Transformation for a single random variable*

If we have a single random variable, Y, related to another random variable u, through the expression

$$Y = f(u) \qquad \text{(transformation function)}$$

and we know the probability for u, we may find the probability of Y by the formula

$$P(Y_i) = P(u_i) \cdot \left| \frac{du}{dY} \right|$$

where $P(Y_i)$ = probability of Y assuming the value Y_i
   $P(u_i)$ = probability of u assuming the value u_i

$\left|\dfrac{du}{dY}\right|$ = derivative of the transformation function solved for u,

$u = f^{-1}(Y)$,

where f^{-1} denotes the inverse of the original function $f(Y)$.

(2) *Transformation for two random variables jointly dependent*

Suppose we have two jointly dependent variables

$$Y_1 = f_1(u_1, Y_2)$$

$$Y_2 = f_2(u_2, Y_1)$$

Thus we may write

$$\left.\begin{array}{l} Y_1 = f_1(u_1, u_2) \\ Y_2 = f_2(u_1, u_2) \end{array}\right\} \quad \text{(transformation functions)}$$

The joint probability of any values of both variables may be computed by the formula

$$P(Y_{1i}Y_{2j}) = P(u_{1i}u_{2j}) \cdot \left|\frac{\partial(u_1, u_2)}{\partial(Y_1, Y_2)}\right| \quad \begin{array}{l} (i = 1, 2, \ldots, n) \\ (j = 1, 2, \ldots, n) \end{array}$$

where $P(Y_{1i}, Y_{2j})$ = joint probability of any two values of Y_1 *and* Y_2, that is, probability of Y_1 assuming the value Y_{1i} *and* Y_2 assuming the value Y_{2j} simultaneously.

$P(u_{1i}, u_{2j})$ = joint probability of any two values of u_1 *and* u_2, that is, probability of u_1 assuming the value u_{1i} *and* u_2 assuming the value u_{2j} contemporaneously.

$\left|\dfrac{\partial(u_1, u_2)}{\partial(Y_1, Y_2)}\right|$ = *Jacobian determinant* of the partial derivatives of the transformation functions, solved for u, that is, derivatives of

$$u_1 = f_1^{-1}(Y_1, Y_2) \quad \text{and} \quad u_2 = f_2^{-1}(Y_1, Y_2)$$

The Jacobian determinant in our example of two jointly dependent Y's is

$$\left|\frac{\partial(u_1, u_2)}{\partial(Y_1, Y_2)}\right| = \begin{vmatrix} \dfrac{\partial u_1}{\partial Y_1} & \dfrac{\partial u_1}{\partial Y_2} \\ \dfrac{\partial u_2}{\partial Y_1} & \dfrac{\partial u_2}{\partial Y_2} \end{vmatrix}$$

Jacobian determinants are usually denoted by $|J|$.

(3) *Generalisation of the transformation procedure for* $Y_1, Y_2, \ldots, Y_k$ *jointly dependent variables.*

Suppose we have k jointly dependent variables

$$\left. \begin{array}{l} Y_1 = f_2(u_1, u_2, \ldots, u_k) \\ Y_2 = f_2(u_1, u_2, \ldots, u_k) \\ \quad \cdot \quad \cdot \quad \cdot \quad \cdot \quad \cdot \\ Y_k = f_k(u_1, u_2, \ldots, u_k) \end{array} \right\} \quad \text{(transformation functions)}$$

$$\cdot \qquad \cdot$$

The joint probability of the k variables assuming any values *contemporaneously* is

$$P(Y_1, Y_2, \ldots, Y_k) = P(u_1, u_2, \ldots, u_k) \cdot \left| \frac{\partial(u_1, u_2, \ldots, u_k)}{\partial(Y_1, Y_2, \ldots, Y_k)} \right|$$

where $P(Y_{1i}Y_{2j} \ldots Y_{kn})$ = joint probability of any values of all Y variables, that is, probability of Y_1 assuming the value Y_{1i}, of Y_2 assuming contemporaneously the value Y_{2i} and so on.

$P(u_{1i}, u_{2j}, \ldots, u_{kn})$ = joint probability of any values of all u variables, that is probability of u_1 assuming the value u_{1i}, of u_2 assuming contemporaneously the value u_{2i} and so on.

$\left| \dfrac{\partial(u_1, u_2, \ldots, u_k)}{\partial(Y_1, Y_2, \ldots, Y_k)} \right| = |J| =$ Jacobian determinant, or determinant of partial derivatives of all the transformation functions (solved for the u's)

that is

$$|J| = \begin{vmatrix} \dfrac{\partial u_1}{\partial Y_1} & \dfrac{\partial u_1}{\partial Y_2} \cdots & \dfrac{\partial u_1}{\partial Y_k} \\[2mm] \dfrac{\partial u_2}{\partial Y_1} & \dfrac{\partial u_2}{\partial Y_2} \cdots & \dfrac{\partial u_2}{\partial Y_k} \\[2mm] \cdot \quad \cdot \quad & \cdot \quad \cdot \quad & \cdot \quad \cdot \\[2mm] \dfrac{\partial u_k}{\partial Y_1} & \dfrac{\partial u_k}{\partial Y_2} \cdots & \dfrac{\partial u_k}{\partial Y_k} \end{vmatrix}$$

18.3.2. TRANSFORMATIONS AND MAXIMUM LIKELIHOOD ESTIMATION

The above transformation rules are often used in maximum likelihood estimation so as to simplify computations. We will illustrate the application of the transformation procedure with the simple linear model

$$Y = b_0 + b_1 X + u$$

where $u \sim N(0, \sigma_u^2)$, $E(u_i u_j) = 0$, and the regressor X is nonstochastic. We want to obtain maximum likelihood estimates of b_0 and b_1 from a sample of n values on Y and X. We will attempt the estimation by the transformation procedure.

We may rewrite the function in the form

$$u = Y - b_0 - b_1 X$$

From this expression we see that, given the observations of the sample (X_1, Y_1), (Y_2, X_2), etc., the values of u will depend on the values which we assign to b_0 and b_1. For example if the values of X and Y observed in the sample are as shown in table 18.1, the assignments of b_0 and b_1 indicated in the last three columns would imply the corresponding values of u.

Table 18.1. Values of u_i with different sets of b_i values

$n = 10$	Given observations of sample		Assumption (A) $b_0 = 0$ $b_1 = 2$	Assumption (B) $b_0 = -2$ $b_1 = 1$	Assumption (C) $b_0 = 3$ $b_1 = -1$
	Sample values of Y	Sample values of X	$u_i = Y_i - 2X_i$	$u_i = Y_i + 2 - X_i$	$u_i = Y_i - 3 + X_i$
1	5	2	$u_1 = 1$	$u_1 = 5$	$u_1 = 4$
2	8	4	$u_2 = 0$	$u_2 = 6$	$u_2 = 9$
3	6	1	$u_3 = 4$	$u_3 = 7$	$u_3 = 4$
4	7	3	$u_4 = 1$	$u_4 = 6$	$u_4 = 7$
5	9	5	$u_5 = -1$	$u_5 = 6$	$u_5 = 11$
6	10	6	$u_6 = -2$	$u_6 = 6$	$u_6 = 13$
7	11	4	$u_7 = 3$	$u_7 = 9$	$u_7 = 12$
8	8·5	4	$u_8 = 0·5$	$u_8 = 6·5$	$u_8 = 9·5$
9	9·5	5	$u_9 = -0·5$	$u_9 = 6·5$	$u_9 = 11·5$
10	7·5	3	$u_{10} = 1·5$	$u_{10} = 6·5$	$u_{10} = 7·5$

Thus any assignment of values to b_0 and b_1 implies a set of values for u, given the particular sample of values of Y and X. Among all possible values of b_0 and b_1 we choose those which maximise the likelihood function of the sample observations.

To find the likelihood function of the sample observations it is convenient to start from the likelihood function of the u values, since we know that $u \sim N(0, \sigma_u^2)$. We can subsequently transform the total probability of the n values of u into the total probability of the n values of X and Y of the sample, by using the transformation function

$$Y = b_0 + b_1 X + u$$

or

$$u = Y - b_0 - b_1 X.$$

The probability for each u_i, given that it is normally distributed with zero mean and variance σ_u^2, is

$$P(u_1) = \frac{1}{\sigma_u \sqrt{2\pi}} \cdot \exp\left\{-\frac{1}{2}\left(\frac{u_1 - 0}{\sigma_u}\right)^2\right\}$$

$$P(u_2) = \frac{1}{\sigma_u \sqrt{2\pi}} \cdot \exp\left\{-\frac{1}{2}\left(\frac{u_2 - 0}{\sigma_u}\right)^2\right\}$$

$$. \; . \; . \; . \; . \; . \; . \; . \; . \; . \; . \; . \; .$$

$$P(u_n) = \frac{1}{\sigma_u \sqrt{2\pi}} \cdot \exp\left\{-\frac{1}{2}\left(\frac{u_n - 0}{\sigma_u}\right)^2\right\}$$

The total probability of all the u's of the sample, or the likelihood function of the u's, is

$$L = \left[\left\{\frac{1}{\sigma_u \sqrt{2\pi}}\right\}^n \cdot \exp\left\{-\frac{1}{2}\Sigma\left(\frac{u_i}{\sigma_u}\right)^2\right\}\right]$$

From this expression we may obtain the total probability (that is the likelihood function) of all the observations of Y and X, by using the transformation rule

$$P(Y_1, Y_2, \ldots, Y_n) = P(u_1, u_2, \ldots, u_n) \cdot \left|\frac{\partial(u_1, u_2, \ldots, u_n)}{\partial(Y_1, Y_2, \ldots, Y_n)}\right|$$

Thus the likelihood function for the sample observations is

$$L^* = \left\{\frac{1}{\sigma_u \sqrt{2\pi}}\right\}^n \cdot \left[\exp\left\{-\frac{1}{2}\Sigma\left(\frac{u_i}{\sigma_u}\right)^2\right\}\right] \cdot \left|\frac{\partial(u_i)}{\partial(Y_i)}\right|$$

But in our particular example the derivatives appearing in the main diagonal of $|J|$ are

$$\frac{\partial u_1}{\partial Y_1} = \frac{\partial u_2}{\partial Y_2} = \ldots = \frac{\partial u_n}{\partial Y_n} = 1$$

and the off-diagonal elements of $|J|$ are equal to zero.

Hence the value of the Jacobian determinant is equal to unity and the likelihood function is

$$L^* = \left[\left\{\frac{1}{\sigma_u \sqrt{2\pi}}\right\}^n \cdot \exp\left\{-\frac{1}{2}\Sigma\left(\frac{u_i}{\sigma_u}\right)^2\right\}\right]$$

$$= \sigma_u^{-n}(\sqrt{2\pi})^{-n} \cdot \exp\left\{-\frac{1}{2\sigma_u^2}\Sigma(Y_i - b_0 - b_1 X_i)^2\right\}$$

or, taking logs to the base e:

$$\log L = -n \log \sigma_u - \frac{n}{2}\log(2\pi) - \frac{1}{2\sigma_u^2}\Sigma(Y_i - b_0 - b_1 X_i)^2$$

We have three unknown parameters to estimate: σ_u^2, b_0, b_1. To obtain their maximum likelihood estimates we take the partial derivatives

$$\frac{\partial \log L}{\partial \sigma_u} \qquad \frac{\partial \log L}{\partial b_0} \qquad \frac{\partial \log L}{\partial b_1}$$

and equate to zero

$$\frac{\partial \log L}{\partial \widehat{\sigma}_u} = -\frac{n}{\sigma_u} + \frac{1}{\sigma_u^3} \Sigma (Y_i - b_0 - b_1 X_i)^2 = 0$$

$$\frac{\partial \log L}{\partial \widehat{b}_0} = -\frac{1}{2\sigma_u^2} \Sigma 2 (Y_i - b_0 - b_1 X_i)(-1) = 0$$

$$\frac{\partial \log L}{\partial \widehat{b}_1} = -\frac{1}{2\sigma_u^2} \Sigma 2 (Y_i - b_0 - b_1 X_i)(-X_i) = 0$$

These three equations, if solved, give the maximum likelihood estimates of b_0, b_1 and σ_u^2.

The two last equations are the same as the two normal equations of the OLS method. Once again we see that if the assumptions of OLS are satisfied *the least squares estimates are identical to those of the maximum likelihood estimates.*

18.4. LIMITED INFORMATION MAXIMUM LIKELIHOOD

The Limited Information Maximum Likelihood (LIML) is another method for obtaining consistent estimates of the coefficients of an overidentified structural equation. It is a generalisation of the instrumental variables method. It is based on the same idea of purging the endogenous variables, which appear as explanatory in the particular equation, from their random component, so that they become non-stochastic and hence independent of the random term u of the particular structural equation. The method of limited information maximum likelihood (LIML), however, is more general than the method of instrumental variables, because it uses all the predetermined variables in the structural system, thus avoiding the arbitrariness of selecting some of these variables as instruments while ignoring the others.

Limited information is similar to two-stage least squares in that both methods make use of all the predetermined variables in the entire model in order to estimate the structural parameters of a single equation, and in that neither limited information nor two-stage least squares require a detailed knowledge of the structure of all the other equations of the model. What is required in both methods is *knowledge of all the predetermined variables of the model* irrespective of the equations in which they appear. There are, however, differences between these two methods which will be discussed at the end of this section.

The method of LIML may be outlined as follows.

We make the following assumptions concerning the particular structural equation whose coefficients we want to estimate:

(1) The equation contains only a part of the total number of the endogenous variables of the entire system.

(2) The equation contains only a part of the total number of the predetermined (exogenous and lagged values) of the entire system.

(3) The equation is overidentified.

(4) We know all the predetermined variables of the system.

(5) The other structural equations of the system are linear and their disturbance terms $(u_1, \ldots, u_n)$ are normally distributed and each one of them is serially independent (non-autocorrelated). However, the random terms of the various equations may be correlated: the method of LIML allows for contemporaneous dependence of u variables of the various equations. We do not require any other information about the other equations of the model.

Step I. We express the endogenous variables of the particular equation as a function of *all* the predetermined variables in the entire system, that is we take the reduced-form of the equations referring to the endogenous variables appearing in the particular equation.

For example, assume we have a system of three equations in three endogenous and four predetermined variables. The particular equation whose coefficients we want to estimate is

$$y_1 = \beta_2 y_2 + \gamma_1 x_1 + \gamma_2 x_2 + u_1 \tag{18.1}$$

where the y's denote the endogenous variables

the β's denote the parameters of endogenous variables

the x's denote the predetermined variables

the γ's denote the parameters of predetermined variables

u_1 is the random variable of the structural equation. It is normally distributed and serially independent.

This equation is overidentified; because

$K = 7$	$K - M > G - 1$
$M = 4$	$(7 - 4) > (3 - 1)$
$G = 3$	$3 > 2$

The reduced-form equations will refer to y_1 and y_2 only (that is they are only a part of the complete reduced-form model, which would comprise as many equations as the number of endogenous variables in the entire model).

Thus

$$y_1 = \pi_{11} x_1 + \pi_{12} x_2 + \pi_{13} x_3 + \pi_{14} x_4 + v_1$$

$$y_2 = \pi_{21} x_1 + \pi_{22} x_2 + \pi_{23} x_3 + \pi_{24} x_4 + v_2$$

The v's (reduced-form random terms) are linear functions of the random terms of all structural equations, and of the structural parameters. Since the structural random variables $(u_1, u_2 \ldots u_g)$ are normally distributed and serially independent by assumption, the v's will have the same properties. (See H. Theil, *Economic Forecasting and Policy*, 1958.)

Given that the structural equation is overidentified we cannot obtain unique values of the structural coefficients $(\beta_2, \gamma_1, \gamma_2)$ from the reduced-form coefficients. However, we could arrive at unique estimates if we impose some restrictions on some coefficients. This is the second stage of the method of LIML.

Step II. To establish the necessary restrictions on the parameter estimates we multiply each of the reduced-form equations through by the structural coefficient of the relevant endogenous variable and we subtract these transformed equations from the reduced-form equation of the structural equation. In our example the first reduced-form equation is multiplied through by 1 and the second by β_2, the structural coefficients of y_1 and y_2 in the original equation. Thus we obtain

$$y_1 = \pi_{11}x_1 + \pi_{12}x_2 + \pi_{13}x_3 + \pi_{14}x_4 + v_1$$

$$\beta_2 y_2 = \beta_2 \pi_{21}x_1 + \beta_2 \pi_{22}x_2 + \beta_2 \pi_{23}x_3 + \beta_2 \pi_{24}x_4 + \beta_2 v_1$$

Subtracting the second expression from the first we obtain

$$y_1 - \beta_2 y_2 = (\pi_{11} - \beta_2 \pi_{21})x_1 + (\pi_{12} - \beta_2 \pi_{22})x_2 + (\pi_{13} - \beta_2 \pi_{23})x_3$$
$$+ (\pi_{14} - \beta_2 \pi_{24})x_4 + (v_1 - \beta_2 v_2).$$

or

$$y_1 = \beta_2 y_2 + (\pi_{11} - \beta_2 \pi_{21})x_1 + (\pi_{12} - \beta_2 \pi_{22})x_2 + (\pi_{13} - \beta_2 \pi_{23})x_3$$
$$+ (\pi_{14} - \beta_2 \pi_{24})x_4 + (v_1 - \beta_2 v_2)$$

The original structural equation may be rewritten in a slightly different way so as to include all the predetermined variables, that is we may include the 'absent' predetermined variables in the structural equation with zero parameters. In our example the structural equation may be written in the form

$$y_1 = \beta_2 y_2 + \gamma_1 x_1 + \gamma_2 x_2 + 0 \, x_3 + 0 \, x_4 + u_1$$

Comparing this equation with the above derived expression for y_1 we see that we have two equations for y_1 in terms of the same explanatory variables but with different coefficients; hence the following relationships must hold if the two equations are to be consistent

$$(\pi_{11} - \beta_2 \pi_{21}) = \gamma_1$$
$$(\pi_{12} - \beta_2 \pi_{22}) = \gamma_2$$
$$(\pi_{13} - \beta_2 \pi_{23}) = 0$$
$$(\pi_{14} - \beta_2 \pi_{24}) = 0$$

and the random terms must be related by the expression

$$(v_1 - \beta_2 v_2) = u_1$$

The above four relations which must hold between the structural parameters and the reduced-form coefficients are the restrictions which we actually impose on our system of reduced-form equations so as to obtain unique values for the structural parameters. From the examination of the above restrictions we see that they may be classified in two types.

(a) The first type of restrictions concern the relationships between the π's and the structural parameters (γ's) of the predetermined variables which appear explicitly in the original equation. They are imposed so that the estimates of the γ's, which will be obtained from the LIML method, are compatible with the specification of the original equation and the π's of the reduced-forms.

(b) The second type of restrictions on the relationships between π's and the structural parameters concern the parameters of 'absent' predetermined variables. It is clear that the structural coefficients of 'absent' variables are zero. Thus any estimate of these coefficients which will be obtained from the LIML method must also be zero.

Step III. We form the likelihood function for the random terms $(v_1, v_2 \ldots)$ of the reduced-form equations. For this we need to know the distribution of the v's. We saw that these random terms are linear functions of all the random variables of the original model $(u_1, u_2, \ldots, u_n)$. Given that the latter are normally distributed and serially independent, the v's will have the same properties, in other words the v's are normally distributed and serially independent. However, there may be correlations between the v's of various equations. Hence the distribution of the v's will be the normal distribution for for jointly dependent variables.

In our example the joint distribution of v_{1i} and v_{2i} is[1]

$$f(v_1 v_2) = \frac{1}{\sigma v_1 \sqrt{2\pi}} \quad \frac{1}{\sigma v_2 \sqrt{2\pi}} \cdot \frac{1}{\sqrt{1 - r^2_{v_1 v_2}}}$$
$$\exp\left[-\frac{1}{2(1 - r^2_{v_1 v_2})} \left\{ \frac{v_1^2}{\sigma_{v_1}^2} + \frac{v_2^2}{\sigma_{v_2}^2} - \frac{2r_{v_1 v_2} \cdot (v_1)(v_2)}{\sigma_{v_1} \sigma_{v_2}} \right\} \right]$$

(π in this expression is the constant 3.14).

Simplifying the notation and rearranging we obtain

$$f(v_1 v_2) = \frac{1}{(2\pi)(\sigma_1)(\sigma_2)\sqrt{1 - r^2}} \cdot \exp\left[-\frac{1}{2(1 - r)^2} \left\{ \frac{v_1^2}{\sigma_1^2} + \frac{v_2^2}{\sigma_2^2} - \frac{2r(v_1)(v_2)}{\sigma_1 \sigma_2} \right\} \right]$$

where v_1, v_2 = disturbance terms of reduced-form equations
r^2 = the correlation coefficient between v_1 and v_2
σ_1^2, σ_2^2 = the variance of the disturbance terms v_1 and v_2.

The above function gives the probability of v_1 and v_2 assuming any particular values v_{1i} and v_{2i} contemporaneously. Given that for a sample of n observations

[1] See L. R. Klein, *A Textbook of Econometrics*, p. 48.

we have n values for each v_1 and v_2, the likelihood function for all the values of the sample becomes

$$L = \left\{ \frac{1}{(2\pi)(\sigma_1)(\sigma_2)\sqrt{1-r^2}} \right\}^n \cdot \exp \left\{ -\frac{1}{2(1-r^2)} \sum_{i=1}^{n} \left(\frac{v_{1i}^2}{\sigma_1^2} + \frac{v_{2i}^2}{\sigma_2^2} - \frac{2rv_{1i}v_{2i}}{\sigma_1\sigma_2} \right) \right\}$$

Taking logs of this expression we obtain

$$\log L = -n \log(2\pi) - n \log \sigma_1 - n \log \sigma_2 - \frac{n}{2}\log(1-r^2) -$$

$$-\frac{1}{2(1-r^2)} \sum_{i=1}^{n} \left[\frac{v_{1i}^2}{\sigma_1^2} + \frac{v_{2i}^2}{\sigma_2^2} - \frac{2rv_{1i}v_{2i}}{\sigma_1\sigma_2} \right]$$

We know that

$$v_1 = y_1 - \sum_{j=1}^{4} \pi_{ij}x_j \qquad (j = 1, 2, 3, 4)$$

$$v_2 = y_2 - \sum_{j=1}^{4} \pi_{2j}x_j$$

Substituting in the $(\log L)$ likelihood function we get (for our example)

$$\log L = -n \log(2\pi) - n \log \sigma_1 - n \log \sigma_2 - \frac{n}{2}\log(1-r^2) -$$

$$-\frac{1}{2(1-r^2)} \sum \left[\frac{(y_1 - \sum_{1}^{4}\pi_{ij}x_j)^2}{\sigma_1^2} + \frac{(y_2 - \sum_{1}^{4}\pi_{2j}x_j)^2}{\sigma_2^2} - \frac{2r(y_1 - \sum_{1}^{4}\pi_{1j}x_j)(y_2 - \sum_{1}^{4}\pi_{2j}x_j)}{\sigma_1\sigma_2} \right]$$

This is the final form of the likelihood function for all the v_{1i}'s and v_{2i}'s of the sample. The likelihood function for models with more y's in each relationship is highly complex.

Step IV. We maximise the likelihood function (of the reduced-form v's) subject to the restrictions imposed (in Step II) on the relationships among the parameters. Thus the method of LIML boils down to the maximisation of a constrained function. The mathematical problem involved is to maximise the likelihood function of the reduced-form disturbances, subject to some constraints on the coefficients of the particular structural equation. The limited information estimates are those values of β's, π's, σ_v's and the covariances of v's which maximise the likelihood function (L) and at the same time satisfy the set of restrictions on the parameters.

The solution of constrained functions is quite complicated. Fortunately a simpler method for the estimation of the LIML coefficients has been established, which may be outlined as follows.

Firstly. We rewrite the original equation as

$$\beta_1 y_1 + \beta_2 y_2 = \gamma_1 x_1 + \gamma_2 x_2 + u_1 \tag{18.2}$$

Although β_1 in our example is equal to 1, we retain it in our analysis for generality. If we were to estimate the second equation of the structural model, $y_2 = f(y_1, y_3, \ldots, y_g; x_1, x_2, \ldots, x_k)$ we would set $\beta_2 = 1$, and so on.

Secondly. We estimate the reduced form equations of the y's appearing in the particular function on *all the exogenous variables* of the entire model. In our example we have two reduced forms

$$y_1 = \pi_{11} x_1 + \pi_{12} x_2 + \pi_{13} x_3 + \pi_{14} x_4 + v_1$$

$$y_2 = \pi_{21} x_1 + \pi_{22} x_2 + \pi_{23} x_3 + \pi_{24} x_4 + v_2$$

which can be estimated by applying OLS.

Multiplying the first reduced equation by β_1 and the second by β_2 and summing the two resulting forms we find

$$\beta_1 y_1 + \beta_2 y_2 = \beta_1 (\pi_{11} x_1 + \pi_{12} x_2 + \pi_{13} x_3 + \pi_{14} x_4) +$$
$$+ \beta_2 (\pi_{21} x_1 + \pi_{22} x_2 \pi_{23} x_3 + \pi_{24} x_4) + (\beta_1 v_1 + \beta_2 v_2)$$

The random component of this expression is $\beta_1 v_1 + \beta_2 v_2$. Hence the unexplained variation in y_1 and y_2 together, after eliminating the influence of all the exogenous variables is

$$\sum_i^n (\beta_1 v_{1i} + \beta_2 v_{2i})^2 = \Sigma (\beta_1^2 v_{1i}^2 + \beta_2^2 v_{2i}^2 + 2\beta_1 v_{1i} \beta_2 v_{2i})$$

or $\left[\begin{array}{l}\text{unexplained variation in } y_1 \text{ and } y_2 \\ \text{using all the exogenous } X\text{'s}\end{array}\right] = \beta_1^2 \Sigma v_{1i}^2 + \beta_2^2 \Sigma v_{2i}^2 + 2\beta_1 \beta_2 \Sigma v_{1i} v_{2i}.$

The reduced residuals v_1 and v_2 are estimated from the above reduced functions and the values $\hat{v}_1$ and $\hat{v}_2$ may be substituted in the expression of the unexplained variation, to yield an expression involving the unknown β's:

$$\boxed{\begin{array}{l}\text{unexplained variation} \\ \text{using all } X\text{'s}\end{array} = \beta_1^2 \Sigma \hat{v}_{1i}^2 + \beta_2^2 \Sigma \hat{v}_{2i}^2 + 2\beta_1 \beta_2 \Sigma \hat{v}_{1i} \hat{v}_{2i}}$$

Thirdly. We estimate the reduced form equations of the y's on *those X's* (exogenous variables) *which appear explicitly* in the original structural equation. In our example we have only two explicit exogenous regressors X_1 and X_2, hence the reduced forms are

$$y_1 = \pi_{11}^* x_1 + \pi_{12}^* x_2 + w_1$$

$$y_2 = \pi_{21}^* x_1 + \pi_{22}^* x_2 + w_2$$

which can be estimated by OLS. Multiplying through these equations by β_1 and β_2 respectively and summing the two resulting forms to get

$$\beta_1 y_1 + \beta_2 y_2 = \beta_1 (\pi_{11}^* x_1 + \pi_{12}^* x_2) +$$

$$+ \beta_2 (\pi_{21}^* x_1 + \pi_{22}^* x_2) + (\beta_1 w_1 + \beta_2 w_2)$$

The random component in this expression is $(\beta_1 w_1 + \beta_2 w_2)$, and hence the unexplained variation in y_1 and y_2 together, after eliminating the influence of the explicit exogenous variables X_1 and X_2, is

$$\Sigma(\beta_1 w_{1i} + \beta_2 w_{2i})^2 = \beta_1^2 \Sigma w_{1i}^2 + \beta_2^2 \Sigma w_{2i}^2 + 2\beta_1 \beta_2 \Sigma w_{1i} w_{2i}$$

The unexplained variance terms w_1 and w_2 can be substituted for their reduced form estimates $\hat{w}_1$ and $\hat{w}_2$ to give

$$\boxed{\begin{array}{l} \text{unexplained variation} \\ \text{using only the explicit} = \beta_1^2 \Sigma \hat{w}_{1i}^2 + \beta_2^2 \Sigma \hat{w}_{2i}^2 + 2\beta_1 \beta_2 \Sigma \hat{w}_{1i} \hat{w}_{2i} \\ \text{exogeneous } X\text{'s} \end{array}}$$

It should be noted that the unexplained variation from the second set of reduced form equations is greater than the unexplained variation from the first set, in which we included *all* the exogenous X's, given that the greater the number of regressors the higher is the explained variation and hence the smaller is the unexplained variation.

Fourthly. We form the ratio of the two unexplained variances, setting the larger in the numerator. This is called the 'unexplained-variance ratio' and is usually denoted by l

$$l = \frac{\text{residual variance using the explicit exogenous } X\text{'s}}{\text{residual variance using all exogenous } X\text{'s}}$$

or

$$l = \frac{\beta_1^2 \Sigma \hat{w}_{1i}^2 + \beta_2^2 \Sigma \hat{w}_{2i}^2 + 2\beta_1 \beta_2 \Sigma \hat{w}_{1i} \hat{w}_{2i}}{\beta_1^2 \Sigma \hat{v}_{1i}^2 + \beta_2^2 \Sigma \hat{v}_{2i}^2 + 2\beta_1 \beta_2 \Sigma \hat{v}_{1i} \hat{v}_{2i}} = \text{variance ratio}$$

Fifthly. We minimise the unexplained-variance ratio with respect to the β's. That is, we choose the values of β's which make the value of l minimum. These estimates of the β's are called Least-Variance-Ratio (LVR) estimates of the structural parameters. The justification of this estimation method is easy to understand intuitively: we choose the estimates β^*'s so that the total variation (in y_1 and y_2 together) should be explained by the explicit present exogenous X's *almost* as well as by all the set of exogenous X's. In other words the β^*'s must take such values that the introduction (into the original function) of the 'absent' predetermined variables should make as small as possible the improvement in the explanation of the variation in the dependent variable.

Sixthly. To minimise the variance-ratio we take the partial derivatives of l with respect to the β's and we equate to zero. In our example

$$\frac{\partial l}{\partial \beta_1} = 0 \quad \text{and} \quad \frac{\partial l}{\partial \beta_2} = 0.$$

The partial differentiation leads to a system of simultaneous equations in which the unknowns are the β's and l. In our example the partial differentiation yields the following results. Let us equate the numerator of the variance ratio to c and the denominator to d so that $l = c/d$.

Now

$$\frac{\partial l}{\partial \beta_1} = \frac{1}{d^2} \left\{ (2\beta_1 \Sigma\hat{w}_{1i}^2 + 2\beta_2 \Sigma\hat{w}_{1i}\hat{w}_{2i})d - c(2\beta_1 \Sigma\hat{v}_{1i}^2 + 2\beta_2 \Sigma\hat{v}_{1i}\hat{v}_{2i}) \right\} = 0$$

$$\frac{\partial l}{\partial \beta_2} = \frac{1}{d^2} \left\{ (2\beta_2 \Sigma\hat{w}_{2i}^2 + 2\beta_1 \Sigma\hat{w}_{1i}\hat{w}_{2i})d - c(2\beta_2 \Sigma\hat{v}_{2i}^2 + 2\beta_1 \Sigma\hat{v}_{1i}\hat{v}_{2i}) \right\} = 0$$

Since $\dfrac{\partial l}{\partial \beta_1} = \dfrac{\partial l}{\partial \beta_2} = 0$, removing common terms we get

$$\beta_1(\Sigma\hat{w}_{1i}^2 d - \Sigma\hat{v}_{1i}^2 c) + \beta_2(\Sigma\hat{w}_{1i}\hat{w}_{2i}d - \Sigma\hat{v}_{1i}^2\hat{v}_{2i}c) = 0$$

$$\beta_2(\Sigma\hat{w}_{2i}^2 d - \Sigma\hat{v}_{2i}^2 c) + \beta_1(\Sigma\hat{w}_{1i}\hat{w}_{2i}d - \Sigma\hat{v}_{1i}\hat{v}_{2i}c) = 0$$

Dividing both equations by d and rearranging terms we get

$$\beta_1(\Sigma\hat{w}_{1i}^2 - l\Sigma\hat{v}_{1i}^2) + \beta_2(\Sigma\hat{w}_{1i}\hat{w}_{2i} - l\Sigma\hat{v}_{1i}\hat{v}_{2i}) = 0$$

$$\beta_1(\Sigma\hat{w}_{1i}\hat{w}_{2i} - l\Sigma\hat{v}_{1i}\hat{v}_{2i}) + \beta_2(\Sigma\hat{w}_{2i}^2 - l\Sigma\hat{v}_{2i}^2) = 0$$

$$(18.3)$$

This system is satisfied if either $\beta_1 = \beta_2 = 0$, or if the determinant of the terms in parentheses is zero, that is

$$\begin{vmatrix} (\Sigma\hat{w}_{1i}^2 - l\Sigma\hat{v}_{1i}^2) & (\Sigma\hat{w}_{1i}\hat{w}_{2i} - l\Sigma\hat{v}_{1i}\hat{v}_{2i}) \\ (\Sigma\hat{w}_{1i}\hat{w}_{2i} - l\Sigma\hat{v}_{1i}\hat{v}_{2i}) & (\Sigma\hat{w}_{2i}^2 - l\Sigma\hat{v}_{2i}^2) \end{vmatrix} = 0$$

However, β_1 and β_2 are assumed (in our specified model) to be different from zero. Hence we equate the determinant of the known terms of our system to zero, and, expanding, we find

$$(\Sigma\hat{w}_1^2 - l\Sigma\hat{v}_1^2)(\Sigma\hat{w}_2^2 - l\Sigma\hat{v}_2^2) - (\Sigma\hat{w}_1\hat{w}_2 - l\Sigma\hat{v}_1\hat{v}_2)^2 = 0$$

This yields the quadratic equation in l

$$Al^2 + Bl + C = 0$$

where $A = \Sigma \hat{v}_1^2 \Sigma \hat{v}_2^2 - (\Sigma \hat{v}_1 \hat{v}_2)^2$

$B = 2 \Sigma \hat{w}_1 \hat{w}_2 \Sigma \hat{v}_1 \hat{v}_2 - \Sigma \hat{w}_2^2 \Sigma \hat{v}_1^2 - \Sigma \hat{w}_1^2 \Sigma \hat{v}_2^2$

$C = \Sigma \hat{w}_1^2 \Sigma \hat{w}_2^2 - (\Sigma \hat{w}_1 \hat{w}_2)^2$

Solving for l we obtain two values for the variance-ratio. Clearly we choose the smallest l of these values since we aim at the minimum variance-ratio.

Having estimated l and using our assumption that $\beta_1 = 1$ we substitute in the system of equations (either (18.1) or (18.2)) and we solve for the other β's.

In order to obtain estimates of the γ's, we substitute the LVR estimates of the β's in the structural equation, we move all the terms containing endogenous variables in the left-hand side and we apply OLS to the resulting expression. In our example we have

$$y - \beta_2 y_2 = \gamma_1^* x_1 + \gamma_2^* x_2 + u^*$$

Applying OLS we obtain the LVR estimates of the γ^*'s.

Seventhly. It can be shown that the LVR estimates (β^*'s and γ^*'s) are identical to the LIML estimates. It has been established that the likelihood function of the LIML method reduces to the expression

$$L = -\frac{1}{2} \log_e \text{(Variance Ratio)}$$

or
$$L = -\frac{1}{2} \log_e (l)$$

(See T. W. Anderson and H. Rubin, 'Estimation of the Parameters of a Single Equation in a Complete System of Stochastic Equations', *Ann. Math. Statist.*, vol. **20**, 1949, pp. 46–63.) It is clear that when the variance-ratio (l) is minimised, the likelihood function (L) is maximised. Therefore the LIML reduces to the minimisation of the variance-ratio l, and the LVR estimates are identical to the LIML estimates. The justification of the LIML may be explained on the same lines as the rationalisation of the procedure underlying the LVR method.

The extension of the LIML–LVR method to relationships including any number of Y's and X's is straightforward. Assume that the structural equation (in whose measurement we are interested) contains n_1 endogenous y's and j predetermined X's

$$y_1 = \beta_2 y_2 + \beta_3 y_3 + \ldots + \beta_{n_1} y_{n_1} + \gamma_1 x_1 + \gamma_2 x_2 + \ldots + \gamma_j x_j + u_1$$

There are n endogenous and k predetermined variables in the whole structural system ($n_1 < n$ and $j < k$).

Step 1. Compute the reduced forms of the (n_1) endogenous variables using all the exogenous (predetermined) variables of the model

$$y_1 = \pi_{11}x_1 + \pi_{12}x_2 + \ldots + \pi_{1k}x_k + v_1$$

$$y_2 = \pi_{21}x_1 + \pi_{22}x_2 + \ldots + \pi_{2k}x_k + v_2$$

$$\cdot \quad \cdot \quad \cdot \quad \cdot \quad \cdot \quad \cdot \quad \cdot \quad \cdot \quad \cdot$$

$$y_{n_1} = \pi_{n_1 1}x_1 + \pi_{n_1 2}x_2 + \ldots + \pi_{n_1 k}x_k + v_{n_1}$$

The unexplained variation of the y_{n_1}'s using all the X's is

$$\begin{bmatrix} \text{residual variation} \\ \text{using all the } X\text{'s} \end{bmatrix} = \Sigma(\beta_1 v_{1i} + \beta_2 v_{2i} + \ldots + \beta_{n_1} v_{n_1})^2$$

Step. 2. Compute the reduced form equations of the n_1 endogenous variables on the X_j's (that is, the exogenous variables present in the function)

$$y_1 = \pi_{11}^* x_1 + \pi_{12}^* x_2 + \ldots + \pi_{1j}^* x_j + w_1$$

$$y_2 = \pi_{21}^* x_1 + \pi_{22}^* x_2 + \ldots + \pi_{2j}^* x_j + w_2$$

$$\cdot \quad \cdot \quad \cdot \quad \cdot \quad \cdot \quad \cdot \quad \cdot \quad \cdot \quad \cdot \quad \cdot \quad \cdot \quad \cdot \quad (j < k)$$

$$y_{n_1} = \pi_{n_1 1}^* x_1 + \pi_{n_1 2}^* x_2 + \ldots + \pi_{n_1 j}^* x_j + w_{n_1}$$

The unexplained variation of the y_{n_1}'s using only the explicit X's is

$$\begin{bmatrix} \text{residual variation} \\ \text{using only the} \\ \text{present } X\text{'s} \end{bmatrix} = \Sigma(\beta_1 \hat{w}_{1i} + \beta_2 \hat{w}_{2i} + \ldots + \beta_{n_1} \hat{w}_{n_1})^2$$

Step 3. Form the ratio of the two unexplained variances·

$$l = \frac{\Sigma(\beta_1 \hat{w}_1 + \beta_2 \hat{w}_2 + \ldots + \beta_{n_1} \hat{w}_{n_1})^2}{\Sigma(\beta_1 \hat{v}_1 + \beta_2 \hat{v}_2 + \ldots + \beta_{n_1} \hat{v}_{n_1})^2}$$

Minimise the variance-ratio with respect to the β's, thus obtaining the LVR/ LIML estimates β^*'s. The minimisation procedure yields the following system of n_1 equations in which the unknowns are the β^*'s (except for the β of the particular structural equation being estimated, which is set equal to unity) and l

$$\left. \begin{aligned} &\beta_1(\Sigma\hat{w}_1^2 - l\Sigma\hat{v}_2^2) + \beta_2(\Sigma\hat{w}_1\hat{w}_2 - l\Sigma\hat{v}_1\hat{v}_2) + \ldots + \beta_{n_1}(\Sigma\hat{w}_1\hat{w}_{n_1} - l\Sigma\hat{v}_1\hat{v}_{n_1}) = 0 \\ &\beta_1(\Sigma\hat{w}_1\hat{w}_2 - l\Sigma\hat{v}_1\hat{v}_2) + \beta_2(\Sigma\hat{w}_2^2 - l\Sigma\hat{v}_2^2) + \ldots + \beta_{n_1}(\Sigma\hat{w}_2\hat{w}_{n_1} - l\Sigma\hat{v}_2\hat{v}_{n_1}) = 0 \\ &\cdot\,\cdot \\ &\beta_1(\Sigma\hat{w}_1\hat{w}_{n_1} - l\Sigma\hat{v}_2\hat{v}_{n_1}) + \beta_2(\Sigma\hat{w}_2\hat{w}_{n_1} - l\Sigma\hat{v}_2\hat{v}_{n_1}) + \ldots \beta_{n_1}(\Sigma\hat{w}_{n_1}^2 - l\Sigma\hat{v}_{n_1}^2) = 0 \end{aligned} \right\} \quad (18.4)$$

For this system to have a non-trivial solution the determinant of the known terms (= terms in brackets) must be equal to zero.

Expanding this determinant and equating it to zero, we obtain a polynomial in l of degree n_1, which, if solved, will give n_1 roots (values) for l. We choose as our estimate of the variance ratio the smallest of these values ($\hat{l}$) because minimum l implies maximum value of the likelihood function of LIML method.

Step. 4. We substitute $\hat{l}$ in the system of equations (18.4), which then may be solved for the β's (setting also $\beta_1 = 1$). The estimates $\beta_1^*, \beta_2^*, \ldots, \beta_{n_1}^*$ are the values that maximise the likelihood function of the LIML method.

Step. 5. We substitute the estimates $\beta_1^*, \beta_2^*, \ldots, \beta_{n_1}^*$ in the structural equation and bring all the terms including endogenous variables in the left-hand side of this equation

$$(y_1 - \hat{\beta}_2 y_2 - \hat{\beta}_3 y_3 - \ldots - \hat{\beta}_{n_1} y_{n_1}) = \gamma_1^* z_1 + \gamma_2^* z_2 + \ldots + \gamma_j^* z_j + u^*$$

Applying OLS to this expression we obtain estimates of the γ's of the structural equation.

18.4.1. PROPERTIES OF THE LIML ESTIMATES

The estimates obtained from the application of LIML are biased for small samples. However, the estimates are consistent, that is, their bias tends to zero and their distribution collapses on the true value of the parameters as the size of the sample grows infinitely large.

Finally, if the disturbances of the structural model are normally distributed the LIML estimates are asymptotically efficient. (See Theil, *Economic Forecasts and Policy*, p. 232. Also J. Johnston, p. 263.)

18.4.2. ASSUMPTIONS OF THE LIML METHOD

The main assumptions of the method have already been stated on page 440. To sum up:

(1) We assume that the equation which we want to estimate is overidentified. That is, there are predetermined variables which have zero coefficients (are excluded from the particular equation), but are present in the other equations of the model.

(2) We assume that the random variables of all the structural equations are normally distributed. Furthermore, it is assumed that the u of each structural equation is serially independent. However, the random terms of different equations may be contemporaneously interdependent. These assumptions about the random variables of the structural equations enable us to establish similar properties for the reduced-form random terms, v's.

(3) We assume that we know all the predetermined variables of the entire system, irrespective of the equation in which they appear.

18.4.3. SOME NOTES ON THE LIML METHOD

1. We said that the LIML method assumes correct specification of the particular equation, as well as correct knowledge of the predetermined variables of the entire model. If our specification is incorrect, obviously the estimates of

the structural parameters will have some error. The LIML, like all other econometric methods, is sensitive to specification errors.

2. The LIML method ignores information provided by the structure of the other equations of the model. For example consider the following overidentified model

$$D = b_0 + b_1 P + b_2 Y + u_1$$

$$P = a_0 + a_1 S + a_2 W + a_3 C + u_2$$

$$D = S$$

where D = quantity demanded of a particular product
  S = quantity supplied
  P = price
  Y = consumers' income
  W = index of weather conditions
  C = costs of production.

The first equation is overidentified $(K - M > G - 1)$. If we apply the LIML method we would have the following consequences.

(a) The combined influence of W and C on the demand would be taken into account, but their separate impacts are not known.

(b) The indirect effect of any endogenous variable not appearing in the demand function is ignored. For example if there were a third equation relating a third endogenous variable H, to the endogenous variable P then the effect of H on the demand equation operating through P, would be ignored. (See Brennan, *Preface to Econometrics*, p. 407.)

3. The computational procedure of LIML is cumbersome. Certainly it is more complicated than two stage least squares. This is one of the reasons for the preference of econometricians for 2SLS in actual econometric research.

4. There are basic similarities between LIML and 2SLS:

(a) Both methods use all the predetermined variables of the model.

(b) Both methods use part of the information of the entire structural model. Neither method requires knowledge of the complete structure of all the equations of the system.

(c) Both methods are single-equation techniques.

(d) Both methods have the same basic idea, that is, the minimisation of the improvement in the fit which would be achieved if in the particular equation we included the predetermined variables 'absent' from it but appearing somewhere else in the model. Thus both methods use two sets of regressions: *first,* the regressions of the endogenous variables of the particular equation on all the predetermined variables of the system; and *second* the regressions of the endogenous variables on the predetermined variables appearing in the particular equation. From these sets of regressions we obtain two sets of unexplained variances. LIML minimises the ratio of these unexplained variances, while 2SLS minimises the difference between the two sets of residual variances. (See J. Johnston, *Econometric Methods,* 1972, chapter 13.)

(e) Both methods yield consistent and asymptotically efficient parameter estimates.

(f) Both methods belong to the 'k-class' estimators: If $l = k$ the 'k-class' estimators method yields LIML estimators. (See A. Goldberger, *Econometric Theory*, pp. 341–4.)

However, research by Nagar and others has provided some evidence that two-stage least squares may have an advantage over LIML in small samples (see Chapter 21). This reason, coupled by the simpler computational scheme of 2SLS, renders this method more attractive to econometricians.

18.5. FULL INFORMATION MAXIMUM LIKELIHOOD

Full information maximum likelihood is a system-method, that is, this method is applied to all the equations of the model and yields estimates of all the structural parameters contemporaneously. It is a straightforward extension of the maximum likelihood method which we examined in the first section of this chapter.

The method assumes that: (1) we know the complete specification of all the equations of the model, (2) the random variables of the structural equations are normally distributed, with zero means. The u's of different equations may or may not be intercorrelated. If they are independent their covariances will be zero and the computations are greatly facilitated. If, however, the contemporaneous disturbances of the structural equations are correlated, the computations become extremely complicated, since we arrive at nonlinear equations when we differentiate the likelihood function with respect to the variances of the random terms.

We will illustrate the application of FIML with an example. Recall that the various steps in the estimation procedure of the maximum likelihood method are:

Firstly. Formulation of the likelihood function for the random variables of all the equations and for all sample values. Given the sample of size n, for each structural equation we have a set of n values for its random variable.

Secondly. Estimation of the Jacobian determinant for the u's of all structural equations. Recall that the Jacobian is the determinant of partial derivatives of the transformation functions solved for u with respect to the endogenous variables $(Y_1, Y_2, \ldots, Y_G)$.

Thirdly. Application of the transformation rule so as to obtain the likelihood function of the endogenous variables $(Y_1, \ldots, Y_G)$ from the likelihood function of the random terms $(u_1, u_2, \ldots, u_G)$.

Fourthly. Estimation of the partial derivatives of the likelihood function with respect to the structural parameters and the variances of all (G) random terms $(\beta_1, \beta_2, \ldots, \beta_G, \gamma_1, \gamma_2, \ldots, \gamma_k, \sigma_{u_1}^2, \sigma_{u_2}^2, \ldots \sigma_{u_G}^2)$.

Fifthly. Equating of the partial derivatives of the likelihood function to zero and solution of the resulting system of equations for the unknown structural parameters and the variances of the u's.

Sixthly. Estimation of the standard errors (variances) of the parameter estimates.

Example. Assume that we want to estimate the parameters of the following model of income determination

$$C = a_0 + a_1(Y - T) + a_2 Y_{t-1} + u_1 \tag{18.5}$$

$$I = b_0 + b_1 Y + b_2 K_{t-1} + b_3 r + b_4 E + u_2 \tag{18.6}$$

$$M = c_0 + c_1 Y + c_2 P_{t-1} + u_3 \tag{18.7}$$

$$Y = C + I + G + E - M \tag{18.8}$$

where C = consumption expenditure
$\quad I$ = investment
$\quad M$ = imports
$\quad Y$ = income
$\quad T$ = taxation
$\quad K_{t-1}$ = capital stock in $(t - 1)$
$\quad P_{t-1}$ = price level in $(t - 1)$
$\quad Y_{t-1}$ = lagged income
$\quad r$ = interest rate
$\quad G$ = government expenditure on goods and services
$\quad E$ = exports.

Equation (18.5) is the consumption function. Consumption expenditure depends on disposable income and lagged income.

Equation (18.6) is the investment function. Investment is determined by the level of national income, the stock of capital at the end of the previous period, the interest rate, and the level of exports.

Equation (18.7) is the import function. Imports are determined by the level of national income and the price level in the previous period.

Equation (18.8) is the classical definition of national income.

The model is complete, in that it comprises four **equations in four** endogenous variables: C, I, M, Y. There are seven predetermined variables in the system: $G, E, K_{t-1}, T, Y_{t-1}, r, P_{t-1}$.

The model is overidentified: for all the behavioural equations the necessary condition for overidentification is satisfied $(K - M > G - 1)$. We will obtain estimates of the structural parameters with the FIML method.

We first substitute Y in the three behavioural equations. (In any econometric model the first step consists of getting rid of all the definitional equations and identities, by substituting the relevant values in the stochastic (behavioural) equations of the model.)

(1) $$C = a_0 + a_1(C + I + G + E - M) - a_1 T + a_2 Y_{t-1} + u_1$$

$$C(1 - a_1) = a_0 + a_1(I + G + E - M - T) + a_2 Y_{t-1} + u_1$$

and $$C = \frac{a_0}{1 - a_1} + \frac{a_1}{1 - a_1}(I + G + E - M - T) + \frac{a_2}{1 - a_1} Y_{t-1} + u_1^*$$

(2) $\qquad I = b_0 + b_1(C + I + G + E - M) + b_2 K_{t-1} + b_3 r + b_4 E + u_2$

$\qquad I(1 - b_1) = b_0 + b_1(C + G - M) + b_2 K_{t-1} + b_3 r + (b_1 + b_4) E + u_2$

and $\qquad I = \dfrac{b_0}{1 - b_1} + \dfrac{b_1}{1 - b_1}(C + G - M) + \dfrac{b_2}{1 - b_1} K_{t-1} + \dfrac{b_3}{1 - b_1} r + \dfrac{(b_1 + b_4)}{1 - b_1} E + u_2^*$

(3) $\qquad M = c_0 + c_1(C + I + G + E - M) + c_2 P_{t-1} + u_3$

$\qquad M(1 + c_1) = c_0 + c_1(C + I + G + E) + c_2 P_{t-1} + u_3$

and $\qquad M = \dfrac{c_0}{1 + c_1} + \dfrac{c_1}{1 + c_1}(C + I + G + E) + \dfrac{c_2}{1 + c_1} P_{t-1} + u_3^*$

To facilitate the analysis we adopt the following notation. We use Greek letters for the 'composite' coefficients

$$\frac{a_0}{1 - a_1} = \alpha_0 \qquad \frac{a_1}{1 - a_1} = \alpha_1 \qquad \frac{a_2}{1 - a_1} = \alpha_2$$

$$\frac{b_0}{1 - b_1} = \beta_0 \qquad \frac{b_1}{1 - b_1} = \beta_1 \qquad \frac{b_2}{1 - b_1} = \beta_2 \qquad \frac{b_3}{1 - b_1} = \beta_3 \qquad \frac{b_1 + b_4}{1 - b_1} = \beta_4$$

$$\frac{c_0}{1 + c_1} = \gamma_0 \qquad \frac{c_1}{1 + c_1} = \gamma_1 \qquad \frac{c_2}{1 + c_1} = \gamma_2$$

Furthermore, we will denote the endogenous variables by y_G and the predetermined variables by z_k. Thus

$y_1 = C$	$z_1 = G$	$z_4 = T$	$z_7 = P_{t-1}$
$y_2 = I$	$z_2 = E$	$z_5 = Y_{t-1}$	
$y_3 = M$	$z_3 = K_{t-1}$	$z_6 = r$	

Finally we will omit the asterisk from the random terms, for simplicity of presentation. Thus the structural model acquires the form

$$y_1 = \alpha_0 + \alpha_1(y_2 + z_1 + z_2 - y_3 - z_4) + \alpha_2 z_5 + u_1$$

$$y_2 = \beta_0 + \beta_1(y_1 + z_1 - y_3) + \beta_2 z_3 + \beta_3 z_6 + \beta_4 z_2 + u_2$$

$$y_3 = \gamma_0 + \gamma_1(y_1 + y_2 + z_1 + z_2) + \gamma_2 z_7 + u_3$$

Note that in this formulation of the model

$$u_1 = \frac{u_1}{1 - a_1} \qquad u_2 = \frac{u_2}{1 - b_1} \qquad u_3 = \frac{u_3}{1 + c_1}$$

Rearranging we obtain

$$y_1 = \alpha_0 + \alpha_1(y_2) - \alpha_1(y_3) + \alpha_1(z_1) - \alpha_1(z_4) + \alpha_2(z_5) + u_1$$
$$y_2 = \beta_0 + \beta_1(y_1) - \beta_1(y_3) + \beta_1(z_1) + \beta_4(z_2) + \beta_2(z_3) + \beta_3(z_6) + u_2$$
$$y_3 = \gamma_0 + \gamma_1(y_1) + \gamma_1(y_2) + \gamma_1(z_1) + \gamma_1(z_2) + \gamma_2(z_7) + u_3.$$

We may ignore the constant terms $\alpha_0, \beta_0, \gamma_0$ by measuring all variables in deviations from their means

We shall examine only the case where the disturbance terms (u_1, u_2, u_3) are normally distributed, with zero means, constant variance and zero covariances. Furthermore, we assume that the u's of the various relations are uncorrelated with each other (no contemporaneous dependence of the u's). We will apply the transformation procedure for the evaluation of the maximum likelihood function.

For each random variable we have a set of n values, corresponding to our sample deviations:

$$
\begin{array}{cccccc}
u_{11} & u_{12} & u_{13} & \ldots & u_{1n} \\
u_{21} & u_{22} & u_{23} & \ldots & u_{2n} \\
u_{31} & u_{32} & u_{33} & \ldots & u_{3n}
\end{array}
$$

Step I. Formulation of the likelihood function for the u*'s*

Under the above assumptions concerning the u's, the joint probability for all the values of all the random terms becomes

$$P(u_{1i}, u_{2i}, u_{3i}) = [P(u_{1i})] \cdot [P(u_{2i})] \cdot [P(u_{3i})]$$

Given the assumption of zero covariances (serially independent) of the values of each u, we can determine the probability for all the values of each u.

Thus, given $\quad u_1 \sim N(0, \sigma_{u_1}^2)$ and $E(u_{1i}u_{1j}) = 0$

$$u_2 \sim N(0, \sigma_{u_2}^2) \quad \text{and} \quad E(u_{2i}u_{2j}) = 0$$

$$u_3 \sim N(0, \sigma_{u_3}^2) \quad \text{and} \quad E(u_{3i}u_{3j}) = 0$$

we have

$$P(u_1) = \left\{ \frac{1}{\sigma_{u_1}\sqrt{2\pi}} \right\}^n \cdot \left[\exp\left\{ -\frac{1}{2}\left(\frac{\Sigma u_{1i}^2}{\sigma_{u_1}^2} \right) \right\} \right]$$

$$P(u_2) = \left\{ \frac{1}{\sigma_{u_2}\sqrt{2\pi}} \right\}^n \cdot \left[\exp\left\{ -\frac{1}{2}\left(\frac{\Sigma u_{2i}^2}{\sigma_{u_2}^2} \right) \right\} \right]$$

$$P(u_3) = \left\{ \frac{1}{\sigma_{u_3}\sqrt{2\pi}} \right\}^n \cdot \left[\exp\left\{ -\frac{1}{2}\left(\frac{\Sigma u_{3i}^2}{\sigma_{u_3}^2} \right) \right\} \right]$$

Consequently the likelihood function for all the values of the u's of the structural model is the product of these probabilities, that is

$$P(u_1, u_2, u_3) = \left\{\frac{1}{\sqrt{2\pi}}\right\}^{3n} \cdot \left\{\frac{1}{\sigma_{u_1}^2} \cdot \frac{1}{\sigma_{u_2}^2} \cdot \frac{1}{\sigma_{u_3}^2}\right\}^n \cdot \left[\exp\left\{-\left(\frac{\Sigma u_{1i}^2}{2\sigma_{u_1}^2} + \frac{\Sigma u_{2i}^2}{2\sigma_{u_2}^2} + \frac{\Sigma u_{3i}^2}{2\sigma_{u_3}^2}\right)\right\}\right]$$

or

$$P(u_1, u_2, u_3) = \left\{\frac{1}{2\pi\sqrt{2\pi}}\right\}^n \cdot \left\{\frac{1}{\sigma_{u_1} \cdot \sigma_{u_2} \cdot \sigma_{u_3}}\right\}^{2n} \cdot \left[\exp\left\{-\left(\frac{\Sigma u_{1i}^2}{2\sigma_{u_1}^2} + \frac{\Sigma u_{2i}^2}{2\sigma_{u_2}^2} + \frac{\Sigma u_{3i}^2}{2\sigma_{u_3}^2}\right)\right\}\right]$$

Step II. Derivation of the likelihood function of the y's from the likelihood function of the u's

To obtain the total probability of all the values of the sample for all endogenous variables we need

(1) *The transformation functions*, that is the relations between the u's and the y's. These are the structural equations, solved for u_1, u_2, u_3

$$u_1 = (y_1) - \alpha_1(y_2) + \alpha_1(y_3) - \alpha_1(z_1) - \alpha_1(z_2) + \alpha_1(z_4) - \alpha_2(z_5)$$

$$u_2 = (y_2) - \beta_1(y_1) + \beta_1(y_3) - \beta_1(z_1) - \beta_4(z_2) - \beta_2(z_3) - \beta_3(z_6)$$

$$u_3 = (y_3) - \gamma_1(y_1) - \gamma_1(y_2) - \gamma_1(z_1) - \gamma_1(z_2) - \gamma_2(z_7)$$

(2) *The Jacobian determinant* of all the values of all the u's, that is, the determinant of partial derivatives of the u's with respect to the y's. The Jacobian determinant in our example is

$$|J|^n = \begin{vmatrix} \dfrac{\partial u_1}{\partial y_1} & \dfrac{\partial u_1}{\partial y_2} & \dfrac{\partial u_1}{\partial y_3} \\[2ex] \dfrac{\partial u_2}{\partial y_1} & \dfrac{\partial u_2}{\partial y_2} & \dfrac{\partial u_2}{\partial y_3} \\[2ex] \dfrac{\partial u_3}{\partial y_1} & \dfrac{\partial u_3}{\partial y_2} & \dfrac{\partial u_3}{\partial y_3} \end{vmatrix}^n = \begin{vmatrix} 1 & -\alpha_1 & +\alpha_1 \\[1ex] -\beta & 1 & +\beta_1 \\[1ex] -\gamma_1 & -\gamma_1 & 1 \end{vmatrix}^n$$

Applying the transformation rule, we are able to find the likelihood function for the y's

$$P(y_{1i}, y_{2i}, y_{3i}) = P(u_{1i}, u_{2i}, u_{3i}) \cdot \left|\frac{\partial(u_{1i}, u_{2i}, u_{3i})}{\partial(y_{1i}, y_{2i}, y_{3i})}\right|$$

Substituting in the above expression we obtain

$$L = |J|^n \cdot \left[\left(\frac{1}{2\pi\sqrt{2\pi}}\right)^n \cdot \left(\frac{1}{\sigma_{u_1} \cdot \sigma_{u_2} \cdot \sigma_{u_3}}\right)^n \cdot \left[\exp\left\{-\left(\frac{\Sigma u_{1i}^2}{2\sigma_{u_1}^2} + \frac{\Sigma u_{2i}^2}{2\sigma_{u_2}^2} + \frac{\Sigma u_{3i}^2}{2\sigma_{u_3}^2}\right)\right\}\right]\right]$$

Taking logs to the base e we obtain

$$\log L = L^* = n \log |J| - n \log \left(2\pi\sqrt{2\pi} \right) - n \log (\sigma_{u_1} \sigma_{u_2} \sigma_{u_3})$$

$$- \frac{1}{2\sigma_{u_1}^2} \Sigma u_{1i}^2 - \frac{1}{2\sigma_{u_2}^2} \Sigma u_{2i}^2 - \frac{1}{2\sigma_{u_3}^2} \Sigma u_{3i}^2$$

Note: If we substitute u_i for the expressions in y_i and z_i of the transformation functions, it is easy to see that the above function gives the joint probability of the sample of endogenous variables, given the predetermined variables. (See Klein, *A Textbook of Econometrics*, p. 104.)

Step III. Maximisation of the likelihood function

To maximise the likelihood function we take its partial derivatives with respect to the β's, α's, γ's and the variances of the σ_u's, and we equate to zero. Thus

$$\frac{\partial L^*}{\partial a_1} = 0 \quad \frac{\partial L^*}{\partial \beta_1} = 0 \quad \frac{\partial L^*}{\partial \beta_3} = 0 \quad \frac{\partial L^*}{\partial \gamma_1} = 0 \quad \frac{\partial L^*}{\partial \sigma_{u_1}} = 0 \quad \frac{\partial L^*}{\partial \sigma_{u_3}} = 0$$

$$\frac{\partial L^*}{\partial \alpha_2} = 0 \quad \frac{\partial L^*}{\partial \beta_2} = 0 \quad \frac{\partial L^*}{\partial \beta_4} = 0 \quad \frac{\partial L^*}{\partial \gamma_2} = 0 \quad \frac{\partial L^*}{\partial \sigma_{u_2}} = 0$$

Performing the partial differentiation we obtain the following general equations

$$\frac{\partial L^*}{\partial \alpha_i} = n \frac{1}{|J|} \cdot \frac{\partial |J|}{\partial \alpha_i} + \Sigma \frac{\partial L^*}{\partial u_1} \cdot \frac{\partial u_1}{\partial \alpha_i} = 0 \qquad (i = 1, 2)$$

$$\frac{\partial L^*}{\partial \beta_i} = n \frac{1}{|J|} \cdot \frac{\partial |J|}{\partial \beta_i} + \Sigma \frac{\partial L^*}{\partial u_2} \cdot \frac{\partial u_2}{\partial \beta_i} = 0 \qquad (i = 1, 2, 3, 4)$$

$$\frac{\partial L^*}{\partial \gamma_i} = n \frac{1}{|J|} \cdot \frac{\partial |J|}{\partial \gamma_i} + \Sigma \frac{\partial L^*}{\partial u_3} \cdot \frac{\partial u_3}{\partial \gamma_i} = 0 \qquad (i = 1, 2)$$

$$\frac{\partial L^*}{\partial \sigma_{u_i}} = -n \frac{1}{\sigma_{u_i}} + \frac{1}{\sigma_{u_i}^3} \Sigma (u_i)^2 = 0 \qquad (i = 1, 2, 3)$$

If the equations of the structural system are not simultaneous, or if they are simultaneous but of the recursive type (for the definition of recursive models see Chapter 14) each equation contains only predetermined variables as explanatory. In this case the terms containing the Jacobian vanish, because $|J| = 1$. However, in most models the endogenous variables are interdependent, $|J| \neq 1$, and hence we must evaluate the Jacobian determinant before proceeding to the above estimation. It is obvious that the Jacobian of the transformation from u_i to y_i is all important for the estimation of the parameters in systems of simultaneous equations.

For each structural parameter we will have an equation of the above general form. Let us examine the equation for one of the structural parameters, for example α_1.

$$\frac{\partial L^*}{\partial \alpha_1} = 0$$

(1) We first differentiate L^* with respect to $\sigma_{u_i}^2$ (for $i = 1, 2, 3$).

$$L^* = n \log |J| - n \log (2\pi\sqrt{2\pi}) - n \log (\sigma_{u_1} \sigma_{u_2} \sigma_{u_3})$$
$$- \frac{1}{2\sigma_{u_1}^2} \Sigma u_{1i}^2 - \frac{1}{2\sigma_{u_2}^2} \Sigma u_{2i}^2 - \frac{1}{2\sigma_{u_3}^2} \Sigma u_{3i}^2$$

$$\frac{\partial L^*}{\partial \sigma_{u_1}} = \frac{n}{\sigma_{u_1}} - \left\{ \Sigma u_{1i}^2 \left(-\frac{1}{\sigma_{u_1}^3} \right) \right\} = 0$$

$$= -\frac{n}{\sigma_{u_1}} + \frac{\Sigma u_{1i}^2}{\sigma_{u_1}^3} = 0$$

or $\qquad \sigma_{u_1}^2 = \frac{1}{n} \Sigma u_{1i}^2$

Similarly $\sigma_{u_1}^2 = \frac{1}{n} \Sigma u_{2i}^2 \quad$ and $\quad \sigma_{u_3}^2 = \frac{1}{n} \Sigma u_{3i}^2$

(2) We substitute $\sigma_{u_1}^2, \sigma_{u_2}^2, \sigma_{u_3}^3$ in L^* and obtain

$$L^* = n \log |J| - n \log (2\pi\sqrt{2\pi}) - n \log (\sigma_{u_1} \sigma_{u_2} \sigma_{u_3}) - \frac{3n}{2}$$

We may rewrite L^* in a slightly different way

$$L^* = n \log |J| - n \log (2\pi\sqrt{2\pi}) - \frac{n}{2} \log (\sigma_{u_1}^2 \sigma_{u_2}^2 \sigma_{u_3}^3) - \frac{3n}{2}$$

$$= n \log |J| - n \log (2\pi\sqrt{2\pi}) - \frac{n}{2} (\log \sigma_{u_1}^2 + \log \sigma_{u_2}^2 + \log \sigma_{u_3}^2) - \frac{3n}{2}$$

(3) We next differentiate L^* with respect to α_1

$$\frac{\partial L^*}{\partial \alpha_1} = \frac{n}{|J|} \frac{\partial |J|}{\partial \alpha_1} - \frac{n}{2} \frac{1}{\sigma_{u_1}^2} \frac{\partial \sigma_{u_1}^2}{\partial \alpha_1}$$

Substituting $\frac{1}{n} \Sigma u_{1i}^2$ for $\sigma_{u_1}^2$ we obtain

$$\frac{\partial L^*}{\partial \alpha_1} = \frac{n}{|J|} \frac{\partial |J|}{\partial \alpha_1} - \frac{n}{2\Sigma u_{1i}^2} \frac{\partial \Sigma u_{1i}^2}{\partial \alpha_1}$$

$$= \frac{n}{|J|} \frac{\partial |J|}{\partial \alpha_1} - \left(\frac{n}{2\Sigma u_{1i}^2} \right) (2\Sigma u_{1i}) \frac{\partial u_1}{\partial \alpha_1} = 0 \qquad (18.9)$$

(4) We evaluate the Jacobian determinant

$$|J| = \begin{vmatrix} 1 & -\alpha_1 & \alpha_1 \\ -\beta_1 & 1 & \beta_1 \\ -\gamma_1 & -\gamma_1 & 1 \end{vmatrix} = \begin{vmatrix} 1 & \beta_1 \\ -\gamma_1 & 1 \end{vmatrix} + \alpha_1 \begin{vmatrix} -\beta_1 & \beta_1 \\ -\gamma_1 & 1 \end{vmatrix} + \alpha_1 \begin{vmatrix} -\beta_1 & 1 \\ -\gamma_1 & -\gamma_1 \end{vmatrix}$$

$$= (1 + \beta_1 \gamma_1) + \alpha_1 (-\beta_1 + \beta_1 \gamma_1) + \alpha_1 (\beta_1 \gamma_1 + \gamma_1)$$

$$= (1 + \beta_1 \gamma_1 + \alpha_1 (-\beta_1 + \gamma_1 + 2\beta_1 \gamma_1)) \qquad (18.10)$$

The partial derivative of the Jacobian with respect to α_1 is

$$\frac{\partial |J|}{\partial \alpha_1} = -\beta_1 + \gamma_1 + 2\beta_1 \gamma_1 \qquad (18.11)$$

(5) We know that

$$u_1 = y_1 - \alpha_1(y_2) + \alpha_1(y_3) - \alpha_1(z_1) - \alpha_1(z_2) + \alpha_1(z_4) - \alpha_1(z_5) \qquad (18.12)$$

Therefore

$$\frac{\partial u_1}{\partial \alpha_1} = -y_2 + y_3 - z_1 - z_2 + z_4 \qquad (18.13)$$

(6) Substituting 18.10, 18.11, 18.12 and 18.13 in 18.9 we find

$$0 = \frac{n(-\beta_1 + \gamma_1 + 2\beta_1 \gamma_1)}{1 + \beta_1 \gamma_1 + \alpha_1(-\beta_1 + \gamma_1 + 2\beta_1 \gamma_1)} -$$

$$- \frac{n\Sigma[y_1 - \alpha_1(y_2 - y_3 + z_1 + z_2 - z_4) - \alpha_2 z_5][-y_2 + y_3 - z_1 - z_2 + z_4]}{\Sigma[y_1 - \alpha_1(y_2 - y_3 + z_1 + z_2 - z_4) - \alpha_2 z_5]^2}$$

Rearranging we find

$$\frac{(-\beta_1 + \gamma_1 + 2\beta_1 \gamma_1)}{\{1 + \beta_1 \gamma_1 + \alpha_1(-\beta_1 + \gamma_1 + 2\beta_1 \gamma_1)\}} \cdot \Sigma\{y_1 - \alpha_1(y_2 - y_3 + z_1 + z_2 - z_4) - \alpha_2 z_5\}^2$$

$$= \Sigma\{y_1 - \alpha_1(y_2 - y_3 + z_1 + z_2 - z_4) - \alpha_2 z_5\} \cdot (-y_2 + y_3 - z_1 - z_2 + z_4)$$

We derive similar equations for all the structural parameters, α_2, β_1, β_2, β_3, β_4, γ_1, γ_2.

We solve the system of these equations and obtain the estimates $\hat{\alpha}_i$, $\hat{\beta}_i$, $\hat{\gamma}_i$.

We next substitute these estimates in the equations of the variances $\sigma_{u_1}^2$, $\sigma_{u_2}^2$, $\sigma_{u_3}^2$, and we obtain maximum likelihood estimates $\hat{\sigma}_{u_1}^2$, $\hat{\sigma}_{u_2}^2$, $\hat{\sigma}_{u_3}^2$.

The solution of the final set of equations is very tedious because it involves nonlinearities in the parameters. (Only in recursive systems is this type of nonlinearity avoided.)

It was assumed in the above illustrative example that the disturbance terms of the various relations of the model are independent. Even under this assumption the computation burden is heavy. If, however, the contemporaneous disturbances are interdependent, we have another source of nonlinearities, which complicates the computations even more.

18.5.1. PROPERTIES OF THE MAXIMUM LIKELIHOOD ESTIMATES

For small samples the maximum likelihood estimates are biased. However, for large samples they possess the desirable properties of efficiency and consistency.

18.5.2. ASSUMPTIONS OF FIML

The method in its most general form is based on two main assumptions, namely:

(1) The FIML assumes *full information*, that is full knowledge of the complete specification of all the equations of the model. We need to know not only all the variables appearing in the model, but also the mathematical form of all the equations.

(2) The FIML assumes that the random disturbances of the various equations of the model are normally distributed with zero means and constant variances.

In some cases the additional assumption of the independence of the u's of the various equations is adopted, so as to avoid nonlinear equations when differentiating the likelihood function with respect to the variances of the random variables.

Finally it is assumed some times that the model is recursive

$$y_1 = f(z\text{'s})$$

$$y_2 = f(y_1, z\text{'s})$$

$$y_3 = f(y_1, y_2, z\text{'s}) \quad \text{and so on}$$

Under the assumption of recursiveness the Jacobian determinant is unity and hence the nonlinearities in the equations of the parameters are avoided.

(H. Wold has argued that most economic phenomena can be presented adequately by recursive systems. See H. Wold and L. Jureen, *Demand Analysis*, New York, Wiley, 1953.)

18.5.3. SOME NOTES ON FIML

1. Despite the desirable properties of efficiency and consistency of the FIML estimates, it should be remembered that those estimates are biased for small samples. We will come back to this point in Chapter 21 of this book, where we will be discussing the choice among alternative econometric techniques.

2. The requirement of complete knowledge of the complete specification of the model is stringent. In most cases of econometric research we are interested in one or two relationships Specification of the entire model in these cases (apart from the difficulties it presents) seems a waste of time. The research

worker may have a pretty good knowledge of the particular relationship in which he is interested, but he may well not have complete knowledge of the model to which this relationship belongs. Furthermore, the size of a model (that is the number of equations which it will include) is quite an arbitrary decision and may well vary.

3. The method involves the formidable task of estimating equations which are nonlinear in the parameters. Furthermore, it requires a large amount of data and extensive computations. Thus it is an expensive method, in data, time and money terms.

4. Finally, the FIML method is more sensitive to specification errors than other estimation methods. The greater the incorrectness of the specification of the equations, the greater is the error imparted in the estimates.

For the above reasons FIML is not frequently applied in econometric research.

19. Three-stage Least Squares

19.1. GENERALISED LEAST SQUARES REVISITED

We have examined this method in the chapters dealing with heteroscedasticity and serial correlation. In this section we examine the method in its general form. This will facilitate the development of the method of three-stage least squares, which will be included in the next section of this chapter.

Generalised least squares has been developed by A. C. Aitken. (See A. C. Aitken, 'On Least Squares and Linear Combination of Observations', *Proc. R. Phys. Soc. Edin.*, vol. 55, 1934–5, pp. 42–8.) It is appropriate for the estimation of models in which the random term u is heteroscedastic ($E(u^2) \neq \sigma_u^2$) or autocorrelated ($E(u_i u_j) \neq 0$).

The method, as applied in actual econometric research, boils down to the application of OLS to a set of transformed variables. The transformation required in the Y's and the X's depends on the form of heteroscedasticity or of serial correlation. If the type of heteroscedasticity or the relation between the successive values of u is known *a priori* or established by econometric experimentation, we use this information to transform the original relation, so that the standard assumptions of least squares are satisfied. It can be shown that such a transformation is always possible.

Before showing the procedure of Aitken's transformation we will examine the philosophy behind the method of generalised least squares. This will be facilitated if we examine the relationship between OLS and the maximum likelihood method.

We saw that OLS is based on the principle of the minimisation of the sum of squared residuals

$$\Sigma e^2 = \Sigma(Y_i - \hat{b}_0 - \hat{b}_1 X_i)^2$$

We also established that this sum of squared residuals is identical to the expression that appears in the exponent of the likelihood function of the n sample observations except for the term $1/2\sigma_u^2$ which, under the assumption of normality, zero mean, constant variance and zero covariance of the error term u, can be taken out of the summation in the exponent and left out of the differentiation. The joint probability of the n sample values of Y is

$$\text{Likelihood function} = \left\{ \frac{1}{\sigma_u \sqrt{2\pi}} \right\}^n \exp\left\{ -\frac{1}{2\sigma_u^2} \Sigma(Y_i - b_0 - b_1 X_i)^2 \right\}$$

The likelihood function is maximised when the negative exponent is minimised, that is, when

$$\Sigma(Y_i - b_0 - b_1 X_i)^2$$

is minimum.

This expression is identical to the sum of squared residuals which we minimise when applying OLS. Therefore the OLS estimates are identical to the maximum likelihood estimates, provided that u satisfies the standard assumptions.

Examining the residual sum of squares we see that all observations are treated symmetrically, in the sense that all are given equal weights: each observation is given a weight dependent only on the deviation of Y_i from its mean. Thus we say that in OLS we minimise an unweighted sum of squares.

However, if $E(u^2) \neq \sigma_u^2$ (heteroscedastic u's), or if $E(u_i u_j) \neq 0$ (serially correlated u's), the unweighted sum of squares is inappropriate. Each sample observation should be given a different weight, and the appropriate procedure is to minimise a *weighted* sum of squared residuals, where the weights are chosen to incorporate the effects of the various products ($u_i u_j$, or u_i^2). This is done by the method of generalised least squares, which, for this reason, is also called Weighted Least Squares (WLS) method.

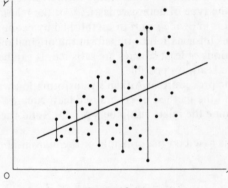

Figure 19.1

For example in the case of positive heteroscedasticity the variance of u increases with increasing values of the variables (figure 19.1). It is clear that as the scatter of observations widens, values of X and Y on the right in this diagram give a less precise indication of where the true regression line lies. Therefore we should give less attention to these observations than to the more precise ones depicted on the left of the diagram. This is achieved by dividing the deviations (i.e. the residuals $Y_i - \hat{Y}_i$) by the value of the corresponding variance of u. Instead of applying OLS which minimises the sum

$$\Sigma(Y_i - \hat{b}_0 - \hat{b}_1 X_i)^2$$

we apply generalised least squares which minimises the 'generalised' sum

$$\Sigma \left[\frac{(Y_i - \hat{b}_0 - \hat{b}_1 X_i)^2}{\sigma_{u_i}^2} \right]$$

In this sum each squared deviation is weighted by a factor $1/\sigma_{u_i}^2$, so that as $\sigma_{u_i}^2$ increases the weight $1/\sigma_{u_i}^2$ decreases, and thus less attention is given to the less precise deviations on the right. In this way observations with large variances (less reliable observations) are 'discounted' in the process of fitting the regression line.

This procedure is based on the maximum likelihood function, which, of course, assumes a different form when heteroscedasticity and/or autocorrelation of the u's occurs. Thus if the variance of the u's is not constant but changes with the observations X_i, we cannot take $\sigma_{u_i}^2$ out of the summation in the exponent of the likelihood function. With heteroscedasticity present in the structural equation the likelihood function is

$$L = \frac{1}{(\sqrt{2\pi})^n \prod_{i=1}^{n} \sigma_{u_i}} \cdot \exp \left[-\frac{1}{2} \Sigma \left\{ \frac{(Y_i - b_0 - b_1 X_i)^2}{\sigma_{u_i}^2} \right\} \right]$$

We observe that the sum in the exponent of the likelihood function is identical with the 'generalised' sum of squared residuals which is minimised by the method of GLS.

Similarly when the u's are autocorrelated (but homoscedastic), the expression to be minimised in applying GLS is

$$\Sigma e_i^2 + \sum_{i}^{n} \sum_{j \neq i}^{n} c_{ij} e_i e_j$$

where c_{ij} is a sum of relevant terms involving the covariances of the u's. This 'generalised' sum of weighted squares and cross products is the expression which, on the assumption of normality of u, would appear in the exponent of the likelihood function. (See E. Kane, *Economic Statistics and Econometrics*, pp. 358–9. Also R. Wonnacott and T. Wonnacott, *Econometrics*, 1970, pp. 322–6.)

In general the method of GLS involves the minimisation of some expression which includes the residuals properly weighted. If the assumption of homoscedasticity and/or serial independence of the u variable does not hold in any particular equation the correct procedure is to weight the elements of the sum of squared deviations before minimising this sum. The weights are defined by the variances and covariances of the u's, which are not known in practice. Thus for the application of GLS Aitken has suggested an alternative approach, namely the transformation of the variables of the original model so as to produce a new model which satisfies the standard assumptions of the random variable and to which OLS can be applied.

The principle underlying the transformation is easy to understand.

With heteroscedastic random variable the original model is

$$Y = b_0 + b_1 X_1 + \ldots + b_k X_k + u\{f(X_1, X_2 \ldots X_k)\}$$

Obviously the variance of this random variable is not constant, but varies with the X's. If we know the form of $f(X_1, X_2, \ldots, X_k)$ we may divide the original model through by it and thus achieve the required transformation

$$\frac{Y}{\{f(X_1, X_2, \ldots, X_k)\}} = b_0 \frac{1}{\{f(X_1, X_2, \ldots, X_k)\}} + \ldots + u$$

With the transformation we obtain homoscedastic u term (see Chapter 9).

Similarly with autocorrelated u's the original model is

$$Y_t = b_0 + b_1 X_{1t} + \ldots + b_k X_{kt} + \{f(u_{t-1}, u_{t-2} \ldots)\}$$

Again the appropriate transformation depends on the form of autocorrelation, that is on the relationship between the successive values of u. If this is known we may proceed with the transformation of the original model and apply OLS to the new model whose error term will be 'corrected' for serial correlation (see Chapter 10).

Thus the crucial problem for the application of GLS is to estimate the form of the relationship between the u's. It has been suggested in Chapters 9 and 10 that the best way is to use the e's of the original model and experiment with various forms of heteroscedasticity or autocorrelation; then to choose between the alternative formulations on the basis of the statistical criteria of the estimates of the autocorrelation coefficients (ρ's) or of the coefficients of the hetero-scedasticity relationship.

It can be proved that the estimates of the GLS method are unbiased (as are indeed the estimates of OLS even when the assumptions of homoscedasticity and serial independence are violated) and efficient, that is will have smaller sampling variances than OLS or other unbiased linear eastimates: the GLS estimates are BLUE under circumstances that OLS estimates are not. (See J. Johnston, *Econometric Methods,* 2nd Edition, p. 210.)

19.2. THREE-STAGE LEAST SQUARES

(A. Zellner and H. Theil, 'Three-stage Least Squares: Simultaneous Estimation of Simultaneous Equations', *Econometrica*, vol. 30, 1962, pp. 54–78.)

Three-stage least squares (3SLS) is a systems method, that is it is applied to all the equations of the model at the same time and gives estimates of all the parameters simultaneously. This method was developed by Theil and Zellner as a logical extension of Theil's 2SLS. It involves the application of the method of least squares in three successive stages. It utilises more information than the single-equation techniques, that is, it takes into account the entire structure of the model with all the restrictions that this structure imposes on the values of the parameters. The single-equation techniques make use only of the variables appearing in the entire model, but they ignore the restrictions set by the structure on the coefficients of other equations, as well as the con-temporaneous dependence of the random terms of the various equations. In simultaneous equations models it is almost certain that the random variable of any equation, u_i, will be correlated with the random variable of other equations. This fact is ignored by single-equation methods. Of course the computations of 3SLS, and of other systems techniques, are much more complicated and the data requirements are enormous: in a single-equation technique we may use a small sample, since for each equation we use the same sample anew; in a simultaneous-equation model we estimate all the parameters at the same time, so that the sample must contain more observations than the total number of parameters of the entire system.

We will use the same notation as in the previous section, that is we will denote the endogenous variables with y's and the predetermined (exogenous) variables with x's.

Three-stage least squares is a straightforward extension of 2SLS, and involves the application of least squares in three stages. The first two stages are the same as 2SLS except that we deal with the reduced-form of all the equations of the system. The third stage involves the application of generalised least squares, that is, the application of least squares to a set of transformed equations, in which the transformation required is obtained from the reduced-form residuals of the previous stage.

The assumptions of the three-stage least squares may be stated briefly as follows.

(1) The complete specification of the entire system is correctly known. We need know not only the variables which appear in each equation but also its mathematical form.

(2) The random term of each equation is serially independent (non-autocorrelation).

(3) The random variables of the various relations of the system are con-temporaneously dependent. If the random variables of the various relations are independent, the 3SLS reduces to the 2SLS. (See A. Goldberger, *Econometric Theory*, p. 352.) However, taking into account the nature of economic phenomena and the simplifications which we adopt in specifying the econo-metric models, we may well expect the u's to be contemporaneously correlated, that is $E(u_iu_j) \neq 0$, where i *refers to the* ith *equation and* j *to the* jth *equation.* We have seen that for various reasons we include explicitly in a relationship only the most important three or four explanatory variables, leaving the influence of the other, less important, variables to be absorbed by the random variable of the relation. If some variables are omitted from more relations of the system it is inevitable that the u's of these relations are correlated and hence the application of 3SLS is appropriate. Application of 2SLS under these circum-stances would ignore part of the information included in the entire system and hence the estimates of the parameters would be less efficient.

(4) The system is overidentified. If some equations are underidentified we attempt to render them identifiable by changing their specification, or we drop

them. We also drop identities and definitional equations after using them to eliminate the relevant variables from the system. (See A. Goldberger, *Econometric Theory*, p. 348.)

Suppose that we are left with a system in G endogenous and K predetermined variables. There are G equations in the system of the form

$$y_1 = b_{12}y_2 + b_{13}y_3 + \ldots + b_{1G}y_G + \gamma_{11}x_1 + \ldots + \gamma_{1K}x_K + u_1$$

$$y_2 = b_{21}y_1 + b_{23}y_3 + \ldots + b_{2G}y_G + \gamma_{21}x_1 + \ldots + \gamma_{2K}x_K + u_2$$

$$y_G = b_{G1}y_1 + b_{G2}y_2 + \ldots\ldots\ldots + \gamma_{G1}x_1 + \ldots + \gamma_{GK}x_K + u_G$$

Pre-multiplying each equation by the K predetermined variables we obtain a system of KG equations, that is, we have K forms for each one of the G equations.

The set of K forms for the first structural equation is

$$x_1 y_1 = b_{12}(x_1 y_2) + b_{13}(x_1 y_3) + \ldots + b_{1G}(x_1 y_G) + \gamma_{11}(x_1^2) + \ldots + \gamma_{1K}(x_1 x_K) + x_1 u_1$$

$$x_2 y_1 = b_{12}(x_2 y_2) + b_{13}(x_2 y_3) + \ldots + b_{1M}(x_2 y_G) + \gamma_{11}(x_1 x_2) + \ldots + \gamma_{1K}(x_2 x_K) + x_2 u_1$$

$$x_K y_1 = b_{12}(x_K y_2) + b_{13}(x_K y_3) + \ldots + b_{1G}(x_K y_G) + \gamma_{11}(x_1 x_K) + \ldots + \gamma_{1K}(x_K^2) + x_K u_1$$

Set of K forms for the second structural equation

$$x_1 y_2 = b_{21}(x_1 y_1) + b_{23}(x_1 y_3) + \ldots + b_{2G}(x_1 y_G) + \gamma_{21}(x_1^2) + \ldots + \gamma_{2K}(x_1 x_K) + x_1 u_2$$

$$x_2 y_2 = b_{21}(x_2 y_1) + b_{23}(x_2 y_3) + \ldots + b_{2G}(x_2 y_G) + \gamma_{21}(x_1 x_2) + \ldots + \gamma_{2K}(x_2 x_K) + x_2 u_2$$

$$x_K y_2 = b_{21}(x_K y_1) + b_{23}(x_K y_3) + \ldots + b_{2G}(x_K y_G) + \gamma_{21}(x_1 x_K) + \ldots + \gamma_{2K}(x_K^2) + x_K u_2$$

The set of K forms for the Gth structural equation is

$$x_1 y_G = b_{G1}(x_1 y_1) + b_{G2}(x_1 y_2) + \ldots + \gamma_{G1}(x_1^2) \quad + \ldots + \gamma_{GK}(x_1 x_K) + x_1 u_G$$

$$x_2 y_G = b_{G1}(x_2 y_1) + b_{G2}(x_2 y_2) + \ldots + \gamma_{G1}(x_1 x_2) + \ldots + \gamma_{GK}(x_2 x_K) + x_2 u_G$$

$$x_K y_G = b_{G1}(x_K y_1) + b_{G2}(x_K y_2) + \ldots + \gamma_{G1}(x_1 x_K) + \ldots + \gamma_{GK}(x_K^2) \quad + x_K u_G$$

We observe that the disturbances of these equations are heteroscedastic, since the composite random terms (u^*'s $= x_i u_j$'s) tend to change together with the x variables (see Chapter 9). Hence the appropriate method for the estimation of the parameters of the system is generalised least squares. The transformation required involves the variances and the covariances of the original error terms (u's), which however are unknown. We may obtain an estimate of these covariances by applying 2SLS to each one of the structural equations of the original model. Thus we have the following three stages of estimation.

Stage I. In the first stage we estimate the reduced-form of all the equations of the system

$$y_1 = f(x_1, x_2, \ldots, x_k)$$
$$y_2 = f(x_1, x_2, \ldots, x_k)$$
$$y_G = f(x_1, x_2, \ldots, x_k)$$

We thus obtain estimated values of the endogenous variables, $\hat{y}_1, \hat{y}_2, \ldots, \hat{y}_G$.

Stage II. We substitute the above calculated values of the endogenous variables in the right-hand side of the structural equations and apply least squares to the transformed equations. We thus obtain the 2SLS of the b's and the γ's, which we use for the estimation of the error terms of the various equations. We find a set of G errors

$$e_1, e_2, e_3, \ldots, e_G$$

each corresponding to the error term (u) of the respective structural equation. Of course for each equation we have n values of the error term (n being the sample observations).

The variances and covariances of the estimated error terms may easily be computed by the usual formula of the covariance

$$\hat{\sigma}_{e_1 e_2} = \frac{\Sigma e_{1i} e_{2i}}{n}$$

$$\hat{\sigma}_{e_1 e_3} = \frac{\Sigma e_{1i} e_{3i}}{n} \qquad \text{and so on.}$$

The complete set of the variances and the covariances of the error terms is as follows

$$
\begin{vmatrix}
\hat{\sigma}_{e_1}^2 & \hat{\sigma}_{e_1 e_2} & \hat{\sigma}_{e_1 e_3} \cdots \hat{\sigma}_{e_1 e_G} \\
\hat{\sigma}_{e_2 e_1} & \hat{\sigma}_{e_2}^2 & \hat{\sigma}_{e_2 e_3} \cdots \hat{\sigma}_{e_2 e_G} \\
\vdots & & \ddots & \vdots \\
\hat{\sigma}_{e_G e_1} & \hat{\sigma}_{e_G e_2} & \cdots \hat{\sigma}_{e_G}^2
\end{vmatrix}
=
\begin{vmatrix}
\frac{\Sigma e_1^2}{n} & \frac{\Sigma e_1 e_2}{n} \cdots \frac{\Sigma e_1 e_G}{n} \\
\frac{\Sigma e_1 e_2}{n} & \frac{\Sigma e_2^2}{n} \cdots \\
\vdots & & \ddots \\
\frac{\Sigma e_1 e_G}{n} & \cdots & \frac{\Sigma e_G^2}{n}
\end{vmatrix}
$$

Stage III. We use the above variances and covariances of the error terms in order to obtain the transformations of the original variables for the application of generalised least squares (GLS).

The presentation of the computations of this stage becomes extremely complicated with the use of simple algebra and summations and will not be presented here. The interested reader is referred to more advanced textbooks of econometrics.

19.2.1. PROPERTIES OF THE 3SLS ESTIMATES

1. The 3SLS estimates are biased but consistent.

2. They are more efficient than 2SLS, since in their estimation we use more information than in 2SLS.

The method is simpler than full information maximum likelihood. However, it requires complete knowledge of the specification of the entire model and a large amount of data. If we are interested in only one relationship of the entire model, 3SLS seems rather a tedious, time consuming approach. Furthermore, it is sensitive to specification error in the equations: a single specification error is transmitted to all the equations of the model.

We said that 3SLS reduces to 2SLS if the random variables are contemporaneously independent. Thus (a) if one is not very sure about the accuracy of the specification of all the equations, or (b) if it seems on *a priori* grounds that the *u*'s are not seriously interdependent, it is preferable to apply 2SLS.

20. Testing the Forecasting Power of an Estimated Model

We said at the beginning of this book that one of the main goals of applied econometric research is to use the estimated model in order to forecast the value of the dependent variables given the values of the explanatory variables. We can predict the value of a variable in two alternative ways: either our forecast is a single value, or we can estimate an interval within which the value of the variable will most probably lie. The first method yields a *point prediction*, the second an *interval prediction.* For example we may predict that the gross national product of the United Kingdom in 1975 will be £45,000 million. This is a point prediction of the GNP. Alternatively we may predict that the gross national product of the United Kingdom in 1975 will be between £44,000 mn and £46,000 mn. This is an example of interval prediction.

Forecasting with an econometric model is a complicated process. In this chapter we will attempt to give a simple exposition of the forecasting procedure starting with a simple example of single-equation regression prediction. In a subsequent section we will illustrate the process of forecasting with an aggregate (multi-equation) econometric model.

20.1. FORECASTING WITH A SINGLE-EQUATION LINEAR REGRESSION MODEL

20.1.1. POINT PREDICTION

Suppose that the relationship between Y and X has been estimated by OLS

$$\hat{Y}_i = \hat{b}_0 + \hat{b}_1 X_i$$

Given the estimates $\hat{b}_0$ and $\hat{b}_1$, and given the value of the explanatory variable X in any period, we may obtain an estimate of the value of the dependent variable by substituting in the estimated regression equation

$$\hat{Y}_F = \hat{b}_0 + \hat{b}_1 \hat{X}_F$$

where Y_F = forecast value of the dependent variable

        X_F = given value of X in the forecast period.

For example if the above function is the consumption function of the United Kingdom and its estimated form is

$$Y_t = 2{,}550 + 0{\cdot}68 \, X_t$$

we can obtain the following point prediction of the level of consumption in 1975, provided the income (X) in that year will be £45,000 mn

$$Y_{1975} = 2{,}250 + 0{\cdot}68 \, (45{,}000) = 33{,}150 \text{ million pounds.}$$

This is known as *conditional forecasting*, because it is based on the condition that the explanatory variable will assume in the forecast period the value X_F. Furthermore this procedure assumes that the structural relationship between Y and X will continue to be the same in the forecast period as it was during the sample period, that is, we assume that the parameters will not change between the two periods.

20.1.2. CONFIDENCE INTERVAL FOR A POINT PREDICTION (INTERVAL PREDICTION)

The need for constructing a confidence interval for a point prediction arises from the fact that when we use an econometric model for forecasting we are making a statistical judgement, which is subject to error. Statistical judgements cannot be precise statements due to their nature. Hence we must construct a confidence interval for such predictions.

The construction of confidence intervals in general has been examined in Chapter 5 (and in Appendix I). For the construction of a confidence interval for the forecast value $\hat{Y}_F$ in particular we must have information on the mean and the variance of the distribution of $\hat{Y}_F$.

(1) We first note that $\hat{Y}_F$ will have a normal distribution since it is determined by $\hat{b}_0$ and $\hat{b}_1$, which have a bivariate normal distribution.

(2) The mean of $\hat{Y}_F$ will be the true value of the forecast

$$Y_F = b_0 + b_1 X_F + u_F$$

(3) As regards the variance of the distribution of $\hat{Y}_F$ we note the following. In the case of a prediction from an econometric function there are two possible sources of variation (error): (a) The estimates of the parameters. In predicting, we do not know the true parameters of the structural relationship, and hence we use their estimates, $(\hat{b}_0, \hat{b}_1)$, which have been obtained from a sample. Hence they are subject to sampling error, which is transmitted to the forecast of the value of the dependent variable. In other words the standard errors of the estimates are a component of the variance of the forecast.
(b) When we use the above method of forecasting we assume that in the period of the forecast the disturbance variable u will assume its mean value, (which is zero by definition). However, in any particular period u may assume a value different from zero, due to the occurrence of a random event. We cannot predict the exact value that u may assume in any particular period, but from the variance of the u term we have a measure of the range within which its values may lie. Hence the variance of the random variable is a second component of the variance of the forecast.

In summary, our point prediction will be associated with a certain variance, due to the sampling errors of the parameter estimates and to the variance of the random variable u.

The variance of the forecast in our single-equation model is given by the formula

$$\text{var}(\hat{Y}_F) = \hat{\sigma}_u^2 \left\{ 1 + \frac{1}{n} + \frac{(X_F - \bar{X})^2}{\Sigma(X_1 - \bar{X})^2} \right\}$$

where $\hat{\sigma}_u^2$ = estimate of the variance of $u = \Sigma e^2/(n - K)$

n = size of the sample

X_F = value of X assumed in the period of the forecast

The standard error of the forecast is then

$$s(\hat{Y}_F) = \hat{\sigma}_u \cdot \sqrt{1 + \frac{1}{n} + \frac{(X_F - \bar{X})^2}{\Sigma(X - \bar{X})^2}}$$

The true value of the dependent variable in the period of the forecast is

$$Y_F = b_0 + b_1 X_F + u_F$$

The estimate of the forecast is

$$\hat{Y}_F = \hat{b}_0 + \hat{b}_1 X_F$$

Subtracting we obtain

$$(Y_F - \hat{Y}_F) = u_F - (\hat{b}_0 - b_0) - (\hat{b}_1 - b_1)X_F$$
$$= (u_F) - \left\{ (\hat{b}_0 - b_0) + (\hat{b}_1 - b_1)X_F \right\}$$

Squaring both sides we obtain

$$(Y_F - \hat{Y}_F)^2 = u_F^2 + \left\{ (\hat{b}_0 - b_0) + (\hat{b}_1 - b_1)X_F \right\}^2 - 2u_F \left\{ (\hat{b}_0 - b_0) + (\hat{b}_1 - b_1)X_F \right\}$$

Taking expected values we have

$$\text{var}(\hat{Y}_F) = E(Y_F - \hat{Y}_F)^2 = E(u_F^2) + E \left\{ (\hat{b}_0 - b_0) + (\hat{b}_1 - b_1)X_F \right\}^2$$

since the expected value of the third term is zero: u refers to the period of the forecast and is independent of the sample u's (i.e. $u_1, u_2, \ldots, u_n$) which influence b_0 and b_1.

By simple algebraic manipulations we obtain

$$\text{var}(\hat{Y}_F) = E(u_F^2) + E \left\{ (\hat{b}_0 - b_0)^2 + (\hat{b}_1 - b_1)^2 X_F^2 + 2(\hat{b}_0 - b_0)(\hat{b}_1 - b_1)X_F \right\}$$
$$= E(u_F^2) + E(\hat{b}_0 - b_0)^2 + X_F^2 E(\hat{b}_1 - b_1)^2 + 2X_F E(\hat{b}_0 - b_0)(\hat{b}_1 - b_1)$$

But

$$E(u_F^2) = \sigma_u^2$$

$$E(\hat{b}_0 - b_0)^2 = \text{var}(\hat{b}_0) = \sigma_u^2 \frac{\Sigma X^2}{n \Sigma(X - \bar{X})^2}$$

$$E(\hat{b}_1 - b_1)^2 = \text{var}(\hat{b}_1) = \sigma_u^2 \frac{1}{\Sigma(X - \bar{X})^2}$$

$$E(\hat{b}_0 - b_0)(\hat{b}_1 - b_1) = \text{cov}(\hat{b}_0 \hat{b}_1) = \sigma_u^2 \cdot \frac{-\bar{X}}{\Sigma(X - \bar{X})^2}$$

Hence

$$\text{var}(\hat{Y}_F) = \sigma_u^2 + \sigma_u^2 \frac{\Sigma X^2}{n \Sigma(X - \bar{X})^2} + \sigma_u^2 \frac{X_F^2}{\Sigma(X - \bar{X})^2} + 2X_F \sigma_u^2 \frac{-\bar{X}}{\Sigma(X - \bar{X})^2}$$

$$= \sigma_u^2 \left\{ 1 + \frac{\Sigma(X - \bar{X})^2 + n\bar{X}^2}{n(\Sigma X - \bar{X})^2} + \frac{X_F^2}{\Sigma(X - \bar{X})^2} - \frac{2X_F \bar{X}}{\Sigma(X - \bar{X})^2} \right\}$$

or

$$\text{var}(\hat{Y}_F) = \sigma_u^2 \left\{ 1 + \frac{1}{n} + \frac{(X_F - \bar{X})^2}{\Sigma(X - \bar{X})^2} \right\}$$

Having established that

$$\hat{Y}_F \sim N\left[Y_F, \sigma_u^2 \left\{ 1 + \frac{1}{n} + \frac{(X_F - \bar{X})^2}{\Sigma(X - \bar{X})^2} \right\} \right]$$

it can be proved[1] that the 95 per cent confidence interval for the true forecast is

$$\hat{Y}_F \pm (t_{0.025}) \left\{ \hat{\sigma}_u \sqrt{1 + \frac{1}{n} + \frac{(X_F - \bar{X})^2}{\Sigma(X - \bar{X})^2}} \right\}$$

or

$$\hat{Y}_F - (t_{.025}) \left\{ \hat{\sigma}_u \sqrt{1 + \frac{1}{n} + \frac{(X_F - \bar{X})^2}{\Sigma(X - \bar{X})^2}} \right\} < Y_F < \hat{Y}_F +$$

$$+ (t_{.025}) \left[\hat{\sigma}_u \sqrt{1 + \frac{1}{n} + \frac{(X_F - \bar{X})^2}{\Sigma(X - \bar{X})^2}} \right]$$

It is clear that the confidence interval for a forecast is more complicated than the confidence interval of a parameter estimate. This is so because the standard error of the forecast is not a constant but depends on the value assumed by the explanatory variable(s) in the period of the forecast.[2] This is better seen from figure 20.1, which shows graphically the confidence interval of a point prediction.

The confidence interval is narrowest at the point of sample means and becomes wider as we move away from these means. The diagram shows clearly that forecasting with an econometric function (model) becomes more uncertain as the values assumed by the explanatory variable(s) for the period of the forecast depart from the mean of the sample, which was used for the estimation of the function.

The extension of the formula of the standard error of the forecast for functions including more explanatory variables is straightforward. If the true relationship between Y and $X_1, X_2, \ldots, X_k$ is linear of the form

$$Y = b_0 + b_1 X_1 + b_2 X_2 + \ldots + b_k X_k + u$$

the variance of the forecast

$$\hat{Y}_F = \hat{b}_0 + \hat{b}_1 X_{1F} + \hat{b}_2 X_{2F} + \ldots + \hat{b}_k X_{kF}$$

will be

$$\text{var}(\hat{Y}_F) = \text{var}(u) + \text{var}(\hat{b}_0) + \sum_{i=1}(\text{var}\,\hat{b}_i)(X_{iF} - \bar{X}_i)^2 + 2\sum_{i<j}(\text{cov}\,\hat{b}_i\hat{b}_j)(X_{iF} - \bar{X}_i)(X_{jF} - \bar{X}_j).$$

[1] See L. R. Klein, *Introduction to Econometrics*, p. 244–51.

[2] See W. Allen Wallis, 'Tolerance Intervals for Linear Regression', *Proceedings of the Second Berkeley Symposium on Mathematical Statistics and Probability*, University of California Press, 1951.

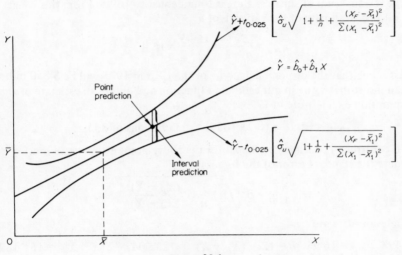

Figure 20.1

This expression is the same as the one derived for the two-variable function except for the third term which includes the covariances of the estimates of the coefficients, which allow for the joint dependence of the b's. See L. R. Klein, *Introduction to Econometrics*, pp. 244–51.

An arithmetic example will illustrate the construction of a confidence interval of a point prediction. Table 20.1 shows the consumption expenditure and income of the USA over the 1957–68 period.

Table 20.1. Consumption and income of the USA (in billions of $)

Year	Consumption expenditure C	Income X
1957	282·3	359·9
1958	291·1	370·1
1959	312·3	394·7
1960	326·5	414·5
1961	336·6	430·8
1962	356·6	458·7
1963	376·6	483·5
1964	402·9	515·5
1965	434·7	557·4
1966	468·3	613·1
1967	494·3	658·9
1968	538·9	721·0

Applying OLS to the data of table 20.1 we obtain the following estimate of the consumption function

$$\hat{Y}_t = 31·76 + 0·71\,X_t \qquad R^2 = 0·998$$
$$(5·39)\ (0·01)$$

The residual sum of squares, Σe^2, is found equal to 169·5. From this we get the following estimate of the variance of u

$$\hat{\sigma}_u = \frac{\Sigma e^2}{n-2} = \frac{169\cdot5}{12-2} = 16\cdot9$$

Assuming that the disposable income of the USA in 1975 will be \$ 850 billion we can insert that value in our estimated function and obtain an estimate of the consumption expenditure in 1975

$$\hat{Y}_{1975} = 31\cdot76 + (0\cdot71)(850) \approx 635 \text{ billions of dollars}$$

To construct a confidence interval for the above point estimate we must compute the standard error of the forecast

$$s_{(\hat{Y}_{1975})} = \hat{\sigma}_u \sqrt{1 + \frac{1}{n} + \frac{(X_F - \bar{X})^2}{\Sigma(X - \bar{X})^2}}$$

The relevant data are

$$\bar{X} = 498 \quad \hat{\sigma}_u = 16\cdot9 \quad n = 12 \quad (X_F - X)^2 = 123{,}904 \quad \Sigma(X - \bar{X})^2 = 151{,}482$$

Hence

$$s_{(\hat{Y}_{1975})} = 16\cdot9 \left(\sqrt{1 + \frac{1}{12} + \frac{123{,}904}{151{,}482}} \right) \approx 2\cdot32$$

Thus the confidence interval of the above point prediction is

$$\hat{Y}_F \pm t_{0.025} \left(s_{(\hat{Y}_{1975})} \right)$$

Given that $t_{0.025} = 2\cdot23$ (with $n - 2 = 12 - 2 = 10$ degrees of freedom) we have

$$635 - (2\cdot23)(2\cdot32) < Y_{F(1975)} < 635 + (2\cdot23)(2\cdot32)$$
$$629\cdot83 < Y_{F(1975)} < 640\cdot17$$

that is the consumption expenditure of the USA in 1975 is expected (with 95 per cent probability) to lie between 630 and 640 millions of dollars (approximately).

20.2. FORECASTING WITH AN AGGREGATE MULTI-EQUATION ECONOMETRIC MODEL

Once the parameters of a structural model have been estimated with any appropriate technique, we can use the model for forecasting, provided we know the values of the predetermined variables in the period of the forecast.

We will illustrate the forecasting process by a simple Keynesian model. In this section we will use the structural parameters for forecasting. The forecasting procedure is greatly facilitated if we use the reduced-form coefficients of the model. However, we will not develop the reduced-form approach, since it is beyond the scope of this textbook. (For an introduction to the forecasting procedure see D. B. Suits, 'Forecasting with an Aggregate Econometric Model', *American Economic Review*, vol. 52, 1962, pp. 104–32.)

Assume we have the following model of income determination.

$$C_t = a_0 + a_1(Y_t - T_t) + u_1$$
$$I_t = b_0 + b_1 Y_t + b_2 Y_{t-1} + u_2$$
$$T_t = cY_t + u_3$$
$$M_t = m_0 + m_1 Y_t + m_2 P_{t-1} + u_4$$
$$Y_t = C_t + I_t + G_t + E_t - M_t$$

The system contains five equations in five endogenous variables, C_t, I_t, T_t, M_t, Y_t. There are four predetermined variables in the model G_t, Y_{t-1}, P_{t-1}, E_t. In total there are nine variables in the model:

$$C_t = \text{consumption expenditure}$$
$$I_t = \text{investment}$$
$$T_t = \text{taxation}$$
$$M_t = \text{imports}$$
$$Y_t = \text{income}$$
$$Y_{t-1} = \text{lagged income}$$
$$P_{t-1} = \text{lagged price level}$$
$$G_t = \text{government expenditure}$$
$$E_t = \text{exports.}$$

The first equation is the consumption function. Consumers' expenditure depends on disposable income.

The second equation is the investment function. Investment is determined by the current level of income as well as by the income in the previous period.

The third equation is a tax revenue function. Revenues from taxation are determined by current income.

The fourth equation is an import function. Imports depend on the level of national income and on the price level of the country lagged one period.

The fifth equation is the usual accounting identity of national income.

Applying the counting rule for identification (see Chapter 15) we see that the four behavioural equations are overidentified. Choosing the method of 2SLS and using time series for the period 1948–1969, we obtain the following estimates of the structural parameters.

$$C_t = 20 + 0.8(Y_t - T_t)$$
$$I_t = 2 + 0.1 Y_t + 0.3 Y_{t-1}$$
$$T_t = 0.2 Y_t$$
$$M_t = 3 + 0.1 Y_t + 0.1 P_{t-1}$$
$$Y_t = C_t + I_t + G_t + E_t - M_t$$

Having estimated the structural parameters we may forecast the values of
the endogenous variables for any period, given that we know the values which
the predetermined variables will assume in that period. Suppose that for the
period of the forecast the exogenous variables will assume the following values

$$G = 20 \qquad Y_{t-1} = 150$$
$$E = 10 \qquad P_{t-1} = 110$$

Inserting these values into the model and transferring all the endogenous
variables in the left-hand side of the equations, we obtain

$$C_t - 0.8\,Y_t - 0.8\,T_t = 20$$
$$I_t - 0.1\,Y_t = 2 + 0.3(150) = 47$$
$$T_t - 0.2\,Y_t = 0$$
$$M_t - 0.1\,Y_t = 3 + 0.1(110) = 14$$
$$Y_t - C_t - I_t + M_t = 20 + 10 = 30$$

This is a system of five equations in five unknowns which are the endogenous
variables C, I, T, M and Y. The system may be solved with any method. Its
solution yields the following forecast values

$$C = 1675 \qquad T = 46.1 \qquad Y = 230.5$$
$$I = 70 \qquad M = 37$$

On the above forecasting procedure we note the following.
Firstly. Any forecast with an econometric model is a *conditional* forecast.
For example the above forecast should be read as follows:
   If the exogenous variables take the values assumed in the forecast period, and
   if the structural parameters remain constant, and
   if the clause '*ceteris paribus*', which was made in estimating the model,
      remains valid for the period of the forecast,
then the endogenous variables will take the values given by the solution of the
structural model.
   In this sense it is apparent that one should not expect the forecast to be
realised. Actually one of the reasons for making forecasts is precisely to avoid
their realisation. For example if taxation and government expenditure are
held constant, and our model forecasts an increase in unemployment due to a
fall in the economic activity, this result is obviously undesirable: the forecast
should not be realised. Thus taxation and/or government expenditure should
change so as to avoid the occurrence of the forecast.
   Secondly. The forecast computed from the above solution is a point forecast.
It is based on the point estimates of the structural parameters, and the random
terms have been set equal to zero (which is their mean value) in the period of
the forecast. However, there are various reasons to expect the actual values of the
endogenous variables to deviate from this 'point' value. Such reasons are:
(a) The random variable u, which was set equal to its mean value of zero in the

forecast period, may assume a value different than zero; (b) The coefficients used in the forecast are not the true parameters, but are estimates of the true parameters obtained from a sample, thus they are subject to sampling error. For these reasons we should construct confidence intervals for the values forecast by an econometric model. (See J. Johnston, *Econometric Methods, 1972*, pp. 152–5.)

Thirdly. If the values assumed by the exogenous variables are not realised in the period of the forecast, obviously the forecast will not be realised.

Fourthly. If the structural coefficients change in the period of the forecast, our model must be modified accordingly, otherwise it is unsuitable for forecasting.

Fifthly. The same holds for the '*ceteris paribus*' clause: if the factors assumed constant when estimating the model (for example tastes, population movements, social changes, etc.) do actually change in the period of the forecast, again our model must be modified before being used for forecasting.

It might be thought that since conditions underlying the structure of the model as well as the structure itself (coefficients) of the model do change, forecasting with econometric models is bound to be inaccurate. Fortunately there are various ways for modifying the model in such a way as to incorporate information which becomes available after the estimation of its coefficients. Some examples will illustrate this point.

Example 1. It is well known that investment functions are bad approximations to the actual behaviour of investors. Assume that we have information of the investment projects directly from a survey of businessmen's plans. Obviously this information is superior to any forecast obtained from an investment function. In this case we may ignore the investment equation and use the above information for forecasting purposes.

Example 2. A lot of information may be incorporated into the model, at least for short-term forecasting (and until a more effective way is found, for example re-computing the function or functions), by adjusting accordingly the constant intercept of the function, that is shifting the function, while keeping its slope(s) constant. For example assume that the government imposes a credit squeeze (or an easing of credit terms). This may well be expected to make the consumption function shift (downwards or upwards). From past experience of similar measures one usually is able to set a (lower or upper) limit to such a shift. This estimated amount of the probable shift is then subtracted (added) to the constant term of the consumption function. It should be noted that this shift is equivalent to ascribing to the u term a value different than its mean value (zero), a procedure perfectly justified from our knowledge that u will not be zero in the period of the forecast.

Example 3. Assume that the taxation laws are changed so as to increase total tax revenue without, however, affecting the marginal tax rate. This means that the slope of the tax equation (which is the marginal tax rate) will be constant, while the constant intercept will increase so as to account for the change in the tax structure. The amount by which the tax revenue will increase is usually estimated by some way or another. This amount is added to the constant term of the tax equation. Again this is equivalent to saying that $u \neq 0$ in the period of the forecast, and in fact that it will assume the value of the estimated change of the tax revenue.

It should be clear from the above examples that an econometric model is not a sterile tool but a highly flexible device, if appropriately used. It can then become a useful tool in policy formulation.

The above forecasting procedure should be repeated if the predetermined variables assume different values. We should include these new values into the structural model and repeat all the computations. Obviously this is a very tedious job when one wants to examine the values which the endogenous variables will assume under different sets of values of the exogenous variables. Fortunately the forecasting procedure may be greatly facilitated by using the reduced-form of the model. For an introduction to this forecasting technique see D. B. Suits, *The Theory and Application of Econometric Models,* Athens 1963, Center of Planning and Economic Research.

20.3. TEST OF SIGNIFICANCE OF THE DIFFERENCE BETWEEN A SINGLE PREDICTION AND THE ACTUAL OBSERVATION

This test is frequently used as a basis for the evaluation of the forecasting power of an econometric model. It is a simple t test similar to the one developed in the preceding paragraph, based on the standard error of the forecast.

We said that the statistic

$$t^* = \frac{Y_F - \hat{Y}_F}{\hat{\sigma}_u \sqrt{1 + \frac{1}{n} + \frac{(X_F - \bar{X})^2}{\Sigma(X - \bar{X})^2}}}$$

has the Student's t distribution with $n - 2$ degrees of freedom.

Instead of Y_F, assume that we have an actual observation on the dependent variable, Y_A, *which is not included in the sample* used for the estimation of the function, and we want to test whether the difference between the observed value of Y and the predicted one from the econometric function ($\hat{Y}_F$) is statistically significant. In other words we want to answer the question: Is the difference compatible with the estimated relationship, or does this difference indicate a significant change in the estimated relationship between Y and X? Formally we want to test the null hypothesis

$$H_0: Y_F = Y_A$$

against the alternative hypothesis $H_1: Y_F \neq Y_A$.

For this purpose we use the sample data as well as the value actually assumed by the explanatory variable, and we compute the observed t^* statistic

$$t^* = \frac{Y_A - \hat{Y}_F}{\hat{\sigma}_u \sqrt{1 + \frac{1}{n} + \frac{(X_F - \bar{X})^2}{\Sigma(X - \bar{X})^2}}}$$

where t^* = observed value of the t statistic
       $\hat{\sigma}_u$ = estimate of the variance of u
       X_F = actual (observed) value of X in the period of forecast
       Y_A = actual (observed) value of Y
       $\hat{Y}_F$ = predicted (forecast) value of Y from the regression.

Subsequently we find the theoretical value of t from the t-Table with $n - 2$ degrees of freedom, that is the value that t would assume if the difference between Y_A and $\hat{Y}_F$ were equal to zero, (with a given probability, for example with 95 per cent probability). We compare the observed t^* with its theoretical value, that is the value of t if the null hypothesis were true, (if there were no difference between Y_A and $\hat{Y}_F$), and decide whether the observed difference $Y_A - \hat{Y}_F$ is significant or not according to the following rule:

If $t^* < t$ we conclude that there is no significant difference between actual and predicted value. The observation is compatible with the estimated relationship. In this case we accept that the predictive power of our model is good.

If $t^* > t$ we conclude that the difference between the actual and predicted value of Y is significant. The observation of Y is not compatible with the relationship which has been estimated.

The difference between the actual and the forecast value of Y may be due to one of the following reasons.

(a) *Abnormal conditions in the period of forecast. u* may assume an exceptionally high value out of the range suggested by its estimated variance. In this case our model is still valid and we do not need to modify or reject it.

(b) *Errors in the value of X_F*. Recall that $\hat{Y}_F$ is a conditional forecast: if X_F contains errors, the forecast value of Y will have errors. Again our model is valid in the sense that the 'poor' prediction is due to errors in X_F and not to wrong specification of the structural relationship.

(c) *Change in the structure of the relationship.* The poor predictive power in this case is due to the fact that the conditions have changed between the sample period and the period of the forecast, so that the estimated relationship between Y and X does not hold any more. In this case the model although valid for the sample period, cannot be used for forecasting, unless modified (restated) and recomputed.

As an illustration of the above test procedure consider the following consumption function of the United States which was estimated for the 1954–65 period. (See E. Kane, *Economic Statistics and Econometrics*, p. 226.)

$$\hat{Y}_t = -3 \cdot 0 + 0 \cdot 928 X_t$$
$$(3 \cdot 5) \ (0 \cdot 01)$$

The disposable income in 1968 was 721 billions of dollars. Using this value we obtain the following estimate of the consumption expenditure for this year

$$\hat{Y}_{F,\ 1968} = -3 \cdot 0 + (0 \cdot 928)(721) \approx 666$$

The actual consumption expenditure in 1968 was 539 billions of dollars. Is the ifference $Y_A - \hat{Y}_F$ significant? Is the predictive power of the 1954–65 function good? Or does the difference suggest a change of the structural relationship between the period 1954–65 and the year 1968? We may answer these questions by performing the above test, using the following data

$$X_A = 721 \qquad Y_A = 539 \qquad \hat{Y}_F = 666$$

$$\hat{\sigma}_u = \sqrt{\frac{\Sigma e^2}{n-2}} = 4 \cdot 48 \qquad \overline{X} = 350 \qquad \Sigma(X - \overline{X})^2 = 3875 \cdot 8$$

The standard error of the forecast $(\hat{Y}_F = 666)$ is

$$\hat{\sigma}_u\left(\sqrt{1 + \frac{1}{n} + \frac{(X_A - \bar{X})^2}{\Sigma(X - \bar{X})^2}}\right) = 4\cdot48\left(\sqrt{1 + \frac{1}{12} + \frac{137{,}641}{3{,}876}}\right) \approx 27$$

Therefore

$$t^* = \frac{Y_A - \hat{Y}_F}{s_{(\hat{Y}_F)}} = \frac{539 - 666}{27} = -4\cdot7$$

The theoretical value of t with $12 - 2 = 10$ degrees of freedom (at the 95 per cent level of significance) is $-2\cdot23$.

Since $t^* < t$ we conclude that the difference between $\hat{Y}_F$ and Y_t is significant. The forecasting power of the consumption function model is poor.

If the structural coefficients must be re-computed, we may either keep the same specification and increase only the sample to include more recent observations, or we may change the specification of the model, or both. Respecification of the function may take various forms, depending on the suspected or known cause of the change in structure. Some examples may illustrate the variety of possible restatements of the original relationship.

(a) One may introduce new observable explanatory variables directly in the function.

(b) One may use more equations and turn his simple model into a multi-equation model.

(c) Changes in the parameters may be measured indirectly by introducing appropriate dummy variables in the original function (see Chapter 12).

(d) If it is known that the coefficients change over time, one may include as a separate explanatory variable 'tX' (where t stands for 'time') in the function, apart from the simple variable X (see Chapter 12).

(e) If the distribution of income is changing, one may split the aggregate income variable into two or more parts, for example Y_1 for wage-income and Y_2 for non-wage income (see Chapter 17).

20.4. EVALUATION OF THE FORECASTING PERFORMANCE OF AN ESTIMATED MODEL

20.4.1. PREDICTION–REALISATION DIAGRAMS

Suppose we have several forecasts from an econometric model and the corresponding realised values of an endogenous variable over several periods. The forecasting performance of the econometric model is judged on the basis of the differences between predictions and realisations. The smaller the differences between predictions (P_i) and actual values (A_i) of the dependent variable, the better the forecasting performance of the model.

We may examine the forecasting performance of a model by using a *prediction–realisation diagram* (figure 20.2). This is a diagram on which we plot the points determined by the predictions and realisations on a certain variable. Along the vertical axis we measure the actual (observed) *changes* in

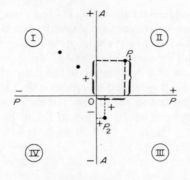

Figure 20.2

the values and along the horizontal axis we plot the predicted changes in values of the variable. Points lying in quadrants II and IV show that the model predicts the direction of the change in the dependent variable correctly. For example point P_1 implies that the model predicted a positive change in the dependent variable and the realised change was actually positive. On the other hand points falling in quadrants I and III show that the forecast was opposite to realisation; the model at point P_2 predicts a positive change (an increase in the value of the variable) while the realised change was negative (the value of the variable decreased). Such points are called *turning point errors*. Points falling in quadrants I and III show a very poor predictive performance of the model. Points falling in quadrants II and IV show that the model predicts correctly the direction of the change. We can say more about the accuracy of the predictions by introducing a 45° line with a positive slope through the origin (figure 20.3). This is called the *line of perfect forecast*: any point on this line shows equality (zero difference) between prediction and

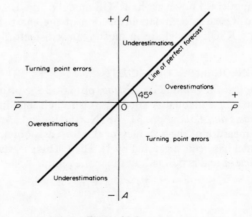

Figure 20.3

actual value. In quadrant II points above the 45° line show that the model underestimated the value of the dependent variable, while points below the 45° line
show that the model overestimated the value of the endogenous variables. On
the contrary in quadrant IV points above the 45° line show overestimation while
points below the line show underestimation of the value of the dependent
variable. The closer the points (defined by predicted and actual values) to the
45° line the better the forecasting performance of the model.

To illustrate the above procedure we plot in figure 20.4 the actual GNP

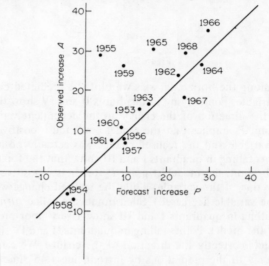

Figure 20.4

of the United States together with its forecast values by the econometric model
of the Research Seminar in Quantitative Economics of the University of
Michigan.[1] This model is known as the RSQE model of the US economy, from
the initials of the Research Seminar. Inspection of the chart shows that the
forecasts from the RSQE model are in most years satisfactorily accurate.

20.4.2. THEIL'S INEQUALITY COEFFICIENT

(H. Theil, *Applied Economic Forecasting*, pp. 26–36, North-Holland 1966.
An earlier version of the inequality coefficient is to be found in H. Theil's,
Economic Forecasts and Policy, pp. 31–48, North-Holland 1962.)

A systematic measure of the accuracy of the forecasts obtained from an
econometric model has been suggested by H. Theil. This measure is called the
inequality coefficient and is defined by the expression

$$U^2 = \frac{\Sigma (P_i - A_i)^2/n}{\Sigma A_i^2/n}$$

[1] Source: D. B. Suits, *Principles of Economics*, 1970, p. 206.

or

$$U = + \sqrt{\frac{\Sigma(P_i - A_i)^2/n}{\Sigma A_i^2/n}}$$

where P_i = predicted (forecast) *change* in the dependent variable
        A_i = actual (realised) *change* in the dependent variable.

The values that the inequality coefficient assumes lie between 0 and ∞

$$0 \leqslant U \leqslant \infty$$

The smaller the value of the inequality coefficient the better is the forecasting performance of the model.

If $P_i = A_i$, then $U = 0$, and we say that with our model we attain perfect forecasts.

If $P_i = 0$, then $U = 1$, and the model forecasts no better than a 'naïve' zero-change prediction.

If $U > 1$ the predictive power of the model is worse than the zero-change prediction. Thus if $U > 1$ it is preferable to accept the zero-change extrapolation that $Y_{t+1} = Y_t$; that is, to assume that there will be no change in the value of the dependent variable between the periods t and $t + 1$.

The numerator of the inequality coefficient is the root mean square prediction error (RMS prediction error) and is the important term in this measure. The denominator is simply a way for achieving the independence of U from the units of measurement of the variables.

Further insight into the sources of the forecast error may be obtained by the following decomposition of the inequality coefficient.

The numerator can be decomposed into three terms each showing a different source of forecast-error:[1]

$$\frac{1}{n}\Sigma(P_i - A_i)^2 = (\bar{P} - \bar{A})^2 + (S_P - S_A)^2 + 2(1 - r_{PA})S_P S_A$$

where $\bar{P}$ and $\bar{A}$ are the means of predictions and actual values

$$\bar{P} = \frac{1}{n}\Sigma P_i \qquad \bar{A} = \frac{1}{n}\Sigma A_i$$

S_P and S_A are the standard deviations of predictions and realisations

$$S_P^2 = \frac{1}{n}\Sigma(P_i - \bar{P})^2 \qquad S_A^2 = \frac{1}{n}\Sigma(A_i - \bar{A})^2$$

and r_{PA} is the correlation coefficient of predicted and realised changes

$$r_{PA} = \frac{\Sigma(P_i - P)(A_i - A)}{n S_P \cdot S_A}$$

---

[1] The rationale of this decomposition is the same as the decomposition of the total variation of any variable, which is the basis of the Analysis of Variance method, developed in Chapter 8.

The three components which form the sources of the forecast error are called *partial inequality coefficients.* The first component shows that the cause of the discrepancy between predictions and realisations is the difference between their means (or central tendencies); it is referred to as the *bias component* of the inequality coefficient. The second component shows that another cause of the discrepancy between P_i and A_i is the difference between their variance; it is referred to as the *variance component* of the inequality coefficient. The third component shows that still another cause of the discrepancy between P_i and A_i is their imperfect covariance; it is called the *covariance component* of the inequality coefficient.

The third source of forecast error is the most dangerous one, in the sense that not much can be done about it: we can never hope that forecasters will be able to produce predictions which would be perfectly correlated with the actual values of the variable. It is natural that $r_{PA} \neq 1$ and hence the 'covariance component' of the prediction error cannot be expected to be zero. The other two sources of error can be reduced in general in the course of time, by the incorporation of additional information in the forecasting process.

A useful way to present the various sources of the forecast error is to divide each component by the total forecast-variation $\Sigma(P_i - A_i)^2/n$. In this way we express each component as a proportion of the total prediction-error. This procedure leads to the following *inequality proportions*

$$\text{bias proportion} \quad U_M = \frac{(\bar{P} - \bar{A})^2}{\Sigma(P_i - A_i)^2/n}$$

$$\text{variance proportion} \quad U_S = \frac{(S_P - S_A)^2}{\Sigma(P_i - A_i)^2/n}$$

$$\text{covariance proportion} \quad U_C = \frac{2(1 - r_{PA})S_P S_A}{\Sigma(P_i - A_i)^2/n}$$

Clearly

$$U_M + U_S + U_C = 1$$

An example. The table below shows the forecast changes P_i from a simple linear regression equation of the imports of a country, and the realised changes of imports (A_i). Is the forecasting performance of our regression model 'good'? To answer this question we compute Theil's inequality coefficient. The relevant terms are included in table 20.2.

$$U^2 = \frac{\Sigma(P_i - A_i)^2}{\Sigma A_i^2} = \frac{101}{256} \approx 0.4$$

and

$$U = \sqrt{0.4} = 0.666$$

Given that the value of the inequality coefficient is low, $(U < 1)$ we conclude that the forecasting performance of the estimated import function (from which the predictions were derived) is fairly good. Decomposition of the forecast error yields the following inequality proportions (given $\bar{P} = 1 \cdot 3$ $\bar{A} = 1 \cdot 4$ $S_A^2 = 23 \cdot 64$ $S_P^2 = 10 \cdot 61$ $S_A = 4 \cdot 86$ $S_P = 3 \cdot 26$ $r_{PA} = 0 \cdot 813$)

Table 20.2. Realised and predicted levels of imports

Forecast period	Predicted change in imports P_i	Actual changes in imports A_i	A_i^2	$(P_i - A_i)^2$	$(A_i - \bar{A})^2$	$(P_i - \bar{P})^2$
1960	+5	+10	100	25	73·96	13·69
1961	+2	+2	4	0	0·36	0·49
1962	−4	−7	49	9	70·56	28·09
1963	0	+4	16	16	6·76	1·69
1964	+1	−3	9	16	19·36	0·09
1965	+4	+6	36	4	21·16	7·29
1966	+7	+4	16	9	6·76	32·49
1967	−2	−4	16	4	29·16	10·89
1968	−2	−1	1	1	5·76	10·89
1969	+2	+3	9	1	2·56	0·49
	$\Sigma P_i = 13$	$\Sigma A_i = 14$	$\Sigma A_i^2 = 256$	$\Sigma(P_i - A_i)^2$ $= 85$	$\Sigma(A_i - \bar{A})^2$ $= 236 \cdot 4$	$\Sigma(P_i - \bar{P})^2$ $= 106 \cdot 1$

$$U_M = \frac{(P - A)^2}{\Sigma(P_i - A_i)^2/n} = \frac{(1 \cdot 3 - 1 \cdot 4)^2}{8 \cdot 5} = 0 \cdot 001$$

$$U_S = \frac{(S_P - S_A)^2}{\Sigma(P_i - A_i)^2/n} = \frac{(3 \cdot 26 - 4 \cdot 86)^2}{8 \cdot 5} = 0 \cdot 301$$

$$U_C = \frac{2(1 - r_{PA})S_A S_P}{\Sigma(P_i - A_i)^2/n} = \frac{2(1 - 0 \cdot 813)(15 \cdot 84)}{8 \cdot 5} = 0 \cdot 708$$

Thus

$$\frac{1}{n}\Sigma(P - A)^2 = (\bar{P} - \bar{A})^2 + (S_P - S_A)^2 + 2(1 - r_{PA})S_P S_A$$

or

$$8 \cdot 5 = 0 \cdot 01 + 2 \cdot 56 + 5 \cdot 92$$

This shows that the error in the forecast is mainly due to the high correlation between P_i and A_i, that is to the source of error about which nothing can be done in order to improve the forecasting performance of the model. For a further discussion of the inequality coefficient the reader is referred to H. Theil's *Applied Economic Forecasting*, North-Holland, 1966.

20.4.3. THE JANUS QUOTIENT

Another measure of the accuracy of the forecasts is the *Janus quotient*[1] defined by the expression

$$J^2 = \frac{\sum\limits_{i=n+1}^{n+m} (P_i - A_i)^2 / m}{\sum\limits_{i=1}^{n} (A_i - P_i)^2 / n}$$

The numerator is the sum of differences between predictions for *future periods outside the sample* which has been used for the estimation of the model, and realisations. The denominator contains the sum of differences of 'predictions' and realisations over the period of the sample.

Conceptually, the Janus quotient refers to the time period $t = n$, that lies.at the end of the sample period and the beginning of the future prediction period. The Janus quotient takes into account both the prediction performance of the model in future periods as well as the 'prediction' performance in the past (sample) periods. Schematically we may present the periods involved in the estimation of the Janus Quotient as follows.

$$i = 1, 2, \ldots, n \qquad i = (n + 1), (n + 2), \ldots, (n + m)$$

```
<------------------------->|<--------------------------------------->
  Sample period  J              Future prediction period
```

The definition of the Janus Quotient shows that J is non-negative. Its values may vary between zero and ∞

$$0 \leqslant J \leqslant \infty$$

Furthermore, it should be clear that if the structure of the model remains in the future the same as in the period of the sample, the Janus Quotient will be approximately equal to unity

$$J \approx 1$$

The higher the value of J the poorer the forecasting performance of the model. Furthermore, values of J higher than unity are suggestive, under certain conditions, of changes in the structure of the model.

EXERCISES

1 Consider the following consumption function estimated from 20 observations.

$$\hat{C}_t = 81 + 0 \cdot 75\ Y$$
$$\quad\quad\quad (0 \cdot 05) \quad\quad\quad\quad R^2 = 0 \cdot 950$$
$$\bar{Y} = 750 \quad\quad \Sigma(Y - \bar{Y})^2 = 7,560 \quad\quad \hat{\sigma}_u^2 = 2 \cdot 3$$

[1] See H. Wold (editor), *Econometric Model Building*, North-Holland, 1964, article by A. Gadd and H. Wold, pp. 229–35.

where Y = disposable income.

Find the value of C in 1980, given that Y_{1980} = 980 billions of dollars. Construct a 95 per cent confidence interval for your forecast.

2. The following equation is the cost function of a firm, estimated on the basis of yearly observations over the 1950–64 period.

$$Y = 2434.6 + 85.70X - 0.03X^2 + 0.00004X^3$$

where Y = total costs (in £), X = output (in arbitrary units).

The output of the firm in 1970 was 1,950 and its cost of production amounted to £295,650.

Test the significance of the difference $Y_F - Y_A$ (at the 95 per cent level).

3. The following table shows the forecasts of the exports (in £ m) of a certain country obtained from two different models and the actual exports. Which model do you think yields better forecasts? (Note that the forecasts refer to the years included in the sample used for the estimation of the export models.)

Year	Actual exports Y_A	Forecast exports from model I Y_{F1}	Forecast exports from model II Y_{F2}
1950	20	30	28
1951	30	25	26
1952	32	28	36
1953	25	28	25
1954	29	25	21
1955	26	30	39
1956	32	30	34
1957	36	39	30
1958	32	34	40
1959	31	30	38

4. Assume that the estimated models in the previous example were used for forecasting the value of exports for the period 1965–70 (a period outside the sample). The forecasts and realised exports are as follows.

Year	Y_A	Y_{F1}	Y_{F2}
1965	38	38	37
1966	42	40	36
1967	46	52	48
1968	50	54	51
1969	52	48	50
1970	54	52	54

Given the above results would you revise your conclusions derived from Exercise 3 concerning the forecasting performance of the two export models?

21. Choice of Econometric Technique Monte Carlo Studies

21.1. GENERAL NOTES

The problem of choice of technique arises from the fact that any relationship of economic theory is almost certain to belong to a system of simultaneous equations, whose parameters may be estimated by various econometric techniques.

We saw that the coefficients of a structural system of simultaneous equations may be obtained either *by single-equation techniques,* that is methods which are applied to one equation of the system at a time, or by *complete systems techniques,* in other words methods which involve the solution of all the equations simultaneously and the estimation of the parameters of all the coefficients of the system at the same time.

The choice of estimation technique depends on many factors such as the purpose for which we embark on the estimation of the model, the identification condition of the equations of our model, the presence of (other) endogenous variables among the set of explanatory variables in any particular equation, the available information concerning the other equations of the system, the importance which the researcher attributes to the various statistical properties of the parameter estimates, the availability of data, the computational complexity of the technique. The choice of estimation method depends also on whether we are interested in the values of the structural parameters or of the reduced form coefficients. We will discuss briefly some of these factors which affect our choice of estimation technique.

21.1.1. IDENTIFICATION CONDITION OF THE MODEL

We saw in Chapter 15 that if the system of simultaneous equations is underidentified, all its structural coefficients cannot be estimated by any econometric method. However, an underidentified system may contain some identified equations, which can be estimated by some econometric technique(s).

If all the equations of a system are exactly identified the whole system is exactly identified and all its coefficients can be estimated uniquely by any of the above mentioned econometric techniques. However, the choice is facilitated by the fact that OLS is then an inferior method (since it yields biased and inconsistent estimates) while the other methods yield identical estimates. Thus the choice of technique for exactly identified models is based on the criterion of

498

simplicity, which shows ILS to be preferred to any of the other techniques. It is only in the case of an equation which contains purely exogenous explanatory variables that OLS is preferred to ILS on the criterion of simplicity, since both methods yield otherwise identical estimates under these circumstances.

If some (or all) the equations of a system are overidentified the whole system is overidentified. Again we are faced with the problem of choice of technique, since overidentified systems may be estimated with any of the techniques examined in this book, with the exception of ILS.

Are the systems of the actual economic world likely to be underidentified, exactly identified or overidentified? An extreme view on this matter is taken by Liu. (See T. C. Liu, 'Underidentification, Structural Estimation and Forecasting', *Econometrica,* vol. **28**, 1960, pp. 855–65.) He argues that most econometric models are incorrectly specified with very few explanatory variables appearing in each equation. The resulting overidentification is fictitious, because there are too many variables missing from each equation. In the actual economic world the relationships include many more variables. Thus Liu suggests that most economic relationships are underidentified and hence it is pointless to attempt the estimation of individual coefficients, because they would not be reliable. Under these circumstances the only meaningful measurement would be the estimation of the reduced-form models with a large number of predetermined variables. The reduced-form coefficients may be obtained by OLS applied to the reduced-form equations and be used for forecasting, despite the fact that the individual structural parameters are not identified.

The opposite view is expressed by the proponents of the recursive systems, for example by Wold and Juréen. (H. Wold and L. Juréen, *Demand Analysis,* New York, John Wiley, 1953.) They suggest that economic theory usually defines the most important explanatory variables of a relationship. There may be many other minor determinants of a dependent variable, but they may well be excluded from the function, simply because each one of them has a negligible effect. Their influence as a whole may well be reflected by the random variable. Under these circumstances economic relationships are overidentified, but they may be adequately presented by recursive models. In this case each equation may be estimated by OLS without any of its defects, provided that one proceeds methodically with the estimation, that is one starts with the equation which includes only exogenous variables and then substitutes gradually in the next equations.

Some econometricians take an intermediate position by accepting that any overidentified system can be rendered exactly identified by adding *significant* or removing *insignificant* variables in the various equations.

It is obvious from the above discussion that identification cannot be discussed *in abstracto.* One has to establish the identification condition of one's model using both theoretical knowledge, judgement and intuition.

It should be stressed once more that the problem of choice of technique becomes important for overidentified systems. The subsequent discussion on the choice of estimation method relates to such systems.

21.1.2. THE PURPOSE OF THE MODEL

The choice of technique depends to a considerable extent on the purpose for which the model is being estimated. We may distinguish three purposes to which a model may be used. (See Chapter 1.)

Firstly. Analysis, i.e. testing economic theory.

In this case the research worker is interested in obtaining as accurate as possible estimates of the individual *structural coefficients* of the model, because these coefficients are the elasticities and other parameters of economic theory.

Secondly. Policy making: evaluation of alternative policy measures.

In this case the research worker is interested in obtaining as accurate as possible estimates of the *reduced-form coefficients* of a model, given that these coefficients are the basis of the estimation of 'policy multipliers' (or impact multipliers). (See D. B. Suits, *The Theory and Application of Econometric Models*, 1963. Also A. S. Goldberger, *Impact Multipliers of the U.S.A. Econometric Model*, 1964.)

Thirdly. Forecasting.

The purpose of the model in this case is the prediction of the magnitude of the endogenous variables, given the values of the predetermined variables, that is, prediction of the values of the endogenous variables on the condition that the predetermined variables will take the assumed values. Conditional prediction is more efficiently conducted by using the reduced form of the model. However, the accuracy of the individual coefficients is of secondary importance. What we want is efficient predictions.

If the purpose of the model is to obtain as accurate as possible values of the individual structural or reduced-form coefficients, the choice of technique has conventionally been based on the statistical properties possessed by the estimates of the various methods. Such desirable statistical properties are: (i) *Consistency* and *efficiency* for large sample estimates. (ii) *Unbiasedness* and *minimum variance* for small sample estimates. In the case of small samples writers have also used a combination of the bias and the variance (or the standard error) of the estimates as criteria for their 'goodness'. Such criteria are *the mean square error* (MSE) and the *proportion of incorrect inferences* that might be made about the importance of some parameter obtained from using a particular technique (see below).

If the purpose of the model is conditional prediction, the choice of technique has been based on the 'predictive performance' of the estimates obtained from the various techniques. When attempting the ranking of the techniques the most common measure of the forecasting performance has been the *mean square error* (MSE) of the forecast or its square root (RMSE)

$$\text{MSE} = \frac{\Sigma(F_i - A_i)^2}{n} \text{ and RMSE} = \sqrt{\frac{\Sigma(F_i - A_i)^2}{n}}$$

Optimal properties of the individual estimates of the coefficients are not a necessary prerequisite for the good predictive performance of a model.

The problem of choice of technique is by no means simple. It has been widely discussed in econometric literature. As yet there is no conclusive evidence as to the ranking of the various econometric techniques. In this chapter we shall present a summary of the main findings of research aiming at the ranking of the various techniques. The ranking of the various econometric methods will be examined in the following sequence.

Firstly. Ranking of econometric techniques according to the properties of the estimates of the *structural parameters*.

Secondly. Ranking of econometric techniques according to the properties of the estimates of the *reduced form* parameters.

21.2. RANKING OF ECONOMETRIC TECHNIQUES ACCORDING TO THE PROPERTIES OF THE ESTIMATES OF STRUCTURAL PARAMETERS

The ranking of the econometric techniques when the purpose of the estimation is to obtain as accurate as possible estimates of the structural parameters depends on the size of the sample and on the correctness of the specification of the model both as to variables included in it and the behaviour of the random variable u. Thus we have a four-fold classification of the various econometric techniques.
1. Ranking according to asymptotic properties:
   (a) Correct specification of model.
   (b) Specification error in the model.
2. Ranking according to small sample properties:
   (a) Correct specification of model.
   (b) Specification error in the model.

21.2.1. RANKING ON THE BASIS OF 'ASYMPTOTIC' PROPERTIES OF THE ESTIMATES OF THE STRUCTURAL PARAMETERS

As criteria for the ranking of the techniques econometricians have traditionally used the asymptotic properties of the coefficient estimates, that is the property of consistency and the property of asymptotic efficiency. These properties have been examined in Chapter 6. We may summarise them as follows.

An estimator $\hat{b}$ is a *consistent* estimator of the true parameter b, if it is asymptotically unbiased and its distribution collapses on the true parameter as the sample size gets sufficiently large. Symbolically, $\hat{b}$ is a consistent estimator of b if

(a) $\lim_{n \to \infty} E(\hat{b}_{(n)}) = b$

and

(b) $\lim_{n \to \infty} [\text{var}(\hat{b}_{(n)})] = 0$

An estimator is *asymptotically efficient* if it is consistent and has a smaller asymptotic variance than *any other consistent estimator* from any other method. Symbolically, $\hat{b}$ is an asymptotically efficient estimator of b if

(a) $\lim_{n \to \infty} E(\hat{b}_{(n)}) = 0$, and $\lim_{n \to \infty} [\text{var}(\hat{b}_n)] = 0$ (consistent)

(b) $[\text{Asym var}(\hat{b})] < [\text{Asym var}(b^*)]$

(where b^* is *any other consistent estimator* of b obtained from another method for any given large sample size).

There is another factor which will be useful in the ranking of the various techniques, namely the general rule that estimators which are obtained from methods using more information are more efficient. In general, it is intuitively clear that the more information we use in estimating a structural parameter, the more efficient the estimate will be, that is the closer we come to the true parameter.

Using the first criterion of consistency, we do not make any substantial progress in our problem of ordering of the various techniques. Because, with the exception of the OLS whose estimates are inconsistent, all other methods examined in this book yield consistent estimates. Thus on the first criterion of consistency we can say that OLS is inferior to the other techniques, but we cannot say anything about which of these other techniques is better.

Using the criterion of asymptotic efficiency, however, we can order the various methods as follows, starting from the least efficient methods and proceeding with methods yielding more efficient estimates.

(a) OLS is clearly inefficient since its estimates are inconsistent.

(b) The method of instrumental variables (IV) uses some of the information of the other equations of the system, that is, it uses some of the predetermined variables included in the other equations of the system.

(c) Two-stage least squares (2SLS) and the limited information maximum likelihood (LIML) methods use the same amount of information: they use all the predetermined variables of the model, and hence they have the same degree of efficiency. Obviously they are more efficient than the instrumental variables method.

(d) Three-stage least squares (3SLS) and the full information maximum likelihood (FIML) methods use more information than any of the previous methods, because apart from all the variables of the system they also use information concerning the mathematical form of the equations (that is, they take into account the structure of all the equations of the system) as well as the contemporaneous dependence of the disturbance variables of the various equations. These two methods have, in general, the same efficiency (asymptotically). However, there is one case in which FIML is more efficient than 3SLS. This rather rare case arises when, before starting the estimation, the researcher has information on the variances and covariances of the random variables of the system. Such information can be exploited more fully by FIML and hence in this event this method is more efficient than 3SLS. However, both these methods are more efficient than the other consistent techniques.

It should be noted that the above ranking of the various econometric methods holds only if the assumptions on which each method is based are satisfied. All methods assume that the specification of the model as to variables included, the mathematical form of the equations, and the distribution properties of the u, is correct (no specification error), that there are no errors of measurement in the variables and that there is no serious multicollinearity in the model. If all these assumptions are satisfied, FIML and 3SLS seem the best methods, since they are the most efficient of all the others. However, these methods are generally more sensitive than the others to specification errors, because an error of specification anywhere in the system affects all the parameter estimates. Given therefore our uncertainty about the correctness of the specification of our model, as well as the errors in variables and the extremely complicated computations of these methods and in particular of FIML, it seems that these methods are the least attractive for econometric research.

Similar considerations about specification errors and the other sources of error hold for the other estimation techniques. In other words the properties of the estimates will not hold if the specification of the model is wrong, or the other sources of error are present. Thus with specification error present the ranking of the various techniques on the basis of their efficiency changes, and it has not as yet been established in an unambiguous way what is the most efficient method when specification error is taken into account. Much more research is required before any definite conclusion can be reached. (See J. Johnston, *Econometric Methods,* 2nd ed., chapter 13.)

21.2.2. RANKING ON THE BASIS OF THE SMALL-SAMPLE PROPERTIES OF THE ESTIMATES OF THE STRUCTURAL PARAMETERS

The theoretical ranking of the various econometric techniques on the basis of the asymptotic properties is important if the sample size is (sufficiently) large. Given that in practice the researcher works usually with small samples, the asymptotic properties of the estimates are of little assistance in his choice of technique. What is important is the ranking of the econometric methods on the merits they have when applied to small samples. Traditionally the ranking has been based on some 'small-sample properties' which are considered as 'desirable' or 'optimal' for the estimates to possess. These properties are (1) unbiasedness, (2) minimum variance, (3) minimum mean square error of the estimators and (4) the proportion of wrong inferences about the significance of the parameters by using a particular econometric method. These criteria have been explained in Chapter 6. We may review them as follows.

Unbiased estimator

An estimator $\hat{b}$ (obtained from a small sample) is an unbiased estimator of the true parameter b if its expected value is equal to the true parameter, that is, if $E(\hat{b}) = b$. Obviously the bias is measured by the difference

$$[E(\hat{b}) - b] = \text{bias}$$

An unbiased estimator is one whose bias is zero, that is one that 'on the average' gives the true value of the parameter.

Minimum variance estimator (or *best estimator*)

An estimator $\hat{b}$ is a minimum variance estimator of the true parameter b if its variance is smaller than *any other* (not necessarily unbiased) estimator b^* obtained from another method, that is if

$$E\{\hat{b} - E(\hat{b})\}^2 \leqslant E\{b^* - E(b^*)\}^2$$

Note that the variance of an estimator is the expected value of the square of the difference of $\hat{b}$ from its own expected value. It is only if $\hat{b}$ is unbiased that $E(\hat{b}) = b$. If $\hat{b}$ is any estimator, not necessarily unbiased, its mean may differ from the true b.

Best unbiased estimator (or *efficient* estimator)

An estimator $\hat{b}$ is a best unbiased estimator if it is unbiased and its variance is smaller than the variance of any *other unbiased estimator* $\tilde{b}$, that is an estimator is BU if

(a) $E(\hat{b}) = b$

and   (b) $\operatorname{var}(\hat{b}) = E[\hat{b} - E(\hat{b})]^2 = E(\hat{b} - b)^2 \leqslant E(\tilde{b} - b)^2$

(Note that both $\hat{b}$ and $\tilde{b}$ are unbiased estimators of b.)

This property is not used for the ranking of the various techniques, because when they are applied to simultaneous (overidentified) systems all methods yield biased estimators (for small samples).

Minimum mean square error

An estimator $\hat{b}$ is a minimum mean square error estimator of the true parameter b if it has a smaller error about the true b than any other estimator b^* (not necessarily possessing any other property), that is if

$$E\{\hat{b} - b\}^2 \leqslant E\{b^* - b\}^2$$

The mean square error (MSE) of an estimator is the expected value of the squared differences of the estimator about the true value b. It has been established in Chapter 6 that the MSE is equal to the sum of the variance of the estimate about its own expected value and the square of the bias

$$\begin{aligned}
\text{MSE} &= E[(\hat{b} - b)^2] \\
&= E[\hat{b} - E(\hat{b})]^2 + [E(\hat{b}) - b]^2 \\
&= \text{variance } \hat{b} + \text{square of bias.}
\end{aligned}$$

Sometimes the square root of the MSE is used as a criterion (RMSE).

From the definition of the MSE it is clear that a biased estimate obtained from some econometric method may have a smaller MSE than an unbiased one obtained from another method — if the former has a smaller variance than the latter so as to compensate for its bias. It is thus evident that the ranking of the various methods will not be the same (in general) but will differ depending upon which of the above criteria one selects for the ordering.

The justification of the use of the MSE as a criterion for judging the adequacy of the various econometric methods is that it is desirable for the estimate to be close to the true value of the coefficient. Thus large deviations of the estimate from the true value (in either direction, that is a higher or lower estimate than the true value) are not desirable. The higher the MSE of an estimate the 'worse' it is considered to be.

The proportion of incorrect inferences that might be made by applying a particular estimation technique

Another criterion which has been recently used for the ranking of various econometric methods is the usefulness (reliability) of the standard errors or the t ratios for judging the statistical significance of the estimates and making inferences about the true values of the structural parameters.

Recall that the traditional tests of significance of the estimates are the standard errors of the estimates ($s_{\hat{b}}$) and the related t ratios

$$t^* = \frac{\hat{b} - b}{s_{\hat{b}}}$$

where b is the hypothesised value of the true parameter. In Chapter 5 we saw that if there are more than 8 degrees of freedom in a sample the t test may be performed approximately by comparing the empirical t^* value with the 'critical value' 2, that is

(a) if $t^* > 2$ (or equivalently if $s_{\hat{b}} < \frac{1}{2}\hat{b}$) we accept the estimate $\hat{b}$ as statistically significant at the 5 per cent level;

(b) if $t^* < 2$ we reject the estimate $\hat{b}$ as statistically insignificant.

Based on this rough application of the t test some researchers have used the percentage of the t ratios with absolute values greater than two, as a criterion for ranking the econometric methods. Others have used more sophisticated procedures for deciding whether the t ratios are a reliable basis for drawing inferences about the true structural coefficients.

The above criterion is a combination of the variance criterion (since $s_{\hat{b}}^2$ = variance of $\hat{b}$) and of the size of the coefficient $\hat{b}$.

Which of the above criteria is the most important? Do we prefer an estimate if it has the smallest bias, the minimum variance, or if it has the smallest MSE? There is no clearcut answer to such questions. There is no law that says that bias or efficiency should be ranked in some unique order. Much depends on the nature of the relationship being studied and the purpose it is going to serve. In some cases the minimum variance may be more desirable than a small bias, while in other cases the least bias may be the most desirable property to be possessed by our estimators. It is obvious that the importance of each criterion is to a certain extent a matter of subjective decision of the econometrician.

The ranking of the various techniques on the basis of their small sample properties differs according to whether there is specification error in the model or not.

Up to this day the small sample properties of the various econometric techniques have been studied from simulated data in what are known as *Monte Carlo Studies*, and not with direct application of the techniques to actual observations. This approach is due to the fact that actual observations on economic variables usually involve multicollinearity, autocorrelation, errors of measurement and most other econometric 'diseases' simultaneously; moreover, when constructing a model, the econometrician is almost certain to make (purposefully for simplicity, or involuntarily from ignorance) some specification error. With specification error superimposed on some or all the other econometric problems simultaneously it is impossible to study and establish the theoretical properties of the various techniques, which by assumption exclude all the above problems. On the other hand with simulation experiments the econometrician can conduct research on the properties of the estimators, because in some sense he can control his experimental data. This approach is the basis of the Monte Carlo Studies to which we now turn.

The design of the Monte Carlo Studies may be outlined as follows.

1. The researcher specifies a model and ascribes specific numerical values to its parameters. For example Basmann postulated the following model in his Monte Carlo experiments

$$-y_1 - 2y_2 + 1 \cdot 5y_3 + 3x_1 \qquad\qquad\qquad\qquad - 0 \cdot 6x_5 + 10 = u_1$$
$$1 \cdot 5y_1 - y_2 \qquad\quad + 0 \cdot 5x_1 + 1 \cdot 5x_2 + 2x_3 - 2 \cdot 5x_4 \qquad + 12 = u_2$$
$$0 \cdot 1y_1 - 4y_2 - y_3 \quad + 1 \cdot 6x_1 - 3 \cdot 5x_2 \qquad\quad + 1 \cdot 2x_4 + 0 \cdot 4x_5 - 5 \; = u_3$$

(See R. L. Basmann, *An Experimental Investigation of Some Small Sample Properties of Generalized Classical Linear Estimators of Structural Equations; Some Preliminary Results,* General Electric Company, Hanford Laboratories, Richland, Washington, 1958, mimeographed.)

The numerical values assigned to the coefficients of the model are defined to be the true structural coefficients.

2. The researcher next specifies the distribution of the u's. In Basmann's example he assumed the u's to be normally distributed with zero means and given covariances.

3. The researcher selects arbitrary values for the exogenous variables (X's).

4. Finally the researcher uses the distributions of the u's and with random drawings from these distributions he obtains values for the u's of each equation.

5. Given the true parameters, the selected values of the explanatory variables and the chosen values of the random term the researcher solves the equations of the model and obtains values for the endogenous variables (y's). These values are called *generated values of the endogenous variables.* For each randomly drawn value of the u's, a new generated value of the endogenous variable is obtained.

With the above procedure the researcher forms small samples (usually of 20 generated observations of endogenous variables) which, together with the selected X values are used to estimate the structural coefficients by various econometric methods.

Such experiments are repeated many times and thus the researcher obtains a large number of estimates of small samples from which he obtains the coefficients for each econometric method. With these values one can approximate the true distribution of the estimates. The average values, $\bar{\hat{b}}$, of the estimates and their variance, $\{\Sigma(\hat{b} - \bar{\hat{b}})^2\}/n$, are computed for each method.

Furthermore, given that the true parameters are 'known' (because they have been defined in the first stage of the experiment), the bias, variance and the MSE can be computed for the estimates of each method.

The most important studies on the small sample properties are cited at the end of this chapter. A detailed survey of the results would require much space and will not be attempted here. Some of the evidence is controversial (see for example the results of Quandt in 1962 and of Summers about multicollinearity). We will present two summary tables which are by no means a complete summary of all the research in this field, but at least they give some idea of the Monte Carlo findings.

In Table 21.1 we summarise the ranking of the various techniques when there is no specification error in the model, while in table 21.2 we give some results when specification error of some sort is present in the model. Both tables refer to studies concerned with the estimation of *structural parameters*.

Table 21.1. Ranking of techniques on the basis of the small sample properties of the estimates of the structural parameters with correct specification of the model

Ranking on the criterion BIAS $(\hat{b} - b)$	Ranking on the criterion VARIANCE $\dfrac{\Sigma(\hat{b} - \bar{\hat{b}})^2}{n}$	Ranking on the criterion RMSE (Root Mean Square Error)	Proportion of incorrect inferences
1. FIML ≈ LIML	1. OLS	1. FIML	1. 2SLS
2. 2SLS	2. FIML	2. 2SLS	2. LIML
3. OLS	3. 2SLS	3. LIML	3. OLS
	4. LIML	4. OLS	

The main conclusions of the above summary table may be outlined as follows:

1. On the criterion of the RMSE the best method is FIML, followed by 2SLS and LIML when there is no specification error in the model.

2. OLS is the poorest method on the criterion of bias and the RMSE. Note that we use here the 'estimated bias' as our criterion, that is the difference between the mean of the estimates and the true value of the coefficients.

3. OLS ranks highest on the criterion of variance, but this has little merit since the variance is measured around a 'wrong' biased mean.

4. On the criterion of the reliability of the t ratios or the standard errors for judging the statistical significance of the estimates 2SLS ranks first, followed by LIML. In general the standard errors of the consistent estimates have been

Table 21.2. Ranking of econometric techniques on the basis of their small sample properties of the estimates of the structural coefficients when various assumptions of the linear regression model are violated.

Criterion of ranking	Omission of variable (alone)	Multi-collinearity (alone)	Multi-collinearity and omission of variable	Auto-correlation (alone)	Auto-correlation and multi-collinearity	Errors of measurement (alone)	Errors of measurement and multi-collinearity	Errors of measurement and auto-correlation	Errors of measurement and auto-correlation and multi-collinearity
BIAS $(\hat{b} - b)$	2SLS ≈ LIML OLS ≈ FIML	2SLS LIML FIML OLS	2SLS FIML OLS LIML						
VARIANCE $\dfrac{\Sigma(\hat{b} - \bar{b})^2}{n}$	OLS FIML 2SLS ≈ LIML	OLS FIML 2SLS LIML	OLS FIML ≈ 2SLS ≈ LIML						
RMSE	2SLS ≈ LIML ≈ OLS FIML	2SLS ≈ FIML OLS LIML	2SLS OLS FIML LIML						
Percentage of t ratios with values greater than 2				2SLS ≈ LIML ≈ OLS	2SLS OLS LIML	LIML 2SLS OLS	LIML 2SLS OLS	LIML ≈ 2SLS OLS	LIML 2SLS OLS

Note. The ≈ sign denotes that the methods 'linked' with it yield almost identical results.

found reliable for making inferences about the true values of the structural coefficients, while the standard errors and the *t* ratios lose their power in OLS. (See J. G. Cragg, 'On the Relative Small Sample Properties of Several Structural Equation Estimators', *Econometrica*, vol. 35, 1967, pp. 89–110.)

The information of table 21.2 suggests that when there is some specification error or strong multicollinearity in the model 2SLS seems in general to have a better performance as compared with the other methods.

Combining the information of tables 21.1 and 21.2 we may tentatively conclude that ordinary least squares yields estimates with the greatest bias. The most serious disadvantage of OLS is that with this method there is a great danger that the econometrician will draw wrong inferences concerning the significance of the various parameters, that is, there is a greater danger with this method of incorrectly accepting coefficients as significant. This is explained by the low variance of OLS estimates as compared with other methods. Thus OLS seems to be the least appropriate method for the estimation of structural parameters of models of simultaneous equations.

However, when multicollinearity (and errors of measurement) is serious in a model, the other (consistent) methods are badly affected in that both the bias and the variances of the estimates increase, so that the gap in performance between OLS and these methods becomes generally smaller.

Among the consistent estimation methods it seems that 2SLS may be considered as the best, since it is also the cheapest and simplest to apply.

21.3. RANKING OF TECHNIQUES WHEN THE PURPOSE OF THE MODEL IS THE ESTIMATION OF 'REDUCED-FORM' PARAMETERS

We said that in many cases the purpose of the estimation is the computation of the reduced-form coefficients (π's) which are the basis for the computation of policy multipliers. With these multipliers one is able to evaluate the effects of alternative government policies on various key endogenous variables.

We said in Chapter 14 that the reduced-form coefficients may be obtained in two ways. The simplest way is to apply ordinary least squares to a system of equations of the form

$$y_i = f(x_1, x_2, \ldots, x_k)$$

where the x's are all the *exogenous* (predetermined) variables of the model. This method is called least squares with no restrictions (LSNR), because it does not take into account the restrictions imposed on the parameters of the structural equations. The second method of obtaining estimates of the π's is to estimate the structural coefficients (b's and γ's) by any econometric method (for example OLS, 2SLS, LIML) and use these estimates for deriving the reduced-form parameters: we must first obtain estimates of the structural b's and γ's and substitute these values into the system of coefficients' relations to obtain the values of the reduced-form parameters, π's (see Chapter 14). This method takes into account all the restrictions on the structural parameters implied in the specification of the structural equations. Both methods yield consistent estimates of the π's. However, the second method incorporates more *a priori* information (that is, the structural restrictions) and hence will be more efficient, at least asymptotically.

In summary the reduced-form π's may be obtained directly by applying the method of LSNR, or indirectly by using the estimates of the structural coefficients estimated by OLS or any one of the consistent econometric techniques. Thus again the econometrician is faced with the problem of choosing among the alternative techniques.

The ranking of the various methods when applied for the estimation of the reduced-form coefficients (π's) is not the same as in the case of their application for the computation of the structural parameters. The studies in the ranking of the techniques according to the 'goodness' of the reduced-form π's provide less conclusive evidence than in the case of the structural parameters. Their results and conclusions are much more tentative. The main findings of these studies are summarised in table 21.3.

Table 21.3. Ranking of techniques on their RMSE for predictions

No specification error	Multi-collinearity	Serial correlation and multi-collinearity	Errors of measurement and multi-collinearity	Serial correlation multicollinearity and errors of measurement
2SLS	FIML	OLS	2SLS $\approx$	2SLS $\approx$
LIML	LIML	2SLS	LIML	LIML
LSNR	2SLS	LSNR	LSNR	LSNR
OLS	OLS	LIML	OLS	OLS

The following tentative conclusions may be drawn from these results.

Firstly. It seems that in general OLS is inferior to the other methods of estimation of reduced-form parameters.

Secondly. When the variables are not strongly multicollinear FIML and LIML show a better performance than 2SLS. However, when multicollinearity is strong 2SLS performs much better, so that taking also into account the simplicity of its computations, this method may still be preferred to the others when estimating the π's.

Thirdly. When autocorrelation is the only source of specification error, the ranking is reversed, and OLS seems to give better results than the other methods.

Fourthly. With errors of measurement in the variables as the only source of mis-specification LIML yields equally good results with 2SLS. OLS is again ranked last.

Fifthly. The same conclusion holds for the case of simultaneous presence of autocorrelation and errors of measurement in the function: 2SLS and LIML give almost identical results, while the estimates of OLS are badly affected.

21.4. GENERAL CONCLUSIONS

The ranking of the various techniques summarised above is based on various Monte Carlo type studies and not on actual economic data. We stress once more that the various studies are not always directly comparable, due to differences in their assumptions about the specification of the model, and that the evidence they provide is by no means conclusive.

The effect of specification error on the parameter estimates obtained from various econometric techniques has not been as yet fully established, neither for large samples nor for small.

On the existing scant evidence it seems that in general OLS is inferior to the consistent methods, although the gap between them may be smaller when various sources of specification error are taken into account.

Among the consistent methods 2SLS seems the best on the basis of its performance when mis-specification of the equation is present, and on its simplicity of computations.

Various studies involving the application of different econometric techniques to different sets of data have shown that perhaps errors of measurement in the variables is much more important than the difference in techniques. It has been found that the variations in parameter estimates are in general much greater between different sets of data than between different methods of estimation. On this evidence various writers have predicted that the results of econometric research will most probably be improved by an improvement in data collecting and processing techniques rather than by improvements or sophisticated refinements in the econometric methods.

Yet given the level of accuracy of a set of data, some methods are more efficient than others. Much work is being done on the lines of the Monte Carlo studies, and it is expected that their results will give more insight into the problem of choice of econometric techniques. (For a detailed discussion of the Monte Carlo studies see J. Johnston, *Econometric Methods,* 2nd edition, 1972, chapter 13.)

The above rankings have been based mainly on the following sources:
(a) A. L. Nagar, 'A Monte Carlo Study of Alternative Simultaneous Equation Estimators', *Econometrica,* vol. **28**, 1960, pp. 573–90.
(b) R. Summers, 'A Capital Intensive Approach to the Small Sample Properties of Various Simultaneous Equation Estimators', *Econometrica,* vol. **33**, 1965, pp. 1–41.
(c) J. G. Cragg, 'On the Sensitivity of Simultaneous Equation Estimators to the Stochastic Assumptions of the Models', *Journal of the American Statistical Association,* 1966, pp. 136–151.
(d) J. G. Cragg, 'On the Relative Small Sample Properties of Several Structural Equation Estimators', *Econometrica,* vol. **35**, 1967, pp. 89–110.

APPENDIX I

Elements of Statistical Theory

APPENDIX I

Elements of Statistical Theory

APPENDIX I

Elements of Statistical Theory

Econometrics is based on statistical theory. The core of statistical theory is *statistical inference* which may be defined as the procedure of drawing conclusions (inferences) about the basic characteristics of all the possible values of a variable (*population*) from a set of observations recorded from the variable (*sample*).

In this Appendix we review some basic concepts of statistical theory. In section A we introduce the necessary definitions, notation and the basic algebraic rules of summations. In section B we review the basic elements of frequency distributions and probability distributions. In section C we discuss the basic characteristics of a population (parameters of the population) and of a sample (sample statistics). In section D we develop the rules for the algebraic manipulation of terms involving population parameters and sample statistics. In section E we outline the procedure of statistical inference. Finally in section F we state the basic laws of probabilities.

This Appendix is meant as a summary revision of the elements of Statistics required for the understanding of the book. Students who did not take a course on Elementary Statistics are referred to D. Bugg, H. Lund *et al.*, *Statistics in the Social Sciences* (North-Holland, 1968), for a systematic introductory treatment of statistical theory.

SECTION A

SUBSCRIPTS AND SUMMATIONS

A.1. SIMPLE SUMMATIONS

A variable may assume various values, which are denoted by subscripts. For example suppose that we have a sample of 10 individuals with information on their income and on the number of their children. We may use the letters X for the variable 'income' and Y for the variable 'number of children', with a subscript to designate the individual to which the particular value of each variable refers:

$$X_1, X_2, \ldots, X_{10}$$
$$Y_1, Y_2, \ldots, Y_{10}$$

where X_i refers to the income of the ith individual and Y_j refers to the number of children of the jth individual.

In order to simplify formulas which involve a large number of values of variables we use the symbol Σ, which is the capital Greek letter sigma (equivalent of the latin letter S) and represents the summation of various values of a variable. Thus:

$$\sum_{i=1}^{n} X_i = X_1 + X_2 + X_3 + \ldots + X_n$$

reads: 'the summation of the values of the variable X from the first value to the nth value of this variable'.

There are three basic rules for the algebraic manipulation of terms including summations of variables.

Rule 1. The summation of the sum (or difference) of two or more variables is equal to the sum (or difference) of their respective summations.

Symbolically we may write this rule as follows

$$\sum_{i=1}^{n} (X_i \pm Y_i) = \sum_{i=1}^{n} X_i \pm \sum_{i=1}^{n} Y_i$$

Proof: $\Sigma(X_i + Y_i) = [(X_1 + X_2 + \ldots + X_n) \pm (Y_1 + Y_2 + \ldots + Y_n)] = \Sigma X_i \pm \Sigma Y_i$

Rule 2. The summation of a constant k, times a variable, x_i, is equal to the constant times the summation of the variable.

Symbolically this rule may be written as

$$\sum_{i=1}^{n} kX_i = k \sum_{i=1}^{n} X_i$$

Proof: $\Sigma kX_i = kX_1 + kX_2 + \ldots + kX_n$

$$= k(X_1 + X_2 + \ldots + X_n)$$

$$= k \Sigma X_i$$

Rule 3. The summation of a constant, k, from 1 to n times, is equal to the product of k times n.

Symbolically we have

$$\sum_{i=1}^{n} k = nk$$

Proof: We may write $\Sigma k = \Sigma(kX_i)$ where all the X's are equal to 1. Thus we have:

$$\Sigma k = \Sigma kX_i = kX_1 + kX_2 + \ldots + kX_n$$

But $X_1 = X_2 = \ldots = X_n = 1$. Therefore

$$\sum_{i=1}^{n} k = k(1) + k(1) + \ldots + k(1) = (k + k + \ldots + k) = nk$$

A.2. DOUBLE SUBSCRIPTS AND SUMMATIONS

Sometimes we want to add various sums. For example assume we have the incomes of 5 individuals from town A, 5 individuals from town B and 5 individuals from town C. We want the total income of all 15 individuals. We may use the letter X for the variable 'income' with two subscripts, X_{ij}, the first (i) referring to the town $(i = 1, 2, 3)$ and the second (j) relating to the individual $(j = 1, 2, 3, 4, 5)$.

The sum of incomes of the 5 inhabitants of town A is

$$X_{11} + X_{12} + X_{13} + X_{14} + X_{15} = \sum_{j=1}^{5} X_{1j}$$

The sum of incomes of the 5 inhabitants of town B is

$$X_{21} + X_{22} + X_{23} + X_{24} + X_{25} = \sum_{j=1}^{5} X_{2j}$$

The sum of incomes of the 5 inhabitants of town C is

$$X_{31} + X_{32} + X_{33} + X_{34} + X_{35} = \sum_{j=1}^{5} X_{3j}$$

The total sum of all (15) incomes is

$$\sum_{j=1}^{5} X_{1j} + \sum_{j=1}^{5} X_{2j} + \sum_{j=1}^{5} X_{3j} = \sum_{i=1}^{3} \sum_{j=1}^{5} X_{ij} = \sum_{j=1}^{5} \sum_{i=1}^{3} X_{ij}$$

In general

$$\sum_{i=1}^{n} \sum_{j=1}^{m} X_{ij} = \sum_{j=1}^{m} \sum_{i=1}^{n} X_{ij} = \sum_{i=1}^{n} (X_{i1} + X_{i2} + \ldots + X_{im})$$

$$= (X_{11} + X_{21} + \ldots + X_{n1}) + (X_{12} + X_{22} + \ldots + X_{n2}) +$$

$$+ \ldots + (X_{1m} + X_{2m} + \ldots + X_{nm})$$

The following rules which involve double summation are useful.

Rule 4.

$$\sum_{i=1}^{n} \sum_{j=1}^{m} (X_{ij} + Y_{ij}) = \sum_{i=1}^{n} \sum_{j=1}^{m} X_{ij} + \sum_{i=1}^{n} \sum_{j=1}^{m} Y_{ij}$$

Proof:

$$\sum_{i=1}^{n} \sum_{j=1}^{m} (X_{ij} + Y_{ij}) = \sum_{j=1}^{m} (X_{1j} + Y_{1j}) \sum_{j=1}^{m} (X_{2j} + Y_{2j}) + \ldots + \sum_{j=1}^{m} (X_{nj} + Y_{nj})$$

$$= \sum_{j=1}^{m} (X_{1j} + X_{2j} + \ldots + X_{nj}) + \sum_{j=1}^{m} (Y_{1j} + Y_{2j} + \ldots + Y_{nj})$$

$$= \sum_{i=1}^{n} \sum_{j=1}^{m} X_{ij} + \sum_{i=1}^{n} \sum_{j=1}^{m} Y_{ij}$$

Rule 5.

$$\sum_{i=1}^{n} \sum_{j=1}^{m} X_i Y_j = \left(\sum_{i=1}^{n} X_i \right) \left(\sum_{j=1}^{m} Y_j \right)$$

Proof:

$$\sum_{i=1}^{n} \sum_{j=1}^{m} X_i Y_j = \sum_{i=1}^{n} (X_i Y_1 + X_i Y_2 + \ldots + X_i Y_m)$$

$$= Y_1 \sum_{i=1}^{n} X_i + Y_2 \sum_{i=1}^{n} X_i + \ldots + Y_m \sum_{i=1}^{n} X_i$$

$$= \sum_{i=1}^{n} X_i (Y_1 + Y_2 + \ldots + Y_m)$$

$$= \left(\sum_{i=1}^{n} X_i \right) \left(\sum_{j=1}^{m} Y_j \right)$$

SECTION B

FREQUENCY DISTRIBUTIONS AND PROBABILITY DISTRIBUTIONS

B.1. POPULATIONS AND SAMPLES

The *population* of a variable X consists of all the conceptually possible values
that the variable may assume. Some of these values may have already been
observed; others may not have occurred, but their occurrence is conceivably
possible. For example the variable 'income per head' may assume any positive
value, from zero to millions of pounds. A very large number of values of
income is observed in any one period. Yet there are infinite other values which,
although not already assumed, may be observed in some other period.

The number of conceptually possible values of a variable is called the *size of
the population*. The size varies according to the phenomenon being investigated.
For example a study of incomes may be conducted at a regional level, at a
country level, at a world-wide level. In the first instance the population
will consist of the incomes of one region; in the second case the population will
consist of the incomes of all the residents of the country; in the third case the
population will comprise the incomes of the residents of all the countries of
the world.

A population may be *finite*, when it consists of a given number of values, or
it may be *infinite*, when it includes an infinite number of values of the variable.
Most of the populations with which we are concerned in econometrics are
infinite.

In most cases we do not know all the values of a population. What we usually
have is a certain number of values that any particular variable has assumed and
which have been recorded in one way or another. Such data form a sample from
the population. *A sample* is a collection of observations on a certain variable.
The number of observations included in the sample is called the *size* of the
sample.

The main object of the theory of statistics is the development of methods of
drawing conclusions about the (unknown) population from the information
provided by a sample.

In order to facilitate the study of populations and samples, statisticians have
introduced various descriptive measures, that is various characteristic values
which describe the important features of the sample or the population. The
most important of these characteristics are the mean, the variance and the

521

standard deviation. To distinguish between samples and populations statisticians use the term *parameters* for the basic descriptive measures of the population and the term *statistics* for the characteristic measures of the sample. Furthermore they use Greek letters for the population parameters and Latin letters for the sample statistics. In summary, the basic descriptive measures of populations and samples are

Population Parameters	*Sample Statistics*
1. Population mean: μ	1. Sample mean: $\overline{X}$
2. Population variance: σ_x^2	2. Sample variance: s_x^2
3. Population standard deviation: σ_x	3. Sample standard deviation: s_x

Before giving the formal definitions of these measures, we will develop the concepts of frequency and probability and their distributions (frequency distributions and probability distributions). Frequency distributions refer to samples while probability distributions are associated with populations.

B.2. FREQUENCY DISTRIBUTIONS

Frequency distributions are associated with samples. If we draw values from a population and record them, we may observe that some values appear more frequently than others in the sample. For example if we are concerned with the population 'income per head of the U.K.', values of £1,500 or £1,600 do appear more often than values of £100 or £1,000,000. The number of times that a certain value appears when we draw observations from a population is called the *absolute frequency* of that value. If for example the income £1,000 is observed 10 times in our drawings from the population of incomes, we say that the value £1000 has an absolute frequency of 10. *Relative frequency* of a particular value is the ratio of the absolute frequency divided by the total number of the observations (n) drawn from the population. If, in our example the total number of observations is 400, the relative frequency of the value $X = £1,000$ is $\frac{10}{400} = 0\cdot025$.

Conventionally the absolute frequency of a value of a variable is denoted by the symbol f_i, where the subscript i refers to the ith value of the variable X.

It should be clear that the total number of observations, or drawings, is equal to the sum of the frequencies of the individual values that have been observed:

$$\sum_{i=1}^{k} f_i = n$$

(k = possible values of the variable X).

Thus the relative frequency of the ith value of X may be written as

$$\begin{bmatrix} \text{relative} \\ \text{frequency} \\ \text{of } X_i \end{bmatrix} = f(X_i) = \frac{f_i}{n} = \frac{f_i}{\Sigma f_i}$$

The sum of all the relative frequencies is equal to unity:

$$\Sigma\frac{f_i}{n} = \frac{1}{n} \Sigma f i = \frac{n}{n} = 1$$

given that $\Sigma f_i = n$.

If we record all the sample values of X with their frequencies we obtain a set of pairs of values with their respective frequencies, which is called the *frequency distribution* (or simply the *distribution*) of the variable X. The frequency distribution is an organised presentation of the observed values of a variable in a sample: it shows the number of observations for each value of the variable in the sample (in the case of a discrete variable) or the number of observations in each interval of values of the variable in the sample (in the case of a continuous variable).

Symbolically the frequency distribution is denoted by $f(X)$ and it gives for each value X_i the relative frequency, $f(X_i)$, with which that value occurs in the set of n observations.

Distributions may be presented in a tabular form, on a graph or with a mathematical formula. Graphically frequency distributions of discrete variables are presented by a *frequency polygon* or a *histogram. An important feature of the histogram is that its area represents the sum of the relative frequencies and hence it is equal to 1.*

An example will illustrate these definitions. Assume that we take a sample of the daily incomes of 1,000 individuals. We observe that 20 individuals have an income of £1 per day; 200 individuals have an income of £2; 540 individuals have an income of £3; 220 individuals have an income of £4; and 20 individuals have an income of £5. This information constitutes the frequency distribution of the variable income. The tabular presentation of this distribution is shown in Table 1.

The graph of the above frequency distribution is shown in figures 1 and 2. On the vertical axis of figure 1 we measure the absolute or the relative frequencies and on the horizontal axis we measure the value of the variable. If the data are not grouped, as in our example, the frequency distribution is presented by vertical lines drawn on top of each value of X to a height equal to the frequency (or the relative frequency). If we join the ends of the vertical lines we form a *frequency polygon.* However, it is more useful to draw the graph of the relative frequencies in a slightly different way. On the horizontal axis we measure single unit intervals, that is, we take classes or class-intervals equal to one unit of X. (In our example we have measured income in single units to begin with.) On top of the unit intervals we draw rectangles with height equal to the relative frequency. These rectangles form the histogram of the frequency distribution (figure 2). The base of each rectangle is (by construction) equal to one unit of X. Consequently the area of each rectangle is equal to the relative frequency of the particular value of X. We know that the sum of the relative frequencies of the values of X is equal to unity. Hence the total area of all the rectangles of the histogram is equal to 1.

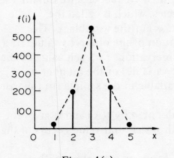

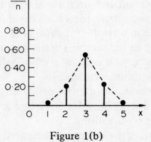

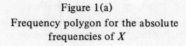

Figure 1(a)
Frequency polygon for the absolute
frequencies of X

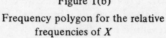

Figure 1(b)
Frequency polygon for the relative
frequencies of X

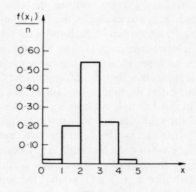

Figure 2
The histogram of the frequency distribution of table 1

Table 1. Frequency distribution of X (daily income)

Values of income (in £) X_i	Absolute frequency f_i	Relative frequency f_i/n
1	20	$\dfrac{20}{1,000} = 0\cdot02$
2	200	$\dfrac{200}{1,000} = 0\cdot20$
3	540	$\dfrac{540}{1,000} = 0\cdot54$
4	220	$\dfrac{220}{1,000} = 0\cdot22$
5	20	$\dfrac{20}{1,000} = 0\cdot02$
Total frequency	$\sum\limits_{i=1}^{n} f_i = 1,000$	$\sum\limits_{i=1}^{n} \dfrac{f_i}{n} = 1$

Heuristically we may think as follows:

The area of a rectangle (A_i) is equal to the product of its height (H_i) times its base (B_i)

$$A_i = H_i \times B_i$$

But H_i = relative frequency of the ith value of $X = f_i$; and $B_i = 1$ by construction, since we took the class interval equal to one unit of X.

Consequently

$$A_i = (f_i/n)(1) = f_i/n$$

The sum of the areas of all rectangles of the histogram is

$$\sum_{i}^{k} A_i = \sum_{i=1}^{n} \frac{f_i}{n} = 1$$

Thus the area of a histogram represents the sum of the relative frequencies and is equal to one.

B.3. PROBABILITY DISTRIBUTIONS

Probability distributions refer to populations and are analogous to the frequency distributions of samples.

Let us first define the concept of probability. It has been observed that as we increase the number of observations from the population of a random variable the relative frequency of any value X_i tends to stabilize at a certain value, which is called the limiting value of the relative frequency or *probability* of the value X_i of the random variable. In other words the *probability* of a value X_i of a random variable is the limiting value of the relative frequency of that value as the total number of observations on the variable approaches infinity, the value which the relative frequency assumes *at the limit* as the number of observations tends to infinity. This is symbolically written as

$$P(X_i) = \lim_{n \to \infty} \frac{f_i}{\Sigma f_i}$$

Sometimes the symbol $f(X_i)$ is used to denote the probability of the value X_i. Each value of a random variable has some probability associated with itself, i.e. there is some probability of observing any value of a variable. The sum of the probabilities of all values, being the sum of relative frequencies (at the limit), is equal to unity.

Probabilities, interpreted as limiting values of relative frequencies, can be estimated from empirical data. Thus in practice we take *the relative frequency as equal to the probability*. It should be however clear that these two concepts are different. The larger the number of observations the closer will the relative frequency be to the probability. For an illustration let us examine the occurrence of male births in the population. We want to find what is the probability that a birth will be the birth of a male. Every year thousands of births are recorded. If we take the total births over, say, a decade all over the world, the number of observations increases considerably. For any practical purpose such a large number of observations may be considered as adequate for the concept of limiting value of the relative frequency, although there is no actual approach of n to infinity. With such calculations it has been found that male births occur with a relative frequency approximately of $\frac{1}{2}$ (or 0·50, or 50 per cent). Thus we say that the probability of a male birth is 0·50.

The probability of any event (or any value of a variable) can assume any value between 0 and 1. Symbolically:

$$0 \leqslant f(X_i) \leqslant 1$$

If the probability of X assuming the particular value X_i is equal to zero this means that the variable cannot assume the value X_i; in other words a probability of zero for X_i suggests impossibility of occurrence of the value X_i. If the probability of a particular value X^* is equal to unity this means that this value does occur at any time, i.e. the value X^* is the only value that the variable can assume. In this case the 'variable' is really a constant. It may assume only the single value X^*. Thus a probability of one corresponds to certainty; that is, the value X^* is certain to occur. Any probability of a particular value X_i between zero and one shows some uncertainty in the occurrence of this particular value of the variable X.

There are several rules for the calculation of the probabilities of one or more values being observed in any particular instance. These rules are known as *laws of probabilities* and are developed in section F below.

We said that a random variable is a variable whose values are associated with some probability of being observed, and that a random variable can be discrete (when it can assume only finite values) or continuous (when it can assume an infinite number of values within any given interval). We shall examine the probability distributions of discrete and continuous variables separately.

B.3.1. *Discrete Random Variables and their Probability Distributions*

If a variable is discrete its values are distinct, i.e. they are separated by finite distances. To each value we may assign a given probability. If X is a discrete random variable which may assume the values $X_1, X_2, \ldots, X_n$, with respective probabilities $f(X_1), f(X_2), \ldots, f(X_n)$, then the entire set of pairs of permissible values together with their respective probabilities is called the *probability distribution* of the random variable X.

The probability distribution is mathematically denoted by a function, $f(X_i)$, which gives the probability of any particular value X_i (of the discrete variable X) being observed. If all the permissible values of X have equal probability of being observed, the probability distribution is called the *uniform* or *rectangular* distribution. For example, in casting an unbiased die each of the permissible values $(1, 2, 3, 4, 5, 6)$ has a probability of $1/6$ of being observed. Thus the probability distribution of the random variable X which denotes the results of casting a die is a uniform distribution. It is shown in table 2 and its graph appears in figure 3.

Table 2. A uniform probability distribution

Probability distribution of variable X = results of casting a die	
Permissible Values of X	Probability of each value: $f(X_i)$
$X = 1$	1/6
$X = 2$	1/6
$X = 3$	1/6
$X = 4$	1/6
$X = 5$	1/6
$X = 6$	1/6
	$\Sigma f(X_i) = 1$

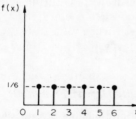
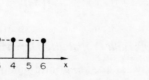
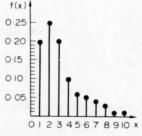

Figure 3. A uniform probability distribution of a discrete variable

Figure 4. A non-uniform probability distribution of a discrete variable

In most econometric applications the variables involved do not have a uniform probability distribution. Each value of the variable has usually its own probability of being observed. For example suppose that we have the random variable X denoting the number of children per family, and that the permissible values of this variable are the positive integers 1, 2, 3, ... 10, each with the probability (estimated from a very large number (sample) of families) shown in table 3.

Table 3. A non-uniform probability distribution

Probability distribution of X_i	
Permissible values X_i	Probability of each value $f(X_i)$
0	0·05
1	0·20
2	0·25
3	0·20
4	0·10
5	0·06
6	0·05
7	0·04
8	0·03
9	0·01
10	0·01
	$\Sigma f(X_i) = 1$

The graph of this non-uniform probability distribution is shown in figure 4.

In many cases we are interested in knowing the probability that the discrete variable X will assume a value less than or equal to a given value. These are called *cumulative probabilities* and are usually denoted by $F(X)$. The cumulative probability is the sum of individual probabilities. For example the probability of a couple having 4 or less children is

$$P(0 \leqslant X \leqslant 4) = P(X = 0) + P(X = 1) + P(X = 2) + P(X = 3) + P(X = 4)$$

$$= 0·05 + 0·20 + 0·25 + 0·20 + 0·10 = 0·80$$

In general if $X_1, X_2, \ldots, X_k, \ldots, X_n$ are successive values of X, then the cumulative probability of the first k values is

$$F(X_k) = f(X_1) + f(X_2) + \ldots + f(X_k) = \sum_{i=1}^{k} f(X_i)$$

B.3.2. *Continuous Random Variables and Probability Density Functions*

If a variable is continuous, it may assume an infinite number of values within any given interval. For example, the variable 'income' can assume infinite values between, say, £10 and £100. In the case of a continuous variable the

probability of any particular value must be zero; that is, $P(X = X^*) = 0$.
However the probability of X assuming values within an interval (X_1 and X_2), no
matter how small this interval might be, is a finite number and can be computed
(by integrals). Thus the fact that $P(X = X^*) = 0$ in the case of a continuous
variable should not be interpreted as meaning that the value X_i^* is impossible.
After all, the variable does assume particular values in any one situation.
Rather $f(X_i^*)$ should be interpreted as the average probability of values very
close in the neighbourhood of X_i^*. (See A. S. Goldberger, *Econometric Theory*,
Wiley, 1964, p. 69.)

The probability distribution of a continuous variable is called *probability
density function* or simply *probability function*. However, in this book we use
the term 'probability distribution' both for discrete and for continuous
variables.

The probability function is mathematically denoted by a continuous function
and graphically presented by a curve. Some typical shapes of probability
functions (distributions) are shown in figure 5.

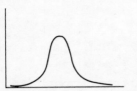

(a) Normal distribution

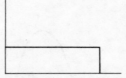

(b) Rectangular or uniform
distribution

(c) Positively skew
distribution

(d) Negatively skew
distribution

(e) U-shaped distribution

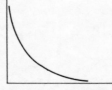

(f) Reverse J-distribution

(g) J-distribution

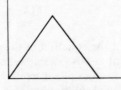

(h) Inverted V

Figure 5

A normal distribution is a symmetrical bell-shaped curve which extends indefinitely in both directions: the curve comes closer and closer to the horizontal axis but never quite reaches it. There is a certain central value of X around which the values of X are clustered symmetrically.

In a rectangular (or uniform) distribution all the values of the variable X are observed with the same probability.

If the majority of values of X are lower than the mean (average) value of X, the distribution is positively skewed; i.e. skewed to the right. If most of the values of X are higher than the mean (average) value of X, the distribution is negatively skewed, i.e. skewed to the left.

An important feature of the curves of probability distributions is that the areas under these curves represent probabilities. *The total area under the curve of a probability distribution*, being the sum of individual probabilities, *is equal to unity*.

For example assume that the probability distribution of a continuous variable X is represented by the curve of figure 6. The probability that X assumes a value

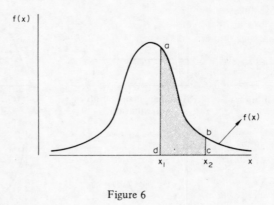

Figure 6

within the interval X_1 to X_2 is given by the shaded area *abcd*. This probability may be computed by integration

$$P(X_1 < X < X_2) = \int_{X_1}^{X_2} f(X)\, dx$$

where $f(X)$ is the equation of the probability function. (The integration in the case of a continuous variable is analogous to the summation of the probabilities of individual values of a discrete variable). Fortunately it will not be necessary to compute probabilities by integrals in econometric applications. Probabilities, when required, will be taken out of particular standard tables, whose use will be explained in subsequent sections.

It should be stressed that the fact that for a continuous variable the probability of any particular value is equal to zero, $P(X = X_i^*) = 0$, does not mean that the value X_i^* is impossible. When we draw a sample from a continuous variable, $P(X_i^*)$ should be interpreted as the average probability of values which are very close in the neighbourhood of X_i (see A. S. Goldberger, *Econometric Theory*, p. 69).

B.3.3. *Joint Probability Distributions*

If we have two random variables X and Y their joint probability, denoted by $f(X_i Y_j)$, is a function which gives the probability that X assumes a given value X_i and Y assumes a given value Y_j, jointly. For example assume that we have the variable X denoting the sex (male or female) of a person, and the variable Y denoting whether the person is a smoker or a non-smoker. Assume that we draw a very large sample of men and women and we find the following probabilities:

P (male and smoker) = $0 \cdot 5$
P (female and smoker) = $0 \cdot 3$
P (male and non-smoker) = $0 \cdot 1$
P (female and non-smoker) = $0 \cdot 1$

This information may be presented in the following tabular form.

Table 4. Joint distribution of X and Y

Values of Y	Values of X		Marginal Probability of Y
	X_1 = Male	X_2 = Female	
Y_1 = smoker	$f(X_1, Y_1) = 0 \cdot 5$	$f(X_2, Y_1) = 0 \cdot 3$	$f(Y_1) = 0 \cdot 8$
Y_2 = non-smoker	$f(X_1, Y_2) = 0 \cdot 1$	$f(X_2, Y_2) = 0 \cdot 1$	$f(Y_2) = 0 \cdot 2$
Marginal Probability of X	$f(X_1) = 0 \cdot 6$	$f(X_2) = 0 \cdot 4$	$1 \cdot 00$

Thus the joint probability of $X = X_1$ *and* $Y = Y_1$ is

$$f(X_1, Y_1) = 0 \cdot 5$$

Similarly, the joint probability of $X = X_2$ *and* $Y = Y_1$ is

$$f(X_2, Y_1) = 0 \cdot 3$$

and so on.

Marginal probability of X_i is the probability of X assuming a specific value X_i irrespective of the value of Y, that is, irrespective of what value Y assumes. In our example the marginal probability of X_1 is

$$f(X_1) = f(X_1, Y_1) + f(X_1, Y_2)$$

$$= \sum_{i=1}^{2} (X_1, Y_i)$$

$$= 0 \cdot 5 + 0 \cdot 1 = 0 \cdot 6$$

Similarly the marginal probability of X_2 is

$$f(X_2) = f(X_2, Y_1) + f(X_2, Y_2)$$

$$= \sum_{i=1}^{2} (X_2, Y_i)$$

$$= 0 \cdot 3 + 0 \cdot 1 = 0 \cdot 4$$

In general, the marginal probability of X_i is given by adding up the corresponding probabilities over all the values of the other variable (Y); and similarly the marginal probability of Y_i is found by summing all the corresponding probabilities of the other variable (X). Symbolically

$$\begin{bmatrix} \text{Marginal} \\ \text{Probability } x_i \end{bmatrix} = f(X_i) = \sum_{j} f(X_i, Y_j).$$

and

$$\begin{bmatrix} \text{Marginal} \\ \text{Probability } y_j \end{bmatrix} = f(Y_j) = \sum_{i} (X_i, Y_j)$$

The extension of the above results to the joint distribution of more than two variables (multivariate distributions) is straightforward.

SECTION C

POPULATION PARAMETERS AND SAMPLE STATISTICS

C.1. POPULATION PARAMETERS

Although the construction of probability distributions and their graphic presentation help in the study of populations, they still involve a lot of tedious work. In order to simplify further the study of populations, statisticians have defined various descriptive measures, i.e. basic characteristic values which describe adequately the basic features of the population. These descriptive measures are called *parameters* of the population or *expected values* (or *mathematical expectations*) of the probability distribution of the variables. The term 'expected value' is used in order to denote the fact that the parameters of the population of a continuous variable are never observed, and those of the population of a discrete variable, although in principle observable, may be impossible to observe in practice because the number of values of the population are not all of them known. Hence we say that we *expect* the population parameters to have a certain (expected) value.

The most common parameters of probability distributions are the following.

1. Measures of location (or of central tendency).

There are various measures of location. The most important is *the arithmetic mean* of the population. The mean is the 'central' or 'average' value of the variable whose population we study. It is denoted by the Greek letter μ.

2. Measures of dispersion (or variation).

There are various measures of dispersion, the most important being the variance and the standard deviation of the population of X. The variance shows how close to the mean the various values of X cluster. The standard deviation is the square root of the variance and gives the average distance of the various values of X from the arithmetic mean.

The variance of a population is denoted by the Greek letter σ_x^2. The population standard deviation then is $\sqrt{\sigma_x^2} = \sigma_x$.

3. Measures of the skewness

Such measures show the degree of symmetry of the distribution around the mean value. Two skew distributions are shown in figures 5(c) and 5(d).

4. Measures of the kurtosis

Such measures show the degree of peakedness or flatness of the distribution of X.

533

Of the above measures the most important are the measures of location and dispersion. Thus when we speak of the parameters of a population we will refer to its mean, variance and standard deviation.

The population mean is called *the expected value* of the population and it is conventionally denoted as $E(X)$ or μ. For a *discrete random variable* the expected value is computed by the sum of the products of the values X_i multiplied by their respective probabilities

$$E(X) = \mu = \sum_{i=1}^{n} X_i f(X_i)$$

where $f(X_i)$ is the probability of the variable X assuming the value X_i.[1, 2] The expected value is the weighted arithmetic mean of the (random) variable X, the weights being the individual probabilities.

Example. Assume that the variable X 'number of children per family' assumes values from zero to ten with the probabilities shown in table 3. The expected value of the random variable X, i.e. the average number of children in a family, is computed as follows:

$$E(X) = \Sigma X_i f(X_i)$$

$$E(X) = (0)(0{\cdot}05) + (1)(0{\cdot}20) + (2)(0{\cdot}25) + \ldots + 10(0{\cdot}01) \approx 3$$

The average number of children in a family in our example is 3, approximately.

The variance of a population is the expected value of the squared deviations of the value of X from their expected mean value

$$\mathrm{var}(X) = \sigma_x^2 = E[X_i - E(X)]^2$$

For a discrete random variable the variance is equal to the sum of the squared deviations of the X's from their expected mean value multiplied by the respective

----

[1] *Proof.*

$$E(X) = \frac{\Sigma X_i f_i}{\Sigma f_i} = \Sigma X_i \frac{f_i}{\Sigma f_i}$$

But

$$\frac{f_i}{\Sigma f_i} = f(X_i) = \text{probability of the value } X_i$$

Therefore $E(X) = \Sigma X_i f(X_i)$.

[2] If the variable is continuous the expected value is given by the same formula by substituting the summation with the integral:

$$E(X) = \int_a^b X f(X)\, dx$$

where $f(X)$ is the probability density function of X.

probabilities of the values of X[1]

$$\text{var}(X) = \sigma_x^2 = \sum_i^n (X_i - \mu) f(X_i)$$

It can be shown that

$$\text{var}(X) = E(X^2) - \mu^2$$

Proof:

$$
\begin{aligned}
\text{var}(X) = \sigma_x^2 &= E[X - E(X)]^2 \\
&= E(X - \mu)^2 \\
&= E(X^2 + \mu^2 - 2X\mu) \\
&= E(X^2) + E(\mu^2) - 2E(X\mu) \\
&= E(X^2) + \mu^2 - 2\mu E(X) \\
&= E(X^2) + \mu^2 - 2\mu^2 \qquad \text{(given } E(X) = \mu) \\
&= E(X^2) - \mu^2
\end{aligned}
$$

The variance shows the way in which the various values of the random variable X are distributed around their expected mean value. The smaller the variance, the closer the cluster of the values of X around the mean and vice versa.

The standard deviation of a population is the square root of the variance. It is denoted by σ_x and is computed from the expression

$$\sigma_x = \sqrt{E[X_i - E(X)]^2} = \sqrt{E(X_i - \mu)^2}$$

Like the variance, the standard deviation is a measure of the dispersion of the values of X around their (population) mean.[2]

[1] If the variable is continuous the variance is given by the same expression by substituting the summation with the integral

$$E(X - E(X))^2 = \int_a^b [X - E(X)]^2 f(X)\, dx$$

where $f(X)$ is the probability density function of X.

[2] The parameters of a population are also called the *moments* of the population. In a distribution of a discrete variable the rth moment about zero is defined as

$$m_r' = \sum_i^n X_i^r f(X_i)$$

and the rth moment about the mean is defined as

$$m_r = \sum_i^n (X_i - \mu)^r f(X_i)$$

The first moment about zero is the mean of the distribution

$$\mu = m_1' = \Sigma X_i f(X_i)$$

The second moment about the mean is the variance of the distribution

$$\sigma_x^2 = \sum_i^n (X_i - \mu)^2 f(X_i) = \sum_i^n (X_i - \mu)^2 P_i$$

If we know the mean μ and the standard deviation σ_x of a population, we have a pretty good idea of the form of its distribution. From the expected value, μ, we know where the distribution is located along the horizontal axis: we know its 'central' point. From the variance or standard deviation we know whether the values of the variable are clustered closely around the mean or are dispersed widely about it. The shape of any distribution depends on the mean and variance of the population of the variable to which the distribution refers. The following results (which are discussed in detail in Section E below) show the extent of information which we have if we know that a population is normal (that is, has a normal distribution) with mean μ and standard deviation σ_x:

68% of the values of X will lie within the interval $[\mu \pm 1\sigma_x]$

95% of the values of X will lie within the interval $[\mu \pm 2\sigma_x]$

99% of the values of X will lie within the interval $[\mu \pm 3\sigma_x]$

Covariance of two random variables

The *covariance* of two random variables is the expected value of the product of the deviations of the variables from their expected values. Symbolically

$$\text{cov}(XY) = E\{[X_i - E(X)] [Y_j - E(Y)]\}$$

which can be shown to reduce to

$$\text{cov}(XY) = E(XY) - E(X)E(Y) \qquad \text{(see p. 542)}$$

C.2. SAMPLE STATISTICS

The parameters of a population can be mathematically measured if we know all the values of the population. However in most cases we do not know all the values of a population. In any particular case what we usually have is a sample from the population. Statisticians have introduced various descriptive measures for samples, which describe the basic features of the sample values, and are called *sample statistics*. The basic statistics of a sample, corresponding to the parameters of the population, are: the sample mean, the sample variance and the sample standard deviation.

The *sample mean* is the average value in the sample. It is designated by $\overline{X}$. The simple arithmetic mean is calculated by adding up the observations of the sample and then dividing the total by the number of observations. Thus

$$\overline{X} = \frac{\sum\limits_{i=1}^{n} X_i}{n}$$

For example suppose that X stands for the incomes of the inhabitants of a country. We choose a sample of 10 individuals and we want to compute the average income.

Suppose that the observations of the sample are as follows:

Individual	x_1	x_2	x_3	x_4	x_5	x_6	x_7	x_8	x_9	x_{10}
Incomes (£ per head)	95	120	80	150	50	130	70	90	110	105

The average income will be

$$X = \frac{\sum_{i=1}^{10} X_i}{n} = \frac{95 + 120 + 80 + \ldots + 105}{10} = \frac{1000}{10} = 100$$

The weighted arithmetic mean is the sum of the products of the X's and their weights, w's, divided by the sum of the weights

$$\overline{X} = \frac{\sum_{i=1}^{n} X_i w_i}{\sum_{i=1}^{n} w_i}$$

Weighted means are widely used in price indexes, or quantity indexes. The weights may be chosen according to the purpose and the nature of the index.

The *sample variance* is a measure of the dispersion of the values of X in the sample around their average value. It is designated by s_x^2. It is computed by the formula.

$$s_x^2 = \frac{\sum_{i=1}^{n} (X_i - \overline{X})^2}{n} = \frac{\sum X_i^2 - n\overline{X}^2}{n} = \frac{\sum X_i^2}{n} - \overline{X}^2$$

For our example the variance of the incomes of ten individuals is

$$s_x^2 = \frac{(-5)^2 + (20)^2 + (-20)^2 + \ldots + (5)^2}{10} = 785$$

Note that in measuring the variance we take the sum of the squares of the deviations of X's from X. This is necessary because the simple sum of the deviations is equal to zero (see p. 529).

The *sample standard deviation* is designated by s_x and is equal to the square root of the variance

$$s_x = \sqrt{\frac{\sum_{i=1}^{n} (X_i - \overline{X})^2}{n}}$$

In the above example the standard deviation is 28.

The sample covariance of two variables

Given any two sets of n sample observations on two variables

$$X_1, X_2, \ldots, X_n$$
$$Y_1, Y_2, \ldots, Y_n$$

we are often interested in measuring their *covariance,* that is, the way in which they change together (co-vary). The covariance is defined as the sum of the products of deviations of X and Y from their means, $\overline{X}$ and $\overline{Y}$ respectively, divided by the number of observations.

$$\text{cov}_{(XY)} = \frac{\sum\limits_{i=1}^{n} (X_i - \overline{X})(Y_i - \overline{Y})}{n}$$

If the variables X and Y are not changing together, if they are independent, their covariance is equal to zero, since the sum of the products of their deviations is zero (see p. 542).

From a population we may draw many samples. A *random sample* of a discrete variable is a sample of observations each of which has the same probability of being drawn from the population. For example if we want a random sample of consumers we may go in the street and ask any one whom we happen to meet on his consumption expenditures. Any individual has the same chance of being included in this sample. If the variable is continuous, a sample drawn from its population is random if the values that are observed are independent (see section F below for the definition of independence of any two events, values).

In most cases in econometrics we use data either in the form of time-series observations or in the form of cross-section observations. These data are considered as being randomly drawn from a hypothetically infinite population. In other words in most cases *the data which econometricians use in their work are considered as random samples from a hypothetically infinite population.*[1] For example a time series of prices of a commodity, say cars, recorded on the market may be considered as a random sample of all possible prices of cars, which form the hypothetically infinite population of car prices.

From the observations of a sample we may compute the sample mean, variance and standard deviation. Once the sample statistics are computed we may make inferences about the population parameters. The basic rules of statistical inference are outlined in section E below.

[1] See M. Brennan, *Preface to Econometrics,* p. 293.

SECTION D

THE ALGEBRA OF EXPECTED VALUES AND SAMPLE STATISTICS

D.1. THE ALGEBRA OF TERMS INVOLVING SAMPLE STATISTICS

Rule 1. The mean value of the sum (or difference) of two variables is equal to the sum (or difference) of their means. Symbolically

$$(\overline{X \pm Y}) = \overline{X} \pm \overline{Y}$$

Proof:
$$\overline{(X + Y)} = \frac{\Sigma(X + Y)}{n} = \frac{\Sigma X + \Sigma Y}{n} = \frac{\Sigma X}{n} + \frac{\Sigma Y}{n} = \overline{X} + \overline{Y}$$

Rule 2. The sum of deviations of a variable from its mean is equal to zero. Symbolically

$$\sum_{i=1}^{n} (X_i - \overline{X}) = \sum_{i=1}^{n} x_i = 0 \quad \text{where } x_i = X_i - \overline{X}$$

Proof: $\Sigma(X_i - \overline{X}) = \Sigma X_i - n\overline{X}$ (given that $\overline{X}$ is a constant)

$$= \Sigma X_i - n\frac{\Sigma X_i}{n} = 0$$

Rule 3. The mean of a variable multiplied by a constant k is equal to this constant times the mean of the variable. Symbolically

$$\overline{kX} = k\overline{X}$$

Proof:
$$\overline{(kX)} = \frac{\Sigma k X_i}{n} = k\frac{\Sigma X_i}{n} = k\overline{X} \qquad \text{(given that } k \text{ is a constant)}$$

Rule 4. The variance of a variable X multiplied by a constant k is equal to the square of the constant times the variance of the variable. Symbolically

$$\text{var}(kX) = k^2 \{\text{var}(X)\}$$

Proof:
$$\text{var}_{(kX)} = \frac{\Sigma(kX - \overline{kX})^2}{n} = \frac{\Sigma(kX - k\overline{X})^2}{n} = k^2\frac{\Sigma(X - \overline{X})^2}{n} = k^2 \{\text{var}(X)\}$$

Rule 5. The variance of the sum of two variables is equal to the sum of the variances plus twice their covariance

$$s^2_{(X+Y)} = s^2_X + s^2_Y + 2\,\text{cov}_{(XY)}$$

Proof:

$$s^2{}_{(X+Y)} = \frac{\Sigma[(X + Y) - (\overline{X + Y})]^2}{n} = \frac{\Sigma[(X - \overline{X}) + (Y - \overline{Y})]^2}{n}$$

$$= \frac{\Sigma\{(X - \overline{X})^2 + (Y - \overline{Y})^2 + 2(X - \overline{X})(Y - \overline{Y})\}}{n}$$

$$= \frac{\Sigma(X - \overline{X})^2}{n} + \frac{\Sigma(Y - \overline{Y})^2}{n} + \frac{2\Sigma(X - \overline{X})(Y - \overline{Y})}{n} = s^2_X + s^2_Y + 2\,\text{cov}_{(XY)}$$

If X and Y are independent, their covariance is zero. Hence, for independent variables

$$s^2_{(X + Y)} = s^2_X + s^2_Y$$

Rule 6. The mean of a constant is the constant itself. Symbolically

$$\overline{k} = k$$

Proof:

$$\overline{k} = \frac{\sum\limits_{i=1}^{n} k}{n} = \frac{nk}{n} = k$$

Rule 7

$$\sum_{i=1}^{n} x_i^2 = \sum_{i=1}^{n} X_i^2 - n\overline{X}^2$$

Proof:

$$\Sigma x^2 = \Sigma(X - \overline{X})^2 = \Sigma(X^2 + \overline{X}^2 - 2\overline{X}X)$$
$$= \Sigma X^2 + n\overline{X}^2 - 2\overline{X}\Sigma X$$
$$= \Sigma X^2 + n\overline{X}^2 - 2n\overline{X}^2 = \Sigma X^2 - n\overline{X}^2$$

Rule 8

$$\sum_{i=1}^{n} x_i y_i = \sum_{i=1}^{n} X_i Y_i - n\overline{X}\overline{Y}$$

Proof:

$$\Sigma xy = \Sigma(X - \overline{X})(Y - \overline{Y}) = \Sigma(XY - \overline{X}Y - \overline{Y}X + \overline{X}\overline{Y})$$
$$= \Sigma XY - \overline{X}\Sigma Y - \overline{Y}\Sigma X + n\overline{X}\overline{Y}$$
$$= \Sigma XY - n\overline{X}\overline{Y} - n\overline{Y}\overline{X} + n\overline{X}\overline{Y} = \Sigma\overline{X}Y - n\overline{X}\overline{Y}$$

D.2. THE ALGEBRA OF EXPECTED VALUES

There are several rules for the algebraic manipulation of expressions involving expected values, which are used in several chapters. The most important of these rules are listed below.

Rule 1. The mathematical expectation of a sum (or a difference) of two random independent variables is the sum (or difference) of their individual expected values.

Let X and Y be two random variables with independent population distributions. We then may write symbolically

$$E(X \pm Y) = E(X) \pm E(Y)$$

Proof: $E(X + Y) = \sum\limits_{i} \sum\limits_{j}(X_i + Y_j) f(X_i, Y_j) = \sum\limits_{i} \sum\limits_{j} X_i f(X_i, Y_j) + \sum\limits_{i} \sum\limits_{j} Y_j f(X_i, Y_j)$

$$= \sum_{i} X_i \sum_{j} f(X_i, Y_j) + \sum_{j} Y_j \Sigma f(X_i, X_y)$$

But $\sum\limits_{j}' f(X_i, Y_j) = f(X_i) =$ marginal probability of X_i

and $\sum\limits_{i} f(X_i, Y_j) = f(Y_j) =$ marginal probability of Y_j

Therefore $E(X + Y) = \sum_i X_i f(X_i) + \sum_j Y_j f(Y_j) = E(X) + E(Y)$

Rule 2. The expected value of a constant is equal to that constant. Symbolically we may write

$$E(k) = k$$

Proof: $E(k) = \sum_i k f(k) = k \sum f(k) = k$

given $\sum f(k) = $ sum of probabilities $= 1$

Rule 3. The expected value of a random variable multiplied by a constant is equal to the constant times the expected value of the variable. Symbolically we may write this rule as follows

$$E(kX_i) = kE(X)$$

Proof: $E(kX_i) = \sum (kX_i) f(X_i) = k \sum X_i f(X_i) = k \, E(X)$

Rule 4. The variance of the sum of two variables is equal to the sum of the individual variances plus twice their covariance:

$$\text{var}(X + Y) = \text{var}(X) + \text{var}(Y) + 2 \, \text{cov}(XY)$$

or

$$\sigma^2_{(X + Y)} = \sigma^2_X + \sigma^2_Y + 2 \, \text{cov}(XY)$$

Proof: $\begin{aligned}\text{var}(X + Y) &= E[(X + Y) - E(X + Y)]^2 \\ &= E\{[X - E(X)] + [Y - E(Y)]\}^2 \\ &= E[X - E(X)]^2 + E[Y - E(Y)]^2 + 2E\{[X - E(X)][Y - E(Y)]\} \\ &= \text{var}(X) + \text{var}(Y) + 2 \, \text{cov}(XY)\end{aligned}$

Rule 5. The expected value of the product of two *independent variables* is equal to the product of the expected values of the two variables:

$$E(XY) = E(X) E(Y)$$

Proof: $E(XY) = \sum_i \sum_j X_i Y_j f(X_i, Y_j)$

Since X and Y are independent their joint probability $f(X_i, Y_j)$ is equal to the product of their individual probabilities (see section F):

$$f(X_i, Y_j) = f(X_i) f(Y_j)$$

Therefore

$$E(XY) = \sum_i \sum_j X_i Y_j f(X_i) f(Y_j)$$

$$= [\sum_i X_i f(X_i)] [\sum_j Y_j f(Y_j)]$$

$$= E(X) E(Y)$$

Rule 6. If X and Y are two independent random variables their covariance is equal to zero:

$$\text{cov}(XY) = 0 \qquad \text{for independent variables}$$

Proof: $\quad \mathrm{cov}(XY) = E\left\{[X - E(X)]\,[Y - E(Y)]\right\}$

$\qquad\qquad\qquad = E\left\{XY - YE(X) - XE(Y) + E(X)\,E(Y)\right\}$

$\qquad\qquad\qquad = E\,(XY) - E(X)\,E(Y)$

By rule 5, for independent variables

$\qquad E(XY) \quad = E(X)\,E(Y)$

Therefore

$\qquad \mathrm{cov}(XY) \quad = E(X)\,E(Y) - E(X)\,E(Y) = 0$

Rule 7. If X is a random variable and a and b are constants, then

$$\mathrm{var}(aX + b) = a^2\,\mathrm{var}(X)$$

Proof: $\mathrm{var}(aX + b) = E\left\{(aX + b) - E(aX + b)\right\}^2$

$\qquad\qquad\qquad = E\left\{(aX + b) - [aE(X) + b]\right\}^2$

$\qquad\qquad\qquad = E\,[aX + b - a\mu - b]^2$

$\qquad\qquad\qquad = a^2 E(X - \mu)^2 = a^2\,\mathrm{var}(X)$

Rule 8 The expected value of the sum of products of two variables is equal to the sum of the expected values of the products. Symbolically

$$E\left(\sum_{i=1}^{n} X_i Y_i\right) = \sum_{i=1}^{n} [E(X_i Y_i)]$$

Proof: $\quad E\left(\sum_{i=1}^{n} X_i Y_i\right) = E(X_1 Y_1 + X_2 Y_2 + X_3 Y_3 + \ldots + X_n Y_n)$

$\qquad\qquad\qquad = E(X_1 Y_1) + E(X_2 Y_2) + \ldots + E(X_n Y_n)$

$\qquad\qquad\qquad = \sum_{i=1}^{n} [E(X_i Y_i)]$

Rule 9 The expected value of the squared sum of products of two variables is

$$E\left(\sum_{i=1}^{n} X_i Y_i\right)^2 = E\left[\sum_{i=1}^{n} X_i^2 Y_i^2 + 2 \sum_{i \neq j} X_i X_j Y_i Y_j\right]$$

Proof: $\quad E\left(\sum_{i=1}^{n} X_i Y_i\right)^2 = E[X_1 Y_1 + X_2 Y_2 + X_3 X_3 + \ldots + X_n Y_n]^2$

$\qquad\qquad\qquad = E(X_1^2 Y_1^2 + X_2^2 Y_2^2 + \ldots + X_n^2 Y_n^2 +$

$\qquad\qquad\qquad\quad + 2X_1 X_2 Y_1 Y_2 + 2X_1 X_3 Y_1 Y_3 + \ldots]$

$\qquad\qquad\qquad = E\left[\sum_{i=1}^{n} X_i^2 Y_i^2 + 2 \sum_{i \neq j}^{n} X_i X_j Y_i Y_j\right]$

SECTION E

ELEMENTS OF STATISTICAL INFERENCE

Statistical inference may be of two kinds, *estimation* and *hypothesis testing.* Estimation is concerned with obtaining numerical values of the parameters from a sample. Hypothesis testing is concerned with passing a judgement on some assumption which we make (on the basis of economic theory or from any other source of information) about the true value of a population parameter. Both types of statistical inference utilise the information of a sample for drawing some conclusions about the parameters of the population, but each type of inference uses this information in different ways. In estimation we use some formulae in which we substitute the observations of the sample in order to obtain a numerical estimate of the population parameters (see below). In hypothesis testing we begin with some assumption about the true value of the population parameter, and then we use the information of the sample to compute a certain *test statistic* with which we will decide whether to accept or reject the assumption (hypothesis) which we made about the true population parameter.

E.1. ESTIMATION

The parameters of the populations of economic variables are unknown, since most of these populations include an infinite number of values. Even when the populations are finite, the number of values they include is very large and, although observable in theory, all of them are not known in practice. Estimation aims at the evaluation of the unknown basic parameters of the populations from the information of a sample. There are various methods of estimation; the most important are the following.

The method of moments, which involves the estimation of a population parameter from the corresponding sample statistic. Let us examine the estimation of the two basic population parameters, the mean μ and the variance σ_x^2, from the sample statistics $\overline{X}$ and s_x^2.

(a) The mean of the sample is an unbiased estimate of the population mean,

$$E(\overline{X}) = \mu$$

Proof

The population mean is $E(X_i) = \mu$

The sample mean is $\overline{X} = \sum_i^n \dfrac{X_i}{n} = \dfrac{1}{n}\sum_i^n X_i$

543

Taking expected values we find

$$E(\bar{X}) = \frac{1}{n} \sum_{i}^{n} E(X_i) = \frac{1}{n} \sum_{i}^{n} \mu = \frac{1}{n} n\mu = \mu$$

(b) The variance of the sample however is a biased estimate of the population variance, that is, $E(s_x^2) \neq \sigma_x^2$

Proof

The population variance is $E(X - \mu)^2 = \sigma_x^2$

The sample variance is $s_x^2 = \dfrac{\sum (X_i - \bar{X})^2}{n}$

Taking expected values we find

$$E(s_x^2) = E \left\{ \frac{1}{n} \sum (X_i - \bar{X})^2 \right\} = E \left\{ \frac{1}{n} \sum [(X_i - \mu) - (\bar{X} - \mu)]^2 \right\}$$

$$= E \left\{ \frac{1}{n} \sum (X_i - \mu)^2 + \frac{1}{n} \sum (\bar{X} - \mu)^2 - 2(\bar{X} - \mu) \frac{1}{n} \sum (X_i - \mu) \right\}$$

$$= E \left\{ \frac{1}{n} \sum (X_i - \mu)^2 + (\bar{X} - \mu)^2 - 2(\bar{X} - \mu)^2 \right\}$$

$$= \frac{1}{n} \sum E(X_i - \mu)^2 - E(\bar{X} - \mu)^2$$

But $E(X_i - \mu) = \sigma_x^2$, and $E(\bar{X} - \mu)^2 = \sigma_{\bar{x}}^2 = \dfrac{\sigma_x^2}{n}$. (For a proof of this result see below,

p. 553.) Therefore

$$E(s_x^2) = \frac{1}{n} \sum \sigma_x^2 - \frac{\sigma_x^2}{n} = \frac{n\sigma_x^2}{n} - \frac{\sigma_x^2}{n}$$

$$E(s_x^2) = \sigma_x^2 \ \frac{n-1}{n}$$

Clearly $E(s_x^2) \neq \sigma_x^2$. However, we may obtain an unbiased estimate of the population variance from the sample variance as follows. We found

$$E(s_x^2) = \frac{n-1}{n} \sigma_x^2$$

Rearranging we get $\qquad \dfrac{n}{n-1} E(s_x^2) = \sigma_x^2$

$$\frac{n}{n-1} E \left[\frac{\sum (X - \bar{X})^2}{n} \right] = \sigma_x^2$$

$$\frac{n}{n-1} \cdot \frac{1}{n} \sum E(X - \bar{X})^2 = \sigma_x^2$$

and

$$E\left[\frac{\Sigma(X - \overline{X})^2}{n - 1}\right] = \sigma_x^2$$

Thus an unbiased estimator of the population variance from the sample observations may be obtained by the formula

$$\hat{\sigma}_x^2 = \frac{\Sigma(X_i - \overline{X})^2}{n - 1}$$

Note the difference between the sample variance as a descriptive measure of the dispersion of the sample observations from their mean

$$s_x^2 = \frac{\Sigma(X_i - \overline{X})^2}{n}$$

and the unbiased estimate of the population variance obtained from the sample observations

$$\hat{\sigma}_x^2 = \frac{\Sigma(X_i - \overline{X})^2}{n - 1}$$

If the sample is small the subtraction of the unity from the denominator makes a lot of difference to the estimate $\hat{\sigma}_x^2$. However, if n is large the sample variance is a satisfactory approximation to the population variance (the bias involved in s_x^2 is unimportant for large samples, usually for $n > 30$).

The other two important methods of estimation are the *least squares method* and the *maximum likelihood method* which are explained in detail in Chapters 4 and 18. In this Appendix we will examine systematically the procedure of hypothesis testing. For this it is necessary to develop the basic concepts and theorems of sampling theory.

E.2. ELEMENTS OF SAMPLING THEORY

Sampling theory is concerned with establishing relationships between the distributions of populations and distributions of sample statistics (for example the relationship between the population distribution and the distribution of the sample mean, or the relationship between the population distribution and the distribution of the sample variance).

The basis of sampling theory is the normal distribution, which we will examine first. We will next introduce four basic distributions: (a) the Standard Normal distribution, (b) the χ^2 distribution, (c) the t distribution, (d) the F distribution. These are distributions of corresponding statistics, the z, t, χ^2 and F statistics. These statistics are formulae (expressions) which transform the units of the original population parameters into units of the sampling distribution of these statistics. The probabilities for these distributions have been computed by various writers and have been tabulated. Thus by using the appropriate transformation procedure one can find the probabilities of the original distribution of X or of the sampling distributions indirectly instead of estimating these probabilities directly from the original or sampling distributions which usually involve highly complex expressions.

THE NORMAL DISTRIBUTION

A normal distribution is a bell-shaped curve which extends indefinitely in both directions. It is symmetrical round the mean of the variable, whose values are measured on the horizontal axis (figure 7).

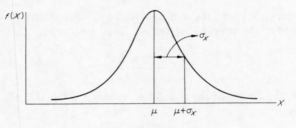

Figure 7

The vertical axis depicts the value of the probability density function $f(X_i)$.

The equation of the normal curve is

$$f(X_i) = \frac{1}{\sqrt{2\pi\sigma_x^2}} \cdot \exp\left\{-\frac{1}{2}\left(\frac{X_i - \mu}{\sigma_x}\right)^2\right\}$$

where $f(X_i)$ = the probability of X assuming the value X_i
     μ = the mean of the variable X
     σ_x = the standard deviation of X
     π = 3·14 = the ratio of the circumference of the circle to its diameter
     e = 2·71828, the base of the natural logarithms

From the above equation it is obvious that a normal curve is completely determined if we know its mean μ and standard deviation σ_x, since all the other coefficients appearing in the equation are known constants.

Any normal curve will be bell-shaped and symmetrical round its mean, but its actual form (height and width) will differ according to the value of its mean μ and its standard deviation σ_x. In figure 8 both curves are normal, they both have the same mean $\mu = 5$, but the inner curve has a smaller standard deviation than the outer curve ($\sigma_{x_1} < \sigma_{x_2}$). In figure 9 two normal curves are depicted with different means ($\mu_1 < \mu_2$) and different standard deviations ($\sigma_{x_1} < \sigma_{x_2}$). If we know the mean μ and the standard deviation σ_x, we can draw the normal curve, by assigning various values to X and computing the respective value of $f(X)$.

The areas under the normal curve are probabilities of X assuming various values. The total area under the curve is equal to unity, because it is the sum of all the probabilities of X assuming all its possible values (from $-\infty$ to $+\infty$ in the case of the normal curve).

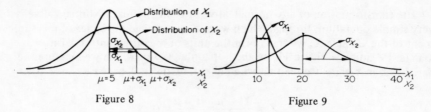

Figure 8   Figure 9

THE STANDARD NORMAL DISTRIBUTION (OR GAUSS DISTRIBUTION)

It should be obvious that the probability of X_i will be different according to the form of the curve. In figure 10 we see that the probability of X taking a value between 10 and 15 ($P\{10 < X < 15\}$) is bigger for the distribution A, as compared to the distribution B. Consequently in order to find the probability

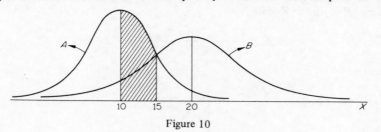

Figure 10

of X assuming a value between X_a and X_b we should compute a separate table for each normal curve, giving the relevant probabilities according to the values of the mean μ, and standard deviation, σ_x, of the variable. Fortunately this is not necessary because we can transform any normal curve into a standard form, which is called *Standard Normal Distribution,* or Gauss Distribution. The Standard Normal Distribution is the probability distribution of a variable Z which has a normal distribution with zero mean and unit variance

$$Z \sim N(0, 1)$$

The probabilities of the various values of Z have been tabulated by Gauss and are shown in Table 1 of Appendix IV.

The standardisation procedure may be outlined as follows. If a variable X has a normal distribution with mean μ and variance σ_x^2, then the statistic

$$Z_i = \frac{X_i - \mu}{\sigma_x} \sim N(0, 1)$$

where X_i = the values of the variable X, whose distribution we want to convert into units of the Standard Normal Curve.

μ = the mean of the distribution of X.

σ_x = the standard deviation of X.

The transformation of any normal curve into the Standard Normal Curve is a very simple operation, through which we actually change the scales of measurement of the variable X: we transform the units of measurement of X into standard Z units. In figure 11, on the horizontal axis of which we measure the variable X in x-units, we see that when $X = \mu$, then $Z = 0$, because

$$Z_i = \frac{X_i - \mu}{\sigma_x} = \frac{\mu - \mu}{\sigma_x} = 0$$

Similarly, if $X = \mu + \sigma_x$, then

$$Z_i = \frac{X_i - \mu}{\sigma_x} = \frac{(\mu + \sigma_x) - \mu}{\sigma_x} = 1$$

In the same way we see that when $X = \mu + 2\sigma_x$ on the X-scale, the corresponding value on the Z-scale is 2,

$$Z_i = \frac{X_i - \mu}{\sigma_x} = \frac{(\mu + 2\sigma_x) - \mu}{\sigma_x} = 2$$

and so on.

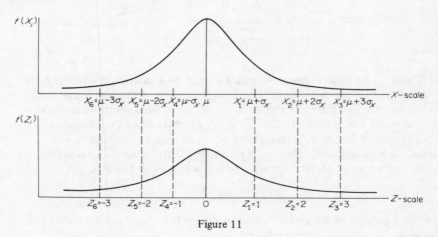

Figure 11

We will show that the probability of $X \sim N(\mu, \sigma_x^2)$ assuming any value between X_1 and X_2 is equal to the probability of Z assuming any value between Z_1 and Z_2 where

$$Z_1 = \frac{X_1 - \mu}{\sigma_x} \quad \text{and} \quad Z_2 = \frac{X_2 - \mu}{\sigma_x}$$

Proof. The general formula for the transformation of X units into Z units is

$$Z_i = \frac{X_i - \mu}{\sigma_x}$$

Now from $Z = \dfrac{X - \mu}{\sigma_x}$ $\longrightarrow$ we obtain $X = \sigma_x Z + \mu$

similarly $Z_1 = \dfrac{X_1 - \mu}{\sigma_x}$ $\longrightarrow$ yields $\quad X_1 = \sigma_x Z_1 + \mu$

and $\quad Z_2 = \dfrac{X_2 - \mu}{\sigma_x}$ $\longrightarrow$ gives $\quad X_2 = \sigma_x Z_2 + \mu$

We want to prove that

$$P(X_1 < X < X_2) = P(Z_1 < Z < Z_2)$$

Substituting X, X_1 and X_2 in this expression we find

$$P(X_1 < X < X_2) = P\{(\sigma_x Z_1 + \mu) < (\sigma_x Z + \mu) < (\sigma_x Z_2 + \mu)\}$$

Subtracting from all three terms μ we obtain

$$P(X_1 < X < X_2) = P(\sigma_x Z_1 < \sigma_x Z < \sigma_x Z_2)$$

Finally dividing all terms by σ_x we find

$$P(X_1 < X < X_2) = P(Z_1 < Z < Z_2)$$

where

$$Z_i = \frac{X_i - \mu}{\sigma_x}$$

Thus the probability that X lies between X_1 and X_2 is equal to the probability that the standard normal (Z) variable lies between

$$Z_1 = \frac{X_1 - \mu}{\sigma_x} \quad \text{and} \quad Z_2 = \frac{X_2 - \mu}{\sigma_x}$$

With the above transformation we avoid the tedious task of constructing separate tables of normal curve areas for each pair of values of μ and σ_x. We need only the table giving the areas (probabilities) under the Standard Normal Curve. The Normal Curve Table is reproduced on page 579. If in a given problem we want to determine an area under a normal curve whose mean and standard deviation are μ and σ_x, we have only to change the X's to Z's and then use the Standard Normal Table.

Examples for the use of the Standard Normal Table

Example 1. The Standard Normal Curve Table shows the area (probability) to the right of any particular value of Z. For example if $Z = 1\cdot96$ the area to the right of this value is $0\cdot025$ (figure 12). This is interpreted as follows: the probability of Z_i assuming any value greater than $1\cdot96$ is $0\cdot025$ (or $2\cdot5$ per cent). Symbolically

$$P\{Z_i > 1\cdot96\} = 0\cdot025$$

Example 2. The Standard Normal Curve Table does not contain areas (probabilities), corresponding to negative values of Z. Since the normal curve is

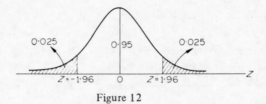

Figure 12

symmetrical, the area for negative values is the same as the area for positive values. For example the area to the left of $Z = -1\cdot96$ is $0\cdot025$.

Example 3. Suppose we want the area (probability) between $Z = 0$ and any positive value Z_i . We subtract the corresponding (to this Z_i) area from $0\cdot50$, so that the area between $Z = 0$ and any positive value Z_i is $0\cdot50$ minus the tabular value corresponding to Z_i. For instance the area $0 < Z_i < 2$ is found as follows.

(a) The area to the right of the zero mean is $0\cdot50$.
(b) The area to the right of $Z = 20$ is $0\cdot0228$
(c) Therefore the area between $Z = 0$ and $Z = 2$ is

$$0\cdot5000 - 0\cdot0228 = 0\cdot4772.$$

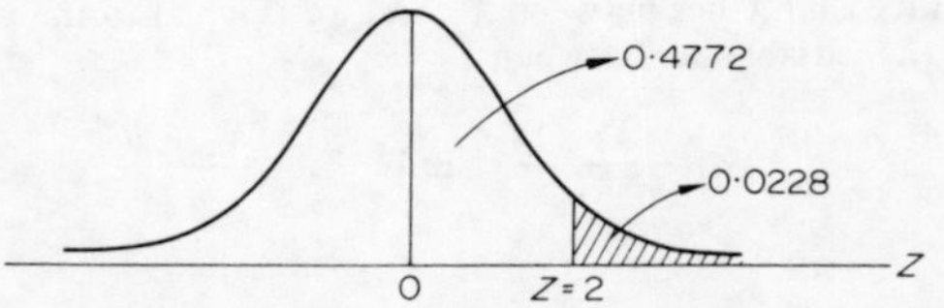

$$P\{0 < Z_i < 2\} = 0\cdot4772$$

Figure 13

This reads: the probability of Z assuming a value bigger than 0 but smaller than 2 is $47\cdot7$ per cent.

Example 4. Assume $X \sim N(\mu, \sigma_x^2) \sim N(10, 4)$. We want to find the probability that X will assume a value lying between $X_1 = 8$ and $X_2 = 12$.

We work as follows

$$Z_1 = \frac{X_1 - \mu}{\sigma_x} = \frac{8 - 10}{2} = -1$$

$$Z_2 = \frac{X_2 - \mu}{\sigma_x} = \frac{12 - 10}{2} = +1$$

We know that $P(X_1 < X < X_2) = P(Z_1 < Z < Z_2)$. From the Standard Normal Table (p. 579) we find the probabilities

$$P(Z > 1) = 0\cdot159 \quad \text{and} \quad P(Z < -1) = 0\cdot159$$

Therefore $P(-1 < Z < 1) = 1 - (0.159 + 0.159) = 0.682$
Therefore $P(8 < X < 10) = P(-1 < Z < 1) = 0.682$

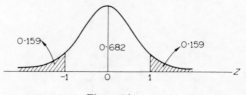

Figure 14

SOME BASIC RESULTS OF THE STANDARD NORMAL CURVE

From the Standard Normal Curve Table we see that:

the area between $Z = 0$ and $Z = 1$ is 0.3413;
the area between $Z = 0$ and $Z = 1.96$ is 0.475;
the area between $Z = 0$ and $Z = 3$ is 0.498.

These results are shown in figure 15.

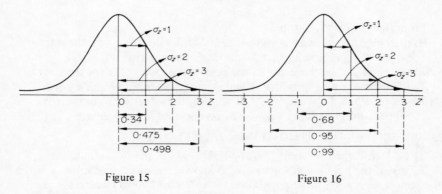

Figure 15   Figure 16

Since the Z distribution is symmetrical with unit standard deviation we can state the following very important results (shown in figure 16).
   (a) The range 0 ± 1 contains 68 per cent of the values of Z (or, the probability of Z taking a value between -1 and $+1$ is 0.68.)
   (b) The range 0 ± 1.96 contains 95 per cent of the values of Z (or, the probability of Z taking a value between -1.96 and $+1.96$ is 0.95).
   (c) The range 0 ± 3 contains 99 per cent of the values of Z (or, the probability of Z assuming a value between -3 and $+3$ is 0.99).

The above results apply to any normal distribution. This is easily understood if we look back at the transformation formula $Z_i = (X_i - \mu)/\sigma_x$ and the explanation of the change of scales of units.

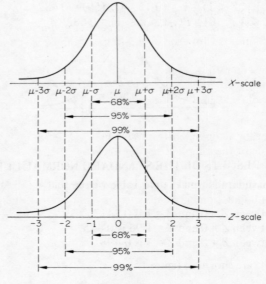

Figure 17

From figure 17 it is clear that:

(i) the range $\mu \pm \sigma_x$ contains 68 per cent of the values of X (or, there is 68 per cent probability that X will take a value between $\mu \pm \sigma_x$);

(ii) the range $\mu \pm 2\sigma_x$ contains 95 per cent of the values of X (or there is 95 per cent probability that X will assume a value between $\mu \pm 2\sigma_x$);

(iii) the range $\mu \pm 3\sigma_x$ contains 99 per cent of the values of X (or there is 99 per cent probability that X will assume a value between $\mu \pm 3\sigma_x$).

CONDITIONS FOR THE APPLICATION OF THE Z STATISTIC

The Z transformation statistic is applicable only in the following cases.

Firstly, if the population variance σ_x^2 is known, irrespective of the size of the the sample. *Secondly,* if the population variance is unknown but the sample is large ($n > 30$); because in this case the sample estimate of the unknown population variance s_x^2 is a good approximation to σ_x^2 (see page 545).

If none of these conditions is fulfilled we cannot use the Z statistic and the standard normal distribution for conducting tests of significance. However, if the parent population is normal (and the sample small, $n < 30$) we can apply another transformation procedure, based on Student's t distribution, which is examined in a subsequent section.

BASIC THEOREMS OF RANDOM SAMPLING: SAMPLING DISTRIBUTIONS

The basic tool of hypothesis testing is the sampling distribution, that is the probability distribution of the sample mean. The concept of the sampling distribution of the sample mean may be explained as follows.

We assume that we draw (hypothetically) an infinite number of samples each of size n from the population of values of the variable X, which has a normal distribution with mean μ and variance σ_x^2.

This step is known as *hypothetical repeated sampling.*

Next we assume that for each (hypothetical) sample we compute the sample mean $\bar{X}_i$.

Thus we have an infinite number of sample means, one for each sample, which form the (hypothetical) population of sample means. The distribution of the sample mean is called the *sampling distribution,* and its parameters are designated by

$\bar{X}$ = mean of the sampling distribution
$\sigma_{\bar{x}}^2$ = variance of the sampling distribution
$\sigma_{\bar{x}}$ = standard deviation of the sampling distribution.

Statisticians have established the following two important theorems which relate the true population parameters to the parameters of the sampling distribution.

Theorem 1

If we have a population of a variable X that has a normal distribution with mean μ and variance σ_x^2, and if repeated random samples, all of size n, are taken from this population and for each sample we compute the sample mean $\bar{X}_i$, the theoretical distribution of the sample means (the sampling distribution of the mean) will be normal with the same mean of the population, μ, and variance equal to σ_n^2/n.

Symbolically, if $\qquad\qquad X_i \sim N(\mu, \sigma_x^2)$

then $\qquad\qquad\qquad\qquad \bar{X}_i \sim N(\mu, \sigma_{\bar{x}}^2 = \sigma_x^2/n)$

We will not attempt to establish the normality of the sampling distribution since this requires the use of complicated expressions. Normality will be assumed here. It is important to stress that normality of the sampling distribution is crucial, because it is required for the use of the Standard Normal Curve Table to situations involving sample statistics (see below).

We will derive the mean and the variance of the sampling distribution.

(1) The mean of the sampling distribution is equal to the population mean

$$\bar{X} = E(\bar{X}_i) = \mu$$

Proof

Each of the n observations of the sample may be considered as n distinct variables, each possessing the same distribution as X, that is

$$X_1 \sim N(\mu, \sigma_x^2)$$
$$X_2 \sim N(\mu, \sigma_x^2)$$
$$\cdot \qquad \cdot$$
$$\cdot \qquad \cdot$$
$$\cdot \qquad \cdot$$
$$X_n \sim N(\mu, \sigma_x^2)$$

In other words we may think of X_1 as representing all the possible values of X that can be observed when drawing the first observation of the sample, X_2 as representing all possible values of X when drawing the second observation of the sample, and so on.

Now we want to prove that the mean of the distribution of the sample means is equal to the population mean. By the definition of the mean

$$E(\bar{X}_i) = E\ \frac{1}{n}\Sigma X_i\ = E\frac{1}{n}(X_1 + X_2 + \ldots + X_n)$$

$$= \frac{1}{n}\{\,E(X_1) + E(X_2) + \ldots + E(X_n)\}$$

$$= \frac{1}{n}(\mu + \mu + \mu + \ldots + \mu) = \frac{1}{n}\sum_i^n \mu = \frac{1}{n}(n\mu) = \mu$$

(2) The variance of the sampling distribution is equal to the variance of the population divided by the size of the samples, n

$$\sigma_{\bar{x}}^2 = \sigma_x^2/n$$

Proof

By definition

$$\text{var}(\bar{X}) = \sigma_{\bar{x}}^2 = \text{var}\left(\frac{1}{n}\Sigma X_i\right)\ = \frac{1}{n^2}\Sigma\ \text{var}\ X_i$$

$$= \frac{1}{n^2}\{\,\text{var}(X_1) + \text{var}(X_2) + \ldots + \text{var}(X_n)\}$$

$$= \frac{1}{n^2}\sum_i^n \sigma_x^2 = \frac{1}{n^2}n\sigma_x^2 = \sigma_x^2/n$$

Clearly the standard deviation of the sampling distribution decreases as n increases. This means that when n is large, a sample mean will be a more reliable estimate of μ. When n becomes large we have more information and the sample mean can be expected to be closer to the mean of the population.

We said that the normality of the sampling distribution is crucial for statistical inference. We also said that the normality of the sampling distribution is secured if the parent population (from which the samples are drawn) has a normal distribution. However, for most populations we cannot be sure about the exact form of their distribution and therefore the above theorem may not be applicable. Yet we can derive similar results for the sampling distribution of $\bar{X}_i$ even when the population, from which the samples are drawn, is not normal. This we can do by making use of a second theorem, which is known as Central Limit Theorem.

Theorem 2. Central Limit Theorem

If the size of the sample is large ($n \rightarrow \infty$) the theoretical sampling distribution of $\bar{X}_i$ will be close to a normal curve regardless of the shape of the distribution of the basic (parent) population. Symbolically if $\qquad\qquad\qquad\qquad\qquad X \backsim N(\mu, \sigma_x^2)$

then $\qquad\qquad\qquad\qquad\overline{X}_i \rightarrow N(\mu, \sigma_x^2/n) \qquad$ for $n \rightarrow \infty$

The Central Limit Theorem is more powerful than may appear at first sight, because although the approximation is derived for $n \rightarrow \infty$ a good approximation is generally obtained for quite small values of $n (n > 30)$.

The standardisation procedure with the Z statistic applies for the distribution of sample means. That is, we can calculate the probabilities of getting various values of $\overline{X}_i$ by using the Z transformation formula. For example suppose we have a sample of size 36 from a population, with $\mu = 48$ and $\sigma_x = 12$ and we want to find the probability of $\overline{X}$ lying between 49 and 50 (figure 18). We compute the corresponding Z values for $\overline{X}_1 = 49$ and $\overline{X}_2 = 50$.

$$Z_1 = \frac{49 - 48}{12/\sqrt{36}} = 0.50$$

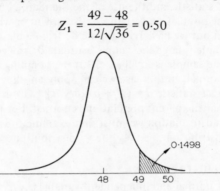

Figure 18

From the Standard Normal Curve Table (p. 659) we find

$$P(Z > 0.50) = 0.3085$$

Similarly,

$$Z_2 = \frac{50 - 48}{12/\sqrt{36}} = 1.00$$

and from the Standard Normal Curve Table we see that

$$P(Z < 1) = 0.1587$$

Thus $P\{49 < \overline{X} < 50\} = P\{0.50 < Z < 1.00\} = 0.1498$

Summary of sampling distribution theorems

Theorem I. If $X_i \sim N(\mu, \sigma_x^2)$, $\qquad$ then $Z = (X_i - \mu)/\sigma_x \sim N(0, 1)$

If $\overline{X}_i \sim N(\mu, \sigma_{\overline{x}}^2 = \sigma_x^2/n)$, then $Z = \dfrac{\overline{X}_i - \mu}{\sigma_x/\sqrt{n}} \sim N(0, 1)$

Theorem II. Central Limit Theorem. If $X_i \nsim N(\mu, \sigma_x^2)$ then

$$\overline{X}_i \rightarrow N(\mu, \sigma_x^2/n) \quad \text{and} \quad Z_i \rightarrow \frac{\overline{X}_i - \mu}{\sigma_x/\sqrt{n}} \rightarrow N(0, 1) \qquad \text{as } n \rightarrow \infty$$

(In practice the approximation of the sampling distribution to a normal shape is good for $n > 30$.)

In actual applied problems we do not have many samples; we usually work with one sample and hence we have one sample mean only. However, we consider that this sample mean has been drawn from a hypothetical repeated sampling process, which gives a sampling distribution with the above character-istics (mean μ, and standard deviation $\sigma_{\overline{x}} = \sigma_x/\sqrt{n}$).

We said that the Z statistic and the use of the Standard Normal Curve is applied only when the population variance σ_x^2 is known, or when the population variance is not known but we have its estimate $\hat{\sigma}_x^2$ from a big *sample* ($n > 30$), because when the sample is large the sample estimate $\hat{\sigma}_x^2$ is a good estimate of σ_x^2. However, when the sample is small ($n < 30$) the sampling distribution (of $\overline{X}$'s) will not be normal. In this case we can apply another transformation, based on the Student's t statistic, $t = (X_i - \mu)/\{\hat{\sigma}/\sqrt{n}\}$ (with n $-$ k *degrees of freedom*) provided that the parent population is normal. For the formal exposition of the t transformation we must first examine the meaning of another theoretical distribution, namely the χ^2 distribution.

THE CHI-SQUARE (χ^2) DISTRIBUTION

If we have a set of normal and independent variables, $X_1, X_2, \ldots X_\nu$, and we normalise them by taking their respective standard normal values

$$Z_1 = \frac{X_1 - \mu_1}{\sigma_1} \sim N(0, 1) \qquad Z_2 = \frac{X_2 - \mu_2}{\sigma_2} \sim N(0, 1) \ldots Z_\nu = \frac{X_\nu - \mu_\nu}{\sigma_\nu}$$

the sum of the squares of the normalised variables has a Chi-square (χ^2) distribution

$$\chi^2 = \Sigma Z_i^2 = \Sigma \left(\frac{X_i - \mu_i}{\sigma_{x_i}} \right)^2$$

with ν degrees of freedom. The number of degrees of freedom is equal to the number of independent variables. The chi-square distribution is skewed to the right, starts from the origin and extends to $+ \infty$ to the right tail (figure 19). As n increases the χ^2 distribution becomes more and more symmetric.

The mean and variance of a χ^2 distribution with ν degrees of freedom are

$$E(\chi^2) = n$$

$$\text{var}(\chi^2) = 2n$$

The chi-square distribution is tabulated for up to 30 degrees of freedom. The

χ^2 table is cumulative: it gives the probability of χ^2 assuming a value higher than a certain figure, given the number of degrees of freedom and the level of significance. The χ^2 table is reproduced on page 661. The table includes only values of χ^2 above which we find 5, 2·5, 1 and 0·5 per cent of the area under the curve. Symbolically we write $\chi^2_{0.025}$ for the value of χ^2 to the right of which

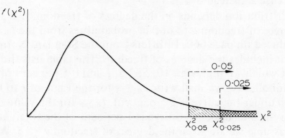

Figure 19

lies 2·5 per cent of the total area under the curve, $\chi^2_{0.05}$ for the value of χ^2 to the right of which lies 5 per cent of the total area under the curve, and so on. Thus if the degrees of freedom are 10 we see from table 3 of Appendix III that $\chi^2_{0.05} = 18\cdot3$. This means that the probability is 5 per cent that χ^2 will assume a value higher than 18·3 given that we have 10 degrees of freedom,

$$P\{18\cdot3 < \chi^2 < \infty\} = 0\cdot05 \qquad (\text{for } \nu = 10)$$

Apart from its use in forming the t statistic, the Chi-square distribution has many other applications. (See T. Yamane, *Statistics,* pp. 613–41.)

THE STUDENT'S t DISTRIBUTION

If a variable Z_i has a standard normal distribution with zero mean and unit standard deviation, $Z_i \sim N(0, 1)$, and another variable V^2 has an independent χ^2 distribution with ν degrees of freedom, then the quantity $t = Z\sqrt{\nu}/V$ has a Student's t distribution with ν degrees of freedom.

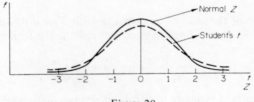

Figure 20

The characteristics of the t distribution may be summarised as follows.

(1) The t distribution is a bell-shaped distribution symmetric about zero (with zero mean). In general it has a variance greater than 1, but the variance approaches 1 as the sample size increases.

(2) The range of values of t is $-\infty < t < +\infty$.

(3) The t distribution is flatter than the normal distribution. This means that the area at the tails is larger for the t distribution than for the standard normal distribution (figure 20).

(4) As the sample size (n) becomes larger, the t distribution approaches the standard normal distribution. In fact if $n > 30$ one makes a very small error if one decides to use Z instead of t.

(5) The t distribution depends on the degrees of freedom, that is we need to know the degrees of freedom ν to obtain probabilities from the t table. The t table is reproduced on page 660. It differs from the Standard Normal Curve Table in that it includes the degrees of freedom. The table lists the values of t to the right of which we find, e.g., 10, 5, 2·5, 1 and 0·5 per cent of the area under the curve. Symbolically, we shall write $t_{0.025}$ for the value of t to the right of which the area under the curve is 2·5 per cent, $t_{0.01}$ for the value of t to the right of which the area under the curve is 1 per cent of the total, and so forth. For example assume we are given the degrees of freedom $\nu = 15$. We can find from the t table the values of t that correspond to various probabilities. (a) For $\nu = 15$, $t_{0.025} = 2·131$, and since the t distribution is symmetrical the value $-t_{0.025} = -2·131$, (b) For $\nu = 15$, $t_{0.05} = 1·753$ and $-t_{0.05} = -1·753$. These results may be stated as follows

$$P\{-2·131 < t < 2·131\} = 0·95 \qquad \text{with 15 degrees of freedom}$$

$$P\{-1·753 < t < 1·753\} = 0·90 \qquad \text{with 15 degrees of freedom}$$

The same results are shown graphically in figure 21.

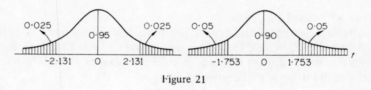

Figure 21

The transformation of the units of a normal variable X_i and its sampling distribution $\bar{X}_i$ into t units is implemented by applying the formulae

$$t = \frac{X_i - \mu}{\hat{\sigma}_x} \quad \text{and} \quad t = \frac{\bar{X}_i - \mu}{\hat{\sigma}_x/\sqrt{n}}$$

where $\hat{\sigma}_x$ is the unbiased estimate of the unknown population variance from a small sample ($n < 30$)

$$\hat{\sigma}_x^2 = \frac{\Sigma(X_i - \bar{X})^2}{n - 1}$$

The t transformation is appropriate if the parent population is normal with unknown variance and the sample with which we are working is small ($n < 30$).

This is so because, in forming the t statistic, $t = (Z\sqrt{v})/V$, the true variance σ_x^2 of the population is eliminated and we are left with a formula which includes the unbiased estimate of the population variance $\hat{\sigma}_x^2$.

Let us examine how σ_x^2 is eliminated from the t statistic.

(1) From the theory developed on p. 547 we know that

if
$$X_i \sim N(\mu, \sigma_x^2)$$

then
$$Z_i = \frac{X_i - \mu}{\sigma_x} \sim N(0, 1)$$

(2) It can be shown that if X is normally distributed with variance σ_x^2, and s_x^2 is the sample variance, $\dfrac{\Sigma(X_i - \bar{X})^2}{n}$, based on a random sample of size n, then the ratio $\dfrac{ns_x^2}{\sigma_x^2}$ has a χ^2 distribution with $n - 1$ degrees of freedom. (See P. G. Hoel, *Introduction to Mathematical Statistics*, Wiley, 1954, pp. 218–19.)

Let
$$V^2 = \frac{ns_x^2}{\sigma_x^2} = \sum_{i=1}^{n} \left(\frac{X_i - \bar{X}}{\sigma_x} \right)^2 \sim \chi^2 \quad \text{with } v = n - 1 \text{ degrees of freedom}$$

(3) It can be shown that Z_i and V^2 have independent distributions. (See P. G. Hoel, op. cit.) Hence we can substitute for Z_i and V in the expression of the t statistic and obtain

$$t = \frac{Z\sqrt{v}}{V} = \frac{Z}{\sqrt{V^2/v}}$$

$$= \frac{(X_i - \mu)/\sigma_x}{\sqrt{\dfrac{1}{n-1}\Sigma\left(\dfrac{X_i - \bar{X}}{\sigma_x}\right)^2}} = \frac{X_i - \mu}{\sqrt{\dfrac{\Sigma(X_i - \bar{X})^2}{n-1}}}$$

But the expression in the denominator is the unbiased estimate of the population variance $\hat{\sigma}_x^2$.

Hence
$$t = \frac{X_i - \mu}{\hat{\sigma}_x}$$

Thus the unknown population variance σ_x^2 has been eliminated and we are left with the sample estimate $\hat{\sigma}_x^2$ which can be computed from the observations of the sample with the formula

$$\hat{\sigma}_x^2 = \frac{\Sigma(X - \bar{X})^2}{n - 1} \qquad \text{(see page 545)}$$

In summary

(1) If
$$X \sim N(\mu, \sigma_x^2)$$
$$\bar{X} \sim N(\mu, \sigma_x^2/n)$$

(2) If σ_x^2 is known, or if it is unknown but $n > 30$, then the appropriate transformation is

$$Z_i = \frac{X_i - \mu}{\sigma_x} \qquad \text{for } X_i\text{'s}$$

and

$$Z_i = \frac{\overline{X}_i - \mu}{\sigma_x/\sqrt{n}} \qquad \text{for } \overline{X}_i\text{'s}$$

(3) If σ_x^2 is unknown and the sample is small ($n < 30$) the appropriate transformation is

$$t = \frac{X_i - \mu}{\hat{\sigma}_x} \qquad \text{for } X_i\text{'s}$$

and

$$t = \frac{\overline{X}_i - \mu}{\hat{\sigma}_x/\sqrt{n}} \qquad \text{for } \overline{X}_i\text{'s}$$

In this case the parent population must be normal.

THE F DISTRIBUTION

If two variables have *independent* chi-square distributions, χ_1^2 and χ_2^2, with ν_1 and ν_2 degrees of freedom respectively, the statistic

$$F = \frac{\chi_1^2/\nu_1}{\chi_2^2/\nu_2}$$

has an F distribution with ν_1 and ν_2 degrees of freedom.

The F statistic usually involves the ratio of two independent estimates of variances, and the F distribution is used to test the equality of these estimates. For this reason the F statistic is often called the *variance ratio*

$$F = \frac{\hat{\sigma}_1^2}{\hat{\sigma}_2^2} = \text{variance ratio}$$

with ν_1 and ν_2 degrees of freedom.

The F distribution has a skewed shape (figure 22). The value of F is always positive. The range of values of F is $0 \leqslant F \leqslant + \infty$. The values of the F distribution

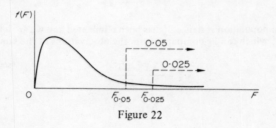

Figure 22

with various degrees of freedom (and various levels of significance) have been tabulated by Dr Snedecor and are reproduced on pp. 663–4. The degrees of freedom ν_1' and ν_2, depend on the way in which we obtain the estimates of the two variances appearing in the numerator and the denominator of the F ratio. The F table gives the probabilities of the right-hand tail. Given that the F

distribution is not symmetrical, the values of the left-hand tail cannot be directly deduced from the regular F table. To avoid complicated calculations statisticians have adopted the following convention. For a two-tailed test the F ratio is always evaluated with the larger estimate of the variance in the numerator and the smaller estimate in the denominator. (See Bugg, Henderson *et al., Statistical Methods in the Social Sciences*, North-Holland, Amsterdam, 1968, p. 282.) With this convention the F ratio is always greater than unity. If the two variance estimates are close to each other their ratio will approach the value of one. The greater the difference between the two variances the greater the value of the F ratio. Thus, in general, high values of F suggest that the difference between the two estimates is significant. However, when conducting a *two-tail test* we must halve the value of our level of significance in looking at the regular F table. For example if we choose the 5 per cent level of significance for a two-tail test we take the value $F_{0.025}$ (with the appropriate degrees of freedom) as our critical value of F.

There is a formal relationship between the t and the F statistics as applied in regression analysis, which is explained in Chapter 8.

E.3. HYPOTHESIS TESTING

The procedure for testing a hypothesis concerning the value of population parameters includes the following steps.
  (1) Formulate the null and alternative hypotheses.
  (2) Choose the level of significance of the test.
  (3) Choose the location of the critical region.
  (4) Choose the appropriate test statistic (for example Z, t, χ^2, F) and find from the relevant tables the critical value(s) of the chosen statistic, that is the value(s) that defines the boundary of the critical region.
  (5) Compute, from the sample observations, the observed value (or sample value, or empirical value) of the chosen statistic, using the relevant formula (for example $Z^* = (X - \mu)/\sigma_x$, or $t^* = (X - \mu)/\hat{\sigma}_x$).
  (6) Compare the sample value of the chosen statistic with the theoretical (tabular) value(s) that define the critical region. If the observed value of the statistic falls in the critical region we reject the null hypothesis. Otherwise we accept the null hypothesis.

We will examine the above stages of hypothesis testing in some detail.

Step 1. Formulate the Null Hypothesis (H_0) and the Alternative Hypothesis (H_1)

We said that the aim of statistical inference is to draw conclusions about the population parameters from the sample statistics. In econometrics, using a set of observations, we obtain estimates of the parameters of economic relationships. We next wish to test their statistical reliability, that is to apply some rule which will enable us to decide whether to accept our estimate or to reject it. To make such a decision the best way is to compare the estimate with the true value of the population parameter. However, the population parameter is unknown. Under these circumstances how are we going to make the decision whether to accept or reject the sample estimate given that we do not have the appropriate yardstick (that is the true population parameter) for making the comparison required? To bypass this difficulty we make some assumption about the value of the true population parameter and use our sample estimate in order to decide whether our assumption is acceptable or not. *A hypothesis is an assumption which we make about a population parameter.* The hypothesis which we wish to test (on the basis of the evidence of our sample estimate) is called the *null hypothesis*, because it implies that there is no difference between the true parameter and the hypothesised value, or the difference between the true value and the hypothesised value is nil. Symbolically $H_0: \mu = \mu_0$.

In most applications it is difficult to hypothesise any special value for the true population parameter. What is worse, we may find that a very large number of hypothetical values are compatible with our sample estimate and in this case we run into the problem of choosing among these possible hypotheses. To avoid these problems it has become customary in econometrics to make the hypothesis that the true population parameter is equal to zero. That is the null hypothesis typically takes the form

$$H_0: \mu = 0$$

or, in the case of parameters of economic relationships,

$$H_0: b_i = 0$$

The *alternative hypothesis* (H_1) is an alternative assumption about the population parameter, a counter proposition to the null hypothesis. It is conventionally denoted by H_1 and may take one of the following forms

(a) $H_1: \mu \neq \mu_0$ (or $H_1: b_i \neq 0$)

(b) $H_1: \mu > \mu_0$ (or $H_1: b_i > 0$)

(c) $H_1: \mu < \mu_0$ (or $H_1: b_i < 0$)

The form in which we express the alternative hypothesis is important in defining the location of the rejection region or critical region of the test. For the purpose of conducting the test of a certain hypothesis concerning the population parameter we divide the whole set of the values of the population into two regions. The *acceptance region* includes the values of X which have a high probability of being observed, and the *rejection region* or *critical region* includes the values of the population which are highly unlikely, that is they have a low probability of being observed. Conventionally in econometrics we consider that highly unlikely values of a variable are those values whose total probability is less than 5 per cent or 1 per cent, that is those values which define an area of the probability distribution equal to 0·05 or 0·01. These probabilities are called *level of significance of the test*.

Step. 2. Choose the Level of Significance of the Test

In making a decision one can never be 100 per cent sure that one will make the right decision. In making any decision we are liable to commit one of the following types of error.

Type I Error: We reject the null hypothesis, when it is actually true.

Type II Error: We accept the null hypothesis, when it is actually false.

It is obvious that we want this probability (of 'being wrong') to be small. Thus we assign a low value to this probability, and we call it the *level of significance* of our test. Choosing a certain level of significance involves our specifying the probability of committing a Type I error. Usually we determine (specify) a value of the level of significance equal to 5 per cent (and more rarely 1 per cent). When we choose the 5 per cent level of significance, we tolerate to make the wrong decision (of rejecting the null hypothesis when it is actually true) five times in a hundred.

Step 3. Choose the Location of the Critical Region

We said that the critical region includes the values of the variable which have a low probability of being observed, that is a (total) probability of 5 per cent or 1 per cent. In other words the critical region includes the values which correspond to the level of significance. The critical region may be chosen either at the right end (right tail) of the distribution of the variable, or at the left tail, or half at each end of the distribution (see figure 23). In the first and second cases, we say that we conduct a *one-tail test*, in the third case we say that we conduct a *two-tail test*.

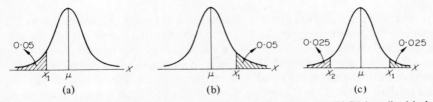

Figure 23. (a) Left-tail critical region at 5 per cent level of significance; (b) Right-tail critical regions at 5 per cent level of significance; (c) Two-tail critical region at 5 per cent level of significance.

The decision of whether to choose a one-tail or a two-tail critical region depends on the form in which the alternative hypothesis is expressed. If the alternative hypothesis is of the form

$$H_1 : \mu \neq \mu_0 \qquad (\text{or } H_1 : b_i \neq b_i^*)$$

we choose a two-tail critical region. If the alternative hypothesis is of the form

$$H_1 : \mu > \mu_0 \qquad (\text{or } H_1 : b_i > b_i^*)$$

we choose a right-tail critical region. Finally if the alternative hypothesis is of the form

$$H_1 : \mu < \mu_0 \qquad (\text{or } H_1 : b_i < b_i')$$

we choose the left tail of the distribution as the critical region of our test.[1] The following rule of thumb may summarise the above statements regarding the choice of the location of the critical region. Choose the location of the critical region on the basis of the direction at which the inequality sign points:

if $>$, choose the right tail as the critical region;

if $<$, choose the left tail as the critical region;

if $\neq$, choose a two-tail critical region.

In econometrics it has become customary to choose a two-tail critical region, although a one-tail test would be preferable on *a priori* economic considerations (see pp. 85 and 90).

Step 4. Choose the Appropriate Test Statistic

In econometrics the most common test statistics are the Z, t, and F statistics. The choice among them depends on the type of test which we want to conduct, on the size of the sample and on the information which we have about the population variance.

(a) If we know the variance of the parent population we may apply the Z transformation statistic, irrespective of the normality of the population and irrespective of the sample size.

(b) If the variance of the parent population is unknown, but the size of the sample is large ($n > 30$), we may still apply the Z statistic since the estimate of the population variance from a large sample is a satisfactory estimate of the true σ^2.

(c) If the variance of the parent population is unknown and our sample is small ($n < 30$) we may apply the t statistic provided that the parent population is normal. For the application of the t statistic normality is crucial.

(d) In econometric research the population variance (σ_u^2) is one of the unknowns of the estimated model. Furthermore, the samples usually available are small ($n < 30$). Thus for testing the reliability of the estimates, $\hat{b}$'s, we may apply the t statistic, or the F statistic. It has been established that

$$t^2 = F$$

(see Chapter 8).

(e) The F statistic is used for conducting various tests of significance in econometric applications. The most important of these tests have been explained in Chapter 8.

·It should be clear that the choice of the test statistic aims at the transformation of the units of the variable into units of the chosen statistic, through the corresponding transformation formula. For example

$$t = \frac{X_i - \mu}{\hat{\sigma}_x} \quad \text{or} \quad Z = \frac{X_i - \mu}{\sigma_x}$$

[1] The above results concerning the choice of the location of the critical region are based on the examination of the power functions of tests. See T. Yamane, *Statistics*, pp. 196–226.

The transformation enables us to find the probability of the variable assuming any value within a certain range indirectly by using the results (established in section E.2)

$$P\{X_1 < X < X_2\} = P\{Z_1 < Z < Z_2\}$$

where

$$Z_i = \frac{X_i - \mu}{\sigma_x}$$

or

$$P\{X_1 < X < X_2\} = P\{t_1 < t < t_2\}$$

where

$$t_i = \frac{X_i - \mu}{\hat{\sigma}_x}$$

Having chosen the level of significance, the location of the critical region, and the test statistic, we may use the relevant table of the probability of this statisic and find its critical values, that is the values which define the boundaries of the critical region.

Example. Assume that we have estimated the following consumption function of a certain country for the period 1950−70

$$\hat{C} = 165\cdot3 + 0\cdot74\,Y$$

$$(43\cdot2)\quad(0\cdot20)$$

where the numbers in brackets are the standard errors of the $\hat{b}$'s. We wish to test the statistical significance of the estimated marginal propensity to consume $\hat{b}_1 = 0\cdot74$.

The null and alternative hypotheses are

$$H_0 : b_1 = 0$$

$$H_1 : b_1 \neq 0.$$

We choose the 5 per cent level of significance for our test, that is we specify that 5 times out of hundred we may make the wrong decision (of rejecting H_0 when it is actually true).

Since the alternative hypothesis is expressed in the customary form of $b_i \neq 0$, we choose a two-tail critical region. Each tail will correspond to half the chosen level of significance, that is, the area of each tail is $0\cdot025$ (or $2\cdot5$ per cent).

Given that the population variance (σ_u^2) is unknown and our sample is small ($n = 21 < 30$) we will apply the t statistic. From the t table we find the critical values of t, that is, the values which define the boundaries of the critical region. In our example the critical values of t (tabular values) will be those that cut off $2\cdot5$ per cent of the area of the t distribution. From the t table we find:

$$-t_{0\cdot025} = -2\cdot093 \quad \text{and} \quad +t_{0\cdot025} = +2\cdot093$$

(with $n - 2 = 19$ degrees of freedom). The critical region of our example is shown in figure 24.

Step 5. Compute the Sample Value of the Chosen Test Statistic

Using the sample information we compute the *sample value (or observed value)* of the chosen test statistic, which we denote with an asterisk (for example

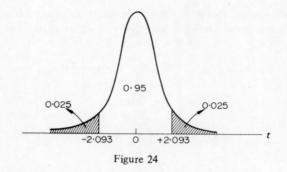

Figure 24

t^*, F^*) to distinguish it from the *critical value* or *theoretical value* or *tabular value* of the statistic which is defined in step 4.

In our example the observed (sample) value of the chosen t statistic is

$$t^* = \frac{\hat{b}_1 - 0}{s_{(\hat{b}_1)}} = \frac{0.74}{0.20} = 3.7$$

Step 6. Compare the Sample Value of the Chosen Statistic with its Critical Value

The final step of our test is to compare the observed value of the chosen statistic (as estimated in step 5) with the critical (tabular) value of this statistic, as defined in step 4.

If the observed value (t^*, F^*) falls in the critical region (for example $t^* < -t_{0.025}$ or $t^* > +t_{0.025}$) we reject the null hypothesis and we infer that $b_i \neq 0$, that is we accept the alternative hypothesis. This of course does not imply that our estimate $\hat{b}_i$ is the correct value of the population parameter b_i. Rejection of the null hypothesis suggests merely that the true b_i has a value different from zero (see below section E.4).

If the observed value (t^*, F^*) falls outside the critical region (for example $-t_{0.025} < t^* < t_{0.025}$) we accept the null hypothesis, that is, we infer that the true population parameter b_i is zero.

In our example $t^* = 3.7$. Clearly $t^* > t_{0.025}$ and hence we reject the null hypothesis: the true population b_i has a value different from zero.

E.4. CONFIDENCE INTERVALS – INTERVAL ESTIMATION

We have concluded in the preceding paragraph that when we reject the null hypothesis we actually accept that our estimate is significantly different from zero, that is, the estimate of the parameter is obtained from a sample drawn from a population, whose true parameter is different from zero. Rejection of the null hypothesis, however, does not mean that our sample estimate is the correct estimate of the true parameter; it simply implies that the true parameter has some value different from zero. The null hypothesis test does not by itself determine how close to the true parameter our estimate is. In order to establish, as a further result, how close to the true parameter our estimate lies, we should construct *confidence intervals* of the true parameter, that is find the range of values, round the estimate, within which (with a given probability) the true value of the population parameter will fall. This is known as *interval estimation*.

In this section we will examine how we construct confidence intervals of the true parameters, using our sample estimate and its standard deviation. Suppose that from a random sample we obtain $\overline{X} = 4$. We wish to establish how close to the population mean our estimate is. The population mean is unknown, but we assume that we know its standard deviation σ_x, or that we have a large sample from which we can get a satisfactory estimate of the standard deviation.

We know from the Central Limit Theorem that

$$Z_i = \frac{\overline{X}_i - \mu}{\sigma_{\overline{x}}} \rightarrow N(0, 1) \qquad \text{as } n \rightarrow \infty$$

where
$$\sigma_{\overline{x}} = \frac{\sigma_x}{\sqrt{n}}$$

Furthermore, from the Z table we find that the range $0 \pm 1 \cdot 96$ contains 95 per cent of the values of Z, or the probability of Z taking a value between $-1 \cdot 96$ and $1 \cdot 96$ is 95 per cent. This may be written

$$P\{-1 \cdot 96 < Z < 1 \cdot 96\} = 0 \cdot 95$$

Substituting $Z = (\overline{X}_i - \mu)/\sigma_{\overline{x}}$ we obtain

$$P\left\{-1 \cdot 96 < \frac{\overline{X} - \mu}{\sigma_{\overline{x}}} < 1 \cdot 96\right\} = 0 \cdot 95$$

Subtracting $\overline{X}$ from all terms of the inequality we find

$$P\{\overline{X} - 1 \cdot 96(\sigma_{\overline{x}}) < \mu < X + 1 \cdot 96(\sigma_{\overline{x}})\} = 0 \cdot 95$$

This result reads: the probability that the true parameter μ will be in the interval $\overline{X} \pm 1 \cdot 96(\sigma_{\overline{x}})$ is $0 \cdot 95$.

Thus when we construct the interval $\overline{X} \pm 1 \cdot 96(\sigma_{\overline{x}})$ we can be sure with a probability of 95 per cent that this interval will include the true value of the population parameter μ. This is the reason why the interval

$$\overline{X} \pm 1 \cdot 96(\sigma_{\overline{x}})$$

is called the 95 per cent confidence interval of the true population parameter.

Example. A university lecturer wishes to estimate the average marks gained by the students of his university which form a finite population. A random sample of size $n = 36$ is selected and the sample mean is found to be $\overline{X} = 56$. The standard deviation of the marks of all the students (population) is known to be $\sigma_x = 4$. Therefore the sample standard deviation will be

$$\sigma_{\overline{x}} = \sigma_x/\sqrt{n} = 4/6 \approx 0 \cdot 67$$

The 95 per cent confidence interval will be

$$56 - (1 \cdot 96)(0 \cdot 67) < \mu < 56 + (1 \cdot 96)(0 \cdot 67)$$

Thus the true (population) average marks scored by the students of the university in question will most probably (with a probability of 95 per cent) lie between 54·69 and 57·31.

E.5. SOME NOTES ON THE MEANING OF 'DEGREES OF FREEDOM'

The concept of "degrees of freedom" is very important in performing tests of the reliability of estimates obtained from a sample. We will attempt to explain it with various illustrations.

Let us assume that we want to select various values in order to form a set of such values. The set may be a sample of values on a variable, such as

$$X_1, X_2, \ldots, X_n$$

or it may be a set of deviations of the n values of a variable from their mean:

$$(X_1 - \overline{X}), (X_2 - \overline{X}), \ldots, (X_{n-1} - \overline{X}), (X_n - \overline{X})$$

In order to form a particular set of values we select its various item-components. In some cases we are free to select all the n items of the set, while in others our freedom is limited by the knowledge of some of the values of the set. For example in choosing the n values of a random variable for a sample, we are free to choose all these values. Knowlege of any of the values does not tell us anything about the other values of the sample. Any value of the variable X is chosen withour reference to the values of the other members of the sample. The n items consist of free choices: we have n degrees of freedom in our choice.

Assume next that we want to form the set of n deviations of the n values of X from their mean $\overline{X}$. We know the n values of X and therefore we know their mean $\overline{X}$ which is computed by the formula

$$\frac{\Sigma X_i}{n} = \overline{X}.$$

We said that the sum of the deviations from the mean is always equal to zero: $\Sigma(X_i - \overline{X}) = 0$. Hence if we know $n - 1$ of the deviations, the nth is automatically determined. For example if we have 4 observations and we know that the three deviations are 5,   3, 2, then the 4th deviation from the mean must be equal to −4. In any set of n deviations from a sample mean, all but one can be chosen arbitrarily: the nth must assume such a value as to bring the sum to zero. Thus in this case we can choose only $n - 1$ items of our set: we have $n - 1$ degrees of freedom. We have lost one degree of freedom in computing $\overline{X}$ from the sample.

In general, we may say that degrees of freedom is the number of elements (of a set) that can be chosen freely, or the number of variables that can vary freely. (See D. B. Suits, *Statistics,* Rand-McNally, 1963, p. 62–3.)

SECTION F

BASIC LAWS OF PROBABILITY

In many cases we wish to calculate the probability of two (or more) events occurring at the same time. Any two events may be (a) dependent, (b) independent, (c) mutually exclusive and (d) mutually not exclusive.

Independent events. Two events are said to be independent if the occurrence of one event is not connected in any way with the occurrence of the other. The occurrence of event A does not depend on whether B has occurred or not. For example:

- (a) Casting a die twice: the result of the first throwing is independent of the result of the second throwing.
- (b) The sex of the children of a family: the sex of the second child is independent of the sex of the first child.
- (c) The results of a horse-race and a boxing match are two independent events.
- (d) Tossing a coin twice: The result of the second toss is independent of the result of the first toss.

Mutually exclusive events. Two events are mutually exclusive if the occurrence of A precludes the occurrence of B. In other words the two events cannot occur together. For example:

- (a) The results of a fooball match between Wales and Scotland. There can be either a win or a loss by the Welsh team or an equal result.
- (b) The results of tossing a coin once. Heads and tails are the two possible results, which are obviously mutually exclusive.
- (c) The results of drawing a card from a pack. When we draw a card from a pack we may have 52 mutually exclusive events: the 'result' of the card precludes the appearance of any other card.
- (d) The result of an examination. One either passes or fails. Thus the 'pass' and 'fail' are two mutually exclusive events.

Dependent Events. Two events are said to be dependent if the occurrence of the one is connected in some way with the occurrence of the other. For example:

- (a) The results of drawing two cards from a pack, one at a time, without replacement. The result of the second card depends on the first, because when the first card is drawn there are only 51 cards left from which we have to draw the second card.

569

(b) Drawing two red balls from a bag which contains 10 red and 10 white balls. If the first ball drawn is red and is not replaced, the probability of the second ball drawn is affected, since now there are only 19 balls in the bag, and of them only 9 are red.

Not mutually exclusive events. Two events are said to be not mutually exclusive when they may occur at the same time: The occurrence of the one does not preclude the occurrence of the other. For example:

(a) Drawing a card from a pack. What is the probability of the card being either a spade or a king? These two results are not mutually exclusive since a king can be the king of spades.

(b) Electing the mayor of a town. What is the probability of the mayor being either a female or a catholic? These two events are not mutually exclusive, since a female can be a catholic.

There are four basic laws of probability.

1. *Addition rule* (Mutually exclusive events)

If two events A and B are mutually exclusive, the probability of either A or B occurring is the sum of their respective probabilities. Symbolically we may write this law as follows:

$$P(A \text{ or } B) = P(A) + P(B)$$

For example assume that we throw a die and we want to find the probability of either a two (event A) or a six (event B) appearing. These events are mutually exclusive because if the die shows up two, the occurrence of a six is precluded. Therefore the probability of either A or B is the sum of the individual probabilities:

$$P(A) = \tfrac{1}{6}$$
$$P(B) = \tfrac{1}{6}$$
$$P(A \text{ or } B) = P(A) + P(B) = \tfrac{1}{6} + \tfrac{1}{6} = \tfrac{2}{6}$$

The same rule can be extended to the occurrence of three or more mutually exclusive events.

2. *Multiplication rule* (Independent events)

If two events are independent the probability of both A and B occurring simultaneously is the product of their individual probabilities. Symbolically we have

$$P(A \text{ and } B) = P(A) \cdot P(B)$$

For example let A be the winning of a cricket match by an English team playing against an Australian team, and B the winning by a black horse in a horse-race. What is the probability of both these results occurring?

The two events are obviously independent. Assume that the English and Australian teams are equally good, so that the probability of England winning is $\frac{1}{2}$ (or 50 per cent). Furthermore assume that in the horse-race there are 5 horses running, all of equally good shape, so that the probability of the black horse winning is $\frac{1}{5}$. Thus

$$P(A) = \frac{1}{2}$$

$$P(B) = \frac{1}{5}$$

and $P(A \text{ and } B) = P(A) \cdot P(B) = \frac{1}{2} \times \frac{1}{5} = \frac{1}{10}$

The same rule may be extended to the occurrence of three or more independent events.

3. *Multiplication rule* (Dependent events)

If two events are dependent on each other (jointly dependent) the probability of both occurring (joint probability) is the probability of one event multiplied by the probability of the other, given that the first event has occurred. Symbolically we have

$$P(A \text{ and } B) = P(A) \cdot P(B/A)$$

The term $P(B/A)$ designates the *conditional probability* of B, that is, the probability of B occurring, given that A has already occurred.

For example suppose that we draw two cards from a pack of 52 cards. What is the probability of both cards being clubs? For the first card to be a club the probability is

$$P(A) = \frac{13}{52}$$

given that there are 13 clubs in a pack. Suppose the first card drawn is actually a club and that we do not return the card to the pack. Under these circumstances the probability of the second card being a club depends on the first event in two ways: (a) since the first card is a club, there remain only 12 cards in the pack; (b) since the first card is not returned to the pack there are only 51 cards left from which to draw the second card. Thus

$$P(B/A) = \frac{12}{51}$$

Therefore the joint probability of A and B occurring simultaneously is

$$P(A \text{ and } B) = P(A) \cdot P(B/A) = \frac{13}{52} \cdot \frac{12}{51}$$

The above rule may be extended to the joint occurrence of more than two dependent events.

4. *Addition rule* (Events not mutually exclusive)

If two events are not mutually exclusive, the occurrence of either A or B means the occurrence of either A or B or both A and B. The probability of either A or B is given by the formula:

$$P(A \text{ or } B) = P(A) + P(B) - P(A \text{ and } B).$$

For example suppose a composer of pop-songs decides to choose a singer from a group of singers consisting of males and females, some of them foreigners. Their names are put in a hat and the composer draws one of them at random. He wishes the singer to be either a female or a foreigner (of either sex) so as to make the performance more exciting. What is the probability that his wish will be fulfilled and that he will hit on the name of a female (event A) or a foreigner (event B)? These two events are not mutually exclusive since a female singer may also be a foreigner. Assume that the total group includes ten singers, five male and five female, two male foreigners and two female foreigners.

Event A is the selection of a female singer

Therefore $$P(A) = \frac{5}{10}$$

Event B is the selection of a foreign singer irrespective of sex

Therefore $$P(B) = \frac{4}{10}$$

However, A and B may occur simultaneously, hence

$$P(A \text{ and } B) = P(A) \cdot P(B) = \frac{5}{10} \cdot \frac{4}{10} = \frac{20}{100} = \frac{2}{10}$$

(A and B being independent)

Therefore $P(A \text{ or } B) = P(A) + P(B) - P(A \text{ and } B)$

$$= \frac{5}{10} + \frac{4}{10} - \frac{2}{10} = \frac{7}{10}$$

The rule can be extended to more than two not mutually exclusive events.

APPENDIX II

Determinants and the Solution of Systems of Equations

APPENDIX II

Determinants and the Solution of Systems of Equations

Although the notation of determinants looks somewhat complex, their use is very simple. The solution of the simplest simultaneous equations is simplified still further by the use of determinants.

In this Appendix we will explain the meaning of determinants and their use in the solution of systems of equations. No proofs will be given.

1. DEFINITION

Suppose that we have a system with two equations in two unknowns, y and x:

$$a_1(x) + b_1(y) = k_1 \tag{1}$$
$$a_2(x) + b_2(y) = k_2 \tag{2}$$

where a_1, b_1, a_2, b_2, k_1 and k_2 are known constants.

The simplest way to arrive at the solution of this system is to multiply the first equation by b_2 and the second by b_1; subtract the resulting expressions, thus eliminating the terms involving y; solve for x; substitute back into one of the original equations and find the value of y. This procedure yields

$$x = \frac{k_1 b_2 - k_2 b_1}{a_1 b_2 - a_2 b_1} \quad \text{and} \quad y = \frac{k_2 a_1 - k_1 a_2}{a_1 b_2 - a_2 b_1}$$

We observe that the denominator is the same in both expressions and is computed from products of the coefficients of x and y. We may write the coefficients in an array

$$\begin{vmatrix} a_1 & b_1 \\ a_2 & b_2 \end{vmatrix}$$

from which it is obvious that the denominator can be obtained by taking the product indicated by the downward sloping arrow ($a_1 b_2$) and then subtracting the product indicated by the upward sloping arrow ($a_2 b_1$). Similarly we may write the numerators as arrays of coefficients

$$\begin{vmatrix} k_1 & b_1 \\ k_2 & b_2 \end{vmatrix} = k_1 b_2 - k_2 b_1 \quad \text{and} \quad \begin{vmatrix} a_1 & k_1 \\ a_2 & k_2 \end{vmatrix} = a_1 k_2 - a_2 k_1$$

Thus the solution of the above simple system may be written in the form

$$x = \frac{\begin{vmatrix} k_1 & b_1 \\ k_2 & b_2 \end{vmatrix}}{\begin{vmatrix} a_1 & b_1 \\ a_2 & b_2 \end{vmatrix}} \quad \text{and} \quad y = \frac{\begin{vmatrix} a_1 & k_1 \\ a_2 & k_2 \end{vmatrix}}{\begin{vmatrix} a_1 & b_1 \\ a_2 & b_2 \end{vmatrix}}$$

We refer to arrays of this kind as *determinants,* because they help in the *determination of the solution of systems.*

In general a *determinant* is a square array of numbers used in the determination of the solution of a system of simultaneous equations.

The *order* of a determinant is the number of its rows (or its columns, since the array is square). For example the determinants in the above illustration are of second order (each has two rows and two columns). The determinant

$$\begin{vmatrix} a_1 & b_1 & c_1 \\ a_2 & b_2 & c_2 \\ a_3 & b_3 & c_3 \end{vmatrix}$$

is of order 3, and so on.

2. EXPANSION OF A DETERMINANT

Expansion of a determinant is the computation of its value. Before explaining the process of the evaluation of a determinant we will give some essential definitions.

First let us introduce a more general notation for the elements of a determinant

$$\begin{vmatrix} a_{11} & a_{12} & a_{13} \dots a_{1n} \\ a_{21} & a_{22} & a_{23} \dots a_{2n} \\ \cdot & \cdot & \cdot & \cdot \\ \cdot & \cdot & \cdot & \cdot \\ \cdot & \cdot & \cdot & \cdot \\ a_{n1} & a_{n2} & a_{n3} \dots a_{nn} \end{vmatrix}$$

This is a determinant of order n. In this notation each element is characterised by two subscripts; the first indicates the row in which the element appears; the second indicates the column in which the element appears. Thus a_{21} is the element in the second row and first column; in general, a_{ij} is the element in the ith row and the jth column of the determinant.

The *principal diagonal* of a determinant consists of the elements in the determinant which lie in a straight line from the upper left-hand corner to the lower right-hand corner.

The *minor of an element* belonging to a determinant of order n is the determinant of order $n - 1$ obtained by deleting the row and column which contain the particular element. For example in the fourth order determinant

$$\begin{vmatrix} a_{11} & a_{12} & a_{13} & a_{14} \\ a_{21} & a_{22} & a_{23} & a_{24} \\ a_{31} & a_{32} & a_{33} & a_{34} \\ a_{41} & a_{42} & a_{43} & a_{44} \end{vmatrix}$$

the minor of the element a_{43} is obtained by removing the row and column containing this element

$$\text{minor of } a_{43} = \begin{vmatrix} a_{11} & a_{12} & a_{14} \\ a_{21} & a_{22} & a_{24} \\ a_{31} & a_{32} & a_{34} \end{vmatrix}$$

Clearly the minor is of a lower order than the order of the determinant. Traditionally the minor of an element is denoted by a capital letter with the same subscripts as the given element. For example the minor of a_{43} is denoted by A_{43}.

The *cofactor of an element* belonging to a determinant is its minor preceded by a + or − sign according as the sum of the subscripts of the element is even or odd.

For example the cofactor of a_{43} is $-A_{43}$ since $(4 + 3) = 7$, an odd number.

In general the cofactor of the a_{ij} element may be denoted as

$$(-1)^{i+j} A_{ij}$$

where $(-1)^{i+j}$ is positive when the sum $i + j$ is even
$(-1)^{i+j}$ is negative when the sum $i + j$ is odd.

The expansion (value) of a determinant may be obtained by using the cofactors (presigned minors) of its elements, as follows:

(1) Choose any row (or column). To avoid confusion the student is advised to choose always the first row.
(2) Multiply each element in the chosen row (or column) by its cofactor.
(3) Add algebraically the products obtained in the previous stage.

For example let us expand the determinant

$$\begin{vmatrix} 3 & 4 & 7 \\ 2 & 1 & 3 \\ 7 & 2 & 1 \end{vmatrix} \quad \text{or} \quad \begin{vmatrix} a_{11} & a_{12} & a_{13} \\ a_{21} & a_{22} & a_{23} \\ a_{31} & a_{32} & a_{33} \end{vmatrix}$$

The cofactors of the elements of the first row are

(1) $(-1)^{1+1} A_{11} = + \begin{vmatrix} 1 & 3 \\ 2 & 1 \end{vmatrix}$

(2) $(-1)^{1+2} A_{12} = - \begin{vmatrix} 2 & 3 \\ 7 & 1 \end{vmatrix}$

(3) $(-1)^{1+3} A_{13} = + \begin{vmatrix} 2 & 1 \\ 7 & 2 \end{vmatrix}$

The value of the determinant is the sum of products of the elements of the chosen (first) row multiplied by their cofactors

$$a_{11}[(-1)^{1+1} A_{11}] + a_{12}[(-1)^{1+2} A_{12}] + a_{13}[(-1)^{1+3} A_{13}]$$

$$= (3) \cdot \begin{vmatrix} 1 & 3 \\ 2 & 1 \end{vmatrix} + (4) \cdot (-1) \cdot \begin{vmatrix} 2 & 3 \\ 7 & 1 \end{vmatrix} + (7) \cdot \begin{vmatrix} 2 & 1 \\ 7 & 2 \end{vmatrix}$$

$$= (3)(1-6) - (4)(2-21) + (7)(4-7)$$

$$= (-15) + 76 - 21 = 40$$

The expansion of a determinant of higher order becomes increasingly complicated as the order increases. For example let us evaluate the fourth order determinant

$$\begin{vmatrix} a_{11} & a_{12} & a_{13} & a_{14} \\ a_{21} & a_{22} & a_{23} & a_{24} \\ a_{31} & a_{32} & a_{33} & a_{34} \\ a_{41} & a_{42} & a_{43} & a_{44} \end{vmatrix}$$

We choose the first row and proceed with the computation of the cofactors of its four elements

(i) Cofactor of element $a_{11} = (-1)^{1+1} A_{11} = + \begin{vmatrix} a_{22} & a_{23} & a_{24} \\ a_{32} & a_{33} & a_{34} \\ a_{42} & a_{43} & a_{44} \end{vmatrix}$

This cofactor is a determinant of order 3 and must be further expanded. We choose its first row and find the cofactors of its three elements. Thus

Cofactor $a_{11} = + A_{11} = \begin{vmatrix} a_{22} A_{22} + (a_{23})(-A_{23}) + a_{24} A_{24} \end{vmatrix}$

$$= \left\{ a_{22} \begin{vmatrix} a_{33} & a_{34} \\ a_{43} & a_{44} \end{vmatrix} - a_{23} \begin{vmatrix} a_{32} & a_{34} \\ a_{42} & a_{44} \end{vmatrix} + a_{24} \begin{vmatrix} a_{32} & a_{33} \\ a_{42} & a_{43} \end{vmatrix} \right\}$$

$$= a_{22}(a_{33} a_{44} - a_{43} a_{34}) - a_{23}(a_{32} a_{44} - a_{42} a_{34}) + a_{24}(a_{32} a_{43} - a_{42} a_{33})$$

(ii) Cofactor of $a_{12} = -A_{12} = - \begin{vmatrix} a_{21} & a_{23} & a_{24} \\ a_{31} & a_{33} & a_{34} \\ a_{41} & a_{43} & a_{44} \end{vmatrix}$

$$= - \left\{ +a_{21} \begin{vmatrix} a_{31} & a_{33} \\ a_{41} & a_{43} \end{vmatrix} - a_{23} \begin{vmatrix} a_{31} & a_{34} \\ a_{41} & a_{44} \end{vmatrix} \right.$$

$$\left. + a_{24} \begin{vmatrix} a_{31} & a_{33} \\ a_{41} & a_{43} \end{vmatrix} \right\}$$

$$= - \left\{ \begin{array}{l} (a_{21}) (a_{33} a_{44} - a_{43} a_{34}) \\ -a_{23} (a_{31} a_{44} - a_{41} a_{34}) + \\ + a_{24} (a_{31} a_{43} - a_{41} a_{33}) \end{array} \right\}$$

(iii) Cofactor of $a_{13} = +A_{13} = \begin{vmatrix} a_{21} & a_{22} & a_{24} \\ a_{31} & a_{32} & a_{34} \\ a_{41} & a_{42} & a_{44} \end{vmatrix}$

$$= \left\{ a_{21} \begin{vmatrix} a_{32} & a_{34} \\ a_{42} & a_{44} \end{vmatrix} - a_{22} \begin{vmatrix} a_{31} & a_{34} \\ a_{41} & a_{44} \end{vmatrix} \right.$$

$$\left. + a_{24} \begin{vmatrix} a_{31} & a_{32} \\ a_{41} & a_{42} \end{vmatrix} \right\}$$

(iv) Cofactor $a_{14} = -A_{14} = - \begin{vmatrix} a_{21} & a_{22} & a_{23} \\ a_{31} & a_{32} & a_{33} \\ a_{41} & a_{42} & a_{43} \end{vmatrix}$

$$= - \left\{ a_{21} \begin{vmatrix} a_{32} & a_{33} \\ a_{42} & a_{43} \end{vmatrix} - a_{22} \begin{vmatrix} a_{31} & a_{33} \\ a_{41} & a_{43} \end{vmatrix} \right.$$

$$\left. + a_{23} \begin{vmatrix} a_{31} & a_{32} \\ a_{41} & a_{42} \end{vmatrix} \right\}$$

$$= - \left\{ \begin{array}{l} -a_{21} (a_{32} a_{43} - a_{42} a_{33}) \\ -a_{22} (a_{31} a_{43} - a_{41} a_{33}) \\ + a_{23} (a_{31} a_{42} - a_{41} a_{32}) + \end{array} \right.$$

The value of the fourth order determinant is the sum of the products of the elements of its first row times their respective cofactors

$$|\Delta| = a_{11} A_{11} - a_{12} A_{12} + a_{13} A_{13} - a_{14} A_{14}$$

The procedure for expansion becomes formidable as the order of the determinant increases. Fortunately there are various properties related to the determinants by means of which the expansion procedure can be greatly facilitated. For the benefit of the reader who is interested in simplified computational aspects we will state without proof the most important properties.

3. PROPERTIES OF DETERMINANTS

Property 1

If the rows and columns are interchanged, the value of the determinant remains unchanged; for example

$$\begin{vmatrix} a_1 & b_1 & c_1 \\ a_2 & b_2 & c_2 \\ a_3 & b_3 & c_3 \end{vmatrix} = \begin{vmatrix} a_1 & a_2 & a_3 \\ b_1 & b_2 & b_3 \\ c_1 & c_2 & c_3 \end{vmatrix}$$

$$\begin{vmatrix} 2 & 3 & 4 \\ 1 & 2 & 3 \\ 5 & 6 & 7 \end{vmatrix} = \begin{vmatrix} 2 & 1 & 5 \\ 3 & 2 & 6 \\ 4 & 3 & 7 \end{vmatrix}$$

Property 2

If all the elements in a row (or column) are zero, the value of the determinant is zero. For example

$$\begin{vmatrix} a_1 & b_1 & c_1 \\ 0 & 0 & 0 \\ a_3 & b_3 & c_3 \end{vmatrix} = 0 .$$

Property 3

If any two rows (or columns) are identical the value of the determinant is zero. For example

$$\longrightarrow \begin{vmatrix} 2 & 3 & 4 & 2 \\ 1 & 2 & 3 & 2 \\ 4 & 5 & 6 & 2 \\ 1 & 2 & 3 & 2 \end{vmatrix} = 0$$

The same property may be stated in an equivalent way. If a row is a multiple of another row the value of the determinant is zero.

Property 4

If any two rows (or columns) are interchanged, the determinant changes sign. For example

$$\begin{vmatrix} 2 & 3 & 2 & 4 \\ 1 & 2 & 3 & 2 \\ 5 & 4 & 3 & 2 \\ 1 & 2 & 3 & 4 \end{vmatrix} = - \begin{vmatrix} 2 & 4 & 2 & 3 \\ 1 & 2 & 3 & 2 \\ 5 & 2 & 3 & 4 \\ 1 & 4 & 3 & 2 \end{vmatrix}$$

Property 5

If all the elements in a row (or column) are multiplied by the same number k, the value of the determinant is multiplied by k. For example

$$\begin{vmatrix} a_1 & kb_1 & c_1 \\ a_2 & kb_2 & c_2 \\ a_3 & kb_3 & c_3 \end{vmatrix} = k \begin{vmatrix} a_1 & b_1 & c_1 \\ a_2 & b_2 & c_2 \\ a_3 & b_3 & c_3 \end{vmatrix}$$

The same property may be stated as follows: If any row (or column) has a factor k common to all its elements, then this factor may be removed, the determinant being k times the new one.

Property 6

If to all the elements of a row (or column) we add a constant multiple of any other row (or column) the value of the determinant is not changed. For example

$$\begin{vmatrix} a_1 & b_1 + ka_1 & c_1 \\ a_2 & b_2 + ka_2 & c_2 \\ a_3 & b_3 + ka_3 & c_3 \end{vmatrix} = \begin{vmatrix} a_1 & b_1 & c_1 \\ a_2 & b_2 & c_2 \\ a_3 & b_3 & c_3 \end{vmatrix}$$

Property 7

If all the elements of a row (or column) of a determinant are expressed as the sum of two (or more) terms, the determinant can be expressed as the sum of two (or more determinants). For example

$$\begin{vmatrix} a_1 + k_1 & b_1 & c_1 \\ a_2 + k_2 & b_2 & c_2 \\ a_3 + k_3 & b_3 & c_3 \end{vmatrix} = \begin{vmatrix} a_1 & b_1 & c_1 \\ a_2 & b_2 & c_2 \\ a_3 & b_3 & c_3 \end{vmatrix} + \begin{vmatrix} k_1 & b_1 & c_1 \\ k_2 & b_2 & c_2 \\ k_3 & b_3 & c_3 \end{vmatrix}$$

Some examples will show how the evaluation of a determinant is simplified by the use of these properties. For example given the determinant

$$\begin{vmatrix} 3 & 1 & 2 & 1 \\ 2 & 7 & 3 & 4 \\ 7 & 15 & 8 & 9 \\ 5 & 10 & 5 & 0 \end{vmatrix}$$

Subtracting from the third row twice the second row (this operation leaving the value of the determinant unchanged) we find

$$\longrightarrow \begin{vmatrix} 3 & 1 & 2 & 1 \\ 2 & 7 & 3 & 4 \\ 3 & 1 & 2 & 1 \\ 5 & 10 & 5 & 0 \end{vmatrix} = 0$$

since two rows are identical.

In general, by the application of the above properties we should try to get as many zeros into a determinant as possible, preferably all in the same row or the same column. For example consider the determinant

$$\begin{vmatrix} 1 & 2 & 3 & 4 \\ 4 & 3 & 2 & 1 \\ 6 & 4 & 4 & 6 \\ 1 & 1 & 1 & 1 \end{vmatrix}$$

Subtract four times the last row from the third row

$$\begin{vmatrix} 1 & 2 & 3 & 4 \\ 4 & 3 & 2 & 1 \\ 2 & 0 & 0 & 2 \\ 1 & 1 & 1 & 1 \end{vmatrix}$$

Take two out of the determinant as a common factor of the third row

$$2 \begin{vmatrix} 1 & 2 & 3 & 4 \\ 4 & 3 & 2 & 1 \\ 1 & 0 & 0 & 1 \\ 1 & 1 & 1 & 1 \end{vmatrix}$$

We may now choose the third row as the basis for the evaluation of the determinant, since we will have to evaluate only two cofactors, those of the elements in circles. With some practice in the application of these properties one can acquire a considerable skill in the evaluation of determinants.

CRAMER'S RULE FOR THE SOLUTION OF SIMULTANEOUS LINEAR EQUATIONS

We will illustrate this method by starting with an example of a system of three linear equations in three unknowns. Assume that we have the following system in the three unknowns X, Y, Z

$$a_{11}X + a_{12}Y + a_{13}Z = k_1$$
$$a_{21}X + a_{22}Y + a_{23}Z = k_2$$
$$a_{31}X + a_{32}Y + a_{33}Z = k_3$$

The determinant of the coefficients of the unknowns is

$$\begin{vmatrix} a_{11} & a_{12} & a_{13} \\ a_{21} & a_{22} & a_{23} \\ a_{31} & a_{32} & a_{33} \end{vmatrix}$$

Firstly. The denominator of the expressions which form the solution is the above determinant of the coefficients of the unknowns.

Secondly. The numerator in the solution for each unknown is the same as the determinant of the coefficients, with the exception that the column of coefficients of the particular unknown is replaced by the column of constants on the right hand side of the system of equations.

Thus, if we denote the determinant of the coefficients by $|\Delta|$, the solution of the system is

$$X = \frac{\begin{vmatrix} k_1 & a_{12} & a_{13} \\ k_2 & a_{22} & a_{23} \\ k_3 & a_{32} & a_{33} \end{vmatrix}}{|\Delta|} \qquad Y = \frac{\begin{vmatrix} a_{11} & k_1 & a_{13} \\ a_{21} & k_2 & a_{23} \\ a_{31} & k_3 & a_{33} \end{vmatrix}}{|\Delta|} \qquad Z = \frac{\begin{vmatrix} a_{11} & a_{12} & k_1 \\ a_{21} & a_{22} & k_2 \\ a_{31} & a_{32} & k_3 \end{vmatrix}}{|\Delta|}$$

Cramer's rule for the solution of n simultaneous linear equations in n unknowns is exactly analogous to the rule given for the preceding case of $n = 3$.

Given n linear equations in n unknowns, $x_1, x_2, \ldots, x_n$

$$a_{11}x_1 + a_{12}x_2 + a_{13}x_3 + \ldots + a_{1n}x_n = k_1$$
$$a_{21}x_1 + a_{22}x_2 + a_{23}x_3 + \ldots + a_{2n}x_n = k_2$$
$$\cdot \quad \cdot \quad \cdot \quad \cdot \quad \cdot \quad \cdot \quad \cdot \quad \cdot \quad \cdot$$
$$a_{n1}x_1 + a_{n2}x_2 + a_{n3}x_3 + \ldots + a_{nn}x_n = k_n$$

Let $|\Delta|$ be the determinant of the coefficients of the unknowns $x_1, x_2, \ldots, x_n$, i.e.

$$|\Delta| = \begin{vmatrix} a_{11} & a_{12} \ldots a_{1n} \\ a_{21} & a_{22} \ldots a_{2n} \\ \cdot & \cdot \quad \cdot \quad \cdot \quad \cdot \\ a_{n1} & a_{n2} \ldots a_{nn} \end{vmatrix}$$

Denote by $|\Delta_j|$ the determinant with the jth column (which corresponds to the coefficients of the unknown x_j) replaced by the column of the coefficients on the right-hand side of the equations of the system. Then

$$x_1 = \frac{|\Delta_1|}{|\Delta|}, \qquad x_2 = \frac{|\Delta_2|}{|\Delta|} \ldots, \; x_j = \frac{|\Delta_j|}{|\Delta|}, \ldots, \; x_n = \frac{|\Delta_n|}{|\Delta|}$$

(for $\Delta \neq 0$)

For example the solution to the system

$$3x_1 + 4x_2 + 3x_3 + 2x_4 = 7$$
$$3x_1 + 3x_2 + 2x_3 + 3x_4 = -3$$
$$2x_1 - 3x_2 - 4x_3 + 1x_4 = 6$$
$$3x_1 + 1x_2 - x_3 \qquad\qquad = 0$$

is the following

$$|\Delta| = \begin{vmatrix} 3 & 4 & 3 & 2 \\ 3 & 3 & 2 & 3 \\ 2 & -3 & -4 & 1 \\ 3 & 1 & -1 & 0 \end{vmatrix} = 13$$

$$|\Delta_1| = \begin{vmatrix} 7 & 4 & 3 & 2 \\ -3 & 3 & 2 & 3 \\ 6 & -3 & -4 & 1 \\ 0 & 1 & -1 & 0 \end{vmatrix} = 311 \qquad |\Delta_2| = \begin{vmatrix} 3 & 7 & 3 & 2 \\ 3 & -3 & 2 & 3 \\ 2 & 6 & -4 & 1 \\ 3 & 0 & -1 & 0 \end{vmatrix} = -477$$

$$|\Delta_3| = \begin{vmatrix} 3 & 4 & 7 & 2 \\ 3 & 3 & -3 & 3 \\ 2 & -3 & 6 & 1 \\ 3 & 1 & 0 & 0 \end{vmatrix} = 456 \qquad |\Delta_4| = \begin{vmatrix} 3 & 4 & 3 & 7 \\ 3 & 3 & 2 & -3 \\ 2 & -3 & -4 & 6 \\ 3 & 1 & -1 & 0 \end{vmatrix} = -151$$

Then

$$x_1 = \frac{|\Delta_1|}{|\Delta|} \qquad x_2 = \frac{|\Delta_2|}{|\Delta|} \qquad x_3 = \frac{|\Delta_3|}{|\Delta|} \qquad x_4 = \frac{|\Delta_4|}{|\Delta|}$$

$$x_1 = \frac{311}{13} \qquad x_2 = \frac{477}{13} \qquad x_3 = \frac{456}{13} \qquad x_4 = \frac{-151}{13}$$

An example with regression analysis

Given the relationship

$$Y = b_0 + b_1 X_1 + b_2 X_2 + u$$

The normal equations are

$$\Sigma Y = \hat{b}_0 n + \hat{b}_1 \Sigma X_1 + \hat{b}_2 \Sigma X_2$$
$$\Sigma X_1 Y = \hat{b}_0 \Sigma X_1 + \hat{b}_1 \Sigma X_1^2 + \hat{b}_2 \Sigma X_1 X_2$$
$$\Sigma X_2 Y = \hat{b}_0 \Sigma X_2 + \hat{b}_1 \Sigma X_1 X_2 + \hat{b}_2 \Sigma X_2^2$$

Given a sample of n observations on Y and X we can obtain values of the unknown $\hat{b}$'s. Assume that the sample yields the following sums of squares and products (with $n = 10$)

$$|\Delta| = \begin{vmatrix} n & \Sigma X_1 & \Sigma X_2 \\ \Sigma X_1 & \Sigma X_1^2 & \Sigma X_1 X_2 \\ \Sigma X_2 & \Sigma X_1 X_2 & \Sigma X_2^2 \end{vmatrix} = \begin{vmatrix} 10 & 2 & 8 \\ 7 & 1 & 3 \\ 1 & 6 & 4 \end{vmatrix} = 138$$

Also $\Sigma Y = 15$, $\Sigma YX_1 = 25$, $\Sigma YX_2 = 12$. Then

$$|\Delta_0| = \begin{vmatrix} \Sigma Y & \Sigma X_1 & \Sigma X_2 \\ \Sigma X_1 Y & \Sigma X_1^2 & \Sigma X_1 X_2 \\ \Sigma X_2 Y & \Sigma X_1 X_2 & \Sigma X_2^2 \end{vmatrix} = \begin{vmatrix} 15 & 2 & 8 \\ 25 & 1 & 3 \\ 12 & 6 & 4 \end{vmatrix} = 766$$

$$|\Delta_1| = \begin{vmatrix} n & \Sigma Y & \Sigma X_2 \\ \Sigma X_1 & \Sigma X_1 Y & \Sigma X_1 X_2 \\ \Sigma X_2 & \Sigma X_2 Y & \Sigma X_2^2 \end{vmatrix} = \begin{vmatrix} 10 & 15 & 8 \\ 7 & 25 & 3 \\ 1 & 12 & 4 \end{vmatrix} = 737$$

$$|\Delta_2| = \begin{vmatrix} n & \Sigma X_1 & \Sigma Y \\ \Sigma X_1 & \Sigma X_1^2 & \Sigma X_1 Y \\ \Sigma X_2 & \Sigma X_1 X_2 & \Sigma X_2 Y \end{vmatrix} = \begin{vmatrix} 10 & 2 & 15 \\ 7 & 1 & 25 \\ 1 & 6 & 12 \end{vmatrix} = -883$$

Therefore

$$b_0 = \frac{|\Delta_0|}{|\Delta|} = \frac{766}{138} \approx 5\cdot 55$$

$$b_1 = \frac{|\Delta_1|}{|\Delta|} = \frac{737}{138} \approx 5\cdot 34$$

$$b_2 = \frac{|\Delta_2|}{|\Delta|} = \frac{-883}{138} \approx -6\cdot 39$$

APPENDIX III

Exercises and Questions

Solutions to the problems of this Appendix and the individual chapters of the book can be obtained from the author on request.

University of Waterloo,
Department of Economics,
Waterloo, Ontario
Canada.

APPENDIX III

Exercises and Questions

CHAPTER 2   METHODOLOGY OF ECONOMETRIC RESEARCH

2.1. What types of criteria would you use to evaluate the results of an estimated relationship? Which of these criteria are more important?

2.2. Show that in the linear demand function

$$D = b_0 + b_1 P + u \qquad (b_1 < 0)$$

the slope (b_1) is a component of the price elasticity of demand.

2.3. Show that in the following demand function

$$D = b_0 \cdot P^{b_1} \cdot u \qquad (b_1 < 0.)$$

the coefficient b_1 is the price elasticity of demand. (Such demand functions are called *constant elasticity* functions.)

2.4. Economic theory postulates exact relationships between economic variables. Consider the following economic relationships.

Demand function: $D = b_0 + b_1 P + b_2 Y$
where D = quantity demand; P = price; Y = income

Supply function: $S_x = b_0 + b_1 P_x + P_x + b_2 P_f$
where S_x = quantity supplied; P_x = price; P_f = price of factor inputs

Consumption function: $C = b_0 + b_1 Y$
where C = consumption expenditure; Y = disposable income

Liquidity preference: $L = b_0 + b_1 r + b_2 Y$
where L = demand for money; r = interest rate; Y = gross national product

Cost function: $C = b_0 + b_1 X$
where C = total cost; X = total output

(i) What is the meaning of exact relationships?
(ii) What is the economic meaning of the coefficients $(b_0, b_1, b_2,$ etc.) in each one of the above relationships?
(iii) What would you expect the sign (and magnitude) of the coefficients $(b$'s) to be in each of the above cases?

2.5. Let Q denote the quantity demanded and P the price of the commodity.

Compute the price elasticity of demand at the prices specified:

(a) Demand function $Q = 200 - 20P$
Compute the price elasticity when $p = 8, p = 5, p = 2$
(b) Demand function $Q = 100/P = 100 \cdot P^{-1}$
Compute the price elasticity when $p = 100, p = 20, p = 2$
(c) Demand function $Q = 1000 - P^2$
Compute the price elasticity when $p = 30, p = 20, p = 10$

2.6. Assume a linear demand curve of a firm

$$X = b_0 - b_1 P$$

Derive the marginal revenue curve, and comment on its shape and slope. Verify the statement of economic theory that the slope of the MR curve is one-half that of the linear demand curve.

2.7. The market demand function for commodity x is

$$X = 200 - 20\sqrt{P}$$

(a) Find the marginal revenue function for a monopolist who produces x.
(b) Find the marginal revenue when $P = 4$.
(c) Find the price elasticity when $P = 4$.

2.8. Consider the following two models of total cost of production of a certain commodity

(a) Linear cost function $\quad C = b_0 + b_1 X + u$
(b) Non-linear cost function $C = b_0 + b_1 X - b_2 X^2 + b_3 X^3 + u$

where C = total cost
X = total output of the commodity

Assume that the above models were estimated from a cross-section sample of fifty firms and gave the following results

(a) $C = 10{,}000 + 8X$
(b) $C = 2{,}000 + 10X - 0.02X^2 + 0.001X^3$

Find the average variable cost, the marginal cost and the total average cost functions for each of the above models and comment on their shapes in view of the postulates of the traditional theory of costs.

2.9. Consider the Cobb–Douglas production function

$$X = b_0 \cdot L^{b_1} \cdot K^{b_2} \cdot u$$

where X = output; L = labour input; K = capital input;
u = random variable absorbing mainly the influence of omitted explanatory variables.

(a) Interpret the coefficients b_1 and b_2.

(b) Find the marginal product functions of the two factors of production. Are the marginal products constant? Explain.

2.10. Consider the following demand function for university jackets (that is, jackets bearing the name of the university)

$$Q = b_0 + b_1 P + u$$

(a) Interpret the coefficients b_0 and b_1, defining their sign.
(b) How would your interpretation of the parameters of the demand function change if you knew that the demand for university jackets is strongly affected by the amount of money awarded for scholarships?
(c) Make a list of some important variables which have been omitted from the above demand function and discuss how you would expect changes in these factors to 'shift' the demand function.

2.11. Assume that the true consumption function is $C = f(Y_d, W, D, A, L, r)$

where C = consumption expenditure
Y_d = personal disposable income
W = wealth of the population
D = distribution of income
A = age composition of population
L = liquid assets of the population
r = level of interest rates

(a) If a researcher estimates the simple function

$$C_t = b_0 + b_1 Y_d + u$$

what does he implicitly assume about the 'omitted' determinants (regressors) of the consumption expenditure?
(b) Indicate how you would expect changes in each of the omitted variables to 'shift' the simple consumption function.

2.12. Assume that the aggregate consumption function is

$$C = b_0 + b_1 Y + u$$

(a) Interpret the coefficients b_0 and b_1.
(b) Write the aggregate savings function corresponding to the above consumption function and interpret its coefficients.
(c) Define the relation between the coefficients of the consumption and savings function.

2.13. It is often argued that large corporations are leaving the big cities and relocate to surrounding rural areas because taxes in the cities are higher than taxes in the surrounding areas.

Assume that we have a cross-section of the average size of assets (A) of firms from different cities at a point in time. Set up a linear regression model to express the above hypothesis.

2.14. Assume that the true investment function is

$$I_t = b_0 + b_1(\Pi_t) + b_2(r_t) + b_3(K_{t-1}) + u_t$$

where I_t = investments expenditure in period t
                Π_t = profits in period t
                r_t = long-term interest rate
        K_{t-1} = stock of capital existing at the end of $t - 1$.

Express your *a priori* expectations regarding the sign of the coefficients of the above relationship, including b_0.

2.15. The Keynesian liquidity preference implies that the demand for money to hold (M) is a decreasing non-linear function of the interest rate (r), *ceteris paribus*. Furthermore Keynes discussed the possibility of the 'liquidity trap', a situation in which the demand for money becomes very large (infinitely large) if the interest rate approaches a given low level. Write a liquidity preference function incorporating the above hypotheses, assuming that the liquidity trap occurs at $r = 0.01$.

2.16. Assume that the number of firms that locate in a given province depends on the *relative* tax rate of that province. However, the larger the number of firms that locate in a province, the higher the pollution rate in that province. Express these hypotheses in suitable regression models, stating your *a priori* expectations about the sign of the coefficients of these models.

CHAPTER 3   CORRELATION THEORY

3.1. Would you expect a positive, negative or zero linear correlation to exist between the population of values of each of the following pairs of variables?

(a) Number of households and total population, in different towns.
(b) Ages of husbands and their wives.
(c) Number of firms going bankrupt per year and percentage increase in national income per year.
(d) Hat size and intelligence.
(e) Years of education and income earned.
(f) Total cost of production and level of output.
(g) Average cost of production and level of output.
(h) Quantity of butter demanded and price of butter.
(i) Quantity of butter supplied and price of butter.
(j) Quantity of butter demanded and price of margarine.

3.2. The following table shows how ten students, arranged in alphabetical order, were ranked according to their achievements in the class exercises and the final examination of a statistics course.

Class exercises	8	3	9	2	7	10	4	6	1	5
Final exam	9	5	10	1	8	7	3	4	2	6

(a) Can we infer from the above information that there is any marked relationship between achievements in class exercises and in final exam?
(b) Test the hypothesis that the true rank correlation coefficient is significantly different from zero at the 5 per cent level.

3.3. Interpret the following results, obtained from samples on the relevant variables

(a) $r_{yx} = 0.89$ where Y = road accidents; X = consumption of beer
(b) $r_{yx} = 0.95$ where Y = road accidents; X = wages & salaries (wage-bill)

3.4. (a) If from a sample of observations on Y and X we find $r = 0$, can we infer that there is no relationship between X and Y? Why?
(b) What can we infer from such a finding? Give examples of your own to illustrate your answers.

3.5. The following table shows the grades of ten students selected at random in two short quizzes, one in micro-economics and one in macro-economics.

Grade on micro-quiz	6	5	8	8	7	6	10	4	9	7
Grade on macro-quiz	8	7	7	10	5	8	10	6	8	6

(a) Compute the correlation coefficient between the two sets of quiz grades and comment on its value.
(b) Using the above information, test the hypothesis that there is no correlation between the degree of knowledge of micro- and macro-economics.

Intermediate results:

$$\Sigma(X - \bar{X})(Y - \bar{Y}) = 13 \quad \Sigma(X - \bar{X})^2 = 30 \quad \Sigma(Y - \bar{Y})^2 = 24.5.$$

3.6. Assume you are given the estimated relationship $Y = 10 - 6X$. Show that the correlation coefficient

$$\rho_{xy} = \frac{\text{cov}(XY)}{\sigma_x \cdot \sigma_y} \text{ is equal to } -1.0.$$

3.7. Show that the correlation coefficient is a symmetric expression; that is

$$r_{YX} = r_{XY}.$$

3.8. The following table shows the sales of a company in ten districts and the total disposable income of the inhabitants of these districts.

District		A	B	C	D	E	F	G	H	I	J
Sales	Y	15	16	17	18	20	20	22	24	23	25
Disposable total income ($ million)	X	9	13	14	15	16	16	17	19	20	21

Can the company use the disposable income as a basis for setting sales quotas in the ten districts?

(Hint: test the significance of the correlation coefficient between sales and disposable income.)

Intermediate results:

$$\Sigma X^2 = 2{,}674 \quad \Sigma Y^2 = 4{,}108 \quad \Sigma XY = 3{,}306$$

3.9. Using the following data, show that the correlation coefficient between Y and X is identical to that between the variables

$$Y^* = \frac{Y - 125}{5} \quad \text{and} \quad X^* = \frac{X - 48}{4}$$

Y_i	125	80	100	140	160-	135
X_i	44	36	40	48	60	56

Can you explain the above results?

3.10. 'An R^2 of 1 guarantees a perfect fit, but an R^2 not equal to 1 does not rule out a perfect fit.' Explain under what conditions this statement is true.

3.11. A market research team asks two experts to *rank* ten brands of beer in order of preference. Their rankings are as follows:

Brands of beer	A	B	C	D	E	F	G	H	I	J
Ranking by first expert	10	9	1	4	3	8	5	2	6	7
Ranking by second expert	8	7	1	3	2	10	5	6	9	4

(a) Show that the rank correlation coefficient between the ranks given by the two experts is $r' = 0.71$.

(b) Interpret this result.

(c) Construct a 95 per cent confidence interval for r' at the 5 per cent level of significance, assuming $\rho' = 0$.

3.12. Assume that ten men assigned to a particular task in a manufacturing plant were given two aptitude tests. After they had been on the job for some period of time the production manager was asked to rank the employees from first to tenth with regard to their value to the company.

The firm wants to identify the test whose results are more closely correlated with the ranking of the production manager. Future recruits will then be required to take only this test, and the other will be discontinued.

The results of the two tests and the ranking of the production manager are shown in the following table.

Worker	A	B	C	D	E	F	G	H	I	J
Score test A (out of 100)	96	98	79	78	84	90	76	60	62	44
Score test B (out of 100)	78	72	60	72	64	84	62	56	44	40
Ranking by manager	1	2	3	4	5	6	7	8	9	10

Which test will the firm choose for its future recruits?

3.13. The following table includes the rankings of ten courses (offered in the Department of Economics) by two students, one studying economics and one studying economics and mathematics.

(a) Can you infer from this data that the ten courses are equally popular among students?

	Course 701	Course 710	Course 715	Course 721	Course 731	Course 732	Course 750	Course 703	Course 711	Course 700
Student's A Ranking	8	3	7	4	2	6	9	1	5	10
Student's B Ranking	10	6	3	2	8	9	1	7	4	5

(b) Interpret the meaning of the obtained rank correlation coefficient.
(c) Test the statistical significance of the rank correlation coefficient, at the 1 per cent level of significance.

3.14. Show that if X and Y are independent, then they are uncorrelated.

CHAPTER 4   THE SIMPLE LINEAR REGRESSION MODEL AND THE OLS METHOD

4.1. The following table includes the price and quantity demanded of the product of a monopolist over a six-year period.

Year	1970	1971	1972	1973	1974	1975
Quantity (In thousand yards)	8	3	4	7	8	0
Price (In $ per yard)	2	4	3	1	3	5

(a) Estimate the demand function for the oligopolist's product, assuming this function is linear. Comment on the values of the estimated coefficients ($\hat{b}_0$ and $\hat{b}_1$) on the basis of economic theory.

(b) Estimate the average elasticity of demand.

(c) Estimate the elasticity of demand at the price 4.

(d) Forecast the level of demand if price rises to $6. Comment on your forecast.

   4.2. (a) Show that the value of the average price elasticity of the following estimated demand function

$$\hat{Q} = 950 - 25P$$

   is −0·5, given $\bar{Q} = 500$ and $\bar{P} = 10$.

(b) Using the above information obtain the price elasticity of demand for $P = 20$.

   4.3. The following table includes data on the quantity supplied for exports of commodity x and its price.

Year	1963	1964	1965	1966	1967	1968	1969	1970	1971	1972
Quantity supplied (millions tons) (Y)	5	4	3	4	7	9	8	10	8	2
Export price (X) ($ per ton)	2	4	2	3	8	7	6	8	7	3

(a) Test the hypothesis that the quantity supplied and price are positively related, by estimating the supply export function $Y = b_0 + b_1 X + u$. Interpret your results.

(b) Show that $\hat{b}_1$ is a part of the price elasticity of supply, and obtain a numerical value for the latter.

(c) A government department makes independent estimates of the export price in future years. It is estimated that in 1978 the price will be $8 and in 1988 it will be $12. Use these price estimates to forecast the export volume of commodity x in 1978 and in 1988.

   (Hint: You must consider the explanatory factors which are omitted from the function. Is it likely that these factors will behave in the future in the same way as in the sample period? You must also consider the value of r^2.)

Intermediate results:

$$\Sigma X = 50 \qquad \Sigma X^2 = 304 \qquad \Sigma XY = 353 \qquad \Sigma Y = 60 \qquad \Sigma Y^2 = 428$$

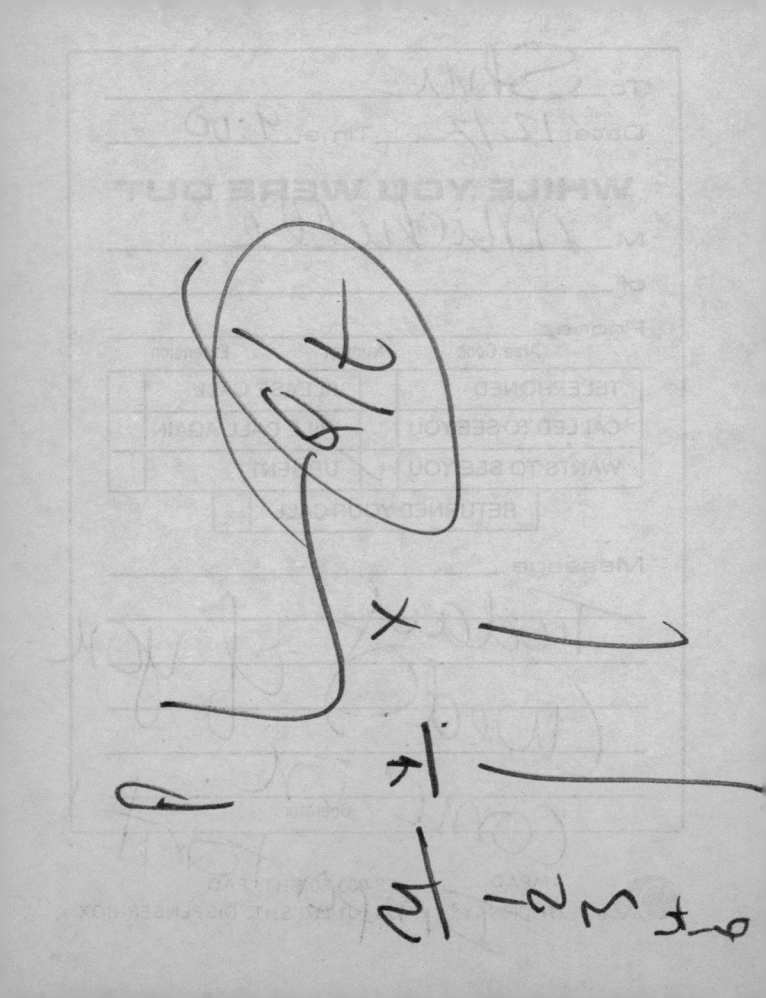

To Shu

Date 12/17 **Time** 9:02

WHILE YOU WERE OUT

M _Michelle_

of _____

Phone _____

	Area Code	Number	Extension

TELEPHONED		PLEASE CALL	
CALLED TO SEE YOU		WILL CALL AGAIN	
WANTS TO SEE YOU		URGENT	✓
RETURNED YOUR CALL			

Message _Todays if you could if you came in_

Operator _____

4.4. Given the linear regression model

$$Y_t = b_0 + b_1 X_t + u_t \qquad (t = 1, 2, \ldots, n)$$

derive the distribution of Y, stating clearly your assumptions.

4.5. The following table includes the total cost and the level of output of firm A over a ten-year period.

Year	1966	1967	1968	1969	1970	1971	1972	1973	1974	1975
Quantity produced (000 of units)	40	42	48	55	65	79	88	100	120	140
Total cost (000 dollars)	150	140	160	170	150	162	185	165	190	185

Given the following intermediate results

$$\Sigma X = 777 \qquad \Sigma Y = 1,657 \qquad \Sigma XY = 132,938 \qquad \Sigma X^2 = 70,903$$
$$\Sigma Y^2 = 277,119$$

(a) Estimate the linear cost function $C = b_0 + b_1 X$
(b) Find the AVC, the MC, and the ATC, and plot them roughly on a graph.
(c) How would you use linear regression to test the hypothesis that the AVC (as well as the MC and ATC) are non-linear, having the U-shape of traditional theory? Write down the set of normal equations that you would require in this case.

4.6. How can we estimate the coefficients of the two-variable model

$$Y_t = b_0 + b_1 X_t + u_t$$

when all the observations on the explanatory variable are identical?

4.7. Distinguish carefully between the following concepts

(a) The *true relationship* between X and Y
(b) The *true regression* line
(c) The *estimated relationship*
(d) The *estimated regression* line.

Use a graph to illustrate your answer.

What assumptions do we make about the random term u? Why are these assumptions necessary?

4.8. Prove that the estimated regression line

$$\hat{Y} = \hat{b}_0 + \hat{b}_1 X$$

passes through the point of the means $(\bar{Y}, \bar{X})$.

4.9. The following table includes information on the consumption expenditure and incomes for twenty individuals during 1974.

Person	1	2	3	4	5	6	7	8	9	10
Consumption $	15,600	6,400	9,200	14,900	7,200	7,600	7,200	7,200	7,900	8,800
Income $	16,300	6,800	8,600	15,300	8,700	7,800	7,300	8,300	9,400	10,800

Person	11	12	13	14	15	16	17	18	19	20
Consumption $	15,400	4,100	11,100	2,400	11,500	4,200	6,700	12,100	11,100	4,700
Income $	18,600	5,100	11,600	2,700	11,800	4,600	5,400	12,900	13,300	5,900

(a) Estimate the consumption and saving functions using this cross-section sample, and plot them on a graph.

Intermediate results:

$$\Sigma X = 191,200 \qquad \Sigma Y = 175,300 \qquad \Sigma X^2 = 2,165,180,000$$
$$\Sigma XY = 1,973,670,000 \qquad\qquad \Sigma Y^2 = 1,813,469,000$$

(b) What is the marginal propensity to consume (MPC) and the marginal propensity to save (MPS)?
(c) Forecast the level of consumption expenditure at the mean income.
(d) Forecast the level of savings for an individual whose income in $20,000.

4.10. Consider the linear regression model

$$Y_t = b_0 + b_1 X_t + u_t \tag{1}$$

Suppose that there are no data on X_t, but we know that $Z_t = a_0 + a_1 X_t$, where a_0 and a_1 are arbitrary known constants.

Using the available Z_t data, we can estimate

$$Y_t = c_0 + c_1 Z_t + u_t \tag{2}$$

Find the relationship between the coefficients of (1) and (2). Hence show how from the estimates $\hat{c}_0$ and $\hat{c}_1$ you can obtain estimates of the original model ($\hat{b}_0$ and $\hat{b}_1$).

4.11. Assume that from a sample of n observations on Y and X we estimate the regressions

$$Y_t = b_0 + b_1 X_t + u_t$$

and

$$X_t = c_0 + c_1 Y_t + v_t$$

(a) Show that $r_{xy}^2 = r_{yx}^2$.
(b) Show that $(b_1).(c_1) = r_{xy}^2 = r_{yx}^2$.

4.12. Consider the following model

$$Y_t = b_0 + b_1 X_t + u_t \tag{1}$$

where u depends on X in the following way

$$u_t = b_2 X_t^2 + v_t \qquad (2)$$

where v_t is a random variable which is independent of X and satisfies all the other assumptions of the linear regression model.

Which assumptions of the linear regression model are violated in (1)?

4.13. The following regression model has been used in a cross-section study of the grades of students

$$G_i = b_0 + b_1 Y_i + u_i \qquad (1)$$

where G_i = average grade of the ith student

$\qquad Y_i$ = income of the parents of the ith student

(a) List the main factors that are absorbed in this model by u_i.
(b) In view of your answer in (a) above, how would you modify the above model to make it more realistic?
(c) If you do not modify (1), what assumptions of the linear regression model would you expect to be violated?
(d) Using the cross-section data of the following table, test the hypothesis that the grades of students are explained by their parents' income.

n	1	2	3	4	5	6	7	8	9	10
Exam grades	90	80	60	70	40	60	70	50	50	40
Parents' income ($)	25,000	21,000	15,000	15,000	9,000	12,000	18,000	6,000	12,000	8,000

4.14. Prove that the estimated slope of the regression of Y on X will be equal to the reciprocal of the estimated slope of the regression of X on Y only if $r^2 = 1$. (Hint: Recall that $r_{yx}^2 = r_{xy}^2$.)

4.15. In the two-variable model $\quad Y_t = b_0 + b_1 X_t + u_t \quad$ prove that

(a) $\Sigma x_i e_i = 0 \qquad$ (where $x_i = X_i - \bar{X}$)
(b) $\Sigma X_i e_i = 0$.

4.16. Assume that the true relationship between Y and X is

$$Y_t = b_0 + b_1 X_t + u_t$$
$$E(u_t) = 0 \qquad t = 1, 2, \ldots, n.$$

An investigator attempts to estimate b_1 by running a regression of Y on X without an intercept term.

(a) Show that the estimate of b_1 will be biased.
(b) Derive an algebraic expression for the bias.
(c) Under what conditions would the bias be zero?

4.17. It is believed by the 'monetarist school' that the level of income is determined by the quantity of money.

(a) Using the U.S.A. data of the following table, test the validity of this hypothesis. The variables are measured in billions of dollars.

Year	1966	1967	1968	1969	1970	1971	1972	1973	1974	1975
GNP	753·0	796·3	868·5	935·5	982·4	1,063·4	1,171·1	1,306·6	1,413·2	1,516·3
Money supply	175·7	187·3	202·2	208·8	219·6	233·8	255·3	270·5	283·1	294·8

Source: *Economic Report of the President* (Washington, D.C.).

(b) Interpret the intercept and slope of the regression line.
(c) If the government wants to raise the level of income to \$2,000, at what level should it set the money supply? Explain.

Intermediate results:

$\Sigma X = 2,331 \cdot 1$ $\Sigma Y = 10,806 \cdot 3$ $\Sigma X^2 = 558,721 \cdot 6$ $\Sigma Y^2 = 12,301,463 \cdot 2$
$\Sigma XY = 2,616,249 \cdot 4$

4.18. Show that the least-squares estimator $(\hat{b}_0)$ of the model

$$Y_t = \hat{b}_0 + u_t \qquad (t = 1, 2, \ldots, n)$$

is given by the mean of Y, i.e.

$$\hat{b}_0 = \bar{y}.$$

Prove that, if u satisfies the standard assumptions,

(a) $E(\hat{b}_0) = b_0$, i.e. $\hat{b}_0$ is unbiased

(b) $\operatorname{var}(\hat{b}_0) = \sigma_u^2 \left(\dfrac{1}{n}\right)$

4.19. Consider the following alternative models of a demand function for a certain commodity.

Model A	$D_t = b_0 + b_1 P_t + b_2 Y_t + u_t$
Model B	$D_t = a_0 \cdot P_t^{a_1} \cdot Y_t^{a_2} \cdot e^{u_t}$

where D = quantity demanded
Y = personal income
P = price of the commodity

(a) Obtain an expression for the price elasticity for each of these models.

(b) Express each of the above models in a form which incorporates the assumption of 'no money illusion' of the traditional theory of demand.

(c) From economic theory it is known that several determining factors of the demand are omitted from the above models. Name some of these omitted variables and, concentrating on the linear model, explain the effects of such omissions on the assumptions of the linear regression model.

4.20. It is being recently argued that the rate of inflation depends, among others, on the rate of direct and indirect taxes. To test this 'tax-inflation' hypothesis a researcher sets up the model

$$\dot{P}_t = b_0 + b_1 t_{p,t} + b_2 t_{s,t} + u_t$$

where $\dot{P}$ = percentage change in the price level

t_p = tax rate on personal income

t_s = indirect taxation rate

(a) Do you consider this model adequate for testing the 'tax-inflation' hypothesis? (Hint: Consider which factors are absorbed by u, and whether the *ceteris paribus* assumption implied by this specification is valid.)

(b) In view of your answer in (a), what assumptions of the linear regression model are violated?

CHAPTER 5   STATISTICAL TESTS OF SIGNIFICANCE OF THE OLS ESTIMATES

5.1. (a) Compute r^2 for the demand function of Exercise 4.1 and test its statistical significance at the 5 per cent level.

(b) Calculate the standard errors of the coefficients of the demand function of Exercise 4.1. Then test the null hypothesis $b_i = 0$ at the 5 per cent level.

(c) Construct a 95 per cent confidence interval for the true slope of the demand function of Exercise 4.1.

5.2. (a) Obtain r^2 for the supply function of Exercise 4.3 and test its statistical significance at the 5 per cent level.

(b) Test the statistical significance of the coefficients $\hat{b}_0$ and $\hat{b}_1$ ($H_0 : b_i = 0$) using a 5 per cent level of significance.

5.3. (a) Obtain r^2 for the cost function of Exercise 4.5 and test its statistical significance at the 1 per cent level of significance.

(b) Test the null hypothesis $b_1 = 0$ at the 1 per cent level of significance.

(c) Construct a 99 per cent confidence interval for b_1.

5.4. (a) Obtain r^2 for the consumption function of Exercise 4.9 and test the null hypothesis $\rho = 0$, at the 5 per cent level of significance.

(b) Is the estimate of the marginal propensity to consume significantly different from 1 at the 5 per cent level of significance?

(c) Construct and interpret a 95 per cent confidence interval for the marginal propensity to consume.

5.5. Given the following estimated consumption function

$$\hat{C}_t = 5{,}000 + 0{\cdot}8\,Y_t \qquad\qquad r^2 = 0{\cdot}95$$

s.e. $\qquad\qquad\qquad$ (500) $\quad$ (0·09) $\qquad\qquad n = 15$

where C = consumption expenditure; Y = income.

(a) Evaluate the above-estimated function on the basis of (i) the available economic theory, (ii) the traditional statistical criteria r^2 and t tests on the b's. Conduct also the t test for r^2. (Use $\alpha = 5$ per cent).
(b) Estimate the savings function.
(c) Estimate the MPC and MPS.
(d) Interpret the constant intercepts of the consumption and savings functions.
(e) Forecast the level of consumption and the level of savings for 1980, if in that year income is \$200,000.
(f) Under what conditions would you expect your forecast to be accurate?

5.6. Prove that r_{yx}^2 remains unchanged if a linear transformation is made on both variables, such as

$$Y_t^* = a_0 + a_1\,Y_t \qquad \text{and} \qquad X_t^* = c_0 + c_1 X_t$$

where a_0, a_1, c_0, c_1 are arbitrary constants. (Hint: Show that r^2 from the regression $Y = f(X)$ is equal to r^2 from the regression $Y^* = f(X^*)$.)

5.7. In the two-variable model $Y_t = b_0 + b_1 X_t + u_t$ prove that

$$r^2 = \hat{b}_1^2 \cdot \frac{\Sigma x^2}{\Sigma y^2}$$

5.8. (a) How is the correlation coefficient useful in regression?
(b) Prove that

$$r^2 = 1 - \frac{\Sigma e_i^2}{\Sigma y_i^2}$$

where $y_i = (Y_i - \bar{Y})$.

5.9. From the following sample of ten yearly observations a researcher wants to estimate the demand function for second-hand T.V. sets.

No. of T.V. sets (Y)	543	580	618	695	724	812	887	991	1186	1940
Price (in $) $\quad(X)$	61	54	50	43	38	36	28	23	19	10

The researcher is in doubt as to the mathematical form of the demand function.

He estimates two alternative forms and his results are given below:

Linear demand function

$$Y = b_0 + b_1 X + u$$
$$\hat{Y} = 1704 - 22 \cdot 3X \qquad r^2 = 0 \cdot 76.$$

Standard error $\qquad (4 \cdot 4)$

Constant elasticity demand function

$$Y = b_0 \cdot X^{b_1} \cdot u$$

or $\qquad \log_e Y = \log_e b_0 + b_1 (\log_e X) + \log_e u$

$$(\widehat{\log_e Y}) = 9 \cdot 12057 - 0 \cdot 69(\log_e X) \qquad r^2 = 0 \cdot 99.$$

Standard error $\qquad (0 \cdot 02)$

(a) Estimate the price elasticity for each of the above functions.
(b) Calculate the value of t for the regression *slopes*.
(c) Which of the two functions is statistically more satisfactory (on the basis of the traditional statistical criteria)?
(d) Which of the two functions is more satisfactory on the basis of economic theory?
(e) Forecast (obtain an estimate of) the demand for second-hand T.V. sets for the price $P = \$8$ from each of the above functions.

5.10. What is being tested by the null hypothesis in regression analysis? Use a numerical example of your own (a hypothetical estimated function from economic theory) to illustrate your answer.

5.11. What information does the estimate $\hat{b}_i$ give us about the true value of the parameter b_i?

5.12. It has been shown that in the model $Y_t = b_0 + b_1 X_t = u_t$

$$\text{var} (\hat{b}_0) = \sigma_u^2 \left(\frac{\Sigma X^2}{n \Sigma x^2} \right).$$

Prove that the variance of $\hat{b}_0$ may also be computed by the expression

$$\text{var} (\hat{b}_0) = \sigma_u^2 \left(\frac{1}{n} + \frac{\bar{X}^2}{\Sigma x^2} \right).$$

5.13. In Chapter 5 (page 75) we established that

$$\hat{b}_1 = b_1 + \frac{\Sigma x_i u_i}{\Sigma x_i^2}$$

Show that

$$\text{var}\,(\hat{b}_1) = \sigma_u^2 \,\frac{1}{\Sigma x_i^2} + 2 \sum_{i \neq j} \frac{x_i x_j}{(\Sigma x_i^2)^2} \cdot E(u_i u_j)$$

which reduces to the formula

$$\text{var}\,(\hat{b}_1) = \sigma_u^2 \,\frac{1}{\Sigma x^2}$$

if the assumption of zero autocorrelation and homoscedasticity hold.

5.14. Given the two-variable model $Y_t = b_0 + b_1 X_t + u_t$, prove that the t test of the null hypothesis on the slope ($H_0 : b_1 = 0$) is identical with the t test on r under the null hypothesis $\rho = 0$.

5.15. A researcher estimated the following *per capita* consumption functions, using the ten-year period 1947–56.

(a) Austria $\left(\dfrac{C}{N}\right) = 2 \cdot 251 + 0 \cdot 481 \left(\dfrac{Y_d}{N}\right)$ $\qquad\qquad r^2 = 0 \cdot 990$

 (thousands of Austrian schillings *per capita*)

(b) Italy $\left(\dfrac{C}{N}\right) = 0 \cdot 384 + 0 \cdot 541 \left(\dfrac{Y_d}{N}\right)$ $\qquad\qquad r^2 = 0 \cdot 986$

 (hundreds of Italian lire *per capita*)

(c) Sweden $\left(\dfrac{C}{N}\right) = 13 \cdot 535 + 0 \cdot 392 \left(\dfrac{Y_d}{N}\right)$ $\qquad\qquad r^2 = 0 \cdot 843$

 (hundreds of Swedish kronor *per capita*)

(d) United Kingdom $\left(\dfrac{C}{N}\right) = 0 \cdot 950 + 0 \cdot 392 \left(\dfrac{Y_d}{N}\right)$ $\qquad r^2 = 0 \cdot 893$

 (hundreds of pounds sterling *per capita*)

(e) United States $\left(\dfrac{C}{N}\right) = 6 \cdot 991 + 0 \cdot 334 \left(\dfrac{Y_d}{N}\right)$ $\qquad\qquad r^2 = 0 \cdot 790$

Relative to the null hypothesis $H_0 : b_1 = 0$ the value of the t ratios for the above consumption functions are

Austria: $t = 31 \cdot 43$ $\qquad$ Italy: $t = 26 \cdot 15$ $\qquad$ U.K.: $t = 8 \cdot 63$
Sweden: $t = 6 \cdot 97$ $\qquad$ U.S.A.: $t = 5 \cdot 81$

Consider whether the above results are consistent with the hypothesis that the marginal propensity to consume (out of disposable *per capita* income) in all these countries is in fact $0 \cdot 50$.

5.16. Show that if by applying OLS to the model $Y_t = b_0 + b_1 X_t + u_t$ we find $r_{yx}^2 = 0$, then $\hat{b}_1 = 0$.

5.17. Prove that $\text{cov}\,(\hat{b}_0 \hat{b}_1) = -\bar{X}\,\dfrac{\sigma_u^2}{\Sigma x^2}$, assuming that the standard stochastic assumptions of the linear regression model are valid.

$$\left(\text{Hint: cov}\,(\hat{b}_0\hat{b}_1) = E(\hat{b}_0 - b_0)(\hat{b}_1 - b_1)\right.$$

$$(\hat{b}_0 - b_0) = -\bar{X}\,\frac{\Sigma xu}{\Sigma x^2} + \bar{u}$$

$$\left.(\hat{b}_1 - b_1) = \frac{\Sigma xu}{\Sigma x^2}\cdot\right)$$

CHAPTER 6   PROPERTIES OF THE OLS ESTIMATES

6.1. The OLS slope of the two-variable model $Y_t = b_0 + b_1 X_t + u_t$ has the following properties:

1. $E(\hat{b}_1) = b_1$, unbiasedness

2. $\text{var}\,(\hat{b}_1) = \sigma_u^2\,\dfrac{1}{\Sigma x_i^2}$

3. Best linear unbiasedness (BLU)

4. $\hat{b}_1$ has a normal distribution

5. $\hat{b}_1$ is consistent.

State the assumptions of the linear regression model used to obtain each property.

6.2. Distinguish carefully between the members of each of the following pairs of properties:
(a) Unbiasedness and consistency
(b) Consistency and asymptotic efficiency
(c) Efficiency and minimum variance
(d) Asymptotic efficiency and BLUE
(e) Unbiasedness and minimum MSE
(f) Consistency and zero MSE.

6.3. Among the properties of unbiasedness and efficiency (or minimum variance) which would you consider more important? Why?

6.4. 'Unbiasedness is most desirable when it is combined with low variance. Similarly, low variance is most desirable when it is combined with unbiasedness.' Explain, drawing appropriate graphs to illustrate your answer.

6.5. 'Compared to minimum MSE, unbiasedness is a relatively unimportant property.' Discuss.

6.6. Since (in the two-variable model $Y_t = b_0 + b_1 X_t + u_t$) the standard error of the regression coefficient b_1 varies inversely with the variance of X, we can improve the significance of the estimated parameter by selecting values of X at the end-points of the range of possible values. Explain why this is true, and discuss whether such a procedure is desirable.

6.7. (a) What is a biased estimate?

(b) Show that $\hat{b}_1 = b_1 + \dfrac{\Sigma x_i u_i}{\Sigma x_i^2}$ and explain under what conditions $\hat{b}_1$ would be biased, i.e. $E[(\hat{b}_1) - b_1] \neq 0$.

(c) What is a consistent estimate? What conditions must be fulfilled for an estimator to be consistent? Illustrate your answer with an appropriate diagram.

6.8. Consider the model

$$Y_t = b_0 + b_1 X_t + u_t \qquad\qquad (t = 1, 2, \ldots, n)$$

where u satisfies the basic stochastic assumptions

   u is random
   $E(u) = 0$
   $E(u)^2 = \sigma_u^2$ constant (homoscedasticity)
   $E(u_i u_j) = 0 \qquad (i \neq j) \qquad$ (serial independence).

How would the properties of $\hat{b}_1$ be affected in the following cases:
(a) The number of observations (n) is increased.
(b) The variance of X (dispersion of values of X) increases.
(c) All the X's have the same value.
(d) $E(u)^2 = 0$?

CHAPTER 7   MULTIPLE REGRESSION AND OTHER EXTENSIONS OF THE SIMPLE LINEAR REGRESSION MODEL

7.1. The quantity supplied of a commodity X is assumed to be a linear function of the price of x and the wage rate of labour used in the production of x. The population supply equation is given as

$$Q = b_0 + b_1 P_x + b_2 W + u$$

where Q = quantity supplied of x
   P_x = price of x
   W = wage rate

Using the sample data of the following table,

(a) Estimate the parameters by OLS.
(b) Test the statistical significance of the individual coefficients at the 5 per cent level.
(c) What percentage of the total variation in the quantity supplied is explained by both P_x and W?
(d) Compute the price elasticity of supply at the mean price and mean quantity traded.

$Y = Q$	20	35	30	47	60	68	76	90	100	105	130	140	125	120	135
$X_1 = P_x$	10	15	21	26	40	37	42	33	30	38	60	65	50	35	42
$X_2 = W$	12	10	9	8	5	7	4	5	7	5	3	4	3	1	2

Intermediate results:

$\Sigma Y = 1{,}281$ $\Sigma X_1 = 544$ $\Sigma X_2 = 85$

$\Sigma X_1 Y = 53{,}665$ $\Sigma X_1^2 = 22{,}922$ $\Sigma X_1 X_2 = 2{,}568$

$\Sigma X_2 Y = 5{,}706$ $\Sigma Y^2 = 132{,}609$ $\Sigma X_2^2 = 617$

7.2. (a) Transform the following non-linear models into a linear form which can be estimated by the OLS method

(i) $Y_t = b_0 + b_1 (X_1 X_2) + b_2 \sqrt{X_1} + b_3 X_2^{-1} + u_t$

(ii) $\log_e Y_t = b_0 + b_1 e^{x_1, t} + b_2 \left(\dfrac{1}{3 + X_{1,t} X_{2,t}} \right) + u_t$

(iii) $Y_t = b_0 \cdot X_1^{b_1} \cdot X_2^{b_2} \cdot e^u$

(iv) $Y_t = b_0 + b_1 X_{1,t} + b_2 X_{1,t}^2 + b_3 X_{1,t}^3 + u_t$

(b) Write the set of normal equations for each of the transformed models.

7.3. If you were to estimate the following relationships

(a) Imports $= f$ (gross domestic product)
(b) Price level $= f$ (wage level)
(c) Supply of commodity $x = f$ (price of x)

which mathematical form would you choose: a linear function, a log-linear function, or would you use the first differences of the variables? Explain.

7.4. The total investment function for the economy as a whole is assumed to be of the form

$$I = b_0 \cdot r^{b_1} \cdot e^u$$

where I = investment
r = interest rate.
The following sample is given

I ($ billion)	9·0	5·5	8·5	4·0	3·5	2·5	3·0	1·5	1·2	1·8	1·5
r (per cent)	2	3	2	4	5	6	4	6	8	7	9

(a) Estimate the parameters of the investment function by OLS.

(b) Test the statistical significance of the coefficients at the 1 per cent level of significance.

(c) Construct a 95 per cent confidence interval for b_1.

Intermediate results (in $\log_e$):

$\Sigma(\log_e I) = 12 \cdot 2770$ $\qquad\qquad$ $\Sigma(\log_e r) = 16 \cdot 6730$

$\Sigma(\log_e I)^2 = 18 \cdot 5591$ $\qquad\qquad$ $\Sigma(\log_e r)^2 = 27 \cdot 9610$

$\Sigma(\log_e I)(\log_e r) = 15 \cdot 1223$.

7.5. In the three-variable model, expressed in deviations of the variables from their mean, show that

$$\sum_{i=1}^{n} e_i x_{1i} = \sum_{i=1}^{n} e_i x_{2i} = 0$$

7.6. Prove the following expression of the adjusted coefficient of multiple determination

$$\bar{R}^2 = 1 - \left[\frac{\Sigma e^2/(n-k)}{\Sigma y^2/(n-1)} \right]$$

7.7. Consider the three-variable model, expressed in deviations from the means

$$y_t = b_1 x_{1t} + b_2 x_{2t} + u_t.$$

Prove that the estimate $\hat{b}_1$ from applying OLS to the above model is equal to the estimate which we can obtain by regressing y^* on x_1^*

where $y^* =$ residuals from the regression $y = \alpha x_2 + v$

$\qquad x_1^* =$ residuals from the regression $x_1 = cx_2 + w$

(where v and w are random terms satisfying the usual assumptions).

7.8. Explain how you would use linear regression to estimate the coefficients of the following non-linear relationships

(a) $X = b_0 . L^{b_1} . K^{b_2} . e^u$.

This is a Cobb–Douglas production function, with $X =$ output; $L =$ labour input; and $K =$ capital input.

(b) $C = b_0 + b_1 X + b_2 X^2 + b_3 P_f + u$.

This is a cost function, with $C =$ total cost; $X =$ output and $P_f =$ price index of factor prices.

Write in each case the set of normal equations required for the application of the linear regression.

Exercises and Questions

(c) Show that in case (a) the coefficients b_1 and b_2 are constan
output with respect to labour input and capital input respe
(d) Define the *a priori* (economic-theoretical) signs of the coeff
each one of the above two functions.

7.9. The following table includes information on the quantity uemanucu ui
a certain commodity, its price, and consumers' income.

Year	1961	1962	1963	1964	1965	1966	1967	1968	1969	1970
Quantity demanded (tons) (Y)	59,190	65,450	62,360	64,700	67,400	64,440	68,000	72,400	75,710	70,680
Price (X_1)	23·56	24·44	32·07	32·46	31·15	34·14	35·30	38·70	39·63	46·68
Income (X_2) (1,000 $)	76,200	91,700	106,700	111,600	119,000	129,200	143,400	159,600	180,000	193,000

(a) Estimate a linear and a log-linear demand function.
(b) Estimate the income and price elasticities for each of the above types of
demand function.
(c) Calculate the t statistic for the regression slope of each function.
(d) Which of the two functions is more satisfactory (i) on *a priori* grounds;
(ii) on statistical grounds?
(e) Forecast the demand for the particular commodity at $X_1 = 50$ and
$X_2 = 200,000$ from each of the two estimated functions.

Intermediate results (original variables):

$\Sigma Y = 670,330·0$ $\Sigma X_1 = 338·13$ $\Sigma X_2 = 1,310,400·0$

$\Sigma X_1 Y = 22,895,663·0$ $\Sigma X_1^2 = 11,863·72$ $\Sigma X_1 X_2 = 46,579,743·0$

$\Sigma X_2 Y = 89,307,903,000$ $\Sigma Y^2 = 45,150,718,300$ $\Sigma X_2^2 = 184,593,140,000$

Intermediate results (in $\log_e$):

$\Sigma(\log_e Y) = 111·1054$ $\Sigma(\log_e X_1) = 35·0156$

$\Sigma(\log_e X_2) = 117·4488$ $\Sigma(\log_e Y)^2 = 1234·4897$

$\Sigma(\log_e X_1)^2 = 123·0020$ $\Sigma(\log_e X_2)^2 = 1380·2043$

$\Sigma(\log_e Y)(\log X_1) = 389·1466$ $\Sigma(\log_e X_1)(\log_e X_2) = 411·7895$

$\Sigma(\log_e Y)(\log X_2) = 1305·0915$

7.10. (a) Interpret and evaluate the following estimated functions on the
basis of (a) the available information from economic theory,
(b) the traditional statistical criteria (r^2, and t tests on the $\hat{b}$'s).

(i) *Estimated demand function* for domestically produced automobiles

$$\hat{D}_x = 1584 - 12P_x + 18P_f + 0 \cdot 6Y \qquad r^2 = 0 \cdot 88$$

s.e.   (320) (3)   (2)   (0·1) $n = 30$

where D_x = demand for domestically produced cars
P_x = price of domestically produced cars
P_f = price of imported cars
Y = disposable income

(ii) *Estimated savings function*

$$\hat{S} = -5 \cdot 000 + 0 \cdot 2Y \qquad r^2 = 0 \cdot 95$$

Standard errors: (500) (0·02) $n = 15$

where S = savings; Y = income

Estimate the MPC and MPS.
Estimate the level of savings for 1978 if in that year income is $200,000.

(b) Estimate the demand for domestically produced cars if $P_x = 3,000$, $P_f = 2,500$, $Y = 250,000$.
(c) Estimate the average price elasticity, cross-elasticity, and income elasticity, given $\bar{D}_x = 60,000$ $\bar{P}_x = 4,000$ $\bar{P}_f = 3,000$ $\bar{Y} = 150,000$.

CHAPTER 8   REGRESSION AND ANALYSIS OF VARIANCE

8.1. The savings function for the economy as a whole is given as

$$S_t = b_0 + b_1 Y_{t-1} + b_2 r_t + u$$

where S_t = aggregate saving in year t
Y_{t-1} = national income in year $t - 1$
r_t = interest rate in year t.

The sample data are given in the following table:

Year	1965	1966	1967	1968	1969	1970	1971	1972	1973	1974	1975
S_t	20	25	25	30	33	38	35	45	43	50	55
Y_t	100	110	130	140	160	170	170	200	240	250	260
r_t	0·02	0·02	0·03	0·02	0·03	0·04	0·03	0·04	0·04	0·05	0·05

(a) Estimate by OLS the parameters of the savings function.
(b) Test the additional variation of r using the ANOVA table.

(c) Test the overall significance of the savings function.
(d) Compute the marginal propensity to consume and the marginal propensity to save.
(e) Forecast the level of savings at $Y_{t-1} = 300$ and $r = 0.8$.

Intermediate results:

$\Sigma S = 399$	$\Sigma Y = 1930$	$\Sigma S^2 = 15{,}707$
$\Sigma SY = 76{,}010$	$\Sigma Y^2 = 369{,}700$	$\Sigma r = 0.37$
$\Sigma Sr = 14.58$		$\Sigma r^2 = 0.0137$
		$\Sigma rY = 70.70$

8.2. The following table includes the output (Y), the labour industry (L), and capital input (K) of fifteen firms of the chemical industry.

Firms	Output (1000 tons) Y	Labour (hours) L	Capital (machine hours) K
1	60	1100	300
2	120	1200	400
3	190	1430	420
4	250	1500	400
5	300	1520	510
6	360	1620	590
7	380	1800	600
8	430	1820	630
9	440	1800	610
10	490	1750	630
11	500	1950	850
12	520	1960	900
13	540	1830	980
14	410	1900	900
15	350	1500	800
	$\Sigma Y = 5{,}340$	$\Sigma L = 24{,}680$	$\Sigma K = 9{,}520$

(a) Using these data, estimate the following Cobb–Douglas production functions

(i) $Y = b_0 . L^{b_1} . e^u$; (ii) $Y = b_0 . L^{b_1} . K^{b_2} . e^u$.

Intermediate results (in the logs to base e):

Let $Y^* = \log_e Y$	$L^* = \log L$	$K^* = \log K$
$\Sigma Y^* = 86.15$	$\Sigma L^* = 110.89$	$\Sigma K^* = 95.96$
$\Sigma Y^* L^* = 638.34$	$\Sigma L^{*2} = 820.12$	$\Sigma K^{*2} = 615.70$
$\Sigma Y^* K^* = 553.85$	$\Sigma Y^{*2} = 500.18$	$\Sigma L^* K^* = 710.14$

(b) Construct an ANOVA table to test:
   (i) The overall significance of the regression $Y = f(L, K)$.
   (ii) The significance of the improvement in the fit from the introduction of K as an additional explanatory variable.
(c) Estimate the marginal product of labour and capital (at the mean values $\bar{Y}, \bar{K}, \bar{L}$).
   8.3. (a) Express the Cobb–Douglas production function $Y = f(L, K)$ in a form that incorporates the assumption of constant returns to scale. (This is the restricted form of the production function.)
(b) Using the data of Exercise 8.2 and the following intermediate results, test the assumption of constant returns to scale.

Intermediate results:

$$\Sigma(\log_e Y/K) = -9{\cdot}8059 \qquad \Sigma(\log_e L/K) = 14{\cdot}9191$$

$$\Sigma(\log_e Y/K)^2 = 8{\cdot}1792 \qquad \Sigma(\log_e L/K)^2 = 15{\cdot}5418$$

$$\Sigma(\log_e Y/K)(\log_e L/K) = -9{\cdot}9495.$$

   8.4. Given two samples $n_1 = n_2$ covering different time periods, from which we estimate two export functions (one for each period) of the form

$$E_t = b_0 + b_1 P_t + b_2 P_{w,t} + b_2 T_t + u_t$$

where P_t = price of exports
$P_{w,t}$ = price of competing 'world' exports (i.e. exports of other countries)
T = tariffs in countries of destination.

Applying the Chow test we find that we reject the null hypothesis.

(a) State the null hypothesis which has been rejected.
(b) Interpret the economic implications of the rejected hypothesis.
(c) Which b's precisely change (are unstable) over time?
   8.5. Given the following observations on output (X), capital input (K) and labour input (L) for ten knitting firms, test the hypothesis that there are constant returns to scale. (Variables are measured in arbitrary units.)

Firms	1	2	3	4	5	6	7	8	9	10
Output (Y)	15·9	20·0	25·1	39·8	25·2	63·1	50·1	79·4	15·8	31·6
Labour	12·6	15·8	25·2	50·1	31·6	63·1	79·5	39·8	15·8	39·9
Capital	31·7	25·2	31·6	25·1	31·7	50·2	31·6	126·0	19·9	15·8

If you accept the hypothesis of constant returns to scale, what can you conclude about the shape of the average variable cost, the average total cost and the marginal cost?

Intermediate results (in logs to the base e):

Let $Y^* = \log_e Y$ $\qquad L^* = \log_e L$ $\qquad K^* = \log_e K$

$\Sigma Y^* = 34\cdot53$ $\qquad \Sigma L^* = 34\cdot54$ $\qquad \Sigma K^* = 34\cdot77$ $\qquad \Sigma Y^{*2} = 122\cdot17$

$\Sigma Y^* L^* = 122\cdot01$ $\qquad \Sigma L^{*2} = 122\cdot80$ $\qquad \Sigma K^{*2} = 123\cdot83$

$\Sigma Y^* K^* = 122\cdot07$ $\qquad\qquad\qquad\qquad \Sigma L^* K^* = 120\cdot94$

Let $\log_e(Y/K) = X_1$ $\qquad$ and $\qquad \log_e(L/K) = X_2$

$\Sigma X_1 = -0\cdot2296$ $\qquad\qquad \Sigma X_2 = -0\cdot2331$ $\qquad \Sigma(X_1)^2 = 1\cdot8593$.

$\Sigma X_1 X_2 = 2\cdot8209$ $\qquad \Sigma(X_2)^2 = 4\cdot7410$

8.6. It is often hypothesised that the marginal propensity to consume declines as income increases. Assuming that you have a cross-section sample on the disposable income and consumption expenditure of a large number of families (randomly selected), explain how you could use the Chow test to investigate this hypothesis.

8.7. The Keynesian liquidity preference (demand for money to hold) is a function relating the amount of money (M) to the interest rate (r) and the level of income (Y). It is commonly assumed that the demand for money is equal to the supply of money: $M_D = M_s$. Using the above information and the data of the following table, estimate the liquidity preference function for Canada

$$M^*_{D,t} = b_0 + b_1 r^*_t + b_2 Y^*_t + u^*_t$$

where
$\qquad M^*$ = percentage change in $M = \Delta \log M$
$\qquad r^*$ = percentage change in $r = \Delta \log r$
$\qquad Y^*$ = percentage change in $Y = \Delta \log Y$.

Year	M millions of \$	r_1 long-run interest rate	r_2 short-run interest rate	Y millions of \$
1945	3,514	2·93	0·36	11,850
1946	3,996	2·61	0·38	12,026
1947	3,943	2·57	0·41	13,768
1948	4,335	2·96	0·41	15,613
1949	4,422	2·83	0·48	16,462
1950	4,330	2·78	0·55	18,167
1951	4,375	3·26	0·80	21,230
1952	4,658	3·59	1·07	23,759
1953	4,558	3·68	1·69	24,724
1954	4,920	3·14	1·44	24,644
1955	5,248	3·08	1·62	27,149
1956	5,186	3·61	2·92	30,071
1957	5,392	4·17	3·76	32,403
1958	6,080	4·22	2·04	33,398
1959	5,890	4·86	4·75	35,472
1960	6,190	5·06	3·32	36,808
1961	6,960	5·03	2·82	38,060
1962	7,190	5·03	4·00	41,054

Intermediate results:

$\Sigma M^* = 0.7159$ $\Sigma r_1^* = 0.5410$ $\Sigma r_2^* = 2.4079$ $\Sigma Y^* = 1.2427$

$\Sigma M^* r_1^* = -0.0060$ $\Sigma r_1^{*2} = 0.1645$ $\Sigma r_2^{*2} = 2.3013$ $\Sigma Y^{*2} = 0.1235$

$\Sigma M^* r_2^* = -0.1095$ $\Sigma r_1^* Y^* = 0.0823$ $\Sigma Y^* r_2^* = 0.2735$ $\Sigma M^{*2} = 0.0754$

$\Sigma M^* Y^* = 0.0364$.

(a) Evaluate your results on the basis of *a priori* statistical and econometric criteria.
(b) Does the choice between using the long-run and the short-run interest rate have any effect on your results?
(c) Explain why, in this example, the Chow test gives more information than usually.

8.8. The following table shows the imports, the national income and the relative price of imports (all measured in index form) of a certain country.

Year	1965	1966	1967	1968	1969	1970	1971	1972	1973
Imports (Y)	100	106	107	120	110	116	123	133	137
National income (X_1)	100	104	106	111	111	115	120	124	126
Relative price of imports (X_2)	100	99	110	126	113	103	102	103	98

Intermediate results:

$\bar{Y} = 1,052$ $\bar{X}_1 = 113$ $\bar{X}_2 = 106$

$\Sigma y^2 = 1,260.89$ $\Sigma x_1^2 = 650$ $\Sigma x_2^2 = 648$

$\Sigma x_1 y = 874$ $\Sigma x_2 y = -79$ $\Sigma x_1 x_2 = -112$

Construct an ANOVA table to test (a) the overall significance of the regression $Y = f(X_1, X_2)$, (b) the significance of the improvement in the fit from the introduction of X_2 as an additional explanatory variable.

8.9. (a) The following is a model of the demand for money

$$M_D = b_0 + b_1(i) + b_2(Y) + b_3(L) + u$$

where M_D = quantity of money demanded
   i = interest rate
   Y = national income
   L = stock of liquid assets (other than money) e.g. savings, time deposits.

Using time series data for the period 1919–57 for the U.S.A., a researcher estimated the following function:

$$M_D = 0.003 - 0.261\ (i) + 0.530\ (Y) + 0.367\ (L)$$

s.e. $\qquad\qquad (0.009)\ (0.112)\qquad (0.101)\qquad (0.102)$

$$\Sigma y^2 = 0.1903 \qquad\qquad R^2 = 0.579.$$

Evaluate these results on the basis of economic (*a priori*), statistical and econometric criteria

(b) In order to test the stability of the function over the long 38-year period used in the sample, the researcher divided the observations into two sub-samples and fitted the following regressions.

Period 1920–39:

$$M_D = 0.008 - 0.180\ (i) + 0.517\ (Y) + 0.281\ (L)$$

s.e. $\qquad\qquad (0.013)\ (0.15)\qquad (0.122)\qquad (0.150)$

$$\Sigma y_1^2 = 0.0927 \qquad\qquad R_1^2 = 0.697$$

Period 1939–57:

$$M_D = -0.013 - 0.419\ (i) + 0.936\ (Y) + 0.587\ (L)$$

$$\Sigma y_2^2 = 0.0805 \qquad\qquad R_2^2 = 0.479$$

The discrepancies between the coefficients of these equations suggest a change in the economic structure.

Perform the Chow test in order to evaluate the hypothesis of an unchanging structure of money demand. (State clearly your H_0 and H_1 hypotheses.)

8.10. A researcher wishes to test the hypothesis that in the model

$$Y_t = b_0 + b_1 X_t + u_t \qquad\qquad (t = 1, 2, \dots, n)$$

$b_0 = 2b_1$.

(a) Would a straightforward application of OLS to the above model be the best procedure?

(b) Outline a formal test for the restriction $b_0 = 2b_1$.

8.11. The Phillips Curve implies that there is a negative relationship between the percentage change in wages and the unemployment rate.

(a) Do the data of the following table support the existence of the Phillips-Curve relationship?

Year	1957	1958	1959	1960	1961	1962	1963	1964	1965	1966
% change in wages	5.0	3.2	2.7	2.1	4.1	2.7	2.9	4.6	3.5	4.4
Unemployment %	1.6	2.2	2.3	1.7	1.6	2.1	2.6	1.7	1.5	1.6

(b) Is your conclusion compatible with the following additional information?

Year	1967	1968	1969	1970
% change in wages	4·0	7·7	5·7	9·5
Unemployment %	2·5	2·5	2·5	2·7

8.12. In order to test the hypothesis that there is no difference in the MPC (marginal propensity to consume) of 'manual workers' and 'white-collar employees' a research team estimated the following consumption functions:

Manual workers: Sample size $n_1 = 35$

$$\hat{C}_1 = 120 + 0.90\,Y \qquad r_1 = 0.92 \qquad \Sigma(C_1 - \overline{C}_1)^2 = 3,251$$
$$(32)\ (5.6)$$

(The numbers in brackets are the t values for the $\hat{b}$'s.)

White-collar employees: Sample size $n_2 = 30$

$$\hat{C}_2 = 160 + 0.82\,Y \qquad r_2^2 = 0.95 \qquad \Sigma(C_2 - \overline{C}_2)^2 = 4,532$$
$$(23)\ (8.5)$$

(The numbers in brackets are the t values for the $\hat{b}$'s.)

Combined sample consumption function: Sample size $n = 30 + 35$

$$\hat{C} = 250 + 0.70\,Y \qquad r^2 = 0.92 \qquad \Sigma e^2 = 16,320$$
$$t_{\hat{b}} \qquad (5.3)\ (6.2)$$

On the basis of the above results, can we accept the hypothesis that there is no difference between the MPC of the two groups? (Use a 5 per cent level of significance.)

8.13. Show that $F^* = \dfrac{R^2/(K-1)}{(1-R^2)/(n-K)}$, and explain the hypothesis being tested by this statistic.

8.14. Consider the model

$$Y_t = a_0 + a_1 X_{1,t} + a_2 X_{2,t} + a_3 X_{3,t} + a_4 X_{4,t} + u_t.$$

Assume you have a sample of 20 observations and you want to test the null hypothesis

$$H_0: a_0 = 5 \qquad 2a_0 + 3a_1 = 4 \qquad a_0 + 2a_1 + a_3 = 7.$$

(a) Outline the procedure which you would adopt to test the above hypothesis.
(b) Find the values of the restricted parameters (hence, the number of restrictions).

(c) Find the degrees of freedom of the restricted form, of the unrestricted form, and of the F ratio (which is appropriate for this test).
(d) Write the restricted form of the above model.

CHAPTER 9   THE ASSUMPTION OF CONSTANT VARIANCE OF u

9.1. The following table includes annual consumption and disposable income in Belgium, 1951–62 (in billions of Belgian francs).

Year	1951	1952	1953	1954	1955	1956	1957	1958	1959	1960	1961	1962
C_t	297·0	303·8	308·1	325·2	339·8	338·6	358·5	358·0	378·7	391·7	413·1	432·8
$Y_{d,t}$	331·4	333·2	338·1	360·4	378·2	375·7	398·6	410·2	417·7	445·9	462·7	486·8
e_t	−3·34	1·94	2·12	0·46	0·08	0·98	1·62	−8·64	5·75	−4·98	2·29	1·71

Source: *United Nations Yearbook of National Accounts Statistics.*

The OLS estimate of the consumption function is

$$\hat{C}_t = 21 \cdot 5 + 0 \cdot 841 \ Y_{d,t} \qquad R^2 = 0 \cdot 992$$
$$\text{s.e.} \qquad (9 \cdot 4) \ (0 \cdot 024) \qquad F = 1265 \cdot 9$$

The residuals are shown in the third row of the above table.

(a) Plot the residuals and comment on the assumption of homoscedasticity.
(b) Test for heteroscedasticity, using Spearman's rank correlation coefficient, r'.
(c) Test for heteroscedasticity, using the Goldfeld and Quandt test (omitting the two observations for 1955 and 1957, in order not to exclude the two critical years 1958 and 1960).
(d) Compare the results of the two tests.
(e) Re-estimate the consumption function, assuming $\sigma^2_{u_t} = \sigma^2_u \cdot Y^2_{d,t}$ (where σ^2_u = constant) and compare your results with the OLS results.
(f) Is there heteroscedasticity in the re-estimated model?

9.2. Consider the following model

$$Y_t = b_0 + b_1 X_t + u_t \tag{1}$$

where u depends on X in the following way

$$u_t = b_2 X_t^2 + v_t \tag{2}$$

where v_t is a random variable which is independent of X and satifies all the other assumptions of the linear regression model.

Which assumptions of the linear regression model are violated in (1)?

9.3. (a) If $\sigma_{u_i}^2 = k^2 [f(X)]$ (where k is a constant), what are the consequences on the OLS estimates?

(b) Show how heteroscedasticity is eliminated if we apply OLS to the transformed model:

$$\frac{Y}{\sqrt{f(X)}} = \frac{b_0}{\sqrt{f(X)}} + b_1 \frac{X}{\sqrt{f(X)}} + \frac{u}{\sqrt{f(X)}}\ .$$

(c) Assuming $\sigma_{u_i}^2 = k^2 \cdot X^2$ (where k is constant), show that the corrective solution implied by (b) is equivalent to the application of weighted least squares (WLS); that is, to the minimisation of the sum of weighted residuals

$$\sum_{i=1}^{n} \frac{e_i^2}{\sigma_{u_i}^2} = \sum_{i=1}^{n} e_i \frac{1}{\sigma_{u_i}^2}\ .$$

(d) What are the weights used in the above case? Are these weights appropriate for dealing with heteroscedastic u's? Explain.

9.4. Discuss the most likely pattern of heteroscedasticity in the following cases.

(a) From a cross-section sample of family expenditures a researcher wants to estimate the food expenditure function

$$E_i = b_0 + b_1 Y_i + b_2 S_i + u_i \qquad (i = 1, 2, \ldots, n)$$

where E_i = food expenditure of the ith household
$\quad\quad\ Y_i$ = disposable income of the ith household
$\quad\quad\ S_i$ = size of the ith household.

(b) The short-run production function of a firm is given by the linear function

$$X_t = b_0 + b_1 L_t + u_t$$

where X = output
$\quad\quad L$ = labour input

It is known that there are frequent breakdowns of the production process if the installed plant is combined with more than fifty workers.

(c) From a cross-section sample of firms a researcher wants to estimate the cost function

$$C_i = b_0 + b_1 X_i + u_i$$

where C_i = total cost of the ith firm
$\quad\quad\ X_i$ = total output of the ith firm.

(Assume that this is a long-run cost function.)

(d) An investigator estimates the following demand function for crude oil from a cross-section of countries being at different stages of economic development

$$Q_j = b_0 + b_1 \,(\text{GDP})_j + u_j$$

where Q_j = demand for crude oil by the jth country

GDP$_j$ = gross domestic product of the jth country.

9.5. Suppose we have the following data on average daily sales of newspapers (Y), population (X_1), and gross domestic product (X_2) for ten different countries.

Country	1	2	3	4	5	6	7	8	9	10
Y_i (millions)	0·2	102·0	2·9	41·5	4·8	3·7	0·8	4·2	1·8	45·0
X_{1i} (millions)	2·3	180·2	7·8	140·1	15·2	21·3	5·7	86·8	14·9	543·1
X_{2i} ($ billion)	0·8	743·2	14·5	110·4	20·2	15·6	3·0	15·3	5·7	115·2

(a) Give some economic reasons to explain why in the above cross-section sample there is heteroscedasticity.

(b) Estimate the newspaper sales function $Y = b_0 + b_1 X_1 + b_1 X_2 + u$ by OLS.

(c) Test for homoscedasticity, using Spearman's rank correlation coefficient.

(d) Assuming that the pattern of heteroscedasticity is

$$\sigma^2_{u_i} = k^2 \cdot X^2 \qquad \text{(where } k^2 \text{ is constant)}$$

transform the original data and re-estimate the newspaper sales function. Compare your results with the OLS estimates.

(e) Do the OLS residuals justify the assumed pattern of heteroscedasticity?

Intermediate results:

$\Sigma Y = \quad 206·9$ $\Sigma X_1 = \quad 1,017·5$ $\Sigma X_2 = \quad 1,043·9$
$\Sigma X_1 Y = 49,204·84$ $\Sigma X_1^2 = 355,597·26$ $\Sigma X_2^2 = 578,943·31$
$\Sigma X_2 Y = 85,845·81$ $\Sigma X_1 X_2 = 214,141·13$ $\Sigma Y^2 = \quad 14,217·95$

9.6. Consider the consumption function to be of the form

$$C_t = b_0 + b_1 Y_t + b_2 A_t + u_t$$

where $\quad C_t$ = consumption expenditure
$\qquad Y_t$ = personal disposable income
$\qquad A_t$ = liquid assets of consumers
$\qquad E(u_t) = 0$
$\qquad \text{var}\,(u_t) = \sigma^2_u \cdot Y_t^2$ (where σ^2_u is a constant).

(a) Transform the above model into one in which the disturbance term is homoscedastic.

(b) Prove that the variance of the disturbance term of the transformed model is equal to σ^2_u, and, hence, the transformed model is homoscedastic.

(c) Write the normal equations required for the estimation of the transformed model.

9.7. Suppose we want to estimate the investment function from a cross-section sample of firms whose annual sales vary from $100,000 to $10 million. The chosen model is

$$I_{j,t} = b_0 + b_1 S_{j,t-1} + b_2 F_{j,t} + u_{j,t}$$

where $I_{j,t}$ = investment of the jth firm in period t
  $S_{j,t-1}$ = sales of the jth firm in period $t-1$
  $F_{j,t}$ = internal funds (from retained profits) of the jth firm in period t

Do you expect this model to be homoscedastic? Why?

9.8. Would you expect to find heteroscedasticity in the random terms of the following two (different) models of savings function?

MODEL A: $S_i = b_0 + b_1 Y_i + u_i$

MODEL B: $\dfrac{S_i}{Y_i} = b_0 \dfrac{1}{Y_i} + b_1 + v_i$

where S_i = savings of the ith household
  Y_i = disposable income of the ith household

  $v_i = \dfrac{u_i}{Y_i}$ = disturbance (random) term of the second model.

9.9. Assume that the price of shares in the stock market is described by the following model

$$P_j = b_0 + b_1 D_j + b_2 R_j + u_j \qquad (j = 1, 2, \ldots, n)$$

where P = price of share of the jth firm
  D_j = dividend of the jth firm
  R_j = retained profits of the jth firm.

(a) If a cross-section sample of large and small firms is used for the estimation of this model, explain why heteroscedasticity is almost certain to exist, arising both from D_j and R_j.
(b) Discuss how you would proceed to explore the pattern of heteroscedasticity in this case.
(c) Outline the 'corrective solution' which you would adopt, and show that this solution eliminates heteroscedasticity.
(d) A researcher used the following transformed model for estimating the stock-price function

$$\left(\frac{P}{D}\right)_j = b_0 \frac{1}{D_j} + b_1 + b_2 \frac{R_j}{D_j} + \frac{u_j}{D_j}.$$

What are his implicit assumptions regarding heteroscedasticity? Relate your answer to section (a) above.

9.10. Assume that a researcher wants to test the hypothesis that large firms are more profitable than small firms. He considers two models

(i) $\Pi_j = b_0 + b_1 A_j + u_j$ $\qquad (j = 1, 2, \ldots, n)$

where Π_j = total profits (in dollars) of the jth firm
A_j = value of total assets of the jth firm

(ii) $\dfrac{\Pi_j}{A_j} = b_0 + b_1 A_j + u_j$

where Π_j/A_j = rate of profit of the jth firm.

(a) In which model is heteroscedasticity more likely? Explain.
(b) Would you choose the transformed model

$$\frac{\Pi_j}{A_j} = b_0 \frac{1}{A_j} + b_1 + \frac{u_j}{A_j}$$

instead of model (ii) for testing the stated hypothesis? Why?

CHAPTER 10 AUTOCORRELATION

10.1. The following table shows the quantity supplied (Y) and the price (X) of a certain commodity. The variables are measured in arbitrary units.

Year	1960	1961	1962	1963	1964	1965	1966	1967	1968	1969	1970	1971	1972	1973	1974
Y_t	2	2	2	1	3	5	6	6	10	10	10	12	15	10	11
X_t	1	2	3	4	5	6	7	8	9	10	11	12	13	14	15
e_t		1.37	0.46	−0.45	−2.36	−1.27	−0.18	−0.09	−1.00	2.08	1.17	0.27	1.36	3.44	−2.46	2.37

(a) Estimate the supply function $Y_t = b_0 + b_1 X_t + u_t$, using the following intermediate results.

$\overline{Y} = 7 \qquad \overline{X} = 8 \qquad \Sigma X_t Y_t = 1095$

$\Sigma x_t^2 = 280 \qquad \Sigma y_t^2 = 274 \qquad \Sigma X_t^2 = 1240$

(b) Find the t-ratios for $\hat{b}_0$ and $\hat{b}_1$ and conduct tests of significance at 5 per cent level.
(c) Estimate the arc elasticity of supply. Also the point elasticity at the price of 10.

(d) Test the overall significance of the regression, using the F statistic.

(e) Using the regression residuals (given in the last row of the above table), test for autocorrelation, using the Durbin–Watson d statistic. Draw an appropriate graph for this test and state the null and alternative hypotheses. (Use $\alpha = 5$ per cent.)

(f) From your findings in (e) above can you definitely conclude that there is no autocorrelation in the residuals? Explain.

10.2. We give below three examples in which at least one of the assumptions of the linear regréssion model are violated.

For each of these examples:

(a) Indicate which assumption(s) is violated

(b) Discuss the effects of these violations on the OLS estimates (on their values and their standard errors)

(c) Discuss briefly appropriate 'corrective' solutions for remedying the violation(s)

Example 1

Assume that a firm's production decision is described by the function

$$S_t = b_0 + b_1 P_t + u_t$$

(where S_t = quantity produced; P_t = price; u_t = random disturbance).

It is further known that, whenever anything causes the firm to 'overproduce' in the period $(t - 1)$, the managers will cut the production in period (t). (Hint: 'overproduction' is reflected by a positive value of the random variable, while 'underproduction' is reflected by a negative value of this variable.)

Example 2

Assume that the firm's production decision is described by the function

$$S_t = b_0 + b_1 P_t + b_2 t + u_t$$

(Where t = time; the other variables are defined in example 1.)

Assume further that the managers react to 'overproduction' in the same way as in the previous example.

Example 3

Suppose that the consumption–income behaviour of a cross-section of families is described by the function

$$C_t = b_0 + b_1 X_t + u_t.$$

It is well known that families in the low-income brackets have rigid spending– savings habits (due to their low income), while families in high-income brackets have very flexible consumption–savings patterns.

10.3. From a times-series sample of twenty-two observations a researcher estimated the following import function

$$M_t = -4030 + 0.406 \, (GNP)_t - 57.2 \, t \qquad R^2 = 0.546$$
$$\text{s.e.} \qquad (0.086) \qquad (59.8) \qquad F = 15.3$$

where M = imports
     GNP = gross national product
      t = time trend

(a) Interpret these results on the basis of *a priori* (economic) and statistical criteria.

(b) What economic factors could explain the negative trend?

(c) The residuals from the above import function are included in the following table.

n	1	2	3	4	5	6	7	8	9	10	11
e_t	260	29	148	−57	−76	−181	40	−81	−89	22	81

n	12	13	14	15	16	17	18	19	20	21	22
e_t	293	−56	−31	−198	−157	−363	−346	−82	161	182	501

From the examination of the residuals, can you conclude that the standard errors of the estimates of the coefficients are reliable? (Hint: Examine the incidence of autocorrelation by conducting an appropriate test.)

(d) Using the result of the previous section, indicate how you can improve the estimated relation between imports and GNP.

    10.4. (a) What autocorrelation scheme is assumed when we estimate a function by using the first differences of the variables? Explain.

(b) What are the implications in case (a) if we do not supress the intercept?

    10.5. Consider the model $Y_t = b_0 + b_1 X_t + u_t$, where u_t is autocorrelated with a first-order autoregressive scheme $u_t = \rho u_{t-1} + v_t$.
(v_t = random term, satisfying all the usual assumptions).

(a) Show that the OLS estimate $\hat{b}_1 = \dfrac{\Sigma xy}{\Sigma x^2}$ is unbiased despite the presence of autocorrelation.

(b) Show that the formula $\text{var}(\hat{b}_1) = \sigma_u^2 \dfrac{1}{\Sigma x^2}$ is not valid (and hence not applicable), because of the serial correlation in the u's.

    10.6. The following table includes the annual consumption expenditure and disposable income in Japan for the twelve-year period 1951−62 (in billions of Yen).

Year	1951	1952	1953	1954	1955	1956	1957	1958	1959	1960	1961	1962
C_t	2863·2	3511·4	4216·9	4667·7	4973·2	5427·2	5886·6	6196·6	6704·9	7514·6	8584·7	9955·7
$Y_{d,t}$	3522·2	4257·1	4774·0	5252·1	5734·0	6352·2	6995·2	7302·6	8244·7	9458·2	11099·9	12687·7
e_t	−377·8	−232·2	91·7	189·6	139·3	110·5	121·6	191·1	17·4	−68·7	−210·6	−11·8

Source: *United Nations Yearbook of National Accounts Statistics.*

The OLS estimated consumption function is

$$\hat{C}_t = 603 + 0·738 \, Y_{d,t} \qquad r^2 = 0·940.$$
$$\text{s.e.} \qquad (152) \ (0·020)$$

The OLS residuals are recorded in the third row of the above table.

(a) Test for a first-order autoregressive scheme using the Durbin–Watson d statistic (at the 5 per cent level of significance).
(b) Obtain an estimate of ρ:
   (i) From the expression $d \cong 2(1 - \rho)$
   (ii) From the residuals $e_t = \rho e_{t-1} + v_t$
   (iii) From Durbin's two-step method.
(c) Use the above estimates to transform the original data and re-estimate the consumption function (for each of the three transformations).
(d) Compare critically the OLS results with those obtained from the three transformed models.
   10.7. The following table shows the values of expenditure on clothing (Y), total expenditure (X_1), and the price of clothing (X_2). The variables are measured in arbitrary units.

Year	1960	1961	1962	1963	1964	1965	1966	1967	1968	1969
Clothing expenditure (Y)	3·5	4·3	5·0	6·0	7·0	9·0	8·0	10·0	12·0	14·0
Total expenditure (X_1)	15	20	30	42	50	54	65	72	85	90
Price of clothing (X_2)	16	13	10	7	7	5	4	3	3.5	2
e_t		−0·16	0·43	0·12	−0·22	−0·50	1·25	−1·31	−0·24	−0·43	1·07

Applying OLS we obtain the following results

$$\hat{Y}_t = -1.92 + 0.160\,(X_1) + 0.198\,(X_2) \qquad R^2 = 0.95$$

s.e. $\qquad\qquad (0.03) \qquad\quad (0.18)$

(a) Evaluate the results on *a priori* criteria.
(b) Evaluate the statistical significance of the results (at the 5 per cent level of significance), using
  (i) The t-ratios of the $\hat{b}$'s
  (ii) The F ratio for the overall regression
(c) Using the residuals (shown in the last row of the above table), test for auto-correlation, using the Durbin–Watson $\underline{d}$ statistic. State clearly the null and alternative hypotheses and draw a graph for this test. (Use $\alpha = 5$ per cent, $d_u = 1.65$, $d_L = 0.90$.)
(d) Test for heteroscedasticity, using Spearman's rank correlation coefficient r'. Test the statistical significance of r' (at $\alpha = 0.05$).

10.8. Consider the following quarterly data on consumption of steel and gross national product of a certain country. (Variables are measured in arbitrary units.)

Year	Quarter	Consumption of steel (Y)	GDP (X)	e_t
1965	1	385	443·6	10·84
	2	390	445·6	12·90
	3	398	444·5	22·52
	4	396	450·3	12·01
1966	1	368	453·4	−20·55
	2	365	453·2	−23·25
	3	364	455·2	−27·18
	4	374	448·2	−6·91
1967	1	372	437·5	6·79
	2	371	439·5	2·86
	3	387	450·7	2·42
	4	407	461·6	6·42
1968	1	406	468·6	−4·86
	2	432	479·9	4·56
	3	431	475·0	10·75
	4	425	480·4	−3·18
1969	1	445	490·2	2·44
	2	437	489·7	−4·83
	3	427	487·3	−11·31
	4	417	483·7	−16·02
1970	1	430	482·6	−1·41
	2	453	497·8	−0·72
	3	470	501·5	10·85
	4	489	511·7	14·88

The estimated regression line is

$$\hat{Y} = -277 \cdot 0093 + 1 \cdot 4679\,X \qquad R^2 = \quad 0 \cdot 866$$
s.e. $\qquad\qquad\qquad (0 \cdot 12) \qquad\qquad\qquad F = 141 \cdot 69$

(a) Using a 5 per cent critical region, determine whether there is a significant linear first-order autocorrelation.
(b) Can you give economic reasons for the observed autocorrelation?
(c) Estimate the first-order autocorrelation coefficient ρ by the two-step Cochrane–Orcutt method.
(d) Using the estimate $\hat{\rho}$, apply OLS to an appropriately transformed model so as to eliminate the first-order autocorrelation.

10.9. The following table shows the value of imports (Y), the level of gross national product (X_1), and the price index of imported goods (X_2), over the twelve-year period 1960–71 for a certain country.

Year	1960	1961	1962	1963	1964	1965	1966	1967	1968	1969	1970	1971
Y (imports)	57	43	73	37	64	48	56	50	39	43	69	60
X_1 (GNP)	220	215	250	241	305	258	354	321	370	375	385	385
X_2 (price index)	125	147	118	160	128	149	145	150	140	115	155	152
Estimated Y_t	54·3	49·5	56·6	47·4	55·8	50·2	53·4	51·9	54·9	60·4	52·1	52·7

(a) Are X_1 and X_2 meaningful explanatory variables of Y on *a priori* grounds
    (i) If Y = imports of consumer goods
    (ii) If Y = imports of intermediate commodities.
(b) State your *a priori* expectations regarding the signs and magnitudes of the coefficients of X_1 and X_2.
(c) Applying OLS to the above data we obtain the following import function

$$\hat{Y}_t = 75 \cdot 40 + 0 \cdot 02537\,(X_1) - 0 \cdot 21329\,(X_2) \qquad R^2 = 0 \cdot 088$$
s.e. $\qquad\qquad (0 \cdot 05) \qquad\qquad (0 \cdot 25) \qquad\qquad \Sigma e^2 = 1401 \cdot 22$

Evaluate these results on the basis of the standard statistical criteria $(t - \text{ratios}, R^2, \text{ANOVA})$.

Using the information of the last column of the above table, test for autocorrelation, using the Durbin–Watson d statistic.

Draw the appropriate graph for this test, indicating clearly on it the critical d_u and d_L values. (Use $d_u = 1 \cdot 65$ and $d_L = 0 \cdot 90$.)

What is the null hypothesis tested by the Durbin–Watson statistic?

Would you apply the D–W test if you suspected that the u's were autocorrelated as follows

$$u_t = \rho u_{t-3} + v_t$$

What test would you use in this case?

(d) How would you proceed if you wanted to test the hypothesis that the u_t's exhibit a second-order autoregressive scheme?

10.10. A researcher used OLS to estimate the following demand for money function for the U.S.A. over the 39-year period 1919–57.

$$\log \frac{M}{P} = b_0 + b_1 \log(i) + b_2 \log \frac{Y}{P} + b_3 \log \frac{L}{P} + u$$

$$\widehat{\log \frac{M}{P}} = 2 \cdot 310 - 0 \cdot 761 \log(i) + 0 \cdot 008 \log \frac{Y}{P} + 0 \cdot 012 \frac{L}{P}$$

s.e. $\qquad\qquad (0 \cdot 11) \quad (0 \cdot 44) \qquad\quad (0 \cdot 001) \qquad\quad (0 \cdot 006)$

where M = quantity of nominal money demanded
$\quad i$ = interest rate
$\quad L$ = nominal amount of liquid assets
$\quad P$ = price index (to deflate nominal values, so as to eliminate changes in purchasing power).

The residuals (e_t) showed that

$$\sum_{t=1}^{39} e_t^2 = 1 \cdot 0567 \qquad \sum_{t=2}^{39} (e_t - e_{t-1})^2 = 0 \cdot 2240.$$

On the basis of this information, the researcher decided to re-estimate the demand for money function, using the first differences of the original variables.

(a) Calculate the Durbin–Watson d statistic.
(b) Does the value of d justify the 'first-differences' solution, adopted by the researcher?

10.11. (a) 'Autocorrelation is a problem that arises when using time-series data, not when using cross-section data.' Explain.
(b) If the d statistic assumes a value close to zero in a cross-section sample, what can we infer from this finding?

10.12. (a) Show algebraically that the limiting values of the Durbin–Watson d statistic cannot be smaller than zero and greater than 4.
(b) Show that in the case of the first-order autocorrelation the test of the null hypothesis $H_0 : \rho = 0$ is equivalent to the test of the null hypothesis $H_0 : d = 2$.
(c) Draw a graph showing the position of the critical region (in a two-tailed test) of the Durbin–Watson d statistic and comment on this region.

10.13. Using forty quarterly observations a researcher estimated the following model of the determination of prices of shares in the U.K.

$$Y = b_0 . X_1^{b_1} . X_2^{b_2} . e^u$$

where $Y = P$ = ordinary shares price index of *The Financial Times*.
$\quad X_1$ = GDP = gross domestic product
$\quad X_2$ = gross earnings of firms; that is, earnings before interest payments and tax payments (EBIT).

The estimated share-price function is

$$\log_e (\hat{P})_t = -5 \cdot 10 + 0 \cdot 72 \log_e (GDP)_t + 0 \cdot 50 \log_e (EBIT)$$

s.e. $(0 \cdot 22)$ $(0 \cdot 34)$ $R^2 = 0 \cdot 751.$

The forty residuals (e_t) are included in the following table.

n	1	2	3	4	5	6	7	8	9	10
e_t	0·008	0·053	0·169	0·027	0·071	0·068	0·053	0·024	0·056	−0·076

n	11	12	13	14	15	16	17	18	19	20
e_t	−0·104	−0·159	−0·111	−0·095	−0·075	−0·018	−0·206	−0·142	−0·190	−0·137

n	21	22	23	24	25	26	27	28	29	30
e_t	−0·016	−0·022	0·069	0·197	0·204	0·279	0·196	0·066	0·040	0·066

n	31	32	33	34	35	36	37	38	39	40
e_t	0·020	−0·148	−0·076	−0·151	−0·137	−0·020	−0·020	−0·049	0·138	0·047

(a) Construct an ANOVA table to test the overall significance of the estimated stock-price function.

(b) Compare your finding in (1) above with the conclusions which you can draw by an examination of the standard errors of the $\hat{b}$'s.

(c) By simple inspection of the residuals find out whether there is positive or negative autocorrelation in the u's.

(d) Verify your findings in (3) by estimating the Durbin–Watson d statistic.

(e) Obtain an estimate of ρ, assuming a first-order autoregressive scheme. (Use (i) the d^* value, (ii) the expression $\rho = \Sigma e_t e_{t-1} / \Sigma e_{t-1}^2$.)

(f) Outline the way in which your estimate $\hat{\rho}$ would be of use in improving the estimated function. Explain.

10.14. A researcher wants to use quarterly data to estimate the model

$$Y_t = b_0 + b_1 X_t + u_t \qquad (t = 1, 2, \ldots, n)$$

It is known that the random terms in the same quarters of successive years are serially correlated

$$u_t = \rho u_{t-4} + v_t \qquad (t = 1, 2, \ldots, n)$$

where v_t is a random term satisfying all the usual assumptions. An estimate of ρ can be obtained from the OLS residuals of the original model, e_t's, by regressing e_t on e_{t-4}; that is

$$e_t = \rho e_{t-4} + v_t$$

where

$$\hat{\rho} = \frac{\sum\limits_{t=4}^{n} e_t e_{t-4}}{\sum\limits_{t=4}^{n} e_{t-4}^2}$$

(a) Given this estimate, find an appropriate transformation of the original model so as to remove the serial correlation.
(b) Show that your transformation includes a random term which is not serially correlated with a fourth-order autoregressive scheme.

10.15. A researcher, using time-series data for the period 1954–65, estimated the following consumption function:

$$\hat{C} = -3\cdot0 + 0\cdot9277\,X$$

The following table includes the data used and the residual errors:

Year	1954	1955	1956	1957	1958	1959	1960	1961	1962	1963	1964	1965
Consumption (C) (billions of $)	236	254	267	281	290	311	325	335	355	375	401	431
Income (X) (billions of $)	257	275	293	309	319	337	350	364	385	405	437	469
e_t		0·52	1·82	−1·87	−2·71	−2·99	1·30	3·25	0·26	0·78	2·23	−1·45	−1·14

(a) Test for autocorrelation (at the 5 per cent level of significance), using the Durbin–Watson d statistic. State clearly the null and alternative hypotheses and draw a graph to illustrate your test.
(b) Test for heteroscedasticity, using the Spearman's rank-correlation coefficient.
(c) Outline the corrective solution which you would adopt if heteroscedasticity is found significant in (b).
(d) Outline a method that you would adopt if you were to obtain an estimate of the autoregressive structure of the residuals:
  (i) for a first-order autoregressive scheme
  (ii) for a second-order autoregressive scheme.

10.16. Show that, if we decided to use first differences of the variables in order to avoid autocorrelation, it is necessary to suppress the intercept, because the presence of an intercept in a function expressed in the first differences of the variables *incorporates* the assumption that the dependent variable is affected by an autonomous trend.

10.17. Assume that the short-run production decision of a firm is given by the model

$$Y_t = b_0 + b_1 X_t + u_t$$

where Y_t = output; X_t = labour input.

Suppose further that whenever anything causes the firm to 'overproduce' in the period $t-1$ (a fact indicated by $u_{t-1} > 0$), the firm will tend to 'underproduce' in period t (a fact indicated by $u_t < 0$).

(a) Identify which assumption(s) of the linear regression model is violated.

(b) Indicate the effects of these violations on the OLS estimate of the slope coefficient and its standard error.

(c) Discuss briefly the appropriate 'corrective solution' in this case.

10.18. In Exercise 2 of Chapter 8 (p. 172) the estimated linear demand function is

$$D = b_0 + b_1 P + b_2 Y + u$$

$$\hat{D} = 62471 \cdot 55 - 969 \cdot 28\,P + 0 \cdot 2849\,Y \quad R^2 = 0 \cdot 903$$
$$t_{\hat{b}_i} \qquad\qquad (-3 \cdot 06) \quad (4 \cdot 93) \qquad F = 32 \cdot 58$$

The residuals are

e_1	e_2	e_3	e_4	e_5	e_6	e_7	e_8	e_9	e_{10}
$-2156 \cdot 08$	$540 \cdot 63$	$572 \cdot 48$	$1894 \cdot 39$	$1216 \cdot 23$	$-1751 \cdot 79$	$-1113 \cdot 28$	$1966 \cdot 59$	$365 \cdot 66$	$-1534 \cdot 83$

The Durbin–Watson $\underline{d}$ statistic is $1 \cdot 63$.

(a) Is there autocorrelation in the function? (Note that the d-table starts for $n = 15$. Since your sample is $n = 10$, use as the critical value of $d_u = 1 \cdot 65$.) Draw a graph, illustrating your Durbin–Watson test, stating clearly your H_0 and H_1.

(b) Obtain an estimate of ρ from the expression $d \cong 2\,(1 - \rho)$.

(c) Obtain an estimate of ρ using Durbin's two-step method. Compare this estimate with the one obtained in (b) above and comment on their difference.

(d) Use $\hat{\rho}$ obtained in (b) above to transform the original data and re-estimate the demand function (in linear form) with the transformed data

$$D_t^* = b_0 + b_1 P_t^* + b_2 Y_t^* + v_t$$

(This is the method of Generalised Least Squares, GLS.)

(e) Compare the OLS estimates with the GLS estimates and comment on the differences in results.

10.19. Consider the investment model

$$I_t = b_0 + b_1 (S_t - S_{t-1}) + b_2 r_t + u_t$$

$$u_t = \rho_1 u_{t-1} + \rho_2 u_{t-2} + v_t$$

where I = investment $\quad r$ = interest rate
$\quad\quad\quad S$ = sales $\quad\quad v$ = random term satisfying the usual assumptions

(a) Outline a method for obtaining estimates of ρ_1 and ρ_2 of the second-order autocorrelation.

(b) Write the transformed variables which you would use in order to eliminate the assumed pattern of autocorrelation.
(c) Show that your transformation in (b) eliminates the second-order autocorrelation.

10.20. Assume that we have the following true model

$$Y_t = 50 + X_t + u_t \qquad (t = 1, 2, \ldots, 20)$$

(the model assumes that the true slope is equal to 1). The u's are serially correlated as follows

$$u_t = u_{t-2} + v_t$$

where v_t is a random variable satisfying all the usual assumptions. It is known that $u_0 = -6$ and $u_{-1} = +5$.

(a) Suppose that the values of X_t are defined by the relation $X_t = t$. Assume also that all the v's (in the artificial sample) are equal to zero. Under these conditions generate a sample of twenty points (twenty values of Y_t and twenty values of X_t).
(b) Use the generated sample to estimate the model $Y_t = b_0 + b_1 X_t + u_t$ by OLS.
(c) Does the Durbin–Watson d statistic warn us about the existence of the above autoregressive scheme of the u's? Why?
(d) Because of autocorrelation, the OLS method is not appropriate for estimating the model. Find the transformation of the original data corresponding to the assumed autoregressive scheme.
Can we apply OLS to the transformed data and re-estimate the model?
(e) Test whether the estimate b_1^* obtained from the original data is in fact equal to 1.

10.21. A researcher estimated the following log-linear money-demand function, using data for the 39-year period 1937–75.

$$(\log M) = \log b_0 + b_1 (\log r) + b_2 (\log Y) + b_3 \log (L) + u$$

where M = supply of money (= demand for money)
$\quad r$ = interest rate
$\quad Y$ = income
$\quad L$ = liquid assets

$$\log M = 2 \cdot 310 - 0 \cdot 761 \ (\log r) + 0 \cdot 008 \ (\log Y) + 0 \cdot 012 \ (\log L)$$
s.e. $\qquad (0 \cdot 110) \ (0 \cdot 444) \qquad (0 \cdot 001) \qquad (0 \cdot 006)$

$R^2 = 0 \cdot 884; \quad r_{(\log M)(\log L)} = 0 \cdot 81$

The pattern of the regression residuals, reproduced below, suggests that there is strong evidence of positive first order autocorrelation in the estimated function.

Year	Residual	Year	Residual	Year	Residual	Year	Residual
1937	−0·0764	1947	−0·1126	1957	0·0851	1967	0·1546
1938	0·0359	1948	−0·1426	1958	0·1836	1968	0·0354
1939	−0·0250	1949	−0·1400	1959	0·1668	1969	0·0125
1940	−0·0844	1950	0·0958	1960	0·1671	1970	0·0240
1941	−0·1073	1951	−0·0883	1961	0·2263	1971	−0·0915
1942	−0·0919	1952	−0·0274	1962	0·1708	1972	−0·1900
1943	−0·0990	1953	−0·0229	1963	0·2270	1973	−0·2580
1944	−0·1254	1954	0·0435	1964	0·2927	1974	−0·3360
1945	−0·1396	1955	0·0555	1965	0·3098	1975	−0·3306
1946	−0·1933	1956	0·1086	1966	0·2872		

(a) Compute the Durbin–Watson $\underline{d}$ statistic and verify the above statement.

(b) Obtain an estimate of ρ

  (i) from the expression $d \cong 2(1 - \rho)$

  (ii) from the expression $\hat{\rho} = \Sigma e_t e_{t-1} / \Sigma e_{t-1}^2$.

(c) Test whether the estimate $\hat{\rho}$ from the second expression is significantly different from 1, i.e. $H_0 : \rho = 1$.

(d) If you accept H_0 in the previous question, what procedure would you adopt in order to avoid the consequences of autocorrelation?

CHAPTER 11

11.1. (a) Using the hypothetical observations of the following table, show that multicollinearity makes the coefficient of X_1 unstable and increases its standard error

n	1	2	3	4	5	6	7	8
Y	9	5	8	6	8	5	9	6
X_1	9	4	8	7	8	4	9	7
X_2	7	2	4	3	4	2	7	3

(b) Is this a general result of multicollinearity?

Intermediate results:

$$\Sigma Y = 56 \qquad \Sigma X_1 = 56 \qquad \Sigma X_2 = 32$$
$$\Sigma Y X_1 = 414 \qquad \Sigma X_1^2 = 420 \qquad \Sigma X_2^2 = 156$$
$$\Sigma Y X_2 = 246 \qquad \Sigma X_1 X_2 = 248 \qquad \Sigma Y^2 = 412$$

11.2. What are relevant indicators of the seriousness of multicollinear X's?

11.3. (a) Outline Frisch's Confluence Analysis as applied in exploring the pattern of multicollinearity.

(b) Would you omit an explanatory variable if it is found to be detrimental (in the Frisch sense)?

(c) In what sense is Frisch's approach superior to the Glauber and Farrar test?

11.4. Consider the model

$$Y_t = b_0 + b_1 X_{1t} + b_2 X_{2t} + b_3(X_{1t} - X_{2t}) + a_4 X_{1t} X_{2t} + u_t$$

Under the assumptions of the linear regression model, which parameters can and which ones cannot be estimated? Explain.

11.5. The omission of an important explanatory variable from a function imparts a 'mis-specification bias' in the estimates of the coefficients of the included variables.

Derive an algebraic expression to show the nature and the determinants of this bias.

11.6. Consider the following linear production function of an economy

$$X_t = b_0 + b_1 L_t + b_2 K_t + u_t$$

where X_t = quantity of output produced in t

L_t = 'quantity' of labour (e.g. hours)

K_t = 'quantity' of capital (e.g. machine hours)

(a) Which assumptions of the linear regression model are likely to be violated in this single-equation model?

(b) Suppose that capital is omitted from the function. Explore the bias which will be imparted in $\hat{b}_1$, taking into account that this is a model of the production process *over time*. Would the bias in $\hat{b}_1$ be the same if you had a *cross-section* of firms from the same industry? Why?

11.7. Assume that the true investment function is

$$I_t = b_0 + b_1(\Pi_t) + b_2(r_t) + b_3(K_{t-1}) + u_t$$

where I = investment expenditure

Π = profits

r = interest rate

K_{t-1} = stock of capital existing at the end of the previous period

(a) Express your *a priori* expectations regarding the sign of the coefficients of the above relationship, including b_0.

(b) Derive an expression measuring the specification bias that would be imparted in b_1 if r and K were mistakenly omitted from the investment function.

(c) Will b_1 be under-estimated or over-estimated by the omission of the above two variables?

11.8. Assume that a researcher estimates the aggregate consumption function with the simple model

$$C_t = b_0 + b_1 Y_{d,t} + u_t$$

where C_t = consumption expenditure

$Y_{d,t}$ = disposable personal income

It is known, however, that aggregate consumption is affected by many other factors. The most important of these other determinants are

N = population	L = liquid assets
M = money supply	A = total assets
r = interest rate	W = total wealth
P = general price level	

Explain the effects on the value of b_1 of the violation of the *ceteris paribus* clause for each one of the above variables.

11.9. Assume that the consumption behaviour of a cross-section of families is estimated by the model

$$Y_j = b_0 + b_1 X_j + u_j$$

where Y_j = consumption expenditure of the jth family
X_j = disposable income of the jth family

(a) We observe that two important regressors are omitted: liquid assets, and size of family.
(b) It is known that families with small incomes have very similar and rigid spending habits, while high-income families have very dissimilar and flexible spending habits.
(c) Given (a) and (b) which assumption(s), of the linear regression model are violated?
(d) What are the consequences of these violations on the OLS estimate of b_1?
(e) Discuss appropriate 'corrective' solution(s).

11.10. A wine producer knows that the amount of wine that goes sour (Y) depends on the amount of chemical used (X_1) and the length of fermentation time (X_2). The producer suspects that the use of greater quantities of chemicals can speed up the wine-production process.

To test this hypothesis the producer hires an econometrician and provides him with the following information for sixty-seven producing periods:

$$\Sigma(Y - \bar{Y})^2 = 1\cdot16 \qquad \Sigma(Y - \bar{Y})(X_1 - \bar{X}_1) = -8$$
$$\Sigma(X_1 - \bar{X}_1)^2 = 100 \qquad \Sigma(X_2 - \bar{X}_2)^2 = 100$$
$$\Sigma(X_1 - \bar{X}_1)(X_2 - \bar{X}_2) = -80 \qquad \Sigma(Y - \bar{Y})(X_2 - \bar{X}_2) = 100$$

The researcher estimated the functions

$$y = b_1 x_1 + u$$

and

$$y = b_1 x_1 + b_2 x_2 + v$$

(where u and v are random disturbances) and found that the value of b_1 in the first regression was different than that obtained from the second regression.

Estimate the two regressions and explain the difference in the two estimates of b_1, deriving an appropriate expression for measuring this difference.

11.11. Consider the model (in deviation form)

$$y_t = b_1 x_{1,t} + b_2 x_{2,t} + u_t \qquad (t = 1, 2, \ldots, n)$$

If X_1 and X_2 are *orthogonal* (i.e., $r_{x_1 x_2} = 0$), show that the estimates $\hat{b}_1$ and $\hat{b}_2$ obtained from applying multiple regression to the above model are identical with the estimates b_1^* and b_2^* obtained from the simple regressions

$$y = b_1 x_1 + v$$

and

$$y = b_2 x_2 + w$$

(where v and w are random terms satisfying the usual assumptions).

11.12. Consider the following Cobb–Douglas production function

$$X_t = b_0 . L_{1t}^{b_1} . L_{2t}^{b_2} . K_t^{b_3} . e^{u_t}$$

where L_1 = unskilled workers
L_2 = skilled workers
K = capital input
u = random term
e = base of natural logarithms

Assume that the total labour force of the firm in all periods is 2,000 workers, that is $L_1 + L_2 = 2{,}000$ for all t. Can we estimate the parameters of the production function?

11.13. Assume that there are n commodities and that the demand for commodity 1 depends on its own price, the prices of the remaining commodities, the general price level, measured by the simple average of all prices,

$$P_G = \frac{\displaystyle\sum_{i=1}^{n} P_i}{n}$$

and income. The demand function may be written as

$$D_1 = b_0 + b_1 P_1 + b_2 P_2 + \ldots + b_n P_n + a P_G + c Y + u$$

Can we estimate the parameters of this demand function? Why?

11.14. The following table shows the quantity demanded of a certain commodity, its price, and consumers' income. The variables are measured in arbitrary units.

Year		1965	1966	1967	1968	1969	1970	1971	1972	1973	1974
Demand	(Y)	3·5	4·3	5·0	6·0	7·0	9·0	8·0	10	12	14
Price	(X_1)	16	13	10	7	7	5	4	3	3·5	2
Income	(X_2)	15	20	30	42	50	54	65	72	85	90

(a) Discuss the effects of multicollinearity on the basis of the following results.

(i) $r_{X_1 X_2} = -0.943$

(ii) $Y_t = b_0 b_1 X_1 + u_t$

$\hat{Y}_t = 12.4879 - 0.6536 (X_1)$ $s_{\hat{b}_1} = 0.121$ $R^2 = 0.784$
                                                                                                  $F^* = 28.97$
                                                $t_{\hat{b}_1} = -5.38$ $d = 0.72$

(iii) $Y_t = b_0 + b_2 X_2 + u_t$

$\hat{Y}_t = 1.2179 + 0.12738 (X_2)$ $s_{\hat{b}_2} = 0.011$ $R^2 = 0.942$
                                                                                                  $F^* = 130.76$
                                                $t_{\hat{b}_2} = 11.44$ $d = 1.96$

(iv) $Y_t = b_0 + b_1 X_1 + b_2 X_2 + u$

$\hat{Y}_t = -1.9194 + 0.19841 (X_1) + 0.16062 (X_2)$ $R^2 = 0.950$
$\qquad\qquad (0.19) \qquad\qquad (0.03)$ $F^* = 67.04$
                                                                                            $d = 2.64$

(b) Explain the specification bias in model (ii), in which 'income' is omitted, and in model (iii), in which 'price' is omitted, by referring to an appropriate expression measuring the specification bias.

(c) Would you omit X_2 because it is *detrimental* in the Frisch sense? Why?

11.15. Consider the model

$$Y_t = b_0 + b_1 X_t + b_2 X_t^2 + u_t.$$

Does this model have perfect multicollinearity? (Hint: Write the normal equations and examine whether they are linearly independent.)

11.16. Consider the following demand for money function

$$M_D = b_0 + b_1 X_1 + b_2 X_2 + b_3 X_3 + u$$

where $X_1 = r_t$ = interest rate
$\qquad X_2 = r_{t-1}$ = lagged interest rate as a measure of 'habits' or 'inertia'
$\qquad X_3 = r_t - r_{t-1}$ = a measure of expectations, based on the most recent
$\qquad\qquad\qquad\qquad$ change in r.

(a) Show that we have perfect multicollinearity between the variables.

(b) Which coefficients cannot be estimated without further information?

(c) Verify that perfect multicollinearity is shown by the fact that the normal equation corresponding to X_3 is equal to the difference of the two normal equations corresponding to X_1 and X_2.

11.17. From a sample of fifty observations the following log-linear demand functions for commodity x were estimated

$$\widehat{\log_e Q_t} = 2.8 + 1.30 (\log_e Y_t) \qquad\qquad R^2 = 0.93$$
s.e. $\qquad\qquad\qquad (0.06)$

$$\log_e \widehat{Q}_t = 3 \cdot 5 + 0 \cdot 85 \ (\log_e Y_t) - 1 \cdot 40 \ (\log_e P_t) \qquad R^2 = 0 \cdot 98$$

s.e. $\qquad\qquad\qquad (0 \cdot 08) \qquad\qquad (0 \cdot 32)$

where Q = quantity demanded of $\underline{x}$
$\quad\quad Y$ = disposable income
$\quad\quad P$ = price of $\underline{x}$.

(a) Evaluate the results on *a priori* and statistical criteria.
(b) Explain the difference of the income coefficient in the two models.
(c) Referring to the appropriate expression of the specification bias in the coefficient of income, can you name a commodity for which $\hat{b}_1$ in the first function would be lower than $\hat{b}_1$ in the second function?
(d) If there is no 'money illusion' and it is known that the coefficient of price is equal to -1, what would you expect the value of the estimate of the income coefficient to be?

11.18. Assume that *the true* demand function of commodity z is linear of the form

$$Q_{z,\,t} = b_0 + b_1 P_{z,\,t} + b_2 Y_t + u_t$$

where Q_z = quantity demanded
$\quad\quad P_z$ = price of commodity z
$\quad\quad Y$ = personal disposable income
$\quad\quad u$ = random term, satisfying the usual assumptions.

Suppose that Y_t is mistakenly omitted from the demand function.

(a) Derive an expression for the specification bias imparted in $\hat{b}_1$. (Use general notation for the variables.)
(b) Under what conditions will $\hat{b}_1$ be upwardly biased? Under what conditions will $\hat{b}_1$ be downwardly biased?
(c) What is the most plausible type of bias in $\hat{b}_1$ on *a priori* economic criteria?

11.19. From economic theory we know the above function excludes several important explanatory variables. The most obvious omission is the price of other commodities, P_0. Explain the effects of this omission on the assumptions of the linear regression model.

CHAPTER 12 ERRORS IN VARIABLES; TIME AS A VARIABLE; DUMMY VARIABLES

12.1. An economist wants to estimate the tax-revenue function

$$T_t = b_0 + b_1 (\text{GDP})_t + u_t$$

where $\quad T$ = government tax revenue
$\quad\quad$GDP = gross domestic product

It is known that GDP has errors of measurement, and the investigator decides to use the instrumental-variables (IV) method using as an instrument the number of cars registered. The relevant data are included in the following table.

Year		1966	1967	1968	1969	1970
Tax revenue	(Y) \$ million	3	2	5	6	4
GDP	(X) \$ billion	4	1	7	8	5
Cars registered (Z)	millions	5	1	9	6	4

(a) Estimate the tax-revenue function by OLS.
(b) Estimate the tax-revenue function by IV. Compare the two estimated functions.
(c) Is Z a good instrumental variable for GDP?

12.2. Consider the true model

$$Y_t = b_0 + b_1 X_t + u_t$$

where X_t has no measurement errors.

Assume that our sample observations on X have errors of measurement, so that what we observe is

$$X'_t = X_t + v_t$$

where v_t is a random variable satisfying all the usual stochastic assumptions and in addition it is independent of u_t.

(a) Write the regression model relating Y_t to X'_t
(b) What assumptions of the linear regression model are violated in this case?
(c) What are the consequences of the violation of these assumptions on the properties of the OLS estimates.
(Hint: Recall which assumptions are necessary for the derivation of each basic property.)

12.3. We may test changes in the coefficients of a function over time (a) by using dummy variables, (b) by using time t in the function, (c) by applying a Chow test. Outline each of these methods, stating the hypothesis being tested in each case.

12.4. It is known that purchases of new cars are higher in spring and in autumn. Given the model

$$A_t = b_0 + b_1 Y_t + b_2 P_t + u_t$$

where A = number of new cars purchases
Y = disposable income
P = price of cars.

Show how the seasonal variation in car purchases can be taken into account by appropriately defined dummy variables, if the model is to be estimated by quarterly data.

12.5. Assume that the seasonal variation in the car purchases are due to seasonal fluctuations of costs and prices of cars. Would you proceed with seasonal adjustment of your data (either by using dummy variables, or other methods) when estimating the demand for new cars with quarterly data? Explain.

12.6. In estimating the following relationships from quarterly data, do you think that seasonal adjustments of the data is necessary?

(a) Number of new houses started $= f$ (price of houses, interest rates).
(b) Strawberry consumption $= f$ (price of strawberries, income).
(c) Ice cream consumption $= f$ (price of ice cream, income).
(d) Ice cream consumption $= f$ (price of ice cream, income, temperature).

12.7. It is known that the level of investment is determined by the change of sales over the previous year and by businessmen expectations. Given the model

$$I_t = b_0 + b_1(S_t - S_{t-1}) + u_t,$$

show how you could use a dummy variable to take into account expectations, assuming that changes in expectations do not affect the slope of the investment function.

12.8. Assume that expectations do not only shift the investment function but also change its slope. Use dummy variables to test this hypothesis.

12.9. Consider the demand for compact-size cars

$$C = b_0 + b_1 Y + b_2 P + u$$

Using time t, construct a model for the demand of compact cars to test the following hypotheses.

(a) The demand for compact cars declines autonomously over time.
(b) The slopes b_1 and b_2 change over time.
(c) All coefficients change over time.
(d) If all coefficients change over time, what alternative procedure could you adopt to test this hypothesis?

12.10. Consider the model

$$Y_t = b_0 + b_1 X_{1,t} + b_2 X_{2,t} + u_t$$

Test the hypothesis that the relationship between Y and X_2 is non-linear, by an appropriately constructed dummy variable.

12.11. Explain the 'dummy variable trap'. Illustrate your answer with an example of your own.

12.12. It is argued that whenever studies are published linking lung-cancer to smoking, the demand for cigarettes declines.

The following table includes the quantity of cigarettes bought (Y), cigarette price (X_1) and the level of disposable income during 1961–70. (Variables are measured in arbitrary units.)

It is known that two tobacco studies have been published during this decade, one in 1965 and one in 1970.

Year	1961	1962	1963	1964	1965	1966	1967	1968	1969	1970
Cigarettes bought	16·1	17·3	19·9	20·4	20·5	22·0	24·0	24·7	25·7	24·5
Price	70	69	62	70	62	63	62	64	65	67
Income	22 97	26·02	26·43	26·67	26·11	25·87	26·34	24·92	25·49	26·42

Using the above information and an appropriately constructed dummy variable, test the hypothesis of the lung-cancer scare caused by smoking.

Intermediate results:

$\Sigma Y = \quad 215 \cdot 1 \qquad \Sigma X_1 = \quad 654 \qquad \Sigma X_2 = \quad 257 \cdot 24$

$\Sigma Y X_1 = 14{,}020 \cdot 3 \qquad \Sigma X_1^2 = 42{,}872 \qquad \Sigma X_2^2 = 6{,}628 \cdot 04$

$\Sigma Y X_2 = \quad 5{,}544 \cdot 45 \qquad \Sigma X_1 X_2 = 16{,}812 \cdot 42 \qquad \Sigma Y^2 = 4{,}721 \cdot 75$

12.13. Suppose that investment plans (I_t) depends on profits (Π_t) and on the rate of interest (r_t) if the latter exceeds $0 \cdot 06$. If r_t is less than $0 \cdot 06$, I_t depends only on profits. Express this relationship in a testable regression model.

12.14. Given the model

$$Y_t = b_0 + b_1 X_{1,t} + b_2 X_{2,t} + u_t$$

(a) Show how you would modify this model to show that there is an autonomous growth in Y.

(b) Show how you would modify this model to show that the slope of X_1 changes autonomously over time.

12.15. Consider the problem of estimating the demand for 'Harlequin' books from a cross-section sample of consumers from all regions of Canada.

(a) Can you estimate the price elasticity of demand from this sample? Why?

(b) Can you estimate the income elasticity from this sample? Why?

(c) It is a widespread belief that 'Harlequin Romances' are read only by women, and their demand is slightly higher in urban areas as compared to rural areas. Construct appropriate dummy variables measuring the explanatory variables 'Region' and 'Sex'.

(d) Write the demand function for the jth individual in the sample:

    (i) If the jth individual is a woman from an urban area.

    (ii) If the jth individual is a woman from a rural area.

    (iii) If the jth individual is a male from Toronto.

12.16. Given the following demand function for food

$$D_t = b_0 + b_1 P_t + b_2 Y_t + u_t$$

where D = demand for food
$\quad\quad P$ = price of food
$\quad\quad Y$ = income.

(a) Express your *a priori* expectations regarding the sign of the coefficients of the above relationship, including b_0.
(b) Construct appropriate dummy variables to express the fact (or hypothesis) that the food function shifts downwards and becomes less elastic (with respect to price *and* income) in periods of wage and price controls.

12.17. Consider the model

$$Y = a_0 + a_1 X_1 + a_2 X_2 + u \quad\quad \text{in region 1}$$
$$Y = b_0 + b_1 X_1 + b_2 X_2 + u \qu\quad \text{in region 2}$$
$$Y = c_0 + c_1 X_1 + c_2 X_2 + u \quad\quad \text{in region 3}$$

(a) Outline the procedure for testing the null hypothesis $H_0 : a_2 = b_2 = c_2$ (i.e. the coefficient of the second variable is the same in all regions).
(b) What is assumed about the disturbance terms in the three regions?

CHAPTER 13   LAGGED VARIABLES. DISTRIBUTED LAG MODELS

13.1. Consider the investment function

$$I_t = a + b_0 X_t + b_1 X_{t-1} + b_2 X_{t-2} + \ldots + b_7 X_{t-7} + u$$

where X_t = sales in period t.
Assume that the lag scheme is of the 'inverted-V' type, with the following weights

$$\tfrac{1}{10} \quad \tfrac{1}{8} \quad \tfrac{1}{6} \quad \tfrac{1}{5} \quad \tfrac{1}{3} \quad \tfrac{1}{7} \quad \tfrac{1}{9} \quad \tfrac{1}{12}$$

Outline the procedure for estimating the coefficients of the original investment function.

13.2. (a) Can you make any suggestions as to the likely pattern of the distributed lag for the explanatory variables in the following relationships?
   (i) Demand for wine = f (income, advertising)
   (ii) Investment = f (sales, profits).

(b) Having decided the pattern of the distributed lag, assign arbitrary weights to the lagged values of the X's to form an appropriate 'weighted' variable W. Show next how you would obtain values for the coefficients of the original model. (Concentrate on the investment function for this part.)

13.3. (a) Outline the method of the Almon lag scheme assuming that a certain function $Y = f(X)$ includes six lags, and that the degree of the 'approximation polynomial' is 3.

(b) How would you proceed if you wanted to find out whether the 'approximation polynomial' is of degree 4?

13.4. From economic theory we know that the level of current consumption is affected by the current and past levels of income

$$C_t = f(Y_t, Y_{t-1}, Y_{t-2}, Y_{t-3}, \ldots)$$

Use a Koyck transformation to derive an appropriate model of the above consumption function. State clearly the assumptions of the Koyck transformation, and discuss their plausibility for the particular model of the consumption function.

13.5. Assume that the rate of investment depends on the current interest rate and on the interest rate in the previous six quarters.

Set up an Almon scheme of this investment model, assuming that the 'approximation polynomial' is of degree 2.

13.6. Consider the distributed-lag model

$$Y_t = a + b_0 X_t + b_1 X_{t-1} + \ldots + b_8 X_{t-8} + u_t.$$

Assume that an investigator wants to estimate this model by the Almon scheme with a polynomial of degree 4. Using a sample of sixty observations, the investigator obtains the following estimates of the coefficients of the approximation polynomial

$$\hat{a}_0 = 0 \cdot 5 \qquad \hat{a}_1 = 2 \cdot 5 \qquad \hat{a}_2 = 2 \qquad \hat{a}_4 = -5.$$

Calculate the values of the coefficients of the original lagged model.

13.7. Show under what conditions Koyck's distributed lag model can provide a solution to the problem of multicollinearity.

13.8. The following table includes data on the consumption and personal income of Canada over the 1940–75 period (at constant prices). Assume that the consumption function is of the form

$$C_t = b_0 X_t + b_1 X_{t-1} + b_2 X_{t-2} + \ldots + b_8 X_{t-8} + u_t$$

where X = personal income.

(a) Write the time series of the W variables implied by the Almon scheme, given that the 'approximation polynomial' is of degree 2.

(b) Estimate the function

$$C_t = a_0 W_0 + a_1 W_1 + a_2 W_2 + v_t$$

where the a's are the coefficients of the 'approximation polynomial'

(c) Test the hypothesis that the 'approximation polynomial' is of degree 3.

(d) Use the $\hat{a}$'s from (b) or (c) above to obtain estimates of the b's of the Canadian consumption function.

Year	C_t	X_t	Year	C_t	X_t
1940	9,768	10,499	1958	23,723	25,247
1941	10,323	11,312	1959	24,812	25,880
1942	10,614	13,433	1960	25,607	26,701
1943	10,850	13,812	1961	25,930	26,904
1944	11,382	14,638	1962	27,073	28,935
1945	12,384	14,838	1963	28,319	30,202
1946	13,814	15,431	1964	29,668	31,237
1947	14,837	15,791	1965	31,087	33,208
1948	14,647	16,326	1966	32,331	34,970
1949	15,379	16,756	1967	33,703	36,360
1950	16,511	17,573	1968	35,706	38,252
1951	16,438	18,310	1969	37,161	39,833
1952	17,249	19,251	1970	37,427	40,378
1953	18,429	20,180	1971	39,160	43,107
1954	18,984	20,031	1972	42,011	46,807
1955	20,499	21,551	1973	44,438	49,559
1956	21,602	22,911	1974	44,818	50,106
1957	22,623	23,909	1975	48,603	55,215

(e) Estimate a simple Keynesian consumption function

$$C_t = b_0 + b_1 X_t + u_t.$$

Evaluate the results on the basis of the usual statistical criteria.
(R^2, F, t-ratios, Durbin–Watson d statistic.)

(f) Estimate the consumption function with a Koyck geometric lag (given $C_{1939} = 9,089$) $C_t = b_0 + b_1 X_t + b_2 C_{t-1} + v_t.$
Evaluate the results, using the standard statistical criteria.

(g) Compare your estimated functions:
  (i) The simple Keynesian consumption function
  (ii) The consumption function with Koyck geometric lag
  (iii) The consumption function with the Almon lag scheme.

Intermediate results:

$n = 36$ $\Sigma X_t = 969,453$ $\Sigma C_{t-1} = 848,396$
$\Sigma C_t = 887,910$ $\Sigma X_t^2 = 31,324,356,220$ $\Sigma C_{t-1}^2 = 24,006,564,610$
$\Sigma C_t^2 = 26,286,206,300$ $\Sigma C_t C_{t-1} = 25,113,882,580$
$\Sigma C_t X_t = 28,678,883,660$ $\Sigma C_{t-1} X_t = 27,395,836,690$

CHAPTER 14   SIMULTANEOUS EQUATION MODELS

14.1. (a) What is the simultaneous equation bias? How does it arise?
Illustrate your answer with an example of an economic model of
simultaneous relations.

(b) Can we use OLS for estimating equations belonging to a system of simultaneous relations? Why?

14.2. Consider the model

$$L_t = a_0 + a_1 W_t + a_2 S_t + u_1 \tag{1}$$

$$W_t = b_0 + b_1 L_t + b_2 P_t + u_2 \tag{2}$$

where L = the amount of labour employed
$\quad\quad W$ = the water rate
$\quad\quad S$ = sales
$\quad\quad P$ = a measure of the productivity of labour.

(a) Define the endogenous and exogenous variables.
(b) Obtain the reduced-form coefficients of the above model; that is, the π's of the following equations

$$L = \pi_{10} + \pi_{11} S + \pi_{12} P + v_1$$

$$W = \pi_{20} + \pi_{21} S + \pi_{22} P + v_2$$

(c) Show that π_{11} can be split into two effects: a direct effect and an indirect effect on sales (S) on employment (L). Explain the way in which S affects L indirectly.

14.3. Define recursiveness and explain how this property is related to the question of identification.

CHAPTER 15   IDENTIFICATION

15.1. Given the following market model

$$D = b_0 + b_1 P + u$$

$$S = a_0 + a_1 P + v$$

$$D = S$$

(a) Show that both equations are under-identified.
(b) Show the effect of the inclusion of an additional variable (e.g. W = weather conditions) in the supply function, as far as the identification state of both equations is concerned.
(c) Under what conditions would both equations be identified?

15.2. Given the following macro-model of income determination:

$$C_t = a_0 + a_1 Y_t + a_2 T + u$$
$$I_t = b_0 + b_1 Y_{t-1} + v$$
$$T_t = c_0 + c_1 Y_t + w$$
$$Y_t = C_t + I_t + G_t$$

(a) Define the endogenous and exogenous variables.
(b) Examine the identification state of the three behavioural equations.
(c) Show that if we impose the restriction $a_1 = a_2$, the consumption function becomes identified.

15.3. Consider the two market models for beef

Model I $P = b_0 + b_1 Q + b_2 Y + u$ (demand)

$\qquad\quad Q = a_0 + a_1 P + b_2 Z + v$ (supply)

Model II $P = b_0 + b_1 Q + b_2 Y + b_3 W + u$ (demand)

$\qquad\quad Q = a_0 + a_1 P + b_2 Z + v$ (supply)

where Y, Z and W are exogenous variables.

(a) Show that the first system is exactly identified and explain why the most appropriate estimating method is ILS.
(b) Show that the second model is over-identified.
(c) Show that the imposition of the restriction $a_1 = 0$ serves to identify uniquely the second structural model, and under these conditions the supply equation can be estimated by OLS, while the demand function could be estimated by ILS. Are OLS estimates of the supply function biased *or* unbiased (when $a_1 = 0$)? Why?

15.4. Consider the following market models

Model I $Q_D = b_0 + b_1 P + b_2 t + u$

$\qquad\quad Q_S = c_0 + c_1 P + c_2 W + v$

Model II $Q_D = b_0 + b_1 P + u$

$\qquad\quad Q_S = c_0 + c_1 W + v$

Model III $Q_D = b_0 + b_1 P + u$

$\qquad\quad Q_S = c_0 + c_1 P + c_2 W + c_2 t + v$

(where t = time and W = weather index; both are exogenous).

(a) Derive the reduced-form equations for each of these models.
(b) Define the condition of identifiability of each structural equation.

CHAPTER 16   SIMULTANEOUS EQUATION METHODS

16.1. Consider the following model of the coffee market

$$Q_D = b_0 + b_1 P + b_2 Y + u$$

$$Q_S = a_0 + a_1 P_{t-1} + a_2 W + v$$

$$Q_D = Q_S$$

where Q = quantity of coffee
$\quad P$ = price of coffee
$\quad W$ = weather index (e.g. inches of rainfall)
$\quad Y$ = income.

(a) Verify that the demand equation is over-identified.
(b) Is the supply function identified?
(c) Using the data of the following table, estimate the demand for coffee by OLS and by 2SLS. (Variables are measured in arbitrary units. It is known that $P_0 = 19$.) Are the differences in results surprising?

n	Q	P	Y	W
1	11	20	8·1	42
2	16	18	8·4	58
3	11	22	8·5	35
4	14	21	8·5	46
5	13	27	8·8	41
6	17	26	9·0	56
7	14	25	8·9	48
8	15	27	9·4	50
9	12	30	9·5	39
10	18	28	9·9	52

Intermediate results:

(1) *For OLS*

$n = 10$

$\Sigma Q = 141$ $\Sigma P = 244$ $\Sigma Y = 89$

$\Sigma QP = 3,459$ $\Sigma P^2 = 6,092$ $\Sigma Y^2 = 749·94$

$\Sigma QY = 1,261·2$ $\Sigma YP = 2,188·8$ $\Sigma Q^2 = 2,041$

(2) *For 2SLS*

$n = 9$ (Given $P_0 = 19$)

$\Sigma P_{t-1} = 216$ $\Sigma W = 425$ $\Sigma Y = 80·9$

$\Sigma P_{t-1}^2 = 5,308$ $\Sigma W^2 = 20,551$ $\Sigma P = 224$

$\Sigma P_{t-1} Y = 1,955·7$ $\Sigma WY = 3,823$ $\Sigma Y^2 = 729·33$

$\Sigma P_t P_{t-1} = 5,462$ $\Sigma WP_{t-1} = 10,286$

$\Sigma WP = 10,519$

16.2. (a) Find the identification condition of each equation of the model of Exercise 14.2.

(b) Outline a method for estimating the first equation of Exercise 14.2 *alone*. Explain your choice of the estimation method.

16.3. Consider the following model of the market of a certain commodity

$$Q_D = b_0 + b_1 P_t + u_t$$

$$Q_S = a_0 + a_1 W_t + v_t$$

$$Q_D = Q_S$$

where Q = quantity of the commodity
P = price of the commodity

(a) Define the endogenous and exogenous variables.
(b) Define the identification condition of the behavioural equations.
(c) Do you notice any special characteristic of this model which affects our choice of estimating technique?
(d) What estimation methods are appropriate for the coefficients of the model?

16.4. Consider the following model of wage—price determination

$$W_t = b_0 + b_1 (UN)_t + b_2 P_t + u_t$$

$$P_t = a_0 + a_1 (M)_t + a_2 (UN)_t + a_3 W_t + v_t$$

where W = *percentage change* in wages
P = *percentage change* in prices
M = *percentage change* in money supply
UN = rate of unemployment

(a) Establish the identification condition of each equation.
(b) Outline the appropriate method for the estimation of the identified equation.

16.5. Consider the aggregate model

$$C_t = b_0 + b_1 Y_t + b_2 C_{t-1} + u_t$$

$$I_t = a_0 + a_1 Y_t + a_2 Y_{t-1} + a_3 r_t + v_t$$

$$Y_t = C_t + I_t.$$

(a) Define the endogenous and exogenous variables.
(b) Establish the identification condition of the behavioural equations.
(c) Choose the most appropriate technique for the estimation of the identified equations.

16.6. Prove that for an exactly identified equation ILS and 2SLS give identical results.

16.7. Consider the simple aggregate model

$$C_t = b_0 + b_1 Y_t + u_t$$

$$I_t = c_0 + c_1 r_t + v_t$$

$$Y_t = C_t + I_t$$

where C = aggregate consumption
I = aggregate investment
Y = aggregate income
r = rate of interest.

Endogenous variables: C, I, Y. Exogenous variable: r. u and v are independent and satisfy the usual assumptions of zero mean, constant variance, serial independence and normality.

(a) Given the following information from a sample of twenty observations estimate the reduced-form equations for C and Y.

$$\Sigma(C - \bar{C})(r - \bar{r}) = -12 \qquad \Sigma(Y - \bar{Y})(r - \bar{r}) = -16 \qquad \Sigma(r - \bar{r})^2 = 4$$
$$\bar{C} = 55 \qquad\qquad \bar{Y} = 60 \qquad\qquad \bar{r} = 3$$

(b) Compute the ILS estimates of the parameters of the consumption function.
(c) Which estimation method would you adopt for the investment function? Why? What additional information if any would you require for the estimation of the investment function?

   16.8. Consider the model

$$Y_1 = b_0 + b_1 X_1^2 + b_2 Y_2 + u$$
$$Y_2 = c_0 + c_1 X_1 + c_2 Y_1 + v$$

(a) Establish the identification condition of each equation.
(b) Derive the reduced-form system.
(c) Outline the most appropriate method for estimating the structural parameters of the model.

   16.9. Consider the model

$$L = b_0 + b_1 W + b_2 X + u$$
$$W = a_0 + a_1 L + a_2 Pr + v$$

where L = amount of labour employed
  W = wage rate
  X = sales
  Pr = index of labour productivity

(a) Define the endogenous and exogenous variables.
(b) Establish the identification condition of each equation.
(c) Derive the reduced-form system.
(d) Which technique would you choose for the estimation of the structural parameter?

   16.10. Consider the following model, expressed in deviations of the variables from their means.

$$y_1 = b_1 y_2 + u$$
$$y_2 = c_1 y_1 + c_2 x_1 + v$$

Use the following observations (which are given in deviation form)

y_1	y_2	x_1
-4	2	-2
0	3	-1
3	2	0
1	-7	3

Estimate the first equation

(a) by OLS, (b) by ILS, (c) by 2SLS and compare your results. Which method is the most appropriate in this case? Why? Which method would you adopt for estimating the second equation? Why?

16.11. Consider the following simple model of an economy

$$C = a_0 + a_1 Y + u_1$$

$$I = b_0 + b_1 \Pi + u_2$$

$$Y = C + I + G$$

where C = consumption
Y = national income
I = investment
Π = profits
G = government expenditures

(Endogenous variables C, I, Y.)

(a) Verify that the consumption function is over-identified.
(b) Can we estimate the investment function by OLS? Why?
(c) Using the data of the following table, estimate the consumption function by OLS and by 2SLS. (Variables are measured in $ millions.) Compare the results of the two methods.

Year	Y	C	I	Π	G
1966	484	311	75	29	97
1967	504	325	75	27	104
1968	520	335	72	27	113
1969	560	355	83	31	122
1970	591	375	87	33	128
1971	632	401	94	38	137
1972	685	433	108	47	144
1973	750	466	121	50	162
1974	794	492	116	47	185
1975	866	537	126	50	203

Intermediate results (exercise 16.11):

$\Sigma Y = 6,386$ $\Sigma C = 4,030$ $\Sigma I = 957$ $\Sigma \Pi = 379$
$\Sigma Y^2 = 4,233,094$ $\Sigma C^2 = 1,677,100$ $\Sigma I^2 = 95,365$ $\Sigma \Pi^2 = 15,211$
$\Sigma YC = 2,664,176$ $\Sigma CI = 399,488$ $\Sigma I\Pi = 38,038$ $\Sigma \Pi G = 55,597$
$\Sigma YI = 634,795$ $\Sigma C\Pi = 159,082$ $\Sigma IG = 139,543$ $\Sigma G = 1,395$
$\Sigma Y\Pi = 252,876$ $\Sigma CG = 585,944$ $\Sigma G^2 = 205,445$
$\Sigma YG = 931,504$

16.12. Consider the following simple aggregate model

$$C_t = b_0 + b_1 Y_t + u_t$$
$$I_t = c_0 + c_1 r_t + c_2 Y_t + v_t$$
$$Y_t = C_t + I_t$$

where the variables are defined as in exercise 16.7.

(a) Given the following intermediate results (computed from a sample of twenty observations), estimate the coefficients of the reduced-form of C and Y.

$$\Sigma(C - \bar{C})(r - \bar{r}) = -12 \qquad \Sigma(Y - \bar{Y})(r - \bar{r}) = -16 \qquad \Sigma(r - \bar{r}) = 48$$
$$\bar{C} = 26 \qquad\qquad \bar{Y} = 30 \qquad\qquad \bar{r} = 12$$

(b) Compute the ILS estimates of the parameters of the consumption function.
(c) How would you proceed in order to estimate the investment function?

16.13. Consider the following model of a market

$$Q_D = b_0 + b_1 P + b_2 Y + u$$
$$Q_S = c_0 + c_1 P + v$$
$$Q_D = Q_S$$

(a) Derive the reduced-form of the model.
(b) Establish the identification condition of the behavioural equations.
(c) Given the following information (from a sample of twenty observations), estimate the ILS estimates of the supply function

$$\Sigma(P - \bar{P})(Y - \bar{Y}) = 10 \qquad \Sigma(Y - \bar{Y})^2 = 100 \qquad \bar{P} = 5 \qquad \bar{Y} = 42.5$$

(d) Assume the following values for the parameters of the demand function

$$b_0 = 1, \qquad b_2 = -1, \qquad b_2 = 0.2$$

Estimate the ILS estimates of the supply function.
(e) What are the properties of the estimates of the supply function if you obtain them (i) by OLS, (ii) by ILS.
(f) Can you estimate the parameters of the demand function by ILS? Why?
(g) If the parameters of the demand function are unknown, can you estimate the supply function by ILS?

16.14. Consider the aggregate model

$$C = b_0 + b_1 Y_d + u$$
$$G = \bar{G} \quad T = \bar{T}$$
$$Y_d = Y - T = Y - \bar{T} = \text{personal disposable income}$$
$$T = C + \bar{I} + \bar{G}$$

(a) Derive the reduced-form of the consumption function.
(b) Show that the consumption function can be estimated by the ILS method, using as explanatory variable the personal savings.

16.15. Using the result $S = \bar{I} + \bar{G} - \bar{T}$ of the previous exercise and the data of Exercises 9.1 and 10.6, re-estimate the Belgian and Japanese consumption function by ILS. Test the ILS regressions for evidence of autocorrelation and heteroscedasticity.

16.16. Given the closed aggregate econometric model

$$C = b_0 + b_1 Y + u$$

$$I = \bar{I}$$

$$Y = C + \bar{I}$$

(a) Derive the reduced-form equations of the model.
(b) Derive the system of relationships between the structural and the reduced-form coefficients.
(c) Using the data of the following table, estimate the consumption function with OLS and with ILS. Compare the two estimated functions.

t	Consumption (Y)	Income (X_1)	Investment (X_2)
1	14·069	20·880	6·811
2	14·467	21·720	7·253
3	14·268	22·303	8·035
4	14·195	22·169	7·974
5	14·837	23·178	8·341
6	15·447	24·065	8·618
7	16·088	24·800	8·712
8	16·233	25·256	9·023
9	16·578	25·762	9·184
10	17·008	25·891	8·883
11	17·747	26·885	9·138
12	18·445	28·162	9·717
13	18·877	29·118	10·241
14	19·285	29·468	10·183
15	20·127	30·678	10·551
16	20·835	32·363	11·528
17	21·243	33·185	11·942
18	21·681	33·848	12·167
19	22·135	34·528	12·393
20	22·662	35·600	12·938
21	22·741	36·306	13·565
22	23·396	37·034	13·638

Intermediate results:

$\Sigma Y = 402 \cdot 36$ $\Sigma X_1 = 623 \cdot 20$ $\Sigma X_2 = 220 \cdot 83$
$\Sigma Y^2 = 7{,}569 \cdot 49$ $\Sigma X_1^2 = 18{,}216 \cdot 64$ $\Sigma X_2^2 = 2{,}303 \cdot 89$
$\Sigma X_1 Y = 11{,}741 \cdot 12$ $\Sigma X_1 X_2 = 6{,}475 \cdot 52$ $\Sigma Y X_2 = 4171 \cdot 627$

16.17. Consider the model (in deviation form)

$$y_1 = b_1 y_2 + u_1$$

$$y_2 = c_1 y_1 + c_2 x_1 + c_3 x_2 + u_2$$

(a) Establish the identification condition of each equation.
(b) Given the following data

$y_1 = Y_1 - \bar{Y}_1$	$y_2 = Y_2 - \bar{Y}_2$	$x_1 = X_1 - \bar{X}_1$	$x_2 = X_2 - \bar{X}_2$
−4	2	−2	−1
0	3	−1	2
3	2	0	−1
1	−7	3	0

Estimate the first equation by 2SLS. Why is this method more appropriate than the ILS method in this case?

16.18. Consider the following inflation model

$$W_t = a_0 + a_1 P_t + u_t$$

$$P_t = b_0 + b_1 W_t + b_2 X_1 + b_3 X_2 + v_t$$

where W_t = rate of change of wages
P_t = rate of change of prices
X_1 = rate of change of prices of imports
X_2 = rate of change of aggregate demand.

Endogenous variables: W, P
Exogenous variables: X_1, X_2

(a) Establish the identification condition of each equation and of the entire model.
(b) Can we estimate the structural coefficients of both equations? Why
(c) Explain why ILS cannot be applied to estimate the coefficients of the wage equation.
(d) Apply OLS and 2SLS to estimate the wage equation using the following data and intermediate results. Compare the estimates of the two methods.

n	W	P	X_1	X_2
1	8·2	12·8	−2	5
2	−2·1	−6·3	−4	−1
3	4·3	4·2	1	3
4	−1·2	−4·6	−2	−2
5	6·0	7·9	2	2

Intermediate results:

$$\hat{P} = 1·19 + 1·61 X_1 + 1·38 X_2$$

(e) Find R^2 of the wage equation and the standard error of $\hat{a}_1$ (from the second stage of 2SLS).

(f) Test the null hypothesis $H_0 : a_1 = 0$ against the alternative hypothesis $H_1 : a_1 \neq 0$ given $\Sigma e_t^2 = 1 \cdot 55$ (from the second stage regression). Use a 5 per cent level of significance.

16.19. The following table includes twenty-four yearly observations on sales of steel, gross national product, and expenditure on housing construction.

n	Y steel sales	X_1 GNP	(Z) Housing construction
1	385	443·6	20·7
2	390	445·6	20·2
3	398	444·5	19·9
4	396	450·3	20·0
5	368	453·4	19·8
6	365	453·2	19·6
7	364	455·2	20·8
8	374	448·2	22·8
9	372	437·5	24·9
10	371	439·5	25·4
11	387	450·7	24·7
12	407	461·6	23·8
13	406	468·6	23·6
14	432	479·9	22·1
15	431	475·0	21·1
16	425	480·4	20·7
17	445	490·2	20·8
18	437	489·7	21·1
19	427	487·3	21·7
20	417	483·7	22·6
21	430	482·6	23·1
22	453	497·8	23·9
23	470	501·5	24·2
24	489	511·7	23·9

(a) Estimate the demand for steel $Y_t = b_0 + b_1 (\text{GNP})_t + u_t$ by applying OLS.

(b) Given the possibility of simultaneous equation bias, estimate the demand for steel by the instrumental variables method, using housing construction as an instrument.

(c) Is housing construction a good choice as an instrumental variable?

Intermediate results:

$n = 24$

$\Sigma Y = 9,839$ $\Sigma X_1 = 11,231 \cdot 7$ $\Sigma Y^2 = 4,061,197$

$\Sigma Y X_1 = 4,620,814 \cdot 2$ $\Sigma X_1^2 = 5,267,389 \cdot 2$ $\Sigma Z = 531 \cdot 4$

$\Sigma Y Z = 218,166 \cdot 2$ $\Sigma X_1 Z = 248,835 \cdot 5$

CHAPTER 17   MIXED ESTIMATION METHODS

17.1. Using the following hypothetical data, apply the 'pooling technique' to obtain estimates of the coefficients of the linear demand function for bread

$$E_{Br} = b_0 + b_1 P_{Br} + b_2 Y_d + b_3 P_c + u$$

where E_{Br} = expenditure on bread
P_{Br} = price of bread (index)
Y_d = personal disposable income
P_c = price of cookies and cakes (index)

Family budget data

Family unit	Expenditure on bread (Y)	Family income (X_1)	Family size (X_2) (equivalent adults)
1	11·5	1,100	3·5
2	14·1	900	4·0
3	8·0	1,800	2·0
4	13·0	1,000	3·8
5	8·5	2,000	2·2

Time series data

Year	Expenditure on bread (Y)	Price of bread (X_1)	Personal disposable income	Price of cookies and cakes (X_2)
1961	60·1	100	12,300	100
1962	61·0	95	12,900	103
1963	61·1	110	13,800	102
1964	61·5	112	14,900	101
1965	62·0	114	16,000	98

17.2. It is commonly believed that the MPC of wage-earners is higher than the MPC of non-wage-earners. Assuming that you have *cross-section* data on the disposable income and consumption expenditure of a number of families, indicate how you could use the *Chow test* to investigate this hypothesis.

17.3. Indicate how you could test the above hypothesis from a time-series sample by imposing an appropriate restriction on the relationship between the MPC of the two groups (wage-earners and non-wage-earners).

17.4. Explain how the method of pooling together cross-section and time-series data can 'solve' the problem of multicollinearity. Use examples of your own to illustrate your answer.

17.5. Show that the 'pooling' technique is a special case of restricted least squares.

17.6. Using the following hypothetical data, apply the 'pooling technique' to obtain estimates of the coefficients of the log-linear demand function for beef.

$$E_B = b_0 \cdot Y^{b_1} \cdot P_B^{b_2} \cdot P_L^{b_3} \cdot e^u$$

where E_B = expenditure on beef
          Y = personal disposable income
         P_B = price of beef
         P_L = price of lamb

Family budget data

Family unit	Expenditure on beef (Y)	Family income (X_1)	Size of family (X_2)
1	20·5	1,204	2·3
2	27·5	1,426	3·1
3	14·1	914	1·4
4	25·0	1,300	3·5
5	16·0	1,000	2·0

Time-series data

Year	Expenditure on beef (Y)	Disposable income	Price of beef (X_1)	Price of lamb (X_2)
1967	320	85	100	100
1968	326	89	90	105
1969	359	97	115	90
1970	400	100	95	115
1971	420	140	130	80

APPENDIX IV

Statistical Tables

Table 1. Areas under the Normal Curve

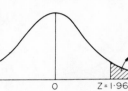

Example

$$Z = \frac{X - \mu}{\sigma}$$

$P(Z > 1\cdot 96) = \cdot 0250$

z	·00	·01	·02	·03	·04	·05	·06	·07	·08	·09
0·0	·5000	·4960	·4920	·4880	·4840	·4801	·4761	·4721	·4681	·4641
0·1	·4602	·4562	·4522	·4483	·4443	·4404	·4364	·4325	·4286	·4247
0·2	·4207	·4168	·4129	·4090	·4052	·4013	·3974	·3936	·3897	·3859
0·3	·3821	·3783	·3745	·3707	·3669	·3632	·3594	·3557	·3520	·3483
0·4	·3446	·3409	·3372	·3336	·3300	·3264	·3228	·3192	·3156	·3121
0·5	·3085	·3050	·3015	·2981	·2946	·2912	·2877	·2843	·2810	·2776
0·6	·2743	·2709	·2676	·2643	·2611	·2578	·2546	·2514	·2483	·2451
0·7	·2420	·2389	·2358	·2327	·2296	·2266	·2236	·2206	·2177	·2148
0·8	·2119	·2090	·2061	·2033	·2005	·1977	·1949	·1922	·1894	·1867
0·9	·1841	·1814	·1788	·1762	·1736	·1711	·1685	·1660	·1635	·1611
1·0	·1587	·1562	·1539	·1515	·1492	·1469	·1446	·1423	·1401	·1379
1·1	·1357	·1335	·1314	·1292	·1271	·1251	·1230	·1210	·1190	·1170
1·2	·1151	·1131	·1112	·1093	·1075	·1056	·1038	·1020	·1003	·0985
1·3	·0968	·0951	·0934	·0918	·0901	·0885	·0869	·0853	·0838	·0823
1·4	·0808	·0793	·0778	·0764	·0749	·0735	·0721	·0708	·0694	·0681
1·5	·0668	·0655	·0643	·0630	·0618	·0606	·0594	·0582	·0571	·0559
1·6	·0548	·0537	·0526	·0516	·0505	·0495	·0485	·0475	·0465	·0455
1·7	·0446	·0436	·0427	·0418	·0409	·0401	·0392	·0384	·0375	·0367
1·8	·0359	·0351	·0344	·0336	·0329	·0322	·0314	·0307	·0301	·0294
1·9	·0287	·0281	·0274	·0268	·0262	·0256	·0250	·0244	·0239	·0233
2·0	·0228	·0222	·0217	·0212	·0207	·0202	·0197	·0192	·0188	·0183
2·1	·0179	·0174	·0170	·0166	·0162	·0158	·0154	·0150	·0146	·0143
2·2	·0139	·0136	·0132	·0129	·0125	·0122	·0119	·0116	·0113	·0110
2·3	·0107	·0104	·0102	·0099	·0096	·0094	·0091	·0089	·0087	·0084
2·4	·0082	·0080	·0078	·0075	·0073	·0071	·0069	·0068	·0066	·0064
2·5	·0062	·0060	·0059	·0057	·0055	·0054	·0052	·0051	·0049	·0048
2·6	·0047	·0045	·0044	·0043	·0041	·0040	·0039	·0038	·0037	·0036
2·7	·0035	·0034	·0033	·0032	·0031	·0030	·0029	·0028	·0027	·0026
2·8	·0026	·0025	·0024	·0023	·0023	·0022	·0022	·0021	·0020	·0019
2·9	·0019	·0018	·0018	·0017	·0016	·0016	·0015	·0015	·0014	·0014
3·0	·0013	·0013	·0013	·0012	·0012	·0011	·0011	·0011	·0010	·0010

Table 2. Percentage Points of the *t* Distribution

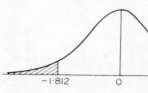

Example

For $\nu = 10$ degrees
of freedom:

$P(t > 1\cdot812) = 0\cdot05$
$P(t < -1\cdot812) = 0\cdot05$

ν \ α	·25	·20	·15	·10	·05	·025	·01	·005	·0005
1	1·000	1·376	1·963	3·078	6·314	12·706	31·821	63·657	636·619
2	·816	1·061	1·386	1·886	2·920	4·303	6·965	9·925	31·598
3	·765	·978	1·250	1·638	2·353	3·182	4·541	5·841	12·941
4	·741	·941	1·190	1·533	2·132	2·776	3·747	4·604	8·610
5	·727	·920	1·156	1·476	2·015	2·571	3·365	4·032	6·859
6	·718	·906	1·134	1·440	1·943	2·447	3·143	3·707	5·959
7	·711	·896	1·119	1·415	1·895	2·365	2·998	3·499	5·405
8	·706	·889	1·108	1·397	1·860	2·306	2·896	3·355	5·041
9	·703	·883	1·100	1·383	1·833	2·262	2·821	3·250	4·781
10	·700	·879	1·093	1·372	1·812	2·228	2·764	3·169	4·587
11	·697	·876	1·088	1·363	1·796	2·201	2·718	3·106	4·437
12	·695	·873	1·083	1·356	1·782	2·179	2·681	3·055	4·318
13	·694	·870	1·079	1·350	1·771	2·160	2·650	3·012	4·221
14	·692	·868	1·076	1·345	1·761	2·145	2·624	2·977	4·140
15	·691	·866	1·074	1·341	1·753	2·131	2·602	2·947	4·073
16	·690	·865	1·071	1·337	1·746	2·120	2·583	2·921	4·015
17	·689	·863	1·069	1·333	1·740	2·110	2·567	2·898	3·965
18	·688	·862	1·067	1·330	1·734	2·101	2·552	2·878	3·922
19	·688	·861	1·066	1·328	1·729	2·093	2·539	2·861	3·883
20	·687	·860	1·064	1·325	1·725	2·086	2·528	2·845	3·850
21	·686	·859	1·063	1·323	1·721	2·080	2·518	2·831	3·819
22	·686	·858	1·061	1·321	1·717	2·074	2·508	2·819	3·792
23	·685	·858	1·060	1·319	1·714	2·069	2·500	2·807	3·767
24	·685	·857	1·059	1·318	1·711	2·064	2·492	2·397	3·745
25	·684	·856	1·058	1·316	1·708	2·060	2·485	2·787	3·725
26	·684	·856	1·058	1·315	1·706	2·056	2·479	2·779	3·707
27	·684	·855	1·057	1·314	1·703	2·052	2·473	2·771	3·690
28	·683	·855	1·056	1·313	1·701	2·048	2·467	2·763	3·674
29	·683	·854	1·055	1·311	1·699	2·045	2·462	2·756	3·659
30	·683	·854	1·055	1·310	1·697	2·042	2·457	2·750	3·646
40	·681	·851	1·050	1·303	1·684	2·021	2·423	2·704	3·551
60	·679	·848	1·046	1·296	1·671	2·000	2·390	2·660	3·460
120	·677	·845	1·041	1·289	1·658	1·980	2·358	2·617	3·373
∞	·674	·842	1·036	1·282	1·645	1·960	2·326	2·576	3·291

Source: This table is abridged from Table III of Fisher & Yates: *Statistical Tables for Biological, Agricultural and Medical Research* published by Oliver & Boyd Ltd., Edinburgh, and by permission of the authors and publishers.

Table 3. Percentage Points of the χ^2 Distribution

Example

For $\nu = 10$ degrees of freedom:

$P(\chi^2 > 15\cdot99) = \cdot10$

ν	$\cdot995$	$\cdot99$	$\cdot975$	$\cdot95$	$\cdot90$	$\cdot75$	$\cdot50$	$\cdot25$	$\cdot10$	$\cdot05$	$\cdot025$	$\cdot01$	$\cdot005$
1	$0\cdot0^4393$	$0\cdot0^2157$	$0\cdot0^2982$	$0\cdot0^23$	$0\cdot0158$	$0\cdot102$	$0\cdot455$	$1\cdot323$	$2\cdot71$	$3\cdot84$	$5\cdot02$	$6\cdot63$	$7\cdot88$
2	$0\cdot0100$	$0\cdot0201$	$0\cdot0506$	$0\cdot103$	$0\cdot211$	$0\cdot575$	$1\cdot386$	$2\cdot77$	$4\cdot61$	$5\cdot99$	$7\cdot38$	$9\cdot21$	$10\cdot60$
3	$0\cdot0717$	$0\cdot115$	$0\cdot216$	$0\cdot352$	$0\cdot584$	$1\cdot213$	$2\cdot37$	$4\cdot11$	$6\cdot25$	$7\cdot81$	$9\cdot35$	$11\cdot34$	$12\cdot84$
4	$0\cdot207$	$0\cdot297$	$0\cdot484$	$0\cdot711$	$1\cdot064$	$1\cdot923$	$3\cdot36$	$5\cdot39$	$7\cdot78$	$9\cdot49$	$11\cdot14$	$13\cdot28$	$14\cdot86$
5	$0\cdot412$	$0\cdot554$	$0\cdot831$	$1\cdot145$	$1\cdot610$	$2\cdot67$	$4\cdot35$	$6\cdot63$	$9\cdot24$	$11\cdot07$	$12\cdot83$	$15\cdot09$	$16\cdot75$
6	$0\cdot676$	$0\cdot872$	$1\cdot237$	$1\cdot635$	$2\cdot20$	$3\cdot45$	$5\cdot35$	$7\cdot84$	$10\cdot64$	$12\cdot59$	$14\cdot45$	$16\cdot81$	$18\cdot55$
7	$0\cdot989$	$1\cdot239$	$1\cdot690$	$2\cdot17$	$2\cdot83$	$4\cdot25$	$6\cdot35$	$9\cdot04$	$12\cdot02$	$14\cdot07$	$16\cdot01$	$18\cdot48$	$20\cdot3$
8	$1\cdot344$	$1\cdot646$	$2\cdot18$	$2\cdot73$	$3\cdot49$	$5\cdot07$	$7\cdot34$	$10\cdot22$	$13\cdot36$	$15\cdot51$	$17\cdot53$	$20\cdot1$	$22\cdot0$
9	$1\cdot735$	$2\cdot09$	$2\cdot70$	$3\cdot33$	$4\cdot17$	$5\cdot90$	$8\cdot34$	$11\cdot39$	$14\cdot68$	$16\cdot92$	$19\cdot02$	$21\cdot7$	$23\cdot6$
10	$2\cdot16$	$2\cdot56$	$3\cdot25$	$3\cdot94$	$4\cdot87$	$6\cdot74$	$9\cdot34$	$12\cdot55$	$15\cdot99$	$18\cdot31$	$20\cdot5$	$23\cdot2$	$25\cdot2$
11	$2\cdot60$	$3\cdot05$	$3\cdot82$	$4\cdot57$	$5\cdot58$	$7\cdot58$	$10\cdot34$	$13\cdot70$	$17\cdot28$	$19\cdot68$	$21\cdot9$	$24\cdot7$	$26\cdot8$
12	$3\cdot07$	$3\cdot57$	$4\cdot40$	$5\cdot23$	$6\cdot30$	$8\cdot44$	$11\cdot34$	$14\cdot85$	$18\cdot55$	$21\cdot0$	$23\cdot3$	$26\cdot2$	$28\cdot3$
13	$3\cdot57$	$4\cdot11$	$5\cdot01$	$5\cdot89$	$7\cdot04$	$9\cdot30$	$12\cdot34$	$15\cdot98$	$19\cdot81$	$22\cdot4$	$24\cdot7$	$27\cdot7$	$29\cdot8$
14	$4\cdot07$	$4\cdot66$	$5\cdot63$	$6\cdot57$	$7\cdot79$	$10\cdot17$	$13\cdot34$	$17\cdot12$	$21\cdot1$	$23\cdot7$	$26\cdot1$	$29\cdot1$	$31\cdot3$
15	$4\cdot60$	$5\cdot23$	$6\cdot26$	$7\cdot26$	$8\cdot55$	$11\cdot04$	$14\cdot34$	$18\cdot25$	$22\cdot3$	$25\cdot0$	$27\cdot5$	$30\cdot6$	$32\cdot8$
16	$5\cdot14$	$5\cdot81$	$6\cdot91$	$7\cdot96$	$9\cdot31$	$11\cdot91$	$15\cdot34$	$19\cdot37$	$23\cdot5$	$26\cdot3$	$28\cdot8$	$32\cdot0$	$34\cdot3$
17	$5\cdot70$	$6\cdot41$	$7\cdot56$	$8\cdot67$	$10\cdot09$	$12\cdot79$	$16\cdot34$	$20\cdot5$	$24\cdot8$	$27\cdot6$	$30\cdot2$	$33\cdot4$	$35\cdot7$
18	$6\cdot26$	$7\cdot01$	$8\cdot23$	$9\cdot39$	$10\cdot86$	$13\cdot68$	$17\cdot34$	$21\cdot6$	$26\cdot0$	$28\cdot9$	$31\cdot5$	$34\cdot8$	$37\cdot2$
19	$6\cdot84$	$7\cdot63$	$8\cdot91$	$10\cdot12$	$11\cdot65$	$14\cdot56$	$18\cdot34$	$22\cdot7$	$27\cdot2$	$30\cdot1$	$32\cdot9$	$36\cdot2$	$38\cdot6$
20	$7\cdot43$	$8\cdot26$	$9\cdot59$	$10\cdot85$	$12\cdot44$	$15\cdot45$	$19\cdot34$	$23\cdot8$	$28\cdot4$	$31\cdot4$	$34\cdot2$	$37\cdot6$	$40\cdot0$

Table 3. Percentage Points of the χ^2 Distribution (*contd.*)

P \ ν	·995	·99	·975	·95	·90	·75	·50	·25	·10	·05	0·25	·01	·005	P \ ν
21	8·03	8·90	10·28	11·59	13·24	16·34	20·3	24·9	29·6	32·7	35·5	38·9	41·4	21
22	8·64	9·54	10·98	12·34	14·04	17·24	21·3	26·0	30·8	33·9	36·8	40·3	42·8	22
23	9·26	10·20	11·69	13·09	14·85	18·14	22·3	27·1	32·0	35·2	38·1	41·6	44·2	23
24	9·89	10·86	12·40	13·85	15·66	19·04	23·3	28·2	33·2	36·4	39·4	43·0	45·6	24
25	10·52	11·52	13·12	14·61	16·47	19·94	24·3	29·3	34·4	37·7	40·6	44·3	46·9	25
26	11·16	12·20	13·84	15·38	17·29	20·8	25·3	30·4	35·6	38·9	41·9	45·6	48·3	26
27	11·81	12·88	14·57	16·15	18·11	21·7	26·3	31·5	36·7	40·1	43·2	47·0	49·6	27
28	12·46	13·56	15·31	16·93	18·94	22·7	27·3	32·6	37·9	41·3	44·5	48·3	51·0	28
29	13·12	14·26	16·05	17·71	19·77	23·6	28·3	33·7	39·1	42·6	45·7	49·6	52·3	29
30	13·79	14·95	16·79	18·49	20·6	24·5	29·3	34·8	40·3	43·8	47·0	50·9	53·7	30
40	20·7	22·2	24·4	26·5	29·1	33·7	39·3	45·6	51·8	55·8	59·3	63·7	66·8	40
50	28·0	29·7	32·4	34·8	37·7	42·9	49·3	56·3	63·2	67·5	71·4	76·2	79·5	50
60	35·5	37·5	40·5	43·2	46·5	52·3	59·3	67·0	74·4	79·1	83·3	88·4	92·0	60
70	43·3	45·4	48·8	51·7	55·3	61·7	69·3	77·6	85·5	90·5	95·0	100·4	104·2	70
80	51·2	53·5	57·2	60·4	64·3	71·1	79·3	88·1	96·6	101·9	106·6	112·3	116·3	80
90	59·2	61·8	65·6	69·1	73·3	80·6	89·3	98·6	107·6	113·1	118·1	124·1	128·3	90
100	67·3	70·1	74·2	77·9	82·4	90·1	99·3	109·1	118·5	124·3	129·6	135·8	140·2	100
Z_a	-2·58	-2·33	-1·96	-1·64	-1·28	-0·674	0·000	0·674	1·282	1·645	1·960	2·33	2·58	Z_a

For $\nu > 100$ take $\chi^2 = \frac{1}{2}(Z_a + \sqrt{2\nu - 1})^2$. Z_a is the standardised normal deviate corresponding to the α level of significance, and is shown in the bottom of the table.

Source: This table is abridged from 'Table of percentage points of the χ^2 distribution' by Catherine M. Thompson, *Biometrika*, vol. 32, 1941, pp. 187–191, and is published here by permission of the author and editor of *Biometrika*.

Table 4A. Values of $F_{0.05,\,\nu_1,\,\nu_2}$

Example
For $\nu_1 = 9$, $\nu_2 = 12$ degrees of freedom
$P(F > 2.80) = 0.05$

ν_1 = degrees of freedom for numerator

ν_2	1	2	3	4	5	6	7	8	9	10	12	15	20	24	30	40	60	120	∞
1	161	200	216	225	230	234	237	239	241	242	244	246	248	249	250	251	252	253	254
2	18.5	19.0	19.2	19.2	19.3	19.3	19.4	19.4	19.4	19.4	19.4	19.4	19.4	19.5	19.5	19.5	19.5	19.5	19.5
3	10.1	9.55	9.28	9.12	9.01	8.94	8.89	8.85	8.81	8.79	8.74	8.70	8.66	8.64	8.62	8.59	8.57	8.55	8.53
4	7.71	6.94	6.59	6.39	6.26	6.16	6.09	6.04	6.00	5.96	5.91	5.86	5.80	5.77	5.75	5.72	5.69	5.66	5.63
5	6.61	5.79	5.41	5.19	5.05	4.95	4.88	4.82	4.77	4.74	4.68	4.62	4.56	4.53	4.50	4.46	4.43	4.40	4.37
6	5.99	5.14	4.76	4.53	4.39	4.28	4.21	4.15	4.10	4.06	4.00	3.94	3.87	3.84	3.81	3.77	3.74	3.70	3.67
7	5.59	4.74	4.35	4.12	3.97	3.87	3.79	3.73	3.68	3.64	3.57	3.51	3.44	3.41	3.38	3.34	3.30	3.27	3.23
8	5.32	4.46	4.07	3.84	3.69	3.58	3.50	3.44	3.39	3.35	3.28	3.22	3.15	3.12	3.08	3.04	3.01	2.97	2.93
9	5.12	4.26	3.86	3.63	3.48	3.37	3.29	3.23	3.18	3.14	3.07	3.01	2.94	2.90	2.86	2.83	2.79	2.75	2.71
10	4.96	4.10	3.71	3.48	3.33	3.22	3.14	3.07	3.02	2.98	2.91	2.85	2.77	2.74	2.70	2.66	2.62	2.58	2.54
11	4.84	3.98	3.59	3.36	3.20	3.09	3.01	2.95	2.90	2.85	2.79	2.72	2.65	2.61	2.57	2.53	2.49	2.45	2.40
12	4.75	3.89	3.49	3.26	3.11	3.00	2.91	2.85	2.80	2.75	2.69	2.62	2.54	2.51	2.47	2.43	2.38	2.34	2.30
13	4.67	3.81	3.41	3.18	3.03	2.92	2.83	2.77	2.71	2.67	2.60	2.53	2.46	2.42	2.38	2.34	2.30	2.25	2.21
14	4.60	3.74	3.34	3.11	2.96	2.85	2.76	2.70	2.65	2.60	2.53	2.46	2.39	2.35	2.31	2.27	2.22	2.18	2.13
15	4.54	3.68	3.29	3.06	2.90	2.79	2.71	2.64	2.59	2.54	2.48	2.40	2.33	2.29	2.25	2.20	2.16	2.11	2.07
16	4.49	3.63	3.24	3.01	2.85	2.74	2.66	2.59	2.54	2.49	2.42	2.35	2.28	2.24	2.19	2.15	2.11	2.06	2.01
17	4.45	3.59	3.20	2.96	2.81	2.70	2.61	2.55	2.49	2.45	2.38	2.31	2.23	2.19	2.15	2.10	2.06	2.01	1.96
18	4.41	3.55	3.16	2.93	2.77	2.66	2.58	2.51	2.46	2.41	2.34	2.27	2.19	2.15	2.11	2.06	2.02	1.97	1.92
19	4.38	3.52	3.13	2.90	2.74	2.63	2.54	2.48	2.42	2.38	2.31	2.23	2.16	2.11	2.07	2.03	1.98	1.93	1.88
20	4.35	3.49	3.10	2.87	2.71	2.60	2.51	2.45	2.39	2.35	2.28	2.20	2.12	2.08	2.04	1.99	1.95	1.90	1.84
21	4.32	3.47	3.07	2.84	2.68	2.57	2.49	2.42	2.37	2.32	2.25	2.18	2.10	2.05	2.01	1.96	1.92	1.87	1.81
22	4.30	3.44	3.05	2.82	2.66	2.55	2.46	2.40	2.34	2.30	2.23	2.15	2.07	2.03	1.98	1.94	1.89	1.84	1.78
23	4.28	3.42	3.03	2.80	2.64	2.53	2.44	2.37	2.32	2.27	2.20	2.13	2.05	2.01	1.96	1.91	1.86	1.81	1.76
24	4.26	3.40	3.01	2.78	2.62	2.51	2.42	2.36	2.30	2.25	2.18	2.11	2.03	1.98	1.94	1.89	1.84	1.79	1.73
25	4.24	3.39	2.99	2.76	2.60	2.49	2.40	2.34	2.28	2.24	2.16	2.09	2.01	1.96	1.92	1.87	1.82	1.77	1.71
30	4.17	3.32	2.92	2.69	2.53	2.42	2.33	2.27	2.21	2.16	2.09	2.01	1.93	1.89	1.84	1.79	1.74	1.68	1.62
40	4.08	3.23	2.84	2.61	2.45	2.34	2.25	2.18	2.12	2.08	2.00	1.92	1.84	1.79	1.74	1.69	1.64	1.58	1.51
60	4.00	3.15	2.76	2.53	2.37	2.25	2.17	2.10	2.04	1.99	1.92	1.84	1.75	1.70	1.65	1.59	1.53	1.47	1.39
120	3.92	3.07	2.68	2.45	2.29	2.18	2.09	2.02	1.96	1.91	1.83	1.75	1.66	1.61	1.55	1.50	1.43	1.35	1.25
∞	3.84	3.00	2.60	2.37	2.21	2.10	2.01	1.94	1.88	1.83	1.75	1.67	1.57	1.52	1.46	1.39	1.32	1.22	1.00

ν_2 = degrees of freedom for denominator

Abridged from M. Merrington and C. M. Thompson, 'Tables of percentage points of the inverted beta (F) distribution', *Biometrika*, vol. 33, 1943, p. 73. By permission of the *Biometrika* trustees.

Table 4B. Values of $F_{0.01}$, ν_1, ν_2

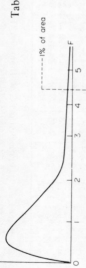

-----1% of area

Example
For $\nu_1 = 9$, $\nu_2 = 12$ degrees of freedom
$P(F > 4.39) = 0.01$

ν_1 = degrees of freedom for numerator

ν_2 = degrees of freedom for denominator

$\nu_2 \backslash \nu_1$	1	2	3	4	5	6	7	8	9	10	12	15	20	24	30	40	60	120	∞
1	4052	5000	5403	5625	5764	5859	5928	5982	6023	6056	6106	6157	6209	6235	6261	6287	6313	6339	6366
2	98.5	99.0	99.2	99.2	99.3	99.3	99.4	99.4	99.4	99.4	99.4	99.4	99.4	99.5	99.5	99.5	99.5	99.5	99.5
3	34.1	30.8	29.5	28.7	28.2	27.9	27.7	27.5	27.3	27.2	27.1	26.9	26.7	26.6	26.5	26.4	26.3	26.2	26.1
4	21.2	18.0	16.7	16.0	15.5	15.2	15.0	14.8	14.7	14.5	14.4	14.2	14.0	13.9	13.8	13.7	13.7	13.6	13.5
5	16.3	13.3	12.1	11.4	11.0	10.7	10.5	10.3	10.2	10.1	9.89	9.72	9.55	9.47	9.38	9.29	9.20	9.11	9.02
6	13.7	10.9	9.78	9.15	8.75	8.47	8.26	8.10	7.98	7.87	7.72	7.56	7.40	7.31	7.23	7.14	7.06	6.97	6.88
7	12.2	9.55	8.45	7.85	7.46	7.19	6.99	6.84	6.72	6.62	6.47	6.31	6.16	6.07	5.99	5.91	5.82	5.74	5.65
8	11.3	8.65	7.59	7.01	6.63	6.37	6.18	6.03	5.91	5.81	5.67	5.52	5.36	5.28	5.20	5.12	5.03	4.95	4.86
9	10.6	8.02	6.99	6.42	6.06	5.80	5.61	5.47	5.35	5.26	5.11	4.96	4.81	4.73	4.65	4.57	4.48	4.40	4.31
10	10.0	7.56	6.55	5.99	5.64	5.39	5.20	5.06	4.94	4.85	4.71	4.56	4.41	4.33	4.25	4.17	4.08	4.00	3.91
11	9.65	7.21	6.22	5.67	5.32	5.07	4.89	4.74	4.63	4.54	4.40	4.25	4.10	4.02	3.94	3.86	3.78	3.69	3.60
12	9.33	6.93	5.95	5.41	5.06	4.82	4.64	4.50	4.39	4.30	4.16	4.01	3.86	3.78	3.70	3.62	3.54	3.45	3.36
13	9.07	6.70	5.74	5.21	4.86	4.62	4.44	4.30	4.19	4.10	3.96	3.82	3.66	3.59	3.51	3.43	3.34	3.25	3.17
14	8.86	6.51	5.56	5.04	4.70	4.46	4.28	4.14	4.03	3.94	3.80	3.66	3.51	3.43	3.35	3.27	3.18	3.09	3.00
15	8.68	6.36	5.42	4.89	4.56	4.32	4.14	4.00	3.89	3.80	3.67	3.52	3.37	3.29	3.21	3.13	3.05	2.96	2.87
16	8.53	6.23	5.29	4.77	4.44	4.20	4.03	3.89	3.78	3.69	3.55	3.41	3.26	3.18	3.10	3.02	2.93	2.84	2.75
17	8.40	6.11	5.19	4.67	4.34	4.10	3.93	3.79	3.68	3.59	3.46	3.31	3.16	3.08	3.00	2.92	2.83	2.75	2.65
18	8.29	6.01	5.09	4.58	4.25	4.01	3.84	3.71	3.60	3.51	3.37	3.23	3.08	3.00	2.92	2.84	2.75	2.66	2.57
19	8.19	5.93	5.01	4.50	4.17	3.94	3.77	3.63	3.52	3.43	3.30	3.15	3.00	2.92	2.84	2.76	2.67	2.58	2.49
20	8.10	5.85	4.94	4.43	4.10	3.87	3.70	3.56	3.46	3.37	3.23	3.09	2.94	2.86	2.78	2.69	2.61	2.52	2.42
21	8.02	5.78	4.87	4.37	4.04	3.81	3.64	3.51	3.40	3.31	3.17	3.03	2.88	2.80	2.72	2.64	2.55	2.46	2.36
22	7.95	5.72	4.82	4.31	3.99	3.76	3.59	3.45	3.35	3.26	3.12	2.98	2.83	2.75	2.67	2.58	2.50	2.40	2.31
23	7.88	5.66	4.76	4.26	3.94	3.71	3.54	3.41	3.30	3.21	3.07	2.93	2.78	2.70	2.62	2.54	2.45	2.35	2.26
24	7.82	5.61	4.72	4.22	3.90	3.67	3.50	3.36	3.26	3.17	3.03	2.89	2.74	2.66	2.58	2.49	2.40	2.31	2.21
25	7.77	5.57	4.68	4.18	3.86	3.63	3.46	3.32	3.22	3.13	2.99	2.85	2.70	2.62	2.53	2.45	2.36	2.27	2.17
30	7.56	5.39	4.51	4.02	3.70	3.47	3.30	3.17	3.07	2.98	2.84	2.70	2.55	2.47	2.39	2.30	2.21	2.11	2.01
40	7.31	5.18	4.31	3.83	3.51	3.29	3.12	2.99	2.89	2.80	2.66	2.52	2.37	2.29	2.20	2.11	2.02	1.92	1.80
60	7.08	4.98	4.13	3.65	3.34	3.12	2.95	2.82	2.72	2.63	2.50	2.35	2.20	2.12	2.03	1.94	1.84	1.73	1.60
120	6.85	4.79	3.95	3.48	3.17	2.96	2.79	2.66	2.56	2.47	2.34	2.19	2.03	1.95	1.86	1.76	1.66	1.53	1.38
∞	6.63	4.61	3.78	3.32	3.02	2.80	2.64	2.51	2.41	2.32	2.18	2.04	1.88	1.79	1.70	1.59	1.47	1.32	1.00

Abridged from M. Merrington and C. M. Thompson, 'Tables of percentage points of the inverted beta (F) distribution', *Biometrika*, vol. 33, 1943, p. 73. By permission of the *Biometrika* trustees.

Table 5A. Significance Points of d_L and d_U: 5%

n	$k' = 1$		$k' = 2$		$k' = 3$		$k' = 4$		$k' = 5$	
	d_L	d_U	d_L	d_U	d_L	d_U	d_L	d_U	d_L	d_U
15	1·08	1·36	0·95	1·54	0·82	1·75	0·69	1·97	0·56	2·21
16	1·10	1·37	0·98	1·54	0·86	1·73	0·74	1·93	0·62	2·15
17	1·13	1·38	1·02	1·54	0·90	1·71	0·78	1·90	0·67	2·10
18	1·16	1·39	1·05	1·53	0·93	1·69	0·82	1·87	0·71	2·06
19	1·18	1·40	1·08	1·53	0·97	1·68	0·86	1·85	0·75	2·02
20	1·20	1·41	1·10	1·54	1·00	1·68	0·90	1·83	0·79	1·99
21	1·22	1·42	1·13	1·54	1·03	1·67	0·93	1·81	0·83	1·96
22	1·24	1·43	1·15	1·54	1·05	1·66	0·96	1·80	0·86	1·94
23	1·26	1·44	1·17	1·54	1·08	1·66	0·99	1·79	0·90	1·92
24	1·27	1·45	1·19	1·55	1·10	1·66	1·01	1·78	0·93	1·90
25	1·29	1·45	1·21	1·55	1·12	1·66	1·04	1·77	0·95	1·89
26	1·30	1·46	1·22	1·55	1·14	1·65	1·06	1·76	0·98	1·88
27	1·32	1·47	1·24	1·56	1·16	1·65	1·08	1·76	1·01	1·86
28	1·33	1·48	1·26	1·56	1·18	1·65	1·10	1·75	1·03	1·85
29	1·34	1·48	1·27	1·56	1·20	1·65	1·12	1·74	1·05	1·84
30	1·35	1·49	1·28	1·57	1·21	1·65	1·14	1·74	1·07	1·83
31	1·36	1·50	1·30	1·57	1·23	1·65	1·16	1·74	1·09	1·83
32	1·37	1·50	1·31	1·57	1·24	1·65	1·18	1·73	1·11	1·82
33	1·38	1·51	1·32	1·58	1·26	1·65	1·19	1·73	1·13	1·81
34	1·39	1·51	1·33	1·58	1·27	1·65	1·21	1·73	1·15	1·81
35	1·40	1·52	1·34	1·58	1·28	1·65	1·22	1·73	1·16	1·80
36	1·41	1·52	1·35	1·59	1·29	1·65	1·24	1·73	1·18	1·80
37	1·42	1·53	1·36	1·59	1·31	1·66	1·25	1·72	1·19	1·80
38	1·43	1·54	1·37	1·59	1·32	1·66	1·26	1·72	1·21	1·79
39	1·43	1·54	1·38	1·60	1·33	1·66	1·27	1·72	1·22	1·79
40	1·44	1·54	1·39	1·60	1·34	1·66	1·29	1·72	1·23	1·79
45	1·48	1·57	1·43	1·62	1·38	1·67	1·34	1·72	1·29	1·78
50	1·50	1·59	1·46	1·63	1·42	1·67	1·38	1·72	1·34	1·77
55	1·53	1·60	1·49	1·64	1·45	1·68	1·41	1·72	1·38	1·77
60	1·55	1·62	1·51	1·65	1·48	1·69	1·44	1·73	1·41	1·77
65	1·57	1·63	1·54	1·66	1·50	1·70	1·47	1·73	1·44	1·77
70	1·58	1·64	1·55	1·67	1·52	1·70	1·49	1·74	1·46	1·77
75	1·60	1·65	1·57	1·68	1·54	1·71	1·51	1·74	1·49	1·77
80	1·61	1·66	1·59	1·69	1·56	1·72	1·53	1·74	1·51	1·77
85	1·62	1·67	1·60	1·70	1·57	1·72	1·55	1·75	1·52	1·77
90	1·63	1·68	1·61	1·70	1·59	1·73	1·57	1·75	1·54	1·78
95	1·64	1·69	1·62	1·71	1·60	1·73	1·58	1·75	1·56	1·78
100	1·65	1·69	1·63	1·72	1·61	1·74	1·59	1·76	1·57	1·78

Note: k' = number of explanatory variables excluding the constant term.
Source: J. Durbin and G. S. Watson, 'Testing for Serial Correlation in Least Squares Regression', *Biometrika*, vol. 38, 1951, pp. 159–77. Reprinted with the permission of the authors and the *Biometrika* trustees.

Table 5B. Significance Points of d_L and d_U: 1%

n	$k' = 1$		$k' = 2$		$k' = 3$		$k' = 4$		$k' = 5$	
	d_L	d_U	d_L	d_U	d_L	d_U	d_L	d_U	d_L	d_U
15	0·81	1·07	0·70	1·25	0·59	1·46	0·49	1·70	0·39	1·96
16	0·84	1·09	0·74	1·25	0·63	1·44	0·53	1·66	0·44	1·90
17	0·87	1·10	0·77	1·25	0·67	1·43	0·57	1·63	0·48	1·85
18	0·90	1·12	0·80	1·26	0·71	1·42	0·61	1·60	0·52	1·80
19	0·93	1·13	0·83	1·26	0·74	1·41	0·65	1·58	0·56	1;77
20	0·95	1·15	0·86	1·27	0·77	1·41	0·68	1·57	0·60	1·74
21	0·97	1·16	0·89	1·27	0·80	1·41	0·72	1·55	0·63	1·71
22	1·00	1·17	0·91	1·28	0·83	1·40	0·75	1·54	0·66	1·69
23	1·02	1·19	0·94	1·29	0·86	1·40	0·77	1·53	0·70	1·67
24	1·04	1·20	0·96	1·30	0·88	1·41	0·80	1·53	0·72	1·66
25	1·05	1·21	0·98	1·30	0·90	1·41	0·83	1·52	0·75	1·65
26	1·07	1·22	1·00	1·31	0·93	1·41	0·85	1·52	0·78	1·64
27	1·09	1·23	1·02	1·32	0·95	1·41	0·88	1·51	0·81	1·63
28	1·10	1·24	1·04	1·32	0·97	1·41	0·90	1·51	0·83	1·62
29	1·12	1·25	1·05	1·33	0·99	1·42	0·92	1·51	0·85	1·61
30	1·13	1·26	1·07	1·34	1·01	1·42	0·94	1·51	0·88	1·61
31	1·15	1·27	1·08	1·34	1·02	1·42	0·96	1·51	0·90	1·60
32	1·16	1·28	1·10	1·35	1·04	1·43	0·98	1·51	0·92	1·60
33	1·17	1·29	1·11	1·36	1·05	1·43	1·00	1·51	0·94	1·59
34	1·18	1·30	1·13	1·36	1·07	1·43	1·01	1·51	0·95	1·59
35	1·19	1·31	1·14	1·37	1·08	1·44	1·03	1·51	0·97	1·59
36	1·21	1·32	1·15	1·38	1·10	1·44	1·04	1·51	0·99	1·59
37	1·22	1·32	1·16	1·38	1·11	1·45	1·06	1·51	1·00	1·59
38	1·23	1·33	1·18	1·39	1·12	1·45	1·07	1·52	1·02	1·58
39	1·24	1·34	1·19	1·39	1·14	1·45	1·09	1·52	1·03	1·58
40	1·25	1·34	1·20	1·40	1·15	1·46	1·10	1·52	1·05	1·58
45	1·29	1·38	1·24	1·42	1·20	1·48	1·16	1·53	1·11	1·58
50	1·32	1·40	1·28	1·45	1·24	1·49	1·20	1·54	1·16	1·59
55	1·36	1·43	1·32	1·47	1·28	1·51	1·25	1·55	1·21	1·59
60	1·38	1·45	1·35	1·48	1·32	1·52	1·28	1·56	1·25	1·60
65	1·41	1·47	1·38	1·50	1·35	1·53	1·31	1·57	1·28	1·61
70	1·43	1·49	1·40	1·52	1·37	1·55	1·34	1·58	1·31	1·61
75	1·45	1·50	1·42	1·53	1·39	1·56	1·37	1·59	1·34	1·62
80	1·47	1·52	1·44	1·54	1·42	1·57	1·39	1·60	1·36	1·62
85	1·48	1·53	1·46	1·55	1·43	1·58	1·41	1·60	1·39	1·63
90	1·50	1·54	1·47	1·56	1·45	1·59	1·43	1·61	1·41	1·64
95	1·51	1·55	1·49	1·57	1·47	1·60	1·45	1·62	1·42	1·64
100	1·52	1·56	1·50	1·58	1·48	1·60	1·46	1·63	1·44	1·65

Note: k' = number of explanatory variables excluding the constant term.

Source: J. Durbin and G. S. Watson, 'Testing for Serial Correlation in Least Squares Regression', *Biometrika*, vol. 38, 1951, pp. 159–77. Reprinted with the permission of the authors and the *Biometrika* trustees.

Select Bibliography

TEXTBOOKS ON ECONOMETRIC THEORY

1. Christ, C., *Economic Models and Methods*, Wiley, 1966.
2. Goldberger, A. S., *Econometric Theory*, Wiley, 1964.
3. Johnston, J., *Econometric Methods*, 2nd edn, McGraw-Hill, 1972.
4. Klein, L. R., *A Textbook of Econometrics*, Row-Peterson, 1953.
5. Kmenta, J., *Elements of Econometrics*, Macmillan, New York, 1971.
6. Malinvaud, E., *Statistical Methods in Econometrics*, North-Holland, 1966.
7. Theil, H., *Principles of Econometrics*, North-Holland, 1972.
8. Wonnacott, R. J., and Wonnacott, T. H., *Econometrics*, Wiley, 1970.

TEXTBOOKS ON STATISTICAL THEORY

1. Bugg, D., Henderson, M. A., *et al.*, *Statistical Methods in the Social Sciences*, North-Holland, 1968.
2. Freund, J., and Williams, F., *Modern Business Statistics*, Pitman, 1959.
3. Mood, A. M., and Graybill, F. A., *Introduction to the Theory of Statistics*, McGraw-Hill, 1963.
4. Suits, D. B., *Statistics*, Rand-McNally, 1963.
5. Yamane, T., *Statistics*, 2nd edn, Harper International, 1970.
6. Yule, G. U., and Kendall, M. G., *An Introduction to the Theory of Statistics*, 14th edn, Griffin, 1950.

CHAPTERS 1–7

1. Anderson, R. L., and Bancroft, T. A., *Statistical Theory in Research*, McGraw-Hill, 1952, chapters 1–16.
2. Relevant chapters of general textbooks on Econometric Theory.
3. Ramsey, J. B., 'Tests for Specification Errors in Classical Linear Least Squares Regression Analysis', *Journal of the Royal Statistical Society*, Series B, vol. 31, 1969, pp. 350–71.
4. Theil, H., 'Specification Errors and the Estimation of Economic Relationships', *Review of the International Statistical Institute*, vol. 25, 1957, pp. 41–51.

CHAPTER 8–ANALYSIS OF VARIANCE

1.   Scheffé, H., *The Analysis of Variance,* Wiley, 1959.
2.   Chow, G. C., 'Tests of Equality between Sets of Coefficients in Two Linear Regressions', *Econometrica,* vol. 28, 1960, pp. 591–605.
3.   Fisher, F. M., 'Tests of Equality between Sets of Coefficients in Two Linear Regressions: An Expository Note', *Econometrica,* vol. 38, 1970, pp. 361–6.

CHAPTER 9–HETEROSCEDASTICITY

1.   Goldfeld, S. M., and Quandt, R. E., 'Some Tests for Homoscedasticity', *Journal of the American Statistical Association,* vol. 60, 1965, pp. 539–47.
2.   Glejser, H., 'A New Test for Heteroscedasticity', *Journal of the American Statistical Association,* vol. 64, 1969, pp. 316–23.
3.   Lancaster, T., 'Grouping Estimators on Heteroscedastic Data', *Journal of the American Statistical Association,* vol. 63, 1968, p. 191.
4.   Aitken, A. C., 'On Least-squares and Linear Combination of Observations', *Proceedings of the Royal Society of Edinburgh,* vol. 55, 1935, pp. 42–8.
5.   Kane, E. J., *Economic Statistics and Econometrics,* Harper International, 1968, chapter 14.
6.   Rutemiller, H. C., and Bowers, D. A., 'Estimation in a Heteroscedastic Regression Model', *Journal of the American Statistical Association,* vol. 63, 1968, pp. 552–7.

CHAPTER 10–AUTOCORRELATION

1.   Von Neumann, J., 'Distribution of the Ratio of the Mean Square Successive Difference to the Variance', *Annals of Mathematics and Statistics,* vol. 12, 1941, pp. 367–95.
2.   Durbin, J., and Watson, G. S., 'Testing for Serial Correlation in Least-squares Regression', *Biometrika,* vol. 37, pp. 409–28, and vol. 38, pp. 159, 178, 1951.
3.   Theil, H., and Nagar, A. L., 'Testing the Independence of Regression Disturbances', *Journal of the American Statistical Association,* vol. 56, 1961, pp. 793–806.
4.   Henshaw, R. C., 'Testing Single-equation Least-squares Regression Models for Autocorrelated Disturbances', *Econometrica,* vol. 34, 1966, pp. 646–60.
5.   Durbin, J., 'An Alternative to the Bounds Test for Testing for Serial Correlation in Least-squares Regression', *Econometrica,* vol. 38, 1970, pp. 422–9.
6.   Theil, H., 'The Analysis of Disturbances in Regression Analysis', *Journal of the American Statistical Association,* vol. 60, 1965, pp. 1067–79.

7. Theil, H., 'A Simplification of the BLUS Procedure for Analysing Regression Disturbances', *Journal of the American Statistical Association,* vol. 63, 1968, pp. 242–51.
8. Abrahamse, A. P. J., 'On the Power of the BLUS Procedure', *Journal of the American Statistical Association,* vol. 63, 1968, pp. 1227–36.
9. Kadiyala, K. R., 'A Transformation Used to Circumvent the Problem of Autocorrelation', *Econometrica,* vol. 36, 1968, pp. 93–6.
10. Cochrane, D., and Orcutt, G. H., 'Application of Least-squares Regressions to Relationships Containing Autocorrelated Error Terms', *Journal of the American Statistical Association,* vol. 44, 1949, pp. 32–61.
11. Sargan, J. D., 'Wages and Prices in the United Kingdom: A Study in Econometric Methodology', pp. 65–63 in P. E. Hart *et al., Econometric Analysis for National Economic Planning,* Butterworth, 1964.
12. Durbin, J., 'Estimation of Parameters in Time-series Regression Models', *Journal of the Royal Statistical Society,* Series B, vol. 22, 1960, pp. 139–53.
13. Griliches, Z., and Rao, P., 'Small-sample Properties of Several Two-stage Regression Methods in the Context of Autocorrelated Errors', *Journal of the American Statistical Association,* vol. 64, 1969, pp. 253–72.
14. White, J. S., 'Asymptotic Expansions for the Mean and Variance of the Serial Correlation Coefficient', *Biometrika,* vol. 48, 1961, pp. 85–94.
15. Griliches, Z., 'A Note on the Serial Correlation Bias in Estimates of Distributed Lags', *Econometrica,* vol. 29, 1961, pp. 65–73.
16. Taylor, L. D., and Wilson, T. A., 'Three-Pass Least-Squares: A Method for Estimating Models with a Lagged Dependent Variable', *Review of Economics and Statistics,* vol. 46, 1964, pp. 329–46
17. Durbin, J., 'Testing for Serial Correlation in Least-squares Regression when some of the Regressors are Lagged Dependent Variables', *Econometrica,* vol. 38, 1970, pp. 410–21.
18. Zellner, A., and Geisel, M. S., 'Analysis of Distributed Lag Models with Applications to Consumption Function Estimation', Paper presented to European Meeting of the Econometric Society, 1968.
19. Liviatan, N., 'Consistent Estimation of Distributed Lags', *International Economic Review,* vol. 4, 1963, pp. 44–52.
20. Wallis, K. F., 'Lagged Dependent Variables and Serially Correlated Errors: A Reappraisal of Three-Pass Least-squares', *Review of Economics and Statistics,* vol. 49, 1967, pp. 555–67.
21. Sargent, T. J., 'Some Evidence on the Small-sample Properties of Distributed Lag Estimators in the Presence of Autocorrelated Disturbances', *Review of Economics and Statistics,* vol. 50, 1968, pp. 87–95.

CHAPTER 11–MULTICOLLINEARITY

1. Frisch, R., *Statistical Confluence Analysis by Means of Complete Regression Systems,* Oslo, 1934.

2.   Farrar, D. E., and Glauber, R. R., 'Multicollinearity in Regression Analysis: The Problem Revisited', *Review of Economics and Statistics,* vol. 49, 1967, pp. 92–107.
3.   Silvey, S. D., 'Multicollinearity and Imprecise Estimation', *Journal of the Royal Statistical Society,* Series B, vol. 31, 1969, pp. 539–52.
4.   Johnston, J., 'An Econometric Model of the United Kingdom', *Review of Economic Studies,* vol. xxix, pp. 29–39, 1961.
5.   Fox, K., *Intermediate Economic Statistics,* Wiley, 1968, chapter 13.
6.   Cohen, B. C., 'The Effects of Multicollinearity on Regression Measures', *Abstract of the Indian Econometric Society,* 1971.

CHAPTER 12.1–ERRORS IN VARIABLES

1.   Wald, A., 'The Fitting of Straight Lines if Both Variables are subject to Error', *Annals of Mathematics and Statistics,* vol. 11, 1940, pp. 284–300.
2.   Bartlett, M. S., 'Fitting a Straight Line when Both Variables are subject to Error', *Biometrika,* vol. 5, 1949, pp. 207–12.
3.   Theil, H., and Van Yzeren, J., 'On the Efficiency of Wald's Method of Fitting Straight Lines', *Review of the International Statistical Institute,* vol. 24, 1956, pp. 17–26.
4.   Durbin, J., 'Errors in Variables', *Review of the International Statistical Institute,* vol. 22, 1954, pp. 23–32.
5.   Hooper, J. W., and Theil, H., 'The Extension of Wald's Method of Fitting Straight Lines to Multiple Regression', *Review of the International Statistical Institute,* vol. 26, 1958, pp. 37–47.
6.   Halperin, M., 'Fitting of Straight Lines and Prediction when both Variables are subject to Error', *Journal of the American Statistical Association,* vol. 56, 1961, pp. 657–69.
7.   Leser, C., *Econometric Techniques and Problems,* Griffin, 1966, chapter 2.

CHAPTER 12.3–DUMMY VARIABLES

1.   Klein, L. R., Ball, R. J. D., *et al., An Econometric Model of the United Kingdom,* Blackwell, 1961.
2.   Stone, R., *The Measurement of Consumers' Expenditure and Behaviour in the United Kingdom, 1920–1938,* Cambridge, 1954, 1961.
3.   Klein, L. R., and Shinkai, Y., 'An Econometric Model of Japan, 1930–1959', *International Economic Review,* vol. 4, 1963, pp. 1–28.
4.   Orcutt, G. H., *et al., Microanalysis of Socioeconomic Systems: A Simulation Study,* Harper & Row, 1961.
5.   Lovell, M. C., 'Seasonal Adjustment of Economic Time Series', *Journal of the American Statistical Association,* vol. 58, 1963, pp. 993–1010.

6. Jorgenson, D. W., 'Minimum Variance, Linear, Unbiased Seasonal Adjustment of Economic Time Series', *Journal of the American Statistical Association,* vol. 59, 1964, pp. 681–724.

CHAPTER 12.4–ESTIMATION FROM GROUPED DATA

1. Prais, S. J., and Aitchison, J., 'The Grouping of Observations in Regression Analysis', *Review of the International Statistical Institute,* vol. 1, 1954, pp. 1–22.
2. Cramer, J. S., 'Efficient Grouping, Regression and Correlation in Engel Curve Analysis', *Journal of the American Statistical Association,* vol. 59, 1964, pp. 233–50.
3. Haitovsky, Y., 'Unbiased Multiple Regression Coefficients estimated from One-way Classification Tables when the Cross Classifications are Unknown', *Journal of the American Statistical Association,* vol. 61, 1966, pp. 720–8.
4. Haitovsky, Y., *Regression Estimation from Grouped Observations,* National Bureau of Economic Research, New York, October, 1967.
5. Orcutt, H., Watts, H. W., Edwards, J. B., 'Data Aggregation and Information Loss', *American Economic Review,* September 1968.

CHAPTER 13–LAGGED VARIABLES–DISTRIBUTED LAG MODELS

1. Koyck, L. M., *Distributed Lags and Investment Analysis,* North-Holland, 1954.
2. Griliches, Z., 'Distributed Lags, A Survey', *Econometrica,* vol. 35, 1967, pp. 16–49.
3. Cagan, P., 'The Monetary Dynamics of Hyper Inflations', in M. Friedman (ed.), *Studies in the Quantity Theory of Money,* Chicago University Press, 1956.
4. Nerlove, M., 'Distributed Lags and Estimation of Long-Run Supply and Demand Elasticities, Theoretical Consideration', *Journal of Farm Economics,* vol. 40, 1958, pp. 301–11.
5. Nerlove, M., 'Estimates of Elasticities of Supply of Selected Agricultural Commodities', *Journal of Farm Economics,* vol. 38, 1956.
6. Nerlove, M., *Distributed Lags and Demand Analysis,* USDA, Agricultural Handbook, No. 141, 1958.
7. Almon, S., 'The Distributed Lag between Capital Appropriations and Expenditures', *Econometrica,* vol. 30, 1965, pp. 178–96.
8. De Leeuw, F., 'The Demand for Capital Goods by Manufacturers: A Study of Quarterly Time Series', *Econometrica,* vol. 30, 1962, pp. 407–23.
9. Lund, P. J., and Holden, K., 'An Econometric Study of Private Sector Gross Fixed Capital Formation in the United Kingdom, 1923–1938', *Oxford Economic Papers,* vol. 20, 1968, pp. 56–73.

10. Tinsley, P. A., 'An Application of Variable Weight Distributed Lags', *Journal of the American Statistical Association*, vol. 62, 1967, pp. 1277–89.

11. Almon, S., 'Lags Between Investment Decisions and their Causes', *Review of Economics and Statistics*, vol. 50, 1968, pp. 193–206.

12. Solow, R. M., 'On a Family of Lag Distributions', *Econometrica*, vol. 28, 1960, pp. 393, 406.

13. Jorgenson, D., 'Rational Distributed Lag Functions', *Econometrica*, vol. 34, 1966, pp. 135–49.

14. Ball, R. J., and Drake, P. S., 'The Relationship between Aggregate Consumption and Wealth', *International Economic Review*, vol. 5, 1964.

15. Houthakker, H. S., and Taylor, L. D., *Consumer Demand in the United States 1929–1970, Analysis and Projections*, Harvard University Press 1966.

CHAPTER 14–SIMULTANEOUS-EQUATION MODELS

1. Suits, D. B., *The Theory and Application of Econometric Models*, Athens, 1963, Center of Planning.

2. Christ, C. F., 'Aggregate Econometric Models: A Review Article', *American Economic Review*, vol. 46, 1956, pp. 385–408.

CHAPTER 15–IDENTIFICATION

1. Fisher, F. M., *The Identification Problem*, McGraw-Hill, 1966.

2. Haavelmo, T., 'The Statistical Implications of a System of Simultaneous Equations', *Econometrica*, vol. 11, pp. 1–12.

3. Koopmans, T. C., 'Identification Problems in Economic Model Construction', *Econometrica*, vol. 17, pp. 125–44.

4. Liu, T. C., 'Underidentification, Structural Estimation and Forecasting', *Econometrica*, vol. 28, pp. 855–65.

CHAPTER 16–SIMULTANEOUS-EQUATION METHODS

1. Sargan, J. D., 'The Estimation of Economic Relationships Using Instrumental Variables', *Econometrica*, vol. 26, 1958, pp. 393–415.

2. Reiersøl, O., 'Confluence Analysis by Means of Instrumental Sets of Variables', *Arkiv for Mathematik, Astronomi och Fysik*, vol. 324, 1945.

3. Theil, H., *Estimation and Simultaneous Correlation in Complete Equation Systems*, The Hague: Central Planning Bureau, 1953.

4. Basmann, R. L., 'A Generalised Classical Method of Linear Estimation of Coefficients in a Structural Equation', *Econometrica,* vol. 25, 1957, pp. 77–83.
5. Theil, H., *Economic Forecasts and Policy,* 2nd edn, North-Holland, 1961, pp. 231–2, 334–6.
6. Goldberger, A. S., 'An Instrumental Variable Interpretation of k-class Estimation', *The Indian Economic Journal,* vol. 13, 1965, pp. 424–31.
7. Nagar, A. L., 'The Bias and Moment Matrix of the General k-class Estimators of the Parameters in Simultaneous Equations', *Econometrica,* vol. 27, 1959, pp. 575–94.
8. Maeshiro, A., 'A Simple Mathematical Relationship among k-class Estimators', *Journal of the American Statistical Association,* vol. 61, 1966, pp. 368–74.
9. Oi, W. Y., 'On the Relationship among Different Members of the k-class *International Economic Review,* vol. 10, 1969, pp. 36–46.
10. Fisher, F. M., 'The Relative Sensitivity to Specification Error of Different k-class Estimators', *Journal of the American Statistical Association,* vol. 61, 1966, pp. 345–56.

CHAPTER 17–MIXED ESTIMATION

1. Durbin, J., 'A note on Regression when there is Extraneous Information about one of the Coefficients', *Journal of the American Statistical Association,* vol. 48, 1953, pp. 799–808.
2. Theil, H., and Goldberger, A. S., 'On Pure and Mixed Statistical Estimation in Economics', *International Economic Review,* vol. 2, 1960, pp. 65–78.
3. Theil, H., 'On the Use of Incomplete Prior Information in Regression Analysis', *Journal the American Statistical Association,* vol. 58, 1963, pp. 401–14.
4. Meyer, J., and Kuh, E., 'How Extraneous are Extraneous Estimates?', *Review of Economics and Statistics,* vol. 39, 1957, pp. 380–93.
5. Wallace, T. D., and Hussain, A., 'The Use of Error Components Models in Combining Cross-section with Time-series Data', *Econometrica,* vol. 37, 1969, pp. 55–72.
6. Balestra, P., and Nerlove, M., 'Pooling Cross-section and Time-Series Data in the Estimation of a Dynamic Model: The Demand for Natural Gas', *Econometrica,* vol. 34, 1966, pp. 585–612.

CHAPTER 18–MAXIMUM LIKELIHOOD METHODS

1. Anderson, T. W., and Rubin, H., 'Estimation of the Parameters of a Single Equation in a Complete System of Stochastic Equations', *Annals of Mathematics and Statistics,* vol. 20, 1949, pp. 46–63.

2. *FIML*
    Sargan, T. D., 'Three Stage Least-Squares and Full Maximum Likelihood
    Estimates', *Econometrica,* vol. 32, 1964, pp. 77–81.

CHAPTER 19–THREE-STAGE LEAST-SQUARES

1. Zellner, A., and Theil, H., 'Three-Stage Least-Squares: Simultaneous
    Estimation of Simultaneous Equations', *Econometrica,* vol. 30, 1962,
    pp. 54–78.

CHAPTER 20–FORECASTING POWER OF A MODEL

1. Ball, R. J. and Burns, T., 'An Econometric Approach to Short-run Analysis
    of the U.K. Economy 1955–1966', *Operational Research Quarterly,* vol. 9,
    1968.
2. Suits, D. B., 'Forecasting and Analysis with an Econometric Model',
    American Economic Review, vol. 52, 1962, pp. 104–32.
3. Suits, D. B., *The Theory and Application of Econometric Models,* Athens,
    1963: Center of Planning.
4. Theil, H., *Applied Economic Forecasting,* North-Holland, 1966.
5. Theil, H., *Economic Forecasting and Policy,* 2nd edn, North-Holland, 1962.
6. Christ, C. F., 'Aggregate Econometric Models: A Review Article', *American
    Economic Review,* vol. 46, 1956, pp. 385–408.

CHAPTER 21–MONTE CARLO STUDIES

1. Ladd, G. W., 'Effects of Shocks and Errors in Estimation: An Empirical
    Comparison', *Journal of Farm Economics,* vol. 38, 1956, pp. 485–95.
2. Wagner, H., 'A Monte Carlo Study of Estimates of Simultaneous Linear
    Structural Equations', *Econometrica,* vol. 26, 1958, pp. 117–33.
3. Basmann, R. L., *An Experimental Investigation of Some Small Sample
    Properties of GCL Estimators of Structural Equations, Some Preliminary
    Results,* General Electric Company, Handford Laboratories, Richland,
    Washington, 1958, mimeographed.
4. Foote, R. J., *Analytical Tools for Studying Demand and Price Structures,*
    US Dept of Agriculture, Agriculture Handbook 146, 1958.
5. Neiswanger, W. A., and Yancy, J. A., 'Parameter Estimates and Autonomous
    Growth', *Journal of the American Statistical Association,* vol. 54, 1959,
    pp. 389–402.
6. Klein, L. R., 'The Efficiency of Estimation in Econometric Models', in
    Essays in Economics and Econometrics, University of North Carolina
    Press, Chapel Hill, N.C., 1960.

7. Nagar, A. L., 'A Monte Carlo Study of Alternative Simultaneous Equation Estimators', *Econometrica,* vol. 28, 1960, pp. 573–90.

8. Quandt, R. E., 'Some Small Sample Properties of Certain Structural Equation Estimators', Econometric Research Program, Princeton, Research Memorandum No. 48, December 1962.

9. Summers, R., 'A Capital Intensive Approach to the Small Sample Properties of Various Simultaneous Equation Estimators', *Econometrica,* vol. 33, 1965, pp. 1–41.

10. Quandt, R. E., 'On Certain Small Sample Properties of k-Class Estimators', *International Economic Review,* vol. 6, 1965, pp. 92–104.

11. Cragg, J. G., 'On the Sensitivity of Simultaneous Equation Estimators to the Stochastic Assumptions of the Models', *Journal of the American Statistical Association,* vol. 61, 1966, pp, 136–51.

12. Cragg, J. G., 'On the Relative Small Sample Properties of Several Structural Equation Estimators', *Econometrica,* vol. 35, 1967, pp. 89–110.

13. Mendis, L. P., 'Small-sample Properties of Some Econometric Estimators: A Simulation Study', 1972, University of Lancaster, unpublished Ph.D. dissertation.

Index

Prior restrictions (*contd*)
  see also *A priori* information *and*
    Mixed estimation
Probability, definitions, 525–6
  laws of, 569–72
Probability distribution, 525–32
Probability limit, 107, 526
Properties of estimators, 100–9
  large-sample, 104–9
  of a model, 29–30
  of OLS estimators, 109–16
  small-sample, 101–4

Qualitative variables, 18, 281–4
  see also Binary variables *and* Dummy
    variables

$\bar{R}^2$, adjusted R^2 for degrees of freedom, 129
R^2, coefficient of multiple determination,
  121, 128
Random disturbance u, 13, 52
  see Stochastic disturbance u *and*
    Random variable u
Random sample, 538
Random variable, 526
Rank condition for identification, 353, 358
Rank correlation coefficient, 40–3
  rest of, 96–7
  see also Spearman's rank-correlation
    coefficient
Rational distributed lag model, 318–19
Rectangular distribution, 527–9
Rectangular weights, 287–8
Recursive system, 340–2
Reduced form, 337–40
Reduced-form method, 369–76
  see also Indirect least squares
Regressand, 12, 48
  see also Dependent variable
Regressors, 12, 48
  see Explanatory variables *and*
    Exogenous variables *also*
    Independent variables
Regression
  simple, 48–67
  multiple, 117–39
Regression line, 48–67
Regression parameters, 48–67, 117–39
Rejection region, 562–4
  see also Critical region
Residual sum of squares, 61, 71
  see also Variation, unexplained
Restricted least squares (RLS), 399–402
  see also Mixed estimation
Restrictions on parameters, 361–5

  see *A priori* information
  also Zero restrictions on parameters

Sample, 521
Sample mean, 536
Sample statistics, 521, 536–7
Sample variance, 537
Sampling distribution, 552–6
  of the OLS estimators, 79–80
Sampling theory, 545–56
Seasonal adjustment, using dummy variables,
  284
Serially correlated error, 200–32
  see also Autocorrelation
Significance level, of a test, 561, 563
Simultaneous-equation bias, 331–6
Simultaneous-equation methods, 20–2,
  369–95, 437–78
Simultaneous-equation models, 331–45
Small-sample properties of estimators,
  100–4
Solow's lag scheme, 316–18
Spearman's rank-correlation coefficient,
  40–3
  test of, 96–7
Specification bias, 253–6
Specification error, 16, 253–6
Specification of a model, 12–22
Standard deviation, 537
  of OLS estimators, 74–81
Standard errors of estimators, 74–6, 79–81
Standard normal distribution, 547–52
Standardisation rules, 547–9, 557–9
Standardised variable, 242–3, 547, 558
Statistic, sample, 536–8
  test, 564–6
Statistical inference, 543–68
Stochastic assumptions of linear regression
    model
  simple model, 55–7
  multivariate model, 118–19
Stochastic disturbance u, 13, 52
  see Random disturbance u
  also Disturbance variable u
Stochastic explanatory variables, 258–9
Stochastic variable, definition, 526
  continuous, 528
  discrete, 527
Stock-adjustment model, 310–13
  see Partial adjustment model
  also Nerlove's partial adjustment model
Structural model, 336–7
Student's t distribution, 86–91, 557–60
Student's t statistic, 86–91, 557–60
Sufficiency, 103